Temples Tour
(South India)

Rajiv Aggarwal

Radhakrishna Prakashan

First Edition : 2024

Published by :
Radhakrishna Prakashan Pvt. Ltd.
G-17, Jagatpuri, Delhi-110 051

Branches : Ashok Rajpath, Opposite Science Collage, Patna-800 006
First Floor, Darbari Building, Mahatma Gandhi Marg, Prayagraj-211 001
1, Anmol, Sorabji Santuk Lane, Dhobi Talao, Marine Lines, Mumbai-400002

Website : www.radhakrishnaprakashan.com
E-mail : info@radhakrishnaprakashan.com

Printed by
Vikas Computer & Printers
Tronica City-201 102 (U.P.)

Price : ₹ 2,500
₹ 10,000 (Set of 4 Volume)

TEMPLES TOUR : SOUTH INDIA
by Rajiv Aggarwal

ISBN : 978-81-978346-3-9
ISBN : 978-81-978346-6-0 (Set)

INDEX

Pamban Bridge
Rameswaram

PREFACE

With kind blessings of my revered parents, forefathers, Shri Kuldevi Shitala Mata of Gurgaon, Shri Ishdevta Marghat Wale Hanuman Baba and the immense compassion of the Supreme God, I have the privilege to write about the Temples, Ponds/Lakes, Trees, Saints and Statues located in the Republic of India. The number of Temples in our country is unlimited and it is not possible to give details of all but I have tried to compile in this book about important & main Temples etc.

During global pandemic Covid-19, in Chaitra Navratri of Vikrami Samvat 2077, a lockdown was imposed in the entire country, in which I felt during the Ashtami Pooja that I should write something about the Temples of my country. I decided that I would write about the major Temples of the whole country & when I started compiling, I felt such pleasurable realisations, which are not possible to be threaded in words. I found that each & every particle of our country is Devbhoomi. I have written this book with the help of official website of 730 Districts (till March 2020) of the country, website of Ministry of Tourism of Government of India & all States, website of Archaeological Survey of India, Wikipedia, official website of Temples, other religious websites, Social Media Handles, many books & articles. In this book, the Temples are sorted alphabetically & they are written according to the pin code in the District/State. In April 2020, when I started compiling the details of temples for this book, there were 730 districts in the country. It took me about 4 years to complete this work & currently there are 785 districts in the country. I have compiled the details of approximately 5500 Temples, hence, in my view, It is the most extensive compilation of Indian Temples in a pack of books.

In this book, I have covered Temples from Andaman to Ajmer, Bodhgaya to Sarnath, Jagannath Puri to Kedarnath, Kanyakumari to Ksheer Bhavani, Koteshwar to Kamakhya, Lakshadweep to Leh, Sammedshikhar to Shravanbelgola & Somnath to Kashi Vishwanath etc. There are various types of Temples such as Ashtavinayak Temples, Buddhist Temples, Char Dham, Chota Char Dham, Eight Mahakshetras of Lord Vishnu, Hot/Perennial Sulphur Springs, ISKCON Temples, Jain Temples, Jyotilinga, Nag Devta Temples, Nava Narasimhas, Nava Thirupathi, Panch Badri, Panch Dwarka, Panch Kannan Kshetrams, Panch Kedar, Panch Prayag, Pancha Narasimha Kshetras, Pancha Rama Kshetras, Pancha Bhoota Sthalam, Pancha Sabhai Temples, Sapta Puris, Seven Baithaks of Pushtimarg (Thakurji), Seven Thakurji of Vrindavan, Shakti Peetha, Shani Parihara Temples, Sindhi Temple, Six Abodes of Lord Murugan, Sun Temples, Trilinga Kshetras & other Temples, Ponds/Lakes, Trees, Saints & Statues of more than 50 foot height.

The Temples of our country have different characteristics and some of the illustrations are : There are Temples known as Bhai-Behan Temple, Devrani-Jethani Temple, Mama-Bhancha Temple, Sas-Bahu Temple. There are two Stepwells; Sasuni Vav and Vahuni Vav in Kaleshwari Group of Monuments at District Mahisagar.

In Morbi, Gujarat, Mani Temple is a symbol of love and in Baramulla, Kashmir, King built Sugandhesha Temple in honour of his wife, whereas to build the Laxmi Narayan Temple in Chamba, Himachal Pradesh, the King has sacrificed his 8 sons. Shri Prem Mandir of Panipat is being founded and operated by women only, which is a symbol of women empowerment since 1920. In Jagannath Temple at Baripara, only ladies can pull the chariot of Maa Subhadra. The villagers of Piplantri, District Rajsamand plant 111 trees every time a girl child is born and the community ensures that these trees survive, attaining fruition as the girls grow up and this noble initiative of the villagers is an example which is part of primary curriculum in Denmark.

In many Temples, the sun rays fall on the vigrahas consecrated in the Temple sometimes on a special festival or once a year or daily. At Gwarighat, Jabalpur, devotees put up problem petitions in Sri Sidh Ganesh Temple. At Arulmigu Masani Amman Temple, Anaimalai in Coimbatore, devotees place their grievances in writing & tie it in the hands of Ambica & it is strongly believed that solution would knock the doors of the applicant within 90 days. If any problem is experienced in other Temples of South India, devotees seek a solution in Rajarajeshwara Temple at Taliparamba through a prasna, which is a traditional way of astrological decision making.

It is interesting to note that half portion of Longwa village of Mon District in Nagaland is in India and half of it is in Myanmar and similarly half portion of Salburdi village of Balaghat District is in Madhya Pradesh and half of it is in Maharashtra and there is another pilgrim place, Goverdhan in Mathura District, whose circumambulation passes through two states i.e. Uttar Pradesh and Rajasthan and in Ramayana Circuit, Chitrakoot Dham has also been divided in two states i.e. Madhya Pradesh & Uttar Pradesh and temples in holy city Rishikesh are located in three Districts i.e. Dehradun, Pauri Garhwal & Tehri Garhwal. Majuli or Majoli is a River Island in the Brahmaputra River and in 2016, it became the first Island to be made a District in India.

Annamalaiyar Temple at Tiruvannamalai, Sri Ekambaranathar Temple at Kanchipuram, Meenakshi Sundareswarar Temple at Madurai, Nellaiappar Arultharum Kanthimathi Amman Temple at Thirunelveli and Saavira Kambada Basadi at Moodabidri are Temple of one thousand pillars and Dharmapuri Fort Temple has the hanging sculptured pillar. There are various Temples having musical pillars.

At Parshwanath Temple in Maksi, Madhya Pradesh, theft is impossible. The age of the Holy Cave of Shri Mata Vaishno Devi is nearly a million years. Lonar Lake in Buldhana, Maharashtra, is 5,76,000 (± 47,000) years old. Lamp lit on Deepawali at Hasanamba Temple in Hassan, Karnataka remains lit till the next Deepawali. Ghee lamp in the sanctum sanctorum of the Calcutta Jain Temple has been kept alight since 1867. At Maa Durga Mandir, Gadiya, District Shajapur, lamps burn with water of Kalisindh River for years. There is a tradition of offering a saree to Goddess Sri Mahalaxmi at Kolhapur from Lord Tirupati Balaji every year.

In Bade Hanumanji Ka Mandir at Hanuman Garh, Firozabad, the temple is 2300 years old and Lord Hanuman has only one eye. In Rajagopala Swamy Temple at Nagapattinam, Lord Hanuman has 3 eyes. In Punnainallur Sree Mahamariamman Temple at Thanjavur, vigraha perspire in summer. Milk turns blue when anointed at Sri Nagnath Swami Temple, Thirunageswaram. Unakoti Heritage site at Kailashahr in Tripura is an ancient Shaivite place of worship with about one crore huge rock reliefs. 10 million Shivalingas are existed in Sri Uma Parthiva Kotilingeshwara Swamy Kshetram at Siddipet. The specialty of Shivalinga at Neelkanth Mahadev Temple in Kalinjar Fort at Banda is that water keeps leaking from it. In the Tapkeshwar Temple of Dehradun, water droplets fall on the Shivalinga from the natural rocks. In Tuti Jharna Mandir at Ramgarh District in Jharkhand, Mother Ganges herself do the anointment of Shivalinga 24x7. In Vaijnath Mahadev Mandir at Anand District, the Shivalinga has 25 holes and holy water continuously comes out from it without knowing the source of water. The fragrance of Tulsi Leaves comes from 2000 years old Shivalinga at Gandheswar Temple, Sirpur. Saraswati River flows directly under the deity's feet at Raghunathji Temple at Devprayag.

It is an astonishing fact that Dhanushkodi in Rameswaram is the smallest town in the world, whereas Sri Lakshmi Narasimha Swamy Temple at Hyderabad has the world's largest Saligram. Highest Temple of Lord Shiva in the world is Tungnath Temple at Chandrashila, Rudraprayag District & highest temple of Lord Krishna in the world is located at Yulla Kunda, Kinnaur District.

The famous Ashokan lion capital at Sarnath became the National Emblem of India and national symbol on the Indian flag, design of Parliament House is taken from the Chausath Yogini Temple at Morena and Rajagopuram of Srivilliputtur Andal Temple is the State Emblem of Tamilnadu. Shiv Khori Cave Shrine at Ransoo in Reasi District is in the shape of Lord Shiva's Damroo. Surya Mandir at Giridih is built in the shape of lotus flower. In Khandwa District, Omkareshwar, the sacred island, is shaped like OM. There are two OM shaped Temples – one at Pali and other at Silvassa. Ramanarayanam at Vizianagram is uniquely built in the shape of a bow and arrow. Trilok Teerth Dham at Badagaon is built in the shape of the Jain Emblem. An 81 ft. Pichchi shaped Guru Mandir is built at Madagondanahalli in Tumkur District.

The colour of the vigraha varies from morning to evening at Prabhasgiri. The vigraha installed in Sri Mahankaleshwara Temple at Hyderabad changes expression every minute. The expression of the vigraha installed in Harsiddi Devi Temple at Rangir in Sagar District and Dharidevi Temple at Pauri Garhwal becomes that of a girl in the morning, of a woman in the afternoon and of an old lady in the evening. At Mata Mundeshwari Temple, Kaimur, the Shivlinga has been made of a stone which changes colour with change in the direction of Sun from dawn to dusk.

It is a religious belief that devotees get relief from fractured bones after having Prasad in Hanuman Temple at Katni District. The Chilkur Balaji Temple in Ranga Reddy District is known as Visa Mandir. In the Mahasu Devata Temple at Hanol Village in Dehradun District, matches are played between the Gods.

The vigrahha of Ambegalu Navaneetha Krishna (crawling Krishna with butter in hand) is believed to be the only vigraha of Lord Sri Krishna in this pose at Mallur in Ramanagara District. Sudama Mandir at Porbandar is the only Temple in India, which is dedicated to the childhood friend and devotee of Lord Krishna, Sudama. Shri Garudan Kavu Kshetram at Allathiyur, Kerala is the only Garuda Temple in India.

At Sirwell Mahadev Temple in Khargone, it is believed that King Ravana offered 10 heads to Lord Shiva. At Arulmigu Chidambaram Thillai Natarajar Temple, western scientists have proved that Lord Nataraja's big toe is the Centre Point of World's Magnetic Equator. Upper right hand's finger of Lord Alarnath at Puri got burned due to hot kheer and it is clearly visible. Mirpur Jain Temple at Sirohi is mentioned in the 'World Encyclopedia of Art'. There is continuous chanting of "Sri Ram, Jai Ram, Jai Jai Ram" since 1st August 1964 in Bala Hanuman Temple at Jamnagar for which it is recorded in the Guinness Book of World Records and also 24x7 "Hare Rama Hare Krishna" chanting in Geeta Vatika at Gorakhpur since 1968.

Our great nation is a paradise for the trekkers as various Temples, Lakes & Mountains are located at high altitude.

In writing this book, I have not used any kind of Artificial Intelligence. I have tried to give maximum details but I am neither a scholar nor am I able to claim any credentials. It is natural to have errors, lack of information and details in this book. I hope that the esteemed readers, during the study of this book, will make me aware of the errors left in it so that they can be removed in future.

In writing this book, I have immense support from my family. I express my gratitude to all of them. In the end, I convey my thanks to Sh. Vivek Narayan Shejwalkar Ji (Member of Parliamant), Sh. Ashok Maheshwari Ji of Rajkamal Prakashan, Sh Krishan Kumar Ji of Ashoka Prakashan, Sh. Vijay Aggarwal Ji & Sh. Ankit Aggarwal of Puja Press, Sh. Lalit Vats and Sh. Narasimhamurthy Ganapathy as without their kind guidance & help, this book cannot be published.

INDIA

India is one of the oldest civilizations in the world with a kaleidoscopic variety and rich cultural heritage. It has achieved all-round socio-economic progress since its Independence. It covers an area of 32,87,263 sq. km. extending from the snow-covered Himalayan heights to the tropical rain forests of the south. As the 7th largest country in the world, India stands apart from the rest of Asia, marked off as it is by mountains and the sea, which give the country a distinct geographical entity. Bounded by the Great Himalayas in the north, it stretches southwards and at the Tropic of Cancer, tapers off into the Indian Ocean between the Bay of Bengal on the east and the Arabian Sea on the west.

Indian Standard Time	GMT + 05:30
Languages	There are 22 different languages that have been recognised by the Constitution of India, of which Hindi is an Official Language.
Capital	New Delhi
Administrative Divisions	28 States and 8 Union Territories.
National Flag	The National Flag is a horizontal tricolour of deep saffron (kesaria) at the top, white in the middle, and dark green at the bottom in equal proportion. At the centre of the white band is a navy blue wheel, which is a representation of the Ashoka Chakra at Sarnath.
National Days	26th January (Republic Day) 15th August (Independence Day) 2nd October (Gandhi Jayanti; Mahatma Gandhi's Birthday)
National Anthem	The National Anthem of India Jana-Gana-Mana, composed originally in Bengali by Guru Rabindranath Tagore, which was adopted in its Hindi version by the Constituent Assembly as the National Anthem of India on 24th January 1950.
National Song	The song Vande Mataram, composed in Sanskrit by Bankimchandra Chatterji, was a source of inspiration to the people in their struggle for freedom. It has an equal status with Jana-Gana-Mana.
State Emblem	The state emblem is an adaptation from the Sarnath's Lion Capital of Ashoka. In the original, there were four lions, standing back to back, mounted on an abacus with a frieze carrying sculptures in high relief of an elephant, a galloping horse, a bull and a lion separated by intervening wheels over a bell-shaped lotus. Carved out of a single block of polished sandstone, the Capital is crowned by the Wheel of the Law (Dharma Chakra).

National Bird	The Indian peacock, Pavocristatus, the National Bird of India, is a colourful, swan-sized bird, with a fan-shaped crest of feathers, a white patch under the eye and a long, slender neck. The male of the species is more colourful than the female, with a glistening blue breast and neck and a spectacular bronze-green tail of around 200 elongated feathers. The female is brownish, slightly smaller than the male and lacks the tail. The elaborate courtship dance of the male, fanning out the tail and preening its feathers is a gorgeous sight.
National Animal	The magnificent tiger, Pantheratigris is a striped animal. It has a thick yellow coat of fur with dark stripes. The combination of grace, strength, agility and enormous power has earned the tiger its pride of place as the national animal of India.
National Flower	Lotus (Nelumbo Nucifera Gaertn) is the National Flower of India. It is a sacred flower and occupies a unique position in the art and mythology of ancient India and has been an auspicious symbol of Indian culture since time immemorial.

The Indian culture varies like its vast geography. People speak in different languages, dress differently, follow different religions, eat different food but are of the same temperament. So whether it is a joyous occasion or a moment of grief, people participate whole-heartedly, feeling the happiness or pain. A festival or a celebration is never constrained to a family or a home. The whole community or neighbourhood is involved in bringing liveliness to an occasion. The Vedic civilization is the earliest civilization in the history of ancient India. It is named after the Vedas, the early literature of the Hindu people. The Vedic Civilization flourished along the River Saraswati, in a region that now consists of the modern Indian states of Haryana and Punjab. Vedic is synonymous with Hinduism, which is another name for religious and spiritual thought that has evolved from the Vedas. The Ramayana and Mahabharata were the two great epics of this period.

BUDDHIST ERA - During the life time of Lord Gautam Buddha, sixteen great powers (Mahajanpadas) existed in 7th and early 6th centuries BC. Among the more important republics were the Sakyas of Kapilavastu and the Licchavis of Vaishali.

GUPTA DYNASTY - After the Kushanas, the Guptas were the most important dynasty. The Gupta period has been described as the Golden Age of Indian history. The first famous King of the Gupta dynasty was Ghatotkacha's son Chandragupta-I. He married Kumaradevi, the daughter of the chief of the Licchavis. This marriage was a turning point in his life. He got Pataliputra in dowry from the Lichhavis. From Pataliputra, he laid the foundation of his empire and started conquering many neighbouring states with the help of the Licchavis. He ruled over Magadha (Bihar), Prayaga and Saketa (east Uttar Pradesh). His kingdom extended from River Ganges to Allahabad. Chandragupta-I also got the title of Maharajadhiraja (King of Kings) and ruled for about fifteen years.

HARSHVARDHANA - With the commencement of 7th century, he ascended the throne of Thaneshwar and Kannauj. By 612 AD, Harshavardhana consolidated his kingdom in northern India. He is well known for his religious toleration, able administration and diplomatic relations.

THE PALAS - Between 8th and 10th centuries AD, a number of powerful empires dominated the eastern and northern parts of India. The Pala King Dharmpala reigned from the late 8th century to early 9th century. Nalanda University and Vikramashila University were founded by Dharmpala.

THE SENAS - After the decline of the Palas, the Sena dynasty established its rule in Bengal. The founder of the dynasty was Samantasena. The greatest ruler of the dynasty was Vijaysena. He was a great scholar and wrote four works including one on astronomy. The last ruler of this dynasty was Lakshamanasena.

THE PRATIHARA - The greatest ruler of the Pratihara dynasty was Mihir Bhoja. He recovered Kanauj (Kanyakubja) by 836 AD and it remained the capital of the Pratiharas for almost a century. He built the city Bhojpal (Bhopal). Raja Bhoja and other valiant Gujara Kings faced and defeated many attacks of the Arabs from west.

THE RASHTRAKUTA - This dynasty, which ruled from Karnataka, is illustrious for several reasons. They were great patrons of art and literature. The encouragement that several Rashtrakuta Kings provided to education and literature is unique and the religious tolerance exercised by them was exemplary.

THE CHOLA EMPIRE OF SOUTH - It emerged in the middle of 9th century, covered a large part of Indian peninsula, as well as parts of Sri Lanka and Maldives Islands. The first important ruler to emerge from the dynasty was Rajaraja Chola-I and his son and successor Rajendra Chola. The Chola Empire finally came to an end with the invasion of Malik Kafur in the early 14th century.

BHAKTI MOVEMENT - An important landmark in the cultural history of medieval India was the silent revolution in society brought about by a galaxy of socio-religious reformers, a revolution known as the Bhakti Movement. This movement was responsible for many rites and rituals associated with the worship of God by Hindus, Muslims and Sikhs of Indian subcontinent. For example, Kirtan at a Hindu Temple, Qawaali at a Dargah (by Muslims) and singing of Gurbani at a Gurdwara are all derived from the Bhakti Movement of medieval India (800-1700). The leader of this Hindu revivalist movement was Adi Shankaracharya, a great thinker and a distinguished philosopher and this movement was propounded by Chaitanya Mahaprabhu, Namadeva, Tukaram, Jayadeva.

HINDUISM

Hinduism in India is as multifarious a religion as it is long standing. Spirituality and symbolism happen to be its two fundamental elements. It is only by visiting the numerous religious destinations within the nation and peeking into their backgrounds that you begin to converge with the thresholds of this centuries' old culture. Hinduism is the world's oldest religion with roots and customs dating back more than 4,000 years. Hinduism embraces many religious ideas. For this reason, it's sometimes referred to as a "way of life". Prominent themes in Hindu beliefs include the four Purusarthas, the proper goals or aims of human life, namely Dharma (ethics / duties), Artha (prosperity / work), Kama (desires / passions) and Moksha (liberation / freedom from the cycle of death and rebirth / salvation). One of the key thoughts of Hinduism is "atman" or the belief in soul. This philosophy holds that living creatures have a soul and they're all part of the supreme soul. Hindus revere all living creatures and consider the cow a sacred animal. Traditionally, the life of a Hindu is divided into four Ashramas (phases or life stages) such as Brahmacharya (student), Grihastha (householder), Vanaprastha (retired) and Sannyasa (renunciation). Hinduism is closely related to other Indian religions including Buddhism, Sikhism and Jainism. There are two primary symbols associated with Hinduism, the Om and the Swastika. The Om symbol is composed of three Sanskrit letters and represents three sounds (a, u and m), which when combined are considered a sacred sound. The word Swastika means "good fortune" or "being happy" in Sanskrit and the symbol represents good luck.

Hindus value many sacred writings as opposed to one holy book. Hindu texts are classified into Sruti ("heard") and Smrti ("remembered"). These texts discuss theology, philosophy, mythology, Vedic yajna, Yoga, agamic rituals and Temple building among other topics. The primary sacred texts, known as the Vedas, were composed around 1500 BC. This collection of verses and hymns was written in Sanskrit and contains revelations received by ancient Saints and Sages. The Vedas are made up of: (1) The Rig Veda; (2) The Samaveda; (3) Yajurveda and (4) Atharvaveda. The Upanishads, the Bhagavad Gita, 18 Puranas, Ramayana and Mahabharata are also considered important texts in Hinduism. Hindu worship, which is known as "puja", typically takes place in the Mandir (Temple). Hindus can also worship at home and many have a special shrine dedicated to certain gods and goddesses. The giving of offerings is an important part of Hindu worship. Additionally, many Hindus take pilgrimages to Temples and other sacred sites in India. Hinduism has many sects and is sometimes divided as (1) Smarta (followers of Lord Brahma and all major deities); (2) Vaishnava (followers of Lord Vishnu); (3) Shaivism (followers of Lord Shiva) and (4) Shaktism (followers of Devi). Hindu practices include rituals such as puja (worship) and recitations, japa, meditation (dhyana), family-oriented rites of passage, annual festivals and occasional pilgrimages. Devas are an integral part of Hindu culture and are depicted in art, architecture and through icons and stories about them, particularly in Indian epic poetry and the

Puranas. Varying lists of avatars of Lord Vishnu appear in Hindu scriptures including the ten Dashavatara of the Garuda Purana and the twenty-two avatars in the Bhagavata Purana, though the latter adds that the incarnations of Lord Vishnu are innumerable. In the goddess-based Shaktism tradition, avatars of the Devi are found and all goddesses are considered to be different aspects of the same metaphysical Brahman and Shakti (energy). While avatars of other deities such as Ganesha and Lord Shiva are also mentioned in medieval Hindu texts.

Smartism centres its worship simultaneously on all the major Hindu deities: Lord Shiva, Lord Vishnu, Shakti, Ganesha, Surya and Skanda. The Smarta tradition is aligned with Advaita Vedanta, and regards Adi Shankara as its founder or reformer, who considered worship of God-with-attributes (Saguna Brahma) as a journey towards ultimately realizing God-without-attributes (nirguna Brahma, Atman, Self-knowledge). Vaishnavism is the devotional religious tradition that worships Lord Vishnu and his avatars, particularly Lord Rama and Krishna. Temple worship and festivals are typically elaborate in Vaishnavism. The Ramayana and Bhagavad Gita along with Lord Vishnu-oriented Puranas provide its theistic foundations. Shaivism is the tradition that focuses on Lord Shiva. Some Shaivas worship in Temples, while others emphasize yoga, striving to be one with Lord Shiva within. Avatars are uncommon and some Shaivas visualize god as half male, half female, as a fusion of the male and female principles (Ardhanarishvara). Shaivism is related to Shaktism, wherein Shakti is seen as spouse of Lord Shiva. Community celebrations include festivals and participation with Vaishnavas in pilgrimages such as the Kumbh Mela. Shaktism focuses on goddess worship of Shakti or Devi as cosmic mother. Devi is depicted as in gentler forms like Parvati, the consort of Lord Shiva; or as fierce warrior goddesses like Kali and Durga. Shaktism is also associated with Tantra practices. Community celebrations include festivals, some of which include processions and idol immersion into sea or other water bodies.

Bhaktimarga is considered in Hinduism as one of many possible paths of spirituality and alternative means to moksha. Hindu Temples and domestic altars are important elements of worship in contemporary theistic Hinduism. Many adherents undertake pilgrimages, which have historically been an important part of Hinduism and remain so today. Pilgrimage sites are called Tirtha, Kshetra, Gopitha or Mahalaya. The process or journey associated with Tirtha is called Tirtha-yatra. According to the Hindu text Skanda Purana, Tirtha are of three kinds: Jangam Tirtha is to a place movable of a sadhu, a rishi, a guru; Sthawar Tirtha is to a place immovable like Saptapuri, Char Dham, Jyotirlingams, Shaktipeethams, Holy Rivers etc. while Manas Tirtha is to a place of mind of truth, charity, patience, compassion, soft speech and soul. Some pilgrimages are part of a Vrata (vow), which a Hindu may make for a number of reasons. It may mark a special occasion, such as the birth of a baby or as part of a rite of passage such as a baby's first haircut or after healing from a sickness. An alternative reason for Tirtha, for some Hindus, is to respect wishes or in memory of a beloved person after his or her death. Other reasons for a Tirtha in Hinduism is to rejuvenate or gain spiritual merit by traveling to famed Temples or bathe in Rivers such as the Ganges. A Hindu Temple is a house of god(s). It is a space and structure designed to bring human beings and gods together, infused with symbolism to express the ideas and beliefs of Hinduism. A Temple incorporates all elements of Hindu cosmology, the highest spire or dome representing Mount Meru – reminder of the abode of Lord Brahma and the centre of spiritual universe, the carvings and iconography symbolically presenting dharma, karma, artha, kama andmoksha. Hindu Temples are spiritual destinations for many Hindus as well as landmarks for arts, annual festivals, rite of passage rituals and community celebrations. Hindu Temples come in many styles, diverse locations, deploy different construction methods and are adapted to different deities and regional beliefs. Two major styles of Hindu Temples include the Gopuram style found in south India and Nagara style found in north India. Other styles include cave, forest and mountain Temples. Yet, despite their differences, almost all Hindu Temples share certain common architectural principles, core ideas, symbolism and themes. Many Temples feature one or more idols (murtis). The idol and Grabhagriha in the Lord Brahma-pada (the centre of the Temple), under the main spire, serves as a focal point (darsana, a sight) in a Hindu Temple. A Temple is a place which is mighty from outside but which is magical inside. It strengthen the devotees with its enlightenments and its divinity and beauty cannot be defined, rather it can just be felt.

❖ ❖ ❖ ❖ ❖

DETAILS OF SPECIAL TIRTHSTHAL

DHAM - Char Dham, 'the four abodes/seats', are the names of four pilgrimage places in India that are widely revered by Hindus that have to be visited in one's lifetime. They are: Badrinath, Rameshwaram, Dwarka and Jagannath Puri. In his different incarnations, Lord Vishnu takes bath in Rameswaram, meditate in Badrinath, feast in Puri and rest in Dwarka. Vaishnavite Hindus believe that visiting these sites helps them to achieve "Moksha" (salvation). The Char Dham defined by the great 8th century reformer and philosopher, Adi Shankaracharya consists of two Vaishnavite, one Shaivite and one mixed site. Geographically speaking the Char Dham makes a perfect square with Badrinath and Rameswaram falling on same longitude and Dwarka (old) and Puri on same latitude, representing the farthest north, east, west and south points of India (at that time, before coastlines changed).

According to Hindu belief, Badrinath became prominent when Nar-Narayan, an avatar of Lord Vishnu, did Tapasya there. At that time, that place was filled with berry trees. In Sanskrit, berries are called "badri", so the place was named Badrika-Van i.e. the forest of berries. The particular spot where the Nar-Narayan did Tapasya, a large berry tree formed covering him to save him from the rain and the sun. Local people believe that Mata Lakshmi became the berry tree to save Lord Narayan. Post-Tapasya, Narayan said, people will always take her name before his name, hence Hindus always refer "Lakshmi-Narayan". It was, therefore called Badri-Nath i.e. the Lord of Berry forest. This all happened in the Sathya/Sath-Yuga. So Badrinath came to be known as the first Dham.

Badrinath Dham, Uttarakhand - Math: Jyotirmath | Seed Mantra: Ayamatma Brahma | Ved: Atharvaveda | Sanyasi Name: Giri, Parvat, Sagar | First Mathadhish: Acharya Totak | Direction: North | Auxiliary Shiva Temple: Kedarnath Jyotirlinga | Kumbh: Haridwar

The second Dham, Rameswaram got its importance in the Treta Yuga when Lord Rama built a Shivalingam here and worshiped it to get the blessings of Lord Shiva. The name Rameswaram means "Rama is Lord".

Rameswaram Dham, Tamil Nadu - Math: Vedant Gyanmath | Seed Mantra: Aham Brahmasmi | Ved: Yajurveda | Sanyasi Name: Bharti, Puri | First Mathadhish: Acharya Sureshwarji | Direction: South | Auxiliary Shiva Temple: Sri Ranganathaswamy Temple | Kumbh: Nashik

The third Dham, Dwarka got its importance in the Dwapara Yuga when Lord Krishna made Dwarka his residence instead of Mathura, his birthplace.

Dwarka Dham, Gujrat - Math: Sharada Math | Seed Mantra: Tatwamasi | Ved: Samaveda | Sanyasi Name: Saraswati, Tirth, Ashram | First Mathadhish: Hastamalak (Prthvidhar) | Direction: West | Auxiliary Shiva Temple: Somnath Jyotirlinga | Kumbh: Ujjain

At the fourth Dham, Puri, Lord Vishnu is worshiped as Jagannath, his Avtar for Kalyuga.

Jagannath Dham, Puri, Odisha - Math: Govardhan Math | Seed Mantra: Prajnanam Brahma | Ved: Rigveda | Sanyasi Name: Arany | First Mathadhish: Padmapad | Direction: East | Auxiliary Shiva Temple: Lingaraj Temple | Kumbh: Prayagraj

CHOTA CHAR DHAM - Nestled among the serene heights of the great Himalayas are four pilgrim-destinations namely Yamunotri, Gangotri, Kedarnath and Badrinath, collectively known as Char Dham. These pilgrimage centres draw the maximum numbers of pilgrims each year, thus becoming the most important hubs of religious travel in the whole of Northern India. Traditionally, the pilgrimage begins from the West and ends in the East. Thus, the Chota Char Dham Yatra commences from Yamunotri, then proceeding to Gangotri and finally to Kedarnath and Badrinath. Each of these four sites is devoted to a specific deity. Yamunotri is dedicated to the Goddess Yamuna who goes along the pilgrims to the high altitudes of the picturesque Rawai Valley. It is believed that a bath in the waters of the Yamuna protects the devotee from untimely death. Gangotri is dedicated to the Goddess Ganga. The shrine overlooks the River Bhagirathi, another name of River Ganga – the name having been derived from the myth of the ancient King Bhagirath's penance that succeeded in bringing her upon the earth from the heaven. Kedarnath is dedicated to Lord Shiva and is also a part of the Panch Kedar. It is the northernmost Jyotirlinga and is close to the source of the holy River Mandakini. Badrinath is dedicated to Lord Vishnu. It is situated on the bank of the River Alaknanda. According to legend, Lord Vishnu meditated here while his consort Lakshmi took the form of a berry (Badri) tree to offer him shade. The Chota Char Dham Yatra is one of the quite accessible yet most arduous journeys. The Yatra route in the Uttarakhand State is usually bustling with activity, especially during the summer. The scenic beauty of the mountains solemnly provides strength to the pilgrims as they move towards their destination.

ISKCON - The International Society for Krishna Consciousness (ISKCON), otherwise known as the Hare Krishna movement, includes five hundred major centres, temples and rural communities, nearly one hundred affiliated vegetarian restaurants, thousands of namahattas or local meeting groups, a wide variety of community projects and millions of congregational members worldwide. Although less than fifty years on the global stage, ISKCON has expanded widely since its founding by His Divine Grace A. C. Bhaktivedanta Swami Prabhupada in New York city in 1966. ISKCON is part of the Gaudiya or Chaitanya Vaishnava tradition, which hails from the eastern regions of India. Gaudiyas place special emphasis on the teachings of 16th Century Saint and Avatar, Sri Chaitanya Mahaprabhu. ISKCON belongs to the Gaudiya-Vaishnava sampradaya, a monotheistic tradition within the Vedic or Hindu culture. Philosophically, it is based on the Sanskrit texts Bhagavad-Gita and the Bhagavat Purana or Srimad Bhagavatam. These are the historic texts of the devotional bhakti yoga tradition, which teaches that the ultimate goal for all living beings is to reawaken their love for God, or Lord Krishna, the "all-attractive one". ISKCON devotees chant God's names in the form of the maha-mantra or the great prayer for deliverance: Hare Krishna, Hare Krishna, Krishna Krishna, Hare Hare/Hare Rama Hare Rama, Rama Rama, Hare Hare. Members of ISKCON practice bhakti-yoga in their homes and also worship in Temples. They also promote bhakti-yoga, or Krishna Consciousness, through festivals, the performing arts, yoga seminars, public chanting and the distribution of the society's literatures.

JYOTIRLINGAM - The Lingam, which is a rounded, upright stone, is used as a symbol of Lord Shiva. Worship of the Lingam is one of the most important aspects of the worship of Lord Shiva. The word "Lingam" actually means a sign or characteristic, so the Shivalingam is a sign of Lord Shiva and helps us to remember him in his formless aspect. The Shivalingam is also considered to be the divine phallus, containing within it the seed of the universe. Together with the yoni or seat on which it rests and which corresponds to the female vulva, the yoni-lingam represents the union of man and woman, Shiva and Shakti, the cosmic spirit in union with the cosmic Prakriti, which brings everything into existence. There are thousands of thousands of Lingams all over India but some of them have a special importance. The most important of these are called Jyotirlingas. Jyoti means 'radiance' and Lingam means the 'Image or Sign' of Lord Shiva; Jyotirlingam, thus, means the Radiant Sign of The Almighty Shiva. There are twelve traditional Jyotirlinga shrines in India, which are titled as Somnatha, Mallikarjuna, Mahakala, Omkara, Kedara, Bhimshankara. Vishvanatha, Tryambaka, Vaidynatha, Nagesha, Rameswara and Ghrushnesha. Most of these are supposed to be self-formed or sprouted out of their own will. A few have been installed by human hands. Every Lord Shiva worshipper dreams of doing a pilgrimage to all these twelve Jyotirlingas at least once in his lifetime. According to Shiva Mahapurana, once Lord Brahma (the god of creation) and Vishnu (the form of God during Preservation) had an argument over supremacy of creation. To settle the debate, supreme God Shiva pierced the three worlds appearing as a huge Infinite Pillar of Light, the Jyotirlinga which later cooled into the Holy Mountain Annamalai (on which the Temple of Arunachaleshvara is located). Lord Vishnu and Brahma split their ways to downwards and upwards respectively to find the end of the light in either direction. Lord Brahma lied that he found out the end, while Lord Vishnu conceded his defeat. This lie of Lord Brahma angered Lord Shiva, making him curse Brahma that even though he is the creator of the universe, he would not be worshiped. The Jyotirlinga is the supreme Shiva, part less reality, out of which Lord Shiva appeared in another form, Lingodbhava. Originally, there were believed to be 64 Jyotirlingas, while 12 of them are considered to be very auspicious and holy. Each of the twelve Jyotirlinga places take the name of the presiding deity, each considered a different manifestation of Shiva. At all these places, the primary image is Lingam representing the beginingless and endless Stambha pillar, symbolising the infinite nature of Lord Shiva.

NAVADURGA - Navadurga or Nabadurga are nine manifestations of the Goddess Durga in Hinduism, especially worshipped during the festival of Navratri where each of the nine manifested forms are venerated respectively for each night. The nine forms of Goddess Durga are: Shailaputri, Brahmacharini, Chandraghanta, Kushmanda, Skandamata, Katyayani, Kaalratri, Mahagauri and Siddhidhatri. Each manifestation is known by her respective name, governing planet, iconography, mantra for invocation (usually repeated 108 times at each sitting during the period of Navratri), dedication day for Navratri and respective prayers.

1. Shailaputri - Shailaputri literally means the daughter (putri) of the mountain (shaila). After performing self-immolation in her form as Sati, the Mother Goddess took birth in the house of the King of Mountains, as the daughter of Lord Himalaya. Also known as Sati, Bhavani, Parvati or

Hemavati, she is the absolute form of Mother Nature and the embodiment of the power of Brahma, Vishnu and Mahadeva. Her governing planet is Moon. Devi Shailaputri is depicted with two hands and has a crescent moon on her forehead. She holds a trident in her right hand & a lotus flower in the left. She rides on Nandi (bull). Her Mantra is: Om Devi Shailaputryai Namah.

2. Brahmacharini - "Brahma" means "the one self-existent Spirit, the Absolute Reality, Universal Self, Personal God, the sacred knowledge". "Charini" means "occupation with, engaging, proceeding, behaviour, conduct, to follow, moving within, going after". She is the goddess of asceticism and penance, as her name is the female equivalent of one who practices Brahmacharya. She is the Mother Goddess born unto Prajapati Daksha as his daughter Sati and later married Shiva. This is her unmarried form. Her other names are Parvati, Aparna, Uma, Patlabati. Her governing planet is Mars. She walks on bare feet, carrying a japa mala in her right hand and a kamandalu in her left hand. Her Mantrais : Om Devi Brahmacharinyai Namah.

3. Chandraghanta - Chandraghanta is made up of the words chandra meaning moon and ghanta meaning bell. She is a powerful form of the Mother Goddess. She adorns her forehead with a half-moon shaped like a bell, which explains the origin of her name. She is the goddess who inspires courage in a person and is always ready for war against demons. When provoked, she can be malevolent to those who invite her wrath, but she remains the embodiment of serenity to her followers. Her governing planet is Venus. Goddess Chandraghanta mounts the tigress. She wears the semi-circular moon(Chandra) on her forehead. The half-moon on her forehead looks like the bell (Ghanta) and hence, her name. She is depicted with ten hands. Goddess Chandraghanta carries Trishul, Gada, sword and kamandalu in her four left hands and keeps the fifth left hand in Varadamudra. She carries a lotus flower, arrow, Dhanush and Japa Mala in Her four right hands and keeps the fifth right hand in Abhaya Mudra. This form of the Mother Goddess is ready for war with all her weapons, to protect the peace and welfare of her devotees. It is believed that the sound of the moon-bell on her forehead drives all types of evil away from her devotees. Her Mantra is: Om Devi Candraghantayai Namah.

4. Kushmanda - Ku means "a little", Ushma means "warmth" or "energy" and Anda taken from the last three words of the Sanskrit word "Brahmand" that means The Universe. After taking the form of Siddhidatri, the Mother Goddess began to live inside the Sun, resulting in liberation of the Sun's energy to the universe. Since then, this form of the Goddess has been known as Kushmanda, namely for her power and capability to live inside the Sun. The glow and radiance of her body is as luminous as that of the Sun. Her governing planet is Sun. Rides on a lioness and has eight hands. She holds a kamandalu, Dhanush, Bada and Kamal in her right hands. Her left hands hold Amrit Kalash (pot of nectar), japa mala (prayer beads), Gada and Chakra - in that order. She created the universe in the flash of her smile and is believed to bestow siddhis (supernatural powers) and nidhis (wealth) to her devotees. She is the avatar of Goddess Parvati. Her Mantra is: Om Devi Kus mandayai Namah.

5. Skandamata – She is Mother of the War God Skanda (Kartikeya). Her governing planet is Mercury. Goddess Skandamata mounts the ferocious lion. She is also recognized as "The Goddess of Fire". She carries baby Skanda in her lap. Lord Skanda (also known as Kartikeya or

Lord Murugan) is the brother of Ganesha. Goddess Skandamata is depicted with four hands. She carries lotus flowers in her upper two hands. She holds baby Skanda in right hand and keeps the left hand in Abhayamudra. She sits on a lotus flower and because of that, is also known as Goddess Padmasana. Devotees who worship this form of the Mother Goddess get the added benefit of blessings of Lord Skanda, the God of War (also known as Kartikeya). Her Mantra is: Om Devi Skandamatayai Namah.

6. Katyayani - To destroy the demon Mahishasura, Parvati incarnated as the daughter of Sage Katyayana, and help the devas. She is known for her anger, vengeance and ultimate victory over the demons. She will bestow boons upon those who worship and revere her with a pure heart if she is pleased. Her governing planet is Jupiter. Goddess Katyayani rides on a magnificent lion and is depicted with four hands. She carries a lotus flower and sword in her left hands respectively and keeps her right hands in Abhayamudra and Varadamudras. Her Mantra is: Om Devi Katyayanyai Namah.

7. Kalaratri - This is the fiercest and the most ferocious form of the Mother Goddess, in which Parvati manifests to destroy the demons Sumbha and Nisumbha. Kalaratri, meaning the night of death (death night). All time, light, emotions, life forms and others all blend into her. She is the death of time and is greater than Kala (time) himself. Her governing planet is Saturn. Her complexion is dark black and She rides on a donkey. She is depicted with four hands. Her right hands are in Abhayamudra and Varadamudra. She carries a sword and deadly iron hook in her left hands. Her Mantra is: Om Devi Kalaratryai Namah.

8. Mahagauri - Mahagauri is known as the Goddess of purity and cleanliness. The man who pleases her, by her grace, all of his flaws, faults and mistakes will be burnt to ashes and he will be redeemed. Due to her extremely fair complexion, she was known as Mahagauri. Her governing planet is Rahu. She rides the bull, just like Goddess Shailaputri. She has four arms, holding a Trishula in one of her right hands and depicts the Abhayamudra with the other right hand. She carries a tambourine or Damaru in one left hand and depicts the Varadamudra or kamandalu in her other left hand. She is known as the forgiving goddess and forgives sinners and purifies them. Her Mantra is: Om Devi Mahagauryai Namah.

9. Siddhidhatri - Siddhidhatri is the one who removes ignorance and she provides the knowledge to realize true reality. The Siddhi that she provides is the realization that only she exists. She is the mistress of all achievements. In the beginning of the universe, Lord Shiva worshiped the unmanifest form of the Mother Goddess, Adi Parashakti for creation. As Adi Parashakti, the Mother Goddess had no form, she thus appeared as Siddhidatri and from the left half of Lord Shiva. It is said that Siddhidatri originated from the form of Ardhanarishvara. Her governing planet is Ketu. She sits on a lotus or rides on a tiger or lion. She is depicted with four hands. She has gada in the one right hand, a chakram in the other right hand, a lotus flower in the left hand and a shankha in the other left hand. She bestows all types of siddhi (supernatural powers) to her devotees and hence is worshipped by humans, ghandarvas, asuras and devas alike. Her Mantra is: Om Devi Siddhidatryai Namah.

SAPTAMATRIKA - The term Matrika refers to the group of mother goddess, the saptamatrika are a group of seven mother goddess who are always depicted together. These goddess are Shakti or the personification of the power of other male gods, who they also derived their names from.

Brahmani : She is the Shakti of Lord Brahma, the creator. She has a body as bright as gold. Her vahana is a Hamsa.

Vaishnavi : She is the Shakti of Lord Vishnu, the preserver. She wears all the ornaments usually worn by Lord Vishnu. Her vahana is Garuda and she holds a conch and chakra in her hands.

Maheshwari : She is the Shakti of Lord Shiva. Her vahana is a Bull. She has four arms and rudraksh.

Kaumari : She is the Shakti of Skanda. Her vahana is Peacock.

Varahi : She is the Shakti of Lord Varaha. She has the face of a boar and complexion of a storm cloud.

Indrani : She is the Shakti of Lord Indra. Her vahana is an Elephant. She carries thunderbolt along with her.

Chamunda : She is the only Matrika who does not have a corresponding male god. Her complexion is dark. She holds a skull in her hands.

SAPTAPURI - It is a list of Seven Holy pilgrimage sites in Hinduism, which bless the pilgrims with Moksha (liberation from the cycle of Birth and Death). The Sapta Puri are places of birth of religious and spiritual masters, places where gods have descended as avatars (incarnations) such as Ayodhya where Lord Rama was born and places considered as Nityatirthas, naturally endowed, with spiritual powers since ages such as Varanasi and Haridwar. Kanchipuram is known for its Kamakshi Amman Temple dedicated to the mother goddess. Dwarka represents the place where Lord Krishna, after leaving Mathura, spent 100 years before he left for his divine abode from here. Mathura is the embodiment of events in the life of Lord Krishna during his childhood and young days. Haridwar with shrines of both Lord Shiva and Vishnu, represents the gateway to Uttarakhand, as the sacred River Ganges emerges from the hills into the plains at this place. Varanasi is the place of salvation, as it is strongly believed that death at this place will bring salvation. Varanasi is the holiest of all and it is favourite to Lord Shiva. In Hinduism, one should visit the major Temples in Varanasi in his/her life. Ujjain, also known by the ancient name Avanti has one of the 12 Jyotirlingas installed in the Mahakaleshwar Temple. Each of these cities is also famous for the spectacular melas or fairs held. Haridwar and Ujjain are famous for the Kumbh Mela held once every 12 years. Marriage festival of Kamakshi at Kanchipuram is a special occasion. Krishna Janmashtami (birthday of Lord Krishna) is a special occasion in Dwarka and Mathura.

SHAKTIPEETHA - The Shakti Peetha are significant shrines and pilgrimage destinations in Shaktism, the goddess-focused Hindu tradition. There are 51 or 108 Shakti Peethas by various accounts, of which between 4 and 18 are named as Maha (major) in medieval Hindu texts. Most of these historic places of goddess worship are in India but there are seven in Bangladesh, three in Pakistan, three in Nepal and one each in China and Sri Lanka. There are 51 Shakti Peethas linking to the 51 alphabets in Sanskrit. The legend behind the Shakti Peethas is that Lord Brahma performed a yajna (Vedic ritual of fire sacrifice) to please Shakti and Shiva. Goddess Shakti emerged, separating from Lord Shiva and helped Lord Brahma in the creation of the universe. Lord Brahma decided to give Shakti back to Lord Shiva. Therefore, his son Daksha performed several yagnas to obtain Shakti as his daughter in the form of Sati. It was then decided that Sati was brought into this world with the motive of marrying Lord Shiva. However, due to Lord Shiva's curse to Lord Brahma that his fifth head was cut off due to his lie in front of Lord Shiva, Daksha started hating Lord Shiva and decided not to let Lord Shiva and Sati get married. However, Sati got attracted to Lord Shiva and finally one day Lord Shiva and Sati were married. This marriage only increased Daksha's hatred towards Lord Shiva. Daksha performed a yagna with a desire to take revenge on Lord Shiva. Daksha invited all the deities to the yajna except Lord Shiva and Sati. The fact that she was not invited did not deter Sati from attending the yagna. She expressed her desire to attend the yagna to Lord Shiva, who tried his best to dissuade her from going. Lord Shiva eventually relented and Sati went to the yagna. Sati, being an uninvited guest, was not given any respect at the yagna. Furthermore, Daksha insulted Lord Shiva. Sati was unable to bear her father's insults toward her husband, so she self-immolated in the yajna. Enraged at the death and insult of his spouse, Lord Shiva in his Virabhadra avatar destroyed Daksha's yagna, cut off Daksha's head but later replaced it with that of a male goat as he restored him to life. Virabhadra didn't stop fighting; he kept raging with anger. Gods prayed to Lord Vishnu. He came there and started fighting him. Still immersed in grief, Lord Shiva picked up the remains of Sati's body and performed the Tandava, the celestial dance of destruction, across all creation. The other Gods requested Lord Vishnu to intervene to stop this destruction, towards which Lord Vishnu used the Sudarshana Chakra, which cut through Sati's corpse. The various parts of the body fell at several spots all through the Indian subcontinent and formed sites which are known as Shakti Peethas today. To complete this massively long task, Lord Shiva took the form of Bhairava. At all the Shakti Peethas, the Goddess Shakti is accompanied by her consort, Lord Bhairava (a manifestation of Lord Shiva).The only exceptional Shakti Peetha is the Vindhyavasini Shakti Peetha, as it is believed that the Shaktipeethas were created on earth, where the body parts of Sati fell, but Vindhyavasini is the place where Devi chose to reside after her birth in Dwapar Yuga as the sister of Lord Krishna. The Kerala Hindus believes that the self-immolation of the Sati happened in the Kottiyoor in Kannur district in Kerala. The annual Kottiyoor Vysakha Mahotsavam is conducted to commemorate the self-immolation of Sati. The Kottiyoor Temple is located on the both banks of the Bavali River.

Sharada Peeth: This Temple is currently non-existent. Only ruins are found in these places. Its ruins are near the Line of Control (LOC) between the Indian and Pakistani-controlled portions of the former princely state of Jammu and Kashmir.

❖ ❖ ❖ ❖ ❖

ANDAMAN & NICOBAR

The Andaman Islands and the Nicobar Islands has separate the Andaman Sea to the east from the Indian Ocean. The Andaman & Nicobar Islands is a union territory of India. Port Blair has one Airport, one major harbour and a number of other small harbours.

Capital	Port Blair
Total Population	4,34,192 (Estimated in 2019)
Total Islands	572
Inhabited Islands	38
Districts	03
Official Language	Hindi, Nicobarese, Bengali, Tamil, Malayalam, Telugu
Animal	Dugong or Sea Cow
Bird	Andaman Wood Pigeon
Tree	Andaman Padauk
Airport	Port Blair

DISTRICT – NICOBAR (Railway Station – No Railway Station Nearby)

S. No.	Temple	Address	Type
1	Indira Point	Great Nicobar Island - 744301	Ramayana Circuit

INDIRA POINT - It is the southern most point of India. A mythological story related to Lord Rama is also prevalent here. The Bay of Bengal looks quite calm from this place, while the Bay of Mannar has strong waves. It is believed that when Lord Rama asked for a way from the sea to go to Lanka, the sea refused to show the way to Lord Rama, after which Lord Rama got angry and took up his bow and arrow. Seeing this, the sea apologized to Lord Rama for his mistake and showed him the way. Since that time the sea on one side is calm and on the other side, there are huge waves.

DISTRICT – SOUTH ANDAMAN (Railway Station – No Railway Station Nearby)

S. No.	Temple	Address	Type
1	Sri Karpaga Vinayakar Temple	Goleghar, Port Blair – 744101	Ganesh
2	Sri Vetrimalai Murugan Temple	Shadipur, Port Blair – 744106	Murugan

SRI KARPAGA VINAYAKAR TEMPLE - Sri Karpaga Vinayakar Temple, which is famous for its architectural values, is one of the most admired locations for the Hindus in Port Blair. Residents of the city believe that all their wishes will come true, if they worship the deity here. Lord Ganesha's Vigraha is built with black clay and adorning glittering ornaments. It is located 2 KMs from Port Blair Airport.

SRI VETRIMALAI MURUGAN TEMPLE - Sri Vetrimalai Murugan Temple is the biggest pilgrimage site of the Andaman Islands for its spectacular nuances of Dravidian architecture and intricate artwork that leave one spellbound as soon as one steps into the Temple arcade. Situated behind the Governor's Place, it is dedicated to Lord Murugan or Karthikeyan- the son of Lord Shiva who is one of the most revered deities of the Tamil folks. The Temple was built in 1926 in the Ross Islands by the British rulers to win the loyalty of the Tamilians. Later, its venue was shifted to the capital city Port Blair post-independence.

ANDHRA PRADESH

The study of history reveals that major portion of the southern India (Dakshina Padham) was extended by Andhra region. Several dynasties ruled over this part of the country. On the 1st of October, 1953, Andhra State came into existence. Kurnool became the capital of the new State. As the rest of the constituents of the Indian Union, Andhra Pradesh too, in its own inimitable way, contributed its own part to the common cultural heritage of India, maintaining at the same time its own individuality.

Capital City	Amaravati
Total Population	49,386,799 (2011)
Districts	26
Official Language	Telugu
Emblem	Poorna Ghatam
Motto	Satyameva Jayate
Animal	Blackbuck
Bird	Rose-ringed Parakeet
Fish	Striped Murrel
Tree	Neem
Flower	Jasmine
Fruit	Mango
Sport	Kabbadi
Festival	Ugadi
Song	Maa Telugu Thalliki
Dance	Kuchipudi
Airport	Cuddapah, Kurnool, Rajahmundry, Tirupati Vijayawada, Vishakhapatnam

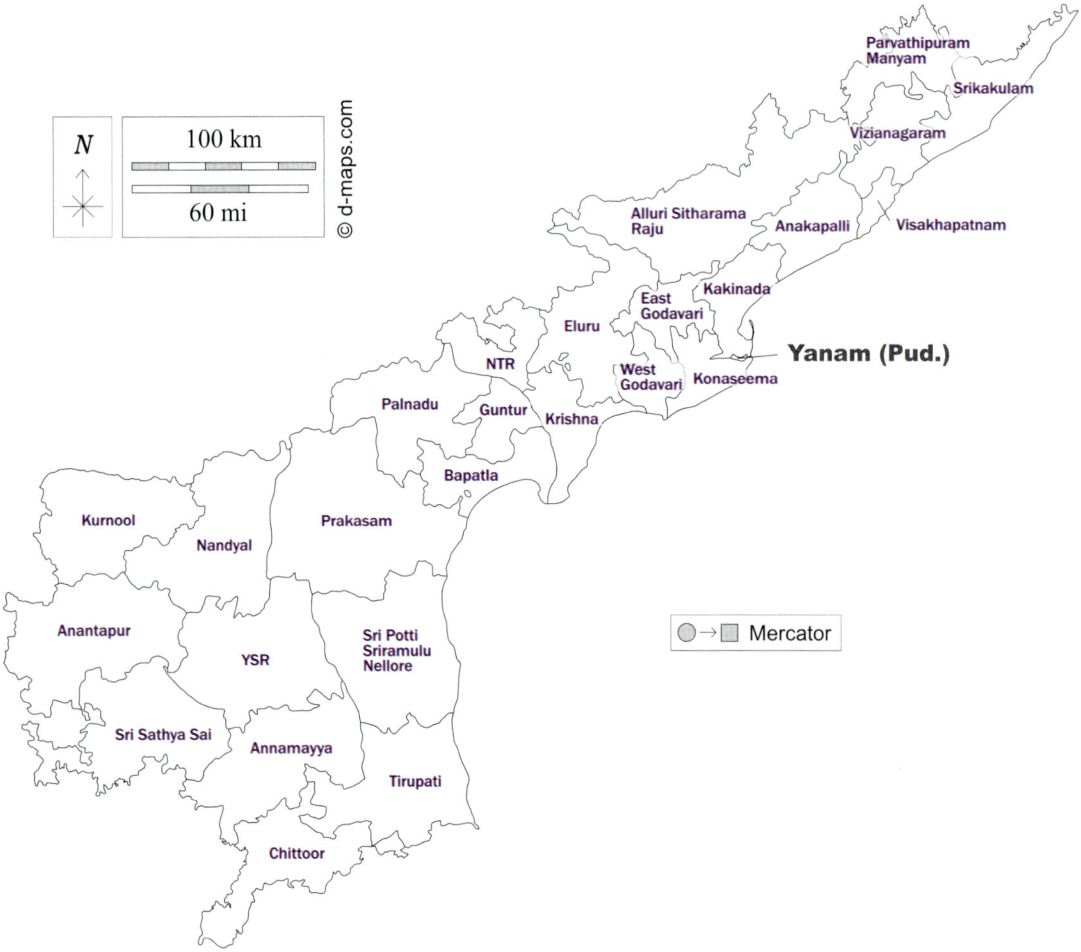
N
100 km
60 mi
© d-maps.com
Parvathipuram Manyam
Srikakulam
Vizianagaram
Alluri Sitharama Raju
Anakapalli
Visakhapatnam
Kakinada
East Godavari
Eluru
Yanam (Pud.)
NTR
West Godavari
Konaseema
Palnadu
Guntur
Krishna
Bapatla
Kurnool
Nandyal
Prakasam
Anantapur
YSR
Sri Potti Sriramulu Nellore
Mercator
Sri Sathya Sai
Annamayya
Tirupati
Chittoor

DISTRICT – ANANTHAPURAMU (Railway Station – Sai P Nilayam/Hindupur/Tadipatri/Kadiri)

S. No.	Temple	Address	Type
1	ISKCON	Hare Krishna Land, N.H.-7, Somaladoddi – 515004	Radha-Krishna
2	Kumbakarna Garden	Penukonda - 515110	Garden, Jain
3	Lord Hanuman Vigraha	Puttaparthi – 515134	Hanuman
4	Sri Sathya Sai Prasanthi Nilayam	Puttaparthi - 515134	Sathya Sai Baba
5	Madhavaraya Temple	Gorantla - 515231	Vishnu
6	Doddeswara Swamy Temple	Hemavathi - 515286	Shiva
7	Veerabhadra Temple	Lepakshi - 515331	Shiva
8	Chintala Venkataramana Temple	Tadpatri – 515411	Vishnu
9	Yadiki Caves	Yadiki Caves - 515408	Cave
10	Sri Ranganatha Swamy Temple	Alurkonda, Tadpatri – 515411	Vishnu
11	Sri Anjaneya Swamy Temple	Gugudu - 515425	Hanuman, Chavdi
12	Thimmamma Marrimanu	Gootibylu – 515521	Banyan Tree
13	Sri Kadiri Laxmi Narasimha Swamy Temple	Kadiri – 515591	Vishnu
14	Sri Laxmi Chennakeshwara Temple	Dharmavaram – 515671	Vishnu
15	Mounagiri Hanuman Temple	Hampapuram - 515722	Hanuman
16	Sri Nettikanti Anjaneya Swami Vari Devasthanam	Kasapuram – 515803	Hanuman
17	Jambu Dweepa	Konakondla – 515842	Jain

ISKCON AT HARE KRISHNA LAND, SOMALADODDI – The Temple is one of the beautiful Temples of ISKCON. The Temple is in the shape of a horse-drawn chariot with statues of four huge horses at the entrance. This Temple is known as the Radha Parthasarathi Temple and was inaugurated in February 2008. The Temple is dedicated to Lord Krishna and is focused on spreading the beliefs of 'Krishna Consciousness', a belief that Lord Krishna is the supreme power, over all others. The beautiful Temple looks even more scintillating at night when lights illuminate its walls. The most cherished festival is Janmashtami, the birthday of Lord Krishna.

PENUKONDA - It is one of the early capitals of the Vijayanagara Empire and the Fort was impregnable during its time. The two most noteworthy sights in the Fort are the "Gagan Mahal", the summer resort of the Kings and "Babayya Darga" a splendid example for communal harmony. Here, Kumbakarna Garden was spread over 5 acres. It has a gigantic statue of the sleeping Kumbakarna, measuring 142 feet in length and 32 feet in height into whose cavernous belly one can walk into it. Several asuras are seen trying to wake up the sleeping giant. The famous Pache Parsvanath Swamy Temple, with vigraha of Lord Parsvanath containing a single green coloured stone (Pacha) is located here. According to the inscription on the vigraha, it was consecrated in A.D. 1359, by a disciple of Mula Sangh Nandisangha's Balatkara Gana, Saraswathi Gachha, Kondakundanvaya's Priyarajaguru Mandalacharya Maghanandi Siddantha Deva. It was once the seat of a Jain Bhattaraka. Also located here is the historic Ajitnath Temple from the same period.

LORD HANUMAN VIGRAHA AT PUTTAPARTHI – It is located on the top of Vidya Giri Hill overlooking the Sri Sathya Sai Prasanthi Nilayam. The height of the Vigraha is 59 Foot.

SRI SATHYA SAI PRASANTHI NILAYAM AT PUTTAPARTHI - It is the abode of Puttaparthy Sri Sathya Sai Baba, drawing devoted disciples from all over the world. The Baba is credited with acute powers. On Sivarathri, on the birth day of the Baba and particularly during Dasara, quite a large number of devotees visit the place. A beautiful mantapa by name" Poornachandra" is constructed in which a large number of Baba devotees would assemble and perform "Bhajana" on festival days. One of the most beautiful structures in Ashram, is the Chaitanya Jyoti Museum, which houses all stories and incidents of the life of Sai Baba, all the way from his early childhood.

Dhanvantari Vigraha - Dhanvantari is the god of Ayurveda & incarnation of Lord Vishnu. He, during the samudramanthan, arose from the ocean of milk with the nectar of immortality. The Govt. of India has declared that Dhanvantari Trayodashi Kumara every year would be celebrated as National Ayurveda Day.

MADHAVARAYA TEMPLE AT GORANTLA - The Temple was built by King Narasimha of the Saluva dynasty of the Vijayanagara empire in Saka 1276 (1354 A.D). The most ornamental and interesting portion of the building is the pillared porch in front. The plain portions of the massive pillars are decorated with bas-relief sculptures representing scenes from Ramayana and Puranas. The entrances are richly carved with Vaishnava figures. The Garbha Griha has a small vigraha of Lord Madavaraya. Large stepped well in front of the Temple is another interesting place within compound, the holy water in the well, famous among locals for skin diseases.

DODDESWARA SWAMY TEMPLE AT HEMAVATHI – The Temple was built during the Pallava Reign. The stone used in making the vigrahas sounds like metal when stuck & is also remarkably polished. A Nandi made of black basalt granite, 8 ft. in length & 4 ft. in height sits at the entrance. There is a 6 ft. tall Lingam installed inside the sanctum sanctorum. The Temple area houses two other Temples dedicated to Lord Shiva called the Siddeswara Swamy Temple & Mallikarjuna Swamy Temple. There is a Museum in side which has rare vigrahas of historical importance of display.

VEERABHADRA TEMPLE AT LEPAKSHI - Built in the 16th CE, the architectural features of the Temple are in the Vijayanagara style with profusion of carvings & paintings at almost every exposed surface of the Temple. It is one of the centrally protected monuments of national importance. There is a very large Nandi about 200 metres away from the Temple which is carved from a single block of stone, which is said to be one of the largest of its type in the world. According to Skanda Purana, the Temple is one of the divyakshetras, an important pilgrimage site of Lord Shiva. The vigrahas on the pillars and walls are of divine beings, saints, guardians, musicians, dancers & 14 avatars of Lord Shiva. Figurines of the Goddesses Ganga & Yamuna flank the entrance to the sanctum. The presiding deity deified in the

sanctum sanctorum is a near life-size vigraha of Veerabhadra, fully armed & decorated with skulls. There is a cave chamber in the sanctum where sage Agasthya is said to have lived when he installed the vigraha of the Linga. Within the Temple complex, on the eastern wing, there is a separate chamber with Lord Shiva & his consort Parvathi carved on a boulder. In another shrine there is an vigraha of Lord Vishnu. Within the Temple precincts, to its eastern side, there is huge boulder of granite stone which has carving of coiled multi-hooded serpent providing an umbrella cover over a Linga.

BUGGA RAMALINGESWARA SWAMY TEMPLE AT TADIPATRI - The Temple is dedicated to Lord Shiva. It is situated on the southern bank of the Penna River. It was built between 1490 and 1509 by Pemmasani Ramalinga Nayudu-I, a Pemmasani Nayaka chieftain of the Gutti-Gandikota region during the reign of the Vijayanagara Empire. The presiding deity is a Linga, considered to be 'swayambhu' (naturally occurring or self originated). The Temple has seven small independent pillars in front of the Lord Vishnu shrine and when struck they produce 'saptaswara' (the seven musical notes). The gopurams of the Temple are unfinished & were described by architectural historian James Anderson as 'wonders'. The Temple consists of a sanctum, ardhmandapa, and mukhamandapa in an axial line. The Temple contains bas relief structures illustrating episodes from Ramayana and Mahabharata. Unlike other Hindu Temples where the deities are east-facing, in this Temple the Shiva linga faces west.

CHINTALA VENKATARAMANA TEMPLE AT TADPATRI - The Temple is dedicated to Lord

Venkateswara, a form of Lord Vishnu, who is referred to as Chintala Venkataramana. It is situated on banks of river Penna which is passing through the town. The Temple is known for its granite sculptures and is classified as one of the Monuments of National importance by Archaeological Survey of India. The Temple has a Garuda mantapa built as Chariot with rotating granite wheels which is similar to the one found in Vithala Temple of Hampi.

YADIKI CAVES - It is midway between Gooty and Tadipatri. The cave system is in the picturesque village of Konapulappadu. The magnificent view of the hillocks, gorges, spring, paddy fields, lake and winding roads enthral every visitor. Geemanugavi Cave is 5 KMs. in length and one can go up to 2 KMs. inside. The intricate design of stalactite and stalagmite formations takes shape of chandeliers, bridges, globes, snakes etc. The sight of some, which glitters like diamonds is amazing. Udamanugavi, another cave, can accommodate 100 people. Kona Ramalingeswara Temple adjacent to the spring adds to the beauty.

SRI RANGANATHA SWAMY TEMPLE AT ALURKONA – The Temple is built on the top of the hill by Yerramaraju, a Chiefttain of Bukkarayalu in 1330. There is a waterfall nearby with perennial spring. It is not only a pilgrim centre but also a picnic spot on account of the scenic beauty of the place. Thousands of pilgrims visit the place all round the year and perform marriages and religious ceremonies. The annual Brahmostavam Festival is being celebrated on Chitra Suddah Pournima (Usually in April) attracts huge congregation.

GUGUDU - The village is situated among the Mutchukota Hills. It is known for its Sri Kullai Swamy, the name of the much venerated saint. Barren women are said to become fertile by paying a visit to the shrine. There is also Sri Anjaneya Swamy Temple near by the abode of Sri Kullai Swamy Chavidi.

THIMMAMMA MARRIMANU AT GUTIBAILU - It is a huge banyan tree and the name of this tree is preserved by the local people since ancient times. The word 'marri' means banyan and 'manu' means tree in Telugu language. Many people visit the place to worship and to let their souls relax in the peaceful ambience. The route is quite exciting while getting here as it goes through fields and little villages.

SRI KADIRI LAXMI NARASIMHA SWAMY TEMPLE AT KADIRI - Kadiri is the holy shrine where Lord Vishnu set foot and handed over the Utsavamoorthis to Brugu Maharshi for his daily worship. Special Poojas are performed during Dassera and Sakranthi. There are several sacred thirthas connected to the Temple.

SRI LAXMI CHENNAKESHWARA TEMPLE AT DHARMAVARAM – It is renowned for its architectural brilliance and for the perennial waterspout and pillars, which produces seven different musical notes when struck. Nearest Railway Station is Dharmavaram.

MOUNAGIRI HANUMAN TEMPLE AT HAMPAPURAM - The Temple is dedicated to Lord Hanuman. The Temple displays millennia of traditional Hindu and Andhra culture, spirituality and architecture. The main monument, at the center of the Temple, is 39 feet (12 m) high, made from a single stone. The Temple is located in a peaceful environment outside of the city with out any disturbances occurring.

SRI NETTIKANTI ANJANEYA SWAMI VARI DEVASTHANAM AT KASAPURAM - Hindu pilgrims from several parts of Anantapur, Kurnool and Bellary districts congregate here in large number specially on Saturdays and worship the deity, besides performing marriages and tonsure ceremonies. Even Muslims of the surrounding areas visit the place and make their offerings to this deity. A huge procession is taken out once in a year on the day next to the Telugu New Year Day. Nearest Railway Station is Guntakal.

JAMBU DWEEPA AT KONAKONDLA - The Jain Mythical cosmo graphical diagram of Jambu Dweepa engraved on a stone on the top of the hill Alchemists at Konakondla village in Vajrakarur Mandal which was identified by Sri R.V. Chakravarthy, Head Master, Parishad High School, Konakondla in the year 1966. The pilgrims, especially south Indian Jain pilgrims are mostly attracted by this Jambu Dweepa. Adjacent to this, there are Kambam Narasimha Swamy Hills, Rasasidda hillock & Kari Basappa hillock. There is a Thirthanka Temple with vigrahas of Thirthankaras on Rasasidda hillock. This may belong to 13th CE A.D. Nearest Railway Station is Guntakal.

DISTRICT – CHITTOOR (Railway Station – Chittoor / Pakala / Vayalpad / Katpadi / Tirupati)

Chittoor is known for its many Temples that offer a sense of tranquillity to its visitors. The landscape is covered with huge igneous rocks and as per legend these rocks are said to have been left by giants who used to play with them. The prime attraction in Chittoor is the Lord Shiva Temple at Kalavagunta, which dates back to 7^{th}century. Other Temples in the area include the Mogileshwara Shiva Temple and the Rama Temple at Venkatagiri. The Rama Temple has jasmine trees in the courtyard, which bloom all year round.

S. No.	Temple	Address	Type
1	Sri Swayambu Varasidhi Vinayakaswamy	Kanipakam - 517131, Irala Mandal	Ganesh
2	Sri Boyakonda Gangamma Vari Devasthanam	Diguvapalli Village, Chowdepalli Mandal – 517257	Mata
3	Sri Lakshmi Narasimha Swamy	Tarigonda - 517291, Vayalpadu	Vishnu
4	Chennakeshava Temple	Sompalem - 517390	Vishnu
5	Sri Pattabhi Rama Swamy	Valmikipuram – 517299	Ram
6	Sri Konetiraya Swamy	Keelapatla - 517408, Gangavaram	Vishnu
7	Sri Prasanna Venkateswara Swamy	Kosuvari Palle - 517418, Tamballapalle	Vishnu
8	Sri Kalyana Venkateswara Swamy	Srinivasa Mangapuram – 517501	Vishnu
9	Sri Bedi Anjaneya Swamy	Tirumala – 517501	Hanuman
10	Sri Bhu Varaha Swamy	Tirumala - 517501	Vishnu (wild boar)
11	Sri Venkateswara Swamy	Tirumala – 517501	Vishnu

S. No.	Temple	Address	Type
12	Alipiri Prasanna Anjaneya Swami	Tirupati – 517501	Hanuman
13	Sri Govindarajaswami	Tirupati -517501	Vishnu
14	ISKCON	Tirupati – 517501	Krishna
15	Sri Kapileswara Swamy	Tirupati – 517501	Shiva
16	Sri Kodanda Ramaswamy	Tirupati – 517501	Ram
17	Sri Tataiahgunti Gangamma Temple	Tirupati - 517501	Mata
18	Sri Ankaala Parameswari	Tiruchanoor - 517503	Mata
19	Sri Padmavathi Ammavari	Tiruchanoor - 517503	Mata
20	Sri Agastheshwara Swamy Temple	Tirupati Road, Thondavada - 517505	Shiva
21	Sri Parasurameswara Swamy Temple	Gudimallam – 517526	Shiva
22	Shiva Temple	Sri Bommarajapuram - 517571	Shiva
23	Sri Kalahastlswara Swamy Vari Devastanam	Sri Kalahasti - 517644	Shiva
24	Kailasakona	Narayanavaram – 517581	Narasimha
25	Sri Vedanarayana Temple	Nagalapuram - 517589	Vishnu

VINAYAKA TEMPLE AT KANIPAKAM – The Temple was constructed in the early 11th CE by the Chola king Kulothunga Chola-I & was expanded further in 1336 by the Emperors of Vijayanagara dynasty. As per legend, it is believed that the deity is Svayambhu. The deity is seen in the well with full of water always. The holy water from the well is offered to the devotees as theertham. A striking & strange feature of the Vigraha is that it is growing in size. At present, we can see the knees & the abdomen of the Vigraha. Long ago there lived two brothers Sankha & Likhita. They were on a pilgrimage to Kanipakam. As the journey was tiring, the younger brother Likhita felt hungry. Disregarding the advice of the elder brother he plucked a mango from the mango grove. Sankha felt bad & reported this to the ruler of that area & pleaded for punishment for the sin committed during pilgrimage. Thus Likhita was punished severely being deprived of both arms. Later they took bath in the river near Kanipakam Temple. Lo Behold! The chopped arms were restored to Likhita as soon as he had a dip in the sacred waters of the river. These incidents lead the ruler to rename the river as 'Bahuda' (Bahu means human arm). Thus the river beside Kanipakam Temple is now known as 'Bahuda River'. Day to day disputes between people is resolved by taking a 'special oath'. The people in the dispute take a holy dip in the Temple tank & swear before the lord. It is taken as gospel truth. There are instances when the person who committed that sin voluntarily agrees as soon as he had the dip & much before entering the Temple itself. It seems the Lord lawns invisibly on the sinner & makes him repent & feel guilty for his sinful deeds.

SRI BOYAKONDA GANGAMMA VARI DEVASTHANAM AT DIGUVAPALLI - The Temple of Goddess Gangamma is one of the many ancient Temples located on top of a mountain. The word "Baikonda" pronounced as "Baa-ee-kon-da" means mountain which has a well. The Goddess resides right besides this well & is believed to be very powerful. The goddess is known to destroy all evil & those who sincerely worship her are bound to succeed. Her Temple is dedicated to the sister of Lord Venkateswara. Devotees come here & make their wishes and once the wish comes true they come back to make an offering to the Goddess which they would have agreed upon once their wish

became true. The water from the well is believed to cure many skin ailments. Local people believe that the Pushkarini water is very powerful & sprinkling it in the field will yield good crop. Devotees can test whether their wishes will be fulfilled by placing a flower on the head of the deity. Locals believe that if the flower falls on the right side it is positive & negative if it falls on the left. The offering for the Goddess is generally a hen or a sheep which will be sacrificed to the Goddess & the meat will be cooked at the same place & shall be eaten by all the family members who would have come along. Once a year the Temple Navartri festival brings in lakhs of people from all over India, particularly the South India.

SRI LAKSHMI NARASIMHA SWAMY TEMPLE AT TARIGONDA - This Temple is said to have built by Sage Durvasa some thousands of years ago. As per the inscriptions, as the presiding deity was found in a pot of butter milk, Tari-Butter Milk, Kunda-Pot, the place became popular as "Tarigonda". According to legend, during the period of Cholas, there used to be a cattle rearer Rama Naidu in Chitticherla village. On a fine day, when he was skimming the buttermilk, he found the lord emerged from it. However, he threw it away thinking as a stone. The same thing repeated on next day also & he repeated the same thing. On that night, Lord appeared in his dream & told him that He was in "Marella Gavi" (hole) located near Tarigonda & asked Rama Naidu to construct a Temple for him with the treasure present in the hole. Rama Naidu who shared his dream with villagers, went to the spot next day & found the treasure in the huge hole & constructed the Temple.

CHENNAKESHAVA TEMPLE AT SOMPALEM - The Temple is truly a Vijayanagara era gem. Among its features, the most striking are the Garuda Sthambha, Kalyana Mantapa, Stone Chariot & the morals depicting episodes of Ramayana. At nearly in 60ft. in height the monolithic pillar is intricately carved with the Makara Mascot and Garuda. There is another Temple in the village which is known as the Kote Chowdeshwari Temple.

SRI PATTABHI RAMA SWAMY TEMPLE AT VALMIKIPURAM - This is a unique Temple, where the presiding deity of Lord Rama is seen along with Sita Devi, Sri Lakshamana, Bharata & Shatrughna. Since, the main deity of Lord Rama holds sword in his hand, the deity is remarkably known as "Pratapa Rama". As per inscriptions, this ancient Temple was built by Sri Jambavantha in Treta Yuga as a mark of his respect towards Lord Rama. After his victory over Ravanasura, Lord Rama returned to Ayodhya & adorned the throne. This Temple is said to have been built in connection with the coronation ceremony of Lord Rama & hence the presence of all his brothers along with Sita Devi is significantly seen in this Temple. The legend also says that Lord Rama expressed himself before Sage Valmiki in this pious place before the later commenced penning Srimad Ramayanam. So this place is named after the sage as "Valmikipuram". The Temple was patronized by Cholas & Vijayanagara rulers & is an architectural marvel. The Temple "Vimanam" is considered here as "Sudarshana Vimanam" & is said to be most powerful.

SRI KONETIRAYA SWAMY TEMPLE AT KEELAPATLA - The significant feature of this Temple is that the presiding deity is a look-like of Tirumala Sri Venkateswara Swamy. According to legend, the presiding deity is said to have been consecrated by Sage Bhrigu. Later, the Temple was constructed by Cholas & then by Vijayanagara rulers. To protect the presiding deity from Muslim invasion, it was preserved safely in the Temple tank & later it was re-consecrated. As the deity was protected in the Temple tank-Koneru, the presiding deity is known as "Konetiraya Swamy".

SRI PRASANNA VENKATESWARA SWAMY TEMPLE AT KOSUVARI PALLE - The presiding deity of this Temple will be seen along with Goddess Padmavathi Devi and the deity is about 5.6 foot in height. History reveals that the deity was consecrated by Vengi Cholas while Sri Achyuta Devaraya built the Temple in the year 1462 AD. This Temple is also known as "Tiruvengalanadha" Temple.

SRI KALYANA VENKATESWARA SWAMY TEMPLE AT SRINIVASA MANGAPURAM - This ancient Temple which is under the control of ASI is maintained by Tirumala Tirupati Devasthanams since 1967 and utsavams & rituals in this Temple are being performed since 1981. Today, this Temple is considered sacred, next to Tirumala Temple. Those who are unable to make it to Tirumala can have darshan of Lord Sri Kalyana Venkateswara Swamy to fulfil their wish. As the name indicates, this Temple carries significance for newlywed couples. Newlyweds offer prayers first in this Temple as this is the place where Lord Sri Kalyana Venkateswara Swamy with Padmavathi Devi stayed for six months, just after their wedding. After celebrating his marriage with Goddess Padmavathi, Lord Venkateswara did not return to Tirumala hills, but instead, he visited the sage Agasthya's ashram to seek blessings. Over the wish of sage Agastya, Lord Venkateswara along with his consort stayed at his ashram which has now become the famous Temple. While returning to the Tirumala Temple, Lord Venkateswara blessed the place with two boons : 1. The newly weds and elderly who are not able to visit Tirumala can get the same benefits through visiting Sri Kalyana Venkateswara Swamy Temple. 2. A devotee who takes part in the Kalyanautsasvam and ties a 'kaappu' on their hand, can find their best, most beloved life-partner or find new happiness from their existing relationship.

SRI BEDI ANJANEYA SWAMY TEMPLE AT TIRUMALA - Sri Bedi Anjaneya Swamy Temple is located exactly to the opposite of Lord Sri Venkateswara Swamy Temple in Tirumala. This ancient Temple enjoys priority after Sri Bhu Varaha Swamy Temple and Lord Sri Venakteswara Swamy Temple. According to the legend, Lord Hanuman in his youthful age wanted to leave Tirumala in search of a camel. This forced his mother Anjana Devi to tie his hands with cuffs and order him to stay in that place till she returned. However, it is believed that Anjana Devi stayed back in Akasa Ganga area and never returned to this place. Hence, the icon of Lord Hanuman in this Temple will be seen in a unique form where both his hands were handcuffed ("Bedi-Cuffs").

SRI BHU VARAHA SWAMY TEMPLE AT TIRUMALA - This Temple is located on the banks of Swami Pushkarini, in the sacred Seven Hills. The presiding deity is Sri Bhu Varaha Swamy, an incarnation of Lord Sri Maha Vishnu in the form of a wild boar. Sri Bhu Varaha Swamy was residing on the hills when Lord Sri Venkateswara Swamy descended onto the earth. According to the legend, Tirumala was originally called "Adivarahakshetra" (dwelling place of Sri Bhu Varaha Swamy). According to Brahmapurana, it is Lord Sri Bhu Varaha Swamy who granted land to Lord Sri Venkateswara Swamy on his request to reside in the sacred Seven Hills. As a thanks giving gesture, Lord Sri Venkateswara Swamy had gifted the privilege of first darshan & first naivedyam to Lord Sri Bhu Varaha Swamy. Thus as per the tradition, it is imperative for the pilgrims to pay a visit to Sri Bhu Varaha Swamy before visiting Lord Sri Venkateswara Swamy.

SRI VENKATESWARA SWAMY TEMPLE AT TIRUMALA - The hill shrine of Tirumala is accredited as being the most visited Temple in India and also in the world as a whole. Located on the picturesque Seshachalam Hill Ranges, this Temple occupies a unique place in our great land of holy shrines. The "Temple Legend" is made out of references from a range of ancient scriptures such as Varaha Purana, Padma Purana, Garuda Purana, Brahmanda Purana, Markandeya Purana, Harivamsa Purana, Vamana Purana, Brahma Purana, Brahmottara Purana, Aditya Purana, Skanda Purana

and Bhavishyottara Purana. These extracts describe the sanctity and antiquity of the deity, Temple and the hills around Tirumala, besides the numerous teerthams, streams and springs that abound them.

Akasa Raja had no children. As part of the yaga, he was ploughing the fields, he found a baby in a lotus flower and named her Alarmelmangai (Lady born in Lotus petals) and adopted her as his daughter. Lord Vishnu reincarnated as Srinivasa (or presented himself after penance in the ant-hill) as the son of an elderly woman-saint Vakula Malika Devi. Vakula Devi was Yasoda in her previous birth, Lord Krishna's foster-mother and was unhappy in that life for not seeing his marriage. As per the boon received from Lord Krishna, she was reborn as Vakula Devi and enjoyed the rare spectacle of witnessing the celestial wedding of the divine couple. In course of time, Princess Padmavati grew up into a beautiful maiden and was visited by Saint Narada. On reading her palm, he foretold that she was destined to be the spouse of Lord Vishnu himself. In due time, Lord Srinivasa on a hunting spree was chasing a wild elephant in the forest. The elephant led him into a garden where Princess Padmavati and her maids were playing. The sight of the elephant frightened them and their Princess. When Lord Srinivasa appeared in front of the Elephant, it immediately turned round, saluted the Lord and disappeared into the forest. Lord Srinivasa noticed princess Padmavathi and enquired about her from her maids. Enthralled by her bewitching beauty, Lord Srinivasa lost interest in other activities and told his foster mother Vakula Devi about his love for Padmavathi. He also revealed his identity as Lord Vishnu and narrated her about her past life as his foster-mother then as Yasodha. Vakuladevi left her hermitage to approach Akasa Raja with the marriage proposal of marriage between Lord Srinivasa and Padmavathi. In the meantime, an anxious Lord Srinivasa came to the city in the disguise of a lady fortune-teller. Princess Padmavathi also lost her heart to Lord Srinivasa and fell ill after returning to the palace. Unable to diagnose her ill-health, the maids invited the fortune-teller into the palace to foretell the future of their princess. When the Lord in the guise of a lady fortune-teller revealed that Padmavathi was born with a cause to marry Lord Vishnu in his current avatar as Lord Srinivasa, she recovered and regaled in joy. As the king heard of this news, Vakula revealed her to the King and asked for his daughter's hand in marriage to her son, Lord Srinivasa. The overjoyed king gleefully agreed and his advisor Bhrihaspati wrote the invitation for the wedding between the two celestial beings of Srinivasa and Padmavathi. Lord Srinivasa called for a conference of the Gods to declare his marriage with Princess Padmavati. According to mythologies, the Lord also obtained a huge loan from Kubera, the god of wealth, towards meeting the expenses for the divine and grand wedding matching his stature as the supreme lord of the universe.

Lord Sri Venkateswara, also known as Venkatachalapati, Srinivasa & Balaji, made Tirumala his abode 5000 years ago. Even before him, it was Lord Varahaswami who had made Tirumala his abode. Since then, many devotees have continued to construct grand entrances on the ramparts of the Temple over generations. In Tirumala, the East facing Sri Varahaswami Temple is located in the North West of Swami Pushkarini. As per legend, Lord Srinivasa sought a gift of land from Sri Varahaswami, which he readily granted. In return, Srinivasa provided him with an agreement deed assuring that he would be paid the 1st darshan, worship and offerings by all the devotees visiting the Temple. This tradition is in practise to this day at Tirumala & Lord Varahaswami continues to receive the age old traditional worship. Even today, all offerings are first made to Lord Varahaswami and then to Lord Sri Venkateswara.

As per strong belief & faith of devotees, some of the facts and secrets of Sree Tirupati Balaji are : a) Shila Toranam is the natural arch of Tirumala Hills & is a National Geo Heritage Monument. It is one of the oldest & rarest geological formation and natural wonders of the world. It is said that the arch is of same height, as the height of the Vigraha of Sree Tirupati Balaji. Sree Vankateswara Swami's face is clearly visible in this natural rock formation. b) Sree Vankateswara is seen standing in the center of the Garbha Griha but his standing in the corner in the right side. The lamps that burn inside the Garbha Griha are never extinguished and no one knows that how many thousands years, they have been burning. c) Their is a village 23 KMs away from the holy Temple and no outsider can enter into this village. Flower, Milk, Ghee, Makhan & all samagri brought from there are offered to Sree Venkateswara. d) Sree Venkateswara has silky hair on his head and does not get entangled in him and he always looks fresh. e) The Vigraha is adorned daily with pachai karpooram, which is highly reactive & leads to crack on a stone but the Vigraha of the Lord remain un-effected. f) The back of the main Vigraha always remain moist. The sound of the wave can be heared after listening carefully. g) After the morning Abhishekam, the Vigraha sweat & the sweat is wiped with a silk cloth. h) The flowers used in the Garbha Griha are never brought out from it and these are immersed in an small water fall that exist behind the Vigraha of Lord without looking back. i) Goddess Laxmi resides on Sree Venkateswara's chest. Every Thursday, Lord Balaji is decorated with Sandalwood at the time of Nijarup darshan. On removing the Sandalwood, Goddess Laxmi comes down on it. j) Garuda is vahana of Sree Venkateswara & surprisingly, there is a hill in Tirumala feature a natural rock formation like Garuda. k) Tirupati Ladoo has a GI Patent.

AKASA GANGA - The blissful waterfalls of Akasa Ganga is one of the most sacred waterfronts in India and lies at the foothills of Venkatadri Tirumala. Visited by everyone who comes to seek the blessings of Lord Venkateshwara, the presiding deity of the city, the waterfall provides water for the Lord's bath as well. The place has been mentioned in the Vedas and it is believed that the falls originated from the holy feet of Lord Venkateshwara. It is said that in the earlier days, the priests of the Temple carried water from here to the Temple in the wee hours of the morning. This custom is still in play but restricted to special occasions only. Devotees come to this waterfalls to bathe as they believe that their sins are washed away when they take a dip in the holy water. Another belief says that if childless parents tie a cradle to a tree near the falls, they will conceive shortly.

ALIPIRI PRASANNA ANJANEYA SWAMI TEMPLE – It is located at the 7th mile on first ghat road. The Temple is dedicated to Lord Anjaneya. The vigraha of Lord Anjaneya is very tall and is located in a scenic environment.

SRI GOVINDARAJASWAMI TEMPLE AT TIRUPATI - Renowned Vaishnavaite Saint Sri Ramanujacharya consecrated this Temple in 1130 AD. Before Lord Sri Govindaraja Swamy, Sri Parthasarathi Swamy was the presiding deity of this Temple. When South India was invaded by Muslim rulers, the presiding deity of Chidambaram, Sri Govindaraja Swamy was brought and kept safely in Tirupati. After the situation at Chidambaram returned to normalcy, the vigraham of Lord Sri Govindaraja Swamy was taken back to Chidambaram from Tirupati. Sri Govindaraja Swamy is the elder brother of Sri Venkateswara Swamy, who accomplished the ever-magnificent marriage between Sri Venkateswara Swamy and Padmavathi Ammavaru. Hence Sri Govindaraja Swamy is considered to be the god who helps you to elevate your wealth and manage the wealth acquired efficiently.

Narasimha Tirtha - The Tirtha is dedicated to Sri Govindaraj Swamy. It is located on the banks of a pond Machineella Gunta. It is believed that the vigraha is very huge and more than 1000 years old and it is the original vigraha of Sri Govindaraj Swamy which was brought from Chidambaram after a conflict between Shaivas & Vaishnavas.

ISKCON AT TIRUPATI – ISKCON has established a famous & magnificent Temple of Sri Radha-Krishna at Tirupati.

SRI KAPILESWARA SWAMY TEMPLE AT TIRUPATI - Kapila Theertham is a famous Saivite Temple and Theertham. The Vigraha is believed to be installed by Kapila Muni and hence Lord Siva here is referred to as Kapileswara. Greatness of Lord Sri Kapileswara was mentioned in the Kulothunga Chola inscriptions. These are the most ancient inscriptions among all the inscriptions found in the Temple and belong to the 10th century. The Temple stands at the entrance to a mountain cave in one of the steep and vertical faces at the foot of the Tirumala hills, where the waters of the mountain stream fall directly into Temple Pushkarini known as "*Kapila Theertham*". A huge stone Vigraha of a seated bull "Nandi", Shiva's steed, greets devotees and passers-by at the entrance to the Temple. According to Temple Legend Kapila Muni had

performed penance to Lord Siva at this place and blessed with the Muni's devotion, Lord Siva and Parvathi presented themselves. The Lingam is believed to be self-manifested. Kapila muni is believed to emerge from the Bilam (Cavity) in the Pushkarini (Theertham) on to the earth. It is believed that persons bathing in it will attain salvation from the cycle of birth and death ('Brahmaloka'). Moreover, those who have never offered Pindam (thidhi or thadhhina) to their departed ancestor souls can do it here and wash off your sins for non-performance of it in past. There are many sub-shrines with-in the main Temple premises. Temples for Kamakshi-concert of Shiva, Vinayaka, Subhramanya, Agasthesswara, Rukmini Satyabhama Sametha Sri Krishna are few among them.

SRI KODANDA RAMASWAMY TEMPLE AT TIRUPATI - The vigrahas of Lord Sri Kodandarama Swamyvaru, Goddess Sita Ammavaru and Sri Lakshmana Swamyvaru were installed during the regime of Chola Emperor. This Temple which has a glorious history of over one thousand years was built by the Chola kings in 10th century A.D. This Temple was well developed by various kings especially by Sri Krishna Deva Raya in 15h century. The symbols and raja mudrikas of Vijaya Nagara dynasty can be seen on the rock walls of the outer mandapas. There is an Anjaneya Swamy Temple located just opposite to the Temple.

SRI TATAIAHGUNTI GANGAMMA DEVI TEMPLE AT TIRUPATI - The Temple is dedicated to village Goddess of Tirupati who is believed to be the sister of Lord Venkateshwara. The Temple is located on the banks of Thathaya Gunta. Ganga Jathara is a very famous local festival and it is held every year in the month of may.

SRI ANKAALA PARAMESWARI TEMPLE AT TIRUCHANOOR - The Temple is an ancient Temple which has been renovated recently. The Temple is dedicated to the Goddess. The Temple is located near Tukeevakam at Tirupati Highway.

SRI PADMAVATHI AMMAVARI TEMPLE AT TIRUCHANOOR - Tiruchanoor, is one of the oldest pilgrim towns, is abode of Goddess Sri Padmavathi Devi, consort of Lord Venkateswara. This pilgrim centre is popularly known as "Alarmelmangapuram" (Alar-Lotus, Mel-top, Manga-Goddess, Puram-town) or Alimelumangapuram. As per legend as Goddess Mahalakshmi emerged on the golden lotus as Padmavathi Devi located at the centre of Padmasarovaram, this place became famous by the name "Alarmelmangapuram". There is a strong belief that the pilgrims should pave visit to Padmavathi & seek

her divine blessings before they visit Lord Venkateswara at Tirumala. The Temple was constructed in the time of Tondaman Chakravarthi, who happens to be the elder brother of Goddess Padmavathi.

SRI AGASTHESHWARA SWAMY TEMPLE AT THONDAVADA – The Temple is a sacred shrine lies at the confluence of three rivers Swarnamukhi, Bhima & Kalyani in Chandragirimandal. The Sivalingam in this Temple was installed by Agasthya Mahamuni. This Temple faces east & has almost all parivaradevathas installed in well-built places. Just opposite the Aalaya & in the middle of River, there is a mandapam. In this, you can see the beautiful vigrahas of Lord Balaji, Ayyappa, Ganapati etc. There is also a small shrine of Lord Rama, Sita, Lakshmana & Anjaneya. Unlike other Temples, here Goddess Maragadhavalli appears to the left hand side of Lord Agastheeshwara Swamy resembling the sitting posture of a Bride and a Bride groom in a marriage. Instead of Navagrahas, the Sapthamathrukas were installed here. They are Kowmari, Vaishnavi, Vaarahi, Bramhi, Mahedri, Mahishwari & Chamundi. Nearest Railway Station is Renigunta.

SRI PARASURAMESWARA SWAMY TEMPLE AT GUDIMALLAM - The Village is situated on the banks of Suvaranamukhi River. The village has a beautiful Shiva Temple. The main importance of the Temple lies in the Linga which is housed in the Garbhagriha. The Gudimallam Temple is considered to be the oldest Shiva Temple identified so far tracing to 3rd CE BC. Legend has it that Parashuram's mother Renuka was suspected of infidelity by her husband Sage Jamadagni. The Sage ordered Parashurama to behead his mother. Parashurama obeyed his father & when Sage Jamadagni wanted to reward his son, Parashurama asked him to bring his mother back to life and she was brought back to life but Parashuram could not overcome guilt of beheading his mother & he felt remorse about his act. As a penance he was advised by other Rishis to worship Lord Shiva at Gudimallam. After searching for several days, Parashurama found the Temple in the middle of a forest. He dug a pond nearby & began his penance. Every day morning a single flower used to appear in the pond & Parashuram offered it to Lord Shiva. To guard the single flower, he appointed Chitrasena, a Yaksha. Chitrasena was actually a manifestation of Lord Brahma. Chitrasena had kept a condition that to guard the flower, he should be given an animal to eat and a pot of toddy. Parashuram agreed to it and he used to hunt an animal for Chitrasena daily. One day when Parshuram went out to hunt, Chitrasena felt tempted to worship Lord Shiva himself. He used the single flower to worship Lord Shiva. An enraged Parashurama attacked Chitrasena when he found the flower missing. Finding the transgression grievous, the Parshuram entered into a fierce fight with the demon. When the vanquished demon was about to be crushed, Lord Shiva appeared and blessed both with their desire of Sayujyamukti – merging in him. Brahma as Chitrasena, Vishnu as Parasurama & Shiva as the Lingam form the Gudimallam Shivalingam.

SHIVA TEMPLE AT SBR PURAM LAKE, PUTTUR - The Temple is dedicated to Lord Shiva. It is located in the middle of the lake. Nearest Railway Station is Puttur.

SRI KALAHASTHEESWARA SWAMY VARI DEVASTHANAM AT SRIKALAHASTI - It is one of the most famous Shiva Temples in South India & is said to be the site where Kannappa was ready to offer both his eyes to cover blood flowing from the Sivalinga before Lord Siva stopped him & granted him mukti. Srikalahasti Temple is famous for its Vayu Linga, one of the Panchabhoota Sthalams, representing wind. The Temple is also regarded as Rahu-KetuKshetra and Dakshina Kailasam. The inner Temple was constructed around 5th CE & the outer Temple was constructed in the 12th CE by the Chola Kings & the Vijayanagara Kings. Samba Siva said to Vayu for his penance, You are qualified for three boons. As per your wish, you will be spread throughout this world. Without you there will be no life. This Linga of mine will forever be known all over through your name & all Suras, Asuras, Garuda, Gaandharvas, Kinneras, Kimpurushas, Siddhas, Saadhvis, humans & others will worship this Lingam. This is the only Temple in India which remains open during Solar & lunar eclipses, while, all other Temples are closed. As per legend, Kalahatiswara was worshipped at this place by Brahma during all four Yugas. Arjuna during Mahabharata is believed to have worshipped the presiding deity. There are other legends attached to this Temple. The 120 ft. high main gopuram & the 100 pillar mandapam were constructed by Krishnadevaraya, the Vijayanagara King in 1516. The presiding vigraha of Lord Shiva in the form of Linga is made of white stone in a shape resembling trunk of elephant. The Temple faces south, while the sanctum faces west. There is a rock cut shrine of Vinayaka below the ground level. Vallaba Ganapathi, Mahalakshmi-Ganpathi & Sahasra Lingeswara are some of the rare images found in the Temple. There is a large shrine of Jnanaprasanammba, the consort of Kalahatisvara. There are smaller shrines in the Temple for Kasi Viswanatha, Annapurna, Suryanarayana, Sadyoganapathi & Subramanya. Nearest Railway Station is Sri Kalahasti.

NARAYANAVARAM GROUP OF TEMPLES -

Kailasakona - Kailasanatha Kona or Kailasa Kona is a beautiful waterfall. A Temple of Lord Shiva and Parvathi is seen nearby. This waterfall is having a height of around 40 feet. The specialty of the falls is that there is water all through the year. The water fall is attracting not only the people of nearby districts but also from Tamilnadu.

Singrikona - The place is famous for an ancient Temple of Sri Lakshmi Narasimha Swamy. The vigraha consecrated in the Garbha Griha is in standing posture which is very rare in the Temples of Sri Lakshmi Narasimha Swamy.

SRI VEDANARAYANA TEMPLE AT NANGALPURAM - The Temple had been built by Raja Krishna Deva Raya. The Temple is also known as Matsya Narayana Temple, as Lord Maha Vishnu is worshiped in the form of Matsya rupam here, the first incarnation. As per Sthalapuranam, Lord Maha Vishnu is Swayambhu here. During Mahapralayam, Lord Maha Vishnu tem Matsya avtaram and appeared before Satyavratha and asked him to save all Vedas from Pralayam. It is also believed that Lord Maha Vishnu in this form destroyed an asura, Somakudu here and retrieved all the Vedas hence Temple is known as Vedanarayana Perumal. Lord Maha Vishnu resides here with Sridevi and Bhudevi. Suryapooja utsavam is one of the important festival in the Temple during which sunrays directly fall at the feet of Lord Perumal on the first day, on the chest on the second day and on the forehead on the third day. This happens once in a year.

DISTRICT – EAST GODAVARI (Railway Station – Kakinada/Rajahmundry/Nidadhavolu)

S. No.	Temple	Address	Type
1	Sai Baba Vigraha	Repuru – 533006	Sai Baba
2	Maa Vishweshwari Shakti Peetha (Durga Kotilingala Veedhi)	Rajahmundry – 533101	Shakti Peetha
3	Markandeya Swamy Vari	Godavari Bund Rd, Mangalavaripeta, Rajahmundry – 533101	Shiva
4	Sri Rangadhamam Temple	Rajahmundry – 533101	Vishnu
5	Sri Umamarkendeyeswara Swamy Temple	Godavari Bund, Rajahmundry - 533105	Shiva
6	Sri Vighneswara Swamy Temple	Ainavalli Village & Mandal – 533211	Ganesh
7	Sri Veeraswara Swamy Vari	Muramalla - 533220, Amalapuram	Shiva
8	Sri Mandeswara Swamy Vari Devasthanam	Kothapeta Mandal, Mandapalli – 533223	Shiva
9	Sri Pallalamma Ammavari Devasthanam	Vanapalli (V), Kothapetha Mandal – 533228	Mata
10	Sri Umakoppeswara Swamy Temple	Kotipalli, Kothapeta Mandal - 533229	Shiva & Parvati
11	Jaganadh Swamy	Ryali - 533236, Amalapuram	Vishnu
12	Lord Venkateswara Swamy Varu	Vadapalli - 533237, Ravulapalem	Vishnu
13	Buddhist Stupa	Adurru – 533247	Buddhist
14	Sri Balaji Balaji Devasthanam	Appanapalli - 533247, Mamidikuduru Mandal	Vishnu
15	Sri Lakshmi Narasimha Swamy Vari Devasthanam	Antarvedi - 533252, Sakhinetipalli Mandal	Vishnu
16	Sri Bhimeswara Swamy Temple	Draksharama, Ramachandra Puram (M) – 533262	Shakti Peetha & Shiva
17	Sri Bapanamma Talli Temple	Seetha Palli - 533288	Mata
18	Sri Lakshmi Narasimha Swamy Temple	Korukonda – 533289	Vishnu

S. No.	Temple	Address	Type
19	Bali-Sugriva Konda	Maredumilli - 533295	Ramayana Circuit
20	Sri Ayyappa Swamy Varu	Kakinada-Rajahmundry Canal Road, Dwarapudi Village - 533341	Ayyappan (Vishnu)
21	Sri Vigneswara Swamu Varu	Bikkavolu - 533343, Kakinada	Ganesh
22	Sri Suryanarayana Swamy Temple	G. Mamidada Village - 533344, Pedapudi Mandal	Sun
23	Sri Talupulamma Ammavari Devasthanam	Lova - 533401, Tuni Mandal	Mata
24	Sri Veera Venkata Satyanarayana Swamy Vari Devasthanam	Annavaram – 533406	Vishnu (Satyanarayan)
25	Sri Srungara Vallabha Swamy Varu	Tholi Tirupati - 533433, Kakinada	Vishnu
26	Sri Hanuman Temple	Yerravaram – 533435	Hanuman
27	Sri Suryanarayana Swami Temple	Pandavula Metta - 533437, Peddapuram	Mahabharat Circuit
28	Sri Chalukya Kumararama Sri Bhimeswara Swamy Vari Temple	Samalkot - 533440, Kakinada	Shiva
29	Sri Prasanna Anjaneya Swamy Temple	Samalkot – 533440	Hanuman
30	Sri Kukkuteswara Swamy Devasthanam	Pithapuram – 533450	Maha Shakti Peetha

SAI BABA VIGRAHA AT REPURU – It is the tallest Vigraha of Sai Baba in the world. Height of the Vigraha is 116 foot. It was completed in the year 2015.

MAA VISHWESHWARI SHAKTI PEETHA AT RAJAHMUNDRY - The Godavari River is sacred to Hindus and has several pilgrimage centers on its banks. It is considered the Dakshin Ganges and Rajahmundry Dakshin Kasi. Godavari River (1465 KMs) is the second longest River next only to the River Ganga. Every twelve years, Pushkaram fair is held on its banks of the river. Godavari Tir Shakti Peeth or Sarvashail is the famous Shakti Peetha where it is said that the Left Cheek of Maa Sati fell and the vigrahas worshiped at this religious place are Vishweshwari (Vishweshi) or Rakini or Viswamatuka (The mother of the whole world) and Lord Shiva as Vatsnabh or Dandapani (The one who holds a staff). The Temple's architecture is splendid. The Temple looks massive, as the Temple's gopuram is at a great height. The gopuram has several images of gods and goddess sculpted on it. There is one puranic reference about Sage Gautama who lived on the Brahmagiri hills at Trayambakeshwar with his wife Ahalya. Sage Gautama, once tried to chase away a cow which ate all the stock of rice in his granary. As the sage was chasing the cow with Durbha grass, the cow fell dead. The sage meditated upon Lord Shiva and wanted to rid himself of

the Gohatya. He requested Lord Shiva to bring the Ganges to purify his hermitage. Lord Shiva was pleased with the worship of Sage Gautama and appeared as Triambaka and brought down River Ganges to Trayambakeshwar. The River is also known as Gautami, as it was brought down by Sage Gautama. The river gets the name Godavari, as the river was brought down to absolve Sage Gautama from the sins of "Gohatya".

MARKANDEYA SWAMY VARI AT RAJAHMUNDRY – It is one of the ancient Temples of Rajahmundry. The Temple was rebuilt in 1818 which shows Lord Shiva along with all other deities in one place. It is located near Ghats of Godavari. Devotees generally have a dip in River Godavari before they enter the Temple.

SRI RANGADHAMAM TEMPLE AT RAJAHMUNDRY - Gowthami Ghat got its name as many rishis performed their 'tapas' on this river bank. Sri Ranganattha is the presiding deity in the Temple. Lord Ranganattha was consecrated in the main sannidhi of this Temple. The other sannidhis in the Temple are Sri Lakshmi Devi, Sri Goda Rangamannar (similar to Sri Villiputthur), Sudarsana Swamy and Vishwaksena. Sri Bhu Neelasametha Kalyana Venkateswara Swamy, twelve Alwar sannidhi and Acharya sannidhis reside in the first floor of the Temple. The specialty of the Temple is that it follows the same tradition and rituals conducted in Srirangam. This Temple was dedicated to Pedda Srimannarayana Jeeyar Swamiji on the occasion of Jeeyar Sathabdi – centenary celebrations.

SRI UMAMARKENDEYESWARA SWAMY TEMPLE AT RAJAHMUNDRY - According to the recitals, a Muni called Mrukhanada dedicated for Meditation with an object of getting children and Lord Siva gave Varam at the choice of Muni to choose a Baby having no husband throughout her life or a Boy surviving 11 years for a sprit of devotion and pious personality. The Muni choosed a Boy at the instance of Lord Siva. Lord Siva gave varam accordingly. The Boy, named Markandaya having the knowledge of his short survival, dedicated his life for Tapasya, installed a Lingam at the place where the Temple is now situates and worshipped the Lingam. On attaining the age of 11 years, Yamah tried to take his life but Lord Shiva came to rescue the Boy and gave varam of total survival of his life. The Boy completely dedicated his life for the worship of Lord Siva and reached Siva and Parvathi Ammavaru. As the Vigraha (Lingam) and Ammavaru are stated to have installed by Muni Markandeya, the Temple is popularly known as Sri Markendeyeswara Swamy Varu. According to the records, the Temple was managed by Sri Raja Raja Narendhra, Cholas and subsequently by Reddy Rajas. It was installed about 194 years back. The Temple is an ancient and historical one in both East and West Godavari Districts. His holiness Kanchi Kama Koti Peethadhipathi, Sree Srungeri Peethadhipathi, Kurthalam Peethadhipathi and Saraswathi Jayendaraswamy have visited that Temple and worshipped Lord Siva and Ammavaru.

LORD SIDDI VINAYAKA SWAMY TEMPLE AT AINAVILLI - In the midst of the lush – green fields of the River Godavari, the Konaseema area reminds one of the sanctity and sacred feeling described in the Vaastu Sastra. In this area of Konaseema is Ainavilli, where the "siddi Vinayaka Temple" is situated. As mentioned in "kshetra Purana", before performing Daksha Yagna, Daksha Prajapati was supposed to have performed puja of Vinayaka at this place for its successful completion. There is another story that Vyasa Maharshi, during the beginning of his tour of the South had installed the

Son of Parvati at this place and this age old "Siddi Vinayaka" is reputed to fulfill the wishes of his devotees. In a spacious & elevated area, this Temple of Vinayaka stands with Vigraha facing south. With two gopurams and gates, one can approach Vinayaka from the south and Sri Visveswara Swamy from the East. In the same compound is situated Sri Devi, Bhudevi with Sri Kesava Swamy. By the side are situated Sri Annnapurna Devi. Sri Kalabhairava Swamy and Kshetrapalaka are situated by the side. It is the belief and practice of the people of this area to make a promise in the name of this God.

SRI VEERASWARA SWAMY VARI AT MURAMALLA - Sri Veerabhadra Swamy was born brightly to demolish Daksha Yagna. After demolition of Dakshyagna, with advice of Lord Maha Vishnu, he again alived Daksha and the Daksh Yagna was successfully completed. Even after completion of Yagna, Sri Veerabhadra Swamy could not leave his anger and so he was full in fire that was caused with the Yoga Sakthi of Sathi Devi. To pacify Sri Veerabhadra Swamy, the saints and the devotees went to Vaikunta and requested Sri Maha Vishnu to pacify Veerabhadra Swamy. On their request Maha Vishnu went to Veerabhadra Swamy in the disguise of Narasimha to pacify Veerabhadra Swamy but Sri Veerabhadra Swamy caught hold of Maha Vishnu tightly. Then Maha Vishnu who was in Narasimha disguise has gone to Brahma Loka and informed Lord Brahma Deva about Veerabhadra Swamy. Then Thrimurtulu requested Adiparasakthi to pacify Veerabhadra Swamy who was in harsh stage. Then she has sent one of her Kala by name Bhadrakali (Out of 16 Kalas) on earth to pacify Veerabhadra Swamy but it was in vain. Then she was shrink in the nearby water tank and came out in the disguise of a young lady and went near Veerabhadra Swamy. After seeing her, Veerabhadra Swamy was pacified. Then they both got married in the way of Gandharva Vivaham. All the Maha Munis have erected Ashramas called Muni Mandali which was turned in the name of Muramalla after many years. From then onwards, all the Maha Munis are performing Gandarva Vivaham to Lord Veerabhadra Swamy in the disguise of Nitya Kalyanam, which is continuing till today. Accordingly, the devotees are performing marriages to their daughters. If the marriages to their daughters are delayed parents are performing marriages to Sri Veerabhadra Swamy so that the marriage of their daughter will be performed early. The Nitya Kalyanam of Sri Veerabhadra Swamy will be witnessed not only by the devotees but it is in vogue that Munis like Agastya, Sukudu, Viswamitra, Vasista, Gowtama, Bhargava, Vyasa, Bharadwaj, Marichidu, kasyapudu, Markendeyudu and Narada will also witness this Kalyanam.

SRI MANDESWARA (SANESWARA) SWAMY VARI DEVASTANAM AT MANDAPALLI - This place was the holy ashram of the sage Dhadhichi Maharshi. This hermit Dhadhichi has done a supreme sacrifice of donating his valuable spinal cord for the mighty and powerful weapon popularly known as the Vajrayudha of Lord Indra, which was employed to kill the deadly asuraas. The weapons wielded by the eight suras in the eight directions called astadikpalakas, killed innumerable ghostly demons. To avenge the death of these demons certain other demons called Aswadha and Pippala invaded the area and brought about untold hevoc. At last the eminent hermit "Agasta" living in South India obliging the prayers of the people and their king assured them of the death of these

aganist in the hands of "Lord Sani", the son of the Sun god. Further they appealed Sani deva to protect them by putting an end to these terrible monsters "Aswadha and Pippala ". Sani made up his mind to kill the monsters for which he had to wage a war for one long year and killed them. As a mark of this glorious victory, he installed an Vigraha of "Lord Siva" here. This installation of Sivalinga became necessary for atoning sins of kings that belonged to Kasyapa Dynasty. So in obidence to the scared advice of the Maharushis, Sani atoned the sin of Brahma hatya by installing and adoring Lord Siva. After that Sani declared that whoever worship this Linga by offering the dear gingelli oil etc. would be blessed. He further said that he would bless such devotees obviating all evils that befall them due to the curse satru. For this reason, Lord Eswara is popularly known as Saneswara of Mandeswara. So people offer gingelli products which are dear to Sani who is the deity here.

PALLALAMMA AMMAVARU DEVASTHANAM AT VANAPALLI - This Temple is one of the greatest Temples of Deities in Andhra Pradesh and having much power. Vanapalli village is situated by the side of "Gowthami River". There is verdict in this area that at the time of digging the main canal from Rajahmundry to Kundaleswaram (Via) Vanapalli, it was thought by Sir Arthur Cotton that the Temple of Sri Pallalamma Ammavaru will obstruct the way of Canal and wanted to dismantle it. At this time Sri Ammavaru appear in the dream of Sir Arthur Cotton and told him that her Temple will not obstruct the way of canal and that he can continued to dig the canal without dismantling the same and that she will extend her sakthi also during the period of digging. Thus, Sir Arthur Cotton has completed the digging of canal and pay his respects to Goddess with great devotion. It is seen that a Vigraha of "Jackal" is under the feet of Sri Pallalamma Ammavaru and Sri Ammavaru is seated herself by putting her leg on the other leg. It is also seen that the Vigraha of "Ganapathi" is facing "South" which is very important for this Temple. Pooja and Archanakaryakramams are being performed in this Temple as per tradition of "Gramadevatha Agama Sastra".

LORD UMA KOUPPULINGESWARA SWAMY TEMPLE AT KOTIPALLI - The Vigraha installation of the Lord was done by Maharshi Agastya. The Lord here is being called Sri Uma Koppulingeswara Swamy. In the past when Maharshi Agastya was performing penance on the banks of the River Kowsiki near Palvalapuram, the Kalyana Mahotsavam of Parvathi & Parameswara was taking place for the good of the world. Agastya wanted to witness the Kalyana Mahotsavam. Before performing Daksha Yagna, Daksha Gods like Indra who were on the mountain of Himavat were afraid that if Agastya came to witness the Kalyanotsavam, pralaya would take place. So they sent viswabrahma to persuade Agastya not to go to

Himavat Parvatha. Viswabrahma told Agastya that the Kalyanotsava of Parvathi & Parmeswara was over and he had seen it. Agastya was surprised and wanted to see the Kalyanotsava with his divyadrishti. Then Parvathi & Lord Parameswara appeared in the divyadrishti of Agastya in the traditional marriage (turmeric-coated) clothes. Agastya prayed the Lord to appear before him. The Lord appeared before Agastya along with Parvathi. Agastya wanted Parvathi &

Parmeswara to remain on one peetam in the pilgrim center of Palvalapuram. The Lord fulfilled the wish of Agastya. No where can the Lord Parameswara be seen on Ekapeetam with Parvathi as here. Later this pilgrim center became famous as Lolla Agasteswara Swamy pilgrim center. The Lord began to be called as Koppulingeswara because he wore hair around his head. Even today one can see the magnificent Linga of the lord with hair around it in the sacred Temple. The State Archeological Department registered five monuments (Rajagopuram, Swamivarimandapam and some vigrahas on pillars etc.) and the same was exhibited in front of entrance gate of the Temple.

JAGANADH SWAMY TEMPLE AT RYALI - It is an enchanting place situated between the Rivers Vashista and Gowtami. In this Temple the exquisite Vigraha of Jaganadh Swamy is made of black stone. It has Maha Vishnu in front and Jagan Mohini on back side and can also catch a glimpse of ten incarnations of concerts, Thumbara, Narada, Rambha, Urvasi, Garuda, Ganga and many more. The flow of Akasha Ganga at the feet of Sri Maha Vishnu can be seen here. This shrine is referred as "Swayambhu". As per Bhagavatam, Lord Vishnu takes the guise of Mohini to rescue Devatas against Rakshasas during Samudra Manthana for getting Amrutam (holy divine nectar). During equally distributing the Amrutham among Devatas and Rakshasas, Mohini works in favour of Devatas and avoids the nectar by giving to Rakshasas. Lord Eshwara (Shiva) sees Mohini and falls in love with her. Lord Shiva comes to know that Mohini is the guise of Lord Vishnu when a flower falls from the plait of Mohini. This place where the flower has fallen is named Ryati meaning FALL in Telugu. Lord Shiva is worshipped as Uma Kamandaleswara because on the back side, Lord Brahma consecrated the Sivalingam with his Kamandalam. The Mahavishnu is consecrated as Mohini at the back side and hence worshipped as Sri Jaganmohini Keshava Swamy. The Temples of Lord Shiva and Lord Vishnu face each other in East and West direction, a rare feature to see at Ryali. The shrine of Sri Jaganmohini is a joy to see.

LORD VENKATESWARA SWAMY VARU AT VADAPALLI – It is a very old and famous Temple of Andhra Pradesh. The deity is made of Errachandanam wood. The roof around the Temple is filled with Govindanamaalu. It is believed that Lord Venkateswara is pleased and fulfills their wishes if the devotees perform 11 pradakshinas. It is also called Konaseema Tirupati.

ADURRU - It is a 2400 years old Buddhist site located on the west of Vianetaya. Amongst the 3 most popular Buddhist Stupas in the world, the first is in Adurru, the second is in Ranchi and the last one in Sarnath. The famous Mahastupa was built like giant wheel with 17 feet diameter.

SRI BALAJI BALAJI DEVSTHANAM AT APPANAPALLI – It is situated on the holy banks of River Vynateya and has attained the reputation as second Tirupathi of Konaseema being the abode of Lord Bala Balaji. The founder of the present Bala Balaji Devasthanam is Sri Molleti Ramaswamy, an ardent devotee of the Lord of the seven hills. One night, he saw in his dream that the Lord ordering him to go ahead with his Samkalpa of building a Temple for the Lord at Appanapalli without coming to Tirupathi with the share of profit in his business for the Lord annually. Accordingly, Sri Ramaswamy at once installed the photos of Sri Sri Sri Venkateswara Swamyvaru and his consort Padmavathi Ammavaru in his coconut shop in 1966. In the course of time, pilgrims in thousands started pouring in and Appanapalli occupied a place of devotional importance in the pilgrim map. It is indeed a point of great surprise and beyond any body's comprehension to explain how the devotee Ramaswamy could serve free meal to one and all including Milk to infants besides Medical aid. "It is all His will". On 18th March 1970, the foundation stone for the construction of the New

Temple was laid by Sri Ramaswamy amidst the chanting of Mantras by the Vedic Scholars. His Holiness Sri Sri Sri Tridandi Srimanarayana China Jeeyar Swamyvaru installed the vigrahas of the Lord and his consort.

SRI LAKSHMI NARASIMHA SWAMY AT ANTHARVEDI - Sage Vasista, after mingling the Goutami branch of the Godavari into the Sea, established his Ashram here. Lord Brahma, to get freed from the sins he had committed against Lord Sankara, performed Rudrayaga and installed Lord Neelakantheswara here. As this place was made a stage or "Vedik" to perform the Yagya, it was named as "Antarvedi". After commencement of Kaliyuga, Antervedi was a Jungle where Kesavadas, a cow-herd used to graze his cows daily. A reddish brown cow of the herd to go lonely in the jungle and used to shed her milk on the hill behind a bush. On her returning home, Kesavadas was not given milk by the cow. One day he watchfully followed that cow and astonished to see the scene that was daily happening. He could not get sleep that night. At last when he could some how merge himself in to sleep, Lord Narahari appeared on him in dream and said to him to build a Temple for him there. The next morning Kesavadas told this to the Villagers. A Brahmin scholar of the village, who had a sound knowledge of the shastras, could guess the God appeared to Kesavadas in dream to be Lord Narasimha who was once erected and worshipped. The Villagers made a survey of the ant-hill area, where the cow daily used to shed her milk and dug the area after offering coconuts to the Lord. They found a stony sculptured form of the Lord Narasimha. They build a Temple there and that place become one of the most popular shrines in the later ages. On an auspicious day, the foundation stone was laid on a first step for the reconstruction of the Temple in 1923. Some time later once a fisherman was fishing his net in the Raktakulya River. He found a marble saligrama instead of fish. He carelessly threw it back into the water and again spread his net. He found the same stone as many times as he was fishing at different spots in the river. Being afraid of this incident, he angrily dashed it to the ground, then there was a strange continuous blood flow from the stone. With surprise and fear, he prayed the Lord and fell senseless there. The Lord appeared to him in dream and said that he only appeared in the waters of Raktakulya River as Kurmavatra in marble and asked him to take him to the Temple and install him at the Abode of Lord Narasimha telling the priests as his works to celebrate the "Nityabhisheka" formalities to him along with Lord Narasimha there. The fisherman did so. This stony form Kurma incarnation of the Lord can be seen available even today at Antarvedi Devasthanam. It is said that there will be no re-birth on taking a dip at these

places and on offering charities there. Performing ceremonial formalities to the ancestors at this holy-shrine is equivalent to these done at Gaya and Ganges. Antarvedi has the sea in the East and the South the Godavari in the West and the Raktakulya River in the North. Antarvedi is said to be the second Varanasi by the grace of the Lord. A mere wish to visit this holy place will bless the devotees with desired results. Thus the great glory of the shrine is boundless. There are five important spots of this Holy shrine namely : 1. The Sea; 2. The Sagar Sangam; 3. The Vasishta River; 4. The Raktakulya River & 5. The Chakrateertham. Nearest Railway Station is Palakollu.

MAHASHAKTIPEETH – SRI BHIMESWARA SWAMY TEMPLE AT DRAKSHARAMAM - Draksharama is situated on the eastern banks of the River Godavari. It means the Abode of Daksha Prajapathi, Father-in-law of Lord Siva. The history of the Sacred Pilgrimage is exhaustively dealt within the 'Skanda Purana' of Sri Vyasa. Out of eighteen 'Ashta Dasa Peethas', Sri Manikyamba of Draksharama is the Twelfth. As per legend Daksya Yagya & Sati's self-immolation, left cheek of Sati fell here. This Holy Pilgrimage is one of the rare few, where the God and Goddess are equally important. One is Varanasi in Northern India with Viswanatha and Annapurna. Second is Srisailam in Southern India with Sri Mallikharjuna and Bramaramba and third is Draksharama with Bhimanatha and Manikyamba. There are many mythological anecdotes scattered in many of the sacred puranas about the 'Swayambhu' aspect of the Lord's existence here. One of many is for once who is curious to know that Bhimanatha came down from Kailasa and settled here at the request of Parvathi herself who happened to be the daughter of Dakhsa. The historical aspect of the Temple goes from the thirteenth century onwards. This Temple is one of the "Pancharamas". This is an ancient and holy pagoda. This Temple is a protected Monument. The wealth of inscriptions and epigraphical details that can be glanced from the inscriptions on the walls of this Temple are a paradise for the epigraphist and the historian.

SRI BAPANAMMA TALLI TEMPLE AT SEETAPALLI – It is located in dense forest and is a famous Temple. It is mostly considered safe to travel during the day time.

SRI LAKSHMI NARASIMHA SWAMY AT KORUKONDA - It is an ancient historic Temple known as Vaishnava Divya Kshetram. It is dedicated to Lord Vishnu. It is a 'Swayambhu' Vigraha situated at the top of a hill which can be accessed through long flight of 650 steps. The Temple was constructed 800 years ago. There are two Temples out of which one is Swayambhu and another is Prathishta Deity. It is really wonder and mankind could not be instate either the deity or any other stone which is about 120 mts. height, the Temple have got much Shilpa Soundaram around it. There are number of Sila – Sasanams appeared in the Temple and as well as on the top hill of the Temple. The great poet Sri Srinatha in his poetry prayed the God stated, this Korukonda is "Vedadri".

BALI-SUGRIVA KONDA AT MAREDUMILLI FORESTS - The Maredumilli forests are rich in biodiversity which form part of the Eastern Ghats. The Jungle star campsite is located adjoining the Valamuru River with the stream flowing on 3 sides overlooking the Bali-Sugriva Konda which is believed to be the battle ground of Bali-Sugriva during the Ramayana period.

SRI AYYAPPA SWAMY VARU, ANDHRA SABRIMALAI AT DWARAPUDI - This is a replica of Swamy Ayyappa Temple at Kerala. It is said that the devotees who cannot go to Sabarimala (Kerala) can offer their prayers here. There are many other Temples located in the same premises. There is a large vigraha of Harihara known as Shankaranarayana wherein Hari represents Lord Vishnu & Hara represents Lord Shiva. Nearest Railway Station is Dwarapudi.

SRI VIGNESWARA SWAMI VARU AT BIKKAVOLU - Bikkavolu Temple is dedicated to Lord Vinayaka. The main deity inside the Temple is 7 foot tall. This is a "Swayambhu" deity. It is believed that the Vigraha was installed during 849 AD and has been increasing year by year. Here the devotees whisper their wishes in lord's ear. The other fascinating thing is that the water that comes out from bottom portion of left leg of the lord.

KODANDARAMA TEMPLE AT GOLLALA MAMIDADA - The Temple is dedicated to Lord Rama, the incarnation of Lord Vishnu. It was built on the banks of Tulyabhaga (Antharvahini), a tributary of Godavari. The Temple is notable for its unique architecture and two huge gopurams which stand at 160–170 feet and 200–210 feet. The Temple gopurams are adorned with intricately carved vigrahas depicting scenes from Ramayana, Mahabharata, and Bhagavatam. The construction of the Temple began in 1889 when brothers Dwarampudi Subbi Reddy and Rami Reddy donated five acres of land and built a small Temple with wooden vigrahas of Lord Rama and Sita. Later Kovvuri Basivi Reddy, a local philanthropist took over the Temple in 1920. A larger Temple was built in 1939. The two gopurams were constructed in 1948–50 and 1956–58. The Temple is also known as 'Chinna Bhadradi' or the 'Little Bhadrachalam'. It is one of the two most popular Rama Temples in Andhra Pradesh along with Kodandarama Temple in Vontimitta. Sri Rama Navami is the most prominent festival celebrated at the Temple & features an annual wedding ceremony of Lord Rama & Sita. Other important festivals celebrated at the Temple are Vaikunta Ekadasi and Vijayadasami.

SRI SURYANARAYANA SWAMY TEMPLE AT GOLLALA MAMIDADA - Gollala Mamidada in Peddapudi Mandal is a well known pilgrimage centre for the last hundred years. It is situated on the banks of the river "Thulya Bhaga" (Antharvahini). Sri Suryanarayana Swamy Temple was incepted by late Sri Kovvuri Basivi Reddy Garu in the year 1920. The performance of rituals in this Temple is in accordance with Sri Vyshanava Samradaya. This Temple has gained much importance in Andhra Pradesh as the tenets are of Vyshanava Sampradaya.

SRI TALUPULAMMA AMMAVARI DEVASTHANAM AT TUNI MANDAL – The Temple is wedged between 2 heavily forested hillocks. Truck owners as well as car owners, particularly those who live in the Godavari and North Coastal Districts share a special bond with this Temple as they believe strongly that Goddess Thalupulamma Thalli will protect them from accidents, dangers and will also help in earning profits. The truck owners pitch tents at the foot of the hillock Temple and offer animal sacrificies and paint their vehicle registration numbers on the walls with devotion. Most of the people, who buy new vehicle, make sure to visit this Temple and get their vehicles blessed by the Goddess. Legend has it that the great Sage Agastya was so enchanted and drawn by the scenic splendor and tranquility of this place that he settled down here and meditated. He respectively named these mountains as "Darakonda and Teegakonda". One can see, even now, a perennial stream flowing down from the "Darakonda Hill".The deity Thalupulamma Thalli is said to be a "Swayambhu" (self-incarnate). She is called Thalupulamma Thalli because "the mere thought" (thalapu) of her is enough for the Goddess to grant boons for her devotees. The Goddess is so kind hearted, so compassionate that she doesn't wait for her devotees to come to her. Just one mere thought of her and she rushes to her devotees and grants them whatever they pray for, ask for. To access this Temple one must climb a long and steep flight of steps starting from the ornate entrance getaway that leads up to the sanctum of Goddess Thalupulamma Thalli. While climbing these long and steep flights of steps, the devotees halt for a few minutes at an intermediary landing where they worship Lord Vighneswara and other deities present there. Unlike other Temples which close at 8:00 P.M / 9:00 P.M, the Thalupulamma Thalli Temple closes early at 6:00 P.M. None stay back. This is because the wild animals who inhabit that hillock roam about at night which makes it quite unsafe for the pilgrims. It is also believed that the Goddess Thalupulamma Thalli frequents this hillock at night. Nearest Railway Station is Tuni.

LORD SRI VEERA VENKATA SATYA NARAYANA SWAMY VARI AT ANNAVARAM - Annavaram is one of the most famous Holy Shrines in India and enjoying second place after Tirupati in Andhra Pradesh. The Temple is built in the Dravidian style. The glory and richness of Lord Satyadeva was widely described in Revakhanda of Skandapuranam. The presiding deity Lord Satyadeva with his consort Sri Anantha Lakshmi on one Side and with Lord Siva on the other side took his abode on Ratnagiri, which is named after Ratnakara, son of Meru, the king of holy mountains. Like in all Divyakshetrams as surrounded and followed by holy rivers, Sri Satyanarayana Swamy at Annavaram is also followed by sacred Pampa

River touching the feet of the hill. Lord Satyadeva, the god of truth, is showering his eternal blessings on mankind in his beautiful manifested form of the Divine Trinity namely Hari Hara Hiranya Garbha Thrimurtyatmaka. It is believed that the place was known for constant food distribution (free feeding) by the benevolent people of the locality and that therefore the place was called by the name Annavaram. Enriched by the installation of Srimathripathvibhuti Vykhunta Maha Narayana Yantra, which plays a dominant and important role with the power of attraction of both money and men (Dhana Janakarsha), the Peetham of Swamyvaru is highly adorned with the installation of Panchayatana, befitting the glory and sanctity of the deity. This famous yantra is a unique one, the like of which does not exist any where else in India. The Temple of Sri Veera Venkata Satyanarayanaswamy is the main Temple on the Ratnagiri hill. There are also a Temple of Sri Rama and the shrines of Vana Durga and Kanaka Durga nearby. The Temple of gramadevatha "Nerellamma" is in the village at the foot of the hill. The main Temple is constructed in the form of a chariot with the four wheels at each of the four corners. The Vigraha is about 13 foot high in a cylindrical form, the base being in the lower sanctum representing Lord Brahma and the top is in the upper sanctum representing Lord Vishnu. The middle portion represents Lord Siva. The Temple is in two floors; the ground floor contains the yantra and the peetham of the Lord. On the four sides of the yantra there are four deities namely Ganapati, Suryanarayanaswamy, Bala Tripurasundari and Maheswaraswamy which constitutes panchayathanam. Lord Sri Rama is considered to be the Kshetra Palaka of this holy abode of the Lord Satyadeva. Nearest Railway Station is Annavaram.

SRI SRUNGARA VALLABHA SWAMY VARU AT THOLI TIRUPATI - This Temple is 9000 years old and it is said that there are 108 Tirupatis throughout the country and this is the first of all. There are 3 major and unique things we can witness: 1. Smiling posture of Lord Venkateswara; 2. Lord will be seen as small Venkatesa for Children and Big Venkatesa for Elders (various sizes of Lord is visible to people) & 3. Sankha and Chakra are in altered positions in comparison with Lord Balaji of Tirupati. It is also called Toli Tirupati.

SRI RAMALAYA PRASANNANJANEYA SWAMY TEMPLE AT YERRAVARAM – It is one of the biggest Lord Hanuman Vigraha. Height of the Vigraha is 97 ft. Nearest Railway Station is Pithapuram.

SRI SURYANARAYANA SWAMI TEMPLE AT PANDAVULA METTA – As per Mahabharata legend, during 'Aranyavasa', Pandavas have spent some time in Peddapuram on a hill, which was located in between Bay of Bengal and the River Godavari. Only Koya people were there. The Pandava brothers arranged a tunnel to Rajahmundry from this hill through which they used to have river bath. This hill was named after their name as "Pandavula Metta". The height of Pandavula Metta is about 200 Ft. After some time, they left the hill for Rameswaram. Till today, we can find Pandava names and Draupathi name in Koya people. The entrance of the tunnel is there today. The rest of the tunnel was disturbed in the Yuga changes. People constructed Temple on the hill and arranged 108 steps to the hill. There are also two natural caves on the hill facing east. "Bheemunipadalu' (prints of Bheema's feet, the brother of Pandavas) can be seen on a hill rock behind Temple. One can experience excellent sea breeze in all seasons, as the sea (Bay of Bengal) is just 22 KMs away. The area around the Temple is surrounded by mango, plam & other trees & Tapioca plantation giving well laid green carpet beside the serene beauty & sanctity of the deity.

SRI CHALUKYA KUMARARAMA SRI BHIMESWARASWAMY VARI TEMPLE AT SAMALKOT - It is famous and one of the 'Pancharamas'. This was built in the 9th century. Lord Bhimeswara Swamy appears as Ekashila Shiva Linga along with Ekashila Nandi. Darshan of Shiva Linga is at first floor, along with Goddess Shri Bala Tripura Sundari and Pushkarini (lake) can be seen. It is one of the centrally protected monuments of national importance. The limestone Linga, installed in the shrine, is 16 foot tall that it rises from the pedestal on the ground floor and enters the second floor by piercing the roof, where the Rudrabhaga is worshipped. The Temple resembles the other Pancharama Temple at Draksharama which is also called Bhimeswara Alayam. The construction of the Temple was started in AD 892 and was completed during AD 922.

SRI PRASANNA ANJANEYA SWAMY TEMPLE AT SAMALKOT - It is one of the biggest Lord Hanuman Vigraha. Height of the Vigraha is 97 foot.

MAHASHAKTIPEETH – SRI KUKKUTESWARA SWAMY DEVASTHANAM AT PITHAPURAM - It is the brief history of Padagaya Kshetram, which is one of the important Astadasa Peetha's. It is described in the third chapter of Bheema Khanda and of Skandapurana. As the seat place (Peetha) of Satidevi has fallen on this place, hence, it is called Pithapuram. It is equally holy and sacred place with 'Kedaram' in North-India and 'Kumbhakonam' in South-India. This place was visited by the Sage Vyasa with his disciples. The primal deity of this is lord Shiva in the form of Cock. This Shakti Peetham is famous with the name of Puruhutika. Sripada Sri Vallaba was born as

Dattatreya Swamy in this place. So, it has become the main Avatara Kshetram of Dattatreya. Sri Raja Rajeswari Devi is a powerful Goddess being worshipped in this Pithapuram Temple. It is believed that this Goddess fulfill all our desires. She is also called Kumara Gananadhamba as she sits in between her two sons Kumara Swamy on one side and lord Ganesha on the other side. It is said that "Pinda Pradanam" performed here acquires Salvation. The last rights performed here is equal to the rights performed at Kasi. Nearest Railway Station is Pithapuram.

DISTRICT – GUNTUR (Railway Station – Vijayawada / Bapatla / Narasaraopet)

S. No.	Temple	Address	Type
1	Amareswara Swamy Temple	Amaravathi - 522020	Shiva
2	Amravathi Museum	Amaravathi – 522020	Buddhist
3	Dhyana Buddha Vigraha	Amaravathi – 522020	Buddhist
4	Bhavanarayana Swamy Temple	Baptala – 522101	Vishnu
5	Jain Temple	Ponnur - 522124	Jain
6	Sri Vasudasa Ashramam	Nadigaddapalem, Tsundur, Tenali - 522318	Rama
7	Sri Narasimha Temple	Kedavaram – 522411	Narasimha (Vishnu)
8	Jeeyar Educational Trust	Sithanagaram – 522501	Vishnu
9	Undavalli Caves	Undavalli – 522501	Vishnu, Jain
10	Sri Panakala Lakshmi Narasimha Swamy Temple	Mangalagiri - 522503	Vishnu
11	Kapotheswara	Chejrala - 522661	Shiva

AMARESWARA SWAMY TEMPLE AT AMARAVATHI - Amaravathi is named after its famous Temple of Amareswara Swamy, which enshrines the Swayambhu Linga. The Temple was constructed in the 8th century. This is dedicated to Lord Shiva and houses a Shiva Lingam of fifteen foot high, which is one of the tallest Sivalingam in India and it is said that Sivalinga was growing up in size. This is one among the panchalingalu (pancharama) and one of biggest Temple in Andhra Pradesh. The Temple is situated at the highest place on the banks of River Krishna. In general, rivers flow in west to east direction but in Amaravati Hill, the Krishna River flows in the north-south direction. This is something unique and so it is considered holy place. The Temple walls are adorned with various inscriptions elucidating different dynasties that reigned over the region. On the four sides of the Amaravati Temple are large gopurams in a usually Dravidian architectural style. The Temple contains three concentric circles. While the first circle houses the Temples of Mahishasura Mardini,

Veerabhadraswamy, Omkareswara Swamy, Guru Dattareya, and Agasteswara Swamy, the second circle contains the Temples of Vinayaka, Kalabhairava, Anjaneya, Nagendraswamy, Kumaraswamy along with the Vigraha of Lord Krishna under a

tree. The third circle is a bit above the second circle and comes with the Temples of Kasi Viswanatha, Mallikarjuna, Pushpadanteswara Swamy and Kalahasthiswara. At the heart of these three circles is the deity of Amaralingeswara Swamy.

AMARAVATHI MUSEUM AT AMRAVATHI - Amaravathi Museum, formerly known as Andhra Nagari (Amaravati), is one of the most important Buddhist sites in the country. Acharya Nagarjuna built India's largest Stupa here more than 2000 years ago. It is considered to be the most sacred pilgrimage centre for Buddhists in South India.

DHYANA BUDDHA VIGRAHA AT AMARAVATHI - The Vigraha was commissioned in 2003 and completed in 2015. The height of the Vigraha is 125 Foot. It is situated on the banks of Krishna River with eight pillars on a Lotus pandal. The eight pillars signifies path for salvation followed by Buddha, four zones for noble truths and five ayaka pillars for stages of life.

BHAVANARAYANASWAMI TEMPLE AT BAPATLA - The Temple is one of the most ancient Temples (1400 years old). This Temple is said to belong to Mauryan period and the presiding deity is Bhavanarayanaswami. The name of the town Baptala derives its name from the presiding deity of this Temple, Bhavanarayana Swami. The Baptla town was also called Bhavapuri during the time of Mauryan Empire. It is one of the centrally protected monuments of national importance.

JAIN TEMPLE AT PONNUR - The Temple is believed to be very old & famous. Acharya Kundkund Dev visit this place very frequently to get his diet.

Sri Veera Anjaneya Swamy Temple at Ponnur - The Temple is dedicated to Lord Anjaneya Swamy. The vigraha of Lord Anjaneya Swamy is 24 ft. tall and is made of black stone. There are number of other shrines nearby the Temple. Devotees visit the place in large numbers particularly on various special occasions.

SRI VASUDASA ASHRAMAM AT NADIGADDAPALEM - Initially, the vigrahas of Lord Sri Rama along with his family were consecrated by Vasudasa Swamy in early 1900s. Later Pedda Jeeyar Swamiji developed the Temple and consecrated deities of Lord Rama Darbar in 1956. In 1972, Pedda Jeeyar Swamiji performed Sri Lakshmi Narayana Mahakrathu with 1000 kundas in Thirumala. In the 12 Yagasalas, Sri Pedda Jeeyar Swamiji installed and empowered 12 Lakshmi Narayana Dhruva Murthis in that Mahakrathu. All those Dhruva Murthis were consecrated in 12 Temples across in the country including Nepal. One of those twelve Lakshmi Narayana Murthis was installed in Nadigaddapalem – thus Lord Lakshmi Narayana Perumal was added to Lord Rama's family. There is Ramayana Stupam installed by Sri Pedda Jeeyar Swamiji. Out of the 108 Svadhyaaya Jnana Yajnams, the 28th Jnana Yajnam was performed in Nadigaddapalem. This Temple became even more significant when Sri Pedda Jeeyar Swamiji's Brundavanam was consecrated here. Every day Aradhana and Nithya Annadanam programs are conducted. It is of common knowledge and belief that whoever circumambulates around the Brundavanam will have their questions answered and their wishes will be fulfilled.

SRI NARASIMHA TEMPLE AT KETHAVARAM – The Temple is an ancient Temple. It is situated in a dense forest area. The place is also known as Kattaram and Kedaram in the scriptures. Kethavaram was named after the King Ketha Varma who ruled this region. River Krishna is too deep in this region. The presiding deity is a Swayambhumurthi. Lord Narasimha graces the devotees with Mother Mahalakshmi. There is also a shrine for Sri Anjaneya in this Temple. While digging the land here for a tank, one worker was hit by a stone and it began bleeding. Testing the rock, it turned to be a diamond rock. Further digging brought out some vigrahas also. Hence, Lord Narasimha is praised as Vajralaya, vajram meaning diamond.

JEEYAR EDUCATIONAL TRUST AT SITHANAGARAM - The auspicious hill Sri Vijaya Kiladri is situated on the banks of Krishna River. This divine hill "Adrirajam" is an abode to all Gods and specifically is the place where Arjuna performed penance. The sacred hills possess great importance and radiate spectacularly with the waves of the Krishna River rippling over the shores. In 2017, Lord appeared as Archa in 9 forms to bless all beings with His compassion on this Hill. It happened purely due to the divine 'Sankalpam' of Pedda Jeeyar Swamiji and motivation of HH Chinna Jeeyar Swamiji. The nine Temples are: Ashtalakshmi Devalayam, Bhu Varaha Swamy, Kodanda Rama Swamy Alayam, Sri Krushna Perumal Sannidhi, Sri Lakshmi Narasimha Swamy, Sudarshana Narasimha Perumal, Vaikuntta Narayana Perumal, Sri Venkateshwara Swamy Sannidhi, Vishwaksena Alwaracharya Sannidhi. According to science of Vaastu, if there is a water body to the North of any place, then it brings immense good fortune. Tirumala has the 'Pushkarini' to the North of its main Temple and Sri Rangam has the River Cauvery flowing on all three sides of its Temple. Likewise, the Kiladri hills, it is surrounded by River Krishna on its three sides. The Vastu Science has predicted that due to such favourably placed water bodies, the auspicious hills Vijaya Kiladri shall bring great welfare and prosperity to the entire state and country – just like Sri Rangam and Tirumala.

UNDAVALLI CAVES - Dating back to 7th century, the Undavalli Caves, carved out of a single sandstone, are a prime example of India's rock-cut architectural heritage. The inviting design of the caves speaks volumes about the advanced architectural skills of the ancient Viswakarma architects and Temple builders. The caves are said to have been associated with the influential Vishnukundina dynasty, which ruled over important parts of India between 420 AD and 620 AD. These caves are a fine specimen of Gupta architecture as well, and the detailed design on the second floor reflects Chalukyan architecture. The largest cave has four floors and houses a huge Vigraha of Lord Vishnu in a reclining posture. It is said that this sculpture was carved out of a single block of granite. The first storey of the caves houses sculptures of Jain Tirthankaras that suggest that they once served as a home for Jain monks. The walls on the first floor are covered with stunning frescoes that depict scenes from mythological stories. The facade of the third floor hosts numerous sculptures that include depictions of lions and elephants. Nearby is another unique cave dedicated to Lord Brahma, Lord Vishnu and Lord Shiva. The architecture and green surroundings of the Undavalli Caves will remind you of Bhubaneswar's Udaygiri Caves.

SRI PANAKALA LAKSHMI NARASIMHA SWAMY TEMPLE AT MANGALAGIRI – It is a Vaishnavite Temple & one of the eight sacred places of Lord Vishnu in India. It is situated at the foot of auspicious Hill in Mangalagiri. It has one of the highest gopurams in South India & only one of its type in this part of India. It is 153 ft. in height & 49 ft. wide and has eleven storeys. Mangalagiri means The Auspicious Hill. This place is one of the 8 important Mahakshetrams in India. Lakshmi Devi has done tapas on this hill. This shape of the hill looks like an elephant. From all the directions, the hill appears in the elephant shape only. It is believed that Lord Rama while departing for Vaikuntam after completing his mission in that incarnation advised Lord Anjaneya to stay at Mangalagiri & after obtaining his blessings to remain in this world for ever. Lord Anjaneya took his adobe at Mangalagiri as Kshetrapalaka. On the right side of the steps, there is a stone inscription by Sri Krishnadeva Raya of Vijayanagar & a little further up, the foot prints of Mahaprabhu Chaitanya are to be seen. Midway on the steps there is a Temple of Lord Panakala Lakshmi Narasimhaswamy, there is only the face with the mouth widely opened. A dhwajasthambham was erected in front of the Temple in 1955. Behind the Temple, there is the Temple of Sri Lakshmi to the west of which there is a tunnel which is believed to lead to Vundavalli caves on the banks of the Krishna. It will be interesting to note that even a single ant is not traceable near the Lord nor around the Temple in spite of the offering of so much jaggery water to the Lord. There is a legend about the offering of the panakam (jaggery water) to the Lord. It is said that the hill was once a volcano. Sugar or jaggery water, it is said, neutralizes sulphur compounds found in a volcano and prevents a volcanic eruption. The Lord that has established himself on the hill is in the form of Narasimha (man-lion) which Lord Vishnu assumed to kill Hiranyakasipu, a rakshasa father of Prahlada, a great devotee. He is also called as Sudarsana Narasimhaswamy. The legend says that Namuchi, a Rakshasa after great penance obtained a boon from Brahma that he would not be killed by anything that is either wet or dry. He began to harass Indra and the Devathas. Encouraged and supported by Lord Vishnu, Indra commenced destroying the army of Rakshasa Namuchi, who did in a cave in Sukshmakaram (small size) giving up his

sthulakaram (Physical manifestation). Indra dipped Sudarsanam, the disc of Lord Vishnu in the foam of the ocean and sent it into the cave. Lord Vishnu manifesting himself at the centre of the disc destroyed the Pranavayuvu (life breath) of the Rakshasa with the fire of his exhalation. He thus got the name of Sudarsana Narasimha. The blood that flowed from the body of the Rakshasa seemed to have formed into a pool at the foot of the hill which is known hill. The Devathas themselves were unable to withstand the fire of the anger of the Lord and they prayed for appeasement. The Lord took amrutam & cooled down. It was in Krithayugam. The Lord said that he would be satisfied with ghee in Threthayugam, with milk in Dwaparayugam & with panakam in Kaliyugam. Hence, the Lord is called in Kaliyugam as Panakala Lakshmi Narasimhaswamy.

KAPOTHESWARA TEMPLE AT CHEJERLA - The Temple here is dedicated to Lord Siva and dates to the 4th or 5th century AD. This is probably the only Temple in the whole of India dedicated to Lord Siva as Kapotheswara. The prime sanctum houses Lord Kapoteswara in the form of Shiva Linga. The barrel vaulted eka-talavimanam is apsidal or gaja-prishtavimanam (shape of an elephant back) with apsidal salashikara. It is believed by scholars that the vimana was originally Buddhist Chaitya and was modified for purposes of Shiva worship. The legend of Kapotheswara is related to Lord Shiva's self-sacrificed part of his body to an eagle to save a pigeon (Kapotha) that took refuge with him. The Temple is erected to this pious king under the title 'Kapotheswara.'. Interestingly, in the white marble Vigraha of Shiva Linga, even today you will find large pits / cavities as if portions have been scooped or cut out and these are said to be the places of the body from which the Lord cut off his own flesh in order to save the life of the Kapotha. Also on top of Shiva Lingam, there are still two large vertical cavities. The water used for ablution of Shiva Linga drained through one of these cavities. Surprisingly the smell of raw flesh is felt & blood oozes from the cavities occasionally. The Sanskrit inscription of Mahendaravarma Pallava-I (600 - 620 A.D.) is seen on the face of the slab fixed behind Nandi Mandapa in front of the prime sanctum.

DISTRICT – KRISHNA (Railway Station – Vijayawada/Machilipatnam/Repalle)

S. No.	Temple	Address	Type
1	Sri Durgamalleswaraswamy Varla Devastanams	Indrakeeladri, Vijayawada – 520001	Mata
2	Mogalrajapuram Caves	Moghalrajapuram – 520020	Shiva
3	Panduranga Swamy Temple	Keera Pandhari Kshetram, Chilakalapudi, Machilipatnam – 521002	Panduranga Vithal
4	Sai Baba Temple	Zilla Court Centre, Machilipatnam – 521002	Sai Baba
5	Sri Lakshmi Narayana Swami Temple	Avanigadda - 521121	Rama
6	Sri Subrahmanyeswara Swamivari Devasthanam	Mopidevi – 521125	Shiva
7	Paritala Anjaneya Temple	Paritala – 521180, Vijayawada	Hanuman
8	Shivalayam Temple	Kanchikacherla - 521180	Shiva

S. No.	Temple	Address	Type
9	Sri Yogananda Lakshmi Narasimha Swamy Devasthanam	Vedadri – 521457, Jaggayyapet Mandal	Narasimha (Vishnu) & Shiva

KANAKA DURGA TEMPLE AT VIJAYAWADA – The Temple is situated on the banks of River Krishna. Sri Kanakadurgamma is swayambhu. It is one of the largest Temples in India & 2nd largest Temple in Andhra Pradesh. The Temple is built in Dravidian style of architecture. In the Krithayuga, Goddess Durga killed Mahishasura. Then goddess Durga shined on the Keela Mountain in the form of Mahishasura Mardini as she had given boon to keela. On this mountain, Goddess Durga had been glowing with the lighting of crores of suns with golden colour. On the left side of Durga Devi, there is "Sri Chakaram" & beside that there is a Ganapati. Kanaka Durgamma has 8 arms with Chakra, Conch, Bow & Arrow, Sword, Spear, Club, Trident, Thunderbolt & Lotus. Here Durga is on the right side of Malleswara as against the tradition of Goddesses taking their position on the left of their consorts. This shows that Shakthi is predominant on the Indrakeeladri. This is the only Temple in the world where the main deity are decorated in forms of Sri Saraswati, Sri Mahalakshmi, Sri Bala Tripurasundari, Sri Rajarajeswari, Sri Mahishasuramardini, Sri Durga Devi, Sri Annapurna Devi, Sri Gayatri, Sri Lalitha Tripura Sundari. Adi-Sankaracharya visited the Temple and installed the Srichakra & initiated worship of Kanaka Durga in vedic ways & avoided animal sacrifice. One of these hills is called Indrakeela, which is a famous hill mentioned in the Mahabharata as the place where the Arjuna obtained from Lord Siva an important weapon called Pashupastra. The aspect of Lord Siva who appeared before Arjuna for granting him the boon is Kirata or the hunter. The Temple of Vijayeswara is attributed to Arjuna to commemorate the event of obtaining Pashupastra. The shrine has the representation of this & many other events of Mahabharata depicted in sculpture form.

MOGALRAJAPURAM CAVES AT MOGHALRAJAPURAM - It has five rock cut sanctuaries dating back to the 5th century AD and out of these five, only one is in good condition. The Mogalarajapuram Temple has an 'Ardhanarisvara' Vigraha which is thought to be the earliest in South India and one of its kind. One of the caves has an overhanging cornice with artificial windows. The vigrahas of Lord Natarajaand Vinayaka in one cave are still in good condition compared to the other worn out images of deities. It is also a place of archaeological importance.

PANDURANGA SWAMY TEMPLE AT MACHILIPATNAM – The Temple is devoted to Lord Panduranga Vithal. The Vigraha of the god measures around 3 foot in height and he shares similarity with the childhood appearance of Lord Krishna. The Vigraha is decorated with ornaments and wears a diamond-studded crown. A Vigraha of Sri Abhayanjaney Swami is placed in front of the Vigraha. The main entrance of the Temple has a tower. The Panduranga Swamy Temple is flanked

by a prakaram on all its three sides, which feature the images of the disciples of Sri Panduranga Vithal. Just beside the entrance of the Temple, there is another Temple that houses the images of Rukmini, Radha and Satyabhama. There are 108 sub-Temples within the Temple complex. Pilgrims visit the Panduranga Swamy Temple during the Karthika Pournima to take a dip in the sea (Samudra Snanalu). There is also an increase in tourist inflow at the site on Ashadha Shudda Ekadashi.

SAI BABA TEMPLE AT MACHILIPATNAM - The Sai Baba Vigraha is a single masterpiece in which he is seen sitting on two tigers with a tortoise under his foot. The 54-foot-high and 36-foot-wide Vigraha is made of cement was built way back in the year 2007.

SRI LAKSHMI NARAYANA SWAMI TEMPLE AT AVANIGADDA - The Temple is dedicated to Lord Rama. It was constructed by King Kulotunga Chola - II in 1065 CE. It is believed to be the second tallest Temple structure in AP, as the height of the Gopuram is 99 ft. with 7 Kalashas on it. The Temple is built in the shape of a chariot depicting architectural style of Chola Kings. It is also believed that at this place, Maa Sita learned the Vedic knowledge from Vasistha Maharishi. The Temple also houses a shrine for Sri Daasa Anjaneya Swami.

SRI SUBRAHMANYESWARA SWAMIVARI DEVASTHANAM AT MOPIDEVI - The Lord is in the form of Lingam. It is famous for 'Childless Couples for Childbirth', Sarpa Dosha Nivarana Pooja, Rahu Ketu Dosha Pooja & Anapathya Dosha Pooja for the relief of vision, Ear related problems, cure for skin related diseases, good life partner & Annaparasanna. Devotees strongly believe that if couple sleep in Mopidevi Temple for a night, they will be blessed with children.

PARITALA ANJANEYA TEMPLE AT VIJAYAWADA - The Vigraha of Lord Hanuman is the tallest in the world. The Vigraha was installed in the year 2003 and stands 135 foot tall. The Vigraha is taller than Christ the Redeemer Vigraha in Rio de Janeiro, Brazil (38 m including 8 m pedestal) and attracts many devotees, both foreign and domestic. The tallest Lord Hanuman Vigraha outside India is at Carapichaima, Trinidad and Tobago, which is 85 ft tall. The Temple has a shrine of Lord Rama - Sita - Lakshman, the Devi and Lord Anjaneya.

SHIVALAYAM TEMPLE AT KANCHIKACHERLA - The Temple is dedicated to Lord Shiva. The Temple is one of the tallest Temples of Lord Shiva in Andhra Pradesh. The Temple has been built in the shape of Shivalinga & is having carvings on surface of it.

SRI YOGANANDA LAKSHMI NARASIMHA SWAMY DEVASTHANAM AT VEDADRI - It is one of the Pancha Narasimhar Kshetrams in Andhra Pradesh. This holy shine is called "Vedadri". The Temple structure is conventional being brightly coloured & ornamented with a variety of images. There is a beautiful image of Narasimha Swami in yoga posture. The Temple has beautiful Raja Gopuram with images of gods and goddesses carved on it. The lower portion of Dwajasthambam is seen inside the mandapam. "Bramhandpurana" says that Somaksura a demon of Yore stole the four Vedas from Lord Bramha & hide himself in the Ocean. Lord Bramha then approached Lord Srimannarayana & prayed for the restoration of Vedas. Lord Srimannarayana in 'Matsyavathara' entered the Ocean, killed the demon Somakasura & brought back the Vedas intact. The Vedas, in human form thanked the Lord & prayed to stay with them on their heads. There upon the Lord munificently granted their Prayer but said that they would do that only after killing another demon Hiranya Kasapa & saving his son prahalda. The Lord also assured the Vedapurushas that he would stay with them as panchamurthy only. So saying the Lord bid them till such time to remain in the river Krishnaveni as Saligrama Mountain. Lord told them that Krishnaveni also prayed to allow her to worship him every day & that he has granted her the boon. According to the bid of the Lord, the Vedapuras has remained in Krishnaveni as Saligrama Mountain. Later, the Lord incarnated himself as 'Narasimha' killed the mighty demon Hiranya Kasapa & saved Prahalda & ever since stayed as Jwala Narasimha on the mountain head at Vedadri. Then Lord Bramha requested Jwala Narasimha to stay in Sathya Loka as Saligrama Narasimha, so the Lord went to Sathya Loka as Saligrama Narasimha. Later on, the Lord, at the request of Rishis like Rishya Srugna & kinga like Mann, stayed in the middle of the mountain as Yogananda Narasimha Swamy & at the request of the Garudas, the Lord stayed as Veera Narasimha & as per the prayer of Vana Devatha, the Lord is pervading the mountain as Laxmi Narasimha. Thus the Lord existing in 5 forms different from each other called Pancha Narasimha namely (Jwala, Saligrama, Veera, Yogananda & Laxmi Narasimha).

DISTRICT – KURNOOL (Railway Station – Tadipatri/Kurnool City/Nandyal/Markapur/Adoni)

S. No.	Temple	Address	Type
1	Sri Nimishimba Devi Temple	Kurnool - 518001	Mata
2	Sri Bugga Ramalingeswaram Swami	Kalvabugga Village – 518002, Orvakal Mandal	Shiva
3	Sanganeswara Temple	Kurnool - 518002	Shiva
4	Shridi Sai Baba	Kothapeta – 518004	Saibaba

S. No.	Temple	Address	Type
5	Sun Temple	Gani Village – 518010	Sun
6	Srisaila Devasthanam	Srisailam – 518101	Mahashakti Peetha & Jyotirlinga
7	Sri Panikeswara Swamy	Panyam – 518118	Shiva
8	Belum Caves	Belum - 518122	Buddhist
9	Sri Lakshmi Narasimha Swamy	Kollimigundla – 518123	Narasimha (Vishnu)
10	Sri Chennakesava Swamy	Owk Village – 518124	Vishnu
11	Yaganti Swamy	Yaganti – 518124, Banganapally	Shiva, Parvati & Nandi
12	Sri Lakshmi Jagannadha Gattu Cave Temple	Laxmipuram Village – 518218	Jagannath (Vishnu)
13	Valmiki Caves	Boyavandlapalle – 518221	Cave
14	Adoni Fort	Adoni Town – 518301	Veerabhadra
15	Sri Ramalayam	Peddathumbalam – 518302	Rama, Jain
16	Sri Chowdeswari Devi	Nandavaram – 518343	Mata
17	Sri Urukunda Eranna Swamy Temple	Urukunda - 518344	Narasimha (Vishnu)
18	Manthralayam	Adoni – 518345	Sri Raghavendra Swamy Samadhi
19	Sangameswaram	Nandikotkur – 518401	Saptanadi, Shiva & Mahabharat Circuit
20	Sri Rupalasangameswara Jagannatha Gattu Temple	Sangameswaram, Nandikotkur – 518401	Shiva
21	Sri Suryanarayana Swamy Temple	Nandikotkur – 518401	Sun
22	Kolanu Bharathi Temple	Kottapalle – 518422	Saraswati Mata & Shiva
23	Koulutla Chennakesava Temple	Kappatralla – 518465	Vishnu & Shiva
24	Sri Mahanandeeswara Swamy Vari Devasthanam	Mahanandi 518502, Nandyal	Shiva
25	Sri Omkareswara Swamy Temple	Omkaram, Honkaram - 518502	Shiva
26	Eguvu Ahobilam & Diguvu Ahobilam	Ahobilam – 518545, Via Allagadda	Narasimha (Vishnu)
27	Sri Lakshmi Maddileti Narasimha Swamy	R.S. Rangapuram Village – 518598	Narasimha (Vishnu)

SRI NIMISHIMBA DEVI TEMPLE AT KURNOOL - Goddess Nimishamba is considered as the incarnation of Goddess Parvathi, the consort of Lord Shiva. There is a belief that Goddess Nimishamba is going to remove all the problems and troubles of her devotees within a minute. That is why she is called Nimishamba. Nimisha means a minute & Amba is the name of Goddess Parvathi. It would be of interest to note that marriage proposals which have been dragging on for years, get clicked immediately after visiting this shrine. There is a festival on "Nimishamba Jayanthi", which is celebrated on Vaishaka Shuddha Dasami of every year. There will be 'Homa' celebrations like Durga Homa, Chandika Homa during Navaratri and special poojas are done to the Goddess on Vijayadashami day. Special Pooja is offered on major festival days like Shivaratri, Ugadi, and Deepavali.

SRI BUGGA RAMALINGESWARAM SWAMY AT KALVABUGGA VILLAGE - It is estimated to have been constructed between 1490 & 1509. It is located on the banks of Penna River. The presiding deity is Lord Shiva in the form of Ramalingeswara Swamy. Five Lingas are in this Temple complex. According to legend, the Temple has been established, where sage Parasurama lived and performed meditation. The nature springs & hill rows are the main attractions of this Temple. The Temple got the name by a perennial underground stream from which water always keeps flowing into the sanctum sanctorum. In 1983, Sri Jayendra Saraswathi of Kanchi Kamakoti Peetam inaugurated Sri Bramarambha Devi Shrine in this Temple. At the river side, there is a Vigraha of goddess standing by steps. It is believed that when the water level of the Penna River reaches the navel point of that Vigraha, the entire town Tadipatri will be sinking in the water and that leads to the end of the town. The architecture of the Temple shows a mixture of Chalukyan, Chola & Vijayanagar art. The entire Shiva Purana is carved on the walls of the Temple in miniature carvings with elaborate details. Episodes from Hindu epics Ramayana & Mahabharata are also carved on the walls. This Temple has a mini stone chariot similar to the famous chariot of Vittala Temple in Hampi. Devotees celebrate the Sivarathri, Karthikamasam and Bramhostavalu as main festivals.

SANGANESWARA TEMPLE AT JAGANNATHA HILLS, KURNOOL - Sanganeswaram is confluence of two sacred rivers. The Temple is dedicated to Lord Shiva. It is believed that Pandavas visited Sri Mallikarjun Swamy Temple at Srisailam and then came to this place and prayed Lord Shiv here. Dharamaraja Yudishthir asked Bheema to bring a Shivalinga for consecration. By the time, Bheema returned with Shivalinga from Kashi Kshetra, Dharamaraja made a Shivalinga from neem wood and consecrated the same at this place. The other Shivalinga brought by Bheema has been consecrated nearby. This history of Shivalingas at this place is from Yugas.

SHRIDI SAI BABA AT KOTHAPETA - On the bank of the Tungabhadra River, the foundation stone of Nakshatra Saibaba Temple was laid down in the year of 1947 & Saibaba Vigraham was erected in 1951 at the Dasara Navaratriutsav. This is first Temple named as Dakshina Shridi Sai Baba. Sri K. Veera Swami Naidu installed the 4 foot marble Vigraha of Sri Sai Baba. There is a Srichakram inside the Temple, where the Vigraha of Baba is located. Temple is maintaining Akhanda Jyothi (ever lit lamp) since the construction of the Temple. In the Temple premises, there is Nanda deep, Dattatreya Vigraha, dhuni and avadhuta vigrahas. Temple considers the place with Vepa Chettu (neem tree) and Raavi Chettu (Bodhi in Sanksrit, peepal tree) as Gurusthan.

SUN TEMPLE AT GANI VILLAGE – This Sun Temple is at third number in India. It is considered as a prominent Temple of 400 years old. As per the source of historical inscriptions, the Guru Raja Acharya Swamy constructed this Temple by performing yagnam of Lord Sun taking with only one glass milk & 2 bananas daily up to the completion of the yagnam. At last, the Lord Sun came into existence & ordered him to erect Sun Vigraham on particular place & positions. During the construction, one big snake came there and the people worried about the emotional feelings of the gigantic shape of the snake. With worries, the labour on the sight killed the snake. In the dream of the Guru Raja Chari, the snake warned that the snake was myself on the sight so by killing me you will not have male baby and the Temple will be remained ruined for some period. In result of that shapam, this Temple is going to be renunciation. Sri Guru Raja Chari expired himself in this site. Sri Kasi Reddy Nayana started visiting the various places. Last but not least, he visited this Sun Temple. At night in a dream, Sri Guru Raj Chari came and ordered him to rebuild this Temple. On the next day onwards, Kasi Reddy Nayana started his struggle to rebuild this Temple. The followers of Kasi Reddy Nayana also participated in this campaign with faith & named this Temple area as "Brundavanam" and erected Kasi Reddy Nayana Vigraha after passing away Kasi Reddy Nayana.

MAHASHAKTIPEETHA & JYOTIRLINGA – BHARAMARAMBA MALLIKARJUNA AT SRISAILAM

- Located in a picturesque environment of Nallamalai Hills, 'Srisailam', the abode of Siva & Sakthi, is on the right side of the River Krishna. The presiding Deities of this Kshetram - God Mallikarjuna Swamy is one of the twelve Jyothirlinga and Goddess Bhramaramba Devi is one of the eighteen Mahasakthis and both are believed to be self-manifested. The unique feature of this Kshetram is the co-existing of Jyothirlingam & Mahasakthi in one Temple complex, which is the rare and only one of its kind. Parvatha, son of Silada Maharshi is said to have performed penance, pleased Lord Siva and made him agree to live on his body. He also prayed Lord Siva that all the Devathas and sacred waters of all theerthas permanently remain on his top and all the Devotees irrespective of cast or creed visiting the scared place should be blessed with the Moksha. God Siva granted these desired of Parvatha. The Parvatha assumed the shape big Hill 'Srisailam' & Lord Siva lived on its top as Sriparvatha Swamy. According to Hindu Mythology, Goddess Adisakthi acquired the shape of Bhramaram (bee) to kill the cruel demon Arunasura and after words settled at Srisailam as Bhramaramba Devi. It is said that here the neck portion of Sathi Devi was placed during Daksha Yagna and hence this place has become as Shakthi Peetam. In the traditional Hindu mythology, this Kshetram is identified as the Kailasa on the earth and named as Ila - Kailasam. Besides its mythical antiquity, Srisailam is also having a hoary historical antiquity. The inscriptional evidences available at Srisailam are of the 12th century A.D and afterwards, which is very intriguing. There is a common belief is in vogue that this Holy Kshetram exists from time immemorial. According to Agni Puranam, in the Krithayuga the Demon King Hiranyakasyapa did penance at the Kshetram and worshipped God Mallikarjuna Swamy. The Skanda Purana proclaims that in the Trethayuga Lord Sri Rama with Seetha Devi during their banish period has visited this Kshetram and consecrated Sahasra Lingas (One thousand Lingas) here. The Epic literatures clear that in the Dwapara Yuga, Arjuna while his pilgrimage and the Pandavas during their exile spent some time in this Kshetram and worship the Deities. Even now there is a pond at the foot way of Srisailam called as Bheemuni Kolanu. It is also said that Bhagavan Dattatreya did penance at this Kshetram and at now also there is a tree (Sthala Vriksham) in the Temple complex named a Dattatreya Vriksham. In the Kaliyuga the Advaitha Philosopher Adisankara, Siddha Nagarjuna, Veerasaiva Saint Allama Prabhu, Sivasarani Akka Mahadevi spent some time at this Kshetram and worshipped the deities. The existing main Temple is a huge complex consisting of separate Temples of

Mallikarjuna and Bhramaramba, several sub shrines, pillared halls, mandapas, springs etc., This entire complex is fortified by the most impressive Prakaram wall of massive stones. The Prakaram wall contains four Dwaras (principal gates) at four cardinals surmounted by the Gopuras. The eastern entrance is the Mahadwaram. In the inner courtyard, there are Nandimandapa, Veerasiromandapa, the Temple of Mallikarjuna, the Temple of Bhramaramba & all are in a row from east to west. Some of the minor shrines such as the Temple of Vriddha Mallikarjuna, Sahasra Lingeswara, Arthanariswara, Veerabhadra, Uma Maheswara and a group of five Temples named as Pandava Prathista Temples and a row of 9 Temples called as Navabrahma Temples etc. are also located in the inner courtyard.

SRI PANIKESWARA SWAMY AT PANYAM – The Temple is dedicated to Lord Shiva. The origin of the Temple dates back to Chalukya times. Long ago, the land was ruled by King Vishnu Vardhan. The wild animals destroying the crops & villagers. The king chased the wild animals in the forest to protect villagers. While the king was in sleep, his hands fell on the chest of his daughter. Facing himself as sin, he cut his two hands even though his daughter and people objected to do. Then the king decided and kept in a place of snakes. Automatically his hands reappeared. He constructed a Temple on the name of Panikeswara Swamy on the deity provided two hands again to the king.

BELUM CAVES AT BELUM – The Belum Caves is the largest & longest cave system open to the public on the Indian subcontinent, known for its speleothems, such as stalactite & stalagmite formations. The Caves have long passages, galleries, spacious caverns with fresh water and siphons. This cave system was formed over the course of tens of thousands of years by the constant flow of underground water from the now-disappeared river Chitravathi. The cave system reaches its deepest point at the point known as Pataalaganga. Belum Caves have a length of 3,229 m. It is one of the centrally protected Monuments of National Importance. Belum came to scientific attention in 1884 by a British surveyor, Robert Bruce Foote & from 1982 to 1984, a team of German speleologists headed by H. Daniel Gebauer conducted a detailed exploration of the caves. Thereafter in 1988, the state govt. declared the site protected & APTDC developed the caves as a tourist attraction in Feb. 2002. Today, 3.5 KMs of the caves have been successfully explored, though only 1.5 KMs is accessible to visitors. There are 16 different pathways, including the main entrance and there are deposits of quartz in the caves. The caves consist of black limestone. The Lord Buddha Vigraha at Belum Caves spreads an essence of tranquility in the air around it.

SRI LAKSHMI NARASIMHA SWAMY AT KOLLIMIGUNDLA VILLAGE - The shrine of Sri Lakshmi Narasimha is a piece of excellent architecture & workmanship depicting the Vijayanagara style of art. It is situated on the 750 foot height hillock. There is wonderful sculptural representation on the walls of the Temple. The Temple was constructed during the period of Sri Krishnadevaraya. There is an Vigraha of Sri Krishnadevaraya with his two wife, Chinnadevi and Thirumaladevi. This is a famous visiting spot, as one can see pyramid shaped hills which cannot be seen in other places.

SRI CHENNAKESAVA SWAMY AT OWK VILLAGE - The Owk Tirunala is prominent stage of other Tirunalas among the surrounding in Rayalaseema Region. Sri Bhulakshmi and Sri Chennakeshava Swamy are associate God name and fame as fulfilling the wishes of the peoples. With the willingness of Sri Krishnadevaraya, this Temple was constructed by Nalla Thimmaraju, founder of

Owk. An avatar of Adisakti worshiped as Mulama here. There is a big reservoir which was built by the then kings of Owk, namely "Thimmaraju Cheruvu".

SRI YAGANTI UMA MAHESWARA TEMPLE AT BANGANAPALLY – The area is situated amidst natural scenery with caves and water falls around. The presiding deity is Uma Maheswara Swamy popularly known as Yaganti Swamy. This deity is in the form of Vigraha & its tower possess beautiful sculptures. Lord Shiva, Parvati & Nandi are the main deities in this Temple. The most striking scenic at this Temple is huge Nandi of size of 15' X 10' X 8'. This Temple was constructed by King Harihara Bukka Raya of Sangama Dynasty of the Vijayanagara Empire in 15th CE. It was built according to Vaishnavaite traditions. As per legend, the Sage Agastya wanted to build a Temple for Lord Venkateswara on this site. However, the Vigraha that was made could not be installed as the toe nail of the Vigraha got broken. The sage was upset over this & performed a penance for Lord Shiva. When Lord Shiva appeared, he said that the place suits for him better, as it resembles Kailash. Sage Agastya then requested Lord Shiva to stay here with Parvathi Goddess as Lord Uma Maheswara in a single stone, which Lord Shiva obliged. The Saint Veerabrahmendra Swami stayed here for some time & wrote Kalagnanam. A feature of this Temple is its Pushkarini, a small pond of water. Water flows into this Pushkarini from the bottom of hill through the mouth of a Nandi. The water is fresh & sweet, as it comes from the hills. No one knows how the water reaches the pond all year round and this Temple architecture in terms of its sculpture shows the skills of ancient Vishwakarma Sthapathis.

Caves present in and around Yaganti Temple are :

Agastya Cave - This is the cave where Sage Agastya did his penance for Lord Shiva. One can enter the cave by climbing 120 steep steps. An Vigraha of Devi is installed & is worshipped here.

Venkateswara Cave - The damaged Vigraha of Lord Venkateswara is present in this cave. As compared to Agastya Cave, it is easy to climb though the steps are steep. According to the story this Vigraha was present in this cave before the Tirumala Venkateswara Temple was constructed.

Veera Brahmam Cave - Here, Saint Sree Potuluri Veera Brahmendra Swamy wrote some of his Kala Gnaanam. The height of cave is less & one needs to bend half over to enter it.

Growing Nandi - The Yaganti Nandi is believed to be growing in size. It is said that people used to do Pradakshinas (rounds) around it in the past. According to Potuluri Veera Brahmendraswamy, the Basavanna (stone nandi) of Yaganti will come alive and shout when Kaliyuga ends.

Absence of Crows - Legend has it that while the Sage Agastya was performing his penance, crows disturbed him and he cursed that the crows cannot enter the place. As the crow is the Vahana for Lord Shani, it is believed that Shani cannot enter this place.

SRI LAKSHMI JAGANNADHA GATTU CAVE TEMPLE AT LAKSHMIPURAM VILLAGE – The Temple is situated in the midst of hills and forest green valley. Vijayanagara Kings constructed and patronized this Temple. Jagannatha Swamy with Sridevi & Bhudevi are famous in the shape of Lingam (Phallus). At the bottom of the hill, there is Koneru. Chariot festival is famous in this area.

VALMIKI CAVES AT BOYAVANDLAPALLE VILLAGE - The Caves, sculptured by nature thousands of years ago, has recently brought to light. About the details, Caves are found in the Palro Leaf Texts (archives) secured in the Village. Sage Valmiki visited three Caves and worshipped the holy Shivalingam consecrated there. Hence, the Caves came to be known as Valmiki Caves. Sri Narayanappa Tata penanced in these caves for a long time and later entered "Mahasamadhi" at Atakonda village. Actually, the Caves were discovered in 1983. Some time back, four German tourists visited the Caves and explored them to some extent. Since these natives believed that the powerful Lord Shiva in the Caves grants their desires, number of devotees come to the Caves to worship the "Shivalinga". Grand festive spirit is seen during "Mahashivaratri" Festival. The Caves unfold the beauties of natural tours. The entrance to the caves appears like a small hole. If we go down through the hole, we reach a spacious plain. After moving further, we see a galaxy of naturally formed Shivalingas. The wonder is that waterfalls drop by drop incessantly on one of the Lingas. Stones in the form of elephant heads greet us. Among them two appear alike in two different places. After going further down, there are stone carved welcoming Arches, Multi-coloured stones, a 30 feet single stone pillar astonish us. The multi colored stones, water gushing out from the waterfalls with musical sounds, small brooks, the water drops falling rhythmically from the ceiling capture the hearts of the visitors. It is a nature lover's paradise. Visitors go into a devotional trance when they see a Pond called Patala Ganga, a naturally formed Nandi vigraha near the pond and stone "Rudrakshas" on the walls. Devotees dip in the Pond to unburden their sins and worship Nandi for granting their desires. It seems that further, there is a way from the Pond in the water through the Cave but nobody dares to go further. There are beautiful naturally formed sculptures and the inspiring scenery.

ADONI FORT AT ADONI TOWN - The Fort standing on the rocky Granite Hills appears to be an important stronghold of the Vijayanagar Kings. The remains of fortification surrounded by a group of five hills. Inscriptions mention the construction of several Temples at this place during the time of Krishnadevaraya. Sri Veerabhadra Swamy, Yogini Lakshmamma, Sri Venkateswara Swamy, Mangaraya Swamy.

SRI RAMALAYAM AT PEDDATHUMBALAM VILLAGE - Built by Western Chalukyas. Jain religion propagated in the District is one of the historical evidence in Chippagiri, Halivi and Pedda Thumbalam. The Jain Temple reflects style with marble stone with the architecture in Nallagonda Kolanupaka Jain Temple. The new Jain Temple constructed modern style. The Temple has beautiful architecture and there are vigrahas of two Thirthankaras. It is biggest Jain Temple in the District. This Temple was previously Jain Temple right now converted to Ramalayam Temple. This Ramalaya Temple established Sita-Rama, Lakshmana vigrahas. It is one of the biggest North Indian style gopuram established in South India. There are number of sculptures. People believe in that Lord Rama gives good health and wealth. The beautiful Temple is under control of State Archaeology Department and also another historical Thousand Pillar Temple is there.

URKUNDA NARASIMHA SWAMY (ERANNA) TEMPLE AT URKUNDA VILLAGE - Here sanctum sanctorum is a holy Peepal Tree under which, there are vigrahas of Veerabadra Swamy & Lakshmi Narasimha. As per legends, a sage named Hiranya, also popular as Eranna or Veeranna, did several years of penance under a Peepal Tree in Urkunda Village. The grazing cows of the village used to gather around him and he used to spend a lot of time caring them and talking to them. The kind villagers visited him with fruits & food and sought his blessings. It is believed that with his divine power, the Sage cured chronic diseases of the villagers. One day, the villagers could not find Sage Veeranna at his usual place, but instead, there was an Vigraha of Sri Lakshmi Narasimha under the Peepal Tree. They believed that it was Sage Veeranna, who had appeared as Narasimha Swamy. They installed the Vigraha under the Peepal Tree properly & began to worship him as Lakshmi Narasimha.

SRI CHOWDESWARI DEVI TEMPLE AT NANDAVARAM - The famous Temple is one of the many treasures which Andhra Pradesh holds. It is said that the actual deity that was present in the Temple was so fearful to watch with the human eye and the powerful aura it carried made many a heart fail on seeing it. Therefore, the doors of the sanctum were permanently closed & then another deity was made, which resembled posture of the actual deity. There is a Srichakra in front of the deity and devotees can worship with vermilion. Sri Chowdeshwari Devi has been showering grace and blessings on her devotee at all times and more so when they encounter with specific problems and seek her guidance for rightful solutions. According to a legend, the king of Nandavara was a Shakti Upasaka. With the help of Mantra Shakti, the king used to wake up at 4 'O' Clock in the morning, reach Kasi, bath in the holy Ganga & return to his Kingdom before dawn & offer worship to Devi at Nandavara. This was his daily practice. One day, the King took his Queen to Kasi along with him. Rani had her monthly course during their stay at Kasi. This affected the king & he lost his Mantra Shakti. As he was unable to return to his kingdom as usual, the King became restless and worried. While walking along the banks of Ganga being unable to find a solution, he saw a group of Brahmins performing Chandi Homa & went near them. The Brahmins promised to pass on to the king one fourth of what they had acquired as punya which would purify Rani & enable them to return to their kingdom. The king promised to give Jahagirs to them for purposes of their performing Dharmic deeds whenever they approached him. Thus the king got the power from the Brahmins & returned to his kingdom. Years rolled on. There came a terrible famine in Kasi. The Brahmins having remembered the king's promise went to Nandavara & met him. They reminded him of his promise. The king had totally forgotten his promise. From that day onwards, all the efforts of the king started yielding negative results. The Brahmins worshipped Sri Chowdeshwari & requested her to come down to Nandavara as the lonely witness for the king's promise. Devi did as they desired. The king realized his mistake. The dynasty of Brahmins thus settled at Nandavara came to be known as Nandavariks. She is also the family deity of Togataveeras. Nearest Railway Station is Panyam.

MANTHRALAYAM AT ADONI - Mantralayam is situated on the banks of River Tungabhadra. It derived its importance from the Jeevasamadhi of Madhva Saint Sri Raghavendra Swamy. The Choultries and Sanskrit School are the real attracting of these places and draws thousands of devotees from South India particularly Madhvas. Here, the places to see including Raghavendra Swamy Brindavan, the tomb that Swamy entered alive, Panchamuki Anjaneya Swamy Temple and

Venkateswara Swamy Temple. Nearest Railway Station is Manthralayam Road.

SANGAMESWARAM AT NANDIKOTKUR - Sangameswaram is a place where seven rivers joints and known on Saptanadi Sangameswaram. The River Bhadra, Bhavanasi, Bheeravathi, Malyaprabha, Tunga, Veni joins Krishna. It was known that Dharmaraja of Pandavas established Sivalingam at the junction of the rivers. Normally most of the time this Temples is submerged in Srisailam back water. It appears in Summer Season.

SRI RUPALASANGAMESWARA JAGANNATHA GATTU TEMPLE AT SANGAMESWARAM – The Temple got constructed in 8th CE by the Chalukyas. This Temple was rebuilt from Sangameswaram which submerging in the Srisailam project water in the year 1984. It is situated on top of the hills. The Temple has marvellous sculpture. It is the model Temple of Kailasanatha Temple in Ellora Caves. A 50 feet Abhayanjaneya Vigraha was constructed recently on the hill. Devotees celebrate Sivarathri and Karthikamasam as main festival.

SRI SURYANARAYANA SWAMY TEMPLE AT NANDIKOTKUR - The Temple was constructed by Chanikyas in 1080 AD. During the reign of Prataparudra of Kakatiya dynasty, Nandikotkur was a place in Navanandi circle. There are Navanandi steps in the village. Sirisinga Deva, a governor of Prataparudra believed to have constructed the Surya Narayana Swamy Temple.

KOLLAM BHARATHI AT KOTHAPALLI - The Temple is the abode of Sri Bharathi. It has an ancient Saraswathi Temple worshipped with the name of Bharathi. In 11th CE, during the region of Janamejayaraju, this Temple was built. A small perennial stream forms a water body (kolanu) near the Bharathi Temple. From the surrounding mountains, River Charughoshini is flowing and absorbed near the feet of Goddess Saraswathi. It is believed that if anybody takes bath in the river, his/her sins will go way. The word "Kolanu" (in Telugu) with usage over the years has become "Kollam". That is how the Temple is known as "Kollam Bharathi". In the same Temple complex also has seven Temples dedicated to Siva (Sapta Linga Kshetram). It also has beautiful waterfalls. This Temple is nestled in the hills of Nallamala forest. This Temple is facing towards north and it is also Garbha Gudi and Mukha Mantapas. In front of the Temple, Srichakradharini is present as special event. Here Kolan-Bharathi is located on blooming lotus in the Aasanos Padmaasana and her

Jatamakuta. This goddess has hangings and necklaces up to belly and has four hands with Abhayahasta and Ankusha in right hand and books in the left hand. She has Aksharamala and Paasankusa. It is believed that those children, who are not mentally developed according to age, will take the darshan of the goddess and after darshan, their intelligence will be developed.

KOULUTLA CHENNA KESAVA TEMPLE AT KAPPATRALLA – It is located in a reserved forest. Along with Koulutla Chenna Kesava Temple, there are additional Shiva Temples in this shrine such as Mallikarjuna Swamy, Bramarambika & Vijaya Vinayaka Temple; Lord Dakshinamurthy Temple & Lord Viswanatha Temple. King Parikshith (the grandson of Arjuna) ruled over Hastinapura after Pandavas retired to Kailasa. One day, while on a hunting trip to the forest, Parikshith was thirsty. He found a saint in deep meditation. He asked for water and the Rishi (saint) did not reply. Parikshith got frustrated and played a prank by putting a dead snake around the neck of the Rishi. He was cursed by the Rishi that he would die of a snake bite within a week; he died consequently at the hands of the Naga prince Takshaka. When Janamejaya (the son of Parikshith) became the King, he wanted to avenge the death of his father and performed Sarpa Yagya (serpent penance). Saint Vasista asked Janamejaya to perform consecration (Prathista) of Vishnava Temples to redeem the sins of killing innocent snakes. Consequently, a Chennakesava Vigraha was consecrated in Koundinya Ashrama to perform regular pujas. After many years, the Vigraha was covered by an anthill (putta). In the 11th century AD, Golla Koulutla observed that his cow was letting her milk flow to the anthill. That night, Lord Chennakesava (Vishnu) appeared in his dream & told him to remove the anthill & re-consecrate his Vigraha. Koulutla dutifully followed the instructions and from then, the deity is known as Koulutla Chennakesava Swamy.

SRI MAHANANDEESWARA SWAMY VARI DEVASTHANAM AT NANDYAL - It is an ancient Temple dates back over 1,500 years. The inscriptions of 10th CE tablets speak of the Temple being repaired & rebuilt several times. The Temple is famous for its fresh water pools, called Kalyani or *Pushkarni*. The architecture of the Temple shows the strong presence of the Chalukya Kings in this region. The pools of Temple shows the skill of the Vishwakarmas. The main Temple is surrounded by three pools: two small pools at the entrance and one big pool inside the Temple itself. A peculiarity of the water source is that it has a constant flow irrespective of the change of seasons. The water source originates at the Garbhagruha just below Swayambhu Linga. One can touch the water near the Shiva Linga. The water is famous for its crystalline and healing qualities and is ever tepid. The outgoing water irrigates 2,000 acres of fertile land surrounding the village. It is a scenic spot having its location to the east of the Nallamalas hill range in a natural set up of ravishing beauty surrounded by thick forest.

SRI OMKARESWARA SWAMY TEMPLE AT OMKARAM – The Temple is dedicated to Lord Shiva. It is situated amidst the thick Nallamalai Forests. The other major sights are Nava Nandi Temples i.e. Surya Nandi, Krishna Nandi and Garuda Nandi. Adding to the serene surroundings is the perennial flow of crystal clear water from perennial springs, the water from which also feeds the Temple tank. Devotees do not leave without taking a holy dip.

SRI LAKSHMI NARASIMHA SWAMY VARI DEVASTHANAM AT AHOBILAM - It is a great religious centre of antiquity. Ahobilam is the place where the Lord Sriman Narayana manifesting as Narasimha from a pillar and killed Hiranyakasipu and saved Prahalada. At upper Ahobilam, worship is offered to Navanarasimha (Nine Forms of Lord Narasimha) whereas at lower Ahobilam, down the hill, the Temple of Prahladavarada is located. The whole complex is in two parts - one called Eguvu Ahobilam (Upper Ahobilam) with Nava Narasimha shrines and the other called Diguvu Ahobilam (Lower Ahobilam) with a single shrine for Lakshmee Narasimha connected by a road, stretching a distance of about 12.8 Kms. from Lower Ahobilam to Upper Ahobilam. Other sites worth seeing are Amruthavalli Tavar Temple, Sannidhi Pushkarini, Bhashyakara Sannindi. Garuda wished for a vision of Lord Narasimha in the form of Avthara. To fulfil his wish, Lord settled in the hills around Ahobilam in nine different forms, which are: - 1. Jwala Narasimha 2. Ahobila Narasimha 3. Malola Narasimha 4. Kroda Narasimha 5. Karanja Narasimha 6. Bhargava Narasimha 7. Yogananda Narasimha 8. Kshatravata Narasimha and 9. Pavana or holy Narasimha. For this reason, this hill came to be known as Garudadri, Garudachalam and Garudasailam. Mahalakshmi took avathar as Senjulakshmi among the Senju, tribal hunters of the hills and married the Lord. The Eastern Ghats are likened to the great serpent Adhisesha basking in the sun with its head (or hood) at Thirumala, its middle at Ahobilam and its tail- end portion at Srisailam - all the three with famous Temples on them. Sri Ahobila Muth, one of the most important Sri Vaishnava religious institutions in India, was established by Sri Athivan Satakopan at the instructions of Lord Lakshmi Nrisimha of Ahobilam. Thirumangai Azhvaar has sung ten verses about this Temple in Periya Thirumozhi.

SRI LAKSHMI MADDILETI NARASIMHA SWAMY AT R.S. RANGAPURAM VILLAGE - The Temple is situated on the banks of Madduleru Vagu, therefore, the God name is Maddileti Swamy. Sri Maddileti Narasimha Swamy Temple is located in natural rock scenario and this location is very beautiful. It is attracting more devotees and also there was beautiful water falls in the name of "Kothula Gundam" and "Thirugudu Gundam". Nearest Railway Station is Rangapuram.

DISTRICT – PRAKASAM (Railway Station – Ongole/Markapur Road/Donakonda/Vinukonda)

S. No.	Temple	Address	Type
1	Sri Nagalaxmi Mata Mandir	Ongole - 523001	Mata
2	Sri Trimukha Durgamba Mahadevi, Sri Barguleshwari Swamy Temple & Kaala Bhairava Swamy	Bhairavakona – 523112	Saraswati Mata & Bhairav
3	Sri Malyadri Lakshmi Narasimha Swamy Vari Devasthanam	Malakonda – 523116, Valetivari Palem	Narasimha (Vishnu) & Mahalakshmi
4	Sri Chennakesava Swamy Temple	Markapuram – 523316	Vishnu
5	Chandavaram Buddhist Site	Jagannadhapuram – 523326	Buddhist

S. No.	Temple	Address	Type
6	Sri Pravathisahita Tripurantakeswara Swamy Temple	Tripuranthakam – 523326	Shiva & Parvati
7	Nemaligundla Ranganayaka Swamy Temple	Thurimella – 523372	Vishnu

SRI NAGALAXMI MATA MANDIR AT SANTHAPETA, ONGOLE - The Temple is famous for worship of Sri Nagalaxmi. Devotees from far & wide visit the Temple to pay there obeisance to the Goddess. Various festival are organised here with great pomp & fervor.

BHAIRAVAKONA – It is a holy place situated in the heart of Nallamala Hills. The name Bhairavakona is originated from the fact that the Temple of Sri Trimukha Durgamba Mahadevi along with Sri Barguleshwari Swamy is present at that place and Bala Bhairava Swamy guards the location. This place is home to an ancient Shiva Temple. There is a waterfall which falls from a height of 200 metres and there are eight Temples carved in the hill there. An interesting feature that attracts devotees to Bhairavakona is that the moonlight falls on the Vigraha of goddess Parvati at a Temple there on Kartik Poornima day. The main deity has three faces in which Goddess Saraswathi Devi is seeing her face in the mirror. The Temple is carved from a single stone.

SRI MALYADRI LAKSHMI NARASIMHA SWAMY VARI DEVASTHANAM AT MALAKONDA – Malyadri is one of the Navanarasimhas (Nine Narasimhas). Malyadri means the Parvatas are arranged as flower mala. The west side of Malyadri has the Ahobhila Narasimha Swamy, northwest side of Malyadri has the Sri Sailam, south side of Malyadri has the Vruchachala Kshetram & Penna River, east side of Malyadri has the Narasimha Swamy of Singarayakonda, North side of Malyadri has the Krishna River. All the devotees of Malyadri give their children names related to Sri Malyadri Narasimha for males and related to Sri Mahalakshmi for females. The Lord has Sudarshana Chakra on one hand, Sanku on one hand, Sri Mahalakshmi is sitting on his thigh so one hand is surrounding her and blessing devotees with one hand. The God gives blessings to Yakshas, Gandharvas, Sidhas and Devamunis on six days (Sunday to Friday). The God gives blessings to Devotees (Manavas) on Saturday only. Sri Mahalakshmi Devi Mata is Goddess of Malyadri. She is on top of the Hill of Malyadri. Here also the God Sri Narasimha and the Goddess Sri Mahalakshmi Devi give blessings to the Devotees.

SRI CHENNAKESAVA SWAMY TEMPLE AT MARKAPUR – It is a famous Temple of Lord Maha Vishnu. Sri Maha Vishnu is the prime deity in this Temple, who is also known as Chenna Kesava Swamy. The deity is accompanied by his consort Goddess Sri Mahalakshmi. Here, the Lord is known

as Kesava as he killed Kesi, a demon. It was established between 1405 -1459 AD under the rule of Vijayanagar. The Temple has marvellous gopurams. It has a huge Galigopuram which stands 135 foot tall, which can be seen from 5 KMs away. The Temple has a 40-pillared Mandapam with the mystic carving of Lord Sri Krishna, Lord Anjaneya, Lord Vighneswara and Goddess Sri Maha Lakshmi along with their Vahanas. The wonderful Kalyana Mandapam of the Temple has 6 musical pillars that create 7 musical notes in its correct "Aaroha" and "Avaroha" when tapped gently with the fingers. The unique feature of this Temple is that every year during the morning of 16th December to 14th January, the sun rays enter the sanctum sanctorum through a window and touch the feet of the deity. This makes the deity's feet glow for 20 minutes. This is a masterpiece of architectural wonder.

CHANDRAVARAM STUPA AT CHANDRAVARAM - It is located on a hill called Singarayakonda, which is on the banks of River Gundla Kamma. It was first discovered by the eminent archaeologist and historian Dr. Veluri Venkata Krishna Sastry. An outstanding stupa with double terraces that was built on a high platform is the main monument. The archaeological site is treasure trove of buildings and objects from the Buddhist period between 2nd Century BC and 2nd Century AD. The Chandavaram Stupa is only next to the Sanchi Stupa in significance and elegance and resembles the famous Dharajaka Stupa at Taxila.

SHRI BALA TRIPURA SUNDARI DEVI TEMPLE AT TRIPURANTAKAM - The name of Tripurantakam came from one of the person who is Tripuantakeswarudu ruled this town and the famous Temples Sri Bala Tripuranthakeswara and Sri Bala Tripurasundari Devi Temples are there. The Temple has old history & real Vigraha of Bala Tripurasundari Devi is installed in the Temple. it's difficult to see the Vigraha because it is very terrible. According to Shiva Purana, Lord Shiva destroyed Tripurasuras (demons ruling three cities) here. After his destruction of the demons and the three cities they inhabited, Lord Shiva was given the name "Tripuranthakeswara" and the place was named "Tripuranthakam". Sri Pravathi Sahita Tripurantakeswara Swamy Temple is on the top of the hill and houses a secret underground passage to Srisailam from the Temple premises. Below the hill, inside a pond, is the Bala Tripura Sundari Temple. She (swayambhu) is the first incarnation of Adiparasakthi. She is believed to reside there in the form of a little girl.

NEMALIGUNDAM RANGANAYAKA SWAMY TEMPLE AT THURIMELLA – It is located in Nallamalla Forest. The main deity Ranganayaka Swamy is in reclining posture. It is believed that those who speaks lies at this Holy Place will be punished.

DISTRICT – SRIKAKULAM (Railway Station – Mandasa Road/Srikakulam Road/)

S. No.	Temple	Address	Type
1	Buddhist Stupta	Danthapuri – 532185	Buddhist
2	Mandasa Vasudeva Perumal Temple	Mandasa - 532242	Vishnu
3	Group of Temples	Baruva - 532263	Shiva, Vishnu

S. No.	Temple	Address	Type
4	Sri Suryanarayana Swamy Vari Devasthanam	Arasavalli – 532401	Sun
5	Srikurmam Kurmanathaswamy Temple	Sri Kurmam – 532404, Gara Mandal	Kurma (Vishnu)
6	Salihundam Buddhist Heritage Site	Salihundam Hill - 532405	Buddhist
7	Hanuman Temple	Madapam - 532421	Hanuman
8	Srimukhalingeswara Temple	Mukhalingam – 532428, Jalumuru Mandal	Shiva
9	Sangameswara Swamy Temple	Sangam – 532462, Vangara Mandal	Triveni Sangam & Shiva

DANTHAPURI - Ancient Buddha Stupa are present in this place. It is believed to be a place of Buddha religion and a siddhardas living place. It is an important archaeological place, called Boudha Gynana Dantha Puri, where the archaeological department found some bricks, pots, wear, terracotta articles, bangles, beads, stone and iron articles. It is elevated in the BC 261 after Kalinga battle by Ashoka Chakravarthi. Kalinga rajas treated as capital of their region. The Boudha Gynana Dantha collected and presented by Arhat Kheru Terudu to Brahmadatta Raja of Kalinga. Brahma Datta Kalinga Raja constructed a monument on Boudha Gyana Dantha at this place so the place is called Danthapuri.

VASUDEVA PERUMAL TEMPLE AT MANDASA - This Place is situated at the foothills of Mahendragiri Hills. The fort is considered to be the highest in South India and it is a place of tourist interest. In this village, the Temple of Varahaswamy attracts the attention of the tourists.

BARUVA - The famous Sri Kotilingeswara Swamy and Janardhana Swamy Temple are located at this place. The River Mahendra Tanaya merges into sea at this place. Thousands of people take sea bath during festivals. Baruva was once an important seaport. Two obelisks, one of black and the other of white, of fifty feet height above the sea level, mark the seaport.

SRI SURYANARAYANA SWAMY VARI DEVASTHANAM AT ARASAVALLI - The famous Sun God Temple is one of the ancient and all among two sun God Temples in India. According to Padmapuranam, Sage Kashyapa installed the Vigraha of Surya at Arasavalli. Therefore, the Surya is of Kashyapa Gotra. He is also termed as planetary King. According to the 'Sthalapuranam', Lord Devendra found this Temple and installed the existing Vigraha of the Sun God, commonly known as Lord Suryanarayana Swamy Varu, with his three consorts Usha, Chaya and Padmini. At the base of the vigrahas are the figures of Mathara and Pingala, the Dwarapalakas and high up are the two divine Saints, Sanaka and Sanadana holding 'Chatrams' (An Umbrella). The Sun God is depicted as riding over a chariot drawn by Anura, the Radhasaradhy. All these figures are exquisitely carved out of a single black finely polished granite stone. The Temple is built in such a way as to make the Sun Rays focus on the feet of the God twice in the year in the months of March and September in the early hours of the day. The rays so focused on the feet of the Vigraha through the five entrance gates of the Temple remain for a few minutes. The Five vigrahas (Panchayatana installed in a particular place in the

Temple) namely: - 1. Aditya 2. Ambika 3. Vishnu 4. Ganesha 5. Maheswara, represent all the faiths. People who are unfortunate enough to suffer from eye and skin diseases visit the Temple and offer their prayers to Sun God. They believe that the God is essentially a God of Health and prayers offered to him would heal their sickness.

KURMANATHASWAMY TEMPLE AT SRIKURMAM - It is dedicated to the Kurma avatar of Lord Vishnu. He is worshipped as Kurmanathaswamy and his consort Lakshmi is worshipped as Kurmanayaki. According to Hindu legend, the presiding deity is believed to have manifested here in the form of a tortoise-shaped deity upon the wishes of Swetha Chakravarthi. Brahma then consecrated the deity with Gopala Yantra. Srikurmam is the only Indian Temple in the world where Vishnu is worshiped in his Kurma avatar. Initially dedicated to Shiva and referred to as Kurmeswara Temple, Ramanuja is said to have converted Srikurmam into a Vaishnavite Temple in the 11th century AD. The deity of Kurmanathaswamy is made of black stone but due to regular applications of sandalwood paste, it appears yellow. The deity is consists of three stone structures. The stone representing the head faces the west; the middle stone represents the body of the tortoise; the small stone at the rear end, covered with swirling circles, represents either the tail of the tortoise or the Sudarshana Chakra. Beside the sanctum sanctorum of Kurmanatha, there is a Temple dedicated to Kurmanayaki in which a deity of Andal is found. Hatakeswara, Karpureswara, Koteswara, Sundareswara, and Pathalasiddheswara are among the Temple's guardian deities. The Temple has two dhvajasthambas, a rarity for a Vaishnavite Temple. 108 ekasila (*single-stone*) pillars, with none resembling each other, bear few inscriptions related to the royal lineages that existed in this area in the past. It is protected by Central Archaeological Department. The Indian postal department issued a stamp featuring the Temple on 11 April 2013. The Sage Durvasa visited the Temple later with his disciples; the event of his arrival was considered significant. Rama's sons Lava and Kusha were said to have worshipped Lord Vishnu as Kurmanatha in Srikurmam. In Dwapara Yuga, Balarama visited the Temple and was denied entry by Bhairava, who was serving as the Temple's Kshetrapalak (guardian deity). Infuriated, Balarama threw Bhairava away from the Temple premises. Kurmanatha came to know this and gave Balarama permission to enter the Temple. Balarama, in resentment, cursed that Srikurmam would be the only Temple where Lord Vishnu would be worshipped in the form of Kurma Narayana. Legends also say that upon Lord Vishnu's request, Anjaneya agreed to guard the Temple. In the Temple's premises, a tortoise park has been built to conserve the adult and young star tortoises, which are found in the foothills and fields of Srikakulam. Srikurmam is the only conservation centre for this species. The Temple is famous for ancestor worship, as it is known as *pitrukshetra*. People believe that their ancestors' souls shall gain salvation if offered prayers here.

SALIHUNDAM BUDDHIST HERITAGE SITE AT SALIHUNDAM HILL - It is situated on the south banks of River Vamsadhara. There are number of Buddhist stupas and a huge monastic complex on a hillock amidst scenic surroundings. The site was first discovered by Gidugu Venkata Rama Murthy in 1919. During excavations relic caskets, four stupas, a Chaityagriha, structural Temples and a number of sculptures reflecting the three phases of Buddhism – Theravada, Mahayana and Vajrayana were found dating back to about 2nd century BC to 12th century AD. The vigrahas of 'Tara' and Marichi were discovered at this site and it is believed that from here, Buddhism spread to Sumatra and other far-eastern countries.

HANUMAN TEMPLE AT MADAPAM - The Temple is dedicated to Lord Hanuman. It is located on the banks of Vamsadhara River. The vigraha of Lord Hanuman is in standing posture and it has a massive height of 171 ft. which is believed to be the tallest vigraha of Lord Hanuman in the world.

SRIMUKHALINGESWARA TEMPLE AT MUKHALINGAM – The Temple was built by Kamarnava–II in 8th century AD of the Eastern Ganga dynasty. The Temple is dedicated to Lord Shiva, which is located on the left banks of River Vamsadhara. Elegantly carved, this Temple is a group of three Temples dedicated to three forms of Lord Shiva namely, Mukhalingeswara, Bhimeswara and Someswara. The Temple is built in Indo-Aryan style. One can witness marvellous sculptures, carvings and intricate architecture here. The architecture of the Temple is so elegant that one just cannot move eyes from it. As you observe closely, you can see that every piece and corner of the Temple is as excellent as the other. At the entrance, which is a huge arched gate, you are welcomed by two lions on each side of the few stair-cases. The first gate takes you to the outer prakara have where there is a Nandi in a mandapam.

SANGAMESWARA SWAMY TEMPLE AT SANGAM – It is a Triveni Sangam, where River Nagavali, Suvarnamukhi and Vegavati confluence takes place. It is similar to one well known in Allahabad. The Sangameswara Temple located here is one of the five Linga Kshetras. Thousands of devotees gather here on Maha Sivaratri Festival.

DISTRICT – SRI POTTI SRIRAMULU NELLORE (Railway Station – Nellore/Sri Kalahasti)

S. No.	Temple	Address	Type
1	Sri Thalpagiri Ranganadha Swamy Temple	Nellore - 524001	Sri Kashyapa Maharishi
2	Vedagiri Laxmi Narasimha Swami Temple	Komarapudi - 524004	Narasimha (Vishnu)
3	Alghu Malluru Krishna Swamy Temple	Mannar Polur – 524121	Vishnu
4	Sri Chengalamma Temple	Sullurupeta - 524121	Mata
5	Venkatagiri Fort	Venkatagiri – 524132	Shiva
6	Sri Mallikarjuna Swamy Kamakshi Tai Temple	Jonnawada - 524305	Shiva-Parvati
7	Sri Pensusila Lakshmi Narasimha Swamy Devasthanam	Penchalakona, Rapur Mandal - 524414	Narasimha (Vishnu)

SRI TALPAGIRI RANGANATHASWAMY TEMPLE AT NELLORE – The Temple is more than 600 years old. This Temple is situated on the banks of the River Pennar and is marked by a huge 29 Mts tall Galigopuram with seven gold kalasams and its architectural splendour. The annual Rath Yathra of the God is a much awaited ritual in Nellore. On the bank of River Pennar, Sri Kashyapa Maharshi performed yagna and as a fruit of his penance conferred upon him the gift of establishing himself as Ranganadha Swamy at Nellore in 7th century by Pallava Ruler Sri Rajaraja Narendra. Subsequently, in 13th century Sri Jatha Varma has offered precious stones and metal to Lord Ranganadha Swamy. On the south side, Sri Ranganayaki Lakshmi Devi Temple and beautiful mirror dais exists, on the west, there is sacred Pennar River and towards north, there is Sri Andal Ammavari Temple.

VEDAGIRI LAKSHMIMARASIMHA SWAMY DEVASTANAM AT NARASIMHAKONDA – The Temple came into being nearly 500 years ago. According to the rock inscriptions, this Temple was built by the Pallava King Narsimha Varma in the ninth century. Legend goes that the Sage Kashyapa established the Temple on the bank of River Pinakini and the vedic scripture, Brahmapurana reveals that the seven sages (Saptarishis) performed 'yagnam' (Sacrifice) on the top of Narasimhakonda. The seven (Koneru) tanks were renovated with Mandapas on the hilltop. Every year 'Brahmotsavams' are celebrated here in the month of May.

ALGHU MALLURU KRISHNA SWAMY TEMPLE AT MANNAR POLURU – The Temple is existing right from the time of Telugu Chola Rulers. It was built in the 17th century by Bangaru Yadama Nayudu, the living place of mallayodas or wrestlers. According to a legend, it was here that Lord Sri Krishna defeated Jambavantha in a duel and married his daughter Jambavati and that Lord Maha Vishnu deflated the bloated ego of Garutmata here alone. Apart from the Vigraha of Satyabhama and Jambavati, the two consorts of Lord Krishna, the Vigraha of Jambavantha creating the illusion of shedding tears are bound to amaze the viewers. One cannot help marvelling at the sculptural splendour exuded by the vigrahas of the beauties.

CHENGALAMMA TEMPLE AT SULLURUPET - Goddess Chengalamma Parameswari manifested herself in the village of Sullurupet and the Temple for her was built on the banks of the Kanlangi River. 400 years old Chengalamma Tree in the Temple premises acts as a boon giver to all devotees. As per records, it was established during the fourth and fifth centuries. People also refer to her as the village Goddess. With the passage of time, she is being worshipped regularly by devotees as Chengalamma. There is no doors in the Temple and Temple is open 24 hours. Chengalamma Thalli and her Vigraha in the Temple premises faces the sea. Goddess Chengalamma has enormous powers. ISRO Scientists visit Sri Chengalamma Parameswara for blessings before launching any satellite. Devotees turn up in large number to witness Chengalamma Jataraa. Nearest Railway Station is Sullurupeta.

VENKATAGIRI FORT – It was constructed in the year 1775 AD. The majestic fort was originally known as Kalimilli and was ruled by Gobburi Polygars under Vijaynagar Empire who were defeated by Recherla Venkatadri Naidu. The many Temples present here include Kashi Vishwanth Temple, Ramalingeswra Swami Temple, Prasanna Venkateswara Swami Temple among others that add to the value of the place. Today, the place is popular with the tourists not only for their interest in culture and history of the place but for eco-tourism. This is why the fort is now a famous trekking and camping destination. Nearest Railway Station is Venkatagiri.

SRI MALLIKARJUNA SWAMY KAMAKSHI TAI TEMPLE AT JONNAWADA – The Temple is located on the banks of River Pennar. In Tretayuga, Mahamuni Kashyapa performed yagna and pleased Lord Mallikarjuna Swamy, thus this place is named as 'Yagnavatika Jonnawada'. Sri Mallikarjuna Swamy Kamakhsi Tai grant to the innumerable devotes their desires, as their God head. Since then he continues conferring boons and his blessings on his devotees. The

Goddess Kamakshi is believed as an incarnation of Shakti. A 'Sri Chakram' was installed here by Sri Jagadguru Sankaracharya. Pilgrims take a holy dip in the Lake known as Kachpateertham, near the Temple, which washes away all their bad karma.

SRI PENSUSILA LAKSHMI NARASIMHA SWAMY DEVASTHANAM AT PENCHALAKONA - This is a very ancient sacred place. Lord Narasimha manifested himself here as a huge of rock in 'Yoga mudra' (in an entwined contemplative posture) and hence it acquired the name of 'Pensusila' (huge rock) and in course of time became famous as 'Penchalakona'. Legend has it that after slaying the demon Hiranya Kasipa, Lord Narsimha bathed in Penchalakona and withdrew that 'Avatara' of Narasimha shedding his anger and ferocity. The Lord here goes by the name of Somasila Narasimhaswamy and has become one of the Nava Narasimhas (nine manifestations). People believe that because the Sage Kanva resided in this area in the past, the river flowing here acquired the name Kanva Nadi and that with efflux of time, it became Kandaleru. It is also learnt that the Temple was renovated in the 10thcentury. Nearest Railway Station is Gudur.

DISTRICT – VISAKHAPATNAM (Railway Station – Vishakhapatnam/Simhachalam)

VISAKHAPATNAM - It is home to three scenic hillocks that stand testament to the communal harmony that India is known for. It is a fascinating experience to get to the three hillocks as one gets to visit a Temple, a Mosque and a Church during the same trip. The Ross Hill is home to the Ross Hill Church while the Sringamani Hillock and the Dargah Konda Hillock are home to the Venkateswara Temple and the Baba Ishaq Madina Dargah, respectively. The Temple is said to be two centuries old while the Mosque has been there for as many as 700 years. The magnificent Church at Ross Hill is more than a century old and its impressive white building stands as a fine specimen of Gothic architecture. The hilltops provide splendid views of Visakhapatnam and the port channel. Other Railway Stations are Duvvada/Anakapalle/Narsipatnam Road/Anandapuram.

S. No.	Temple	Address	Type
1	Sri Kanaka Mahalakshmi Temple	Burujupeta, Chengal Rao Peta, Port Area, Visakhapatnam – 530001	Mata
2	Sri Varaha Lakshmi Narasimha Swamy Devasthanam	Simhachalam – 530028	Vishnu
3	Somalingeswara Swamy Temple	Appikonda – 530031	Shiva
4	Kailasagiri	Visakhapatnam – 530043	Shiva & Parvati
5	ISKCON	Sagar Nagar, Visakhapatnam - 530045	Radha-Krishna
6	Thotlakonda Hill	Thotlakonda - 530048	Buddhist
7	Sri Nookambica Ammavari Mandir	Anakapalle - 531001	Mata
8	The Kotilingeswara Aalayam	Panchadarla – 531061	Shiva & Natural Spring
9	Balighattam Brahmalingeswara Temple	Baligattam – 531116	Shiva
10	Borra Caves	Borra Caves – 531149	Caves
11	Sri Laxmi Narasimha Swamy	Bheemunipatnam - 531163	Narasimha
12	Ananta Padmanabha Swami Temple	Padmanabham – 531219	Vishnu

SRI KANAKA MAHALAKSHMI TEMPLE AT PORT AREA – The Temple is boasts of a symmetry driven structure with a strong historical background significance. It is believed that the presiding Vigraha, who is an incarnation of Shri Lakshmi, was the family deity of the rulers of this area at that time and they used to admire her as Ammavari. According to locals, the Vigraha of the presiding deity, Ammavari, was found in the well that was located near the fort of the then Rajas. In the year 1912, it was taken out and placed in the centre of the road. To widen the same road, the Municipal Department thought of shifting the Vigraha to some other place and hence, installed it in the corner of the road. Right after the whole incident i.e., in 1917, the town started suffering from the disease called Plague and so many people died in the village. Seeing the overall condition, people got scared and figured out that it all happened due to the movement of the Vigraha from one place to another and to protect the town from this life-taking disease, they bought the Vigraha back to its original place where it was earlier installed. Owing to re-erection, the village got free of the Plague disease and the villagers had a sign of relief. Since then, the Vigraha of Sri Kanaka Mahalakshmi is worshipped by people with full faith and devotion.

SRI VARAHA LAKSHMI NARASIMHA SWAMY VARI DEVASTHANAM AT SIMHACHALAM - The word Simhachalam means the hill of lion. It is dedicated to Lord Vishnu, who is worshipped here as Varaha Narasimha. As per the Temple's legend (which is divided into 32 chapters), Lord Vishnu manifested in this peculiar form, with a boar head, human torso & a lion's tail, after saving his devotee Prahlada. According to Stalapurana, Prahalada son of Hrinakasyap was the first person to construct a Temple round the Deity. He accomplished this after his father's death at the hands of Narasimha. Except on Akshaya Tritiya, the Vigraha of Varaha Narasimha is covered with sandalwood paste throughout the year, which makes it resemble a Linga. The Temple resembles a fortress from outside with three outer courtyards & five gateways. The architecture is a mixture of the styles of the Kalinga Architecture, Chalukyas & Cholas. It contains a square shrine surmounted by a high tower, a portico in front with a small tower, a square sixteen pillared mandapam facing the portico & an enclosed veranda. All these are richly & delicately carved with conventional and floral ornaments and scenes from the Vaishnavitepuranas. One of the pillars locally known as the Kappasthambam, which is believed to possess great curative powers. There is a stone car with stone wheels & prancing stone horses. The Temple faces west instead of east, signifying victory. The Temple houses a number of sub-shrines and a few mandapams. The religious practices & customs of the Temple are formulated by the Vaishnavite philosopher Ramanuja. Devotees believe that the deity is capable of giving progeny to women and fulfilling the wishes of devotees. The Temple is neither disturbed nor distracted from the age long conventions, traditions & ritualistic performances inspite of many economic, political or religious controversies or conflicts in the region.

SOMALINGESWARA SWAMY TEMPLE AT APPIKONDA - Kapilamahamuni is said to have installed the vigraha of Somalingeswara Swamy in Appikonda. This Temple was built in 1070 by Chola King Kulottunga-I and refereed as Chola Monument. The Temple has assumed religious importance owing to the existence of a Shiva Temple containing a life size bull carved out of black stone. There are also other small Temples around the Shiva Temple but they are covered with sand dunes and their gopurams alone are visible. The Shiva Temple contains inscriptions of the 12th century AD. These inscriptions mention that this village was granted by a Commander in chief of the Cholas for the maintenance of worship in the Temple. This Temple is declared as protected monument by Archaeological Survey of India.

KAILASAGIRI AT VISHAKHAPATNAM – It is one of the prominent hill top parks with panoramic sea view on the East Coast. This has developed as an attractive picnic spot with the seven different beautiful viewpoints to enjoy the serene atmosphere and scenic beauty. It is a favourite location among the filmmakers all over India. The major attraction of the park is Lord Shiva Parvati Vigraha. The Vigraha of Lord Shiva atop the hill stands tall at a height of 40 foot. There is a floral clock, which is one of the biggest of India with a diameter of 10 foot. The floral clock gives an artistic impression on the lush green patches on the backdrop of the Shiva Parvathi Vigraha. The Shanku Chakra Naama measuring up to 40 mts. high, developed by TTD & VUDA is one of the beautiful sights on the hilltop garden and symbolizes the vigraha of Lord Vishnu.

ISKCON AT SAGAR NAGAR, VISAKHAPATNAM - An ISKCON devotee couple, Sri Samba Das and his wife Nitaisevini reached Visakhapatnam in May 1999 with a towering ambition to build a grand Temple complex for Lord Krishna, a project they fondly named "Glory of Andhra". There were many hurdles that he and his fellow ISKCON devotees tackled head on. Just when it seemed that all was lost, an unanticipated benefactor would step in or a solution would materialize and finally in 2005, in the serene environs adjacent to Sagar Nagar, he acquired a piece of land where the Temple is slated to rise. Revenue Minister of A.P. Sri Dharmana Prasad Rao came for the Bhoomi pooja. First phase of Construction of the Ashram building begun on the auspicious day of Akshaya Tritya day. Bordered on three sides by the serene stillness of verdant hills & over-looking the calm blue water of bay of Bengal, situated just a little distance away from the hustle & bustle of the main Visakhapatnam city through the scenic road that hugs the Coast line, you reach ISKCON Visakhapatnam, Hare Krishna Land in Sagar Nagar. The Deities of Sri Sri Radha Damodar and Jagannath Baladev Subhadra are installed in a spacious hall. Adjacent is the Prasadam hall. Behind is a complex that houses the Seminar hall & Guest house for ISKCON Life members. Also in place is a Goshala, where 64 Cows & calves are taken care with utmost love & affection. In the center lies the land ear marked for the Main Temple. Annual festivals like Rathayatra, Janmashtami, Radhashtami, Gaura Purnima, ISKCON Utsav are consistently celebrated with great pomp & show.

THOTLAKONDA HILL – The Hill is best known for a 2,000-year-old Buddhist complex. The complex is a protected monument. The archaeological excavations conducted here revealed a number of relics including 16 votive stupas, 11 rock-cut cisterns, stoned pathways, circular chaitya-grihas, votive platforms, viharas, a mahastupa etc. Several sculptures, silver coins belonging to the Satavahana period (1st century BCE - 2nd century CE), miniature Buddha Padas or models of Buddha's feet were also discovered during the archaeological excavations. The Buddhist complex overlooks the sea. Perched at an altitude of 128 m above sea level, Thotlakonda Hill is not only an idyllic stop for Buddhists.

SRI NOOKAMBIKA AMMAVARI TEMPLE AT ANAKAPALLE - The Temple is dedicated to Goddess Nookambika Ammavari. The King who ruled this area - Sri Kakarlapudi Appala Raju garu, built this Temple to Kakatambika, a family goddess. She would later be called Nookambika or Nookalamma. On "Kottha Amavasya", a day before Ugadi, thousands of people from throughout Andhra Pradesh come to the Temple for worship. The goddess is one of the nine Shakti forms and popularly known as Sri Anagha Devi in ancient days. It is believed that the creator of the universe was Sri Shakti Ammavaru and that the creation took place in the time period from Palguna Bahula Amavasya (the new moon day) to April (new moon day). During this holy period there are a lot of religious rituals and pujas that are performed to Sri Nookambica Ammavaru. Sunday, Tuesday & Thursday are considered auspicious days for performing puja to Sri Nookambika Ammavaru.

THE KOTILINGESWARA AALAYAM AT PANCHADARLA – The village has derived its name from the five Jets of water coming out of five fountains which receive their supplies from a natural perennial spring. Nearby, there is Lingam and other Lingams in 12 rows of 85 each are carved on the main Lingam, which is consequently known as the Kotilingam or Crore of lingams. There are several inscriptions on the pillars of the Mandapam in the Temple and two of them dated in AD 1407 and 1428 contain a genealogy of chiefs who claimed Eastern Chalukya ancestry and bore the Eastern Chalukya titles of Sarvalokasraya and Vishnu Vardana.

BALIGHATTAM BRAHMALINGESWARA TEMPLE AT BALIGATTAM - The Temple is situated at the foot of a small hill on the Western bank of the river. Here the shrine faces the West. Lakshmi Devi Temple is located nearby Brahma Lingeswara Temple. It is interesting to note that this Temple is supposed to have been built by Lord Brahmanand that the river is declared to have been made by Lord Vishnu during his incarnation as a boar (Varaha). Therefore, the river is known as Varahanadi. The deposits of white clay on the river bank are supposed to be the ashes of a sacrifice performed here by Bali, the demon king from whom the village takes its name as Baligattam. The river at this place flows from North to South for a short distance. On account of these peculiarities, the place is considered to be very sacred. Here the shrine like the one at bananas faces to the west. Sri Sri Sri Chidgagananandha Swamy Ashramam is located on Nayanagari Hill near Balighattam. This is one of the historical holy place to visit.

BORRA CAVES - It is also called Borra Guhalu, are situated on the East Coast of India in the Anantagiri Hill range of the Araku Valley. The caves, one of the largest in the country, are situated around 1,400 m above sea level. The Caves are considered the deepest Caves in India. In 1807, the caves were discovered by William King George of the Geological Survey of India. Considered to be one of the largest caves in India, the caves have karstic limestone structures, which extend to a depth of 80 m. A small Temple inside the cave was believed to be constructed by the locals in respect to the religious incident that once happened in the region. According to the popular story narrated by the tribal people residing in this area, a cow which was grazing on the top of the caves dropped through a hole in the roof. When cowherd was searching for the cow, he came across the caves and found a stone inside the cave, which resembled a Shivalingam. Tourists can spot number of bats and golden gecko in these caves. Mosses and brown-to-green algae are some of the popular floras seen inside these caves. The interiors of these caves are installed with sixty three lamps of mercury, sodium vapour and halogen lamps. The destination also has several mica mines; hence a project named Thalipudi Reservoir Scheme is introduced for mining precious stones like rubies.

SRI LAXMI NARASIMHA SWAMY AT BHEEMUNIPATNAM - The Temple is dedicated to Lord Narasimha. The vigraha of Lord Narasimha is located on a hill in a sitting posture giving darshan to each devotee in an open area. There are also Temples located nearby which as per the historical evidences was constructed around 14th century by Mindi Kings and also there are two more Temples in the town of Bhimili, which date back to the times of Chola's as Bheemeswaralayam and Choleswaralayam.

ANANTA PADMANABHA SWAMI TEMPLE AT PADMANABHAM – It is situated on the left bank of the Gosthani River. The Padmanabheswara Swamy Temple is one of the most important Temples of the region. The presiding deity Padmanabha Swamy is said to be the Lord, who readily responds to the desires of his devotees. On the top of the hill which overlooks the place, is the shrine of Padmanabha and the Kalyanostavam of the deity celebrated annually.

DISTRICT – VIZIANAGARAM (Railway Station – Vizianagaram/Vanamgudi)

S. No.	Temple	Address	Type
1	Sri Kanyaka Parameswari Ammavari Temple	Santha Pet, Vizianagaram - 535001	Mata
2	Dwadasi Jyothirlinga Temple	SVN Nagar, Vizianagaram – 535002	Shiva
3	Gnana Saraswathi Devi Temple	SVN Nagar, Vizianagaram - 535002	Mata
4	Gumchi Temple	Vizianagaram – 535002	Hanuman
5	Sri Jagannatha Swamy Temple	Vizianagaram - 535002	Jagannath
6	Sri Pydithalli Ammavari Temple	Vizianagaram - 535002	Mata

S. No.	Temple	Address	Type
7	Subrahmanya Swamy Temple	Phool Bagh Colony, Vizianagaram - 535002	Murugan
8	Vizianagaram Fort	Vizianagaram - 535003	Hanuman, Mata
9	Ramanarayanam	Korukonda Road, Vizianagaram – 535004	Ramayana
10	Punyagiri Temple	S Kota - 535145	Shiva
11	Geeta Bhawan	Govindapuram – 535204	Krishna
12	Kumili Temple	Kumili - 535204	Rama
13	Ibbilingeswara Swamy Temple	Saripalli – 535218	Shiva
14	Ramtheertham Temple	Nellimarla Mandal - 535218	Rama
15	Tripurantaka Swamy Temple	Jamiagraharam - 535250	Shiva
16	Bobbili Venu Gopalaswamy Temple	Bobbili – 535558	Vishnu

KANYAKA PARAMESWARI TEMPLE AT VIZIANAGARAM - It was built in the year 1890 by the Komatis (Trading community) in the honour of a village girl belonging to their community, who committed suicide to protect her honour. The Temple was constructed on the land donated by the Maharaja of Vizianagaram.

DWADASI JYOTHIRLINGA TEMPLE AT VIZIANAGARAM - It is a Temple with prototypes of Dwadasa Jyothirlingas in all over India. Main Vigraha is Sphatika Linga opened everyday evening at 6 PM aarti. It is a peaceful Temple.

GNANA SARASWATI DEVI TEMPLE AT VIZIANGARAM - It is a Temple of Saraswati Ammavaru. In this Temple, Aksharabhyasams are performed daily for Children. It is an exclusive Saraswati Temple in Northeast Andhra.

GUMCHI TEMPLE AT VIZIANAGARAM - It is dedicated to Lord Hanuman. The structure was originally built in 1713 as a post for the guards to protect a nearby lake 'Amma Koneru' (Mother Lake). It was converted to a Temple in the early 20th century, when an Vigraha of Lord Hanuman was found in a nearby well. This is the only Temple in India where the Vigraha of Hanuman has the paws of a monkey.

JAGANNATH TEMPLE AT VIZIANAGARAM - As per traditions, replica of the Vigraha of Lord Jagannadha is immersed into the sea every twelve years by Puri Temple. The Maharaja of Vizianagaram requested the priests of Puri to permit him to bring the replica to Vizianagaram with the intent of installing the vigrahas in a Temple but his request was denied. It is said that a band of loyal followers of the Maharaja's dived into the sea and retrieved the Vigraha on the night of the immersion. This Vigraha was brought to Vizianagaram & installed in the Temple.

SRI PYDITHALLI AMMAVARU TEMPLE AT VIZIANAGARAM - Pydithallamma is village goddess of Vizianagaram Town. It has two Temples Vanam Gudi and Chaduru Gudi. Vanam Gudi Situated opposite to Vizianagaram Railway Station and Chaduru Gudi where Sirimanu Utsav is performed which is at 3 Lantens Junction, Vizianagaram. As per the legend, after completion of Bobbili battle, an Vigraha was found in the west side of Pedda Charuvu of Vizianagaram.

SUBRAHMANYASWAMY TEMPLE AT VIZIANAGARAM - This Temple has a Vigraha 40 foot height.

VIZIANAGARAM FORT AT VIZIANAGARAM - Vijayarama Raju-I laid the foundation of Vizianagaram Fort in 1713 AD on the auspicious day of Vijaya Dashmi. It has a Temple of Lord Hanuman on one side and Goddess Lakshmi on the other. The Goddess is also known as 'Kota Shakti' or the guardian of the fort. The Raja of Vizianagaram would seek blessings of the Goddess before embarking on any military expedition.

RAMANARAYANAM AT VIZIANAGRAM - Ramanarayanam is a spiritual theme park with aesthetic gateway to those seeking solace in spiritual experience. Raising the bar of what one can expect from a theme park, from a great epic and from a spiritual destination, the Ramanarayanam is as unique as it is special. Based on the great epic of Valimiki Ramayana, this theme park is the first-of-its-kind in the country. It is uniquely built in the shape of a bow and arrow as a two-storey complex. With many trees dotting the landscape, one section showcases the sacred trees of Nakshatravanam, Narayanavanam, Raasivanam, Navagrahavanam, Vinayakavanam, Saptarishivanam, Panchavativanam, Panchabhootavanam. These rare trees have been a part of Indian scriptures and some of them were especially brought in from across the country as well. Beautiful mega fountains along the length of the bow transforms spectacle of indescribable proportions. Vibrant in colour, rich in emotions and full of life, the seventy two laminated mouldings were created by thousands of artisans from different parts of the country. They depict 72 episodes from the Valimiki Ramayan with scenes right from the beginning of the epic, Bala Kaanda to Yuddha Kaanda, below each of the 72 laminated/fibre panels. One tip of the arrow, where a Abhayanjaneya stands tall in While a traditional Vishnu it is more spiritual than it is for channelling inner peace, Lord Vishnu and Lord Rama and 18 feet vigrahas of Saraswati surrounded by fountains are some of the seven special fountains that

exquisitely chiselled exists from the gallery at the colossal 60 feet Vigraha of Sri all its grandeur and splendour. Temple is part of the complex, religious. A meditation centre three Temples of Lord Ganesh, with his consort Goddess Sita Goddess Lakshmi and exquisite colourful water stops. Also look out for the are shaped like the 7 asthras or weapons of Lord Rama which are dotted across the arrow.

PUNYAGIRI SHIVA TEMPLE AT AT SRUNGAVARAPUKOTA MANDAL - Sri Dara-Gangamma and Sivalayam is the ancient Temple, which is situated on the hill known as "Punyagiri" in the vally of Eastern Ghats. On the right side of the way to hill, there is a waterfall known as "Chinaputtudara" which is said to be emanate from the Vigraha and develops as natural spring. Large number of devotees and pilgrims congregate for 3 days on the occasion of Mahasivaratri festival. Folklore states that the Pandavas stayed in this forest during their "vanavas" or exile. The Shivalingam in the Punyagiri Temple is washed by the waters of a nearby perennial spring. Traditionally after cremation of the dead, the ashes from the funeral pyre are scattered in this spring and "astikalu" pooja is performed here to provide solace to the soul of the departed. Nearest Railway Station is Srungavarapukota.

GEETA BHAWAN AT GOVINDAPURAM - Amongst the modern Temples in the district, the 'Geeta Bhavan' at Govindapuram deserves special mention. It is a beautifully built monument in the form of Chariot, which attracts a large number of pilgrims. It has a spiritual prayer cum meditation hall where the people come to gain spiritual solace.

KUMILI TEMPLE IN PUSAPATIREGA MANDAL - This small village is famous on account of a huge complex of Temples from ancient time. The Temples are unique with extremely attractive sculptures, paintings on the walls and vigrahas. The story of Ramayana was painted on the walls of the Temples. The Temples within the complex are of Ganapathi, Shiva, Kalika Devi, Navagrahalu, Satyanarayana Swamy, Subramanyeswaraswamy, Seetharamaswamy, Anjaneya Swamy and Venu Gopalaswamy. The entrance to the Temple has carvings of prominent national leaders. Thus the Temple is representative of all the major faiths as well as the patriotic fervour of the country.

IBBILINGESWARA SWAMY TEMPLE AT SARIPALLI - The beautiful and ancient Temple shows influence of the architectural style prevalent during the Kalinga period and is situated on the banks of River Champavati. The Temple is constructed with stones chiselled perfectly to fit each other without any bonding medium. Because of its beauty, the local inhabitants believe that the Temple was constructed by the Gods. This Temple is dedicated to Lord Shiva and is estimated to have been constructed around 1000 AD. Nearest Railway Station is Nellimaria.

RAMTHIRTAM IN NELLIMARIA MANDAL - It is one of the holiest places in India. Ramtirtham is a unique Temple where three major faiths – Jain, Buddhist and Hindu – are represented. The complex is spread over three hills – Bodi Konda, Gurubhakta Konda and Durga Konda – containing Jain and Buddhist relics. Commemorative seals, remains of Chaityas (Prayer Halls) and Stupas (Semi Circular Buildings), dating back to the Buddhist period, have also been found here.It is believed that these hills were the abode of Lord Rama during his exile in the forest. The main Temple is dedicated to Lord Rama and is believed to have been consecrated by Yudhishtira, the eldest of the Pandava Princes of the epic Mahabharat.

TRIPURANTAKA SWAMY TEMPLE AT JAMI - The Tripurantaka Swamy Temple is dedicated to Lord Shiva. Folklore says that the local inhabitants tried to shift the Temple but they could not uproot the Shivalinga. Modern day geologists estimate that the Shivalinga extends more than 179 feet deep into the earth. Over a period, this Temple was forgotten and was lost in a dense overgrown forest. According to folklore, the Pusapati King had a dream in 1698 AD, in which he was intimated about the Temple. After a thorough search in the jungles, the vigrahas of Lord Rama, Sita and Lakshmana were found and were installed in the Temple. Legend states that the Pandavas prayed here and hid their weapons on a 'Jami' tree. The Jami tree at the Tripurantaka Swamy Temple is considered to be holy for its miraculous properties.

VENU GOPALASWAMY TEMPLE AT BOBBILI - The Temple of the family deity – Venugopala Swamy – had been in existence since Bobbili was founded but the present Temple was built by Chinna Ranga Rao, when he took over the reins of Bobbili after the ill-fated war. It is the only Temple in the region where the Gopuram is higher than the main Temple. The base of the Gopuram is made of solid stone while the six stories over it are made of stone and brick masonry. The base of the Gopuram itself is approximately 9 meters high. On festive occasions, the vigrahas of the deities in the Temple are adorned with jewellery made of gold and precious stones, estimated to be worth millions of dollars. The Vasant Mandapam stands aloof in the placid waters of a lake. The Vigraha from the Temple of Lord Venugopala Swamy is brought to the lake annually to celebrate the onset of spring. Legend has it that the Lord enjoys a day of solitude with his wife here. Post sojourn, the Vigraha is installed in Dola Yatra Mandapam on the banks of the lake for a day and then carried back to the main Temple. The mandapams were constructed by Maharaja Krishnadas Ranga Rao, in 1825. Nearest Railway Station is Bobbili.

DISTRICT – WEST GODAVARI (Railway Station – Eluru/Palakollu/Tadepalligudem/Relangi)

S. No.	Temple	Address	Type
1	Sri Bhunila Sameta Sri Janardhana Swamy Kanyakumara Parameshwari Ammanala Temple	Agraharam Road, Main Bazar, Paidichintapadu, Eluru – 534001	Vishnu & Mata
2	Eluru Buddha Park	Eluru – 534001	Buddhist
3	Sri Uma Ramalingeswara Swamy Temple	Achanta – 534123	Rama
4	Sri Uma Vasuki Ravi Someswara Swamy & Natta Ramalingeswara Swamy	Juttiga – 534124 & Natta Rameswaram – 534124 Penumantra Mandal	Shiva
5	Sri Mavullamma Ammavari Temple	Bhimavaram – 534201	Mata

S. No.	Temple	Address	Type
6	Gunpudi Someswara Janardhana Swamy Temple	Gunpudi – 534202, Bhimavaram	Shiva
7	Sri Ellaramma Ammavari Temple	Mandapaka - 534218	Mata
8	Anjaneya Swami Temple	Relangi – 534225,	Hanuman
9	Sri Ksheera Ramalingeswara Swami Temple	Palakol – 534260	Shiva
10	Abbirajupalem Hanuman Vigraha	Doddipatla – 534266	Hanuman
11	Sri Adikesava Embermanar Swamy Temple	Narasapuram – 534275	Vishnu
12	Sri Kotasattemma Ammavari Temple	Thimmaraju Palem Village – 534301 Nidadavole Mandal	Mata
13	Sri Veerabhadra Swamy Temple	Pattiseema – 534315, Polavaram Mandal	Shiva
14	Sri Vasavi Kanyakaparameswari Temple	Penugonda – 534320	Mata
15	Sri Venkateswara Swamyvari Devasthanam	Dwarka Tirumala (China Tirupati) – 534426	Vishnu
16	Maddi Anjaneya Swami Temple	Gurvaigudem – 534447, Jangareddygudem	Hanuman
17	Sri Venkateswara Swamy Temple	Jangareddygudem – 534447	Vishnu
18	Gubbala Mangamma Ammavari Temple	Buttayagudem – 534448	Ramayana Circuit
19	Guntupalli Caves	Guntupalli, Kamavarapukota Mandal – 534449	Buddhist

SRI BHUNILA SAMETA SRI JANARDHANA SWAMY KANYAKUMARA PARAMESHWARI AMMANALA TEMPLE AT ELURU – It is one of the famous and ancient Temple. Here, the Trinity of Lord along with Mata Lakshmi and Parvati are in existence since long. Every village here who were born to Nokkalamma, Polaremma, Sattemma and Mahavishnu as the name Pothuraju.

ELURU BUDDHA PARK AT ELURU - Gaja Vallivari Cheruvu is one of the ancient ponds in the history of Helapuri town (ancient name of Eluru city). During the Chalukyan period. Elephants used to drink water in this pond. A magnificent 74 foot Buddha Vigraha was constructed in the middle of the pond named Gajjalavari Cheruvuand a painting gallery was also created to spread the Buddha's teachings. The pedestal is decorated with famous Amaravathi sculptures along the railings of the foot bridge up to the Vigraha.

SRI UMA RAMALINGESWARA SWAMY TEMPLE AT ACHANTA - This ancient site, Indu Umrameswara Swamy is the main deity. The Temple was built with the walled towers and the Swami's Deepa Navayathas are the wealthiest donors of kings and zamindars. In the mythology of the famous Saptasagara Sanctuary, Gautama Vasishta is situated in the middle of the west of Vasishta "Achanta". Its ancient name is "martyr". Sri Rameswaran Lingusayam Umasamatumuga is the name of Lord Rama Chandra, in the north of the Temple. These features are noteworthy.

SRI UMA VASUKI RAVI SOMESWARA SWAMY & NATTA RAMALINGESWARA SWAMY TEMPLES AT JUTTIGA & NATTA RAMESWARAM - Juttiga & Natta Rameswaram are twin Villages, which has assumed religious importance on account of the Temples of Swayambhulingam known as Sri Uma Vasuki Ravi Someswara Swamy at Juttiga Village and the Lingam which is made of shells and cones named as Natta Ramalingeswara Swamy at Natta Rameswaram Village. These twin places also known as Dakshina Kasi. Every "Sivarathri" Festival, "Edurukolotsavam" is being celebrated at the border place of two villages. Thousands of Pilgrims attend to that celebration.

SRI MAVULLAMMA TEMPLE AT BHIMAVARAM - The Temple history of came to limelight in the year 1880 AD. It is believed that she is laid in Motupallivari Street under couple of Peepal and Neem Tree. Every year in the month of "Jyesta Masa" (third month of auspicious Telugu almanac calendar) on "Paadyami" (new slender crescent moon day), devotees celebrates one month long festival. In 1910 AD, by floods, the Mulavirat (Vigraha of Mavullamma) partially damaged and later it was reinstate by great artist, sculptor, Sri Grandhi Appa Rao. He carved the Mulavirat (Mavullamma Vigraha) from ferocious stature to pleasant present peace form. Nearest Railway Station is Bhimavaram.

GUNUPUDI SOMESWARA JANARDHANA SWAMY TEMPLE AT BHIMAVARAM - This place is well known for the Temple 'Somarama' which is considered as one of the 5 Pancharama Temples. The Shivalingam is called Someshwara, as it is believed that this Lingam has been installed by Lord Rama. The colour of the Linga changes during full moon day and Amavasya. Goddess Annapurna Temple is situated just above the Garbhalayam saying that Lord Shiva holds the Goddess Ganga on his head and this cannot be seen anywhere else in India. Surprisingly, the Goddess has the sacred thread around her neck and a baby near her feet. To the South of the Garbha Gruham, Goddess Adilakshmi can be seen. To the East side, there is a Pushkarini pond which is also called Soma Gundam. Inside the Temple, Lord Anjaneya Swamy, God Kumara Swamy, Navagraha, Sun God, Lord Ganesha can also be seen. This Temple is an old but looks like a new one because of paintings on the walls and sculptures. At the front of the Temple, there is a lotus covered pond called Chandrakundam and there is a large Gopuram at the Temple entrance. In the hall of Temple there is a big Vigraha of Nandi.

SRI ELLARAMMA AMMAVARI TEMPLE AT MANDAPAKA - It is an ancient & famous Temple. It is dedicated to Goddess.

ANJANEYA SWAMI TEMPLE AT RELANGI – It is one of ancient Temple under Ramayana Circuit. This village also has two deities, popularly known as Sri Peda Mantalamba and Sri China Mantalamba. This village has mythological history connected to Ramayana time. Legends say that these two deities were emerged from the yagnakunda conducted by the Brahmarshi Vishwamitra which was guarded by the Princes Rama and Lakshmana.

SRI KSHEERA RAMALINGESWARA SWAMI TEMPLE AT PALAKOL - This place is famous for Lord Siva Temple which is considered as one of the Pancharama Temples. The Gostani River flows through Palakollu and there is a sangam (confluence) near Narsapur with the Godavari River. From here the river empties into the sea at Antarvedi. The Sivalingam (Moola Virat) can be seen from all the four sides through windows in the Garbhaalayam. The Shivaling is a unique milky white in colour and the tallest. There are 72 pillars made of black stone in the Temple mandapa. Inside, the garbhalaya, Gokarneshwara and Vigneshwara alayas are at the left. Kshiralingam is in the center. To the right are Subramanya Swamy and Janardhana Swamyalayas; Nandi is at the centre. Additionally, Sun God, Kashi Vishweshwara, Goddess Parvathi, Goddess Lakshmi, Nagareshwara Lingam, Dundi Vigneshwara, Veera Bhadra, Sapta Matruka, Kanaka Durga, Brahma, Saraswathi, Kumara Swamy, Kartikeya, Mahishasura Mardhini, Nagasarpa, Nataraja, Dattatreya, Kala Bhairava, Nageshwara, Saneeswara, Radha Krishna can also be seen in the Temple. There is a belief that the Sivalingam is installed by Lord Vishnu. The tower is one of the tallest among the Temple towers in Andhra Pradesh. It is believed that staying one day in Kshirarama is equivalent to staying one year in Varanasi. It is one of the centrally protected monuments of national importance. Nearest Railway Station is Palakollu.

ABBIRAJUPALEM HANUMAN VIGRAHA AT DODDIPATLA – It is located on the banks of River Godavari. The height of the Vigraha is 98 foot. Nearest Railway Station is Palakollu.

SRI ADIKESAVA EMBERMANAR SWAMY TEMPLE AT NARASAPURAM - It is a sacred pilgrimage destination for the Vaishnavites. The Temple, constructed over two centuries ago, is reminiscent of the style of the renowned Sri Perambadur Temple in Tamil Nadu. The annual Brahmotsava celebrations conducted in the month of April- May. Nearest Railway Station is Narasapur.

SRI KOTASATTEMMA AMMAVARI TEMPLE AT THIMMARAJU PALEM VILLAGE - In the 13th CE, King Veerabhadra Chalukya, spouse of Rani Rudrama Devi, ruled a part of West Godavari District with Niravadyapuram as a Capital. During his rule, Nidadavolu was designed as Fort & took place several wars. It is believed that the fort was protected by Goddess Kotasattemma. Niravadyapuram became famous during Kakateeya dynasty. Reddi dynasty succeeded after the decline of Kakateeya dynasty. Floods & natural calamities swept away the Temple and the Vigraha of Ammavaru, which immersed in nature and remained unknown for several centuries. In 1934, a local farmer Sri Devulapalli Ramamurthy Sastry was plunging his land & accidently the plunging weapon hit on the Vigraha of Ammavaru. The Goddess appeared in his dream & asked him to construct a Temple for her. Sri Sastry with help of other farmers constructed the Temple & it was surrounded by compound walls. The Temple was administered by Yadavas. The Temple became very famous & people developed more faith as they felt that their wishes are fulfilled by worshipping the Goddess. Nearest Railway Station is Nidadavolu.

SRI VEERABHADRA SWAMY TEMPLE AT PATTISEEMA – The Temple is situated on Devakuta Hill in midst of River Godavari. It is one of the Pancha Kashi Kshetram. Main deities in this Temple are Lord Veera Bhadra Swamy & Goddess Bhadra Kali. Lord Shiva is Self-manifested as Veerabhadreswara Swamy. Goddess Sathi as goddess Bhadra Kali. According to Temple's history Gouthama Buddha did Dhyanam here. According to legend, once mountains used to have wings, when they are landing at that place there so much loss of people & property. So God's king Devendra has cut the wings. So these mountains are called as Devakutadri Mountains or Neeladri Mountains. Mountain's king is Karaveera, his son did penance for Lord Shiva and asked Lord to stay on him. Then Lord gave him word to stay there in the form of Shiva Lingam. As per legend of Daksha Yagya & Sati's self-immolation, Veerabhadra Swamy had settled here in the form of Shivalinga on this hillock and cleaned his pattisam here in River Godavari. From then this place is called as Pattisam or Pattisachala Kshetram. One can see hand prints on Shivalingam on square panel. Nearest Railway Station is Rajahmundry.

SRI VASAVI KANYAKAPARAMESWARI TEMPLE AT PENUGONDA – The Temple finds mention in various ancient religious texts. According to a legend, Vasavi Knayakaparameswari was famous for her beauty. Hearing this, the Chalukyan Ruler Vishnu Vardhan proposed to marry her but being aware if his ignoble intentions, she preferred to end her life by immolation. Soon after, the king's head is believed to have been shattered into thousand pieces. A Temple dedicated to her was then built. Nearby is the Temple Sri Nageswara Swamy, which houses a huge Lingaroopa of the Swamy. An unexplained mystery of this Temple is that the sandalwood paste smeared around the Linga remains fresh and wet till the next morning.

SRI VENKATESWARA SWAMY VARI DEVASTHANAM AT DWARKA TIRUMALA – It is an ancient holy place and a popular pilgrim centre. This pilgrimage centre is called "Dwaraka Tirumala" after the great saint, "Dwaraka" who located the self-manifested Vigraha of Lord "Sri Venkateswara" after severe penance in a 'Valmikam' (ant hill). The devotees call Sri Venkateswara as Kaliyuga Vaikunta Vasa. This place is also called "Chinna Tirupati". It is a great wonder to see the two main vigrahas under one Vimana Sikharam. One Vigraha is a full and complete Vigraha. The other is a half Vigraha of the upper portion of the form of the Lord. The upper portion of the form is a self-manifested Vigraha located by Sage "Dwaraka". The vigrahas of Padmavathi and Nanchari are installed in the Arthamandapa facing east. The saints of the yore felt that the prayers to the Lord are not complete without worshipping His holy feet. So, the saints joined together and installed a full Vigraha behind the self-manifested Vigraha, to worship the feet of the Lord according to Vaikhanasa Agamam. It is believed that the prayers to the smaller Vigraha of the Lord will lead to Moksha and the big form stands for Dharma, Artha and Kama. The most peculiar aspect here is that the hill appearing to be a serpant in form, even to the naked eye, confirms the mythological version that Anantha, the serpent King has taken up this terrestrial form of serpent hill and is carrying God Mallikarjuna on the hood and Lord Venkateswara on the tail, thus creating a happy and harmonious compromise of Vaishnavism and Saivism at a single place. The main Temple is a masterpiece of South Indian Architecture with its five-storied main Rajagopuram facing the south & 3 other gopurams on the other three sides. The Vimana is in Nagara style & old Mukhamantapa is extended to a great extent to suit the present day needs. The Tiru Kalyanotsavam is celebrated twice a year. One for the self-manifested Vigraha in the month of "Vaisakha" & the other for the installed Vigraha in the month of "Aswayuja". Nearest Railway Station is Bhimadolu.

MADDI ANJANEYA SWAMY TEMPLE AT GURVAIGUDEM - Many devotees visit this Temple on Tuesday and offer prayer to Lord Anjaneya Swamy. There is a tradition of walking around the main Temple sanctum 11 times (known as Pradakshina) before going for darshan and your wishes will be fulfilled in a year time.

SRI VENKATESWARA SWAMI TEMPLE AT JANGAREDDYGUDEM - It is also called Parijathagiri Temple. It is a common belief that Jangareddygudem is the only town in Andhra Pradesh where there is a collection of seven mountains other than Tirumala Tirupathi. Due to the presence of large Kalyanamandapam in the Temple, many of the marriages are also taking place in this Temple. Annadhanam, the sacred tradition of offering food also happens every day in this Temple. Srivari Brahmotsavam is conducted annually in this Temple which is celebrated for around nine days.

GUBBALA MANGAMMA AMMAVARI TEMPLE AT BUTTAYAGUDEM - It is said that Lord Rama, Sita and Lakshman stayed here for some time during exile.

GUNTUPALLI CAVES AT GUNTUPALLI - The rock cut caves of Guntupalli is dotted with some of the finest specimens of monolithic and structural Buddhist remains datable to the 3rd-2nd century BC to 5th-6th century AD. The important monuments located are: Rock cut Temple or Vritta Chaitya, large monastery, small monastery, brick Chaitya, ruined Mandapa, stone Stupa and cluster of Votive Stupas.

YSR DISTRICT (Railway Station – Cuddapah/Razampeta/Nandalur)

S. No.	Temple	Address	Type
1	Sri Lakshmi Venkateswara Swamy Vari	Devuni Kadapa – 516001	Vishnu
2	Tallapaka Annamacharya	Rajampet - 516115	Annamayya
3	Sri Chennakesava Swamy Vari	Tallapaka – 516126	Vishnu
4	Parasurama Temple, Gadhadara, Thretheswara	Attirala – 516126	Parasuram
5	Sri Siddeswara Swamy Vari	Tallapaka – 516126, Rajampeta Mandal	Shiva
6	Sowmyanatha Swami Temple	Nandalur - 516150	Shiva, Buddhist
7	Pushpagiri Temple Complex	Pushpagiri – 516162	Vishnu, Shiva
8	Kodandarama Swamy Temple	Vontimitta – 516213	Rama
9	Abhayahasta Anjaneya Temple (Gandi Kshetram)	Gandi – 516216	Hanuman
10	Sidhout Fort	Sidhout Fort - 516237	Shiva, Mata
11	Gandikota Fort	Gandikota Fort – 516434	Vishnu
12	Sri Narapura Venkateswara Swamy Vari	Jammalamadugu – 516434	Vishnu
13	Brahmamgari Matham	Brahmamgari Matham – 516503	

SRI LAKSHMI VENKATESWARA SAMY VARI AT DEVUNI GADAPA - "Devuni Gadapa" means "Entrance or Gateway or Threshold to reach Lord Sri Venkateswara Swamy". This Temple was said to have constructed by Sage Kripacharya. When the hill shrine of Tirumala is called "Varahakshetram". Devunikadapa is known as "Hanumathkshetram". An Vigraha of Anjaneya Swamy is located behind Lord Sri Lakshmi Venkateswara Swamy here. Saint Poet Thallapaka Annamacharya worshipped the lord and eulogised him as Kadaparaya, Venkatadri Kadaparaya. Since olden days, there is a tradition of having Darshan of Lord Sri Venkateswara of Tirumala only after having Darshan of Sri Lakshmi Venkateswara in Devunikadapa. This tradition is continued even today. Muslims also worship Sri Lakshmi Venkateswara on Ugadhi, which is considered to be a unique tradition. According to the Legend, Lord Venkateswara had married one of his consorts, Bibi Nanchari, in an inter-religious event, leading to establishment of close relations between the Hindus & Muslims in Kadapa. The Rathothsavam that is performed every year from Maghasuddha Padyami to Sapthami to the Lord is an eye feast to the devotees.

TALLAPAKA ANNAMACHARYA AT RAJAMPET - He is popularly known as Annamayya. He was a 15th century Hindu Saint & the earliest known Indian musician to compose songs called sankirtanas in praise of the Lord Venkateswara, a form of Lord Vishnu. He took initiation into Vaishnavism and became a Vaishnava in the Ramanujacharya Sampradaya. The musical form of the keertana songs that he composed, which are still popular among Carnatic music concert artists, have strongly influenced the structure of Carnatic music compositions. It is said that Lord Venkateswara came down to listen to him before he took him to Vaikuntha. Annamacharya is remembered for his saintly life and is honoured as a great devotee of Lord Vishnu by devotees and saintly singers. He is believed to have been the avatar of Nandaka, the sword of Lord Vishnu. He is widely regarded as the Padakavitha Pitamaha. His hymns not only convey sweetness but also guide humanlife in word poems, smeared with devotional fragrances and made understandable even to the common man. He protested against social discrimination and inspired the society with his chants of "Srihari" is the conscience of all.

SRI CHENNAKESAVA SWAMY VARI AT THALLAPAKA - "Chennakesava" means the Lord with beautiful hairs. This Temple was constructed some 1200 years ago. The Archa Murthy of Sri Chennakesava Swamy with Sridevi and Bhudevi on the left and right side of his chest respectively was consecrated in the Sanctum Sanctorum of the Temple. Lord Garuda is present in the opposite side facing Lord Sri Chennakesava Swamy. Sri Prasanna Anjaneya Swamy was consecrated as the Kshetrapalaka of this Temple. Dwajasthambham was installed on the top of the Temple Gopuram. Annual Brahmotsavams are performed from Ashadha Suddha Ekadasi to Bahula Chaviti.

PARASURAMA TEMPLE AT ATTIRALA – It is a very sacred place located on the east bank of the River Cheyyeru. It was called Hatyarala and Yethirevula in olden days. The sanctity of the River Cheyyeru was elaborately described in the great epic of Mahabharata in the story of Sankha and Likhita. It is a centre of Vedic culture and famous for its scenic beauty. River Cheyyeru atoned Bhagwan Parasurama from the sin of matricide and gave hands to Likhita, the brother of Sankha a great sage. People believe that Parasurama Temple was once a Buddhist Vidya Kendra, occupied by Saivas first and later by Vaishnavas. Vaishnavas made this place as Parasurama Kshetra. To the south of this Temple, there is a 72 pillared hall and on the eastern side there are two famous Temples on the hill slope dedicated to Gadhadara and Thretheswara. Gadhadara stands on one leg here. The presence of Gadhadara and holy River Cheyyeru, Attirala is considered as sacred as Gaya Kshetram. There is a Jyothistambha, higher up the Temple of Thretheswara, on the top of a hill. Jyothi lighted on festivals is visible to distance of 30 KMs around.

SRI SIDDESWARA SWAMY VARI AT THALLAPAKA - Sri Kamakshi Sametha & Sri Siddeswara Swamy was a Temple dedicated to Lord Shiva constructed nearly 1300 yearly ago. The vigrahas of Mahaganapati, Siddi Ganapati, Sri Siddeswara Swamy, Sri Kamakshi Ammavaru, Sri Valli, Devasenasametha Sri Subramanya Swamy, Sri Chandeeswara, Sri Kalabhairava and Sri Dakshanamurthy were installed inside the Temple premises. The Temple of Sri Veerabhadra Swamy, the Kshetrapalaka is situated in the south western side of the Temple premises. The Navagrahas were consecrated in the north eastern side. Dwajasthambham was located to the eastern side. The Vigraha of an ardent devotee Sri Vekatataiah is present opposite to Lord Siva inside the Temple. The Munikonda (Siddeswara Swamy hill) is present on the western side of the Thallapaka village. Some of the rishis performed penance here to invoke the blessings of Lord Siva who has given them salvation. After attaining salvation, they consecrated Sivalingam and hence the presiding deity is called Siddeswara. The important feature of this Temple is the existence of Jammi tree in the north eastern side. On the top of this tree, peepal and Banyan trees are also found. These are considered as Brahma, Vishnu and Siva existing as a single tree which is a special feature. The devotees believe that if this tree is worshipped, they are blessed with good children.

SOWMYANATHA SWAMI TEMPLE AT NANDALUR – It is located on the west bank of River Cheyyeru. Sowmyanath Swami Temple is a very big Temple. It is a replica of Thiruvannamalai and patronized by Cholas, Pandyas, Kakatiyas, Vijayanagara, Pottapi and Matli Kings. Here most of the inscriptions are in Tamil. Lord Sowmyanatha is installed on an elevated place and attracts pilgrims with his glittering beauty. Once it was a famous Buddhist Centre in Rayalaseema. In 1913, Buddhist caves and viharas were discovered.

PUSHPAGIRI TEMPLE COMPLEX – It is located on the banks of Pennar (Pinakini) River. It is well known for its numerous Temples. Vaishnavas call it as Madhya Ahobhilam and Saivas as Madhya Kailasam. The Amrita Sarovar would be a thrilling experience, according to local legend, about its sanctity – when Garuda was carrying nectar from Indra Loka, one drop of it fell at this place and turned the pool into a sacred one. One day an old farmer vexed with his wretched life jumped into the pool to commit suicide. The fall transformed him into a young man. He was so astonished by this and made his wife and oxen to take dip in the pool. They were also turned into young. The news reached Satya Loka, Brahma invoked the help of Lord Vishnu & Lord Siva and then they instructed Anjaneya to close the pool. Anjaneya dropped a hill in the pool but instead of sinking the hill, it started floating like a flower. Lord Vishnu & Lord Siva decided to clamp their feet at the ends. The imprint of the foot of Siva became famous as Rudrapada and that of Vishnu's as Vishnupada. Pushpagiri is now called as a second Hampi and is one of the important Advaitha Mutts established by Sankaracharya and is the only place in Andhra Pradesh where the holy Peetham of Sankaracharya is located. The largest and best known among Temples is the Chennakesava Temple, which according to the earliest inscriptions found in the Temple complex, dates back to 1298 A.D. The dancing Ganapati and Krishna preaching the Bhagavad Geetha to Arjuna are remarkable pieces of Art. Other Temples of interest here include Trikuteswara, Durga, Shiva, Rudrapada & Devi, which are remarkable for their architectural precision & excellent images.

KODANDA RAMASWAMY TEMPLE AT VONTIMITTA – It was built by the Chola and Vijayanagara Kings. The images of Lord Rama, Lakshmana and Sita are carved on a single piece of rock. Splendid architecturally, it boasts of a towering gateway, a large beautiful sculptured Mandapam with exquisitely carved pillars, an inner chamber and the sanctum. Apart from architecturally gate-way, the large and beautifully sculpted mandapam with 32 pillars called the Madhya Ranga Mandapam leading to inner chamber and sanctum is of a great architectural interest. In fact, the well-known French-traveller, Tavernier, described the Temple as one of the grandest pagodas in the whole of India. According to the legend, Rama,

Lakshmana and Sita spent some time here in the forest during the period of their exile. Once to quench the thirst of Goddess Sita, Lord Rama shot an arrow deep into the earth, upon which sweet water gushed out. Later, with this perennial water spring, two small tanks named Ramathirtham and Lakshmanathirtham were formed.

ABHAYAHASTA ANJANEYA TEMPLE AT GANDI KSHETRAM - The Temple is built on the foot of a hill on the western side of the River Papaghni in the midst of picturesque surroundings. It has gain a great name and fame as Vayu Kshethra. Papaghni River goes in this place from south to north in between two hills. A legend says that Lord Rama visited this place in his return journey from Lanka. To welcome Rama, Vayu, the father of Anjaneya, hung a wreath of golden flowers across the ravine. Before leaving this place Rama carved the figure of Anjaneya on a rock. The people here believe that it is visible to the sacred souls at the approach of their death time. Sir Thomas Manro, the farmer British Governor, was fortunate enough to see it when he passed near that ravine. The devotees from far places visit this Temple in the month of Sravana.

SIDHOUT FORT AT SIDDHAVATAM - Often referred to as the gateway to Srisailam or Dakshina Kasi, Sidhout Fort also encompasses beautifully sculpted Temples inside its premises. These included Siddheswara, Bala Brahma, Ranganayaka Swamy and a Durga Temple that attracts numerous pilgrims.

GANDIKOTA FORT - The Ranganatha and Madhavaswamy Temples, built during the 15th and 16th centuries, are adorned with sculptures and are in an architectural style reminiscent of the Vijayanagara period. Nearest Railway Station is Muddanuru.

SRI NARAPURA VENKATESWARA SWAMY VARI AT JAMMALAMADUGU - Sri Lakshmi Venkateshwara Temple stands as an example of Vijayanagara architecture. It is said that Tallapaka Annamacharya visited this place and all the Sankaracharyas of the Advaita Mutt and the great poet Kshetrayya also visited this place. According to the sthalapuranam, Lord Sri Venkateswara Swamy appeared in the dream of a devotee, Naaraapuraiah and asked for installation of his Vigraha that can be found near Jambulamadugu on the banks of the Penna. The devotee found the Vigraha in Jambulamadugu as directed by Lord Sri Venkateswara Swamy in Jambulamadugu. Immediately, he installed it on a sand heap to the North of the town. Hence, it is called Sri Narapura Venkateswara Swamy Vari Temple. As per the inscriptions found on the stones in the present Temple, the Temple which was consecrated by Naaraapuraiah was dilapidated which was renovated in 1919 with the co-operation of some local devotees. Nearest Railway Station is Jammalamadugu.

SRI POTHULURI VEERA BRAHMANDRA SWAMY (BRAHMAMGARI MATHAM) – Kandimallayapalli is the place where Sri Potuluri Veerabrahmam, who was famous for his predictions and foresight about the future of the world, stayed. He entered Jeeva Samadhi in the year 1693.The walls are covered with the preaching and predictions of Veerabrahmam. The places to be seen are: Siddaiah Jeeva Samadhi; Eswaramma Temple; Poleramma Temple; Veerabrahmam Reservoir (Telugu Ganga Project).

❖ ❖ ❖ ❖ ❖

KARNATAKA

Karnataka has a recorded history of more than 2,000 years. After Independence, the Mysore State was created in 1953, wherein all the Kannada dominant areas under different dispensations were unified and the enlarged Mysore state carved in 1956 and was renamed Karnataka in 1973.

Capital City	Bengaluru
Total Population	6,10,95,297 (2011)
Districts	31
Official Language	Kannada
Motto	Satyameva Jayate
Animal	Indian Elephant
Bird	Indian Roller
State Butterfly	Southern Birdwing
Fish	Carnatic Carp
Tree	Sandalwood
Flower	Lotus
Fruit	Mango
Festival	Mysore Dasara
Song	Jaya Bharata Jananiya Tanujate
Airport	Belagavi, Bengaluru, Hubli, Kalaburagi, Mangalore, Mysuru

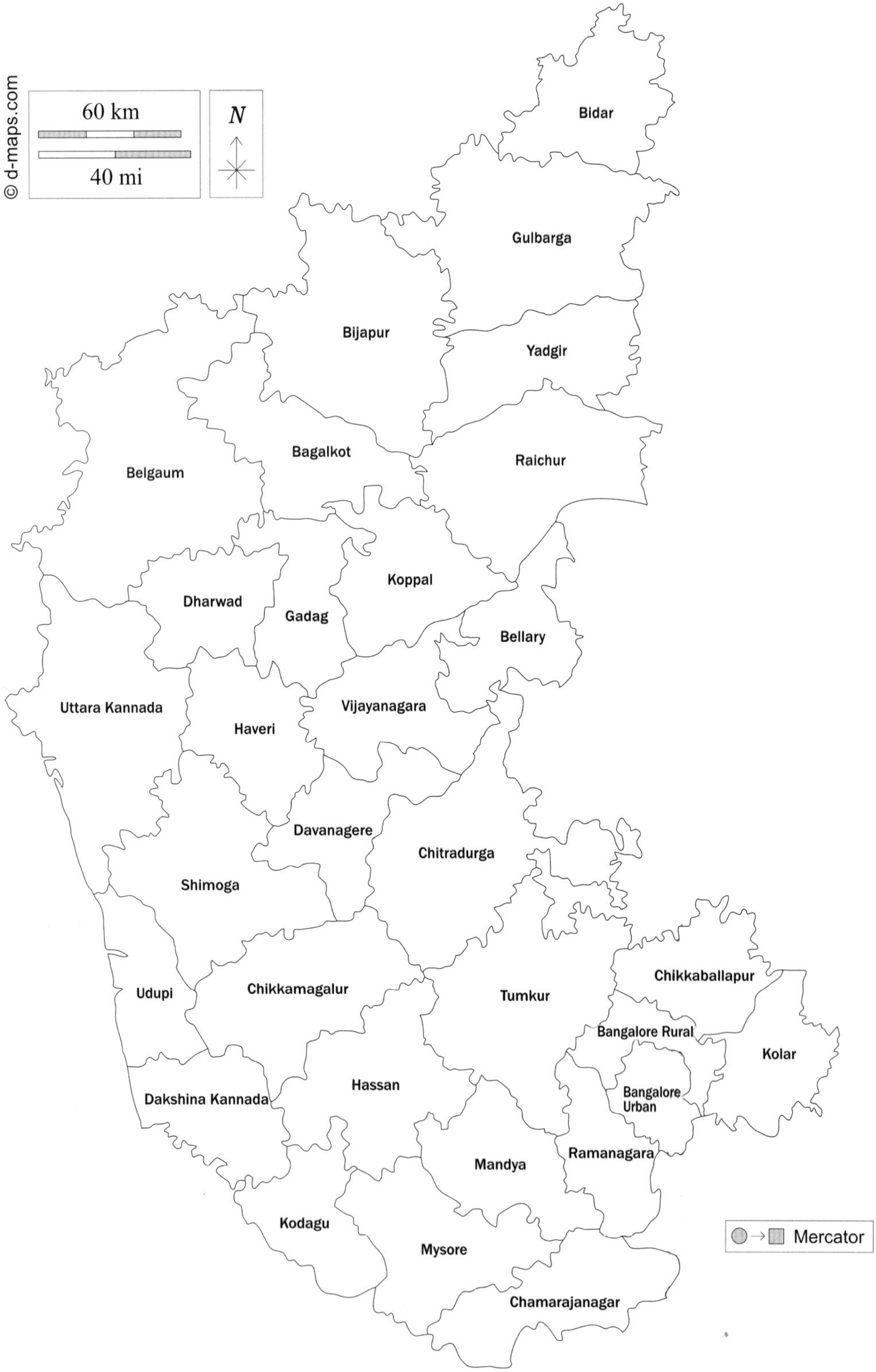
© d-maps.com
60 km
40 mi
N
Bidar
Gulbarga
Bijapur
Yadgir
Raichur
Bagalkot
Belgaum
Koppal
Dharwad
Gadag
Bellary
Uttara Kannada
Vijayanagara
Haveri
Davanagere
Chitradurga
Shimoga
Chikkaballapur
Udupi
Chikkamagalur
Tumkur
Bangalore Rural
Kolar
Bangalore Urban
Dakshina Kannada
Hassan
Ramanagara
Mandya
Kodagu
Mysore
Chamarajanagar
Mercator

DISTRICT – BAGALKOTE (Railway Station – Bagalkot)

S. No.	Temple	Address	Type
1	Kudalasangama	Hungund Taluka – 587112	Saint Basavanna
2	Chikka Sangama	Honnihai - 587116	Sangam
3	Aihole Group of Temples	Aihole – 587124	Mata, Shiva, Sun, Brahma, Vishnu
4	Badami Group of Temples & Caves	Badami – 587201	Shiva, Vishnu, Jain
5	Mahakuta Group of Temples	Mahakoota – 587201	Shiva
6	Pattadakal Group of Temples	Pattadakal – 587201	Shiva, Jain
7	Sri Jagannath Temple	Guledgudd - 587203	Jagannath

KUDALASANGAMA – It is an important centre of pilgrimage for Lingayats. The Krishna and Malaprabha River merges here and flow east towards Srisaila. The Aikya Mantapa or the holy Samadhi of God Basavanna, the founder of the Lingayat sect of Hindu religion along with Linga, which is believed to be self-born (Swayambhu) is here.

CHIKKA SANGAMA AT HONNIHAI - It is a confluence place of Rivers Krishna and Ghataprabha. This place has a Sangamanath Temple with a beautiful architecture. People and devotees from far places visit this place throughout the year.

AIHOLE GROUP OF TEMPLES - Known as the cradle of Temple architecture, Aihole is an experience of time travelling by all means. A quiet village where centuries-old Temples have been let alone to grow old in peace, history rests in equanimity at this former capital of the Badami Chalukyas. Temples from the fifth century to the fourteenth century stand no further than a few yards from another, taking you through a fascinating, evolutionary passage of art and architecture. It has been a part of Hindu mythologies. It has a natural axe-shaped rock on the Malaprabha River bank and a rock in the river show a footprint. Parashurama, the sixth Vishnu avatar, is stated in these legends to have washed his axe here after killing abusive Kshatriyas who were exploiting their military powers, giving the land its red colour. A 19th century local tradition believed that rock footprints in the river were those of Parashurama. There are about 125 Temples divided into 22 groups scattered all over the villages and nearby fields. A large number of prehistoric sites have been found in Morera Angadigalu, near the Meguti hillocks in Aihole.

Durga Temple - The Temple derives its name from Durgadagudi meaning 'Temple near the Fort'. Dedicated to Lord Vishnu, the Temple appears to be a Hindu adaptation of the Buddhist chaitya (hall) with its apsidal end. Standing on a high platform with a 'Rekhanagara' type of Shikhara, it is the most elaborately decorated monument.

Gowda Temple - Close to Ladh Khan Temple & built in the similar lines, the Gowda Temple was dedicated to Bhagavati. Standing on a high moulded base and having about 16 fairly plain pillars, this Temple was probably built even earlier.

Hucchimalli Temple - This appears to be one of the earliest groups of Temples. The sanctum has a northern style "Rekhanagara" tower over it. The vestibule in front of the sanctum was introduced for the first time here.

Konti Group of Temples – These Temples was probably built in the 5th century. The first Temple has panels of Lord Bramha, Shiva & a reclined Vishnu on the ceiling.

Ladh Khan Temple - The experimental nature of Temple building by the Chalukyas is best elaborated in the Ladh Khan Temple, located south of the Durga Temple. Not knowing how to build a Temple, they built it in the Panchayat hall style. The sanctum is built against the back wall and the main shrine has a Shivalinga along with a Nandi. Above the centre of the hall, facing the sanctum, is a second smaller sanctum with vigrahas carved on the outer walls.

Meguti Temple - The only dated monument, the Temple was built atop a small hill in 634 AD. Now partly in ruins, possibly never completed, this Temple provides an important evidence of the early development of the Dravidian style of Architecture. The inscription dating the monument is found on one of the outer walls of the Temple & records its construction by Ravikeerti, who was a commander & minister of Pulakesin-II. Apparently, a Jain Temple is seen from the seated Jain figure here

Ravanphadi Cave - Located south-east of the Hucchimalli Temple, this rock-cut Temple is assigned to 6th CE. The sanctum is provided with a vestibule flanked by carved panels entered through a triple entrance. Despite the variety of vigrahas found here, the Mahishasuramardhini, the great Dancing Shivalinga with Ganesha & Saptamatrikas & the Linga inside the sanctum an overall Shiva application.

Surayanarayana Temple - Located to the north-east of Ladh Khan Temple, the sanctum of this Temple has a 0.6 meter high icon of Lord Surya along with his two consorts Usha & Sandhaya being drawn by horses. The Temple, dating from the 7th – 8th centuries, has a four pillared inner and a 'Rekhanagara' tower over the sanctum.

BADAMI CAVE TEMPLES – It is located on a short distance from the Malaprabha River. Badami, the onetime capital of the Chalukyas, is having several noted Temples, some structural & other rock-cut of the 6th & 7th Century. The foundation of Badami or Vatapi as it was called were laid by Pulakeshi-I and his son Kirtivarman-I beautified the town with Temples & other buildings. Mangalesha, brother of Kiritavarman-I completed the construction of the cave Temples & endowed the Temples with the village on the occasion of the installation of the vigraha of Lord Vishnu.

Badami Caves - This group of 4 cave Temples have been carved out of the hill opposite Badami Fort. Of the four, three are Brahmanical, while the fourth is Jain. Nearly 2000 steps have to be climbed to reach the cave.

Cave-I - This is Shaivite cave. The important carvings in this cave are an 18-armed dancing Lord Shiva, a two-handed Lord Ganesha, Mahishasuramardini, Ardhanareeshwara & Shankarnarayana. The ceiling is adorned by a serpent motif & other carved figures.

Cave-II - This cave has Vaishnavite influence with panels of Trivikrama & Bhuvaraha. On the ceilings are carvings of Anantasayana, Lord Brahma, Vishnu, Shiva & other Ashtadikpalas.

Cave-III - Another flight of steps takes to the third cave, which is the largest & the best of the lot. This cave has carvings pertaining to both Shaivite & Vaishnavite themes. Panels of Trivikrama, Narasimha, Shankaranarayana, Bhuvaraha, Anantasayana & Harihara are engraved in a vigorous style. An inscription found here records the creation of the shrine by Mangalesha in 578 AD. There are some fine bracket figures on the pillars of this cave.

Cave-IV - Lying to the east of cave three, the fourth cave is Jain. There is an vigraha of Bhagwan Mahavira adorning the sanctum. Other carvings here are of Maa Padmavathi & other Thirthankaras. Asteep climb up some steps cut in a crevice between Cave-II &-III leads to the southern part of Badami Fort & to an old gun placed there by Tippu Sultan.

Badami Fort - Strategically situated on top of the hill, the Fort encloses large granaries, a treasury & impressive Temples on top of the northern end of the Hill. Malegitti Shivalaya, perhaps the oldest Temple of the lot, is dedicated to the benign aspect of Lord Shiva as the garland maker. Placed on the summit of a rocky hill, the Temple is built of stone, finely joined without mortar & with Dravidian Tower. The lower Shivalaya has a Dravidian Tower of which only the sanctum remains now.

Agastya Lake - There are some more Temples in Badami town & several of them dotting the banks of a well-built tank locally called the Agasthya Tirtha. Located on the outskirts of the city, the enormous Agastya Lake lies below the Cave Temples. It is said to have been formed in 5th century and many believe that its water has curative properties. The lake is considered holy and devotees take a dip in its waters to wash away their sins. Legend has it that when the Chalukyas ruled the region around Badami, the capital of their kingdom, Vatapi, was carved out of stone and spread around the ravine of the Agastya Lake. It is said that the lake has been named after Sage Agastya of the epic Ramayana.

Banashankari Amma Temple - The Temple is popularly called Banashankari or Vanashankari since it is located in the Tilakaaranya forest. The Temple deity is also called the Shakambhari, an incarnation of the Goddess Parvati. It is also known as Shaktipeeth Shakambhari Devi. There are statues of Bhima, Bhramari, Shatakshi and Ganesha along with mother. The original Temple was built by the 7th century Badami Chalukya Kings, who worshipped the Goddess Banashankari as their tutelary deity. The Goddess Banashankari is the tutelary god for Devanga Community. The Devanga weaver community in particular, holds this goddess in great reverence. Banashankari is also the tutelary deity of some Deshastha Brahmins. The Temple was built initially in the Dravidian architectural style. The rebuilt structure is in the Vijayanagara architectural style. The main structure has a mukha mantapa, ardha mantapa and a sanctum topped by a Vimana. The main sanctum of the Temple has the vigraha of Goddess Banashankari deified in it. The black stone sculpture depicts the Goddess seated on a lioness trampling a demon under her foot. The Goddess has eight arms and holds a trishul, damaru, kapaalpatra, ghanta, Vedic scriptures, khadga-kheta and severed head of demon. There is a water tank in the forefront of the Temple at the entrance, which is locally called as Haridra Tirtha, a corrupted version of the name Harishchandra Tirtha. Lamp towers are seen in the foreground of the Temple on the west bank of the pond and also at the entrance. The tower on the bank of the tank is also an uncommon guard tower which is "reflects the Vijayanagara blend of Hindu and Islamic style". It is called the Victory Tower.The Temple attracts devotees from Karnataka as well as the neighbouring state of Maharashtra. The Temple celebrates its annual festival called Banashankari jatre in the months of January or February. The festival comprises cultural programmes, boat festival as well as a Rath yatra, when the Temple goddess is paraded around the city in a chariot.

Bhutanatha Temple - Dedicated to Lord Shiva, the Temple is one of the two major shrines of the Bhutanatha Group of Temples that extends up to the Agastya Lake. The deity is worshipped here in the Bhutanatha avatar (god of souls). Built in sandstone, the Temple has an open mandapa (hall) that reflects the South Indian Dravidian and North Indian Nagara styles of architecture. The inner shrine is believed to have been built by the Chalukyas in 7th century. At the back of the Temple, the avatars of Lord Vishnu and Jain figures are carved.

SHIVAYOGI MANDIR AT BADAMI – It is a place with spiritual importance located on the banks of the Malaprabha River. It trains and educates the Veershaiva Mathadhipathis and finds an important place for the Veerashaiva Lingayaths. Many enthusiastic devotees joined hands with Sri Hanagal Kumara Swamiji in his social service and establishing Shivayogi Mandira. It was established in 1909 and a 65 ft high chariot is also an attraction.

MAHAKUTA GROUP OF TEMPLES – The group of Temples is an important place of worship for Hindus and the location of a well-known Shaiva Monastery. The Temples are dated to the 6th or 7th century CE and were constructed by the early Kings of the Chalukya dynasty of Badami. The dating of the Temples is based on the style of architecture which is similar to that of the Temples in nearby Aihole and the information in two notable inscriptions in the complex: the Mahakuta Pillar inscription dated between 595–602 CE (written in the Sanskrit language and Kannada script); and an inscription of Vinapoti, a concubine of King Vijayaditya, dated between 696–733 CE and written in the Kannada language and script. Chikka Sangama is a place where Rivers Krishna and Ghataprabha are at confluence and this place has a Sangamanath Temple with a beautiful architecture. People and devotees from far places visit this place throughout the year.

PATTADAKAL MONUMENTS - Once the destination of Kings, Pattadakal was where kingdoms were bestowed upon heirs apparent. The official coronation destination, the Temples at Pattadakal which literally translates into coronation (pattada) stone (kallu) has a collection of Temples that skew towards both the North Indian and South Indian styles of Temple architecture. With sculptures and details intact, these Temples narrate their stories with clarity; stories so powerful, that they resonate across centuries. In total, there are over 150 Hindu, Jain and Buddhist monuments and archaeological discoveries dating from the 4th to 10th century CE in addition to pre-historic dolmens and cave paintings that are preserved at the Pattadakal-Badami-Aihole site.

Galaganath Temple - Built of sandstone, the tower is in the northern "Rekhanagara" style. The Temple was probably never completed. It contains a beautiful sculpture of Shiva in the act of killing the Andhakasura.

Jain Temple - It is built in the Dravidian style. It has some very beautiful sculpture & probably dates from the ninth century.

Jambulinga Temple – A small Temple with a fine figure of the Dancing Shiva with Nandi & Parvathi by his side. Built with a northern style tower, there is a horse-shoe arched projection on its facade.

Kada Siddeshwara Temple - This small Temple, built in the North Indian style, consists of shrine & a hall. There is a fine sculpture which depicts Shiva holding a serpent & trident in his raised arms with Parvathi by his side.

Malikarjuna Temple - Built by Trailokyamahadevi, the queen of Vikramaditya-II, it was originally called Trailokeshwara Temple. It is similar to the Virupaksha Temple but smaller in size. The ceiling has panels of Gajalakshmi & Nataraja with Parvathi. Pillars in the Temple depict the birth & life of Krishna. There are sculptures of Mahishasuramardini (very similar to the one in Mamallapuram) & Ugranarasimha.

Papanatha Temple - Just outside the enclosure is this ornate Temple built about 680 AD. This was an early attempt to develop the northern style of architecture, which was later abandoned in favour of the more balanced Dravidian or Pallava style. It contains impressive sculpted scenes from Ramayana & Mahabharatha.

Sanghameswara Temple - Perhaps the oldest Temple in Pattadakal, it was built by King Vijayaditya & was called Vijayewara after him. Now called Sangameshwara, the Temple is built in Dravidian style & consists of a sanctum, inner passage & a hall. There are sculptures on the outer wall like those of Ugranarasimha & Nataraja.

Virupaksha Temple - The Mallikarjuna & Virupaksha Temples were built by two queens of Vikaramaditya-II to commemorate the victory of the Chalukyas over the Pallavas. As the Virupaksha Temple was built by Queen Lokamahadevi, it was originally called Lokeshwara. The Temple is rich in sculpture like those of Lingodbhava, Nataraja, Ravananugraha & Ugranarasimha. Built in the southern Dravidian style, it is the largest Temple in the enclosure.

SRI JAGANNATH TEMPLE AT GULEDGUDD - The Temple is dedicated to Lord Jagannath. It is mysterious Temple, as during the Bhog Aarti at 10 am sweet rice is offered to Lord Jagannath and when the pot is kept in front of him, it breaks into four pieces mysteriously. It repeats daily & it is assumed that Lord has accepted the offerings.

DISTRICT – BALLARI (Railway Station – Toranagallu/Hosapete)

S. No.	Temple	Address	Type
1	Kumaraswamy Temple	Sandur – 583119	Murugan
2	Hampi Group of Temples	Hampi – 583239	All
3	Group Temples in Talukas	Ballari District	All

KUMARASWAMY TEMPLE AT SANDUR - It is notable for two ancient Hindu Temples which are in the same compound and are both protected monuments. The more famous in religious terms is the Kumaraswami Temple (8th -10th century) believed to be the first abode in south India of Murugan or Karthikeya, the Hindu god of war, son of Parvati and Shiva and brother of Ganesha. To art historians, the Parvati Temple beside it (7th - 8th century) is the more unusual in terms of Hindu Temple architecture.

HAMPI GROUP OF TEMPLES - The austere & grandiose site of Hampi was the last capital of the great Hindu Kingdom of Vijayanagar. Its fabulously rich princes built Dravidian Temples and palaces won the admiration of travellers between the 14th and 16th centuries. Hampi's spectacular setting is dominated by River Tungabhadra, craggy hill ranges and open plains with widespread physical remains. The Krishna Temple Complex, Narasimha, Ganesha, Hemakuta Group of Temples, Achyutaraya Temple Complex, Vitthala Temple Complex, Pattabhirama Temple Complex and Lotus Mahal Complex can be highlighted. The stone chariot in front of the Temple is also testimony to its religious ritual in Hampi. Most of the structures at Hampi are constructed from local granite, burnt bricks and lime mortar. The stone masonry and lantern roofed post and lintel system were the most favoured construction technique. The massive fortification walls have irregular cut size stones with paper joints by filling the core with rubble masonry without any binding material. The majority of the monuments are in good state of preservation and conservation. The Government of India, the Archaeological Survey of India and the Government of Karnataka are responsible for the protection and management of fifty-six Nationally Protected Monuments and the rest of the area covered by 46.8 sq. kms respectively under their respective legal provisions.

ACHYUTARAYA TEMPLE - This is a beautiful & magnificent Temple. It was built in 1534 AD in Vijayanagara architectural style. The Temple is dedicated to Lord Tiruvengalanatha, who is a incarnation of Lord Vishnu. The Temple has a grand entrance.

BADAVILINGA - Located next to the Lakshminarasimha Vigraha, the Badavilinga is 3 meter high and stands permanently in water that flows through an ancient channel.

Hanuman Temple - Whitewashed Hanuman Temple is another famous religious site located on the top of the Anjaneya Hill which is considered as the birthplace of Lord Hanuman.

Hemakuta Hill Temple Complex - This is one of the most famous and prominent Temples in Hampi that is surrounded by a number of beautiful Temples. The Temple is also the perfect place to witness the sunrise and sunset. According to Hindu Mythology, it is believed that this is where Lord Shiva burnt the God of Lust – the Kama with his third eye-fire.

Kodanda Rama Temple - It is a historic Temple. It is believed that Lord Rama had crowned the Sugriva as the King of Kishkinda at this spot. The Temple has 15 ft. tall standing vigrahas of Lord Rama, Sita & Lakshmana which is carved out from a single natural boulder.

Krishna Temple - The beautiful Temple draws visitors not only for spiritual reasons but also for its architectural sights. Said to have been built by King Krishnadevaraya in 1513 AD to celebrate his conquest of the eastern kingdom of Udayagiri or Utkala (in present day Odisha), the Temple's main deity was a Vigraha of Lord Balakrishna (Lord Krishna as infant). This Vigraha is now housed in Chennai's Government Museum. A slab installed inside the courtyard of the Temple tells the tale of the Temple and of the victory. The Temple's carvings standout from that of other structures in Hampi. With mythical lions on pillars and carvings of elephant balustrades flanking the entrances, the Temple is a living work of art. A small pavilion with a rectangular stone container in front of the Temple is said to have been used by devotees to offer grains to the gods.

Lakshmi Narasimha Vigraha - The Lakshmi Narasimha Vigraha, otherwise known as the Vigraha of Ugra Narasimha, was built in the year 1528 AD. This is known to be the awesome 6.7 meters monolith Vigraha seated on a seven hooded serpent in the whole of Hampi. The Vigraha of Lord Narasimha - an incarnation of Lord Vishnu and a half man, half lion- depicts the deity sitting in a cross-legged position in its fierce form.

Sri Malyavanta Raghunathaswamy Hill Temple - The Temple is dedicated to Lord Rama. The Temple has been built in 16th CE of Vijayanagara Era around a boulder. It is one of the most beautiful & stunning architectural marvel. It is believed that Lord Rama along with Lakshman stayed here in the rainy season during their search for Maa Sita. Lord Rama, for the shelter, aimed a arrow in the Malyavant Hill. There is still a cleft on the boulder atop the hill. The Temple has the vigraha which are carved on the face of a massive boulder. Lord Rama & Lakshmana's vigraha are in sitting posture whereas Maa Sita is in standing posture next to them & Lord Hanuman is in a kneeling posture with a great devotion. There is a natural Well towards south of the Temple with vigraha of Lord Krishna playing flute. There is a cave behind the Temple which is dedicated to Lord Shiva. The outer wall of Temple has motifs of fish & marine creatures carved on it.

Rishyamook Hill – This hill relates to Ramayana Circuit and is an ancient hill of Tretayuga. Kurda Rishi has cursed King Bali that if he visits this hill or nearby area he will be dead. Hence his younger brother Sugriva has taken shelter in one of the cave of the hill alongwith his well-wishers.

Sasivekalu Ganesha Temple – The Temple derives its name from the resemblance between Ganesha's belly & a mustard seed which is locally known as Sasivekalu. The Vigraha of Lord Ganesha, which is 2.4 mtrs is seen to have a snake carved around the stomach of Lord Ganesha. The history of the pavilion that surrounds the Vigraha of Lord Ganesha dates back to 1506 AD.

Vijaya Vittala Temple - This 15th century Temple is considered to be one of the largest historical structures in Hampi, which is dedicated to Lord Vittala- an incarnation of Lord Vishnu. The famous Stone Chariot, the huge pillars in the Temple halls and intricate sculptures are the true embodiments of the fascinating architecture. It is the most exquisitely ornate structure on the site and represents the culmination of Vijayanagara Temple architecture. It is a fully developed Temple with associated buildings like Kalyana Mandapa and Utsava Mandapa within a cloistered enclosure pierced with three entrance Gopurams. Equally impressive is the large Ranga Mantapa with 56 musical pillars that resound with musical chimes when struck. In addition to the typical spaces present in contemporary Temples, it boasts of a Garuda shrine fashioned as a granite *ratha* and a grand bazaar street. This complex also has a large *Pushkarani (stepped tank)* with a *Vasantotsavamandapa* (ceremonial pavilion at the centre), wells and a network of water channels.

Virupaksha Temple - Believed to be the oldest functioning Temple in India, Sri Virupaksha Temple is a 7th century Temple dedicated to Lord Virupaksha, an incarnation of Lord Shiva. The Temple is seen to have many inscriptions of Lord Shiva. The Temple was initially a shrine which was later extended into a huge complex during the Vijayanagara rule. The Temple has one big holy place for worship, a hall supported by pillars and 3 antechambers and of all the entrances in the Temple, the eastern gateway is highest one. The ceiling of the Ranga Mantapa is beautifully painted with scenes from the epics and Puranas.

Yantrodharaka Hanuman Temple - The Temple is dedicated to Lord Hanuman. The Temple is located on the top of a Hill on the banks of Tungabhadra River. The Temple had been built in 15th CE. The vigraha of Lord Hanuman is seated in Padmasana posture within the center of Sri Yantra.

BELLARY -

Dammur (T. Bellary) - It is well known for its cave Temple and the Samadhi (tomb) of Venkappa. An annual fair is held here.

Kurugodu (T. Bellary) - At the western end of the village is the Temple of Basaveshwara with a conspicuous modern gopura. Within it, is a large Nandi or Bull of Lord Shiva, which is a monolithic sculpture, about 12 ft in height. Attached to the Temple is Nilamma's Matha held in great esteem. On the site of old Kurugodu, there are also nine old Temples forming one group and a tenth standing alone on the other side of the Hanumanta hill. All these Temples have been constructed of granite without the use of mortar. The inscription in one of them, dated 1175-76 A.D., mentions its erection by a merchant.

Moka (T. Bellary) - The Malleshwaraswamy Temple here attracts a number of pilgrims, especially during the car festival.

HADAGALLI - Keshavaswami Temple was constructed by Rebbaladevi, wife of the Brahmin general Revideva at Poovina-Posavadangile which was the place of her birth. Two of the Temples at this place, Kalleshwara and Keshavaswami, are described in detail in Rea's,"Chalukyan Architecture". The Temples contain some delicate carvings. The vigraha in one of them, dedicated to Yoga-Narayanaswami, is of black-stone and quite exquisitely carved.

Kogali (T. Hadagalli) - The village was also once a Jain centre of considerable importance. Even now there is a Jain Basti (Temple) here with an vigraha of a Teerthankara which is of more than a life-size and in the usual posture of contemplation. There are other Jain relics elsewhere not only in this village but also in neighbouring villages.

Kuruvatti (T. Hadagalli) – It is located on the banks of Tungabhadra River. It is famous for its Chalukyan Temple and its cattle fair. The latter takes place at the time of the car festival about February-March. The Temple is dedicated to Mallikarjuna. It is built of black stone and is elaborately carved. Its chief attractions are two of its door-ways, the east door of the shrine being an especially fine example of the style.

Magala (T. Hadagalli) - It is noted for its Chalukyan Temple of black soap-stone, dedicated to Venugopalaswami. This consists of three shrines opening on to a central mantapa. The door-ways leading to the shrines from the mantapa, especially that on the west, are exquisite in design and workmanship. The ceilings too are probably the finest in the whole series of Chalukyan Temples of the district. There is a Suryanarayana shrine in the premises.

Mailara or Mylara (T. Hadagalli) - It is well-known for the annual festival held every year in February at the Temple dedicated to Lord Shiva in his form of Mailara or Mallari, meaning the defeater of Malla. In the mantapa in front of the door-way leading into the shrine is an elaborately carved torana, the only one to be found in the Chalukyan Temples in this part.

Sogi (T. Hadagalli) - There is a Chalukyan Temple of Kalleshvara in the village.

HARAPANAHALLI - There is a Hanuman Temple and a Jain shrine. There is a Temple of Venkataramanaswami. The most popular Temple in the town is that of 'Uru-Devate' (goddess of the town). The daily worship is done by a person of the Beda caste. In front of it, is an extraordinary collection of snake-stones of various sizes and shapes. A car festival is held in honour of the goddess. The priest on this occasion is a Badagi (carpenter), the office being hereditary in his family. There is a Temple of Mailara Lingappa in the north-west corner of the town, where an annual festival takes place.

Devara-Timmalapum (T. Harapanahalli) - It has a big Temple of Lord Venkateshwara constructed by Dadayya Nayaka, a Palayagar of Harapanahalli. His son Ranga Nayaka also built the unfinished portion of this Temple. There are carved stone vigrahas of these chiefs and their wives in the premises of the Temple. There is also another shrine in the premises of this Temple. The deity of this shrine is called Kannu-Kottappa (meaning healer of eyes). The main Temple has a big gopura which is said to have been built by a Tahsildar of Harapanahalli by name Kandi Seshagiri Rao. The place is known for its annual jatrra (car festival) which is largely attended.

Halavagalu (T. Harapanahalli) - It contains a Chalukyan Temple made of black-stone. It is the plainest of all the Temples of this type in the district.

Kulahalli or Koovlahalli (T. Harapanahalli) - It contains a Temple dedicated to Goni Basappa built in a style which is rather unusual. Goni Basappa was a sanyasi who was held in great esteem in the region.

Nilagunda (T. Harapanahalli) - It contains a small but beautiful Chalukyan Temple dedicated to Bhimeshwara. The Temple never seems to have been completed. The carvings on the ceiling of the central compartment of the mantapa and on the door-way to the central shrine are very attractive. The vigrahas in the shrines of Ananthashayana and Lakshminarayana are also fine examples of Chalukyan work.

Uchchangidurga (T. Harapanahalli) - There is a well-known Temple of Uchchangiamma. The Dasara festival in this Temple is largely attended.

KUDLIGI - There is a prominent Temple of Siddheshwara on a rock.

Chikkajogihalli (T. Kudligi) - The Hanuman and Choudeshwari Temples of the place were renovated.

Gunasagara (T. Kudligi) - It is famous for the vigraha of Gopalakrishna in the local Temple, which is reputed for the excellence of its workmanship.

Ujjini (T. Kudligi) - It is the seat of one of the important religious heads of the Veerashaivas. This ancient religious institution is called Ujjayini Saddharma Peetha. The matha of this guru is the most notable building and a Temple of Siddheshwara. There is a finely carved lotus on the ceiling of one of the compartments of the mantapa in front of the shrine in this Temple.

HOSPET - Jambunatha-Konda is located about 3,000 ft above the sea-level. Half way up, in a very picturesque glen, is the Temple of Jambunatha. There is a mineral spring which is believed to have healing virtues.

Hampi (T. Hospet) – There is a famous Ganigitti Temple. It is a Jain Temple and the tower above its shrine is built in a series of steps, which is the most characteristic of the Jain Temples in this district. According to an inscription on the lamp-post nearby, it was erected by a Jain general named Irugappa in 1385. The Temple of Malyavanta Raghunathaswami is also in existence here. It is built in the Dravidian style. Strange-looking fishes and marine monsters carved along its outer walls are worth noticing. In the innermost shrine of this Temple, is a boulder and the tower of the shrine is perched on the top of this. The Temple of Hazara Ramaswami is believed to have been the private place of worship of the royal family. The outsides of the outer walls of this Temple are covered with courses of sculpture similar to those in the House of Victory. The chief attraction of the Temple is the series of

scenes from the Ramayana carved on two of the inside walls of the mantapa which lies north of the main entrance, and on the wallls of the courtyard adjoining it. Perhaps it was from these carvings that the Temple derived its name ('Hazara Rama' means thousand Ramas). The whole series of carvings is the most noteworthy feature of the Temple.

MALLAPURAM -

Hampasagara (T. Mallapuram) – There is an ancient Temple of Lord Veerabhadraswami.

Kombali (T. Mallapuram) - There is a picturesque Temple of Anjaneya on the bank of the River (now the reservoir). At the time of the annual jatra about the month of December, a large crowd assembles to witness the car festival.

Tambrahalli (T. Mallapuram) – The Ranganatha Temple was constructed about 300 years ago by Obaraya Nayaka who was then the Palayagar of this area. The deity is said to be an udbhavamrurthi. The vigraha of Narayana is lying on a serpent and there is also a Shivalinga beside the deity. There is a step-well which is attached to the Temple. A car festival in honour of the deity is held in the month of Phalguna (about March) on the full moon day.

SANDUR - There is a Temple which is dedicated to Narasimhaswami. The Vitthoba Temple at Sandur has a shrine containing well carved stone pillars and a beautiful ceiling.

Bommaghatta (T. Sandur) - It has an old Temple of Hulikuntiraya (Anjaneyaswamy) which draws devotees not only from Bellary district but also from the neighbouring districts.

Ramanadurga (T. Sandur) - The Ramadeva Temple here is said to be named after Kumara Rama (who had been hidden in this area for some time by Minister Bychappa Nayaka in order to save his life). This is confirmed by an inscription found at the place. The epigraph is dated in the Shaka year 1450 when Krishnadeva Raya was ruling.

SIRUGUPPA - On a bastion of the Fort here, stands an old Temple of Shambhulinga, which is the oldest Temple of the place. The Temple of "Kotturu Basavanna" is a modern structure with a conspicuous gopura. It was built in 1887 by a rich local merchant.

Kenchanagudda (T. Siruguppa) – It is located on the banks of the Tungabhadra River. There is a Temple of Gangadhara. Built into its southern wall, is a long inscription, dated in the year 1708, giving the genealogy of Kenchana Gowda and stating that he built the Temple and the upper fort.

Telckailakota (T. Siruguppa) - The Amareshvara Temple contains an inscription which states that it was built by one Jakka Raya in 1511, as an offering to Lord Shiva and in honour of the king Krishnadeva Raya of Vijayanagara. The Temple, which had been nearly buried in earth and debris, was excavated and provided with a set of steps leading down to it. There is also a Temple of Kadu Siddappa, a saint, and a mantapa under which he is buried. Many miracles are said to have been performed by Kadu Siddappa. It is stated that he brought rain whenever it was wanted, protected the village cattle from wild beasts and on one occasion mounted a wall and made it move about. His help is still invoked when difficulties arise. In the north-eastern part of the village, about two miles away, is a Temple of Hari Mallappa, where a festival and a fair are held annually.

DISTRICT – BANGALORE RURAL (Railway Station – KSR Bengaluru/Dodballapur)

S. No.	Temple	Address	Type
1	Shri Ghati Subramanya Temple	Doddaballapur Taluk, Ghati Subramanya – 561203	Kartikeya, Narasimha
2	Nagadevatha Temple	Devanahalli Fort – 562110	Nagnath

S. No.	Temple	Address	Type
3	Shivagange	Devanahalli – 562110	Shiva
4	The Venugopalaswamy Temple	Devanahalli – 562110	Vishnu
5	Vishwa Shanti Ashram	Arasinakunte Village – 562123	Sant Keshava Das
6	Sri Shanimahathma Temple	Kaggalahalli – 562129	Shani

SHRI GHATI SUBRAMANYA TEMPLE AT DODDABALLAPUR – It is an ancient Temple and is a popular pilgrimage centre. The uniqueness of this Temple is that the prime deity Lord Karthikeya is found together with Lord Narasimha. According to mythology, both vigrahas are believed to have emerged from the earth. It is also an important centre in South India for snake worship. Ghati Subramanya has a recorded history of more than 600 years. It was first developed by the Ghorpade rulers of Sandur. The vigraha of Lord Karthikeya with a seven headed cobra is made from a single stone. It faces eastwards while the vigraha of Lord Narasimha faces westwards. To ensure that both deities are visible to devotees at the same time, a huge mirror was placed in the rear in the sanctum sanctorum. It is believed that on this spot, the deity Lord Subramanya was performing penance in the form of a snake. Lord Subramanya prayed to Lord Narasimha to provide the Naga's family from Lord Vishnu's vehicle, the Garuda, known for his dislike towards serpents. Lord Subramanya's form is that of a seven-hooded snake and it is believed that this is the region where he vanquished Ghatikasura, the demon. Some of the major rituals that can be performed at the Temple include Kuja Dosha, Naga Pratistha, Sarpa Dosha and Nivarana Puja. It is a firm belief of devotees that the Temple should be visited by childless couples so that they may be able to conceive. Another ritual practiced here is the installation of snake vigrahas near the Temple, which is believed to be an auspicious act and offering. Visitors to the Temple are greeted with the sight of thousands of such vigrahas around the complex, planted by devotees.

NAGADEVATHA TEMPLE AT DEVANHALLI – The Temple is the ancestral Temple of a Devanahalli family. The Temple is close to 400 years old and has been recently renovated. It is dedicated to gods of snakes and is located in the Devanahalli Fort.

SHIVAGANGE AT DEVANHALLI - Sri Honnammadevi Temple is inside the cave. Sri Gavi Gangadhareshwara Temple is also inside the cave. Every year in the month of January on the day of Sankranthi festival, the marriage function of Sri Gangadhareshwara and Sri Honnammadevi (Parvathi) is conducted. At that time Ganga holy water will come from the rock at the top of hill and that holy water is used for the dhare ritual (solemnise) of the marriage function. An interesting miracle happens here is that when an abhisheka is performed on Shivalinga with ghee, the ghee turns to butter. Devotees can see the miracle live during abhisheka. It is said that the ghee that turns to butter has medicinal powers and can cure many ailments. According to legend there exists a secret tunnel that extends from the sanctum sanctorum (Garba Griha) of this Temple.

THE VENUGOPALASWAMY TEMPLE AT DEVANHALLI - The small town inside the strong walls of Devanahalli Fort has many Temples. The Venugopalaswamy Temple is one of the oldest among them. The courtyard, with a Garuda Stamba, is spacious and the walls of the Temple depict various scenes from Ramayana and the feats of Lord Krishna as a child and the pillars have beautiful

vigrahas carved on them. On the pillars of the main entrance stand two horsemen with swords unsheathed. The Garbhagriha has a standing Venugopala vigraha of Vijayanagara style. There is a Dravidian style Sikhara over the Temple. The Navaranga has four black-stoned pillars carved with fine relief sculptures on all sides such as hayagriva, dancing female figures with attendant musicians, a conch blower, a kinnara with the lower portion of his body in bird form, a huntress removing a thorn from her leg etc. A teru is the big chariot used to parade the Vigraha of Gopalaswamy around the town once a year.

VISHWA SHANTI ASHRAM AT ARASINAKUNTE - Sri Sadguru Sant Keshava Das established the Ashram in 1982 to promote international peace & understanding. The Ashram has some beautifully designed Temples such as Lakshmi Narayana Temple; Asta Lakshmi Temple; Gayathri Temple; Navagraha Temple; Temple of Santoshi Mata; Seven women depicting seven rivers - Ganga, Yamuna, Godavari, Saraswathy, Narmada, Sindhu and Kaveri; Bhagawath Gita Bodhane, entire Bhagawadh Gita verses are written in Hindi, English and Kannada in 800 granite pieces and fixed on the interior and exterior walls of the Vishwa Roopa Darshan Mandir; The Vishwa Roopa revealed to Arjuna by Lord Krishna & Gitopadesha Chariot, which was designed by the sculptor Kasinath from Shimoga district.

SRI SHANIMAHATHMA TEMPLE AT CHIKKA MADHURE - On the banks of the Madhure Kere Lake, there is a famous pilgrimage centre of Shree Shani Mahathma. The Temple is dedicated to Saturn or Shani Dev, one of the Navagrahas (nine planets) worshiped in the Hindu Temples. The Temple has a typical south Indian style architecture. It has a Gopura like in most of the South Indian Temples. The stunning Dravidian architecture is mind-blowing with many sculptures carved out on the gopuram. The excellent workmanship on the gopuram contains many intricate carvings that are truly alluring. The Temple was built by a farmer called Ganga Hanumaiah to dedicate to Shani Deva to pacify the vengeance and the difficulties in one's life.

DISTRICT – BELAGAVI (Railway Station – Belagavi/Dharwad)

S. No.	Temple	Address	Type
1	Kapileshwara Temple	Shastri Nagar, Shahapur, Belgaum – 590001	Shiva
2	Military Mahadev Temple	Belgaum – 590001	Shiva
3	Shri Vishweshwara Temple	Yellur – 590005	Shiva
4	Belgaum Fort	Belgaum - 590016	Ganesh, Mata
5	Shiva Temple	Ramdurg - 591123	Shiva
6	Kalika Devi Kshetra	Sirsangi - 591126	Mata
7	Sri Renuka Yellamma Devi Temple	Saundatti - Yellamma – 591173	Mata
8	Shree Mauli Devi Temple	Kanakumbi - 591345	Mata
9	Group of Temples in Taluka	Belagavi District	All

KAPILESHWARA TEMPLE AT BELAGAVI - It is said to be one of the oldest Temples in Belagavi. It is called as "Dakshina Kashi" and it is believed that the journey of the 12 Jyotirlingas of India is said to be incomplete without a visit to Kapileshwara. One should visit this Temple during the month of Shravan or on the day of Mahashivratri to enjoy the beauty and feel the religious essence to the fullest extent. There are Temples of Lord Ganesh, Hanuman, Datta, Saibaba in the Temple premises. There is also a Navagraha Mandir situated here. It is known for the first offering to the self-manifested Shivalinga was made by the Sage Kapila and thus, this Temple bears the name Kapileshwara. The Temple interiors are adorned with the depictions from the texts like Linga Purana, Bhagavatam and Gajendra Moksham.

MILITARY MAHADEVA TEMPLE AT CAMP - Situated in the middle of a beautiful and well-kept garden, the Temple is a prime attraction in Belgaum and also one of the city's oldest Temples. The sanctum sanctorum of the Temple houses a large vigraha of Lord Shiva along with a Shivalinga. Two Nandi (bull god) vigrahas can also be seen in front of the Shivalinga. The foundation stone of the Temple was laid in 1954 and it was made open to public in 1955 by Lieutenant General SM Shrinagesh of the Indian Army. The Temple has undergone several renovations and a new dome was built keeping the original style intact. The Temple boasts intricate carvings that are similar to the carvings found in prominent Temples across South India. It has for long been used as a place of worship by Army personnel, which is why it is called the Military Mahadeva Temple.

YELLUR - Located at the foothills of Yellurgad, it is a prime tourist attraction that attracts visitors with its ancient Temples, verdant forests and pristine beaches. The most popular attraction in Yellur is a Lord Shiva Temple, which is said to be more than a thousand years old. The Temple is known as Yellur Shri Vishweshwara Temple and is known for its tender coconut abhishekam through which devotees visiting the Temple pay obeisance to Lord Shiva or Vishweshwara. Devotees from all parts of the country can be seen here offering gold coins and lighting earthen lamps as a ritual to please the presiding deity. Built in the Devayathana style of architecture, the imposing structure of the Temple attracts not only ardent devotees of Lord Shiva but also archaeology and history lovers from all corners of the world. Devotees can also visit the separate shrines of Goddess Annapoorneshwari and Lord Vinayaka, located in the same Temple complex. There's a beautiful lake on the Temple's northern side, along with a Temple dedicated to Goddess Bhagirathi. It is a popular belief that River Ganga once used to flow from the spot where the lake can be seen today.

BELAGAVI FORT AT BELAGAVI - It is an ancient architectural pre-muslim monument where mosques and Temples co-exist in perfect harmony. The Fort was built in the 12th century AD by the local Ratta rulers. At the very entrance, you will find two Shrines; One dedicated to Lord Ganpati and the other to Goddess Durga.

KAMAL BASADI - Located within the Belgaum Fort complex, it is a Jain Temple that was constructed by Bichi Raja, a clergyman of Kartavirya-IV of the Ratta dynasty in 1204 AD. Built in the late Chalukyan style, the Temple is noted for its tower, which is adorned with a huge lotus flower with 72 petals. The roof of the Temple is decorated with vigrahas of 24 Jain Tirthankaras. The sanctum sanctorum houses a black stone Vigraha of Neminatha, the 22nd Tirthankar. It also houses vigrahas of Lord Parshvanath, Lord Adinath and Lord Sumatinath along with vigrahas of the navgrahas or the nine planets. Tourists can also visit the remains of another Jain Temple that was called Chikki Basadi.

SHIVA TEMPLE AT RAMDURG - The Temple is dedicated to Lord Shiva. There is a very huge vigraha of Lord Shiva in padmasana posture which is attracting more & more devotees to visit this holy place & pay their obeisance to Lord Shiva. There is also a huge vigraha of Nandi looking towards Lord Shiva.

KALIKA DEVI KSHETRA AT SIRSANGI - The Temple is dedicated to Goddess Kali. The place was known as Rishishringapura or Hirishingi. As per legend, a Rishi named Vrushya Shrunga was doing severe penance here in the tapovan but demon like Narundasur, Bettasura & Nalundasur disturbed him and upon his request Goddess killed all these demons from this place and Goddess settled down here and a big Temple was construed at this place. Tula Bhara Sewa is very famous here. Ugadi is celebrated here with great pomp & fervor.

YELLAMMA TEMPLE AT SAUNDATTI - The Temple was constructed by Bomappa Naik of Raybag in the year 1514. Situated atop a hill, known as Siddhachal Parvat, near Soundatti, the Renuka Devi Temple is popularly called the Yellamma Devi Temple. Renuka Devi was the wife of Jamadhagni and she was the mother of Parashurama. Her story finds a mention in the Puranas and ancient Indian texts. She is revered as one of the Saptamatrika or seven divine mothers, who protected the earth and its rulers. The goddess is also known as Yelumakkaltai, meaning "the mother of seven children" in Kannada language. She is a cult figure worshiped by the pastoral community of the Dhangar and Kurumbas of southern Maharashtra and North Karnataka. The Temple is built in the Chalukyan and Rashtrakuta Style and the carvings reflect the Jain architecture. There are Temples of Lord Ganesh, Mallikarjun, Parshuram, Eknath, Siddeshwar etc. in the Temple premises. The famous Yellamma Jatra conducted on the full moon day known as the Bharat Hunnime. On this occasion, Goddess Yellamma is worshipped in the manner of Shakti Puja. Devotees from Maharashtra, Goa and Andhra Pradesh also come here apart from people from Karnataka. There are three water tanks or ponds at the back side of the Temple known as Kumkum Kundam, Yoni Kundam, and Arihan Kundam. There is also a sacred well called the Jogal Bhavi;

the water of this well is believed to cure skin diseases. Another location adjacent to the Temple known as Parasurama Kshetra is believed to be the site where Lord Parasurama sat in penance. Another place of worship is the sacred "Yogarbavi Satyabamma Kunda" or tank at the lower end of the hill, where devotees bathe and put on new clothes before proceeding to the Temple for worship. A notable custom observed here is called "Nimmana", which involves the circumambulation of the "Sathyamma Temple" with neem leaves in their mouths. The Temple deity is also known as Jagadamba, meaning "Mother of the Universe" and is believed to be a form of Kali.

SHREE MAULI DEVI TEMPLE AT KANAKUMBI - The Temple is blessed with ultimate beauty of nature at Western Ghats. The Temple is constructed in typical Konkani style of architecture with a two tiered structure with sloping roofs supported by pillars. Adjacent to the Temple, there is an old Well, which is believed to be the birth place of River Malaprabha that flows eastward before joining River Krishna at Kudala Sangama. There is a hidden water fall in the dense forest of Kanakumbi region, which is known as Venezuela of Karnataka. The Surla Falls is a magnificent site ensconced in the lap of Western Ghats.

GROUP OF TEMPLES IN TALUKAS OF BELAGAVI –

DEGAON - It is famous for kadamba style Kamala Narayana Temple of 12th CE. The place name might have originated from its Temples. Devagram or Degaon meaning a village of Gods.

HALASI - It is located in the background of the Western Ghats and was the second capital of the Kadambas of Banavasi. The huge Bhuvaraha Narasimha Temple has tall vigrahas of Varaha, Narasimha, Narayana and Surya. The Archaeological Survey of India is looking after this ancient structure. The place has a fort and Temples of Gokarneshswara, Kapileshwara, Swarneshwara and Hatakeshwara. Halasi has groups of monuments like Kalmeswara, Suvarneswara, Ramalingeswara and Bhuvaraha Temples.

HOOLI - The nice architecture of Hooli Panchalingeshwar Temple is to be adored. It is a protected monument that comes under Archaeological Survey of India. Earlier, during summer afternoons people used to rest in the shade of this Temple because the Temple was made of stone and it was unbelievably cool even in the scorching summer. Opposite the Panchalingeshwara Temple, is the relatively modern Hari Mandir. The Sant Culture or Nath tradition influenced heavily by Jnaneshwar flourished here.

MURGOD - At the time of Mahabharata, it was called Amarkalyan though the name was later changed to Threeshigapura (in Kannada it means Mooru-gudda). Eventually, the name became Murgod. Murgod is the holy place for Saint Basava and Shiva devotees. Shri Mahant Duradhundishwara Math and Shri Shiv Chidambara Mahaswami Punya Kshetra attracts devotees across India. Some other holy places here are "Shri Mallikarjuna Temple" which is built similarly to "Srisaila Mallikarjuna Temple". Its ancient architecture is very attractive. "Pandavar Padi" (Pandavar Hill) - there is a myth that in the time of Mahabharata, Pandavas crossed through this village. "Siddappana Gavi" (Siddappa's Cave) is famous as Yadeyur Siddalingeshwar came to this village and they stayed in this cave. Around the village are "Shri Kshetra Sogal", "Naveelathirth Dam Munavalli".

SOGAL - The name of the place is ascribed to a sage, Sugola Muni, who is believed to have lived in the area but one inscription speaks of "Sovala. Located on a hillside, it has many Temples including the Someshwara Temple, which is of great antiquarian interest. Local folklore states that tigers came to Sogal to listen to the religious teachings. Other legends include a nearby Kalyanmantapa (Temple), where the marriage of Lord Shiva and Parvati is said to have taken place. There is an old Vigraha of Panchanana Shiva and Parvati, wherein Lord Shiva is with basinga and other traditional ornaments. There are Ashtadikpalakas (vigrahas of gods) in this area such as; Yama, Agni, Ishanya and Indra and these artefacts are examples of the artistic accomplishments of the period. To the east of this Temple is the Ajjappana Gudi and a stone Surya-Chandra shrine. Near the Someshwara Temple, there is also small shrine called Girija Temple.

DISTRICT – BENGALURU URBAN (Railway Station – KSR Bengaluru)

S. No.	Temple	Address	Type
1	Muthyalamma Temple	Shivaji Nagar, Bengaluru - 560001	Mata
2	Dharmaraya Swamy Temple	Ganigarpet, Nagarathpete, Bengaluru – 560002	Mahabharat Circuit
3	Sri Lakshmi Narasimha Temple	Malleswaram, Bengaluru – 560003	Narasimha
4	Sri Karanji Anjaneyaswamy Temple	Gandhi Bazaar, Basavanagudi, Bengaluru – 560004	Hanuman
5	The Nandhi Temple	Bull Temple Road, Basavanagudi, Bengaluru – 560004	Nandi
6	Sri Someshwara Swamy Temple	Ulsoor Rd, Someshwarpura, Halasuru, Bengaluru - 560008	
7	Sri Venkateshwara Swamy Temple	Freedom Park, K.G. Road, Bengaluru - 560009	Venkatesh
8	ISKCON	Hare Krishna Hill, Rajajinagar, Bengaluru – 560010	Radha-Krishna
9	Shivoham Shiva Temple	No. 97 Old Airport Road, Bengaluru – 560017	Shiva
10	Srinagar Navashakthi Devi Temple	Chamrajpet, Bengaluru - 560018	Mata
11	Sri Gavi Gangadhareshwara Temple	Gavipuram Extension, Kempegowda Nagar, Bengaluru – 560019	Shiva

S. No.	Temple	Address	Type
12	Hanumanthana Gudda	Hanumanth Nagar, Bengaluru – 560019	Rama, Hanuman
13	Gali Anjaneya Temple	Mysore Road, Byatarayanapura, Bengaluru - 560026	Hanuman
14	Sri Abhaya Anjaneya Swamy Temple	Agara, Bengaluru - 560034	Hanuman
15	Sri Rama Temple	Ejipura, Bengaluru - 560047	Rama, Vishnu
16	Panchamukhi Ganesha Temple	Mysore Road, Kengeri Satellite Town, Bengaluru – 560060	Ganesh
17	Ragigudda Temple	Jayanagar, Bengaluru - 560069	Hanuman
18	Sri Banashankari Temple	S Kariyappa Road, Kanakapura Main Road, Bengaluru - 560070	Mata
19	Sri Anjaneya Temple	Nagarbhavi, Bengaluru - 560072	Hanuman
20	The Art of Living International Center	Udaypura, Bengaluru – 560082	Sri Sri Ravi Shankar
21	Karya Siddhi Anjaneya Temple (Sri Ganapathy Sachidananda Ashrama)	3rd C Main, 7th Cross, Girinagar 2nd Phase, Bengaluru – 560085	Hanuman
22	Sri P. V. Anjaneya Swamy Temple	Mahalakshmi Layout - 560086	Hanuman
23	Sri Devi Karumariamman Temple	Raja Rajeshwari Nagar, Bengaluru – 560098	Mata
24	Shrunga Giri Sri Shanmukha Swamy Temple	BEML, Kempegowda Double Road, 5th Stage, RR Nagar, Bengaluru – 560098	Murugan

MUTHYALAMMA TEMPLE AT SHIVAJI NAGAR, BENGALURU - The Temple is dedicated to Sri Muthyalamma. It is believed that the Goddess bestows special grace upon children who have issues with Baladosha, Balarishta. Several devotees visit the Temple for curing of skin ailments. The Temple is well known for it chariot festival.

SHRI DHARMARAYA SWAMY TEMPLE AT BENGALURU – The Temple is one of the oldest and most famous Temple of Bangalore. The Temple was built over eight hundred years ago by the Thigalas, one of the area's oldest social group. The Temple displays architectural features of buildings from the Western Ganga dynasty, the Pallava dynasty and the Vijayanagara Empire. The first building having been in existence before the current city of Bangalore, which was founded in 1530 by Kempe Gowda-I, when he built a mud fort here. The Temple is built with a gopuram, an ornate monumental entrance tower. Deities worshipped here include Dharmaraya, Krishna,

Arjuna, Draupadi and Bhima. The Karaga festival is celebrated during the months of March and April. On April 9, 2009, Shankar Narayan, as president of the Dharmaraya Swamy Temple Trust and Karaga festivities, became the first woman to lead the festival carrying the ritual pot.

Kote Sri Jalakanteshwara Swamy Temple at Fort, Bengaluru - The Temple is dedicated to Lord Shiva. The Temple is one of the oldest Shiva Temple in Karnataka. There are three Sanctum Sanctorums in the Temple which houses Jalakanteshwara Swamy at the centre in the form of Shivalinga, Maa Parvati to his left & Kailashnatheshwar Swamy to his right. It is placed in such a way only half of the vigraha is visible from the main gate, hence, the Temple is also called Ardhanareeshwara. The Temple is also having a rare Natya Ganesha vigrha and Maa Durga vigraha standing on a ball. There are nine stone pillars which features Navagraha carved on them. It is also believed that unmarried girls gets their married match within 48 days by worshiping at this place. There is also a ritual of offering a necklace made of 108 bengal grams.

SRI LAKSHMI NARASIMHA TEMPLE AT MALLESWARAM - In the Temple, Lord Narasimha is seen alongwith his consort Goddess Lakshmi. There are various morals of Nava Narasimha in the Temple and alongwith depiction of Ramayana on the door. Lord Narasimha is the forth incarnation of Lord Vishnu. He seen in nine forms called as Nava Narasimha. Sri Lakshmi Narasimha is considered as the calmest form.

Sri Gangamma Devi Temple at Malleswaram - The Temple is dedicated to Sri Gangamma or Goddess Ganga, who is also considered to have manifested on Earth as the River Ganga and an incarnation of Shakti. She is believed to be Nada Devathe (Local deity) in Bangalore. A permanent Temple was consecrated in honor of the Goddess in the year 2004. The Temple complex also has smaller shrines for Lord Ganesha, Subramanya and the Navagraha The annual Gangamma Jathre is held in various places across India and the event in Bangalore has been held in and around Malleshwara area since 1928. The Jathre is normally held over a three-day period and see

thousands of devotees arriving from across Bangalore and nearby areas. The Temple and the deity are specially decorated and devotees offer Ragi Ganji (gruel) to the Goddess, along with the traditional flowers, coconut and fruit.

Sri Dakshina Mukha Nandi Theertha Kalyani Kshetra at Malleswaram - It is also known as Nandi Theertha. The Temple has been discovered in 1997 during the excavation of a mound. There is a continuous flow of natural water from the Nandi's Mouth, the source of which is not known. It is believed that it is 7000 years old Temple and a mystery behind its discovery. The Temple houses a Shivalinga.

Sri Venugopala Krishnaswamy Temple at Malleswaram - The Temple is dedicated to Lord Venugopala. The vigraha of Lord Venugopala is in Lord Krishna form having flute in his hands and in standing posture. The vigraha is made of black stone.

KARANJI ANJANEYASWAMY TEMPLE AT BENGALURU - The vigraha of the Lord, which faces north, is approximately of 18 ft. The Lord has the 'choodamani' in his hands depicting one of the scenes from the epic Ramayana. The Temple today stands on the Karanji Lake that existed since the olden times. Upon entrance, a tall flag post dedicated to Lord Garuda welcomes you. The Temple also has carvings that depict various incidents from Ramayana. To the right of the main shrine of Lord Hanuman, is the Temple dedicated to Lord Rama along with Goddess Seetha and his brother Lakshmana. Outside the Temple, there is a huge peepal tree with a lot of vigrahas dedicated to the serpent gods.

THE NANDHI TEMPLE AT BASAVANAGUDI - The Temple was built in 1537 by Kempe Gowda under the in the Vijayanagara architectural style. The bull referred to is a sacred Hindu demi-god, known as Nandi; Nandi is a close devotee and attendant of Lord Shiva. Dodda Basavana Gudi is said to be the biggest Temple to Nandi in the world. The stone monolith vigraha of Nandi is continually covered with new layers of butter, *benne* in the local language of Kannada. There is an vigraha of the elephant-headed Hindu deity Ganesha and another Temple of Lord Shiva close by. The current tower (vimana) over the shrine was constructed in the early 20th century and is adorned with Saivite figures and motifs. Every year on the last Monday and Tuesday of the Hindu month of Karthika Maasa a groundnut fair is held in the Temple premises and groundnut is offered to the deity. This fair is known as 'Kadalekaayi Parishe' in local tongue. As per local legend, a bull was roaming in this region (a few villages then) 500 years ago. The villagers found that every full moon day, their crop of groundnuts vanished mysteriously. They decided to stay on to watch & on a full moon day, they witnessed a huge bull, golden in colour, eyes shining bright like jewels, consume their crop but after this incident, the bull no longer visited their farm. Instead, they found a huge vigraha of a bull appear suddenly on the hill, which was growing at a steady pace. They had to hit a nail in the form of a soolam (trident) to stop its growth.

Sri Digvijaya Lakshmi Narasimha Devaru at Sri Uttaradi Mutt - Historically speaking, Sri Uttaradi Math is the original seat of Jagadguru Sri Madhvacharya. Shri Narayana himself incarnated as Shri Hamsa and adorned the pontifical seat called the Hamsa-Pitha. As he is also known as Uttara, the Math initiated by him came to be known as Uttara-Adi Math (The Math initiated by Sri Uttara). Sri Hamsa initiated Shri Brahma as his first disciple-pontiff and revealed the divine knowledge to him.

SRI SOMESHWARA SWAMY TEMPLE AT SOMESHWARPURA - The Temple is more than 1250 years old. The Temple has 48 intricately carved pillars of Vijayanagara Architecture. The Temple was revamped by the Vijayanagara empire during 16th CE. There are various beautiful carvings on the Temple walls.

Sri Kaliamman Temple at Ulsoor, Bengaluru - The Temple is dedicated to Goddess Kali. The Goddess is also known as Smashana Kali. The vigraha of Maa Kaliamman is Swayambhu. It is believed to be growing insights over the year. As per legend, around 1500 years back, a bairagi was

a devotee of Goddess Kali. Pleased with his devotion, Goddess appeared and decided to stay here as Yogeshwari. When the bairagi was about to die, he buried the vigraha under the soil. Later, the place became a ragi field. A farmer, while ploughing, hit a stone which started bleeding. Goddess Kali descended in a village girl Neeladevi & explained to villagers that Goddess had manifested in the stone. Gradually, a shrine was built here. The vigraha is said to have grown in size slowly from 9 inches to more than 16 inches over the year. There is a huge tree on which the devotees tie threads if they wish for a job, married or wishing for a child.

SRI VENKATESHWARA SWAMY TEMPLE AT FREEDOM PARK - The Temple is dedicated to Lord Venkateshwara who is known as Balaji in the heart of every devotee. The vigraha of Lord Venkateshwara is 25 feet tall and is in standing posture. Devotees visit the place in large numbers particularly on Saturday & special festivals.

ISKCON TEMPLE AT BENGALURU - Built on a hillock, with granite, marble and Korean glass, this huge cultural complex was established to promote Vedic culture and spiritual learning. It houses various deities including Lord Krishna, Balaram and Radha. The annual Rath Yatra (chariot procession) of Lord Krishna and Balaram draws devotees in large numbers. The unique combination of glass and gopuram represents a fusion between majestic traditional styles and bold new aesthetics. The Temple and cultural complex was inaugurated by the then President of India, Dr. Shankar Dayal Sharma on 31st May 1997.

Kailasa Vaikunta Mahakshetra at Rajajinagar - The Temple is dedicated to Lord Vishnu. Lord Vishnu has been consecrated in Ananthashayana posture giving blessings to devotees. The Vigraha of the Lord Vishnu is 20 ft. long. A Shivalinga has also been consecrated in the same precincts, hence, it is also known as Kailasha Vaikunta Mahakshetra. It is a famous and ancient shrine in Bangalore.

SHIVOHAM SHIVA TEMPLE AT OLD AIRPORT ROAD - The Temple is dedicated to Lord Shiva. The Temple is abode of a 65 ft. tall Lord Shiva vigraha seated in a yogic posture. The vigraha is carved out in white marble.

SRINAGAR NAVASHAKTHI DEVI TEMPLE AT CHAMRAJPET, BENGALURU - The Temple is dedicated to Goddess Navashakthi. She is believed to be a form of Goddess Parvathi. The vigraha of Goddess Navashakthi is in Padmasana posture. Devotees visit the Temple in large numbers on Friday & particularly during Navratris.

SRI GAVI GANGADHARESHWARA TEMPLE AT BANGALORE – The Temple also known as Gavipuram Cave Temple is an example of Indian rock-cut architecture. This Temple is dedicated to Lord Shiva. It is famous for its mysterious stone discs in the forecourt. It was built in the 16th century by Kempe Gowda-I, the founder of the city. It was built in recognition after being released from prison of five years by Rama Raya. There are other vigrahas such as Agnimurthi including having two heads, seven hands and three legs. Those who worship this deity will be cured one of the defects of the eye. The Temple is also known for its four monolithic pillars, representing Damaru, Trishul and two fans on the patio. The courtyard of the Temple here contains several monolithic sculptures. On the occasion of Makar Sankranti, Temple witnesses a unique phenomenon in the evening sunlight passes through an arc between the horns of Nandi and falls directly on the Linga inside the cave and illuminating the interior vigraha. Also today the Sun illuminates Shivalinga two times per year - from 13 to 16 January in late afternoons and from 26 November to 2 December. It is a protected monument.

HANUMANTHANA GUDDA AT HANUMANTH NAGAR - Hanumanthana Gudda or Ramanjaneya Gudda means the "Hill of Lord Hanuman". This major Temple is dedicated to Lord Hanuman and was built in 1960s. Two walkways with stairs are available to reach the top of the hill. Inside the Temple, there is an eight foot high vigraha of Lord Hanuman in which the Lord is standing at ease with his weapon, the Gadhe (Gada (mace)). On the top of the Temple, there are giant vigrahas of Lord Hanuman and Lord Rama hugging each other, as it is related they did after the conquest of Lanka. This gigantic vigraha is a symbol of the dedication and loyalty Lord Hanuman showed towards Lord Rama.

GALI ANJANEYA TEMPLE AT MYSORE ROAD, BYATARAYANAPURA - The Temple is dedicated to Lord Hanuman. The Temple has a history of 600 years. In Kannada, Gali means air, hence it is believed that Lord Anjaneya is son of Vayu, the wind god, therefore Lord in this Temple named as Gali Anjaneya. The Temple is very beautiful & the vigraha is in standing posture. There are different Shringars done by the priest of the Temple as per the special occasion.

SRI ABHAYA ANJANEYA SWAMY AT AGARA – It is the tallest vigraha of Lord Hanuman in Bengaluru. The height of the vigraha is 102 ft and the same was established in 2012. The Temple compound has a huge banyan tree making a peaceful space for devotees. The gigantic vigraha of Lord Hanuman is a fiesta to look at and it is simply a spectacular sight.

SRI RAMA TEMPLE AT EJIPURA, BENGALURU - The Temple is dedicated to Lord Rama. The Temple came into limelight when 64 feet high, 25 feet wide monolith statue of Vishwaroopam had been consecrated in the Temple. The vigraha is a colossal slab of granite, weighing 420 tonnes, quarried from a hill in Korakottai village in Tiruvannamalai district, Tamil Nadu. It had been traveled on a vehicle with 240 wheels, as it makes its way to this Temple from Korakottai.

PANCHAMUKHI GANESHA TEMPLE AT KENGERI - It's a renowned Ganapathi Temple with five faces of Lord Ganapathi. We can see Lord Shiva, Ganapathi, Ayapppa, Parvathi under one roof. The outstanding sculptured Temple stands with 30-foot gopuram from ground level covered with gold colour by the 2007 Sri Chakra Committee along with ashram where lots of learners can continue education there while doing the job for the growth of Temples.

Mukthi Naga Mandir at Kengeri - The Temple dates back to app. 200 years old. The world's largest mystic vigraha of Naga has been consecrated in this Temple. The vigraha is believed to be around 16 feet tall. The vigraha is seven headed and is about 56 tonnes in weight and Lord Subramanya is believed to be a form of snake, who is the main deity at the Temple. According to local people, earlier, this place was called as Junjappa Bailu which is named after Junjappa another serpent deity of the locality.

RAGIGUDDA SRI PRASANNA ANJANEYASWAMY TEMPLE AT JAYANAGAR - The Temple is dedicated to Lord Hanuman. The Temple also houses a Shivalinga along with Lord Rama, Sita, Lakshmana, Hanuman shrine in the same precinct. The Temple is on a hillock. There is a smaller Temple dedicated to Lord Ganesha, Navagraha and Goddess Rajarajeshwari at the base of the hillock. It also plays host to the Hindu holy trinity of Lord Brahma, Vishnu & Maheshwara on huge engraved rocks at the side of the Temple. In December every year, the festival of Sri Hanumajjayanthi is celebrated as a 12-day event in grandeur at the Temple.

SRI BANASHANKARI TEMPLE AT S KARIYAPPA ROAD - Sri Banashankari Devi is also known as Sri Shakambari. The Temple is one of the most popular places of worship in Bangalore. It is believed that the Goddess fulfills desires for prayers done in true sincere. The history of the Temple dates back to the year 1915. This Temple was founded by Basappa Shetty. He brought a vigraha of the Goddess from Badami and installed it inside the Temple. The unique features of the Temple is of the fact that the Goddess is worshipped and prayers are offered during Rahukala time. Additionally, it is believed that worshipping the Goddess in Rahukala to overcome all of the hardships as well as paucities of life. This Temple attracts huge number of devotees, particularly on Tuesdays, Fridays as well as Sundays. The prayers to Goddess Banashankari are offered by lighting many oil lamps in semi cut lemon peels, whose pulp have been removed.

Sri Umamaheswara Devalaya at Banashankari - The Devalaya is dedicated to Lord Uma Maheshwara. The Temple has performed many poojas, Homas and Yagnas including the special Koti Bilwarchane which was performed for 30 days with 36 Archaks chanting Shiva Sahasranama and 36 devotees offering Bilwapatra to Lord Shiva. The Temple trust celebrated the silver jubilee year during March, 2013 as it completed 25 years of Pratisthapana of Lord Shiva with grand celebration and fanfare.

Varapada Sree Venkateswara Temple at Devagiri - The Temple is dedicated to Lord Venkateswara. The Temple has two Mahadwaras. The Temple faces West. Lord Venkateshwara is surrounded by Maa Padmavathi & Andal, Ganapathi, Bhakta Anjaneya and Navagrahas. The height of the Rajagopura is 108 feet. It is known to be the highest Gopuram in Bangalore City and surrounding places. Devagiri-gopura Mukha Mantapa is quite spacious to accommodate simultaneous pradakshina of large number of people together. The top of the walls are decorated with pictures and description related to Srinivasa Kalyana. Garbhagudi and its surrounding walls are filled with vigrahas of deities such as Subramanya, Shankara, Venugopala, Seetharama, Lakshminarasimha, Saraswathi and Lakshmi. In front of Mukha Mantapa, Dwajastambha with Garuda as well a spacious Utsava Murthies Hall called Kalyana Mantapa are situated. Vaikunta Ekadashi celebrated once a year has been a very prominent and special celebration exclusive to the Devagiri Temple.

SRI ANJANEYA TEMPLE AT NAGARBHAVI, BENGALURU - The Temple is dedicated to Lord Anjaneya. The vigraha of Lord Anjaneya has been consecrated in a open chamber and the vigraha is in padmasana posture on a hill. The vigraha has been made out of stone and is very beautiful. Devotees visit the Temple in large numbers on Tuesday, Saturday & special festivals.

THE ART OF LIVING - The international headquarters of the Art of Living invite people from all corners of the world. A confluence of old and new, the ashram offers residential courses every week, from a basic one that introduces people to Sudarshan Kriya (a unique breathing technique) to the advanced one that gives them the opportunity to go deeper within oneself. Apart from enjoying meditative walks and exploring the ashram, visitors can also do seva or voluntary work at the ashram. This includes serving food in the kitchen, mopping the premise and taking overall care of

the ashram. A popular attraction is the evening satsang in which many youngsters sing, dance and meditate to songs in praise of various gods and goddesses. The ashram was set up in 1986 and remains a hotspot for those in search of spirituality and solace.

SRI KARYA SIDDHI ANJANEYA SWAMI TEMPLE AT BENGALURU - This is said to be a powerful abode of Lord Hanuman blessed with a splendid architecture. The Temple is known for its rituals and Aaradhanas. A divine space which has witnessed miracles of every kind is a must-visit in the city.

SRI PRASANNA VEERA ANJANEYA SWAMY TEMPLE AT MAHALAKSHMI LAYOUT - The Temple is dedicated to Lord Hanuman. The main Temple is 40 ft. long & 40 ft wide and in the middle, the vigraha of Sri Prasanna Veeranjaneya Swamy is situated. The upper portion is having a dome. Here, the engraved vigraha on the rock depicts a simple figure of Anjaneya in a standing posture. The huge depiction of Sri Prasanna Anjaneya Swamy is magnificent, inspiring & at the same time pleasant on the eyes. The Temple has a separate grand sannathi for Mahalakshmi. The Goddess Mahalakshmi vigraha is 12 ft. high. The vigraha is seated on a 5 ft. lotus. There is a beautiful, pleasant meditation hall with deities Lord Kodanda Rama and Sri Dhyana Anjaneya. Adjacent is a huge library with a wide collection of religious books. On the Magashuddha Trayodashi day, Hanuman Jayanthi pooja is perfomed. This festival goes on for one week. During this festival a variety of cultural programs are held. Annual function is held on Jestashuddha Dashmi, Sri Rama Pattabhisheka, Sri Sitarama Kalyanotsavam, Sathyanarayana Pooja & Lakshmi Pooja are performed.

SRI DEVI KARUMARIAMMAN TEMPLE AT RAJA RAJESHWARI NAGAR - The Temple has been created inside a high fortress. Main Temple is created like a chariot. There are several stone sculptures of Devi in Temple balcony. here is a big Mangal Ghat in the Temple premises. The Temple is run by Sri Mangala Sheethala Devi Charitable Trust. One can have a spectacular view of this Temple from the steps of Sri Shanmukha Temple. The Temple premises is a perfect place for meditation as the area is silent and peaceful.

SHRUNGAGIRI SRI SHANMUKHA TEMPLE AT BENGALURU - Among the two sons of Lord Shiva and Goddess Parvathi, Shanmukha is worshipped in different forms. Shanmukha is seen as a great warrior in the Hindu mythology and is known by various names. He is called as Subrahmanya by the Kannadigas and for Tamilians, he is Murugan. Once the Maha Guru Sri Sri Sri Bharati Thirtha Swamiji of Shringeri Sharadapeetha dreamt about Lord Shanmukha and as per the visions, a beautiful Shanmukha Temple was constructed at Shrungagiri. Here, Lord Subrahmanya is manifested as Shanmukha. The name Shanmukha means 'six faces'. Hence, the Temple tower is adorned by the six faces of Shanmukha. It is one of the exotic Temples in Bangalore. The shrine is 123 ft and the Temple tower (gopura) is about 62 ft. The speciality of this Temple is its Gopura and the crystal dome like structure. The elegant lighting provided for this crystal structure gives a grand look during the evening times. Another speciality of this structure is that of the sensors that attract the sun-rays. These sensors track the sun-rays from morning till evening and make sure they fall on the vigraha of Shanmukha at all times. So, the faces of Shanmukha is bathed in sun during the day time. There are steps leading to the main shrine and around the main deity you would also get to see a museum dedicated to Lord Ganapati in his various forms, sizes and shapes.

DISTRICT – BIDAR (Railway Station – Humnabad/Bidar)

S. No.	Temple	Address	Type
1	Basavakalyan	Basavakalyan – 585327	Basaveshwara
2	Sri Manik Prabhu Temple	Humnabad – 585330	Manik Prabhu
3	Veerbhadreshwara Temple	Humnabad – 585330	Shiva
4	Shri Narsimha Jharna Mandir	Malkapur Road, Mangalpet, Bidar – 585401	Narasimha
5	Papnash Mahadev Temple	Shiva Nagar, Bidar – 585402	Shiva
6	Chidambara Ashram, Shri Siddharudha Matha	Rampure Colony, Bidar – 585403	Shivkumar Swami

BASAVAKALYAN - Once the capital of the Kalyana Chalukyas and the centre of a great social and religious upheaval in the 12th century, Basavakalyan is famed for its cultural heritage. During the time of the social reformer Basaveshwara, it became a seat of learning and an abode of spiritual wisdom. It is renowned for the saints who made the city their home: Basaveshwara, Akka-Mahadevi, Channabasavanna and Siddarama. Various religious places here are: Basaveshwara Temple; Hingulambika Mandir; Munde Pali Hanuman Temple; Sai Baba Temple; Lord Shiva Temple at Narayanpura etc. Sri Basaveswara cave and Akkamahadevi cave have been chiselled and carved in laterite rock-soil. There are Jain vigrahas of the 10th-11th century. There is a vigraha of Allamaprabhu, as the guru of the Basavanna. There is a hillock which is named as Sharana Shaila, where a vigraha of Lord Basavanna of 108 ft was established in the year 2014 on a pedestal.

MANIK PRABHU TEMPLE AT HUMNABAD - It attracts lots of tourists in the Month of December at the time of annual celebrations. On the same occasion every year, a night long classical musical function will be held and till now the likes of Bhimsen Joshi, Zakir Hussain and many others have come here for this annual jatramahotsav.

VEERBHADRESHEWAR JATRA'S AT HUMNABAD & CHANGLARE - Two very ancient Temples of Lord Veerbhadreshwara attract lakhs of tourists in the month of January and November respectively for the yearly Jatra and cart pulling Mahotsav. The Temple at Humnabad was constructed in 1725 and is famous for its moving pillar.

JHARANI NARASIMHA CAVE TEMPLE - Legend has it that Lord Narasimha, an avatar of Lord Vishnu, came to live in this underground cave. There is a beautiful vigraha of Lord Narashimha on a stone wall at the end of the cave. To see the deity, visitors have to wade through a canal of 91 meters. The depth of the water in the channel is generally 1.37 meters. The water inside the cave is perennial. As per Sthala Purana, Lord Narashimha, after killing Hiranyakashipu, killed another demon, Jalasura, who was residing in this cave and was a staunch devotee of Lord Shiva. Demon Jalasura became a stream and flowed in the cave to wash the feet of Lord Narasimha. There is also a Shivalinga inside the cave, which is believed to be worshiped by demon Jalasura.

PAPNASH SHIVA TEMPLE AT BIDAR - As per the local traditional saying, the Shivalinga in this Temple is one of those installed by Shri Ram during the time of his journey back from Lanka. Every year at the time of Shivaratri festival, lot of tourists visit this place. A natural spring flows into a pond in front of the Temple which is called 'Papnasha'.

CHIDAMBARA ASHRAM, SHRI SIDDHARUDHA MATH AT BIDAR - Chidambara Ashram, Shri Siddharudha Math (Gumpa) was built in the year 1986 by Shri Shiv Kumar Swamiji. There are 12 Jyothirlingas on both the sides of Shri Siddharudha vigraha. This is also known as Gumpa. During last three decades, Shri Siddharudha Math (Gumpa) has become the centre of Religious, Educational and Social activities. Lots of devotees has the spiritual thrust in them. A visitor/devotees who visits holy places in Bidar and if he/she do not visit this Temple, his yatra becomes incomplete. Every year lots of devotees from all parts of the India visits to celebrate Sadguru Siddharudha & Shivakumar Mahaswamiji Jayanti.

DISTRICT – CHAMARAJANAGAR (Railway Station – Chamarajanagar)

S. No.	Temple	Address	Type
1	Biligiriranganatha Swamy Temple	B.R. Hills - 571117	Vishnu
2	Himavad Gopalaswamy Temple	Bandipura National Park - 571126	Krishna
3	Sri Male Mahadeshwara Temple	Male Mahadeshwara Hills - 571490	Shiva

BILIGIRIRANGANATHA SWAMY TEMPLE AT B.R. HILLS - The Biligirirangana Hills commonly called BR Hills is a hill range. The area is called Biligiriranganatha Swamy Temple Wildlife Sanctuary or simply BRT Wildlife Sanctuary. It lies at the meeting point of the Eastern and Western Ghats and draws nature lovers from all parts of the country. Blessed with a diverse ecosystem, it gets its name from the Ranganathaswamy Temple perched atop a cliff. Dedicated to Lord Ranganatha, the Temple is a major pilgrimage centre and houses an vigraha of the Lord with his consort Ranganayaki. It attracts a large number of tourists during the month of April when special festivities are held.

HIMAVAD GOPALASWAMY TEMPLE AT BANDIPURA NATIONAL PARK - Himavad Gopalaswamy Betta is a hill at a height of 1450m. It is also the highest peak in the Bandipura National Park. Dense fog predominates and covers the hills round the year and thus gets the prefix Himavadand the Temple of Venugopalaswamy (Lord Krishna) gives the full name of Himavad Gopalaswamy Betta.

SRI MALE MAHADESHWARA TEMPLE AT MM HILLS - Male Mahadeshwara Betta is a pilgrim town, where ancient and sacred Temple of Sri Male Mahadeshwara is a very popular Shaiva pilgrim centre. It is one of the most powerful Shiva Temple. It draws lakhs of pilgrims from the states of Karnataka and Tamil Nadu. Amidst dense forest, the Temple attracts not only the pilgrims but also nature lovers. The height of the hill is about 3000 ft above sea level.

DISTRICT – CHIKKABALLAPUR (Railway Station – Chik Ballapur/Chintamani)

S. No.	Temple	Address	Type
1	Gadidam Sri Venkataramana Swamy Temple	Bagepalli - 561207	Vishnu
2	Naga Devatha Temple	Vidurashwatha - 561208	Naga Devatha
3	Sri Ranganatha Swamy Temple	Rangasthalam, Post Thippanahalli – 562101	Vishnu
4	Bhoga Nandeeshwara Temple	SH-74, Nandi - 562103	Shiva
5	Papagni Math	Skandagiri Hills – 562103	Mutt
6	Yoga Nandeeshwara Temple	Nandi Hills – 562103	Shiva
7	Cave Temple	Chintamani - 562125	Shiva
8	Kaiwara	Kaiwara – 563128	Mahabharat Circuit

GADIDAM SRI VENKATARAMANA SWAMY TEMPLE AT BAGEPALLI - The Temple is dedicated Lord Mahavishnu, who is worshiped as Bhooneeladevi Sahita Prasanna Venkateshwara Swamy. It is believed that the Temple had been built by King Janamejaya son of Parikshit Maharaj. Parikshit Maharaj was cursed by Maharishi Shrigu's son that he will die of a poisonous snake bite. After his death Janamejaya became King and he vows to kill all the snakes and conducted sarpasatra to destroy all snakes. Serpents including Aadisesha prayed for held and Astika Muni came and requested King Janamejaya to stop satram but doshas of destroying serpents remain in him and he became ill. Aadisesha suggested King Janamejaya to built Temples of Lord Vishnu to get relief from the doshas, thus, this Temple was constructed.

NAGA DEVATHA TEMPLE AT VIDURASHWATHA - The Temple is believed to be built by Vidura who after witnessing so much destruction in Mahabharatha war got depressed, Lord Krishna advised him to undertake Tirtha Yatra. He settled here and planted a Ashwatha (Fig Tree) whose stump is still seen here. The Temple is dedicated to Trinity & Nagas. The Temple is unique and rare. People from all over country visit this Temple and install Naga figurines to ward of Naga doshas. It is also believed that the childless couple who have Naga dosha. pray to the stone symbol of serpent and snakes are symbol of fertility. After blessing with a child, the couple place a stone symbol of a snake in the Temple as a mark of gratitude.

SRI RANGANATHA SWAMY TEMPLE AT RANGASTHALA - This village has a beautiful Temple of Lord Ranganatha (Vishnu) in the Vijayanagar style. It is interesting to note that Pratistha of vigrahams of Rangasthala, Sri Rangam & Sri Rangapatna were done on the same day.

BHOGANANDEESHWARA TEMPLE AT NANDI VILLAGE – The village is really a confluence of two Temples and one of the finest examples of Dravidian Temple architecture. It was constructed around 806 AD by Rathnavalli of Bana Dynasty. Sri Arunachaleswara Temple, nearby Bhoganandeeshwara Temple, built out by soap stone, is another example where one can find fine Ganga, Chola, Hoysala style of architecture.

PAPAGNI MATTA AT CHIKBALLAPUR – It is one of the ancient and oldest Mutts of Chickballapur and located at Skandagiri Hills.

YOGA NANDEESHWARA TEMPLE AT NANDI HILLS – It is located 1478 mtr. above sea level. Nandi Hills, earlier known as Nandidurga, was the summer retreat of Tipu Sultan. Attracted by the salubrious climate of this area, the British built spacious bungalows & beautiful gardens. Nearby is the Yoga Nandeeshwara Temple on the Hill.

CHINTAMANI CAVE TEMPLE - The Temple is dedicated to Lord Shiva and Goddess Durga. It is located in Kailasagiri Hills. It is an ancient and famous Temple in the region.

KAIVARA - This town is associated with epic Mahabharatha. Known as Ekchakrapura, this is where the Pandavas lived in exile incognito. Bhima is said to have killed the demon Bakasura, who was tormenting the people. Myth has it that a nearby cave in the hill, contains the corpse of the demon, which supposedly drips blood during Shivaratri. There is a garden complex in Kaivara, containing gardens & musical fountains. Also, in the garden are 5 cottages named after the pandavas & mini zoo with herbarium. The Temples of Amaranarayana & Bhimeshwara as well as Yogi Narayana Ashram are worth a visit.

DISTRICT – CHIKKAMAGALURU (Railway Station – Chikkamagaluru)

S. No.	Temple	Address	Type
1	Sri Chintamani Mahasaraswati Temple	Srinivasa Nagara Road, Chikkamagaluru - 577101	Mata
2	Channakeshava & Siddheswara Temples	Marle – 577102	Vishnu, Shiva
3	Sri Kodandarama Swamy Temple	Hiremagalur – 577102	Ram
4	Sri Anjaneya Temple	Hariharapura - 577120	Hanuman
5	Kalaseshwara Temple	Kalasa – 577124	Shiva
6	Kamandala Ganpati Temple	Koppa - 577126	Ganesha
7	Veerabhadra Temple	Kalhatti Falls, Manchethevaru - 577129	Sage Agasthya
8	Mullayyanagiri & Seetalayyangiri	Mullayanagiri Peak – 577130	Shiva
9	Rambhapuri Peetha	Melpal – Koppa Rd, Lakkavalli Ma – 577131	Shiva
10	Sri Vasanthika Parameshwari Temple	Angadi – 577132	Mata
11	Markandeya Temple	Khandya - 577136	Saint Markandeya
12	Bababydangiri / Dattatreya Peetha	Baba Budan Giri – 577137	Dattatreya
13	The Sri Sharada Peetha	Sringeri – 577139	Adi Shankaracharya
14	Thrikutachala	Belavadi – 577146	Vishnu
15	Adhishakthyathmaka Sri Annapoorneshwari Temple	Srikshetra Horandu, Mudigere Talok – 577181	Mata
16	Amrutheshwara Temple	Arsikere – Shivamogga Main Road, Amruthapura – 577228	Shiva

SRI CHINTAMANI MAHASARASWATI AT CHIKKAMAGALURU - The Temple is dedicated to Goddess Saraswati. The Temple is ancient & famous. It is believed that the Goddess will remove all sufferings & miseries of the devotees and protect them from evils.

MARLE - There are two Temples of the Hoyasala period standing side by side near an ancient tank. The Temples built in 1150 AD are dedicated to Channakeshava and Siddheswara.

SRI KODANDARAMA SWAMY TEMPLE AT HIREMAGALUR - This Temple has been made famous by "Kannada Poojary" Sri Kannan. It is supposed to have been the first Temple in South India dedicated to Sri Rama, Lakshmana & Sita. The Temple is site to be built during Hoysala while most of the extended construction is in Dravidian style. The outer wall of Garbha Griha are sculpted with figures of various forms of Lord Vishnu. According to Sthalpurana, Lord Rama alongwith Lakshmana & Sita gave darshan to Bhagwan Parshuram at this place.

SRI ANJANEYA TEMPLE AT HARIHARAPURA - The Temple is dedicated to Lord Hanuman. Lord Hanuman is also known as Sri Ishta Siddhi Bhaktanjaneya Swamy here. The vigraha of Lord Hanuman is in standing posture with folded hands and is 27 ft. tall. The vigraha had been built by using single stone of black color. Devotees visit this Temple in large numbers for Abhishekam by milk and also on special occasions, there is different shringars done by the priest on the request of devotees.

KALASA - Kalasa is also called "Dakshina Kashi". It has Kalaseshwara Temple. The landscape around is enchanting and one can have the view of the surrounding hill ranges, peaks and eat out at Kalasa View Point.

KAMANDALA GANPATI TEMPLE AT KOPPA - The Temple is dedicated to Lord Ganesha. It is a mystical Temple. The speciality of the Temple is that there is constantly flowing water in front of the Lord Ganesha, which is the origin of Brahmi River. The holy water is believed to be poured by Lord Brahma from his kamandala.

KALHATTHI FALLS - Here the water cascades down 403 ft. The place has legendary association with Sage Agasthya. A Temple dedicated to Lord Veerabhadra by the side of the falls attracts devotees from nearby places. There is accommodation for over night stay. Annual fair takes place during month of March/April. People also trek to the top of falls from Santaveri.

MULLAYYANAGIRI AND SEETALAYYANAGIRI - These are the two places with shrines dedicated to Lord Shiva. Mullayyanagiri is the tallest peak in Karnataka (6317 ft). Two siddhas are supposed to have performed penance at Mullayyanagiri. There are few caves to the left of the Temple. The Temple is called Mullappa Swamy Temple. A little below is Seetalayyanagiri where Seetala Mallikarjuna Temple is situated. Annual fair takes place here.

RAMBHAPURI PEETHA - Situated on the western bank of River Bhadra, this place has the Rambhapuri Peetha, one of the Pancha Peethas of Veershaivas having tradition of more than 1500 years. The Temple of Veerabhadra has rare vigrahas of Veerabhadra and Bhadrakali.

ANGADI - This place is associated with Sala, the founder of the Hoyasala dynasty. The Temple of Sri Vasanthika Parameshwari is situated here, which was the patron deity of the Hoysalas.

KHANDYA-KUDURE ABBI - Khandya has the Temples of Markandeya & Janardhana. Markanda Sage is supposed to have performed penance here. Orthodox Hindus offer ashes of their departed to the Bhadra River for their salvation. The River Bhadra flows past the Temple, dressing the hard stones into different shapes, by constant friction of the loose rocks. The shapes of the stones in the river have resemblance to the horses' hoops which has made this place to be called "Kudure Abbi".

BABABUDANGIRI/DATTATREYA PEETHA - To the north of the city is a hill range called Bababudangiri. It has many peaks, the prominent being Mullainagiri and Deveerammanagiri. Bababudandargah/Dattatreya Peetha is a holy place to both Hindus and Muslims. A cave contains the tomb of Fakir Dada Hayaathmir Khalandar and the sacred padukas of Saint Dattatreya. Annually, Urs for Muslims and Dattajayanthi for Hindus take place at different times with devotion.

SRI SHARADA PEETHA AT SRINGERI - It is a famous pilgrim centre situated on the banks of the River Tunga. Sri Sharada Peetha here is supposed to have been established by Adi Shankaracharya, the proponent of Advaita Philosophy. Vidyashankara Temple built here is a combination of Chola, Dravida, Nagara and Chalukya styles. Sri Sharadamba Temple is another major Temple worth visiting. The name Sringeri is derived from Rishyashringa-giri, a nearby hill that is believed to have contained the heritage of Rishi Vibhandaka and his son Rishyashringa. Rishyashringa appears in an episode in the Bala-Kanda of the Ramayana where a story, narrated by Vasishtha, relates how he brought rains to the drought-stricken kingdom of Romapada. Jagadguru Sri Adi Shankara Bhagavatpada established the first of the four Amnaya Peethams at Sringeri more than twelve centuries ago to

foster the sacred tradition of Sanatana Dharma. Hallowed for all times by Sage Rishyashringa who stayed and performed Tapas here, Sringeri attracted the great Acharya with a remarkable sight. Tradition has it that after the Acharya had dispersed all the non-Vedic creeds prevailing in the country, He was on the look-out for a convenient and holy place where he could establish an institution to spread the truths of Advaita Vedanta. When the Acharya came to Sringeri, he saw an unusual sight on the banks of the Tunga. A cobra was seen spreading out its hood over a frog in labour pains, to give it shadow from the scorching mid-day sun. Struck with the sanctity of the place, which could infuse love between natural adversaries, the Acharya chose this very location to establish His first Math. The Acharya appointed his prime disciple, Sri Sureshwaracharya as the first Acharya of the Peetham. Since then, the Peetham has been blessed with an unbroken Guru Parampara. The ancient Temple of Sri Sharada, the presiding deity of Sringeri has a glorious history. Originally it was an unpretentious shrine with the Murti of Sharada made of sandalwood, installed over the Sri Chakra that Sri Adi Shankara carved on a rock. Subsequently Sri Bharati Krishna Tirtha and Sri Vidyaranya had a Temple built in the Kerala style with timber and tiled roof. Sri Bharati Krishna Tirtha substituted the sandalwood vigraha with the present golden vigraha. The Mahamandapam has huge stone pillars exquisitely carved with deities like Durga, Raja Rajeshwari, Dwarapalakas and Devis which are all sculpted according to the Shilpa Sastras practised in Tamilnadu. In the year 1999, golden chariot was installed at Sringeri. Golden doors were installed and inaugurated at the entrance of' the sanctum sanctorum of Sri Sharada Temple. The eight panels have the figures of Ashta Lakshmi inscribed on them. The Shrine of Sri Vidya Ganapati is located at the South Western side of Sri Vidyashankara Temple. Outside the Shrine of Sri Janardhana Temple, attached to the navaranga, are the shrines of Sri Hanuman and Sri Garuda. Anjaneya, the mighty valorous monkey God, stands to the south of the shrine of Sri Janardana Swami. The Darshan of Goddess Sri Vaageeshwari Devi can be had in the Temple of Jagadguru Sri Vidyaranyar. Sri Adi Shankara has identified and established six pattern of worshiping deities, of which Kaumaram is related to the worshiping of Lord Subramanya. A Temple for Balasubrahmanya Swami was consecrated in 1978 by Sri Abhinava Vidyatirtha Mahaswamigal. The Linga of Sri Chandramoulishwara crystal Linga, radiant like the moon, representing Jnana and bliss, is the principal vigraha of worship. The new addition was the installation of the marble vigraha of Sri Sureshvara behind the centuries old lingam within the sanctum. The goddess Bhavani shrine was built and consecrated by Sri Sacchidananda Bharati and started several festivals including the rathotsava which are being celebrated even to this day. Sri Sachidananda Shivabhinava Nrasimha Bharathiji has constructed a shrine for the founder of the Amneya Peetham, Sri Adi Shankara Bhagawatpada inside the Shardambal Temple complex. The pedestal of the vigraha has four disciples and there is a shivalinga in the front. Sri Abhinava Vidya Thirtha Swamiji had constructed an attractive

vimanam with a stupi constructed over the grabhagriha. The Malayala Brahma Temple is to the right of Sri Sharadamba Temple. The Kshetra Palaka is locally called Malayala Brahma. The Murti of this deity carries a mace and wears padaraksha and is installed to the left of the door of the Sharadamba Temple. To the right of Sri Sharadamba Temple at Sringeri is a shrine dedicated to Rama, Sita and Lakshmana. Special Puja is performed during Rama Navaratri. The vigrahas of Sri Rama Sri Lakshmana and Sri Sita were brought from Aegundi near Hampi during Krishna Devaraya's regime.

Sri Durgamba Temple at Sringeri - The Temple is dedicated to Sri Durgamba Devi. The Temple is believed to be built & consecrated by Adi Shankaracharya. The Temple is located in the remote location, hence the Goddess is famous as Vanadurga. As per legend, when plague disease threatened Sringeri, Sri Sacchidananda Shiva Abhinava Narasimha Bharati prayed to Goddess Durga & with the kind blessings of the Goddess, not a single case of plague occurred in Sringeri. There is also a Shivalinga, which is believed to be a Udbhavalinga in the name of Lord Mallikarjuna. The annual Rathotsava is celebrated here on a grand scale wherein a special pooja of Devi Durgamba is performed by the Jagadguru & farmers offers a part of crop to the Goddess every year as a mark of gratitude.

BELAVADI - It is the place where a triple shrine (Thrikutachala) in which the vigrahas of Sri Venugopalaswamy, Narasimhaswamy and Veera Narayanaswamy are housed. The beauty of the Temple is comparable to the Keshava Temple at Somanathapura. There is an "Udbhava Ganapathi" Temple nearby.

SRI ANNAPOORNESHWARI DEVI AT HORANADU - "Sri Kshetra Horanadu" is situated on the banks of River Bhadra surrounded by the natural vegetation, forest, green lands, and natural beauty of the Western Ghats. The great deity of Adishakthyathmaka Sri Annapoorneshwari's Prathistapana was done by his holiness Agasthya Maharishi several centuries back. The hereditary Dharmakartharu started 400 years back. Till the 5th Dharmakartharu, the Temple was having a very small. The main deity, Annapoorneshwari is made of gold. It is believed that a person who seeks the goddess' blessings would never have any scarcity for food in life. It is believed that Lord Shiva once had a curse and that this curse was reversed when the Lord visited Goddess Annapoorna and sought her blessings. The 5th Dharmakartharu has started renovating the Temple in the year 1962 and completed the Temple with fully dressed stone sculpture according to the vastushilpa, astrology and Hindu mythology and "the

Prathistapana" of Sri Adishakthi Devi and " Punaprathistapana" of Sri Annapoorneshwari was celebrated on the auspicious day of "Akshaya Thadige" in the year 1973 and Mahakumbhabhisheka was performed by his holiness Shrimad Jagadhguru Shankaracharya Sri Sri Abhinava Vidyathirtha Mahaswamiji of Dakshinamnaya Sringeri Sharadapeetam, Sringeri. The 6th Dharmakartharu has constructed the Navagraha Temple and the Prathistapana was performed by his holiness Shrimad Jagadhguru Shankaracharya Sri Sri Bharathitheertha Maha Swamiji of Dakshinamnaya Sringeri Sharadapeetam, Sringeri in the year 1991.

AMRUTHESHWARA TEMPLE AT AMRUTHAPURA - The Temple was built in 1196 CE by Amrutheshwara Dandanayaka under Hoysala King Veera Ballala-II. The Temple is a built according to Hoysala architecture with a wide open mantapa (hall). The Temple has an original outer wall with unique equally spaced circular carvings. The Temple has one vimana (shrine and tower) and therefore is anekakuta design and has a closed mantapa (hall) that connects the sanctum to the large open mantapa. It has beautifully caved pillars and vigrahas of Narayana, Chammundeshwari, Kalabhairava, Saraswathi, Agni and Saligrama are the two important sculptural features. The Ramayana is sculpted on the south side wall on seventy panels with the story proceeding quite unusually in anti-clockwise direction. On the north side wall, all depictions are clockwise, a norm in Hoysala architectural articulation. Twenty five panels depict the life of the Hindu god Krishna and the remaining forty five panels depict scenes from the epic Mahabharata. It is believed that on Shivarathri day, the first rays of the sun fall on the Shivalinga. The Temple has been under the supervision of the Department of Archaeology.

DISTRICT - CHITRADURGA (Railway Station – Chitradurg)

S. No.	Temple	Address	Type
1	Chitradurga Fort	Chitradurga – 577501	18 Temples
2	Prasanna Ganapathi Temple	Holalkere - 577526	Ganesha

CHITRADURGA FORT AT CHITRADURGA - Eighteen Temples were built in the upper Fort. Some

of the well-known Temples were the Hidimbeswara, Sampige Siddeshwara, Ekanathamma, Phalguneshwara, Gopala Krishna, Lord Hanuman, Subbaraya and Nandi. Hidimbeswara Temple displays the tooth of Hidimba, the demon (Rakshasa in Sanskrit). It is said that Hidimba and his sister Hidimbi, a giantess, used to live in this Temple. Hidimbi, who fell in love with Bhima (the second of the Pandava brothers) married him and had a child by him named Ghatotkacha. A large cylinder about 3 metres in circumference and 2 metres high made of iron plates known as Bheri or Drum of Bheema is also located here. Sampige Siddheshvara Temple is at the foot of the hill. In the Gopalakrishna Temple, inscriptions date the vigraha to the early 14th century.In the lower Fort, a Temple dedicated to the tutelary deity of the Nayaka Palegars, the Uchchangiamma or Uthsavamba, was built amidst the rocks of the fort complex on the hill.The Murugarajendra Matha, a famous religious institution of the Lingayats, which was originally located within the fort, is now situated about 2 kilometres to the northwest of Chitradurga.

PRASANNA GANAPATHI TEMPLE AT HOLALKERE - The Temple is dedicated to Lord Ganesha. The Temple had been established in 1475 CE by Guthyappa Nayaka. The Temple contains Lord Ganesha's monolithic vigraha, which is about 20 ft tall. According to local legends, if one worships Lord Ganesha's vigraha with true devotion, their wishes will be fulfilled.

DISTRICT – DAKSHINA KANNADA (Railway Station – Mangalore/Mulki/Subrahmanya Rd)

S. No.	Temple	Address	Type
1	Sri Somanatheshwara Cave Temple	Sri Kshetra Nellitheertha, Neerude Post, Kompadavu Village, Mangalore – 570063	Shiva
2	Kateel Shree Durgaparameshwari Temple	Kateel Post, Mangalore – 574148	Mata
3	Bappanadu Sri Durgaparameshwari Temple	Mulki – 574154	Mata
4	Southadka Sri Ganapathy Temple	Kowkradi – 574198	Ganesh
5	Shree Mahalingeshwra Temple	Puttur – 574201	Shiva
6	Jain Basadis	Belthangady - 574214	Jain
7	Shree Kshetra Dharamasthala	Dakshina Kannada – 574216	Shiva, Jain
8	Shree Kshethra Rajarajeshwari Temple	Polali, Bantwal Taluk – 574219	Mata
9	Saavira Kambada Basadi	Moodabidri – 574227	Jain
10	Shree Narahari Parvata Sadashiva Temple	Panemangalore – 574231	Shiva
11	Kukke Shree Subrahmanya Temple	Subrahamanya Post, Kadaba Taluk – 574238	Nagnath
12	Sri Sahasralingeshwara Teertha Kshethra	Uppinangady - 574241	Shiva
13	Mahathobahara Shree Karinjeshwara Temple	Kavalamudoor Village, Karinja Post – 574265, Bentwal Taluk	Shiva
14	Koragajja Temple	Bolar, Mangalore - 575001	Koragajja
15	Mahatobar Shri Mangaladevi Temple	Mangaladevi, Bolar, Mangalore – 575001	Mata
16	Sharavu Mahaganapathi Temple	Mangalore - 575001	Ganesha
17	Kadri Sri Manjunatha Temple	Vasanth Vihar, Kadri, Mangalore – 575002	Shiva
18	Shree Gokarnanatha Kshethra	Kudroli, Mangalore – 575003	Shiva
19	Shri Mariamma Temple	Urwa, Mangalore - 575006	Mata
20	Kulai Shree Vishnumurthy Temple	Kulai, Mangalore – 575011	Vishnu
21	Shri Ananthapadmanabha Temple	Kudupu Post, Mangalore – 575028	Vishnu

NELLITHEERTHA SOMANATHESHWARA CAVE TEMPLE AT YEDAPADAVU - The Cave Temple is one of the holiest Temple. The main deity of the Temple is Sri Somanatheshwara. The Temple also has Maha Ganapati and Jabali Maharshi as deities here. In typical Tulu-naadu tradition, the Temple also has its set of "Bhootas". Bhootas are considered as the "Ganas" or warrior-assistants of the Gods. The main bhootas of the Nellitheertha Temple are Pili-Chamundi (Pili means Tiger in Tulu), Kshetrapala, Raktheshwari and Doomavathy. The Lingam of Shri Somanatheshwara has been made out of pure Saligramashila and is considered very sacred. There are other artefacts in and around the Temple which are pointers to the past glory of this place. Among them are the "Arasule Mancha" (King's seat), "Arasule Mantapa" (King's abode) and the "Jina Vigraha" (Jain vigraha). The "Nagappa Kere" is a small pond situated to the north of the Temple. Any person, above the age of 5, is allowed to enter the cave irrespective of gender. The main attraction of the Temple is the cave, it is one of nature's wonders. There is a natural Shivalingam in front of the lake and devotees pray and worship the Lingam. The most amazing part of the cave is the fine quality of the mud available inside. It is said that the mud here has healing powers and is treated as prasadam by devotees. Right behind the Shiva Lingam, a second cave starts off. Not many people have ventured into this second cave till date. The name Nellitheertha also has its etymological roots in the cave. Inside the cave, drops of water, in the shape of amla (gooseberries) constantly keep dripping down. In fact, the lake is made up of these drops of water. Hence the name Nelli (Amla) Theertha (holy water). Another unique aspect of the cave is that it is closed for nearly 6 months a year. Though there are religious reasons associated with this (it is said that the cave is open 6 months a year for humans and is meant for Gods and Rishis the remaining 6 months), the point is that the 6 month break each year helps the cave to "rejuvenate". The water freshens up and the animals inside enjoy the lack of disturbance.

KATEEL DURGA PARAMESHWARI AT MANGULURU – The word Kateel or Kateelu is a derivation of two words – 'Kati' meaning Centre and 'Ila' meaning Earth. So, Kateel means the central area of the earth. Geographically, Kateel is located midway between Kanakagiri, the river source, and Pavanje, a joining point of a river to the sea, justifying its name. In this sacred land, Shri Shakthi resides in the form of Durga Parameshawri who is a powerful incarnation of Goddess Parvathi. It is said that the energy here is so pristine and powerful that it can simply rejuvenate the depressed lives to all life, once again. There is a legend attached to the origin of Kateel Durga Parameshwari Temple which dates back to the early days of Kalyug. The Temple's beauty in the middle of the River Nandini, is Devi's divine presence and a drop of devotion in heart, which can create an vigraha of heaven for a moment. The Temple also hosts shrines dedicated to other Gods and Goddesses. To the south of the main sanctum, there is Mahaganapathi and to its right, there is a shrine for shashtra. To the southwest, a shrine for Kshetrapalaka can be found. In the inner yard of the Temple and in the outer yard, two Naga Sannidhis are worshipped along with Brahma in the inner sanctum. It is believed that the divine Mother incarnated in the form of a Linga in the middle of the stream of River Nandini. The single stream divided into two, where Sri Devi emerged as a Linga. After skirting the Linga, the streams reunite and flows as one stream that joins the west sea. Blessed Nandini, rewarded with the privilege of washing for ever the Mother's feet! The Champaka is not liked by the bee for his strong fragrance, so the flower is not used in this shrine of Bhramari, the female bee. The water of tender coconut is the favourite of the Mother, so none in this shrine drinks tender coconut without first offering it to the Mother. The abhisheka (holy shower) with tender coconut is the ultimate of the favourites of the Mother because the Mother appeared as a dancing damsel in the garden of Arunasura in order to kill him. She is fond of the yakshagana dance offered by devotees as service to her.

SRI DURGA PARAMESHWARI AT BAPPANADU, MULKI - Once there was a demon called Darigasura ruling Shonitapura. He had enmity with Devatas and Lord Vishnu. In antagonism and with the intention of defeating the Devatas and Lord Vishnu, he worshiped Lord Brahma and got a boon. With the help of this boon, he defeated Devatas and Lord Vishnu and snatched the ammunitions from Lord Vishnu and handed over that to his wife and told to keep that in worship place. While Lord Vishnu was mourning for his lost ammunitions, Goddess Durgaparameshwari appeared before him in the form of seven angel-women (Sapta-Durgas) and promised to kill a demon. These Sapta-Durgas went to Shonitapura accompanied by one Deity called Guliga. Bhagavathi, one of the Sapta-Durgas appeared before demon Darigasura, while he was on the way to take a bath in the River, in disguised form of an old woman and begged for a meal. Darigasura advised her to go to palace and ask a meal from his wife and also told her to tell him that if she didn't get a meal. Accordingly, Goddess Bhagavathi visited the palace of Darigasura and met his wife but asked for ammunitions of Lord Vishnu to be returned. While wife of Darigasura opposed to return, Bhagavathi willingly and wrongly informed Darigasura that his wife is not ready to give her a meal. Hearing that Darigasura ordered his wife to give Bhagavathi what she wished. Darigasura's wife gave the ammunitions of Lord Vishnu to Bhagavathi accordingly. Knowing deceived by Goddess Bhagavathi, demon Darigasura became furious and declared war against Sapta-Durgas and attacked them in ambush. He defeated Deity Guliga in war but after seven days of furious war, demon Darigasura was defeated by Sapta-Durgas and ultimately, he ran away and took hide in underworld. Goddess Bhagavathi taken form of Bhadra-Kali and began for his search. While demon Darigasura came for offering pooja to Lord Shiva in late evening, Bhadra-Kali found him and slewed him. Bhagavathi then accompanied by her other sister goddesses and Deity Guliga, visited Lord Vishnu and asked for a boat made by sandal wood for a journey from Vaikunta (Great heaven) to Bhooloka (earth) with a intention of settling down in Bhooloka for betterment of earthly people. Lord Vishnu permitted them to take a Sandal wood tree from Vaikunta for preparing a boat. Accordingly, they made a boat and started their journey. Boat came to Bhooloka and crossed Kasaragod, Kumble, Uppala, Pattattur, Manjeshwara, Udyavara, Ullala and Kudroli of southern coast of India. From there it came to Sasihithlu near Mulki town. There, Bhagavathi took tender coconut from one lower caste devotee and wished to settle there only. Goddess Durgaparameshwari emerged symbolically in conjunction point of Shambhavi & Nandini River at Mulki border. In due course, one Muslim merchant viz. Bappa Beary while traveling through Shambhavi River for trading in remote places, his boat suddenly stopped in the middle of the river. While examining the cause he found blood spread over the river water and he deeply felt fear on that. Meantime a divine voice came from the ether ordering him to construct a Temple with the help of Mulki Sawantha (King) and to make pooja by the help of Baila Udupa (Priest). Mulki Sawantha was belonging to Jain religion and a decent ruler. Hearing the incident from Bappa Beary, the King built one Temple with the contribution of many other donors and made Baila Udupa as a chief priest of the Temple. Hence the Temple became Bappanadu Kshetra. The five Lingas are worshipped as Moola Durga, Agni Durga, Jala Durga, Vana Durga & Agra Durga on a single Panipeeta with the vigraha of Durga kept in front. Some of the important festivals celebrated are Karthikapooja Deepothsava, Sharannavarathri, Ugadi & on Fridays special Poojas are offered. Bappanadu Temple has five Rathas & the Brahma Ratha is massive & highly embellished in keeping with its name.

Sri Venkatramana Temple at Mulky - Mulky is the seat of the three deities. Lord Venkataramana originally belong to Karkala and his vigraha was hidden in the Temple tank to save from invaders and the said vigraha had been received by the local devotees and it was installed here. Ugranarsimha is the principle deity and a pride of Gowda Saraswatha Brahmin. On the Mulky Pratistha Poornima, the Lord is bathed with thousands of coconuts to calm him and seek his divine grace. It is also believed that some herbs fell here from Sanjivani Mountain while carrying it by Lord Hanuman.

SOUTHADKA SRI GANAPATHY TEMPLE AT KOKKADA - The uniqueness of the place is Lord Maha Ganapathi is out in the open field without a 'Garbhagudi' & Temple structure. It is surrounded by fascinating greeneries & open round the clock for offering prayers.

SRI MAHALINGESWARA TEMPLE AT PUTTUR - In the long past, three old and very learned Shaiva-cult Brahmins were going through the southern part of India, worshipping a Shivalinga which they got from the Hindu holy 'Kshetra of Kashi '. In their spiritual journey, one day they happened to arrive at a place called 'Gayapada Kshetra' now known as Uppinangady in Puttur Taluk. At Uppinangady, one out of those three Brahmins, divided to move towards Puttur leaving behind the other two and according reached Puttur one evening having the 'Shivalinga' with him. The Brahmins got up early in the next morning and after a holy bath went to the palace of the 'Banga King '; who was ruling this part of the region; for pooja materials. At that time the Banga King did not pay attention to the arrival of this Brahmin, as he was much worried about the labour-pain of his loving sister. However, the minister of the Banga-King, looking at the divine brightness on the face of the Brahmin, made an appeal regarding the problem of the King and on that, the Brahmin worshipped the 'Linga' and blessed the King's sister assuring that she would deliver a baby boy safely. She gave birth to a boy and a god fearing King having felt very happy over the event thanked the Brahmin and arranged for the worship of the Lord. Later on, the Brahmin kept the 'Shivalinga' on land, without a stand or seat, worshipped it and after the pooja, when he lifted the Linga from the land, it would not be detached from the surface of the earth. The Brahmin used all his force to lift the Linga but in vain. Later King's elephant was summoned to lift the

Linga. As the elephant was struggling hard, the Linga grew in to huge proportions (Mahalinga) shattering the elephant into pieces. The different body parts of the gigantic animal spread out in different direction hence, the place where its horn (Khombu) fell came to be called 'Kombettu', Kari fell 'Kariyala, legs fell (kalu) 'Karjala', hand(Kai) fell 'Kaipala' tail fell 'Beedimajalu', head (Tale) fell 'Taleppady' and back (Beri) fell ' Beripadavu'. These are the place names noted and likewise called even today in the surroundings of Puttur and since the elephant fell dead in to the Temple tank, even to this day there is a strong belief that elephants cannot survive drinking the tank water. Nearest Railway Station is Puttur.

JAIN BASADIS AT BELTHANGADY - Venur or Venoor is located on the banks of the Phalguni River. It was once the seat of Jainism and the capital of the Ajila Dynasty. It is on the Dharmasthala-Moodabidri-Karkala route on the coastal religious circuit in the Karnataka. Venur's claim to fame is the monolith of Bhagawan Bahubali also known as Lord Gomateshwara. The single rock vigraha is 38 feet in height and was erected by the Jain ruler Timmanna Ajila in the year 1604. The vigraha is supposed to have been sculptured by Beeru kalkuda. The vigraha stands facing westward on a high platform on the banks of the River Phalguni. This vigraha of Bhagwan Bahubali is one of the five giant monoliths established in Karnataka. There are various Basadis in the area which are related to Tirthankaras.

DHARMASTHALA MANJUNATHA AT DHARMASTHALA - Shri Kshetra Dharmasthala, the land of righteousness and piety, is one of south India's most renowned religious landmarks with a history as old as 800 years. Besides the many Jain Basadis and a museum, the centrepiece of this Temple town is a 39 ft monolith vigraha of Lord Bahubali. The Jain Tirthankara and Lord Manjunatha (Shiva) are worshipped on the same consecrated ground. The Manjunatha Temple, a prominent Shaiva centre, is administered by a benevolent Jain Heggade, whose charity and concern for social welfare have become legendary. Irrespective of caste, creed or religion, pilgrims are given free meals and accommodation. During the annual festival, Laksha Deepotsava held in November-December, one lakh lamps are lit and literary and religious discourses are held. Around the 16 Century, Shri Devaraja Heggade invited Shri Vadiraja Swami of Udupi to visit the shrine. The Swamiji gladly came but refused to accept Bhiksha (food offering) because the vigraha of Lord Manjunatha had not been consecrated according to the vedic rites. Shri Heggade then requested the Swamiji to re-consecrate the Shivalinga himself. Pleased by the observance of the vedic rites and Heggade's charity to all, the Swamiji named the place Dharmasthala, the abode of religion and charity. The Heggade is regarded as the voice of Lord Manjunatha. He is expected to dispense justice, advice and munificence to whoever approaches him with his problems and needs. The Temple has been built following the Kerala Temple architecture. The Temple has a very distinct style of

architecture coupled with a lavish use of wood, stone and metals. The steep and needle like roof is made of wood and is covered with gold-plated copper plates in order to protect the inner skeletal framework from the vigorous monsoons of the Western Ghats. With the novel thought of protecting the Jain legacy, a pious and methodical renovation of the Temple in May 2001 by Shri Veerendra Heggade has made Shri Chandranatha Swamy Basadi, one of the most beautiful edifices in Dharmasthala and the south of India. Standing against the azure blue sky and the lush foliage around it, this Temple clad in white marble is a sight to behold and to cherish, imbibe and nurture the teachings about our mortal life by Shri Chandranatha Swamy, Jain Theerthankara Mahaveer and his disciples.

SRI RAJRAJESWARI TEMPLE AT POLALI, BANTVAL - Shree Kshetra Polali is in the heart of this village surrounded by high hillocks and wide paddy fields. River Phalguni flows from east on the northern side a furlong way from the Temple. It turns left towards south at the back of the Temple in the Western side. This place was being called as Pural and the deity in the Temple was known as Porala Devi in several old records and ancient epigraphs available. It is believed that King Suratha got the Temple constructed, installed the vigraha and placed his own crown on the head of the vigraha. This Temple has been alluded in the Ashokan inscriptions. Queen Chennammaji of Keladi visited Polali and got a grand chariot constructed for the Temple. Polali Chendu is a unique festival in this Temple, which will be performed during annual festival of the Temple. It is not easy to clarify the antiquity and importance of Polali Shree Rajarajeshwari Temple with historical evidences. It is said there were many inscriptions here and there around the Temple. Daily poojas and special poojas in this Temple are done as laid down in Durgagama and Skandagama. The 'Kartikapooja' and the Flower pooja' offered by the devotees are performed only during the time of the daily poojas and not at other times.

SAAVIRA KAMBADA BASADI AT MOODABIDRI - Moodabidri, a Temple town, has a curious connection with the number 18 – it houses 18 Temples with 18 roads that connect the different villages in the vicinity adorned with 18 lakes and also the home to 18 Jain Basadis. The town gets its name from the abundance of bamboo cultivation in the area. In Kannada, 'Mooda' means east while 'Bidri' means bamboo. Saavira Kambada Temple is considered the finest among them. It is a Basadi or Jain Temple noted for its 1000 pillars. The Temple is also known as "Chandranatha Temple" since it honours the Tirthankara Chandraprabha, whose eight-foot ashtadhatu vigraha is worshipped in the shrine. The Basadi was built by Devaraya Wodeyar in 1430. The shrine has a 50 feet tall monolith manasthambha, which was erected by Karkala Bhairava Queen Nagala Devi. From mythical animals to inspirations from Mother Nature – the carvings on the pillars seem to convey various stories and beautifully reflect the art and culture of ancient times. The top two storeys are carved in wood and the lowest one in stone. No wonder, the upper floor is one of the best-kept secrets of the biggest and oldest Jain Temples in Asia! This Temple enjoyed the patronage from different rulers across dynasties like the Chalukya,

Rashtrakuta, Alupa and the Hoysala. Moodabidri is noted for its 18 Jains Temples mentioned as follows:

"Bagada Basadi, Settara Basadi, Hire Basadi, Guru Basadi, Leppada Basadi, Kallu Basadi, Batkana-Thikari Basadi, Pathshala Basadi, Padu Basadi, Kere Basadi, Hosa Basadi, Bitkeri Basadi, Vikram Shetty Basadi, Mahadeva Shetty Basadi, Chola Shetty Basadi, Koti Shetty Basadi, Derma Shetty Basadi, Ammanavara Basadi".

Guru Basadi is the earliest of the Jain monuments built in 714 AD. A black stone vigraha of Bhagwan Parshwanatha, about 11 ft tall, is installed in the sanctum. Here the rare Jain palm leaf manuscripts of 12th century AD, known as 'Dhavala texts', are preserved. This Basadi is also called Siddantha Basadi and Hale Basadi. The Temple also has over 52 vigrahas for worship with the sanctum sanctorum having an vigraha of Parshwanatha which is 3.5 meters high. The Ammanavara Basadi, also known as the Hire Bisadi, is the Temple dedicated to Bhagwan Shanthinatha. The Temple also has vigrahas of Goddess Saraswati and Padmavati along with the 24 Tirthankaras. Shettara Basadi – Vardhamana Swamy Temple is quite an ancient Temple, having been built in the 16th Century. In the Temple, the vigraha of Bhagawan Vardhamana is placed in the centre of the Kayotsarga posture. Bhagwan Vardhamana, also known as Bhagwan Mahavira, was the 24th Tirthankara, hence the Temple is of importance to Jain devotees. There is a Matha at Moodabidri responsible for the upkeep and maintenance of Temples in Moodabidri. It is known as the Jain Varanasi of the South. A Bhattaraka seat exists at Moodabidri responsible for administering the 18 Temples at Moodabidri and the other Temples in the surrounding areas. The name given to the Bhattaraka of Moodabidri is Charukeerthi. Nearest Railway Station is Mulki.

Sri Sita Ram Temple at Ashwathapura - The Temple is dedicated to Lord Rama & Mata Sita. The Temple is ancient and famous. There is an old practice of Nagara Sankeerthane at this Temple.

Konaje Kallu Temple at Padukonaje - The place is a bliss for devotees & an excellent trekking track which is a marvelous hidden treasure. It is also known as 'Karnika Kshethra.' There is Kalabairava and Mahamayi Gudi. The distance between one gigantic granite block to another is a half kilometer. From far, it looks like a monolithic rock. There is a bond between the two granite blocks, which is called 'Boodikere,' where one gets pure water throughout the year. It is at 346 meters above sea level and 244 meters above the base. During monsoon and in winter, one can see Konaje Kallu covered with thick mist. The surrounding area of the Konaje Kallu is a mini-reservoir of the Western Ghats species.

SHREE NARAHARI PARVATHA SADASHIVA AT BANTVAL – The Temple is one of the most ancient and popular pilgrimage situated at Narahari Hill at a height of about 1000 Feet above the sea level. It is also known as the "Kailasa of the Earth". It is believed that Nara and Hari, incarnations of Lord Vishnu, were supposed to have performed the penance at this place. There are ponds atop of the hill in the shape of Shanka (Conch), Chakra (Wheel), Gadha (Weapon) and Padma (Lotus). It is also believed that taking a holy dip in these ponds on Monday of the Karthika month is considered to be sacred. People throng this mountain during Aati Amavasya and Soma Amavasya for Teerthasnana (Dip in the ponds).

Sri Karaneeka Hanumantha Devasthana at Mangaluru - It is a century old Mujarai Temple known for its unique features. In 1830, on learning the hardships faced by Udupi Madhwa Swamiji to perform Madhwa Pooja & Pravachanas independently, Somayya Rao the Deshasta Brahmin sought a necessity of a Madhwa institution in Mangaluru city and built the Temple then. Since Somayya Rao was cleric or Karaneek by profession, the Temple was known Karneeka Hanumantha Devasthana. It is constructed for the Manasa pooja of Shree Vadiraja and Sri Guru Raghavendra who are known for fulfilling the aspiration of common man and also for the preachings of Udupi Madhva Matt Swamijies (pontiff). As such the place is also called as Upadhyaya Mutt and it is believed to be sacred and punya karya to participate in the Jnanayagna of Bhagavata purana being held here for years now. The main deity Lord Anjaneya known as the Mukhya Prana devaru is of Golden color and is considered a rare one of its kind ever seen else where easily as its face is in front ward direction while it is common to see a side ward facing Anjaneya Vigraha at other places. As such the Temple is known as Edirumukhada Anjaneya Temple having Abhaya hasta and Sanjeevini Balli. Aradhana Mahothsava of Sri Sode Vadiraja Theertha Sreepadaru & Mantralaya Guru Raghavendra Theertha Sreepadaru and Hanumantargata Sree Seetharamachandra will be held every year here and Jnanayagna of Bhagavata Purana is carried out continuously for over a years now.

KUKKEY SUBRAMANYA TEMPLE AT KUMARADHARA - Sri Kshetra is located on the bank of River Kumaradhara. Born to annihilate the demonic forces, Kumaraswamy killed Tarakasura and other Asuras in the battle to Kumaraparvatha with his sibling Ganapathi. Devendra had decided to give away his daughter Devasena to him on "Margashira Shudda Shasti". Accordingly the marriage took place on the banks of Kumaradhara Thirtha. Bestowing his grace on "Sarpa Raja" Vasuki, who was doing Thapasya at that time. Kumaraswamy assured to dwell along with Devasena in him. Since then, it is behind that Lord Shanmukha (Skanda) in his spiritual presence is residing with Vasuki in the shrine. Kukke Subrahmanya, one among the seven holy places created by Parashurama, is mythologically and historically famous for "Nagaradhane". Residing with Vasuki, God Subrahmanya showers his divine grace on devotees as the presiding deity of the Kshetra. It is also called "Guptha Kshetra". "Mruthika Prasada" given here is regarded as sacrosanct. The devotees believe that the holy bath in the Kumaradhara Thirtha and Madesnana eradicate dreaded diseases like leprosy. Diseases related to skin, the devotees firmly believe, get cured here. God Subrahmanya has earned an honorific title "Annadana Subbappa". The devotees find solace here after performing "Sarpasamskara", Naga Prathiste", "Ashlesha Bali" for sarpadosha, which causes barrenness / infertility, skin disease, blindness, bhoomidosha etc. In the past Subrahmanya Kshethra, the edicts and Grantha inform, was known as Kukke Pattana. According to Sthala Purana, many Devarushis installed Shivalingas in this Kshetra. Reference to such Shivalingas should be understood as Kukkelinga. The main entrance of the Temple lies to the east. The devotees will enter from west through main Gopuram and enter the inner quadrangle from the east. There is a pedestal in the centre of the sanctum. On the upper Dias there is the vigraha of Shree Subrahmanya and then the vigraha of Vasuki and little lower the vigraha of Shesha.

SRI SAHASRALINGESHWARA TEERTHA KSHETHRA AT UPPINANGADY - The Temple is dedicated to Lord Shiva. This place is famous as Dakshina Kashi. The Temple is located on the confluence of River Kumaradhara & Nethravathi. As per legend, Pandava brother Bheema was once attacked by a giant animal. When Bheem was being chased, he removed a hair and threw it down. The hair turned into a Shivalinga. Bheema continued this act throughout his run. The giant animal was the devotee of Lord Shiva, so he took a pause to worship each Shivalinga. This way Bheem had an escape and his hair turned into around 1000 Shivalingas on the River banks. During heavy rain in rainy season, both rivers unite in front of Sahasralingeshwara. It is an auspicious occasion for the devotees to take Sangam Snan & worship Lord Shiva. Aadishakti took the form of Mahakali to destroy the demon Raktbeej, hence there is a shrine of Goddess Mahakali on the banks of River Nethravathi. Kunkunarchane & Blloaya are offered to Goddess Mahakali. It is also believed that whenever there is an attack by epidermic diseases, devotees worship Goddess Mahakali. People perform last rites of their nears & dears at this place as it is also known as Gayapada Kshetra.

SRI KARINJESHWARA TEMPLE AT KARINJE, BANTVAL - Situated at a height of about 1000 ft from sea level in the midst of lush green Kodyamale Hills, Karinjeshwara is a popular pilgrimage centre. Here the Temple dedicated for Lord Shiva is on the top of a cliff and another Temple, which is dedicated for the Goddess Parvathi is situated in the middle of the way to the cliff. Praised as Rudragiri, Gajaradri, Beema Shaila and Karinja, in different eras, this was the place of reverence from mythological periods. The main Temple of the Lord Shiva is told to have a history which goes back to one thousand years. Stories tell that Sri Ramachandra had visited this place along with his younger brother Lakshman, in respect of which an offering of a large amount of rice is made to the Lord during the noon pooja and it is then poured on a rock slab in front of the Shiva Temple for monkeys. Till today it is the custom among these monkeys that the eldest and bulkies of the bunch named as "Karinja Dadda" takes the first byte of the feast and whoever breaks the rule will be punished by the boss – "The Dadda". Stories also refer back to Dwapara where in pandavas took shelter in the caves around this place during their exile. Gadatheertha a large lake right at the pot of the cliff, assumed to be dug by Beema Senas (gada) stands as a testimony for the story. On the cliff there is another water source created by Arjuna's arrow, named as Varaha Thirtha, along with this there are two other water sources namely Ungusta Theertha and Janutheertha which are respected by the devotees. A holy dip in these water sources on specific days is told to cure away skin diseases. Architectural style of this Shiva Temple is influenced by both Vaishnav and Jain styles of architecture. A stone sculpture on the base of the flag post of the Temple indicates that the Kelady rulers, who were under Vijayanagara kingdom had given royal patronage to this Temple.

KORAGAJJA TEMPLE AT BOLAR - The Temple is dedicated to Daiva Koragajja. One of the most worshipped Daiva throughout Tulunadu is Koragajja. Anything which is lost, any work to be done or any issue to be solved; first and foremost, people recall this divine. Koraga thaniya is the historical figure and not a mythical creation. Dravidian of Indian worship their ancestors, who did extraordinary things for the greater good to their community. Due to which they were recognized and worshipped by their later descendants. Koraga Thaniya who is popularly called Koragajja. Here "Koraga" is the community name and "Ajja" is usually called for old male citizen in Tulu. Even though, he attained divinity during his middle age; people started calling him Ajja because of love & affection towards him.

MANGALA DEVI TEMPLE AT MANGULURU - In Tulunadu, in the 10th century, Kundavarma, the most famous King of Alupa dynasty was ruling. Mangalore was the capital of his kingdom. At that time, there came two sages named Machhendranatha and Gorakanatha from Nepal. They reached Mangalapura crossing the River Nethravathi. The place where they crossed the river came to be known as 'Gorakdandu'. They chose a place near the bank of Nethravathi which was once the centre of activities of Sage Kapila. Hearing about the arrival of the two saints, the king came to meet them. Pleased with the humility and virtues of the king, they brought to his knowledge that his kingdom was a holy place and it was sanctified by the activities of holy saints and sages in the past. They requested him to grant them land so that they could build their hermitage and make it a centre of their religious activities under his protection and patronage. For Kundavarma, it was really a surprise to know that his land had such a hoary history. It was from these saints he came to know that once upon a time, in his land there existed a Temple dedicated to mother Mangaladevi. He heard from them the story of Vikhasini, Andasura, Parashurama and the Temple of Mangaladevi built by Parashurama. The two saints took the king to the places where all these historical events had taken place. They asked the king to dig the place and retrieve the Linga and the Dharapatra symbolising Mangaladevi and install them in a shrine along with Nagaraja for protection. Kundavarma carried out the advice of the two sages. A grand shrine of Sri Mangaladevi stood on the holy place. The two sages' themselves guided and supervised the execution of the work. The Temple attained special significance as Mother Mangaladevi granted special favours especially on maidens. Pious maidens who worship the goddess observing Mangaladharavrata (Swayamvara Parvathi) will have their wishes fulfilled. They get husbands most suited for them. Even today, heads of Kadri Yogirajmutt visit Mangaladevi Temple on the first day of Kadri Temple festival and offer prayer and silk cloth to the Goddess. The sanctum sanctorum houses an vigraha of the goddess where she is seen in a seated posture. Around the main sanctum are shrines dedicated to other deities.

SHARAVU MAHAGANAPATHI TEMPLE AT MANGULURU - The Temple is dedicated to Lord Ganesha. Here Lord Ganapathi manifested himself on the southern wall of the shrine. There is also a shrine of Lord Shiva in the form of Sharabeshwara. The name Sharavu is derived from the word Shara that means arrow, which has an interesting legend attached to it. There was a Tuluva King

Veerabahu. Once he went to forest for hunting. He saw a tiger standing close to a cow and thought that the tiger may attack the cow. Immediately, he shot and arrow at the tiger. Unfortunately, the arrow killed the cow and the tiger escaped. Veerabahu went to Maharishi Bharadwaja who asked him to build a shrine to get relief from Gauhatya. The King build a shrine and installed Shivalingam. It came to be cakked Sharavu & Shivaligam became Sharabeshwara. Lord Ganesha is believed to relief his devotees from their troubles & miseries.

KADRI MANJUNATHA TEMPLE AT MANGALURU - The Kadri Hill is famous for the 11th century historic Kadri Manjunatha Temple with the surrounding tanks with natural springs and laterite caves. It is also known as the Pandava Caves. It was converted to a complete stone structure during the 14th century. The 5 ft bronze vigraha of Lokeshawara is called as oldest vigraha in South India Temples. The vigraha has three faces and six arms and hold flowers in two of the arms. The crown depicts a Dhyani Buddha. The vigraha has an ornate prabhavali and two attendants. There exist two other undated bronze vigrahas of similar craftsmanship, one of them is identifiable as an Avalokiteshwar (called Narayana) and other as Lord Buddha (called Vedavyasa). There are vigrahas of Machendranath, Gorakanath, Shringinath, Lokeshwara, Manjushri and Buddha in the Temple. Another stone inscription in Tulu, Kannada and Malayalam scripts of $12\text{-}13^{th}$century AD is in the Temple. There is a natural spring at an elevated location at the back of the Temple. It is called Gomukha. It is believed that the water flows from Bhageerathi River in Kashi and thereby it gets its name as Kashi Bhageerathi Theertha. It is believed that Parashurama prayed to Lord Shiva for a place to live. Lord Shiva assured Parashurama that if he performed a penance at Kadali Kshethra, Lord Shiva would reincarnate as Manjunatha for the betterment of the world. As per Lord Shiva's orders, Bhagwan Parashurama threw his axe into the sea and created a place for his penance. Yielding to Bhagwan Parashurama's prayers Lord Shiva appeared to him as Manjunatha with Goddess Parvathi and stayed at Kadri. As per the orders of Manjunatha, the Sapthakoti Manthras become the seven Theerthas. The Kadri Kambala (Buffalo race) takes place here in December.

KUDROLI GOKARNATHESHWARA TEMPLE AT MANGULURU – The Temple was built in 1912 by Brahmashree Narayana Guru, the great Philosopher, Saint and social reformer from Kerala. The Temple was built in the Chola Gopuram Style. The main deity of this Temple is Lord Shiva. Navarathri and Shivarathri are the two big festivals celebrated at this Temple. The celebrations at the Temple during Dasara is popularly called as Mangaluru Dasara. As per the Guru's advice, vigrahas of Lord Ganapathy, Lord Subramanya, Goddess Annapoorneshwari, Lord Bhairava, the Navagrahas (Lords of Nine Planets), Lord Shanishwara and Lord Shri Krishna has been installed at the Kshethra. This has helped devotees to worship at all these sannidanams (abode) and seek blessings and solace for their varied problems at one place.

SHRI MARIAMMA TEMPLE AT URWA, MANGALORE - The Temple is dedicated to Goddess Mariyamma. It is believed that Mariyamma and Mangaladevi were sisters. This Temple was built by the Mogaveera community around 800 years ago. Goddess Mariyamma is also referred to as the Goddess of wealth. Annual Maari puja and Dasara are the important festival celebrated there. In Urwa, in the precincts of Mangalore, legend has it that the Goddess appeared in the dreams of one of the Mogaveera staying in Urwa and asked for a residing place in the vicinity and so a Temple was built for the deity. The Mogaveeras have a unique way of thanks giving for this goddess. They make gold ornaments in the form of different variety of fish and the deity is adorned with it, it is one of the oldest and the best known Temples in the district. The gold pendants and necklaces they collectively offer are in the shape of fishes such as "bangude sara" (mackerel necklace), "bhutayi sara" (sardine), "seegadi sara" (prawn) and "maanji sara" (pomfret).

SHREE VISHNUMURTHY TEMPLE AT SURATHKAL - It is an ancient shrine of Lord Vishnu, which has a vigraha estimated to be about 600 years old. The Temple's presiding deity is Shree Vishnumurthy who is another form of Lord Vishnu. Initially no Temple complex was evident but Venkatramana Hebbar, a local archaeologist and historian, found a small shrine in a state of ruin in the forest around 1911. The Temple has been repeatedly renovated and is in use today with an active schedule of worship and festival celebrations. Nearest Railway Station is Surathkal.

ANANTA PADMANABHA TEMPLE AT KUDUPU - This Temple is dedicated to Lord Anantha Padmanabha (another form of Lord Vishnu) and famous for serpent worship. Annual festival Shashti is a famous religious ceremony falls in December. Also Nagarapanchami, a worship of sacrificing the milk to Lord Naga is celebrated with great devotion. Main deity, Lord Anantha Padmanabha, in the main sanctum is faced towards west. Naga Bana (place of serpent deity) though situated in eastern portion of the Temple but it is also faced towards west. There are more than three hundred of Serpent vigrahas in this Naga Bana. Holy pond Bhadra Saraswathi Thirtha is situated left side of the Temple. In front of the Temple, there is one small shrine dedicated to Sub-deity Jarandaya. Inside behind the main sanctum, there lies Sub-deity Shree Devi and Lord Mahaganapathi in southern portion. A holy anthill situated inside the Temple beside which there is a stone vigraha of Lord Subramanya and either side of the main sanctum, there are stone vigrahas dedicated to Jaya and Vijaya (vigrahas of divine watchmen). Outside, in front of the Temple, there lies one Valmika Mantapa either side of which there are Shrines of Ayyappan and Navagriha. Once there was a Brahmin Vedic scholar called 'Kedar' who was very orthodox, kind and religious follower but he was extremely worried of not having a child. Thinking of that the blessing of Saint is ultimate resort for having a child, he wandered everywhere searching one such saint. Finally his search fructified when he came contacted with one such holy Saint called 'Shringa Muni' near a small River 'Bhadra Saraswathi Thirtha'. He prostrated before the saint and placed his reason for worries. Hearing this the saint told him to stay there and start penance to Lord Subramanya who would fulfil your wishes. Kedar accepted the advice of the saint and stood there and started a rigorous penance. Lord Subramanya appeared before Kedar and blessed him with children. Kedar is so happy and expecting a child, he settled near that Bhadra Thirtha River itself duly meditating and worshiping

Lord Subramanya. After some day, wife of Kedar saw a serpent laying eggs and thought even snakes have good fortune of having children and worried too much about her fate comparing to that serpent. Year passed and Kedar's wife became pregnant and couple becomes very happy expecting a child but after nine months, to their and everybody's surprise Kedar's wife delivered three eggs, which was more looking like serpent eggs. Kedar was not happy. Even after rigorous penance if God blessed him with these eggs as children it is nothing but fate and a result of past action. That time he heard a divine voice coming from ether saying that these eggs are nothing but an incarnation of Lord Mahavishnu, Lord Mahashesha and Lord Subramanya for the sake of betterment of the world. It also realized him that he does not have further children and advised him to erect the eggs secretly at the place where he did penance upon Lord Subramanya. It blessed a place and River as a holy spot and whoever takes bath in the river will be blessed with children and freed from all sickness and sin. A divine voice also advised him to stay in that holy place worshiping Lord Anantha Padmanabha and blessed him with salvation at the end of his life. Hearing this voice Kedar became so happy and he kept those eggs in a basket weaved with forest creeps called Kudupu in local language and kept secretly in the place where he meditated upon Lord Subramanya. He spent his rest of life meditating upon Lord Anantha Padmanabha and attained salvation at the end of his life. Now in that place an anthill was grown and the place is well known as Shree Kshetra Kudupu.

DISTRICT – DAVANAGERE (Railway Station – Harapanahalli/Harihar)

S. No.	Temple	Address	Type
1	Group of Temples	Davangere - 577001	Mata, Shiva
2	Group of Temples	Channagiri - 577213	Vishnu, Mata, Lake
3	Group of Temples	Honnali - 577217	Shiva, Rama, Brahma
4	Group of Temples	Belagutti - 577223	Shiva
5	Nagappa Temple	Agasanahalli – 577413	Narasimha
6	Group of Temples	Mayakonda - 577534	Narasimha, Vishnu
7	Group of Temples	Anagodu - 577556	Shiva
8	Hari Hareshwara Temple	Harihar Taluk – 577601	Vishnu, Shiva
9	Kalleshwara Temple	Bagali – 583131	Shiva

GROUP OF TEMPLES AT DAVANAGERE -

Anekonda - The place is known for a beautiful Hoysala style Eshwara Temple.

Davanagere - There are two old Temples of Durgamma and Veerabhadra.

GROUP OF TEMPLES AT CHANNAGIRI -

Chennagiri - The place is popular for an old Hill Fort built by Queen Chennammaji. The Hilltop Fort has a Temple of Bete Ranganathaswami and offers splendid views.

Joladhalu - It is a pilgrimage centre with Amba Bhavani Temple (also known as Kukkvadamma Renuka). The deity is seated on a lion with a trishula and drum in her hands.

Shantisagara - Shantisagara is said to be Asia's second largest Lake. It is a man-made Lake built in 11th or 12th century AD by Princess Shantavva after whom the Lake is named. It was formerly known as 'Sulekere' and provides drinking water to adjacent districts. Veerabhadreshwara Temple, Kali Temple, Sri Siddheshwara Temple and Sri Krishna Temple are major Temples near Shantisagara.

GROUP OF TEMPLES AT HONNALI -

Balleshwara - The place is known for Hoysala era Ballala Lingeshwara Temple on the banks of Tungabhadra River.

Kuruva Island - Kuruvada Gadde is an island in Tungabhadra River with Rameshwara Temple.

Thirtharameswara - Thirtharameswara Temple is popular for its Natural Spring of Holy Water. Thirtharameshwara is one of the few Temples with a shrine dedicated to Lord Brahma.

GROUP OF TEMPLES AT BELAGUTTI -

Belagutti - There are remains of a Fort and an old Siddeshwara Temple.

AGASANAHALLI NAGAPPA TEMPLE AT DAVANGERE - The village has a Temple built for Lord Narasimha in the form of Lord Subramanya. This is a very ancient Temple and the history of the Temple dates back to the age of Saint Agastya who had once visited this village and performed penance. Hence, the village is named Agasanahalli. The sanctum sanctorum has an anthill with the vigraha of Lord Narasimha — naturally formed — which is worshipped here. The Temple complex also has a shrine built for Lord Hanuman. Sightings of a golden colour snake around the Temple by devotees have made this Temple famous. No moon days or Amavasya attract maximum crowd.

GROUP OF TEMPLES AT MAYAKONDA -

Mayakonda - The place is known for Obala Narasimha Temple and Keshava Temple.

Shankaranahalli - The place is home to Ranganathaswami Temple, locally known as Tiruvengalanatha. The Vijayanagara Era design is an exact replica of Temples in Mayakonda.

GROUP OF TEMPLES AT ANAGODU -

Anagodu - The place is known for Siddeshwara Temple.

HARIHARESHWARA TEMPLE AT HARIHAR - The beautifully built Temple of is Lord Vishnu's abode. It was built on during the rule of Shivaji Maharaja. It is also synonymously known as God's Own House. The Temple is surrounded by the hills of Pushpadri, Harihareshwar, Harishinachal and Bramhadri. The Temple is also famous all over the world for its pristine and clean sandy beaches. The main vigraha of Harihara is a conglomeration of Gods Vishnu and Shiva. The features of Lord Shiva are visible in the right hand and Vishnu in the left hand. The Temple has been known as the Kashi of South India. The Temple has a chequered history. A story tells us that Guha, the demon, appeased the creator of the universe and was blessed with a boon. According to this boon, both Shiva (Hara) and Vishnu (Hari) were not able to destroy him using single hand. When he got this boon, he started tormenting devas in Indralok and also the human beings in prithvilok. Since Shiva and Hari together could not destroy him on their own, they united as

Harihara to destroy the demon. This incredible incarnation took place near Kudalore where the two Rivers Tungabhadra and Haridra meet. It is a Protected Monument under Archaeological Survey of India.

Nanditavare - The place is home to Amrita Manikyeshwara Temple built in Hoysala style.

Rajanahalli - The place is home to Bannimahakali Temple, Amba Bhavani Temple and Valmiki Gurupeetha.

KALLESHVARA TEMPLE AT BAGALI – The main Temple was constructed during the reign of the Western Chalukyan King Ahavamalla in 987 AD and consecrated by Duggimayya. Inscriptionally, the main deity is known as Kalideva. The Temple is facing east. The Temple on plan consists of a garbhagriha, an antarala, a mahamandapa with an entrance in the south and east, a huge open sabhamandapa, a shrine for Lord Surya with an astylar mukhamandapa built slightly away from the main entrance, all in east-west orientation. A shrine of Narasimha with an antarala and a passage exists to the north of the sabhamandapa. The sabhamandapa is well-known for its fifty ornate pillars supporting the highly decorated ceiling. The Temple is also known for intricately carved doorways. The eastern end of the sabhamandapa accommodates a couchant bull. There are eight shrines built around the main one. The mahamandapa of the Temple include Lord Shiva, Umamaheshvara, Ganesha, Kartikeya, Surya, Anantashayana, Sarasvati and Mahishamardini. It is protected as a monument of national importance by the Archaeological Survey of India.

DISTRICT – DHARWAD (Railway Station – Hubballi)

S. No.	Temple	Address	Type
1	Navagraha Jain Temple	Varur, Hubli – 581207	Jain
2	Group of Temples in Taluka	Dharwad District	All

NAVAGRAHA JAIN TEMPLE AT VARUR - Navagraha Teertha is one of the major pilgrim spots for the Jain community in India. The Temple features a 61 ft tall monolithic vigraha of the Shri 1008 Bhagavan Parshvanatha and the smaller vigrahas of the other 8 Jain Tirthankaras. The vigraha is the tallest vigraha of the Jain deity Parshvanatha in India and weighs 185 tons. The vigraha stands on a 48-ft high pedestal (109 ft total). It is believed that the graha dhoshas of nine planets can be conciliated by worshiping following nine Tirthankaras. The construction of Navagraha Teertha began in January 2005 and the carving of the monolithic vigraha and other vigrahas alone had lasted one year. The work was supervised by Sri Gunadhar Nandi Maharaj, which was supported by Sri Dharmasena Bhattaraka Swamiji and hundreds of volunteers.

GROUP OF TEMPLES IN TALUKAS OF DHARWAD –

ANNIGERI – It is the birth place of famous Kannada poet Adikavi Pampa. It is well known for the black stone Temple built by the Western Chalukya Empire known as Amruteshwara Temple. It is a Temple of mythological figures supported by 76 columns & has a derasar dedicated to Parshva, the 23rd Tirthankara. Annigeri also has Temples dedicated to Banashankari, Basappa, Gajina Basappa & Hanuman.

There is an ancient Lingayati Temple near the railway station. It also has two Lingayati Mathas.

CHANDRAMOULESHWAR TEMPLE AT HUBBALI - The Chandramouleshwar Temple is a 900 years old Temple built during the Badami Chalukyan era. The Temple is dedicated to Lord Shiva. It houses two big Shivalingas. The main shrine has four entrances in all the four directions. The presiding deity of the shrine, Lord Chandramouleshwar faces east. The other Linga is known as Chaturmukha Linga, literally meaning the four faced Linga.

Nuggikeri Hanuman Temple - The Temple is an ancient Temple in Dharwad. The vigraha of Lord Hanuman is tall & gigantic and it is about 5 ft. in height & made of hard granite coated with senduram. The right hand of the vigraha is in abhayamudra. Both eyes of the vigraha are of Saligram, hence the grace of his kataksham is very powerful. Devotees come from different regions to visit this Temple. The pratishtapana of the Lord Balabheema was done by Sri Vyasatirtha (the chief saint in the court of Sri Krishnadevaraya of Hampi). The deity is vigrahaized by devotees in Dharwad and the surrounding districts of Karnataka and Maharashtra. The Temple management was handed over to the Nuggikeri Desai family, a Deshastha Brahmin family which traces its origins to Indapur in Pune district, by the second Konkanastha Peshwa during the 18th century Maratha Empire. Every year on the auspicious day of Chaitra Suddha Poornima i.e., Hanuman Jayanti, the management organizes a Ratha Mahotsav. Every Saturday thousands of devotees visit the Temple and offer prayers to Lord Hanuman.

SRI SIDDHAROODHA SWAMY MATH AT HUBBALI – Sadguru Siddharoodha Swami was an Indian Hindu guru and philosopher. He lived in the style of an ascetic throughout his life. He condemned practice of casteism and conceived divinity in everything that exists. Considered to be an incarnation of Shiva, he renounced his home and his family ties at the very young age of 6 years and set himself the goal of finding his Satguru or spiritual master. Siddharudha later surrendered himself, as a student, to the realized soul Shri Gajadandaswami and served at his ashram. According to the book Siddharoodh Charitra by Shivadas, he was blessed by his guru and was asked to undertake a pilgrimage with the purpose of helping those in need, dispelling ignorance and revealing the right path to spiritual enlightenment to those who were seeking. Thenceforth, he travelled from Kashmir to Kanyakumari, delivering the right wisdom for spiritual awakening and methodical liberation to all those who were cognizant of his exemplary standards of spiritual practice before setting down at Hubli, where he was quickly recognized for his spiritual knowledge & immaculate sainthood. People sought him out from neighbouring states for solace, satisfaction of desires and spiritual enlightenment. He died at Hubballi in the year of 1929 and was entombed at his ashram. He was believed to be working miracles for his devotees.

Hubbali Railway Station - According to railway officials, the length of the renewed platform at Hubbali Junction is estimated at 1,400 meters, which would be longest in the world.

DISTRICT – GADAG (Railway Station – Gadag)

S. No.	Temple	Address	Type
1	Basaveshwara Vigraha	Gadag – 582101	Saint Basaveshwara
2	Shri Veeranarayana Temple	Gadag, Hanuman Gardi, Agrahar – 582101	Vishnu
3	Trikuteshwar Temple	Tanga Koot, Gadag – 582103	Shiva
4	Dodda Basappa Temple	Dambal - 582113	Shiva
5	Lakkundi Group of Temples	Lakkundi – 582115	Shiva, Jain
6	Someshwara Temple	Lakshmeshwara – 582116	Shiva, Jain

BASAVESHWRA VIGRAHA AT GADAG - The vigraha is situated next to Bhishmakere Lake. Its construction started in 2009 and completed in 2015. This standing Basaveshwara vigraha is 111 feet tall. A relatively miniature Aikya Mantapa of Kudala Sangama is a thoughtful addition. Below the vigraha is a circular chamber housing a small museum of some significant events of Basaveshwara's life. The colourful scenes are depicted in the form of lifesize vigrahas and paintings.

VEERANARAYANASWAMY TEMPLE AT GADAG – The Temple known to have been built around 1117 by the Hoysala Empire King, Vishnuvardhana after his conversion to the Hinduism. The primary deity in Temple is the Lord Narayana (also known as Vishnu). This Temple is one among the Pancha Narayana Temples. It is a beautiful mixture of Chalukya, Hoysala and Vijayanagara sculptures. Garbhagruha and the top tower of the Temple are models of Chalukya sculpture. The main entrance gate of the Temple is of Vijaynagara art. Garuda vigraha is in Namaskara position. Inside the Temple, there are many pillars with artistically carved pictures. The traditional belief says that sitting beneath one of these pillars Mahakavi Kumaravyasa wrote "Karnataka Bharatha Katha Manjari". In Garbhagudi, Shri Veeranarayana vigraha carved in the dark blue shaded stone attracts everyone. Decorated with Kireeta, Karnakundala, Shankha, Chakra, Gadha, Padma and in the robe of Veeragachche, Veeranarayana stands protecting his Bhaktas with Abhayahasta. In his broad bosom is Laxmi at the pedestrian aureole the Dashawathara and at both sides stand Laxmi and Garuda. In the courtyard of this Temple, there are other small Temples of gods and goddesses like Laxmi-Narasimha Temple, Sarpeshwara Temple and so on. The Temple is a protected monument of the Archaeological Survey of India.

TRIKUTESHWAR TEMPLE AT GADAG - The Trikuteshwar Temple, which is also called 'SwayambhuIshwara'. 'Swayambhu Trikuteshwar' is built in 1002 AD. It was designed and built by the acclaimed architect Jakanachari. The main shrine has three Shivalingas representing the Trimurthis Brahma, Shiva and Vishnu. The other shrine is dedicated to the Goddess of Learning, Saraswathi. Decoratively carved walls and pillars, wall panels with beautifully sculpted figures and stonework screens make this Temple very attractive. In an adjacent Temple, there

are three shrines dedicated to Goddess Saraswathi, Gayathri and Sharada. With minute beautiful carvings, 42 pillars stand Sabhamantapa, antarala and the entrance gates are built and decorated with beautifully carved sculptures. vigrahas of dancing Ganapathi, Brahma, Shiva, Vishnu, Karthikeya, Gajalakshmi, Mahakali, Manmatha, Bhairava on both outer and inner walls of the Temple attract everyone. Dancing Ganapathi with six hands, Ashta Matrikas in dancing pose, pairs standing with Shivalinga in their palm vigrahas are also carved. These are the very rare patterns of Chalukya and Hoysala art. On the North-East of the sabhamantapa beautiful Nataraja vigraha stands.

DODDA BASAPPA AT TEMPLE AT DAMBAL - The Temple is dedicated to Lord Shiva. The Temple is one of the finest 12th CE western Chalukyan architectural marvel. The Shivalinga has been consecrated in the Sanctum Sanctorum of the Temple. The Temple consist of Cella, Antarala & Navaranga.

LAKKUNDI GROUP OF TEMPLES – It is paradise of Temples. As per the inscriptions, Lakkundi is also called as 'Lokki Gundi' in the inscription; which was a prominent city a thousand years back. It is a place of antiquarian interest with more than 50 ancient Temples scattered throughout the village, 101 stepped wells which are also called as Kalyani and many inscriptions that are built during the rule of the Chalukyas, Kalachuris, Seuna and Hoysalas. It is also an important Jain centre. There is a Jain Temple dedicated to Mahavira Swami, which is the largest & ancient shrine. It is also noted for its steep wells, artistically built with small, canopied niches inside the walls of several wells that enshrine Lingas. The other attraction of Lakkundi is Sculpture Gallery operated by the Archeological Survey of India.

Kasivisvesvara Temple – It is the most ornate and elaborately furnished. The Temple is Dwikuta having two garbhagrihas, two ardhamantapas and navarangas. On a heightened panipeetha is Shivalinga. Door of the garbhagriha is decorated with carvings and on both sides of the entrance, musicians, dancers and Shilabalikas vigrahas are carved. A vigraha of Narataja with man's skeleton is very interesting to watch. On the East and south of navaranga decorated entrance gates are there. In the middle of the navaranga four pillars with Shiva Purana stories are carved. On other walls also Shivapurana stories and dancing poses of Nataraja and vigrahas of Madanika are carved.

Nanneshwar Temple – The Temple consists of Garbhagraha, half mantapa, navaranga and open mukhamantapa. Shivalinga is installed in the Garbhagraha and at East and South of navaranga there are two entrance gates. The pillars in the navaranga are smooth and glassy in which we can see our reflection. On outer walls are Koshta Panjaras. Main entrance gate of the navaranga has lot of carvings.

LAKSHMESHWARA - It is famous for prolific culture and literature. It is a place with rich heritage in Karnataka hence it is called as Tirulugannada Nadu. Many kings have patronised the place. Adikavi Pampa wrote his famous poetry in Lakshmeshwara. Many Jain Saints and writers have flourished here. They include Devachakra Bhattaraka, Shankanacharya, Hemadevacharya, Padmasena, Tribhuvana Chandra Padmita and Rama Dvacharya. There are many important Temples in this historic town including the Lord Shiva Temple of "Someshwara Temple" of 11th century. It is a splendid specimen of Chalukya architecture. The Temple complex with three main entrances is surrounded by high walls look like a fort. In middle of the Temple complex, there is a Someshwara Temple, surrounded by many small Temples mainly dedicated to Shiva, along the compound wall, built with granite, some halls in the complex meant for resting devotees. There are two ancient Jain Temples (Sannabasadi and Shankabasadi) in the town. It is also home for many smaller shrines, the Kodiyellamma Temple, the Mukha Basavanna shrine and a gigantic vigraha of Suryanarayana.

DISTRICT – HASSAN (Railway Station – Hassan/Arsikere/Mandagere)

S. No.	Temple	Address	Type
1	The Chennakesava Temple	JP Nagar, Belur – 573115	Vishnu
2	Sadashiva Temple	Nuggehalli - 573116	Shiva
3	Bucesvara Temple	Koravangala - 573118	Shiva
4	Halebeedu Group of Temple	Halebeedu – 573121	Shiva, Vishnu
5	Someshwara Temple	Haranahalli - 573122	Shiva
6	Lakshmi Narasimha Temple	Javagal - 573125	Narasimha (Vishnu)
7	Bettada Bhairaveshwara Temple	Sakleshpur - 573134	Bhairav
8	Bhagawan Bahubali Vigraha Gomateshwara	Shravanbela Gola (Rural) – 573135	Jain
9	Sri Hasanamba Temple	Hosaline Road, Ammeer Mohalla, Hassan – 573201	Mata
10	Kondajji Mandir	Salagame - 573219	Vishnu
11	Ishvara Temple	Arasikere - 583125	Shiva

CHENNAKESHAVA TEMPLE AT BELUR - The town is renowned for its Chennakeshava Temple, one of the finest examples of Hoysala workmanship. The Temple was consecrated by the famous Hoysala King Vishnuvardhana to mark his victories in 1116 AD against the Cholas and called the Vijaya Narayana. The Hoysalas used soft

soapstone for their structures as they were found suitable for intricate carvings. Enclosed by a Prakara with a Gopura built in the Vijayanagar style, the Temple stands on a platform or Jagati and looks like a huge casket. The fine workmanship and skill visible in this masterpiece is truly breath-taking. There are more than 80 Madanika sculptures in the Temple, dancing, hunting, standing under canopies of trees and so on. The 4 Madanika figures (striking elegant dancing poses) on the wonderfully engraved columns of Navaranga are unique creations of Hoysala workmanship. The Garbhagriha is stellar in shape & its zigzag walls make the figures of 24 forms of Lord Vishnu look different at different times of the day. It is said that Shantaladevi, the accomplished Queen of King Vishnuvardhana is the model for one of the sculptures in the Vavaranga – Darpana Sundari. The Temples of Kappe Chennigaraya, Soumyanayaki, Andal & other Vaishnava manifestations surround this main Temple.

SADASHIVA TEMPLE AT NUGGEHALLI - The Temple is dedicated to Lord Shiva. The Temple was built around 800 years ago during the rule of King Vira Someshwara. This unusual Hoysala Temple combines Ekakuta structure with a Nagara styled Shikhara.

BUCESVARA TEMPLE AT KORAVANGALA - The Temple is also known as Bucheshwara or Bucheshvara Temple. It is a simple yet elegant specimen of 12th century of Hoysala architecture. The Temple was built in 1173 A.D. by a rich officer called Buci (or Buchiraja) to celebrate the coronation of Hoysala King Veera Ballala-II. By plan, the Temple is a divikuta (two shrines) that face each other. These shrines are connected by a closed mantapa (hall) and an open mantapa. Consequently, one shrine appears much dimmer in lighting than the other. At the eastern end of the complex is a small shrine whose deity is the Bhairava, a form of Lord Shiva. The western shrine facing the east containing an vigraha of Lord Surya. The eastern shrine contains a Linga. The miniature towers (turrets) are in various styles; nagara, dravida, vesara, and bhumija. The large wall vigrahas of deities and their attendants are placed below these decorative towers. These vigrahas include among others; Lord Bhairava, the Goddess Saraswati & Durga, Maheshvara, Narasimha, Brahma, and Venugopala. This Temple is protected as a monument of national importance by the Archaeological Survey of India.

HOYSALESHWARA TEMPLE AT HALEBIDU - The Temple, also referred simply as the Halebidu Temple, is a 12th-century Temple dedicated to Lord Shiva. The Temple is another great example of Temple architecture. It is the largest monument in Halebidu. The twin Temples of Hoysaleshwara & Kedareshwara was built by Vishnuvardhana and Ballala-II of the Hoysala Empire at Halebidu on the banks of a large man-made Lake. Sequences from Ramayana, Mahabharatha & Bhagavatha are depicted on the outer walls of these Temples. The efficiency and experience of the sculpture, who had carved these stories in stone is bewitching. The Temple is a Shaivism tradition monument,

yet reverentially includes many themes from Vaishnavism and Shaktism tradition of Hinduism, as well as vigrahas from Jainism. It has two Nandi shrines outside, where each seated Nandi face the respective Shivalinga inside. The Temple faces east. Both the main Temples and the Nandi shrines are based on a square plan. The Temple was carved from soapstone. It is notable for its sculptures, intricate reliefs, detailed friezes as well its history, iconography, inscriptions in North Indian and South Indian scripts. The Temple artwork provides a pictorial window into the life and culture in the 12th century South India. About 340 large reliefs depict the Hindu theology and associated legends. Outside the southern doorway, in the park, are large vigrahas, among them one is a 6 ft. vigraha of Lord Ganesha. The vigraha was among those which were originally farther out at the Temple premises outer gate and the Hoysala Royal Family members used to pray in front of Lord Ganesha.

SOMESHWARA TEMPLE AT HARANAHALLI - The Temple is an example of 13th century Hoysala architecture. The Temple was built in 1235 A.D. by the Hoysala Empire King Vira Someshwara. A few hundred meters from this Temple is the more ornate Lakshminarasimha Temple which also dates to the same period. The main deity in this Temple is Lord Shiva represented by his universal symbol, the Linga. The Temple is a protected monument under the Karnataka state division of the Archaeological Survey of India.

LAKSHMI NARASIMHA TEMPLE AT JAVAGAL - The place is also called Javagallu. The Temple is an example of mid-13th century Hoysala architecture. The Temple, whose main deity is Lord Narasimha (a incarnation of Lord Vishnu), was built in 1250 A.D. by the Hoysala Empire King Vira Someshwara. The Temple plan is simple and commonly found in other Hoysala Temples. It is a trikuta (three shrined), though only the middle shrine has a superstructure (tower or shikhara) and a sukhanasi (nose or tower over the vestibule). The three equal size shrines are all square in plan and are connected by a common closed hall (mantapa). This Temple is a protected monument under the Karnataka state division of the Archaeological Survey of India.

Bettada Bhairaveshwara Temple at Sakleshpur - The Temple is nestled in the beautiful Western Ghats and offers a panoramic view of the landscape. It is 600 year old Temple. As per legend, the Pandavas stayed here for a short while when they were exiled. The Temple is an excellent spot for those who like the calm and beauty of nature. You can see Pandavar Gudda/Betta & Jenkal Gudda from here.

GOMATESHWARA VIGRAHA AT SHRAVANBELGOLA - The town has been a prominent centre for Jain art, architecture, religion and culture for over two millennia. About two thousand years ago, Bhagawan Bhadrabahu, the earliest among the great Jain Acharyas came to Shravanabelagola from Ujjain with his disciples. Influenced by this ascetic, Chandragupta Maurya, the great emperor who ruled a large part of India, settled in this region, handing over the reins of his kingdom to his son. Wedged between two stark rocky hills, the monolithic vigraha of Lord Gomateshwara, a Jain Saint and an object of worship for centuries, standing atop one of the hills (Indragiri hill), is 18 meters high and is said to be one of the tallest and most graceful monolithic vigrahas in the world. Lord Gomateshwara, also known as Bahubali, was the son of the first Jain Teerthankara, Lord Adinatha. Challenged by his brother Bharatha over the succession to the throne, Lord Bahubali took on Bharatha in a duel that involved three forms – Drishtiyuddha, Mallayuddha and Jalayuddha. Though Lord Bahubali finally emerged victorious, he was overwhelmed by both the enormity and the futility of the desire for material wealth – a pursuit that set brother against brother. He then renounced his kingdom & all other worldly pleasures. Lord Bahubali stood in deep meditation and radiated the glow of spiritual tranquillity. , Prime Minister & commander-in-chief of the Ganga Kingdom, Chavundaraya consecrated the vigraha of Lord Bahubali in a meditative form in 981 AD. Just opposite is the smaller Chandragiri hill where some Jain Temples and tomb of Chandragupta Mourya, famous patron of Jainism can be seen. The biggest Mahamastakabhisheka Festival, an elaborate ritual, held here once every 12 years, attracts devotees from all over the world. Priests climb up to pour hundreds of pots of tender coconut water, turmeric paste, vermilion powder, sugarcane juice, milk, rice flour, kashaya (a herbal concoction), shrigandha (sandal paste), chandana (coloured sandal paste), ashtagandha (eight varieties of sandal paste), saffron, gold and silver flowers, and precious stones over the vigraha's head. A spectacular finale to this splendid ceremony is a shower of flowers from a helicopter.

Akkana Basadi - The Jain Temple was built in 1181 A.D. during the rule of Hoysala Empire King Veera Ballala - II. The Moolnayak of the Temple is the 23rd Tirthankara, Lord Parshavanath. There are various beautifully carved and intricately figures in the Temple.

Chavundaraya Basadi - It as also known as Chamundaraya Basadi or Boppa-Chaityalya. It is one of the fifteen Basadis located on the Chandragiri Hill. The Basadi was erected by Chavundaraya during the rule of Ganga King Marasimha-II and completed by Chavundaraya's son Jinadeva. The vigraha of Lord Neminatha, flanked by Chauri bearers, is believed to be installed by Hoysala period attributing to the characteristics matching Hoysala art. The Temple underwent improvement in the 12th century under the rule of Chola Empire. The pyramidal shikhara crowned with domical finial is example of Chola architecture. This Basadi along with Suparshwanath, Kattale and Chandragupta Basadi is considered the most important for the architecture in Jain Temple complex of Chandragiri Hill. This Temple is built in Dravidian architecture and famous for its artistry. The Temple houses a garbhagriha, pradakshinapatha, open sukansi, navaranga and mukhamandapa. Above the garbagriha is a dvitala vimana. On the first floor of the vimana, houses the vigraha of Lord Parshavanatha installed by Jinadeva in 985 CE. This Temple is the largest shrine in Shravanabelagola with ornamental niches with figures of yakshi and Jain monks in padmasan posture. The architecture of this Temple was influenced by Chalukyan style in Aihole and Badami Temple complex. The Temple also houses an vigraha of Ambika seated under a mango tree with amra-lumbi (mango tree branch) in the right hand and citron in left. The Temple is protected as a monument of national importance by the Archaeological Survey of India.

HASANAMBA TEMPLE AT HASSAN - The main tower at Sri Hasanamba has been newly constructed in Dravidian style. There are three major Temples in the premises of this Temple dedicated to Darbar Ganapati, Hasanamba and Siddeshwara. Another prominent attraction here is the shrine dedicated to Kallappa. The three vigrahas installed here are said to be of three thieves, who had allegedly come to steal the vigraha of the presiding deity, Sri Hasanamba and earned her wrath. Earlier, Hassan was known as Sihmasanapuri and later it got the name of Hassan. It is said that during the rule of Hoysala dynasty in twelfth century AD, an vigraha was found with its face wearing a pleasant smile. Hasana Mukhi or a smiling face was transformed into Hassan. The Hasanamba Temple is opened in the presence of the Deputy Commissioner for only twelve days in a year during Deepavali celebrations. Indrani, Varahi and Vaishnavi are welcomed and worshipped here once a year when Hasanamba Temple is opened. The special feature of this Temple is that the lamp lit this year will be alive till the Temple is reopened next year. Even the flowers retain their freshness for the entire year. Devotees from across south India and Maharashtra visit the Temple. Sri Hasanamba Devi is a goddess of curiosity to all. She's renowned for her unusual mysteries. The Goddess Maheshwari is in the center and Brahmi and Kaumari are on her left and right. In this case there is no type of sculpture, as the ' Agamashastra' is prescribed for a Temple. Yet their three faces are set in golden eyebrows, ears, nose and earrings to quickly recognize these three Goddesses. For the worship of Hasanamba Temple Devi, together with Turmeric and Kumkum, Sindhura is used. In the past and even now, Hassan city's traditional houses do not grind hot chillies or pound them to cook during the open days of the Temple. Not only that, they don't paint walls using lime paste with white clay called jedi. The Temple premises, with an entrance tower (Rajagopura) of about 81 feet, consecrated 101 Lingas in one location, as well as the Siddeshwara Swamy Shrine. The sanctum has a stone with vigraha of Arjuna receiving Lord Shiva's Pashupatastra, with some animals. The Goddess seems to have ensured herself as a village Goddess. Close to this Temple, there are Temples of Doddabasadi

and Virupaksha built almost at that time as well as today's Hasanamba stone Temple. Archaeological experts consider the Hasanamba Temple to be an example of the epitome of the Karnataka Temple architecture. It was originally built in the tradition of the Hoysala dynasty, representing their faith in Jainism. Even the myth behind the Temple's founding is peculiar. Andhakasura, a demon who was unattackable to Lord Brahma's boons, had to be destroyed by Lord Eshwara. It is said that each drop of blood that drops from his body will create a new Andhakasura (a related Rakthabeejasura tale is also in Devimahatmya). To stop this, Goddess Maheshwari was created by Lord Shiva. The other gods have created their female counterparts and sent them to her to assist this female deity as Lord Brahma's Shakthi form Brahmi, Lord Shiva's Shakthi form Maheshwari, Lord Subrahmanya's Shakthi form Kaumari, Lord Vishnu's Shakthi form Vaishnavi, Varaaharoopi's Shakthi form Vaarahi, Indra's Shakthi form Indrani and Mahaadevi herself was in Chamundi form. They thrived with their male counterpart's weapons, ornaments and vaahanas. At the sanctum sanctorum, there is a small stone right in front of the deity's vigraha. The name of this stone is Sose Kallu. A unique story is attached to this stone. A mother-in-law, who used to taunt her daughter-in-law at home every day, pursued her with fury on a day and saw her daughter-in-law standing before the Goddess and meditating. The angry mother-in-law screamed at her saying, "Is the Darshan of Goddess more important to you than household duties?" Also, the mother-in-law took a cup (Chandra Battalu) lying by the side and thrashed it on the daughter-in-law's forehead. The daughter-in-law teared up, "Oh mother Hasanamba, please protect me," unable to bear the pain after being wounded. Moved by the daughter-in-law's plea and loyalty, the mother Goddess, offered her a blessing to stay close to her. The daughter-in-law is said to still reside there in the form of a small stone. The stone, daughter-in-law, is believed to keep moving forward to the extent of a paddy grain every year and it is said that the Kaliyuga will stop the moment she hits the Goddess feet.

KONDAJJI MANDIR AT SALAGAME - The Temple is dedicated to Lord Varadaraja, a form of Lord Vishnu's Janardana aspect. The vigraha of the Lord Varadaraja is 11 ft. tall and it is believed that this tall vigraha was to be enshrined at the Chennakeshava Temple complex but the vigraha was made more than the height that was ordered and it could not make it all the way into the Temple at the right time and was apparently running the risk of being deserted. Ajji (Grandmother in Kannada) decided to buy the vigraha and established it in a Temple at this place, hence it is believed that the village got the name "Kondajji". A very unique thing in the vigraha is that on the right side of the chest of Lord Varadaraja, there is a small impression of Goddess Lakshmi, where Goddess acquires the name as Shrenika. Devotees can climb the loft to perform Abhishekam.

ISHVARA TEMPLE AT ARASIKERE - The Ishvara Temple (also spelt Ishwara or Isvara) dates to 1220 CE rule of Hoysala Empire. The Temple, which is dedicated to Lord Shiva, though modest in size and figure sculpture, is considered the most complex one in architecture among surviving Hoysala monuments because of its ground plan: a 16-point star-shaped mantapa (hall), in addition to an asymmetrical star-shaped shrine, whose star points are of three different types. The Temple faces east as in all Hoysala constructions, uses soapstone (also known as steatite or soaprock) as its basic building material, and is a ekakuta shrine (single shrine or cella) with two mantapas (hall). All three units are connected to form a unity. The sanctum (garbhagriha) enshrines a Linga.

DISTRICT – HAVERI (Railway Station – Haveri)

S. No.	Temple	Address	Type
1	Tarakeshwara Temple	Hangal - 581104	Shiva
2	Galaganath Temple	Galaganath – 581108	Shiva
3	Siddeswara Temple	Haveri – 581110	Shiva
4	Sri Kantesh Hanumantha Temple	Haveri - 581115	Hanuman

TARAKESHWARA TEMPLE AT HANGAL - The name of the Temple is derived from the Tarakeshwara form of Lord Shiva. Even though the credit of construction of this Temple goes to the Kadambas, it was the Kalyani Chalukyas that made significant changes to make it into the form we see today. The Tarakeshwara Temple is a listed monument of the Archaeological Survey of India.

GALAGESHWARA TEMPLE AT GALAGANATH – The Temple also known as Galaganatha Temple. It was constructed during the rule of Chalukyas. It is a breath-taking Shiva Temple with sculptures and intricate carvings.

SIDDHESVARA TEMPLE AT HAVERI – It is a very famous and ancient Temple. The Siddhesvara Temple (also spelt Siddheshvara or Siddheshwara and locally called Purada Siddeshwara) is considered an ornate example of 12th century Western Chalukyan art and is well known for the many loose sculptures of Hindu deities that exist in it. However, inscriptional evidence would suggest that the initial consecration of the Temple was in late 11th century. An interesting aspect about the Temple is that it faces west, instead of facing the rising sun in the east – a standard in Chalukyan constructions.

SRI KANTESH HANUMANTHA TEMPLE AT KADARAMANDALAGI – The Temple is dedicated to Lord Hanuman. Earlier the village was also known as Kanteshpuri. As per legend, several thousands of years ago, Lord Hanuman lived in this village. Once, he saw the son and mistaking it to be a fruit, begin flying towards it. Since then, this village came to be known as Kadaramandalagi which means rays (Kadar) and cluster of rays (mandala). It is believed that King Janmejaya had established this shrine to get rid of his difficulties. Kantesha means Lord full of brightness, hence

Lord Hanuman appears with a front face and sparkling eyes. There is also a small pond on the right side of the Temple where Teppotsava is celebrated with great devotion. Kanakadasa has praised Sri Kantesha in his various poetic compositions.

DISTRICT – KALABURAGI (Railway Station – Kalaburagi/Nalwar/Malkhaid Road)

S. No.	Temple	Address	Type
1	Koranti Temple	Kalaburagi - 585101	Hanuman
2	Sharana Basaveshwara Temple	Kalaburagi – 585102	Sharana Basaveshwara
3	Vaishno Devi Temple	Kalaburagi - 585104	Mata
4	Buddha Vihar	Gulbarga - 585105	Buddhist
5	Shree Kshetra Gangapur	Taluk Afzalpur – 585212	Dattatreya
6	Shri Chandrala Parameshwari Temple	Sannati - 585218	Mata
7	Malkhed Group of Temples	Malkhed - 585292	Saint Sri Javatirtha, Jain
8	Sri Somanatheshwara Temple	Inoli - 585307	Shiva

KORANTI TEMPLE AT KALABURAGI - The Temple is also known as Koranti guarantee Temple, as it is believed that chanting Hanuman Chalisa here makes devotee's prayers answered. The Temple is dedicated to Lord Hanuman. There is a huge vigraha of Lord Hanuman in sitting posture.

SHARANA BASAVESHWAR TEMPLE AT GULBARGA - This Temple has a history of 400 years. The Temple is dedicated to eminent religious teacher & philosopher, Shri Sharana Basaveshwara, a Lingayat Saint of 18th CE, who is known for his Dasoha & Kayaka. The Temple houses his Samadhi at the centre called the garbhagudi. It has a Lake adjacent to it, which attracts many devotees & tourists. A chariot festival, Jatra, is held every year in honour of Sharana Basaveshwara.

VAISHNO DEVI TEMPLE AT RING ROAD, KALABURAGI - The Temple is dedicated to Mata Vaishno Devi. It is a newly built Temple. The Temple looks like a fort having different ways for entry & exit and it is believed to be a replica of Mata Vaishno Devi Cave in Katra, J&K.

BUDDHA VIHAR AT GULBARGA - It has a meditation centre & a Lord Buddha Chaitya. The dome of Buddavihar is built in traditional Buddhist architecture. The dome has an ornamental spire made of panchaloha with a kalasha on top of it also made of panchaloha. Buddha Vihara is surrounded by four 48 ft. tall Ashoka pillars in the four corners in honour of King Ashoka the Great.

DEVALGANGAPUR - It stands on the bank of the River Bhima. The confluence of Bhima & Amaraja rivers are considered extremely holy in this area. Whoever takes bath in Sangam will be free from their sins & their wishes will be fulfilled. There is a Temple in Sangam in which Shree Nrusimha Saraswathy Swamy performed the Anushthaan. The 'Shila Padukas' of Swamy Ji are there at Sangam which everyone can take Darshan. Shree Nrusimha Saraswathy Swamy (1378-1458) is the Purna avatar of Lord Dattatreya. Shreeguru was initially named as Narahari.

Shree Kshetra Ganagapur Dattatreya Temple – It is a very holy place and rich in culture & tradition which is followed by many people around the world as Guru Sthanam. Importance of this Kshetra is explained by Shree Guru which can be seen in "Shree Gurucharitra". This Math is adorned with the Nirguna Paduka's which are unique in nature & look. You never find any other "Nirgun Padukas" all around the globe. These Paduka's are named as Nirgun Padukas for few reasons, Nirgun means formless, without qualities or attributes, an epithet of God who is beyond three. The Aswatha Tree here is as powerful as the Kalpa Vriksha. Near the Aswatha Tree, there are the Papavinasini Teertha, Varanasi Teertha, Rudrapada Teertha, Chakra Teertha, Koti Teertha, Manmadha Teertha etc. There is the Kalleshwara Temple there.

SHRI CHANDRALA PARAMESHWARI TEMPLE AT SANNATI – It is located on the banks of the Bhima River. It is famous for the Chandrala Parameshwari Temple and the excavations by the Archaeological Survey of India in the 1986, wherein terracotta items were found and most importantly numerous limestone panels of sculptures of the ruined 'Maha Stupa' or Adholoka Maha Chaitya (the Great Stupa of the Netherworld) were found.

BUDDHIST SITE AT KAGANAHALLI – It is an important Buddhist site on the banks of River Bhima. It is the place where an ancient Buddhist Mahastupa site was found.

MALKHED -

Uttaradhi Math - The remains of Sri Jayatirtha, one of its most prominent saints in the lineage of Madhvacharya, are buried in a Brindavana here. For the commentary called "Nyaya Sudha", he is popularly known as Teekacharya, a disciple of Akshobhya Tirtha (one of the four disciples of Madhvacharya) and he had converted the Malkhed into the centre of Madhva study. Every year the Aradhana Mahotsava of Jayatirtha held at Malkhed during the month of Ashada.

Jain Bhattaraka Math - The Temple of Lord Neminath having the vigrahas include Tirthankaras, choubisi, Nandishwardvipa & Yakshi. There is a famous panchdhatu shrine with 96 vigrahas. There are other historical vigrahas. The famous Mahapurana (Adipurana & Uttarapurana) was composed here by Acharya Jinasena & his pupil Gunabhadra in 9th CE. Somodeva Suri's Yasastilaka Champu was written here. The mathematics text Ganita Saara Sangraha was written here by Mahaviracharya. The famous Apabhramsha Poet Pushapadanta lived here.

SRI SOMANATHESHWARA TEMPLE AT INOLI - The Temple is dedicated to Lord Somanath. It is located on the bank's of Netravati River. It is believed that the Temple was destroyed couple of centuries ago. The ruins of the Shree Somanatheshwara Durgaparameshwari Temple are on the top of a hill with a scenic view by the side of Nethravathi River. The Temple is reconstructed with natural green surroundings at top of a hill. This is the only place where the river turns north during its course. This Temple is sanctified by the presence of Sri Durgaparameshwari and Sri Ganesh. Villagers say that there are five Somanatha Temples around the area: Ullala, Ammembala, Ira, Inoli, and Konaje. Abbakka Queen of Ullala was an ardent devotee of Sri Somanatha.

DISTRICT – KODAGU (Railway Station – Hassan)

S. No.	Temple	Address	Type
1	Omkareshwara Temple	Madikeri - 571201	Shiva
2	Bhagandeshwara Temple	Bhagamandala - 571247	Triveni Sangam
3	Tala Kaveri	Talacauvery – 571247	River Cauvery

OMKARESHWARA TEMPLE AT MADIKERI - The Temple was built by Lingarajendra-II in 1820 supposedly to atone for killing an innocent Brahmin. The Temple is in the Indo-Saracenic style combining typically Keralite tiled roofs with Islamic domes.

BHAGANDESHWARA TEMPLE AT BHAGAMANDALA – It is a religious place. There is a Triveni Sangama which means confluence of three Rivers i.e. Cauvery, Kannike and Sujyoti. The imposing Bhagandeshwara Temple has a large courtyard and is built in the Kerala style with red- tiled roofs.

TALACAUVERY - It is an important religious place as birth place of sacred River Cauvery. A small shrine with a beautifully decorated silver Shivalinga marks the spot where the mighty river originates. On Tula Sankramana day, which usually falls on 17th October each year, thousands flock here to witness a sudden upsurge of water in the spring, which then bubbles over. Near the Temple stands Brahmagiri peak which offers panoramic views of the mountains.

DISTRICT – KOLAR (Railway Station – Coramandal)

S. No.	Temple	Address	Type
1	Sri Kashi Vishweshwara Temple	Antaragange, Paparajanahalli – 563101	Shiva
2	Kolaramma Temple	Fort Area, Kolar – 563101	Mata
3	Sri Someshwara Temple	Fort Area, Kolar – 563101	Shiva
4	Sri Venkateshwara Temple	Bangaruthirupathi – 563116	Venkatesh
5	Shree Kotilingeshwara Swamy Temple	Ghattiragadahalli – 563121	Shiva
6	Sri Ramalingeswara Swamy Temple	Avani – 563127	Rama, Mata
7	Kurudumale Ganesha Temple	Kurudumale – 563131	Ganesh
8	Narasimha Tirtha	Narasimhatirtha – 563131	Narasimha
9	Virupakshi Temple	Virupakshi – 563131	Vishnu, Mata

SRI KASHI VISHWESHWARA TEMPLE AT ANTARA GANGE - Antara Gange literally means "Ganges from deep" in Kannada. It is, also known as Anthargange, a mountain situated in the Shathashrunga mountain range. It is famous for Sri Kashi Vishweshwara Temple, also known as Kashi of South. The Temple is dedicated to Lord Shiva. In the Temple, there is a pond which gets a continuous flow of underground water from the mouth of a Basava (stone bull). It is believed that drinking water from the pond cleanse one from many diseases. Way to Antar Gange caves is a steep and narrow path behind the Temple to top of the mountain.

KOLARAMMA TEMPLE AT KOLAR - Kolaramma is the presiding deity of Kolar. The Kolaramma Temple is thousand years old and built by the Cholas in the South Indian style. Goddess Parvathi is worshipped as Kolaramma by the people of Kolar. The erstwhile maharajas of Mysore frequently visited this Temple to get the blessings of Kolaramma. The Temple itself has beautifully carved vigrahas and designs all done using the abundantly available granite stones. Another deity of this Temple is Chelamma or the Scorpion Goddess. People believe that by praying at the Chelamma shrine, a person will be guarded from scorpion bites by the deity. Another interesting thing about the Temple is the hundi or the well which is used to collect money offerings from the people and it is a tradition to at least put one coin into the small opening on the floor of the Temple, which apparently is a large hole dug into the earth, one can still hear the clicking sounds of coins accumulated over hundreds of years. A large vigraha of Chamunda flanked by Virabhadra and Ganapati are noteworthy. Facing east, the Temple has an austere mahadvara ornamented with Gajalakshmi in green stone on the lintel while its pillars inside have sculptured figures on all sides. The garbhagriha has stone vigrahas of Saptamatrikas with Dakshinamurti to the right and Vinayaka to the left. The main vigraha of Chamunda faces south and is worshipped as the chief deity Kolaramma.

SOMESHWARA TEMPLE AT KOLAR – It is an ornate of 14th century Vijayanagara era Dravidian style construction. Someshwara, another name of the Lord Shiva, is the presiding deity. The Temple is noted for its tall superstructure (gopuram) over the main entrance (mahadwara). The superstructure is built of brick and stucco. The base of the Temple outer wall (adhishthana) consists of decorative mouldings, with friezes of elephants, dwarfs and lions embellishing the upper mouldings. The Temple is protected by the Archaeological Survey of India as a monument of national importance.

BANGARUTHIRUPATHI - The Temple resembles Tirupathi Venkateshwara. The Temple is situated on a small Hillock and the Lord is facing east. The deity is to be seen through the window carved in western wall. Lord Varaha, Yinayaka, Anjaneya shrines are there on the way to the Temple. Padmavathi Temple is there on another Hillock. There is a big Pond (Kalyani) in front of this complex. Pilgrims congregate is large numbers during Shravana month.

SHREE KOTILINGESHWARA SWAMY TEMPLE AT GHATTIRAGADAHALLI - The place is famous for its 10 million 'Lingas', a stone representation of the Lord Shiva. The word Koti means '10 million in Kannada, the local language of Karnataka. The presiding deity of the Temple is Lord Shiva. The main attraction of the Temple is a huge Linga measuring 108 ft tali and 35 ft tall Lord Nandi vigraha, surrounded by lakhs of small Lingas spread over an area of 15 acres. The Lord Nandi vigraha is installed over a platform which is 60 ft in length, 40 ft in width and 4 ft in height. There are eleven small Temples constructed within the premises for various deities. A water tank is set up close to the Linga used by the devotees to perform Abhisheka.

AVANI - The village has a Temple complex of Ramalingeswara Swamy, Sita Parvati Temple on the Hills and the pillar inscription of Devabarasi, a Nolamba Queen of the first millennium of CE. The Saraswathi Temple of Shankar Mutt is a worthy place for meditation. The Temple complex of Ramalingeswara Swamy has the Temples for Lakshmaneswara, Bharateswara and Shatrughneswara. There are shrines for Bali, Sugreeva and Angada also. Avani is called Dakshina Ittya. The legend says that this is the place of Valmiki Ashrama; where Sita Mata gave birth to Lava and Kusha. To illustrate the point there is "Lava Kusha Linga" Temple here (two Linga vigrahas in one : pannvatta which is a rare phenomenon in shilpa shastra). On the way to the Hills, one can see the natural tank - Dhanushkoti and Horaler Gundu.

KURUDUMALE GANESHA TEMPLE AT MULBAGAL - Kurudumale is a sacred place and is famous for the Ganesha Temple that has attracted people from near and far for years. Home to one of the biggest vigrahas, the Kurudumale Ganesha Temple has a 13½ ft Lord Ganesha vigraha installed within its walls. An architectural marvel whose immense size will take your breath away, the Temple's infamous vigraha is said to be continuously growing. Said to be very powerful, the deity is

visited by people before the commencement of a new job or new phase of their life. It is believed that if a person with pure heart asks for something in the presence of this majestic vigraha, they will achieve what they wish for and great levels of success. As Lord Ganesha is believed to be "Vighnaharta", he will clear all your hurdles and his blessings are always welcome. Ganesh Chaturthi is one of the grandest festival celebrated here.

Garuda Deva Temple - The Temple is dedicated to Lord Garuda which is unique & rare Temple. The vigraha of Lord Garuda is in standing posture having Lord Vishnu on one shoulder & Goddess Lakshmi on the other shoulder. The vigraha has been carved out from a black stone and there are different type of shringars of the vigrahas as per the special occasion. It is also believed that the Temple has remedies for Sarpa Dosha.

Mulbagal - It is also called Mudala Bagilu (The eastern door). There is a Temple complex of Lord Anjaneya. The Lord Anjaneya here is to be decorated with Kedage (screw pine flowers) every day. The vigrahas of Lord Rama – Sita Lakshmana are in this Temple. Lakshmi Narasimha, Venugopala and other deities are housed is the sub-Temples. Tirumala Venkatesha, Kanchi Varadaraja, Tirupathi Govindaraja are also there in this complex. Some beautiful paintings, Dashavathara Kostas can be seen. It has a big outer Gopura

Narasimhatirtha - Sripadaraju Matha and Brindavana of Sripadaru is located at Narasimha Theertha. There is a cave, where Sri Vyasa Rayaru learnt his lessons of Dvaita philosophy. The Yoga Narasimha Swamy on the boulder is Swayambhu. Rathotsava is conducted in the month of Jyeshta.

Virupakshi - Lekkanna Dandesha, a General of Vijayanagara and author of Shiva Tatlva Chintamani, had built this Temple. Apart from the main Temple, which is exquisitely carved and decorated, there is a Temple for Simha Vahana Durga. Goddess Durga is having four arms. A lion is in attendance in front of Goddess Parvathi in the Temple. The beautiful Temple tank is called Manmatha Pushkarini. The enlrance Gopura of the Temple is in good shape and is quite majestic.

DISTRICT – KOPPAL (Railway Station – Hosapete/Munirabad/Koppal)

S. No.	Temple	Address	Type
1	Huligemma Devi Temple	Hosapete - 583201	Mata
2	Chinthamani Temple	Anegundi - 583227	Ramayana Circuit
3	Navabrindavana	Anegundi – 583227	Saints
4	Pampa Sarovar	Hanumanahalli - 583227	Sarovar

S. No.	Temple	Address	Type
5	Mahadeva Temple	Itagi - 583232	Shiva
6	Kanakachalapathi Temple	Kanakagiri - 583283	Vishnu

HULIGEMMA TEMPLE AT HULIGI - The Temple is a 13th century Temple devoted to Goddess Huligemma.

CHINTHAMANI TEMPLE AT ANEGUNDI - It is another treasure trove of ancient history and reminder of the glory of Krishnadevaraya and Vijayanagar Empire. This place is believed to be the maternal home of Bhooma Devi and during Ramayana times, this was Kishkinda, the kingdom of Baali and Sugreeva. There is a very unique Shivalingam with Shree Charka on its top which is very rare.

NAVA BRINDAVANA AT TUNGABHADRA – It has the Samadhis of nine Saints, followers of Madhvacharya and predecessors of Sri Raghavendra.

PAMPA SAROVAR AT HANUMANAHALLI – It is one of the five sacred Sarovar in India. In Hindu mythology, it is regarded as the place where Pampa, a form of Lord Shiva's consort Goddess Parvati, performed penance to show her devotion to Lord Shiva.

MAHADEVA TEMPLE AT ITAGI – The Temple is dedicated to Lord Shiva. It was built in 1112 CE. Soapstone was found in abundance in this regions. This Temple is an articulated structure. It is one of the largest & most ornate Temple built by Kalyani Chalukas. The carvings, sculptures, pillars & towers are proof to the finest of Chalukyan art. It is protected by Archeological Survey of India.

KANAKACHALAPATHI TEMPLE AT KANAKAGIRI - Kanakagiri is an historical place in India. Kanakagiri, known in ancient times as "Swarnagiri". Kanakagiri means a Hill of Gold. Kanakagiri is known to get its present name from Kanaka Muni, a Hindu saint who performed penance there. The Temple is a 16th-century Temple dedicated to Lord Vishnu. The Temple is an example of Dravidian architecture of the Vijayanagara era. The Temple was built by the ruling vassal polyagar (Nayaka or feudal lord). The Temple complex is a large one with spacious halls (mantapa) and massive Yali pillars. Sculpture in the Temple includes those of mythological figures in wood and pilaster, and that of kings and queens in black stone. The popularity of the Temple is supported by a local saying: "people with eyes must see Kanakagiri and those with legs, Hampi", an affirmation that the Kanakachalapathi Temple is a delight to the eyes where as one needs to tread tirelessly to enjoy the architectural wonders of near by Hampi. In the months of February and March, during the Phalguna season, the Temple hosts a popular fair called the "Kanakachalapathi fair" (Jatra). It is a protected monument under the Karnataka state division of the Archaeological Survey of India.

DISTRICT – MANDYA (Railway Station – Mandya/Mandagere/Mysuru/Shrirangapatna)

S. No.	Temple	Address	Type
1	Mallikarjuna Temple	Basaralu - 571416	Shiva
2	Brahmeshvara Temple	Kikkeri – 571423	Vishnu
3	The Laxminarayana Temple	Hosaholalu – 571426	Vishnu
4	Hole Anjaneya Swami	Maddur - 571428	Hanuman
5	Shri Cheluvanarayan Swami & Sri Yoganarasimha Temple	Pandavpura, Melukote – 571431	Vishnu
6	Sri Nambinarayana Swamy Temple	Tonnur - 571434	Vishnu
7	Sri Ranganatha Swamy Temple	Srirangpatna – 571438	Vishnu
8	Sri Adichunchanagiri Mahasamsthana Math	Nagamangala Taluk – 571448	Saint Bala Gangadharanatha
9	Venugopala Swami Temple	Chinakurali - 571455	Vishnu

MALLIKARJUNA TEMPLE AT BASARALU - The Temple is dedicated to Lord Shiva. The Temple was built by Harihara Dhannayaka around 1234 A.D. during the rule of the Hoysala Empire King Vira Narasimha - II. The Temple is highly ornate example of Hoysala architecture. The Temple plan is that of a trikuta (three shrined), though only the middle one has a superstructure (tower or shikhara) and a sukhanasi (nose or tower over the vestibule). The lateral shrines are connected directly to the hall while the middle shrine has a vestibule that connects the sanctum (cella or vimana) to the hall. The decorative plan of the walls of the shrines & the mantapa (hall) is of the "new kind", with two eaves that run around the Temple. The wall panel vigrahas have the same quality of workmanship seen in the more famous Temples at Belur and Halebidu. In the "new kind" of decorative articulation, the first heavy eaves runs below the superstructure & all around the Temple with a projection of about half a meter. The second eaves runs around the Temple about a meter below the first. Between the two eaves are the miniature decorative towers (Aedicula) on pilasters. Below the second eaves are the wall panel of vigrahas of Hindu deities and their attendants in relief. This Temple is protected as a monument of national importance by the Archaeological Survey of India.

BRAHMESHVARA TEMPLE AT KIKKERI - This Temple is a fine specimen of Hoysala architecture. It was constructed in 1171 AD by a lady named Bammare Nayakiti during the rule of the Hoysala King Narasimha-I. The deep indentation of the horizontal courses in the basement and the knife-edge to which the cornices have been brought are interesting points. It is a single celled Temple and has an impressive and lofty stone tower. There is a well-executed vigraha of Vishnu, about four foot high, installed in one of the niches of the navaranga. The madanike figures carved on the capitals of the pillars of the navaranga are of extra-ordinary workmanship and are life-like.

Panchalingeshwara Temple at Govindanahalli - It is also known as Panchalingeshvara. The Temple was constructed around 1238 A.D. during the reign of the Hoysala empire King Vira Someshwara. The name "Panchalingeshwara" literally means "five linga". The famous sculptor of Hoysala times, Ruvari Mallitamma, is known to have made contributions to the Temple. According

to Art Historian, Gerard Foekema, this Temple is a rare example of a panchakuta (lit, five shrines with five towers) construction in Hoysala architecture. The five shrines are built on a north-south axial plan with the sanctums face east. In each shrine, the sanctum is connected to a hall by a vestibule with sukanasi above. A long pillared hall on the east connects the individual mantapa together. The entrance to the Temple complex is via two porched entrances whose ceiling are supported by lathe turned pillars. Irrespective of the number of shrines in the complex, these are standard features in Hoysala Temples. The porches are located in front of the second and third shrines. The decoration on the outer walls of the shrines is modest and comprises miniature decorative towers on pilasters. The wall panel of vigrahas between the eave and the base moldings include some depictions from the Hindu epics. The Temple is a protected monument by the ASI.

LAKSHMI NARAYANA TEMPLE AT HOSAHALLU – It is a magnificent example of Hoysala architecture of 13th century. The intricate carvings in stone depict various vigrahas from the Mahabharata and other epics. The Temple is a trikutachala or three-celled Temple. Only the main cell has a sukhanasi and a tower. Some of the vigrahas carved on the walls are about two and a half ft high. The figures of Panduranga, Dakshinamurti and Mohini are particularly noteworthy. Groups of dancing ladies with accompaniments in impressive poses adorn the capitals of the pillars in the navaranga. An annual jatra called Rangada-habba is held here in honour of Lord Anjaneya in the month of April. It resembles the Holi festival in some respects.

HOLE ANJANEYA SWAMI AT MADDUR - The Temple is dedicated to Lord Anjaneya. The Temple is located along the banks of River Shinsa. It is believed that the Temple is more than 550 years old. It is supposed to be constructed during the reign of Vijayanagara Kings. The vigraha of Lord Anjaneya holds a saugandhika flower in his left hand but right hand held above his head has index and middle fingers longer than the rest of the fingers. This symbolises the Dwaita Philosophy in Vaishnavaite Sect. By this unique feature in the vigraha of Lord Anjaneya, the vigraha represents Anjaneya, Bheema & Madhvacharya. It is strongly believed that if a devotee put some money alongwith coins available here, his wish will be fulfilled.

Important Temples in Maddur -

Varadarajawamy Temple - The Temple is an early Chola or pre-Chola structure. The vigraha of Lord Allalanatha is 12 ft high. The vigraha is elaborately carved both in front and on the back with unusual features which has led to the Kannada saying 'Ella Devara Munde Nodu Allalanathana hinde nodu' - 'All other vigrahas are to be seen from the front but Allalanatha is to be seen from the back'. The Temple was built by king Vishnuvardhana (formerly known as Bitti Deva).

Vidyanatheswara Temple at Vaidyanathapura - The village is situated on the banks of the Shimsha River, a tributary of the Kaveri river and houses the Temple of Vaidyanatheswara. The main presiding deity is Srivaidynatheshwara. As per belief, he is the main protector of Temple and devotees is the Serpent residing in the Temple always, which is safeguarding every devotee coming

to Temple with good faith and noble devotion. Especially panchamrutha abhishekam will be performed twice a day, priests performs abhishekam with wet clothes as per Agama procedures. Legend says that the deity has cured many illnesses and a great solace to his devotees and has been keeping them safe and happy. Being a Temple held with great reverence and faith among the devotees and despite holding a pristine history of uncounted ancience, the main deity Lord Vaidyanatheshwara is Swayambhu Lingam. This Temple is managed by the Deekshit family from time immemorial.

MELKOTE -

SRI CHELUVANARAYAN SWAMI TEMPLE - Melukote is one of the holy and sacred pilgrimages, as it is praised as Badarinath of South India. The holy city is located on the hillock called as Narayanagiri. The main presiding deity is Sri Cheluvnarayana Swamy, who was worshipped by Lord Dattatreya in Kritayuga and acquired the name Vedadri. In Tretayuga, it was known to Narayanadri followed by the name Yadavadri since the deity was worshipped by Sri Krishna & Balarama. In Kaliyuga, the deity was worshiped by the Saint Sri Ramanujacharya well known as Yathiraja Sarvabhowma (king of Yathis) who renovated the Temple.

SRI YOGANARASIMHA TEMPLE - On the top of the hill is an attractive Melkote Narasimha Temple dedicated to Lord Yoga Narasimha. It is believed that the vigraha of Yoga Narasimha Temple at Melkote was installed by Prahlada himself. Krishnaraja Wodeyar - III presented a gold crown to Lord Yoga Narasimha. The Temple infrastructure has a large pond called as Kalyani. The beauty of the steps leading to water and the mantapas built all around are such that it has been captured in many Indian films.

SRI NAMBINARAYANA SWAMY TEMPLE AT TONNUR - The Temple is dedicated to Lord Vishnu. It is known as 1st & oldest Pancha Narayana Kshetra where Indra Deva got relieved from Brahmahatya dosha. The vigraha of Lord Vishnu is believed to be more than 5500 years old. There is a strong belief that who ever visits the Pancha Narayana Kshetram, he gets moksha. There is a lake which is said to have been built under the guidance of Sri Ramanujacharya who named it Trirumalasagara, now called Moti Talab. The devotees believed that this lake has medicinal properties and its water has never dried up since its creation despite severe drought conditions.

SRI RANGANATHASWAMY TEMPLE AT SRIRANGAPATNA - It is learnt that originally Lord rested here looking towards the east. In the town, there are Temple of Sriranganatha, Sri Lakshinarasimha, Sri Gangadereshwara, Sri Jyothirmaheshwara and other small Temples. Among them, the main Temple is that of Sriranganatha. The inner apartment of Sriranganatha Temple was built in 817 AD by a lady, Hambi. The Temple of Lord Thirumala (Srinivasa) was constructed in 894 AD. The vigrahas of Lord Krishna, Sri Pattabhi Rama and Sri Gopala Krishna playing on the flute were installed later on. The water of Cauvery River is similar to the water of the sacred Viraj River which is found in Vykunta. The Temple of Lord Ranganatha is Vykunta itself. Lord Ranganatha has manifested himself in three places in the east at Srirangam, in the south at Ananthashaynam and in the west at Sriangapatna. Once Cauvery performed penance with prayer to Lord Ranganatha, the Lord was pleased with her penance and gave her three benedictions, viz.1) The River would have greater sacredness than the Ganges; 2)The place Srirangapatna would became a Kshetra, a place of pilgrimage and 3) The Ranganatha would settle himself here alone bestowing on his devotees their desires. Lord Ranganatha, then, was worshiped by the Cauvery and he took the form of an vigraha resting on Shree Adishesha. Sri Lakshmi visited the scared vigraha of Lord along with Cauvery and realized the greatness of the Great Lord. She then took bath in the scared river and after worshiping the Lord, took the form of an vigraha on the South East side of the Lord. Realizing the spiritual sacredness of the place, God Brahma, Rudra and others came there and worshiped Lord. Lord Brahma built Temples for the God and the Goddess. All the devas worshiped the Lord Brahma preached the Pancharathna method of worship to Sage Narada in order to worship Lord Ranganatha. The words of Lord Bramha to Sage Narada on the sacredness of this place are notable. No other place in the whole universe is equal in sacredness to this place. The Lord consented to the request of the rishis and graced them by saying that a bath in the Ashtathirtha on the Dasami day on the Thula month gives the devotees their desires as well as moksha.

Devi Nimishamba Temple - The Temple is located on the banks of River Cauvery. It is believed that Devi Nimishamba is an incarnation of Goddess Parvati. The vigraha have been consecrated with Srichakra which is carved on a black stone. The Temple is also having a Balipeetha which is a unique feature of the Temple. A big brass bell hangs in the ceiling of the Temple. After placing balibhojanam on balipeetha, the archaka rings the bell. Crows appear to eat balibhojanam. Devotees offer lemon/lemon garlands to the Goddess, which are placed on Sri Chakra & at the Goddess feet. Lemons are later kept in one's prayer room for few days and then brought in to fresh fallen water, wells or one can consume the lemon juice which is said to bring prosperity to a person. It is also believe that Devi Nimishamba removes obstacles in a minute, as Nimisha means minute in Kannada.

SRI ADICHUNCHANAGIRI MAHASAMSTHANA MATH AT NAGAMANGALA TALUK – It is a Socio-Spiritual centre, which has the history of 1500 years to its credit. Sri Math has been reverberated with the spiritual resonance which is inundated with the Spiritual penance of thousands of Saints and Siddhas. Sri Math has the holy lineage of spiritual masters which was

initiated by Lord Shiva at the end of his deep penance at Sri Kshetra Adichunchanagiri. Dharmapeeta thus established by Lord Shiva, witnessed 70 Jagadgurus the 71st pontiff being His Holiness Jagadguru Sri Sri Sri Dr. Balagangadharanatha Mahaswamiji and 72nd pontiff is His Holiness Jagadguru Sri Sri Sri Nirmalanandanatha Swamiji who is presently heading the Sri Math. After His Holiness Jagadguru Sri Sri Sri Dr. Balagangadharanatha Mahaswamiji, assumed the religious throne as Jagadguru started working towards the society in different areas. Government of India conferred "Padma Bhushan-2010" on swamiji for his out-standing contribution to the society in different field. The Math is having various Temples in Karnataka such as Adihalli Temple; Sri Gangadhareshwara Temple at Bengaluru & Sri Kshetra; Chickballapur Temple; Sri Chowdeshwari Temple at Dasarigatta; Sri Ganesha Temple at BG Nagar & Hassan; Kabali Temple; Seethi Temple; Lord Kalabhyraveshwara Temple at Shimoga; Shimoga Temple and Sri Nagalingeshwara Swamy Temple at Sri Kshetra.

VENUGOPALA SWAMI TEMPLE AT CHINAKURALI (Near Krishna Rajasagara Dam) - The original Temple was built by Hoysala rulers during 12th CE. When the Krishna Rajasagara Dam was constructed, the entire structure and the village where it was situated submerged completely but the complex remained intact & was visible whenever water of the dam recedes. The Temple remained submerged under water for 70 years. It is believed that if devotees are not able to have darshan of their Venugopala, then he comes near them. Sri Hari Khoday of Khoday foundation took the responsibility to relocate & restored the entire Temple complex. The mail vigraha of Sri Venugopala was shifted to the rehabilitated village Hosa Kannambadi before the summeesion.

DISTRICT – MYSURU (Railway Station – Mysuru / Mandya / Nanjangud Town)

Mysore is located in the foothills of Chamundi Hills. It served as capital city of the Kingdom of Mysore for nearly six centuries from 1399 until 1956. The Kingdom was ruled by the Wadiyar dynasty, with a brief period of interregnum in the late 18th century when Hyder Ali and Tipu Sultan were in power. The Wadiyars were patrons of art and culture. Tipu Sultan and Hyder Ali also contributed significantly to the cultural and economic growth of the city and the state by planting mulberry trees introducing silk in the region and fighting 4 Anglo-Mysore wars against the British. The cultural ambience and achievements of Mysore earned it the sobriquet Cultural Capital of Karnataka. Mysore is noted for its heritage structures and palaces, including the Mysore Palace, and for the festivities that take place during the Dasara festival when the city receives many tourists from around the world. It lends its name to various art forms and culture, such as Mysore Dasara, Mysore painting; the sweet dish Mysore Pak, Mysore Masala Dosa; brands such as Mysore Sandal Soap, Mysore Ink; and styles and cosmetics such as Mysore Peta (a traditional silk turban) and the Mysore silk saris. Mysore is also known for its special variety of jasmine flower fondly referred as "Mysore Mallige" and betel leaves.

S. No.	Temple	Address	Type
1	Sri Chamundeshwari Temple	Chamundi Hill, Mysuru – 570010	Shakti Peetha
2	Karyasiddhi Hanuman Temple	G. S. Ashram - 570025	Hanuman
3	Sidlu Mallikarjuna Hill Temple	Bettadapura - 571102	Shiva
4	Gommatagiri	Bilikere - 571103	Jain
5	Monastery	Bylakuppe – 571104	Buddhist
6	Prasanna Chennakeshava Temple	Somanathapura – 571120	Vishnu
7	Keerthi Narayana Temple	Taluk Bettahalli – 571122	Shiva
8	Sri Srikanteshwaraswamy Temple	Nanjangud – 571301	Shiva
9	Jwalamukhi Tripurasundari Temple	Mysuru - 571311	Mata
10	Kodanda Rama Temple	Chunchunakatte - 571604	Rama

MAHASHAKTIPEETHAM – SRI CHAMUNDESHWARI TEMPLE AT MYSURU - 'Chamundi' or 'Durga' is the fierce form of 'Shakti'. The Goddess is believed to be an incarnation of Goddess Parvati, the consort of Lord Shiva. She is the slayer of demons, 'Chanda' and 'Munda' and also 'Mahishasura', the buffalo-headed monster. She is the tutelary deity of Mysuru Maharajas and the presiding deity of Mysuru. For several centuries they have held the Goddess Chamundeswari in great reverence. 'Skanda Purana' and other ancient texts mention a sacred place called 'Trimuta Kshetra' surrounded by eight hills. Lying on the western side is Sri Chamundeshwari Temple, one among the eight hills. In the earlier days, the Hill was identified as 'Mahabaladri' in honour of God Shiva who resides in the 'Mahabaleswara Temple'. This is the oldest Temple on the hills. While going up the hills, a bird's eye view of Mysuru can be seen and several prominent places be spotted. It offers a spectacular scene when the Mysuru Palace and its surroundings are illuminated during the Dasara and other occasions. Blessed by the Goddess, Krishnaraja Wodeyar-III, an ardent devotee of the mother Goddess, presented to the Temple a 'Simha-vahana' (A lion-shaped vehicle) and other animal cars and jewels of value. The cars are used even now for processions on special religious occasions. Besides the Chamundi and Mahabaleswara Temples, there are a few more Temples atop the hills. There are also some interesting spots and the monolith vigraha of 'Nandi' is among them.

While proceeding towards the Chamundi Temple, the vigraha of 'Mahishasura' attracts the visitors. The Temple is of a quadrangular structure built in Dravidian style and it consists of the main doorway, entrance, Navaranga Hall, Antharala Mantapa, Sanctum Sanctorum and Prakara. There is a beautiful seven-tier Gopura or pyramidal tower at the entrance and a 'Vimana' (small tower) atop the sanctum sanctorum. Atop the 'Shikara', the tower at the entrance, are seven golden 'Kalashas'. The tower at the entrance has a small vigraha of Lord Ganesha on the doorway. The doorway is silver-plated and has the vigrahas of the Goddess in different forms. On either side of the

doorway are the vigrahas of 'Dwarapalakas' or door-keepers. As one enters inside, on the right hand side is a small vigraha of Lord Ganesha, the remover of all obstacles. After a few steps, there is a flagstaff, the footprints of the Goddess and a small vigraha of Nandi, facing the sanctum sanctorum. On the right side, before approaching the flag staff, there is an vigraha of 'Anjaneya' attached to the wall. On either side of this entrance are two Dikpalakas, Nandini and Kamalini.

KARYASIDDHI HANUMAN TEMPLE AT G. S. ASHRAM - The Temple is dedicated to Lord Hanuman. The Temple has a beautiful vigraha of Lord Hanuman. Karya means wish or act. Siddhi means realizing. Karya Siddhi Hanuman is one who fulfills your wishes.

Nimbuja Devi Temple AT Mysuru - The Temple is dedicated to Sri Nimbuja Devi. The vigraha of the Goddess is in standing posture. There are various sringars done by the priest on daily basis & during festive season. Devotees visit the Temple in large numbers on Friday & special occasions.

SIDLU MALLIKARJUNA HILL TEMPLE AT BETTADAPURA - The place has traditionally been associated as 'Srigiri' from the times of epics. The hillock representing the last span of Western Ghats is also known as Vijayagiri & Vijayachala. From the lithic records available, Paramabbe, wife of Ganga Bhutuga-I, circa 7th CE AD was ruling from this place known as Kurugal. The Gangas were succeeded by the Cholas, Vijayanagara & Chengalva rulers. The Temple datable to circa 12th CE AD belongs to the Chola-Hoysala period. There are many inscriptions in the Temple. The Temple on the summit of the hill, dedicated to Lord

Mallikarjuna, is reached by climbing nearly 3108 steps. The main shrine comprising of sanctum, ardhamandapa & navaranga is enclosed by a series of pillared structures. There is a gateway in Vijayanagara style with a tallrayagopura at the foot of the hill. The inner ceiling of this gopura has paintings of Vijayanagara times depicting floral designs and pictures. The pillars of the navaranga are short and cylindrical & pilasters on the garbhagriha walls have Chola-Hoysala features. There are huge copper vessels of antiquity here to indicate large scale feeding of pilgrims and the enshrined deity is also called Annadani Mallikarjuna.

GOMMATAGIRI AT BILIKERE - Gommatagiri is an acclaimed Jain centre. The 700-year-old vigraha of Lord Bahubali (also known as Gomateshwara) is erected atop a 50 meter tall hillock called 'Shravana Gudda'. The vigraha is an early Vijayanagara creation in granite. It has serene facial expressions and curly hairs. This Jain centre attracts many pilgrims during the annual "Maha Masthakabhisekha" in September. The local have a belief that the entire region was a bastion of Jainism at least since the 2nd Century BC. The 20 ft. vigraha is very similar to Gommateshwara vigraha in Shravanabelagola (58 ft.) except that it is dwarfed in size.

BYLAKUPPE - Known for handicrafts, incense and carpet factories as well as monasteries, it is one of the largest settlements of Tibetans in the southern part of the country. The most important of monasteries here include Sera Mey and the Great Gompa of Sera Jey. Also located here is the Mahayana Buddhist University with an enormous prayer hall. In the neighbouring settlement is Tashi Lhunpo, which is known as the seat of the Panchen Lama. This place is most famously associated with the Namdrolig Nyingmapa Monastery.

ISKCON - In the year 1999, His Grace Stoka Krishna Prabhu along with few other devotees rented a house in Gokulam to house the deities of Sri Sri Krishna Balarama, which began the journey of ISKCON, Mysuru. A temporary structure was built in the year 2004 and the deities of Sri Sri Krishna Balarama were brought to their new place along with the starting of Akshaya Patra kitchen feeding 2000 school children everyday. The plan for the construction of new cultural centre named "Nava Brindavan Dham" was conceived by His Grace Jai Chaitanya Prabhu and Her Grace Bhaktilatha Devi Mataji in the year 2008. A new Akshaya Patra kitchen was inaugurated in June, 2009 by then Chief Minister of Karnataka B S Yeddyurappa. In year 2012, beautiful marble Deities of Sri Sri Krishna Balarama arrived from Bellary much to pleasure of Mysuru devotees. This was followed by the installation of Utsava Deities of Sri Sri Lakshmi Narasimha on 3rd May 2015. On the auspicious occasion of Vijaya Dashami 11th Oct. 2016, the Bhumi Puja for the Nava Brindavan Dham project was conducted. This was followed by the 'Shilanyas' on 2nd April, 2017 performed by H.E. Vajubhai Rudhabhai Vala, Hon'ble Governor.

NAMDROLING NYINGMAPA MONASTERY - It is the largest teaching centre of Nyingmapa, the lineage of Tibetan Buddhism in the world. The Monastery belongs to the Sangha community and it is here that the teachings of Lord Buddha are preserved intact for worldwide propagation. It was founded by His Holiness Pema Norby Rinpoche in 1963 as the second seat of the Palyul monastery (one of the six great Tibet Nyingma Mother monasteries). The Monastery is home to over 5,000 nuns and monks and also has a retreat centre where 30 monks have undergone an intensive three-year retreat. The Monastery is adorned by several golden paintings. While today it is a resplendent place of worship and meditation, it started off as nothing more than a bamboo structure spread over only 80 sq ft and will leave one amazed with its monumental transformation.

PRASANNA CHENNAKESHAVA TEMPLE AT SOMANATHAPURA - This Temple was built in 1268 by Somanatha, who was general of King Narasimha-III during the Hoysala reign. The exquisitely carved, star-shaped Kesava Temple with triple towers is a perfect example of Hoysala architecture. It is Trikuta Temple with three shrines. The three shrines had vigrahas of Lords Keshava, Janardhana and Venugopala. At the entrance of the Temple, you can see a stone slab with inscriptions on the Temple's history carved on it. The friezes on its outer walls with their intricately carved rows of caparisoned elephants, charging horsemen and mythological birds and beasts will leave you spellbound. Beautifully sculpted vigrahas of gods, goddesses and scenes from the epics, as well as the remarkably ornate ceilings in the pillared hall will take your breath away. Another striking aspect of the Temple is the sixteen different types of ceilings, with each showcasing a different stage that goes during the blooming of plantain. It has been nominated for the status of UNESCO World Heritage Site. Now, it is maintained by the Archaeological Survey of India.

Mudukuthore Mallikarjuna Temple - The Temple is dedicated to Lord Shiva. The Temple is one among the Panchalinga Darshana around Talakadu which is held once in every twelve years. It is believed that Pandava brother Arjuna stayed here for some time and consecrated the Shivalinga and offered Mallika (Jasmine) flowers. There are hundred steps to reach the Temple. There is also a Temple dedicated to Devi Bhramaramba.

TALAKAD - The Kaveri River makes a sharp bend and on the left banks at this turn is Talakad, also known as Talakadu. Talakad is a historic site and of archaeological importance. It's not only a spiritual pilgrimage centre but is a scenic beauty with vast spreads of sand. Talakad came under the Hoysala Empire in the 12th century. Among the Temples of Talakad, the five Lingams believed to represent the five faces of Lord Shiva and the Pancha Pathi are famous. They are Pathaleshwara, Maruleshwara, Arkeshwara, Vaidyanatheeshwara and Mallikarjuna Temples. As a tribute to these

five Shiva Temples, a festival is held once every 12 years called Panchalinga Darshana. The Panchalinga Darshana is held on a new moon day in the month of Karthika when two stars conjoin, the stars of Khuha Yoga and Vishaka. On this day, tradition has it that pilgrims should first bathe in the Gokarna Theertham, worship Gokarneswara & Chandikadevi and then worship Vaidyeshwara, Arkeshwara, Pataleshwara, Maraleshwara, Mallikarjuna and finally worship Kirtinarayana and conclude the pilgrimage in one day.

SRIKANTESHWARA TEMPLE AT NANJANGUD - Nanjangud is famous for its Temple dedicated to Lord Shiva described as Nanjundeshwara. Nanjunda means one who has consumed poison and this legend relates to the churning of the ocean, when Lord Shiva had to consume haalahala. Nanjunda became Vishakanta and also Srikanta for having digested it. Hence the deity is also known as Srikanteshwara, one cures diseases. The town is situated on the banks of the Kapila or Kabini River where a dip in its waters on any momentous occasion is considered to be more meritorious than a dip in the Ganges. It is therefore hailed as Dakshina Kashi. In addition, the waters and the soil around the banks are believed to possess curative properties and thus, Sri Nanjundeshwara is also worshipped as Bhavaroga Vaidya. Tippu Sultan called him Hakim Nanjunda and gifted an emerald Linga and a valuable emerald necklace as votive offerings for having cured his favourite elephant of an eye disease. Referred to as Garalapuri in the Puranas, Nanjangudu has been praised as a holy place sanctified by Parasurama and Gauthama. Parashurama, it is said, prayed for the grace of Srikanteshwara to expiate himself of the sin of beheading his mother Renuka. Folk legends call the place as the dwelling of Nanjayya later identified as Lord Shiva with ballads on Nanjayya describing his romantic interlude with Chamundi of Mysore. The Temple is the biggest Temple in Karnataka. The Mahadvara (main entrance) is seven – storey high and is decorated with seven gold plated Kalasas. A spacious courtyard (Prakara) welcomes hundreds of pilgrims to the divine abode of Lord Shiva and offers a veritable galaxy of stucco figures as it boasts of more than 122 vigrahas including Dikpalas, the largest number of Sculptures relating to Lord Shiva and his various manifestations, several forms of Lord Subramanya, Saptamatrikas and others. There are many exquisite bronze icons that vie for attention and prominent among them are Tandaveshvara, Narayana with Bhudevi, Chandrashekaramurthi, Parvati, Chandikeshvara and others. The inner niches of the Temple wall also depict 32 forms of Ganapathi eulogized in the Mudgala Purana and each is more enchanting than the other. On the banks of the Kapila River is the Parashurama Kshetra and people firmly believe that a pilgrimage to Nanjangudu would be incomplete without a prayer here. There are other Temples dedicated to Gauthama, Ganapathi, Dattatreyaas well as Raghavendra Swami Mutt and Virasaiva Mutts.

Girija Kalyana held in the month of Mithuna (July) is a grand celebration of the marriage of Shiva with Parvati and it is a feast to the eyes to witness both these bejewelled deities resplendent in all their finery. The Temple possesses five exquisitely carved wooden chariots and three among them are pulled on the occasion of Chikka Jathra held in the month of Vrischika (November) and all the five chariots during the Panchamaharathotsava in the month of April. Maha Shivarathri and Navarathri are other festivals celebrated with devotion and fervour on a very grand scale. The Temple is a centrally protected monument.

Jwalamukhi Tripurasundari Temple at Uthanahalli - The Temple is dedicated to Tripura Sundari which means beauty of the three worlds. The Goddess is believed to be the sister of Chamundeshwari Devi. It is also believed that she represent the flaming mouth of jalandhara, the demon whom Lord Shiva crushed to death. When Chamundeshwari Devi was fighting with demon Mahishasura, she observed that from every drop of blood which spilt out of demon Mahishasura, another demon is born, hence she created Tripurasundari to ensure that no blood could be dripped from demon Mahishasura. The vigraha of the Goddess had been consecrated during Wodeyar rule. There is also an utsava vigraha which is made of Panchaloha and the same is installed in the Sanctum Sanctorum. There is also a Temple dedicated to Lord Siddheshwara which is surrounded by a wodden mantapa.

KODANDA RAMA TEMPLE AT CHUNCHUNAKATTE - The Temple is dedicated to Lord Kodandarama. It is an ancient Temple. The uniqueness of the vigraha installed here is that Sita Mata is standing to the right side of Lord Sri Rama instead of the usual left. Legend describes that Lord Rama during his exile period stayed in this place on the behest of the tribal couple Chuncha and Chunchi. It seems during that time, there was not a drop of water here and when Sita Mata wanted to have a bath, Lord Rama instructed Laxmana to facilitate her wish. Laxmana shot an arrow on the rocks and water started gushing out in plenty and she could take her bath. Also in this forest, Lord Rama met Agnatha Rishi and was impressed by his devotion to Lord Narayana, so Lord Rama asked the Rishi to ask for a boon and the Rishi asked Lord Rama that he desired to see Lord Rama with Sita on his right side. The boon was granted and so was the vigraha installed in the same manner. There are two Lord Hanuman Temples, one at the entrance to the Temple and the other after the Temple near the River. The most astonishing feature of this Temple is that even though the falls beside the Temple makes a deafening noise but inside the Sanctum Sanctorum, nothing of the roar can be heard. Brahma Rathotsava is held on the day of Makara Sankranthi every year. The cattle festival, which is one of the biggest in this region, is held during January first week.

DISTRICT - RAICHUR (Railway Station – Raichur)

S. No.	Temple	Address	Type
1	Kurugadde Sripada Srivallabha, Jitamitragadde, Naradaggade & Ramagadde	Kuruvapur - 584102	Saint Srivallabha, Sage Narada, Ramayana Circuit
2	Gabburu Group of Temples	Gabbur - 584113	Hanuman, Vishnu
3	Kalluru Lakshmi Temple	Kallur - 584118	Mata
4	Tryambakeshwara Temple	Kowthal - 584120	Shiva
5	Amareshwara Temple	Devarbhupur, Lingsugur Taluk - 584122	Shiva
6	Group of Temples	Manvi – 584123	Mata
7	Mallikarjun Temple	Maski - 584124	Shiva
8	Ambadevi Temple	Somalapur - 584128	Mata
9	Hanuman Temple	Balaganur – 584138	Hanuman
10	Sri Panchamukhi Hanuman Temple	Gandhal - 584140	Hanuman
11	Sri Rama Mandir	Mukkunda - 584167	Rama, Mata
12	Veerabhadra Temple	Devarsugur – 584170	Shiva
13	Group of Temples	Kadlur - 584170	River Bank

KURUVAPUR - Sripada Srivallabha was an Indian guru of Dattatreyasampradaya who is regarded as the first incarnation of Lord Dattatreya. He was born and lived in Pithapuram. He is considered as one of the first complete Avatars (incarnations) of the deity Dattatreya in Kali Yuga. It is believed that the Avatar Sripada Srivallabha is 'Chiranjeevi' (immortal) and that he took 'Jalsamadhi' in Kuravapura or Kurugaddi, an island on River Krishna. He disappeared since then as a human but still exists in 'Tejorup' (in pure energy form). Sometime after Vallabha disappeared, a Brahmin named Vallabhesh vowed to go to Kuravapur and feed 1,000 Brahmins if he earned more than his usual profit. Near Kuravapur, he encountered bandits in disguise who robbed and beheaded him. Vallabha suddenly appeared from nowhere and killed the bandits with his Trishula; one, who appealed to the saint as Shiva, was spared. Vallabha asked him to reattach Vallabhesh's severed head to his body and brought him back to life. Vallabhesh Brahmin completed his vow and became a disciple of Sripada Srivallabha. Vallabhesh Brahmin is considered the mula-purush (founder) of the Hedgewar family. Sh K. B. Hedgewar, founder of the Rashtriya Swayamsevak Sangh, was a ninth-generation descendant of Vallabhesh.

JITAMITRAGADDE HOLY BATH - Jitamitragadde, another island in the Krishna River, is a sacred place for the Hindus who visit the place all the year round for a holy bath.

KORVA - It is a beautiful island surrounded by the Krishna River. It is looked upon as a holy place and is popularly known as Naradagadde, where Sage Narada is said to have performed penance. It has a Temple dedicated to Narada, a famous Veerashaiva Matha, the samadhi of Vairagya Channabasavaswami who lived about four centuries ago and was well known for his mystic wisdom, a Shivayoga Peetha and a Basavanna Temple. The annual jatra at this place attracts a large number of people and a cattle fair is also held at the time.

RAMAGADDE - It is a beautiful island in the Krishna River. It is looked upon as a holy place. According to a legend, Sri Ramachandra stayed here for a year and consecrated and worshipped a Shivalinga. It has a Veerashaiva Matha.

GABBURU - It is called the Temple town of Raichur District. There are as many as 30 Temples and 28 rock edicts in the town. In ancient times, Gabbur was also known as Garbhapura and Gopuragrama. Many of these Temples were built during the reign of the Kalyani Chalukyas. Some of the prominent Temples of Gabbur are the Hanuman, the Ishwara, the Venkateshwara, the Male Shankara, the Bangara Basappa, the Mahanandeeshwara, the Elu Bhaavi Basavanna and the Boodi Basaveshwara Temple.

KALLUR - It is an archaeological site came into prominence with the discovery of antennae swords in the 1930s, which was the first instance of the Copper Hoard culture being discovered in South India. The earliest finding here has been dated to the Neolithic period. Kallur Mahalaxmi Temple is one of the finest examples of the existence of the power of love, faith, devotion and surrendarence to God. Kallur is also called as "Second Kolhaphur" where Goddess Mahalakshmi dwells. The Temple has vigrahas of both Lord Venkateshwara and Mahalakshmi. It belongs to the Madhwas (a sect of Brahmins-followers of Madhwacharya).

KAVITAL - It has an interesting medieval Temple in the village, called Tryambakeshwara Temple, which has three shrines, two of which contain Lingas. There are two Kannada inscriptions in the Temple and a beautiful vigraha of Mahishasuramardini in one of the two niches in its western wall. All the three shrines are of a uniform size, each being 9 ft deep and 8 ft broad and each one has an ante-chamber. The exterior of the Temple is plain, but the masonry work is very impressive. The shikharas of the shrines, which are of the Dravidian style, have been built up to about two-thirds of their height in dressed stone, while the remaining portion had been completed in brick and lime.

DEVARBHUPUR - It is noted for its Amareshwara Temple. The Temple is beautifully situated amidst hillocks, which have green foliage. Under the auspices of this Temple, annually a big jatra takes place in the month of Phalguna when a cattle fair is also held.

MANVI - Manvi is a place of pilgrimage where several fairs and festivals are held, the chief of which are Karemma Jatra held in January for two days, the Yellamma Jatra held in February for seven days, the Mahamalleshappa Jatra held usually in January and the Sanjeevaraya Jatra held in December. Manvi is also the birth-place of Jagannatha Dasa who spread the bhakti cult.

MASKI - It is a town and an archaeological site located on the bank of Maski River. Maski derives its name from Mahasangha or Masangi. The site came into prominence with the discovery of a minor rock edict of Emperor Ashoka by C. Beadon in 1915. Here is a famous Temple named as Maski Mallikarjun Temple.

SOMALPUR - It is well known for its Ambadevi Temple, situated at the foot of a hill, where annually a fair takes place in the month of Pushya, which is largely attended.

BALAGANUR - Hanumanji Jatra at Balaganurheld in Vaishakha lasts for three days. A cattle show is also held as an adjunct to the religious fair.

Ganadhal - It also spelled as Ganadhala is famous for the Sri Panchamukhi Hanuman Temple where Sri Raghavendra Swamiji did penance for 12 years.

MUKKUNDA - It is located on the banks of Tungabhadra River. It has several ancient Temples including Sri Rama Mandir, Shri Durgamma Temple, the Murari Ranga and the Baajeshwara Temple. The Tungabhadra River surrounds an Eshwara Temple built in Hoysala style during the Sindha dynasty. A Sufi Saint, Khadarlinga Mukkunda is well known and many visitors from surrounding village will come to take the blessings of this saint.

DEVARSUGUR - It is a small village located on the right bank of Krishna River and is mainly famous for Sugureshwara or Veerabhadra Temple. This Temple is known for its annual 'jatra', which is held in the Hindu month of Margashirsha.

KADLUR - Kadlur is looked upon as a sacred place. To the north of this village, the River Bhima joins the Krishna River. According to an inscription found at Chikalparvi, the Vijayanagara King Krishnadevaraya visited this pilgrim center with his family and offered worship.

DISTRICT – RAMANAGARA (Railway Station – Bidadi/KSR Bengaluru)

S. No.	Temple	Address	Type
1	Sri Lakshmi Narasimha Swamy Temple	Sugganahalli - 561101	Narasimha
2	Shiva Temple	Shivagange - 562111	Shiva
3	Ranganathaswamy Temple	Magadi – 562120	Vishnu
4	Sri Kabbalamma Temple	Kabbal – 562126	Mata
5	Revanasiddeshwara Hill	Avverahalli – 562159	Shiva
6	Sri Chamundi Amma	Channapatna - 562160	Mata
7	Anjaneyaswamy Temple	Kengal – 562160	Hanuman
8	Sri Aprameya Devasthana	Malur - 562160	Krishna

SRI LAKSHMI NARASIMHA SWAMY TEMPLE AT SUGGANAHALLI - The Temple is dedicated to Lord Narasimha. The vigraha of Lord Narasimha is very unique as Lord Narasimha's vigraha is in standing posture & facing west unlike every were else. Garuda Devta is also worshipped here daily. It is believed that Shukra Muni have done penance under a Badri tree where the present Temple is situated. Shukra Muni had also darshan of Garuda Devta at this place so Garuda Devta is also worshipped here. Devotees seek relief from skin ailments and other diseases by praying Garuda Devta. Special offerings are made to a cardamom tree in the back yard of the Temple where devotees can have darshan of Lord Narasimha's devine feet. Brahma Rathotsava & Gaurdotsava are major festivals here.

SHIVA TEMPLE AT SHIVAGANGE - The Temple is dedicated to Lord Shiva. There is a Oralakallu Teertha, which is a small Well like formation with devine spring nandi at the top. The speciality of the Temple is that Shivalinga is believed to turns ghee into butter.

RANGANATHASWAMY TEMPLE AT MAGADI - The Rangantha Temple is belongs to Cholas period. The Temple is also built in an elevated placed called Swarnadri Parvata. There is vast prakara with a gateway having tall rajagopura. The garbhagriha has a dravidashikara having

Vijayanagara workmanship. The presiding deity of the Temple is Lord Vishnu in his standing posture, similar to the one in Tirupati. The name of this Temple is actually Paschima Venkatachalapthi Temple as the presiding deity faces west. The area in which the Temple is located is called Tirumale. However nowadays it is more popular as Ranganatha Temple due to the presence of a small vigraha of Rangatha on the Temple wall which is believed to be growing in size every year.

SOMESHWARA TEMPLE AT MAGADI - According to the noted epigraphist and historian B. Lewis Rice, the Someshwara Temple was built by Kempe Gowda-II after coming to power in 1569 A.D. However, there is another view that the Temple was actually built by his descendant Kempavira Gowda-III in 1712 A.D. Notable structures in the large Temple complex include a spacious inner prakara (courtyard) with lofty towers and mantapas (halls). Pillar decor includes motifs of dancing girls, soldiers, birds, and animals such as lions in relief. The complex includes a small shrine for Goddess Parvati, consort of Lord Shiva. A short distance from the complex is a mantapa for Nandi, the vehicle of the Lord Shiva.

SRI KABBALAMMA TEMPLE AT KABBAL - It is one of the most enigmatic shrines in Karnataka, which is dedicated to Goddess Shakti or Kabbalamma. The main deity is represented in a sculpture, the central shrine of the Temple. Other sculptures include that of a Nandi or bull and a small wooden rath or chariot is also one of the attractions in the Temple. From the gateway to the mandapas, the Temple is adorned with intricate stone art, depicting the many representations and stories of the mythology associated with the deity. It is believed that those looking for a good marriage or well-being for their spouse can come and offer prayers at this shrine.

REVANASIDDESHWARA HILL AT AVVERAHALLI - Revanasiddeshwara Betta is a Shaiva Temple in India. It is situated 935 m above sea level. This place is commonly called as SRS Betta. There are 3 Temples on the site - at the top is Revanasiddeshwara Betta, midway is Bheemeshwari (named after the Pandava brother Bheema) and at the base is Renukamba Temple. Sri Revana Siddeshwara is considered as a reincarnation of the great Jagadguru Shri Renukacharya who was ordered by Lord

Shiva to take incarnation on earth to spread Bhakti among the people. With the blessings of Lord Shiva, Jagadguru Renukacharya (also known as Revanaradhya or Revanasiddha) was one of the five acharyas who came in the Kali Yuga to teach and preach Virasaivism. He is aforesaid to possess been born from the Somesvaralinga, however, to possess travelled everywhere to show Virasaivism. The Someshwara Temple is located in Kollipaki. Texts date this legendary Saint to the time of the Ramayana since he was the teacher of the Sage Agastya of Panchavati. This Saint is alleged to possess consecrated thirty million Lingas at the bid of Ravana's brother, Vibhishana, once Ravana's death. He finally established the Rambhapuri Matha. The Renuka gotra of the Virasaivas is known as once him.

SRI CHAMUNDI AMMA AT CHANNAPATNA - The vigraha is dedicated to Sri Chamundi Amma, who is the mother Chamundeshwari Devi of Channapatna. The vigraha is 60 ft. tall and made of five metals such as gold, silver, copper, brass & bronze. The vigraha is 35000 kg. of weight and 18 ft. of mild.

ANJANEYASWAMY TEMPLE AT KENGAL - This Temple was built during the period of Karnataka's 2nd Chief Minister, Sri Kengal Hanumanthaiah, who was also the chief architect of Vidhana Soudha, the legislature building in Bangalore. This Temple is older than 60 years.

Mallur - Mallur is located on the banks of the River Kanva. The village is famous for its Temples of Sri Ramaprameya Swamy, Aravindavalli and Ambegalu Navaneeta Krishna (crawling Krishna) This Temple was built by the Great Chola dynasty, South Indian Tamil rulers may be in the 12th century. The vigraha of Ambegalu Navaneetha Krishna (crawling Krishna with butter in hand), is believed to be the only deity of Lord Sri Krishna in this pose. This vigraha was installed by Vyasaraja (aka Vyasatirtha), who was a prominent saint of Dvaita Vedanta. The famous Kriti (musical composition or song)

"Jagadodharana Adisidale Yashode" was composed by most prominent composer of Carnatic music Purandaradasa in appreciation of the beauty of this vigraha.

DISTRICT – SHIVAMOGGA (Railway Station – Bhadravati/Sagar Jambagaru/Shivamogga)

S. No.	Temple	Address	Type
1	Group of Temples	Shivamogga - 577201	Ganesh, Mata
2	Sri Venkateshwara Swamy Temple	Navile - 577204	Venkatesh
3	Smartha Monastery	Kudli - 577227	Sangam
4	Lakshmi Narasimha Temple	Bhadravati – 577301	Vishnu
5	Aghoresvara Temple	Ikkeri – 577401	Shiva
6	Rameshwara Temple	Keladi – 577401, Sagara Taluk	Shiva
7	Kaitabheshvara Temple	Kubatur - 577413	Shiva
8	Kundadri Hills	Kundadri – 577424	Jain
9	Group of Temples	Nagara – 577425	Shiva, Vishnu
10	Kedareshvara Temple	Balligavi – 577427	Shiva
11	Group of Temples	Bandalike – 577428	Shiva, Jain
12	Group of Temples	Talagunda – 577428	Shiva
13	Group of Temples	Chandragutti – 577429	Mata
14	Sri Kallare Ganapathi Temple	Thirthahalli - 577432	Ganpati
15	Sri Humcha Padmavathi Devi Digamber Jain Temple	SH 1, Humcha – 577436	Jain
16	Sri Pranaveshwara Temple	Talagunda - 577450	Shiva
17	Sarvajna Peetha	Kodachadri, Nagodi - 577452	Adi Shankara
18	Sri Sigandhur Chowdeshwari Kshetram	Tumary - 577453	Mata

SHIVAMOGGA - There are various shrines such as Ganapathi Devasthana in Ramanna Shreste Park, Basaveshwar Temple in Gandhi Bazar, Marikamba Devasthana, Kannika Parmeshwari etc. and it is said that there are 21 or more Ganapathi Devasthanas around Shivamogga city.

SRI VENKATESHWARA SWAMY TEMPLE AT NAVILE - The Temple is dedicated to Lord Venkateshwara. It is an old & famous Temple. There is a special festival on the auspicious occasion of Vaikuntha Ekadashi in addition to various other festivals.

KUDLI - The place where Rivers Tunga and Bhadra embrace and flow together from here, hence, the name Koodali. A cultural place with rich heritage and Temples around. It has a noted Smartha Monastery stated to have been founded in 16th century by Jagadguru Narsimha Bharathi Swamigalu of Sringeri. Within the premises of the Matha, there are shrines of Sharadamba and

Shankaracharya. Outside, there are two Temples of Hoysala times dedicated to Rameshvara and Narasimha. Koodali is also known as Varanasi of the south. It is home to Rushyashrama, Brahmeshwara, Narasimha and Rameshwara Temples. The 600 years old Mutt of Shankaracharya still stands with inscriptions of Hoysala and Okkeri Kings.

LAKSMI NARASIMHA TEMPLE AT BHADRAVATI - It is an 800 years old Temple and dedicated to Lord Vishnu. There is a popular myth related to the formation of the small town of Bhadravathi. It is believed that here Lord Vishnu in the avatar of Varaha rescued Bhudevi. She was held captive under the sea by demon Hirayankasha. As per Holy Scriptures, when Varaha lifted earth with his two tusks, River Tunga and Bhadra were formed. The Temple was constructed by Sir M Vishweshwaraiah, the grandson of an eminent Hoysala monarch, Vishnuvardhana. The sculptures of the Temple also exhibit the daily lifestyle of 13th century along with the vigrahas of musicians and dancers. The Temple consists of other vigrahas of Hindu gods namely, Sri Krishna, Lord Purushottama, Lord Ganesha and Goddess Sharadamba. The vigraha of Lord Narasimha is in a relaxed position protecting his devotee Prahlada. Soapstone has been used to construct the Temple. If you touch the walls, there is a soapy feeling and the stone is really tender. There is a flagpole, known as dwajasthambam in front of the Temple. The stellate tower is another special form of Hoysala architecture. The tiers of the tower step by step diminish in height to form an umbrella. There is a slab in Kannada inscription at the Temple which exhibits the construction details.

Uddhamanjaneya Temple at Gangur - The Temple is dedicated to Lord Anjaneya. The vigraha of Lord Anjaneya is very unique & it is in standing posture & is believed to be growing in size. In the Temple, the devotee is the priest as devotees are allowed to touch the vigraha & worship.

AGHORESVARA TEMPLE AT IKKERI - The Temple is a large structure, built of granite, in a uniquely mixed style that incorporates elements from Vijayanagara architecture, the Karnata Dravida style of the Chalukya dynasty & Hoysala Empire. The Temple faces north & has lofty roof & ornamental doorways on the west, north & east, the north doorway being the best with two elephants at the sides. The Garbha Griha, which is built of huge stones, contains a gigantic pedestal occupying nearly 3/4 of the whole space & sculptured all round with 32 seated female figures called Shakti Peetha. In Sukhanasi is a small translucent Nandi carved out of white spar. The Temple has no navaranga doorway there are two niches, those to the right containing the figures of Ganesha & Subramanya & those to the left figures of Mahishasuramardini & Bhairava. There are intricate carvings on stone walls of the Temple. There are carvings & sculptures such as Temple Relief, Erotica, Figurine, Old Kannada Manuscript, Sculpted Elephant etc. At present it is maintained by ASI.

Marikamba Temple at Sagar - The Temple features the vigraha of the Goddess Marikamba, a form of Durga or Parvati. The Temple was built in the center of the city during the reign of Venkatappa Nayak who ruled over Keladi and Ikkeri kingdom during the 16th century. Marikamba was the family deity of the Nayaka dynasty. Adi Shankaracharya, the philosopher Saint, during one of his tours around South India visited Sagar. During his stay in the town Goddess Marikamba appeared in his dream and told him to establish a Temple for her at this place. He then consecrated the foot prints of the Goddess at the outer limits of the city. Venkatappa Nayaka adopted the deity as his family goddess seeking blessings to attain victory in the battle. After he won the battle, he shifted the footprints of the goddess from the outskirts to a central location in the city and built a Temple to house the footprints. Every three years, in the month of February, a 10-day fair is held. Known as the Marikamba Jathra ('Jathra' means "fair"), it is one of the major festivals of Karnataka. On this occasion, a 16 feet high chariot, colourfully decorated and carrying the vigraha of the vigraha, is taken out on a procession.

RAMESHWARA TEMPLE AT KELADI – Constructed in the Hoysala-Dravida style, the Temple is magnificent with a number of unique features. The Temple built by the ruler Chowdappa Nayaka has three main shrines, namely that of Rameshwara, Parvati and Veerabhadra. The specialty of the Parvati Temple is its exquisite ceiling that is covered with intricate flower patterns carved from wood, of which no two are the same. The Veerabhadra Temple has some really rare sculptures like that of the Gods of the nine planets aka 'Navagraha' as well as the serpent motif or 'Nagamandala'. The vigraha of Daksha Prajapati, featuring goat-head and the awe-inspiring carvings of 'Vastu Purush' (god of structures), are some of the rare examples of artistry found here. The massive 24-feet pillar or Mahasthambha in the backyard which has Ganesha deity with Rani Chennamma paying respects, along with her consorts, is yet another highlight of the Temple.

KAITABHESHVARA TEMPLE AT KUBATUR - The Temple is also spelt Kaitabhesvara or Kaitabheshwara. It is also known as Kotisvara. The Temple was constructed during the reign of Hoysala King Vinayaditya around 1100 AD. The Hoysala ruling family was during this time a powerful feudatory of the imperial Western Chalukya Empire ruled by King Vikramaditya-VI. According to the Archaeological Survey of India, the architectural signature of the Temple is mainly "Chalukyan". Art Historian, Adam Hardy classifies the style involved in the construction of the Temple as "Later Chalukya, non mainstream, far end of spectrum". The building material used is soapstone. The Temple has a single square shaped shrine with an east–west orientation, a vestibule that connects the sanctum to the main large open hall that has a staggered square plan and can be entered from five sides, two lateral and one each in the north, south and east. The walls of the shrine and vestibule stand on a base that is composed of five moldings. The superstructure over the sanctum is four-tiered. It is crowned by a large domed roof that looks like a "helmet" and whose shape follows the shape of the shrine. The "helmet" is the largest sculptural piece in the Temple, it is beautifully carved and well decorated. Atop the dome, is a beautiful water-pot like stone structure that forms the pinnacle of the tower. The sculptures of Mahishamardini, Bhairava and Ganesha can be found on the main tower. The base of the outerwall of the open hall has decorative motifs, pilasters surmounted by miniature decorative pyramidal shaped turrets with gargoyle faced scrolls. The seating area in the hall is treated with floral decorations. The ceilings are ornate and the typical Hoysala style parapet over the eaves has sculptural representations of Ugra Narasimha, Varaha, Garuda and Keshava. The doorjamb at the entrance to the vestibule and sanctum are typically ornate and Hoysala in character, with the lintel displaying a sculpture of "Gajalakshmi". The Temple is protected as a monument of national importance by the Archaeological Survey of India.

KUNDADRI - The place is known as Kundadri hill. This place is also a Jain pilgrimage centre. On reaching the top, you can find Parshwanath Chaityalaya, a stone structure. The Hill is in fact a single gigantic monolithic rock formation with various outgrowths. From the hilltop, you can see the twists and turns of the Thirthahalli - Agumbe road.

Nagara - A 16th century place was also known as "Beendanoor". This place was also capital of Keladi rulers and later on was captured by Hyder Ali. Other places of interest are Shivappanaika Palace, Neelakenteshwara Temple, Devagana Tank and Gudde Venkataramana Swamy Temple.

KEDARESHVARA TEMPLE AT BALLIGAVI - The garbhagriha to the west and south contain the Shivalinga and to the north has an vigraha of the Lord Vishnu. The Temple is connected with the legend of demon Bali according to some lithic records. In its heyday, the Temple attracted a large number of followers of the Kalamukha sect of Shaivism. A four faced vigraha of the god Brahma, which at one time may have been inside the Temple, is on display in a museum within the Temple complex. The Temple is in trikuta style with the shrines facing east, north and south. The western shrine has a vestibule whereas the other two shrines have a "half hall" (ardhamantapa). The Temple is a protected monument of national importance under ASI.

BANDALIKE - The place is famous for Basadis and Temples. Here, you can find sculptures and writings of Rastrakutas and Kadambas period. Other places of interest are Shantinath basadi, Sahasralinga Temple and Someshwara threemurthy Temples.

TALAGUNDA - Several ancient inscriptions are found here. The Pranseshwara Temple is a must see. To the east of Talagunda is "Prabhudeva Gaddige".

CHANDRAGUTTI - It is historical place and pilgrimage centre of Goddess Renukamba. The place was earlier known as Chandragupta Pura, Chandragutti Pete, Gutti Pete. The place is located at 848 metres above sea level on a rocky mountain bed.

SRI KALLARE GANAPATHI TEMPLE AT THIRTHAHALLI - The Temple is dedicated to Lord Ganesha. The Temple is believed to be more than 800 yrs. old. The Temple structure is magnificent and the vigraha of Lord Ganesha of natural stone.

SRI HUMCHA TEMPLE AT SHIMOGA - Sri Humcha Padmavati Devi Jain Temple is a famous Jain Temple. This Temple is called Pomrchcha and Pombucha. In the 7th century, Shri Jinadatt had built this Temple. He was the founder of the Santhara Dynasty. Jaina Math is very popular in Hombucha. It was constructed by the monks. These monks belonged to Nandi Sanga of Kunda Kundanavaya. The Math houses Temples like the Shri Padmavati Temple, Shri Bogara Basadi, Shri Marthanda Basadi, Shri Parshvanatha Temple. The Math is decorated with Lakki trees. This tree is more than 1300 years old. The Lakki Tree will never dry and the water will be constantly oozing out from the point of origin of River Kumudvati. According to the history, King Jinadattaraya came from Mathura. He planned to construct the kingdom and made that place as his capital. While he was travelling back from Mathura, he brought the vigraha of Padmavathi Devi. After a long travel, he reached Hombucha. He was taken the rest under the shadow of Lakki tree. While he saw a dream, he was instructed to build his kingdom in that place. There is another ancient Temple. In the navaranga are placed the peetha/seat and the paduka of the Bhattaraka. On the right side of Navaranga are found two black coloured stone vigrahas of Lord Parshwanatha, one of these vigrahas is in kayotsarga and is very ancient and the other is a new vigraha in padmasana. This vigraha is considered as the only one of its kind in the world as it has the figures of two humans troubling Lord Parshwnanatha while in meditation and the same humans have bowed down to Lord Parshwanatha on either sides of the feet.

SRI PRANAVESHWARA TEMPLE AT TALAGUNDA - The Temple is dedicated to Lord Shiva. The 6.5 ft. tall Shivalinga consecrated in the Temple is believed to be of 4th CE. Ancestors of Kadamba dynasty hailed from Talagunga. The Shivalinga was initially worshiped by Shakavahana and later on the ancestors of Kadamba dynasty worshipped the Shivalinga.

SARVAJNA PEETHA AT KODACHADRI - It is the 10th highest peak of Karnataka. The name "Kodachadri" comes from "Kodacha" or "Kodashi" and "Adri" which in Sanskrit means a Hill of Kutaja or Jasmine flowers. This Peetha is dedicated to Adi Shankracharya as he meditated here. There is another Temple at the foot hills of Kodachadri, which is set to be the moolasthana of Sri Mookambika Devi of Kollur. A 40 ft. iron pillar is erected in front of the Temple standing as a mirror to ancient Indian iron craftmanship.

SRI SIGANDHUR CHOWDESHWARI KSHETRAM AT TUMARY - The Temple is dedicated to Goddess Sigandureshwari. The Temple is located on the banks of Sharavathi River. It is believed that the vigraha of the Goddess had been recovered 300 years ago on the banks of the River. It is believed that the people with land dispute & who loss there valuables come here for solution. The devotees who want to safeguard there land from thieves get a board from the Shrine. There is also a Bhoota Sthana here. It is said that Lord Veerabhadra in this Bhootada Katte is taking care of the security of the place.

DISTRICT – TUMAKURU (Railway Station – Tumakuru)

S. No.	Temple	Address	Type
1	Kote Anjaneya Swami	Tumakuru - 572101	Hanuman
2	Mandargiri Digamber Jain Atishaya Kshetra	Madagondanahalli - 572104	Jain
3	Siddhaganga Mutt	Tumkur – 572104	Shiva
4	Sri Ganesha Temple	Gulur - 572118	
5	Kaidala Keshava Temple	Kaidala – 572118	Vishnu
6	Seebi Narasimha Swamy Temple	Bellavi – 572128	Narasimha
7	Maha Lakshmi Temple	Goravanahalli – 572129	Mata
8	Madhugiri Fort	Madhugiri - 572132	Fort
9	Devarayana Durga	Devarayana Durga – 572140	Mata
10	Siddhalingeshwara Temple	Yediyur - 572142	Shiva
11	Chowdeshwari Temple	Dasarighatta - 572201	Mata
12	Group of Temples	Aralaguppe – 572212	Shiva
13	Hoysala Temples	Turuvekere – 572227	Shiva

KOTE ANJANEYA SWAMI AT TUMAKURU - The Temple is dedicated to Lord Hanuman. The Temple has a 75 ft. tall vigraha of Lord Hanuman at the entrance. The said vigraha was inaugurated in May 2005. The vigraha was consecrated by Sri Vyasaraja. Sri Vyasaraja was Rajaguru of historical Vijayanagar empire. He was also the guru of the likes of Kanakadasa and Purandaradasa. It is believed that over five hundred years ago, Sri Vyasaraja consecrated 732 vigraha of Lord Hanuman throughout India.

MANDARGIRI DIGAMBER JAIN ATISHAYA KSHETRA AT MADAGONDANAHALLI - Mandargiri, also known as Basadi Betta, is a beautiful, round hillock housing a number of Jain Temples that are believed to be 1000 years old. It is an important pilgrimage centre for Jains in Karnataka. Trekking on this monolith is relatively easy as it has around 460 steps that will take you to the top of the hillock. There are three main things here: 1) A Picchi shaped 81 feet Guru Mandir – the first of its kind in Jain history. The Guru Mandir is dedicated to the Digambara Jain ascetic Sri Shantinsagarji Maharaj; 2) The mukha mantapa next to the Pinchi has a tall vigraha of Chandranatha Tirthankara. Looks similar to that of Bahubali – but smaller , was installed recently in 2011 & 3) at the top of this hillock is a Temple complex with 4 small but ancient Temples that date back 800 – 1000 years. Two are dedicated to Bhagwan Chandranatha and the remaining two to Bhagwan Parsavnath.

SIDDHAGANGA MUTT AT TUMKUR – A famous centre for pilgrimage, Siddhaganga has a Temple dedicated to Siddhalingeshwara on a hill rock which is held in high esteem by devotees. At the entrance of this Temple, six shrines can be seen. Near this Temple, amidst scenic surroundings, stands a Veerashaiva Matha. The Matha feeds thousands of students and pilgrims daily. This is one of the important educational centres.

SRI GANESHA TEMPLE AT GULUR - The Temple is dedicated to Lord Ganesha. The vigraha of Lord Ganesha is of black stone and there is another 9 ft. tall clay vigraha of Lord Ganesha which replaced every year. The annual Jathra is held on the third day after the completion of Kartik month.

KAIDALA - Originally named Kridapura, Kaidala acquired its present name because of a supernatural incident believed to have taken place here connected with the legendary sculptor Jakanchary. A flaw was pointed out in masterpiece by this sculptor by another young sculptor called Dankana. This resulted in the senior sculptor cutting off his right hand. On building the Kaidala Keshava Temple, Jakanchary's lost hand was restored and hence the name Kaidala (Kai means Hand in Kannda). To his great surprise, Jakanachary later found that Dankana was his own son. This beautiful Keshava Temple in the Dravidian style contains a 5'6" tall figure of Channigaraya.

SEEBI - This Village contains a beautiful Temple of Lord Narasimha. The terracotta and frescoes of this Temple are of 18th century. According to the renowned British Raj era historian and epigraphist, B. Lewis Rice, legend has it that once a merchant carrying grain on bullocks stopped at Sibi. When a

pot of grain was boiled on a projecting rock, its color turned blood red causing the merchant, his attendants and the buffalos to swoon. While in the unconscious state, the Lord Narasimha appeared in the merchant's dream and informed him that the rock was his abode and that the merchant should build a Temple for him at that spot as atonement for desecrating his abode. A small Temple was thus built by the merchant. In more recent times, the consecration of a larger Temple over the pre-existing shrine was taken up by three wealthy brothers: Lakshminarasappa, Puttanna and Nallappa who were the sons of Kacheri Krishnappa, a Dewan in the court of King Tipu Sultan of the Mysore Kingdom. Story goes that Nallappa had a dream in which the Lord Narasimha promised him eternal happiness if a Temple was raised where it stands today. The completion of the Temple construction took ten years. The main deity of the Temple is Lord Narasimha, an avatar of Lord Vishnu. The tower over the entrance is three tiered and the Temple has a large prakara. The open mantapa leads to a closed mantapa (or navaranga) which has minor shrines for several deities: Lord Rama, Ambegal Krishna, Sriranga, Narasimha, Ganesha and Saptamatrika. The main attraction in the Temple are the mural paintings on the ceiling and walls of the mukhamantapa which depict courtly as well as religious themes such as scenes from the Bhagavata, the Narasimha Purana, the Ramayana & the Mahabharata.

GORAVANAHALLI MAHA LAKSHMI TEMPLE - It is a famous Lakshmi Temple whose vigraha is said to be self-originated. There will be special poojas which will be performed on Friday. Devotees who cannot visit Kolhapur Maha Lakshmi Temple, they visit this Temple and seek blessings from the Goddess. As per Sthala Puranam, a villager Abbayya got the vigraham of Maha Lakshmi & he started worshipping of the Goddess at his home & he was blessed with wealth & all success in life. Abbayya used to feel poor in his home & thus his house was known as Lakshmi Niwasa. Later, his brother started worshipping the Goddess & one day, he had a dream wherein the Goddess asked to construct the Temple for her.

MADHUGIRI - Madhugiri Fort is a single hill and the second largest monolith in entire Asia. The small town is famous for its fort and Temples. Many tourists visit Madhugiri to visit the fort, which is famous for its architecture and was built by the Vijayanagara Dynasty. The fort is perched on a steep slope of the hill.

DEVARAYANA DURGA TEMPLE AT TUMAKURU – It is situated amidst hill and dense forests. In the hilly terrain, there are various holy spots like the Temples of Maa Durga (Fort) & Lord Narasimha built by Mysore rulers in the Dravidian style of architecture, the Sanjivaraya Temple dedicated to Lord Hanuman and the Temple of Kumbhi Narasimha. Near the Narasimha Temple are three sacred ponds called Narasimha Teertha, Parashara Teertha and Pada Teertha. The Pada Teertha is inside a large cave. There is another cave with the vigrahas of Lord Rama, his consort Sita and his brother Lakshmana. Ongoing a little further from the hills, there is a natural spring called 'Namada Chilume'. There are also some other springs nearby. The Rivers Jayamangali and Shimsha originate from these hill ranges.

SIDDHALINGESHWARA TEMPLE AT YEDIYUR - The Temple is dedicated to Lord Shiva. The place was the home of a famous Veerashaiva spiritual teacher and author, Totada Siddhalinga. His Samadhi stands today in the Siddhalingeswara Temple, which is built in Dravidian style. This Temple has a Ratha with six stone wheels. A car festival takes place annually in March-April and lasts a fortnight. This is a pilgrimage centre for Lord Shiva's devotees.

CHOWDESHWARI TEMPLE AT DASARIGHATTA - The Temple is dedicated to Goddess Chowdeshwari. There is a Chowdeshwari Devi Utsava on specific festival days i.e. during Ayudha Pooja & Chowdeshwari Devi Fair.

ARALAGUPPE – There is a famous Kalleshwara Temple in the Ganga-Nolamba style of the 9th century AD. Its ceiling has wonderful dancing Shiva sculpture with musical accompanists and eight Dikpalas surrounding him with all their paraphernalia. There is a Chennakeshava Temple of the Hoysala style. The vigraha of Lord Vishnu in the garbhagriha is magnificent. There are four Ganga Temples at the place.

TURUVEKERE - It was once an 'Agrahara' or 'Rent Free Village' granted to scholarly brahmins in the 13th century AD. It boasts of many fine Hoysala Temples. The Temple of Channakeshava is one of them. It was built by Mahadandanayaka Somanna who also built the famous Somnathapur Temple. The Gangadhareshwara Temple has a Shivalinga with serpent hoods carved in a single piece of stone and is considered an example of fine sculpting. This Temple also a bull finely carved in horne blend, which has retained its shine even today. To the east of the Gangadhareshwara Temple is a large soapstone bell. The Moole Shankareshwara Temple was built during the hoysala rule in 1260 AD.

DISTRICT – UDUPI (Railway Station – Udupi)

S. No.	Temple	Address	Type
1	Chaturmukha Basadi	Karkala – 574104	Jain
2	Sri Venkatramana Temple	Karkala – 574104	Vishnu
3	Durga Devi Temple	Kunjarugiri - 574105	Mata
4	Sri Hale Mariamma Temple	Kaup - 574106	Mata
5	Sri Mahaganapathi Temple	Doopadakatte - 574110	Ganesh
6	Mahalingeshwara Temple	Palimar - 574112	Shiva
7	Sri Mahalakshmi Temple	Uchila - 574117	Mata
8	Sri Ananteshwara Temple	Udupi - 576101	Shiva
9	Jaya Durga Parameshwari Temple	Kannarpady, Udupi - 576101	Mata
10	Udupi Sri Krishna Matha	Thenkpete, Maruthi Veethika, Udupi – 576101	Krishna
11	Sri Puthige Matha	Car Street, Udupi - 576101	Matha
12	Kadiyali Mahishamardini Temple	Udupi - 576102	Mata
13	Uma Maheshwara Temple	Manipal - 576104	Shiva
14	Durgaparameshwari Temple	Herga - 576107	Mata
15	Group of Temples	Barkur - 576210	Hanuman
16	Sri Durgaparameshwari Devastana	Kodi Bengre - 576218	Mata
17	Sri Mookambika Temple	Kundapura Taluk, Kollur – 576220	Mata
18	Sri Durgaparameshwari Temple	Mandarthi – 576223	Mata
19	Sri Guru Narasimha Swamy Temple	Saligrama - 576225	Narasimha
20	Ratteshwara Temple	Rattadi - 576227	Shiva
21	Sri Shankaranarayana Kshetram	Shankaranarayana - 576227	Vishnu
22	Vishnu Temple	Handadi - 576235	Vishnu
23	Anegudde Sri Vinayaka Devasthana	Kumbashi – 576257	Ganesh
24	Sri Gopala Krishna Temple	Hattiangadi - 576283	Krishna

CHATURMUKHA BASADI AT KARKALA – It is a symmetrical Jain Temple and is one of the most famous monuments in Karkala. It was built in the late 16th century by Immadi Bhairarasa Vodeya of the Santhara dynasty in 1586. It has four symmetrical faces and is thus called Chaturmukha Basadi. The Temple has vigrahas of Tirthankara Aranath, Mallinath and Munisuvratnath. This Basadi, completely made of carved granite rocks, is known as Tribhuvana Tilaka Jina Chaityalaya or Ratnatrayadhama from inscriptions. It faces the famous Karkala Bahubali vigraha installed in the year 1432 by Veera Pandya of the Santhara dynasty on the instructions of the Bhattaraka of Karkala, Lalitakeerti.

Varanga - The place is famous for Kere Basadi & there is also a Neminatha Basadi which is just opposite to the Kere Basadi. Varanga is a popular pilgrim center, especially for Jains. This beautiful village houses most ancient and wonderful Basadis (Jain Temples). The main attractions of Varanga are Neminatha Basadi (1200 years old), Chandranatha Basadi (1000 years old), and Kere Basadi (850 years old). These beautiful, picturesque locations are the best way one can relax amidst tranquility. Metro Saga brings to you reasons why you must visit the Basadis of Varanga. A Temple in the midst of a lake, another one on the bank of the lake and another one which houses the Jain Mutt – such is the tranquility found in Varanga. At the Neminatha Temple, two beautifully sculpted elephants greet you, just before the impressive granite entrance. A scene of two elephants garlanding a deity has been carved on the top central portion of this section. Immediately above this, there is a sculpted relief vigraha of a demon face, which is placed for warding off evil forces. Here it is made out of the ornate granite slab of the entranceway, unlike other Temples in Karnataka where these carvings are on brass or bronze. The main attraction of this basadi is 5 feet black vigraha of Lord Neminatha, the 22nd Tirthankara in Padmasana position seating on 'Kamala Peeta' (lotus seat).

SHREE VENKATARAMANA TEMPLE AT KARKALA – It is an ancient Temple having a history of 550 years belongs to Gauda Saraswat Brahmin Samaj. For various reasons Gauda Saraswat Brahmins migrated from Goa and settled in the location of Karkala. They erected a small Temple enshrined Lord Shree Venkataramana and worshiped him for the betterment of their religious, cultural and social welfare. Eventually, devout followers in large numbers thronged this Devasthana (Temple) and the Shrine earned the name of Padu Tirupathi Kshetra. Lord Sri Srinivasa is the presiding deity of the Temple and is popularly known as 'Chappara Srinivasa'. Once a year in a grand and ceremonious procession, Lord Sri Srinivasa is taken out in Golden Mandapa and Lord Shri Venkatramana in the Golden palanquins for Vanabhojana which literally means an outing to the forest in a magnificent Hagalu Utsav, to the eastern part of Karkala.

Shree Vishnu Temple at Karkala – The Temple is ancient and famous. The Temple is believed to be of 10th CE. The Temple is dedicated to Lord Vishnu. In the Grabhagriha of the Temple, there is a tall vigraha of Lord Vishnu in standing posture. The Temple has been an example of architectural style having different carvings.

DURGA DEVI TEMPLE AT KUNJARUGIRI - The Temple is dedicated to Maa Durga. The Temple is built by Bhagwan Parshurama. The vigraha is adorned with beautiful sarees & jewellery. The Temple is situated on a hillock known as Durga Betta. It is also known as Vimanagiri, as it is believed that various gods & goddesses came in vimana when the vigraha was consecrated. The high hill abodes of Maa Durga & Bhagwan Parshurama looks like "Kunjara" i.e. elephant & so it is known as Kunjaragiri. Legend says that after creating Kerala, Bhagwan Parshurama found a pearl which he turned into a nose pin & adorn it on Maa Durga. It is believed that Bhagwan Parshurama is performing penance in the caves below the Durga Betta even now.

SRI HALE MARIAMMA TEMPLE AT KAUP - Since ancient times Kaup is known as "Hoovina Hitthilu". Sri Mariyamma Devi, who is the owner of said place, has been blessing the devotees who come there. The devotion of Goddess Mari was commenced in Tulunadu during 17th century. Basappa Nayaka, one of the prominent rulers of Keladi royal family built a fort "Manoharagadha" on Kapu seashore in 1743. He also constructed a fort in Mallar to Shelter his military (Dandu). Kapu Maripooja is one of the seven rituals of the unilateral Dakshina Kannada district. The other six are - Udupi Paryaya, Bappanadu Dolu, Arasara Kambala, Kavatharu Ayana, Dharmastala Deepotsava and Padubidri Dhakkebali. Maripooja is being offered thrice in a year the suggi Maripooja in the month of March is the most important than the other two Viz at Maripooja Jarde Maripooja.

SRI MAHAGANAPATHI TEMPLE AT DOOPADAKATTE - The Temple is dedicated to Lord Ganesha. The Temple is believed to be more than 100 years old. The vigraha of the Lord Ganesha is of marble and the vigraha is offered rice appams. Two sided Nagashila is a unique feature of this Temple.

MAHALINGESHWARA TEMPLE AT PALIMAR - The Temple is dedicated to Lord Shiva. The Temple consists of Garbhagruha, Pradakshina Patha, Nandi Mantapa, Inner & Outer Pauli, Inner Hajara, Bali Peetha, Dhwaja Stambha. A small Temple of Shastavu is located on left side.

SRI MAHALAKSHMI TEMPLE AT UCHILA - The Temple is dedicated to Goddess Mahalakshmi. She is the Kuldevi of Moghaveera's of coastal Karnataka which is a fishermen community.

SRI ANANTESHWARA TEMPLE AT UDUPI - The Temple is dedicated to Lord Shiva. It is one of the biggest & oldest shrine of Udupi. In the Temple, it is believed that Lord Vishnu enshrined in a Shivalingam. As per legend, King Ramabhoja worshipped Bhagwan Parshurama on a silver pedestal here and Bhagwan Parshurama manifested himself as Ananteshwara. It is believed that Lord Shiva taught Bhagwan Parshurama in various arts of fighting. In Dakshina as guru, Lord Shiva asked Bhagwan Parshurama to reside here in the form of Shivalingam, hence, as an incarnation of Lord Vishnu, Bhagwan Parshurama is worshipped in the Shivalingam & said to be in the heart of Lord Shiva.

JAYA DURGA PARAMESHWARI TEMPLE AT KANNARPADY, UDUPI - The Temple is dedicated to Maa Durga. It is one of the four important Maa Durga Temples in Udupi. The vigraha of the Goddess is two arms & her hands are in a blessing posture. Her vahana, Lion can also been seen in front of the vigraha. The Sanctum of the Temple is built with black granite & this Temple is believed to be more than 5000 years old. The sarovar in the Temple is known as Kanwa Pushkarni as Rishi Kanwa had done penance here. The most important festival of the Temple is Navratri. The Temple is also mentioned in the Skanda Purana.

SRI KRISHNA MATT AT UDUPI – It is the seat of Lord Krishna, which is considered to be one of the holiest places for pilgrimage in southern India. Udupi is first among the seven places of pilgrimages. Surrounding the Sri Krishna Matha are several Temples, the most ancient being made of basic wood

and stone of 1,500 years origin. Thousands of pious devotees throng the Krishna Temple all-round the year to catch a glimpse of Lord Krishna. The unique feature of Shree Krishna Mutt Temple is that the Lord is worshipped only through a window with nine holes called the Navagraha Kitiki. The silver-plated window is exquisitely carved. It has been a tradition in this Temple to worship the Lord only through this window. In the 16th century, during Sri Vaadiraja 's rule, Kanakadasa, an ardent believer of God, came to Udupi to worship Lord Krishna. He was not allowed inside the Temple since he was from a lower caste. Sri Krishna, pleased by the worship of Kanakadasa created a small hole in the back wall of the Temple and turned to face the hole so that Kanakadasa could see him. This hole came to be known as

Kanakanakindi. The sight of the beautiful Muddu Krishna is available to everybody through the Kanakanakindi. Udupi is the birthplace of Sri Madhavacharya, founder of Dwaita Philosophy and one of the three great Acharyas. He is reputed to have discovered the vigraha of Shri Krishna from a ship, which he saved miraculously from the clutches of fatal storm breeding on the sea at Malpe. One day when he was performing his morning prayers on the Malpe shore, he found that a ship sailing in the sea, was in danger owing to rough weather. He with his divine power was able to control the rough weather. Popular belief is that King Rama Bhoja, an ardent follower of Parashurama installed the vigraha of Anantheshwara. Chandreshwara Temple was built in the spot where Chandra (the moon) performed a penance to get rid of the curse of Daksha Prajapathi. The place where Chandra meditated got to be called as Udupi. (Udu = a star and pa = follower) The usual practice in Udupi is to visit Chandreswara, Anantheshwara Temples & then visit Sri Krishna Temple.

SRI PUTHIGE MATHA AT CAR STREET, UDUPI - The Matha had been established for the preaching of the philosophy of Sage Sri Madhvacharya. Among his disciples who were destined to see him and hear him and could call themselves his followers, Shri Upendra Teertha was the most important one whose name finds mention in his Biography "Shri Sumadhwa Vijaya". The main vigrahas worshiped in the Matha are that of Shri Lakshminarasimha & Sri Panduranga (Vittala) which was given to Shri Upendra Tirtha by Shri Madhvacharya. The current Swamiji of the Matha is Shri Sugunendra Tirtha Swamiji.

KADIYALI MAHISHAMARDINI TEMPLE AT UDUPI - The Temple is dedicated to Maa Durga in the form of Mahishamardini. It was established in 7th CE. Th vigraha of the Goddess is of black stone. The vigraha is very powerful & a symbolic representation of good prevailing over evil. The important festival of the Temple is Navaratri which is celebrated with great pomp & fervor.

UMA MAHESHWARA TEMPLE AT MANIPAL - The Temple is dedicated to Lord Shiva & Goddess Parvati. In ancient Temples of South Canara, Lord Shiva & Shakti are worshipped in the form of Linga. The Uma Maheshwara Temple is one of the said Temple and in the Temple there are very fascinating vigrahas of Lord Shiva & Goddess Parvati. It is most popular among students of Manipal.

DURGAPARAMESHWARI TEMPLE AT HERGA - Goddess Durgamarameshwari is affectionately referred to as Hergamma and the Goddess is worshiped in the form of the Linga. The Temple is facing east and consists of Garbhagriha, Tirthamantapa, Pauli, Balipeetha, Dhwajasthambha & Hajara. The Temple is having a beautiful vigraha of Lord Ganesha. Pauli has stone pillars and tiled roof. Hajara is simple with tiled roof. It is one of those Temples which is said to be in existence from time memorial.

Barkur -

Aramane Hanumantha Devasthana - Barkur is the land of 365 Temples & the place was ruled by Alupa Kings. Aramane means Palace in Kannada & Lord Hanuman is protecting the Palace hence it is known as Hanumantha Devasthana. The deity belongs to the 14th CE.

Chowlikere Ganapathy Temple - The Temple was constructed 900 years back during the Chola Period. The Bairagi Ganapathy Temple is entirely hewn out of stone with a slanted stone roof and etched stone pillars. The stone walls of this Temple display beautiful sculptures and it is apparent that this mammoth structure has withstood the ravages of time. The Panchalingeshwara Temple, dedicated to Lord Shiva, is Barkur's largest Temple, & is one of the oldest in the town. Its double-storied gateway, with a pillared verandah on either sides, is most alluring. The rear side of the Temple has an elephant-back-like curvilinear structure. The pillars that surround the circumambulatory path are decorated with carvings depicting mythological characters.

Kathale Basadi - A 20-feet monolithic stone pillar is erected at the entrance. The Temples were elegantly designed with carvings & embellishments. There are three main structures in a courtyard with a victory pillar at the entrance. Archaeologists say that they were built between the 8th & 12th century A.D. Built by the Alupa rulers, the Jain Basadi, unlike most South Indian Temples built in the Dravidian style, does not have a gopuram. The sanctum sanctorum is surrounded by stone walls known as Prangan, with sloping stone pillars over it. The original Bhagwan Mahavira vigraha was destroyed but has been replaced by stone tablets with animal figures that are a later addition. Basadi consists of Navranga with Nagkaali, Shiva, Vishnu & Jain deities. It proves the existence of changing kingdoms with various rulers trying to control the city both politically & in terms of religion.

Shri Venugopala Krishna Temple - The Temple belongs to 14th CE. The Temple is dedicated to Lord Venugopala. Lord Venugopala is the one who is the protector of Cows.

Shri Bappalapura Vinayaka Temple - The Temple is dedicated to Lord Ganesha and here the Lord is known as Eli Ganpathi. It is believed that the Lord has been worshiped in the Temple to save the harvest from rodents during Alupa Dynasty & it is prevalent even now.

SRI DURGAPARAMESHWARI DEVASTANA AT KODI BENGRE - The Temple is dedicated to Goddess Durgaparameshwari. The Temple is old and it was renovated beautifully in 2017. The place is famous for its backwaters and beaches.

SRI MOOKAMBIKA DEVI TEMPLE AT KOLLUR - It is one of the Seven Mukthi Sthala of Karnataka. As per ancient Scriptures and Inscriptions, along with other proofs found in the locality, it is clear that the Kollur Mookambika Temple has been an abode of Devi Shakthi's worship for centuries. The supremacy of the Kollur Kshethram is described in the Skanda Puranam which has the legendary background of Kollur. In an ancient inscription (1481 AD) found here, the source of the Shakthi has been described. Shree Mookambika Devi in the form of Linga is the Adi Shakthi, the creator and the protector of all forms of life. The Sanctum Sanctorum which is in a Quadrangular shape has a tower known as Vimana Gopura which is in the Dravidian Architecture. The tower of the sanctum sanctorum is covered by gold donated by local King centuries ago. The vigraha of Mookambike is very attractive and has four arms, the upper two arms are holding Shankha and Chakra and the palms of the lower two arms are held as blessing the devotees with the Abhaya and Varada Hastha. Around the sanctum sanctorum of Goddess, we can see the retinue deities like Subrahmanya, Dashabhuja Ganapathi, Anjaneya, Chandramouleeshwara and Gopalakrishna. Kings of the "Keladi Dynasty" have been offering a variety of worships to the Goddess. Prominent Kings, Sankanna Nayaka and Shivappa Nayaka had renovated the Temple. They had believed that the Goddess is the symbol of victory. As such whenever they would win a war or drive away their enemies they were devoting the victory and celebrating it before the Goddess. A troll or monster,

known as Kaumhasura, wanted to get a boon from Lord Shiva, that, he should not get death from any living being. To disable him from asking the boon, Vagdevi makes him dumb. Accordingly he became Mookasura or Dumb troll. Due to this, Mookaasura became furious and wanted to take revenge against the Gods. The Gods could not withstand the trouble imparted by him and sought refuge from Devi. In response the Devi had integrated the powers of the Trimurthis and all the Gods into her to put the Mookasura to death and after that, assimilated into the Linga and now exists known as Mookambike and protects her devotees. Since Kola Maharshi had meditated in the Khshethra, which was named as Kolapura. Today it is known as Kollur. Kola Maharshi was fascinated to see a Cow pouring milk onto a linga from her udder, then he started to worship the linga. Since we can see the symbol of the hoof of the cow on the Linga, it shows that the linga has got the godly powers.

SRI DURGAPARAMESHWARI TEMPLE AT MANDARTHI - Long ago, the King Shankachooda was ruling Nagaloka. He had five daughters Devarathi, Nagarathi, Charurathi, Mandarathi and Neelarathi. Once they went to Kailasa with an aspiration of marrying the Lord Subramanya Swamy, son of the Lord Shiva. These Five princesses were stopped by Nandi (Lord Shiva's Devotee) on their way and cursed to become snakes. Instantaneously they were transformed into snakes and fell down to earth. When Vyaghrapada Maharishi who was wandering in the Sahyadri Ghats saw these five snakes caught in the forest conflagration and knew everything about them by his divine insight. He said to the five princes (now Snakes) that their cursed would be removed by a royal person in due course of time. Meanwhile, the King of Avanthi Devavarma, who had been banished and wandering in disguise in the Sahyadri Mountains saw these five snakes and decided to save them. He wrapped the snakes with a piece of cloth and started travelling towards the west. The snakes slid out of the cloth wrapper and reached a nearby termite hill. One of the snakes called "Mandarathi" reached a part of forest, which came to be called as "Mandarthi" later. Devavarma found the vigraha of Durga in Varahi River as was guided to him by the Lord Subramanya Swamy in a dream and consecrated it with all devotion.

SRI GURU NARASIMHA SWAMY TEMPLE AT SALIGRAMA - The place has special importance for those who follow Guru Narasimha as their community deity. Most of the people of Saligrama are Kota Brahmins. The main language spoken in Saligrama is Kannada and Konkani is also spoken here. It was believed that the community followed Guru Narasimha as their spiritual guru instead of following mutts for spiritual guidance as an vigraha of Lord Narasimha appeared in Raja Bhattacharya's dream instructing him to do so. It is believed that the Temple of Guru Narasimha and Lord Anjaneya have records dating back to over a thousand years and nearly four centuries before the time of Jagadguru Sri Shankaracharya. As per Padma Purana, Narada Maharshi originally placed the vigraha of Guru Narasimha in its current place. The annual car festival will be held on 16 and 17 of every January which is attended by thousands of people from all over the state.

RATTESHWARA TEMPLE AT RATTADI - The Temple is dedicated to Lord Shiva. As per legend, Lord Shiva & Lord Vishnu slayed the demon Ratta, hence, it is an ancient abode of Ratteshwara.

SRI SHANKARANARAYANA KSHETRAM - The Temple is dedicated to Lord Shiva. The Temple is a rare Temple where the devotees can see the confluence of Lord Shiva & Lord Vishnu. The place is believed to be one of the seven Bhagwan Parshurama Kshetram. There are Swayambhu Lingams in the form of Udbhava Linga. The Shivalingas is one feet below the ground inside the Sanctum Sanctorum. The Shankaralinga is on the right side and is in round shape. The Narayanalinga is on the left side and is in flat shape with foot prints of Cow on it. There is water around Udbhava Linga and this holy water is called Sudhamrita Tirtha.

VISHNU TEMPLE AT HANDADI - The Temple is famous and ancient. The Temple is dedicated to Lord Vishnu in Janardhana roopa. The Temple belongs to 17th CE.

SRI VINAYAKA TEMPLE AT ANEGUDDE – It is also popularly called as Kumbashi. Anegudde is rewarded one of the seven 'Mukti Sthalas' of Karnataka (Parashuramakshetra). The Temple is dedicated to Lord Vinayaka (Ganesha). Anegudde is the combination of two words - 'Aane' meaning 'Elephant' and 'Gudde', which stands for 'hillock' as it is the abode of the elephant-headed god, Lord Vinayaka. 12 ft tall Anegudde Vinayaka is 'Udbhava Murthi' (Natural Stone), a single stone in the form of very elephant itself. The Tilak on the forehead is made of Sri Gandha (Sandle

Paste) and the God has Swarna Mukha made of 5 KGs of pure Gold. Rest of the Kavacha (vigraha's body) is made of pure Silver. It is also believed that the vigraha of Lord Ganapathi is growing every year.

SRI CHENNAKESHAVA TEMPLE AT KUMBASHI – The Temple is dedicated to Lord Vishnu. The Temple belongs to 11th CE. The vigraha of Lord Vishnu in Chennakeshava form is housed in this humble abode since 11th CE and vigraha is holding Shanka Chakra and Padma Gada in both hands.

SRI GOPALA KRISHNA TEMPLE AT HATTIANGADI - The Temple is dedicated to Lord Gopala Krishna. The Temple is in existence since 13th CE. The Temple is having vigraha of Shi Gopala Krishna in Saligram stone and the Temple is located in a scenic environment. The Temple is with Dashavatara Prabhavali.

DISTRICT – UTTARA KANNADA (Railway Station – Karwar)

S. No.	Temple	Address	Type
1	Sri Channabasavanna Devasthana	Ulavi – 577434	Saint Channabasavanna
2	Ankola Temples	Ankola – 581314	Hanuman, Mata
3	Madhukeshwara Temple	Banavasi – 581318	Shiva
4	Group of Temples	Bhatkal - 581320	All

S. No.	Temple	Address	Type
5	Kavala Caves	Dandeli - 581325	Cave
6	Samsthana Shree Mahabaleshwara Deva	Sri Kshetra Gokarna, Kumta Taluk – 581326	Shiva
7	Sri Tulaja Bhavani Temple	Haliyal – 581329	Mata
8	Tibetan Colony	Mundgod – 581349	Buddhist
9	Shantadurga Temple	Sadashivgad - 581352	Mata
10	Murudeshwar Temple	Murdeshwara – 581353	Shiva
11	Sri Lakshminarayana Mahamaya Temple	P. O. Vandige – 581357, H. M. Road, Ankola	Vishnu-Lakshmi
12	Sri Veeranjaneya Temple	Gersoppa - 581384	Hanuman
13	Shri Maarikamba Temple	Sirsi-Banavasi Road, Sirsi – 581402	Mata
14	Sahasralinga	Sahasralinga – 581402	Shiva
15	Cave Temple	Yana – 581403	Shiva
16	Shri Vinayaka Devaru	Post Melina Idagunji – 581423, Honnavar	Ganesh
17	Kodlamane Shree Vishnumurthy Temple	Kodlamane, Bolkar – 581423	Vishnu

ULAVI – It is an important centre of pilgrimage for people of the Lingayat faith. The Samadhi of Channabasavanna, one of the most revered saints of the Lingayat faith lies here. In the 12th CE, Channabasavanna travelled from Kalyana to Ulavi before he died. Very close to this holy Samadhi is the Akka Nagalambike cave named after Nagalambike, Channabasavanna's mother & Basavanna's sister. The Ulavijathre attracts pilgrims from all over Karnataka.

ANKOLA TEMPLES - Ankola houses many Temples such as famous Honna Raka Temple, beautiful Mahamaya, architectural Venkataramana Temple & traditional Shantadurga (Famously known as Bhumidevathe), Eeshwaradevasthana. Migrated Konkani Saraswats are said to have brought their Kuladevtas with them. They are said to have established the Kuladevata Temples in Ankola. Some of the migrated Goan Deities are Lakshmi Narayan Mahamaya (Nagve Mahmamaya) from the Nagve village, Kundodari Mahamaya (Kudteri Mahamaya) from Curtorim and the Aryadurga Temple from the Anjediva (Aryadweep). The Shantadurga Temple is assumed to be the gram devta of the village is still a question of debate, since many saraswat families do consider it to be their Kuladevta but the locals' state that the deity present is not of Konkani or Goan origin but currently a Dravidian deity.

MADHUKESHWARA TEMPLE AT BANAVASI - It is the first Kannada capital which is ruled by Kadamba dynasty. At present it is announced as one of the rural tourist place by UNDP. The place is known for historical Madhukeshwara Temple. The vigraha is in the honey colour so it is called 'Madhukeshwara'. The noted ancient Kannada poet Pampa describes it as a place where the eyes can see the treasure of nature. It is a place which has harmonized all religions. The River Varada flows from south to north. The Temple has been declared a monument of historical importance by the ASI.

BHATKAL - Bhatkal is sometimes referred to as Mini Dubai. This place is also known as "Al Nawayath". In its early days, it was mainly inhabited by the followers of Jain & Hindu religions, but gradually people from other religions and cultures began to settle there. It was named after Jain Grammarian, Bhattakalanka, who hailed from Hadwalli village, a town on the state highway toward Jog Falls. With Sharavathi River flowing a few miles to the north, the town is located along the shores of the Arabian Sea. Numerous Temples & bases were constructed during the reign of the Saluva dynasty. Vestiges of this period can be found in Mudbhatkal, where a few Temples are still standing as a testament to the magnificence of that era. There are various Temples such as Adike Narayana Temple, Khetapai Narayana Temple, Joshi Shakaranayana Temple, Lakshmi Narayana Temple, Shantappa Nayaka Tirumala Temple & Lakkar Kamti Narayana Temple.

DANDELI -

Kavala Caves - It is one of the historic place in Dandeli. The Caves are limestone caves that came about due to a volcanic activity dating back to ages. These caves are very tiny in dimension and an interesting way to enter them, after climbing down 375 steps, one reaches the Cave entrance and then has to crawl 40 ft deep through winding and have a lot of stalagmite formations. There is a particular huge stalagmite, which is revered by the local people as a Shivalinga. A Temple stands in front of the caves. The naturally formed Shivalinga is a miracle of nature and should not be missed. There is a stone above the Shivalinga, which tickles down water continuously. There is a belief that before there was milk comes out from the stone but now it's changed to water. Some says that it's limewater, which formed this Shivlinga. This place is visited once in a year on the occasion of Mahashivratri. There are more than four caves located in this area, which are naturally build.

SAMSTHANA SHREE MAHABALESHWARA DEVA AT GOKARNA - Srikshetra Gokarna is one of the holiest places in India. The Father of universe Parashiva is in Gokarna in the form of Athmalinga. The Temple is located on the sea shore of the western sea. The Almighty, famous as Mahabaleshwara, is also known as the Sarvabhouma. This is also the place where the most revered Saint Adi Shankaracharya established Shree Ramachandrapura Math, the sacred Jagadguru Peetam. In order to obtain the Athmalinga of Lord Shiva, Ravana performed severe penance at Kailasa and secured the Athmalinga. The Suras frightened by this approached Lord Ganesha & prayed to him to retain the Athmalinga at Gokarna. As the abode of the Athmalinga of Lord Shiva, Gokarna gained worldwide spiritual significance. This holy place is known as Bhookailasa & the Southern Varanasi. In this Temple, all devotees can enter the sanctum sanctorum and have the touch darshan of Athmalinga & can perform Abhisheka with their own hands. Shivaratri Mahotsava is the Car festival when lakhs of people attend and pray for their well being.

Koti Tirtha - It is a holy man-made tank that is considered an important spiritual stopover. The name 'Koti Tirtha' means a thousand springs. It is common practice to take a dip in this pond before visiting the many holy Temples and shrines in the area. Many priests and monks conduct rituals and prayers at the sides of the holy tank, which is spread over an area of six acre. It is surrounded on three sides by colourful Temples and Monasteries. There is a Shivalinga placed at the heart of the pond that is illuminated by light. The calm waters reflecting the Temples as well the coconut trees around create a soothing ambience of reflective spirituality. Legend has it that the mythological bird

Garuda, once picked up Shatashrunga Mountain (abode of Lord Brahma) and flew away with it. When Lord Brahma noticed it, he was livid and immediately ordered Garuda to place it down on earth. Garuda placed it partially on earth and partially in the ocean. While doing so, half of the teerthas on it (one crore) got immersed in water and the remaining one crore were placed on the earth, in Gokarna.

Mahaganapati Temple - It is a humble and unassuming Temple but its size belies its importance for its devotees. Lord Ganesha is the presiding deity and his vigraha faces westwards towards the ocean. There is always a long queue of devotees outside which means that one can finish the pradakshina (circumambulation) in about ten minutes and head over to the Mahabaleshwar Temple, located towards the east. Legend has it that Ravana was successful in removing the atma-lingam (a divine lingam) from Mount Kailash and was taking it with him to Lanka. The gods did not want this journey to be successful and hence pleaded with Lord Ganesha to intervene and save the day. Lord Ganesha knew that wherever the atma-lingam would be lowered to the ground, that spot would become its final resting place on earth. He approached Ravana in the guise of a shepherd when he was crossing Gokarna and tricked him into placing the lingam there. This is why Lord Ganesha is worshipped before the Lingam.

SRI TULAJA BHAVANI TEMPLE AT HALIYAL TALUK - Established on 16th March 1996 by Sri Tulaja Bhavani Education and Dharmadatti Trust, the Temple is thronged by devotees from all over Karnataka and states of Maharashtra and Goa. In the Temple, 4 ft black stone vigraha of Goddess Bhavani was established.

TIBETAN COLONY AT MUNDGOD - Mundgod is a repository of Tibetan life and culture. It showcases the lifestyle and ambitions of the Tibetan refugees and reflects the gradual transformation of a traditional society into modernity. It has been referred to as Mini Tibet.

SADASHIVGAD - The village is significant and picturesque and a popular tourist destination located by the Kali River bridge, which has been built at the confluence of the River and the Arabian Sea. Midway on the Sadashivagad Hill, there is a many centuries old Shantadurga Temple, known for its serenity. From the peak of the Hill, the view of the sun setting in the Arabian Sea is an experience in itself.

MURDESHWARA TEMPLE AT MURDESHWARA - Murudeshwara is sandwiched between the picturesque Western Ghats & the Arabian Sea. Its main attractions are its beach, an awesome Lord Shiva vigraha & a Shiva Temple with Chalukya & Kadamba sculptures built in the Dravidian style of architecture. The Temple is located on a hillock offering you a magnificent view of the sea. Murudeshwara is another name of Lord Shiva. It is famous for the world's second-tallest Shiva vigraha of 121ft. in height. This Temple is built on the Kanduka Hill which is surrounded on three sides by the waters of the Arabian Sea. It is dedicated to Sri Lokankara & a 20-storied gopura is constructed at the Temple. The Temple authorities have installed a lift that provides a

breath-taking view of the 123 ft. Sri Shiva vigraha from the top of the Raja gopura. There is also a Rameshwara Linga at the bottom of the hill. The main deity is Sri Mridesa Linga, also called Murdeshwar. The Linga is believed to be a piece of the original Atma Linga & is about 2 ft. below ground level. The devotees can view the deity by standing before the threshold of the sanctum & the Linga is illuminated by oil lamps. A Shaneswar Temple has been built next to the vigraha of Sri Akshayaguna. Two life-size elephants in concrete stand guard at the steps leading to it. The entire Temple & Temple complex, including the 237.50 ft. tall Raja Gopura, is one among the tallest, was constructed. There are vigrahas of Sun Chariot on side of a park, pool, vigrahas depicting Arjuna receiving Geetopadesham from Lord Krishna, Ravana being deceived by Ganesha in disguise, Shiva's manifestation as Bhaghirnath, descending Ganga, carved around the hill.

SRI LAKSHMINARAYANA MAHAMAYA TEMPLE AT HANUMATTA - The Gaur Saraswat Brahmins, who fled from Goa about 1510 AD, with their family deities came and settled here. They halted at the Temple of Sri Mahishasura Mardini Sri Bhagavathi. In that place, there were also Temples of Sri Veerappa, Sri Honnappa and Sri Hanumantha. The place was called Hanumatta becuase of the Temple of Sri Hanumatha. Before next dawn, a surprising incident took place. The coconut was now surrounded by an ant hill. It was obvious that Sri Lakshminarayana and Sri Mahamaya had desired to stay there permanently. The vigraha of gold in this Temple is taken out for worship once in ten-fifteen years. The punarprathistapana of the Temple took place in 1975.

SRI VEERANJANEYA TEMPLE AT BANGARAMAKKI, GERSOPPA - The Temple is dedicated to Lord Anjaneya. The vigraha had been consecrated by Vedamoorthi, Brahmashree Ganesh Bhat after getting it from Kumta Taluk. The vigraha is in standing posture and both hands are in Namaskar mudra. The tale of the vigraha is in the left to right direction which symbolises Asadhya Sadhaka and Karyasiddhi. There is a unique feature of Darshanam, which is 400 years old tradition, during which Lord is believed to listen the problems of the devotees and speak to them through the mouth of the priest, which takes place on Friday, Saturday, Sunday & Monday excluding Ekadashi, Poornima & Amavasya.

SHRI MARIKAMBA TEMPLE AT SIRSI – It is dedicated to a form of the goddess Durga. It is also known as Doddamma Temple with "Doddamma" denoting the "elder sister" of all Mariammas in Karnataka. The central icon is an eight-armed vigraha of Durga also known by the names Renuka and Yellamma. The Temple was constructed in 1688 AD. The beautiful carvings, the peak and the ancient Kaavi art draw the devotees here. The very sight of Marikamba with a crown studded with diamonds gives solace to the visitors. The fair of the Devi which takes place in alternative years is considered as one of the big fairs of the state. Goddess Marikamba is the family deity of the people of Uttara Kannada and Dakshina Kannada districts.

SAHASRALINGA – It is another place of significance, where Lord Shiva's sculptures carved out of stones thousands of years ago can be found in the middle of a flowing river. The very sound of water moving about is heard in the midst of greenery and all of a sudden River Shalmala comes to the sight of the visitors. The Shalmala moves gently on rocks and in the midst, there are thousand Shivalingas. Where ever one looks he sees Shiva vigrahas. The history reveals that Sode King Arasappa Nayak had made these vigrahas carved for progeny. On the day of Shivaratri, 'Sahasralinga' attracts thousands of devotees.

YANA - It is a quaint village where the luxurious expanse of the Sahyadri Hills is interspersed with two unique rock outcrops that the locals known as the Bhairaveshwar Shikhar and the Mohini Shikhar. The Bhairaweshvar Shikhar is 390 ft high while the Mohini Shikhar is 300 ft high. Both the rock formations are solid black, crystalline Karst limestone. A religious attraction nearby is the Cave Temple below the Bhairaveshwara Shikhara, which contains a Swayambhu Linga. Water drips from the roof just over the Linga and many believe that this increases the sanctity of the place. An interesting part of the annual Shivaratri celebrations here is the car festival that attracts a lot of visitors. Thousands of pilgrims flock to this scenic spot every year.

SHRI VINAYAKA DEVARU AT IDAGUNJI - Idagunji Devasthana is an ancient Temple with a history of more than 1500 years. The Temple is the main attraction receiving more than 1 million devotees per year. Sage Narada along with Valakhilya and other saints wandered westward in search of a suitable place. They came across the Sharavati River which gracefully caressed and consolidated with the ocean. Narada chalked out an exact place located a few miles away to the left of Sharavati. The place was named as Kunjaranya. To add up to the significance of the place, Narada explained that in the past from time to time the Holy Trinity, Hari, Har and Brahma have come to this place to conduct their penance to stop the destruction of the "Asuras" (the demons). He then offered to bring Ganapathi (Vinayaka) along with other Gods including the Holy Trinity. Sage Narada approached Lord Brahma, Vishnu and Maheshwara to attend the "Puja" at Kunjaranya offered by the saints. He also took the liberty of requesting Goddess Parvathi to send her son, Lord Ganapathi to the saints for the removal of obstacles. Lord Ganapathi received the rites, rituals and ceremonious formalities. The great saints and Heavenly beings chanted the hymns in praise of Lord Ganapathi. Ganapathi, magnificently attired, was holding "Modhaka" and "Padma" in his hands. Lord Ganapathi emphasized his decision to stay and gratify the desires of his devotees. He also implied the Gods to leave behind a part of their omniscient power in the various lakes encompassed there. The devotees can attain their hearts desires by dripping into the varied "Theerthas" and by offering pujas to Him. A lake was bestowed to provide water for bathing at Lord Ganapathi's request. It was named as "Ganeshtirth". Kunjaranya which is now renowned as Idagunji.

Kammadev Mahavishnu Temple at Balkur - The Temple is dedicated to Lord Vishnu. The Temple is in existence since 10th CE. There is a vigraha of Lord Ganesha and an ancient Shivalinga has also been consecrated at the Temple.

SHREE VISHNUMURTHY TEMPLE AT KODLAMANE – It is a Tirth Kshetra also called as Shree Parashurama Kshetra. It is located in a hill forest. As per local legend, the Temple was discovered in the middle of dense forest centuries back. A natural stream flows next to the Shree Vishnumurthy Temple, which is called Vishnu Tirth. There is no other place like this anywhere in Brahamanda. The Temple is designed and built on Vedic Hindu Temple architecture. It has Garbhagriha, Antarala, Sandya Mandap, Maha Mandap, Pradakshina, subsidiary Shrines, Bali Peetha and Garuda Stambha. The Garbhagriha is Sanctum sanctorum facing east where presiding deity Lord Vishnumurthy is residing along with other deities which are Lord Maheshwar (in the form of Shiva Linga), Lord Ganapati and Devi Durga. Sacred Saligram are also there which is a symbol of Lord Vishnu. Lord Vishnumurthy is in standing posture with four hands holding Shanka, Chakra, Gada and Padma. The Murthy is carved in sacred black natural stone. After the Antarala in Sandya Mandap there is Kuladevata Sthan who is Shree Kamakshi Devi of Shiroda, a Goddess of Shakti. The walls and pillars of Garbhagudi are beautifully painted in Kaavi art, depicting Dashavatars of Mahavishnu, Ganapati, Saraswati, Hanumatha, Garuda, Temple chariot, palki, flowers etc. On either side of first door of Garbhagudi, there is Jaya-Vijaya beautifully carved in natural black stone. Wood used is Shivani for door frame and jack fruit for door leaf. First door of garbhagudi (door of sandyamandap) has Shree Yoga Narasimha on top & Shree Hanuman on left & Shree Garuda on right side on door frame. Second door which is for Antarala is covered with pure silver and Shree Astha Lakshi on top. Third door which is door of garbhagriha is covered with pure silver with Shree Lakshmi-Narayan to top.

DISTRICT – VIJAYAPURA (Railway Station – Vijayapura)

S. No.	Temple	Address	Type
1	Sahasraphani Parshwanatha Basadi	Vijayapura - 586101	Jain
2	Shree Sundareshwara Lingam Temple	Vijayapura - 586101	Shiva
3	Siddeshwar Temple	Sadashiva Nagar, Vijayapura - 586102	Shiva
4	Shivagiri	Vijayapura – 586104	Shiva

S. No.	Temple	Address	Type
5	Shri Parshwanath Darbar Digamber Jain Atishay Kshetra	Babanagar - 586114	Jain
6	Yalagureshvara Mandir	Yalagur, Muddebiahl - 586212	Hanuman
7	Basavana Bagewadi	Telgi - 586216	Saint Basaveshwara

SAHASRAPHANI PARSHWANATHA BASADI AT VIJAYAPURA - This Jain Temple has a unique vigraha of Lord Parshwanath. The beautifully sculptured vigraha of black stone that is about 1500 years old has a halo of 1008 snake hoods, each of which are interconnected. When the ritual anointing with milk is done, it travels through a maze of tubes before it anoints the head and shoulders of the vigraha. This special ritual is done at 10.00 am on every new moon day (amavasya) and at 9.00 am on every full moon day (Poornima). Covered in an ash filled pit, to escape religious persecution, the vigraha was discovered in the 20th century by a devotee and has now become an important Jain pilgrim centre.

SHREE SUNDARESHWARA LINGAM TEMPLE AT VIJAYAPURA - The Temple is dedicated to Lord Shiva. The Temple is very ancient. The Temple has a Shivalinga with a rare Srichakra.

SIDDESHWARA TEMPLE AT VIJAYAPURA - This Temple, housing the deity of Lord Siddeshwara (Shiva), attracts many devotees from Vijayapura and the surrounding areas.

SHIVAGIRI - The 85-ft tall vigraha of Lord Shiva installed by the T. K. Patil Banakatti Charitable Trust is gradually developing as a pilgrimage place.1500 tonnes vigraha considered as the second biggest vigraha of Lord Shiva in the country. A small vigraha of Shivalinga is installed beneath the big vigraha. "Shiva Charite" is also inscribed in Kannada on the inner walls of the Temple to help the devotees learn the mythological stories related to Lord Shiva.

SHRI PARSHWANATH DARBAR DIGAMBER JAIN ATISHAY KSHETRA AT BABANAGAR - Babanagar Atishaya Kshetra is famous for attractive, unique & ancient vigraha of Lord Parsvanath made of Greenish Black Stone that is miraculous. It is said that in Adilshahi Court this vigraha was placed in the feet of King, this situation was insulting for vigraha. One night, ancestor of present priest of Temple saw a dream and came to know that the Queen of Nawab at that time was suffering from labor pain and if he goes there and gives her water after remembering the name of God in his mind, the Queen will get cured from pain and then in prize he may be able to get that miraculous vigraha easily. That ancestor did the same as per dream and brought the vigraha to his house. Then he constructed the Temple and installed the vigraha in Temple with a function. It is said that power of Parasmani exists in the navel of this vigraha. If a needle was touched to its navel, it turned to gold.

YALAGURESHVARA MANDIR AT YALAGUR - The Mandir belongs to Madhwas (a sect of Brahmins - followers of Madhwacharya). Holy water from Krishna River is used to perform Abhisheka to Yalaguresh. There is a wonderful tradition carried out even as of now that when you want to know if your desired endeavors are going to be fulfil or not, you are asked to sit in-front of Lord & thought that endeavors in your mind and if your endeavors is going to be fulfilled, then a flower on the sacred vigraha falls to his right and if it is not going to be fulfilled, then a flower on the sacred vigraha falls to his left. Hence, it is known as "Speaking Hanumanta". Kartika Utsava/Yalagur Jatra is the biggest event here.

BASAVANA BAGEWADI – It was the birth place of Basaveshwara, the 12th century religious and social reformer and prime minister of the Kalyani Chalukya kingdom. The Temple of Basaveshwara has the shrines of Basaveshwara (Nandi) Sangameshwara, Mallikarjuna and Ganapathi. There are two fine marble vigrahas of Basavanna and his wife.

DISTRICT – YADGIRI (Railway Station – Yadgir)

S. No.	Temple	Address	Type
1	Shri Mailapur Mailarlingeshwar	Yadgiri - 585201	Shiva
2	Siddalingeshwar Temple	Yadgiri - 585201	Shiva
3	Shri Vishwaradhya Temple	Abbetumakur - 585202	Vishnu
4	Chhaya Bhagawati Temple	Jangangaddi - 585219	Mata
5	Shiravala	Shahapur - 585223	Shiva
6	Sleeping Buddha Hill	Shahapur - 585223	Buddhist
7	Shri Venugopala Swamy Temple	Shorapur - 585224	Vishnu
8	Yevur	Shorapur – 585224	Shiva, Jain, Hanuman
9	Kodekal Basavannanavara Gudi	Kodekal - 585237	Saint Basawanna
10	Bhalabhima Sena Temple	Bheemarayana Gudi - 585287	Bhima
11	Shri Kshetra Tintani Mouneshwar Temple	Bandoli - 585290	Saint Mouneshwara

SHRI MAILAPUR MAILARLINGESHWAR TEMPLE AT YADGIRI – It is a famous Temple. The Temple attracts lakhs of devotees every year in "Makara Sankramana" from all over the State.

SIDDALINGESHWAR TEMPLE AT YADGIRI - It is a Panchakuta Temple with four separate "garbhagruha", which is an intricate architecture model arranged in four directions. The ceiling of the navaranga are attractive and the pillars carry beautiful carvings.

ABBETUMAKUR - A famous Temple of Shri Vishwaradhya is located here. The Temple attracts Lakhs of devotees every year in Shivarathri in February-March.

CHAYA BHAGAVATI TEMPLE AT SHORAPUR – On the banks of the mighty Krishna River, there are a set of footprints in a cave Temple for Chaya Bhagavati and the biggest of them is worshiped with great rituals by the villagers. The first rays of the sun always falls on the goddess twice a year. Chaya was the wife of the sun god Surya.

SHIRAVALA THE SOUTH VARANASI – It is a place of historical importance and located on the right bank of River Bhima. Here are almost 20 Temples. Shiravala Temples pertains to the transition phase from Rastrakuta to Kalyani Chalukya and Kalachuri period and some of them are excellent creations. Nagayya and Nannayya Temples are considered as fabulous architectural works of the Rastrakutas.

SLEEPING BUDDHA HILL AT SHAHAPUR - It is made up of 4 small Hills that gives the impression of Sleeping Buddha when viewed horizontally in Southwest direction. It is one of the main attractions of Shahapur town along with Chara Basaveshwara Temple. This is nature's gift and popular attraction of Shahapur, which is located on the banks of Mavina Kere (Pond).

SHRI VENUGOPALASWAMI TEMPLE AT SHORAPUR – It was constructed by Raja Pitambar Bahari Pidda Nayaka (1693-1726) in 1705. It is one of the worthy structures. It has a beautiful and attractive stucco sculptures. The annual fair takes place on Gokulastami. People flock here to witness the spilling of Niru-Okuli from the top of a 35 ft high. Close to the shrine, there is a partially built Temple.

YEVUR - In 11-12thcenturies, Kalyana Chalukya's 22 and 2 of Kalachuri's inscription are reported here. Yevur had attained an important status as educational, religious and cultural centre. Tourists enjoy eye catching architectures, pillar inscriptions, carvings, intricate stones sculptures. Jain Basadi, Someshwara-Sangameshwar Temples Complex, Bhavi Basavanna Temples, Hanumantha Temple etc. are the main Temples.

KODEKAL BASAVANNANAVARA GUDI - Basavanna is well known Saint of truth. Here, he wrote Kala Gnana, which means future happening things.

BHEEMARAYAN GUDI – Here, Bhalabhima Sena is a famous Temple, which attracts lakhs of devotees every year in Sankramana in January.

TINTHINI MOUNESHWAR TEMPLE AT BANDOLI – It is located on the banks of River Krishna. A black stone tortoise adorns the floor of the Temple's main door. The door frame seems ancient. A painting within the Temple area depicts of Jagadguru Mouneshwara with his Temple in the background.

❖ ❖ ❖ ❖ ❖

KERALA

Kerala is noted for its rich culture, heritage and other distinctive characteristics. It was formed on 1st November 1956. Religious tolerance, hospitality, cleanliness, simple life and broad outlook of the people have attracted many a foreigner to the State from time immemorial besides her scenic beauty, pleasant climate and rich natural resources. History has helped Keralites to develop a cosmopolitan outlook. Kerala had contacts with the rest of the world for several centuries in the past

Capital City	Thiruvananthapuram
Total Population	3,34,06,061
Districts	14
Official Language	Malayalam
Motto	Satyameva Jayate
Animal	Elephant
Bird	Hornbill
Fish	Green Chromide
Tree	Coconut Tree
Flower	Kanikonna
Fruit	Jackfruit
Festival	Onam
Airport	Kannur, Kochi, Kozhikode, Thiruvananthapuram

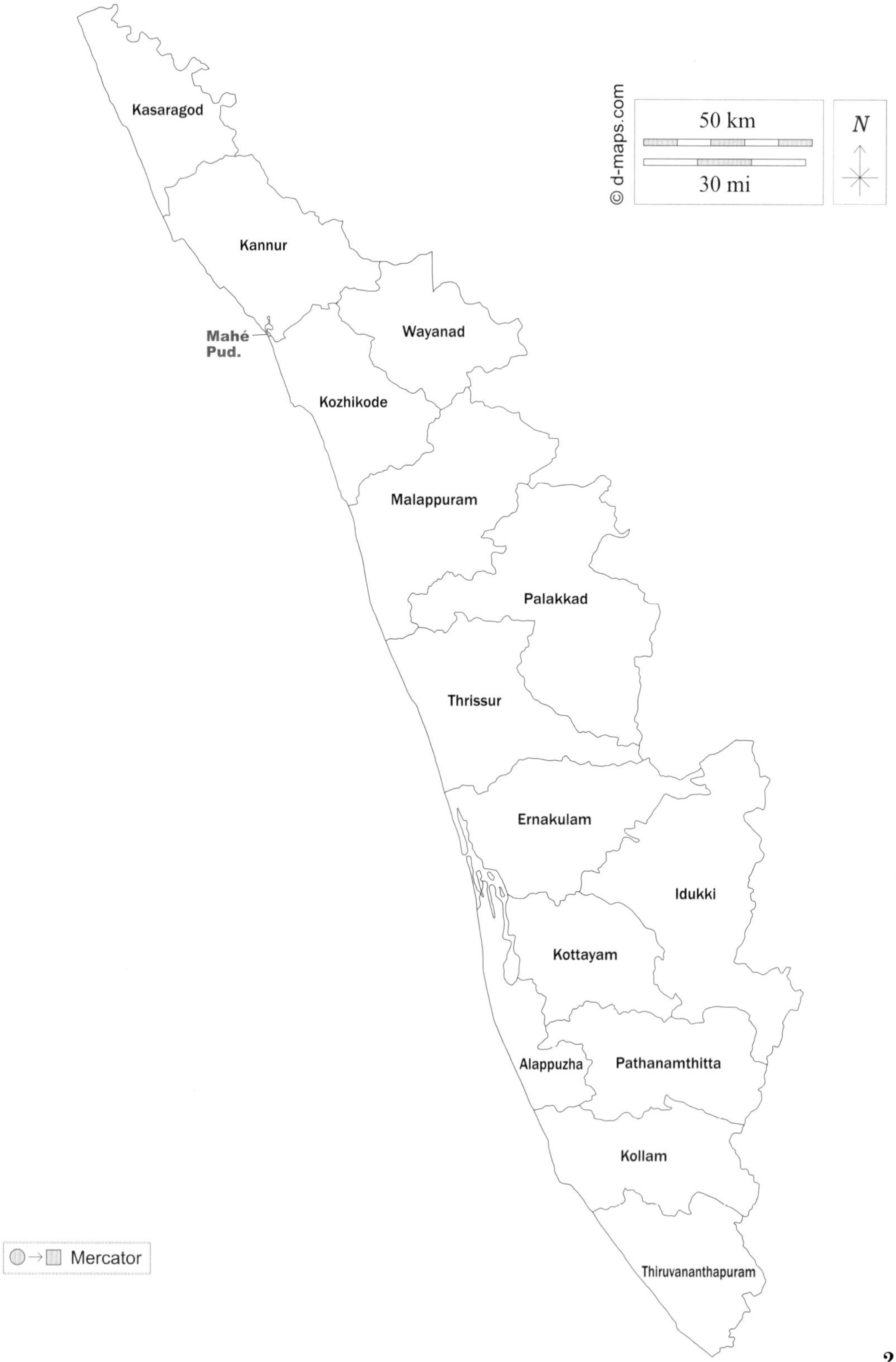
© d-maps.com
50 km
30 mi
N
Kasaragod
Kannur
Wayanad
Mahé
Pud.
Kozhikode
Malappuram
Palakkad
Thrissur
Ernakulam
Idukki
Kottayam
Alappuzha
Pathanamthitta
Kollam
Thiruvananthapuram
Mercator

DISTRICT – ALAPPUZHA (Railway Station – Ambalappuzha/Chengannur/Tiruvalla/Kayankulam)

S. No.	Temple	Address	Type
1	Karthyayani Temple	Cherthala - 688524	Mata
2	Thiruvizha Mahadeva Temple	Thiruvizha - 688530	Shiva
3	Narasimha Kshetra	Thuravoor - 688532	Vishnu
4	Ambalappuzha Sri Krishna Temple	Ambalapuzha - 688561	Krishna
5	Chengannur Mahadevar Temple	Chengannur - 689121	Shiva
6	Maha Vishnu Kshetram	Puliyoor - 689510	Vishnu
7	Chakkulathukavu Sree Bhagavathi Temple	Neerettupram P.O. - 689571	Mata
8	Kandiyoor Sree Mahadeva Temple	Kandiyoor, Mavelikara - 690103	Shiva
9	Sree Nagaraja Swamy Temple	Vetticode - 690503	Nagnath
10	Evoor Major Sri Krishnaswamy Temple	Haripad - 690514	Krishna
11	Mannarasala Sree Nagaraja Temple	Mannarasala P.O. - 690514	Nagnath

KARTHYAYANI TEMPLE AT CHERTHALA - The Temple is dedicated to Goddess Karthyayani. The Prathishta of the Temple was done by Vilwamangalam Swami. As per Sthala Puranam, once Vilwamangalam Swamiyar was passing this area after Prathishta of Padmanabhaswami Temple, he left Devi Chaitanyam and recognise as Karthyayani but Devi seen Vilwamangalam Swami went inside the pond. Swamiji searched for Devi continuously for six days and on seventh day he got hold of Devi's hair. Thus, only Devi's head was Parthisthit here. Devotees do Kozhi Parathal here as an offering to Karthyayani Devi. Chertala Pooram is very famous. It is believed that Devi removes obstacles relating to marriages.

THIRUVIZHA MAHADEVA TEMPLE - In the Temple Lord Shiva is in the form of Lord Kalakandha, which means who swallowed the poison to save the world. It is a famous Temple where people seek the blessings for curing the mad and for those who have poison in their body. The poison is removed by making them vomit the poison by a special ingenious medicine. Abhisheka of the Shivalinga is done with water, tender coconut water, milk, curd etc. The milk abhisheka is done for 1001 times which is a specialty of this Temple. After the abhisheka the vigraha is adorned with the sacred ash and sandalwood paste. In the Temple, there is an vigraha of Lord Vishnu. Payasam Neivedyam is offered to this deity of Lord Vishnu. This Neivedyam of Lord Vishnu is offered to the patients who after taking the medicated milk of morning (pantheeradi pooja) as prasadam to them.

NARASIMHA KSHETRA AT THURAVOOR - It is also known as Thuravoor Mahakshetram. Narasimha Swami & Sudharshana Moorthy has been Prathishthit here as main Deity. As per Sthala Puranam Vigraham of Lord Narasimha was brought from Varanasi. Temple has separate Sannidhi for Vadakkanappan. Sudharshana Moorthy is about 6 ft. Deepawali is famous festival.

SREE KRISHNA TEMPLE AT AMBALAPPUZHA - Built during 17th CE in the typical Kerala architectural style, the Temple is dedicated to Lord Krishna. The Temple is famous all over India for the Pal Payasam, a daily offering of deliciously sweet milk porridge. The Temple is also noted for the performance of Pallipaana performed every 12 years by Velans (sorcerers). The Temple also has a majestic display of paintings depicting the ten avatars of Lord Vishnu. The vigraha is Parthasarthi form of Lord Vishnu, holding a whip in his right hand & a conch in his left. During the raids of Tipu Sultan in 1789, the vigraha of Sri Krishna from the Guruvayoor Temple was brought to Ambalappuzha Temple for safe keeping for 12 years.

Karumady - 'Karumadikkuuttan' is a renowned Buddhist pilgrim centre. There is a special Lord Buddha statue made of solid black granite dates back to 11th century. The site is under the protection of Kerala Archaeology Department. People from across the nation and abroad come here to pay homage and seek blessings, as stories about its wonderful healing properties have spread far and wide.

CHENGANNUR MAHADEV TEMPLE - The Temple is one of the oldest and famous Temple. It is a sprawling Temple complex with a circular Sanctum. Lord Shiva and Parvathi Devi are the main investitures of this Temple. Differing from other Temples, there are two main Shrines in this Temple. Lord Shiva facing East and Devi facing west. The main shrine is a conical copper plated one. Devi's main vigraha is made with an alloy of five metals (panchaloham). The Shivalingam is covered with a gold plate bearing an vigraha of Ardhanareeswara or the Shiva-Shakti manifestation of Shiva. The other sub-investitures of the Temple are Ganapathi, Shasta (Lord Ayyappan), Chandikeswaran, Neelagrivan, Ganga and Naagar. There is also a shrine of Sree Krishna nearby. The interesting belief and festival of this Temple is Triputharattu which is considered as a symbol of fertility. This festival is connected with a menstruation ceremony, which is observed periodically in the Temple. That is why this Temple is also considered as Shakthi Peedam. As per legend of Daksha Yagya and Sati's self-immolation, the loins (Arakkettu) of Devi is said to be fallen here. It is also connected with Mahabharata.

Thrichittatt Mahavishnu Temple at Chengannur - The Temple is dedicated to Lord Mahavishnu. The Temple is one of the 108 Divya Deshams. Lord Mahavishnu is worshiped here as Imayavarappan. As per Sthala Puranam, Pandava brother, Yudhishtira did consecration of the vigraha of Lord here. The Temple is one of the Pancha Mahavishnu where consecration was done by Pancha Pandavas.

MAHA VISHNU KSHETRAM AT PULIYOOR - The Temple is dedicated to Lord Vishnu & it is among the 108 Divya Deshams in Kerala. Here, Lord Vishnu is worshipped at Maya Piran. As per Sthala Puranam, after making Parikshit as the King of Hasthinapur, Pandavas went on a pilgrimage. Pancha Pandavas did Prathishta for Maha Vishnu & prayed for reliving from their sins during Mahabharatha war. One of the Pandavas, Bheema did Prathishta at this Temple. Yudhisthira did Prathishta of Thrichittatt Maha Vishnu Temple. Arjuna did Prathishta of Aranmula Partha Sarathy Temple. Nakula did Prathishta of Thiruanvandoor Maha Vishnu Temple & Sahadeva did Prathishta of Thrikodithanam Maha Vishnu Temple. It is said that Gada used by Bheema in Mahabharata war is still in this Temple because Bheema left this Gada here during his tapasya. It is also said that the Saptha Rishis got mukthi in this Temple.

CHAKKULATHUKAVU SREE BHAGAVATHI TEMPLE - Chakkulathamma is famously known as the Mother who answers the call of her devotees. Countless pilgrims irrespective of caste creed and colour reach the shrine. The benevolent look of Goddess unfolds a thousand lotus flowers of real bhakthi in the minds of devotees. The ancient history of the Temple has some divine connections with the story of Sumbha and Nishumbha referred to in the Devi Mahatmyam. The story goes that two demoniac characters called Sumbha and Nishumbha derived super human powers through rigorous meditation of Lord Brahma. They received a boon that they could be killed only through a battle with woman. Such a condition being almost impossible, Sumbha and Nishumbha conquered Indra and other Devas. Saint Narada feeling pity at the misery of the Gods approaches his father Lord Brahma. He told that only one power could restore power and prosperity to Gods and that power was none other than the very Goddess. Devas accordingly started chanting powerful mantras to appease the Goddess. Echoes of the mantras reached her. Goddess Parvathy grasped the pitiable plight of Devas. There emerged another Goddess from within her as if something comes out of a cover. This was the incarnation of Goddess Durga, having taken a divine form to rescue the Devas from the hardships caused by the asuras. The story culminates in a terrible fight between the "Goddess and Asuras under the leadership of Sumba and Nishumbha. Needless to specify, all the asuras were annihilated by the Goddess. It is believed that the Goddess residing in Chakkulathukavu is a wholesome reaction of this all-pervading Goddess namely Durga. The Temple history that dates back to almost 3000 years. Members of the Illam (Brahmin House) namely Pattamana constructed proper Temple. The vigraha similar to that of Sivalainga, taken out by Sage Narada, was installed in the sanctum sanctorum with all the prescribed ceremonies and Poojas. Diseases were wonderfully cured. Worship of Chakkulathamma sharpens the intellect of children; many places near the Temple have derived their original names from the history of the Temple. For instance, the water in the historical pond of the Temple had the sweetness of jaggery. Water was absorbed into the sand shell which contained the vigraha. So the place around the Temple came to be called as 'Neerattupuram'. The Temple was renovated in 1981. The illuminating vigraha of Vana Durga with the holy eight hands is installed near the original vigraha. Lord Shiva, Sastha, Vishnu, Vinayaka, Muruka, Yakshi, Serpent Gods and Navagrahas are installed as 'Upa Devas'.

KANDIYOOR SREE MAHADEVA TEMPLE – The Temple is an ancient Lord Shiva Temple situated on the banks of Achankovil River. The Temple and region are related to the history of ancient Buddhism in Kerala. It is considered as one among the 108 great Shiva Temples of ancient Kerala

consecrated by Lord Parashurama himself. According to another legend, the Rishi Mrikandu, the father of Rishi Markandeya got an vigraha of Lord Shiva in Kirathamoorthy form while bathing in Ganga. He heard an oracle that the vigraha be placed in a holy and befitting place. The Rishi searching for the apt location came to Kerala and ended up in the bank of Achankovil and established the Temple in Kandiyoor. According to another legend the Temple is located at the site where Lord Shiva cut off Lord Brahma's head. The name Kandiyoor comes from name of Shiva Sri Kantan. It is believed that Lord Parasurama renovated the Temple and gave tanthrik rights to Tharananallur family. The Temple is the earliest Temple about which there is an epigraph about its origin in 823 AD during the reign of Rajasekhara Varman. The primary deity of the Temple is Lord Shiva known as Kandiyoorappan (the ruling deity of Kandiyoor). The deity is east facing. The sanctum sanctorum is two-tiered and there is a platform in the front for devotees, a feature that is of the Hoysala style. The 10 ft Gajaprishta style wall is believed to be constructed by Shiva's Bhothaganas. There are puranic legend stone scriptures in the Temple. The deity worshipped as Dakshinamoorthy in the morning, Umamaheshwaran in the noon, Kirathamoorthy in the evening. Deity is worshipped as Panchmukha from South-West corner of Pradakshina Vazhy by viewing five Thazikakudams of Shiva Temples and as Vaikatappan (ruling deity of Vaikom) during sunset. The sub-deities in the Temple include Lord Vishnu, Parvatheesan, Nagaraja and Nagayakshi, Gosala Krishnan, Sastha, Sankaran, Sreekandan, Vadakkumnathan, Annapoomeswary, Ganapathy, Subramanyan, Moola Ganapathy and Brahma Rakshas of which Sankara, Sreekanda, Vadakkumnadha, Parvatheesa and Mrityunjaya are Shiva himself. There are six Shivalinga Prathishtas in this Temple.

SREE NAGARAJA SWAMY TEMPLE AT VETTICODE - The place is believed to be one of the first two snakes Mandir Envisaged by Bhagwan Parshurama. It is said that the Moorthy for the Mandir was made by Mayasura, the asura architect and the consecration was blessed by the presence of Trinity i.e. Lord Brahma, Vishnu & Shiva. The protector family of this Mandir is Meppallil Illam. It is believed that Bhagwan Parshuram himself has appointed the Meppallil family as the serpent protectors. The Mandir has more than 100 serpent murthis which were brought from various places. The month of Kanni is special in serpent worpship, as it is the month in which the serpents wake from their meditation. It is believed that one who is blessed by the sight of this Mandir procession during Ayilyan festival will be protected from animal poison in coming year.

EVOOR MAJOR SRI KRISHNASWAMY TEMPLE AT HARIPAD - The Temple is dedicated to Lord Krishna. It is said to have originated five millennium ago following Khandava Dahanam. The Temple in its current form is built by Moolam Thirunal. As per legend, Agni, after devouring clarified butter uninterrupted for twelve years from Swetaki's Yagja, suffered a stomach ailment. Lord Brahma advised him to consume the Khandava forest. The forest was abode to Takshaka, the Naga leader and friend of Indra. Whenever Agni tried to consume the forest, Indra, with his thundershowers, stopped him. Agni turned to Arjuna and Lord Krishna for assistance. Agni armed Arjuna with the mighty bow Gandiva which rivalled Pinaka, the bow of Lord Shiva himself. When Arjuna and Lord Krishna arrived at Khandava forest, Kanva Maharishi approached them with a

request to spare his Archa moorthy (a four handed vigraha of Lord Vishnu), Lord Krishna granted the request. Arjuna constructed a Sarakoodam to shelter Agni. Under the Sarakoodam, Agni consumed the forest and was cured of the ailment. Grateful, Agni, expressed his wish to install Arca moorthy in a new Temple there to facilitate worship. As instructed by Sri Krishna, Arjuna fired an arrow to determine an auspicious location for the proposed Temple. The place where the arrow landed was used to construct the new Temple. Evoor is a corrupt form of Eythoor (place where arrow was shot). Lord Krishna performed Prana-Pratishta and Arjuna performed the first pooja. Bhoothanathaswamy (Kiratha Murthy form of Lord Shiva) and Yakshi Amma (Devi Parvathy) were consecrated as the Sub Deities. The remains of burned trees in the locality and names of nearby places, Karippuzha (kari means char), Pathiyoor (corruption of Kathiya Oor-place that burnt), Pandavarkavu, Mannarasala, Kannamangalam (Kanva-Mangalam Kanva's abode) agree with the account. Evoor Bhagavan's Deity is the unique Prayoga Chakra Prathishta. The vigraha of Sri Krishna is in the four armed Lord Vishnu form with Panchajanya Shankha, Sudarshana Chakra and butter in three hands and the fourth arm held on hip. The deity is furious form and Raktha-pushpanjali is a special offering here which is unavailable in Vishnu Temples elsewhere. Ulsava in Evoor Temple starts on first day of makara and continues for ten days. The ulsava begins with the hosting of Garuda printed flag. On the ninth day there is Kala-kettu (decorated effigies of Bulls). The ulsava culminates with Aaraattu (holy bath) after that the flag is lowered and the deity proceeds to Pallikkuruppu (Holy Sleep).

MANNARASALA TEMPLE AT HARIPAD - Of all the places of Serpent worship in the world, there is none that is more benign, owe inspiring & legendary than Mannarasala, as blessed and envisaged by Lord Parasurama, the creator of Kerala. It is not a rare thing to see the same serpent appear in the same location for a number of days in the Temple premises. On the steps of the gatehouse, on the hedgerows, among the creepers; those who perform bhajanam in the Temple can stand very close at any time and pray. The beliefs & rituals associated with the Mannarasala Temple are different from most other Temples & this is one rare Temples where the puja pattern is headed by a Brahmin lady. Legends say that when the Muthassan left for the Cellar, he had given certain rights & instructions to his mother & since then the mother assumes this high position. She should live as a brahmacharini & observe penance. Those who worship me with devotion will have children, will be cured of diseases, will have long life and health & wealth; the men of the family will have the title of 'Vasukisridevi". He reminded that the rituals and customs suggested by Parasurama are inviolable. Valia Amma is the heart and soul of Mannarasala. The resplendent brightness of Valia Amma who has turned into a symbol of Naga deities through fasting & other austerities has not dimmed in the least by now as a result of the performance of rituals & poojas. Pilgrims cannot leave Mannarasala without seeing that fascinating divine glow with their own eyes & feeling contended. The sight of faithful devotees, who come here to seek the blessings of Nagaraja, waiting for long to see the flicker of the eyes of the great mother, so serene and compassionate and filled with blessings, continues even today.

DISTRICT – ERNAKULAM (Railway Station – Ernakulam/Idaplli/Triupunittura/Kurikad/Aluva)

S. No.	Temple	Address	Type
1	Dharmanath Temple	Mattancherry – 682002	Jain
2	Shri Bhavaneeswara Temple	Palluruthy, Kochi – 682006	Shiva, Vishnu
3	Ernakulam Kshetra Kshema Samithi	Kochi – 682011	Shiva

S. No.	Temple	Address	Type
4	Thrikkakara Temple	Edappally – 682024	Vamana (Vishnu)
5	Amrita Institute of Medical Sciences	AIMS Ponekkara – 682041	Saint Sushruta
6	Thamaramkulangara Sree Dharmasastha Temple	Tripunithura P.O. – 682301	Dhanwanthari
7	Sree Poornathrayeesa Temple	Thrippunithura, Ernakulam – 682301	Vishnu
8	Ameda Temple	Udayamperoor - 682307	Mata
9	Chottanikkara Dewaswom	Chottanikkara – 682312	Mata
10	Sri Datta Anjaneya Temple	Alwaye - 683101	Hanuman
11	Aluva Manappuram Mahadeva Temple	Aluva Manapuram, Kochi – 683108	Shiva
12	Vezhamparambu Mana	Karumalloor - 683511	Mana
13	Kottayil Kovilakam	Chendamangalam - 683512	Krishna
14	Kallil Temple	Kunnathunadu Thaluk - 683544	Jain
15	Iringole Forest Temple	Rayamangalam - 683545	Mata
16	Sreekrishna Swamy Temple	Chelamattom - 683550	Krishna
17	Thiru Nayathode Siva Narayana Temple	Nayathode – 683572	Shiva, Vishnu
18	Adi Shankaracharya Temple	Kalady - 683574	Adi Shankaracharya
19	Thirumoozhikkulam Lakshmana Temple	Kurumassery - 683579	Ramayana Circuit
20	Pazhoor Perumthrikkovil	Pazhoor - 686664	Shiva

DHARMANATH TEMPLE AT MATTANCHERRY – The Temple is dedicated to Lord Dharmanath the 15th Tirthankar. It is a renowned & sacred Jain Temple. Its features, different artworks, sculptures and vigrahas of Jain Gods are noteworthy. The Temple is deeply inspired by the Jain Temples of Gujarat and is beautifully tiled by white marbles and other carved structures inside the Temple. The Temple has several blocks designed for prayers and offerings. On entering the premises the first thing pilgrims notice is the imposing Temple gate which is a gateway to the beautiful architecture and splendour of our rich heritage. There is a beautiful picture of Gajalakshmi sitting on the lotus placed over the gates of the Temple. The pillars here are curved elephant trunk brackets quite similar to the Jain Dilwara Temple of Mount Abu. The entire marble interior of the Temple is adorned with artworks and beautifully arranged with the sculptured pillars and vigrahas of Jain Gods and Tirthankars. The walls of the shrines have many Jain holy pilgrimage places depicted in detail. Four additional deities were installed & the entire Temple now has a brand new appearance.

Tirumala Devaswom Temple at Mattancherry - One of the most important Temples in Mattancherry, the Temple is dedicated to Lord Venkatachalapathy. The sanctum sanctorum houses the vigrahas of the Lord with his consorts, Sreedevi and Bhoodevi on either side. Visitors can pay their respects to the shrines of Lord Hanuman, Lord Ganesha, Goddess Mahalakshmi and Garuda, a mythical bird and the vehicle of Lord Vishnu. The Temple sees huge footfalls when many festivals are organised in the months of November and April. The

Temple yard houses vigrahas of Swami Vijayendra Theertha, a philosopher and a king of Vijayanagara. There is a holy tank as Well. Of particular note is a huge bronze bell that is about four ft in diameter and six ft high. It is said that in earlier times, the chiming of the bell could be heard from afar. The Temple was constructed in 1559.

SREE BHAVANEESWARA TEMPLE AT PALLURUTHY, KOCHI – The Temple was developed by Sree Narayana Guru Swamigal in the year 1904. It is dedicated to Lord Shiva and Lord Vishnu with equality. It is the first Temple of the backward classes to have a Golden Mast Swarna Dhwajam. Ernakulam based "Swajanodharani Sabha" submitted a request to Maharaja of Cochin asking for a Temple for Ezhava's. Sambranthi Ayyapan was also a part of this group. Although a bit late, Maharaja of Cochin sanctioned the construction of the Temple subject to a certain conditions. Sree Narayana Guru did the Shiva Linga Prathishta at the Temple. Gurudevan himself appointed his disciple Bava Bharathi as the Melshanthi (head priest) of the Temple. The Temple keeps its doors opened for any devotee, irrespective of his caste or religion even today. The Temple thus symbolizes the path shown by Sree Narayana Guru. The Architecture style of the Temple is moderated style of Architecture. There are many shrines constructed for people who worship the Lords Shiva and Vishnu. The wood carvings inside the interior wall fascinate the tourist toward itself. There is no pond or tank for the devotees to take bath before worshipping the god.

ERNAKULAM SHIVA TEMPLE – The Temple is one of the rare Shiva Temples where God faces sea towards west. Very popular as Ernakulathappan, this Temple is dedicated to Lord Shiva. It was built during the Maharaja rule. The history of the shrine is linked with the history of the city. As per the legend, it was one of the 7 royal Temples of Kochi Maharajas. Arjuna, the pandava performs a severe penance to propitiate Lord Shiva. Pleased with Arjuna's devotion, Lord Shiva accompanied with his consort Sri Parvathi set out from their abode at Kailash to meet Arjuna. Lord Shiva disguises himself as "Kiratha", a tribal hunter before appearing before Arjuna. Just as Lord Shiva appears before Arjuna he sees a wild boar charging towards Arjuna and shoots an arrow at the boar. Arjuna, who is an accomplished archer, also shoots an arrow at the boar. The boar who was in fact a demon named Mookasura in disguise is killed and its original form is revealed. However, dispute arises between Arjuna and Kiratha as to who is the real killer of the animal. A battle ensues between the two, lasting a long time, ultimately resulting in Kiratha's victory over Arjuna. The vanquished Arjuna, unable to even stand up makes a Shiva Linga out of mud and performs a pooja offering flowers. To his surprise, he sees that the flower he offers over the Shiva Linga is falling over the head of Kiratha. Arjuna then realises that Kiratha is none other than his Lord Shiva. Lord Shiva, in his true form, along with Sri Parvathy appears before Arjuna & blesses him. He also gifts him the divine arrow, the "Pasupathastram." Devalan performs his rites here & is redeemed from the curse. At his request the Lord Shiva & Sri Parvathy appear here & exist in the form of Linga. It is this "Gourisankararoopam" that is seen as "Swayambhoolingam".

THRIKKAKARA TEMPLE AT EDAPPALLY – The Temple earlier known as Thirul Kaal Karai, meaning land where the Lord has placed his foot, is the most renowned. Research dates the Temple to be 2000 years or even older. It is the only Temple dedicated to Lord Vamana, who is one of the incarnations of Lord Vishnu. Lord Vamana is believed to have ended the glorious rule of King Mahabali, in the guise of a Brahmin boy. The Temple is also listed as one of the 108 Divya Desams. Many believe that Thrikkakara was the capital of the Mahabali's kingdom. The 10-day Onam festival is flagged off from this Temple with a colourful pageant. Since Onam is the most important festival of this Temple, the Onasadya (Onam feast) is also held in a grand manner. People across all religions participate in the same, celebrating communal harmony in a big way. Earlier, under the reign of the Maharaja of Travancore the Onam festival here was jointly organised by the 61 Naduvazhis (local rulers). The other festivals the Temple observes are Vishu, Diwali, Makar Sankranti, Navratri and Saraswati Puja.

SAINT SUSHRUTA AT AMRITA INSTITUTE OF MEDICAL SCIENCES – There is a 40 ft statute of father of surgery, Saint Sushruta. The two-tiered concrete vigraha, by sculptor Chavara Vijayan, shows Sushruta seated in padmasana posture on a raised pedestal. At its base, there is also a detailed sculpture of the Sage performing surgery on a patient, assisted by a team of physicians.

THAMARAMKULANGARA SREE DHARMASASTHA TEMPLE AT TRIPUNITHURA - Devotees consider this Temple as an extension of the famous Sastha Temple at Chamravattom. According to anecdotes Lord Sastha followed one of his Priests from Morakkala Mana who had shifted to Tripunithura. Lord Sastha assumed the form of a lizard and came with the priest comfortably by sitting on his traditional umbrella made up of palm leaves. Thamaramkulangara Sree Dharmasastha is considered as the incarnation of Lord Dhanwanthari and this is the only one Temple in Tripunithura with Dharmasastha as main deity. Besides Dharmasastha devotees also worship Lord Ganesha and Bhadrakali along with Nagaraja and Brahmasrakshas. A huge Banyan Tree with a pleasing breeze created by its shivering silvery leaves is existed in the Temple. A Nadappura with a traditional flag post adds the beauty of the Temple structure.

SREE POORNATHRAYEESA TEMPLE AT TRIPUNITHURA, KOCHI – The Temple is the only Temple in South India where you can see an odd pose of Lord Vishnu, sitting under the shade of five royal hoods of the divine serpent, Ananthan, whose folded body itself acts as the throne for the God. Devotees worship the almighty here as "Santhaana Gopaala Moorthy" (Savior of infants). Anecdotes say that this beautiful vigraha of Sree Poornathrayeesa was presented to Arjuna by Lord Vishnu, while the former sought the help of the Supreme Being to give rebirth to the ten children of a brahmin (believed to be a member of PuliyannurIllom, ancestral home of the chief priest of the Temple). Arjuna along with the ten children and the holy vigraha returned in his chariot and handed over the children to the brahmin. Later a Temple was built here in memory of this event and the sanctum-sanctorum (Sree Kovil) of this Temple (presently known as Muthukulangara) is in the form of a chariot. Arjuna sent Lord Vighnesha to search for a holy place for the installation of the vigraha

of Lord Vishnu. Devotees consider the ever shining "Valia Vilakku" situated in front of the vigraha, as the oil lamp lighted by Arjuna. Burnt oil of this traditional lamp possesses great medicinal value. The deity, ever since has been living in the minds and hearts of devotees as Santhanagopala Moorthy, blessing the needy, infertile couples with children. Here the divine sculptures in their crude form bear a unique beauty. Representing the Lord of Vaikunta and Yoganarayan, the deity is the Lord incarnate of the triune Vedas. Ensconced with Goddess of Earth, Bhoomi Devi and Goddess of Prosperity, Lakshmi Devi under the umbrella – like hoods of the Serpent King Anantha, the Godhead has been the provider of all the wishes of His devotees.

AMEDA TEMPLE AT UDAYAMPEROOR - The Temple is located on the banks of Vembanad Lake. The Temple is very unique & powerful Sarpa Kavu. Bhagwan Parshurama did Prathishta here. Vilakku, which was lighted by Bhagwan Parshurama, is still seen inside the Temple. The oil from this lamp is given to bhakthas for recovering from illness. Seven forms of Aadi Parashakthi are Sapthamthrukkal. Lord Veerabhadra and Ganesha have Sannidhi here. The main Garbhagriham in the Temple is Sapthamthrukkal. There are Sannidhi to Nagas, Nagayakshi & Lord Vishnu. Sarparadhana is done here. Naga Panchami is famous here. Those who have Nagadosham come here and get relieved of their Doshas.

CHOTTANIKKARA BHAGAVATHY TEMPLE – It is the most important Temple among the 393 shrines spread over 3 Districts of Kerala. The Divine Mother known as Rajarajeswari (Adiparasakthi) is worshipped here in three forms Saraswathy in the morning, Lakshmi at noon and Durga in the evening. There is an vigraha of Mahavishnu on the same pedestal & so the Deity is called Ammenarayana, Devinarayana, Lakshminarayana and Bhadrenarayana also. Along with Lakshmi & Narayana, there are vigrahas of Lord Brahma, Shiva, Ganapathi, Subramanya and Sastha on the same pedestal. Apart from the main deity, the Temple complex consists of Kizhukkavu Bhagavathy Temple, Temple for Sastha, Shiva, Ganapathi, Nagas and other Upa-Devas. "Makom Thozhal" (worship on the Makom day) is the most important festival of the Temple which is celebrated in the month of Kumbham (Feb / March). It is believed that Bhagavathy in her full attire gave darshan to Vilwamangalam Swamiyar on the Makom day and appears on the same day every year for giving darhsan to the devotees in

her special appearance. The Bhadrakaali at Kizhukkavu is believed to exorcise evil spirit from devotees. The golden hued vigraha bedecked with flowers, garlands, jewels and bathed in myriad of light shine splendidly. Sree Mookambika Saraswathy is also believed as present in the Temple in the morning. That is why Mookambika Temple at Kollur opens only after the Goddess Saraswathy returns to their late in the morning. Being present here during Valiyaguruthy on Fridays permanently cures women suffering from mental abnormalities like schizophrenia. An ancient 'Pala' tree standing on the north eastern side of the sanctum sanctorum is covered with long iron nails hammered on by haunted victims with their foreheads.

SRI DATTA ANJANEYA TEMPLE AT ALWAYE - The Temple is located on the banks of River Periyar.

A beautiful entrance to the Temple welcomes the devotees to redress all their grievances. Temple of Lord Sidharaja Dattatreya built in stone is seen at the centre a bit elevated. The deity with a smiling appearance has got Sankh (couch shell), Chakra (discus), Damaru (small drum), Thrissul (trident), Kamandalu (water vessel), Kamadhenu (the divine cow who is capable of fulfilling any wishes of the baktha) and Abhaya Hastha (a hand ready to save, console & redress). The vigraha has six eyes & six hands embracing the devotees and thus stands Sidharaja Dattathreya, the trinity, taking care of the devotees. At the backside of the Temple, on the way for perambulation, is an Oudumbara Vriksha (Malayalam-athimaram). It is a tree which is very very dear to the Lord. Perambulating this tree brings solace and people without children are blessed to have children. It also keeps away the devils and evil forces from your home. The branches of this tree is used for homas and it is a constituents in the Nalpamara (athi, ethi, peral, arrayal), an ayurvedic medicine for skin care. On to the left of the main Temple is the Temple of Mahaganapathy with all the charisma and abhayamudra (a gesture showing ready to solve, save) assuring to remove all the physical, mental and spiritual obstructions experienced by the devotees. On the right side is the Temple of Karyasidhi Anjaneya. The construction of the Karyasidhi Anjaneya Temple as wished by Sri Swamiji started in 1998. The vigraha of Lord Anjaneya made at Sucheendram was brought in a procession with receptions at various Temples of Kerala. Referring to the then newly constructed air port at Nedumbassery (Kochi International Airport), swamiji wished that let Lord Hanuman, the son of air, protect the airport. The sanctum sanctorum of Lord Anjeneya consists of Lakshmana, Sree Ramachandra and Seethe Devi. An vigraha of Nagendra is consecrated along with Karyasidhi Anjeneya. vigrahas of Navagrahas in front of Lord Anjaneya Temple was also consecrated in 2001 by Sri Swamiji. To the left of the Temple, there is the prayer hall and GuruMandira (the place where Sri Swamiji resides during his visits) and there is a bath ghat at river Periyar for the physical and spiritual hygene of the devotees.

ALUVA MANAPPURAM MAHADEVA TEMPLE – It is located on the banks of the Periyar River. The Temple is illuminated during the Aluva Sivarathri, which is celebrated here annually, and is a sight to behold.

VEZHAMPARAMBU MANA AT PARAVOOR - Centuries back Paravoor King invited two Brahmin twins from Puliyannur in Kannur district and entrusted Thantric charge of Peruvaram Mahadeva Temple. The Paravoor King and the King of Alangot were not in good terms. Alangot King employed all the methods at his command to destroy Paravoor King but proved no use. At last he resorted to invoking an evil force "Krithika" was sent to Paravoor King to finish him. The Brahmin twins had an intuition of what was going to happen and they forced by their Thantric power Krithika to return. The place where the twins confronted the evil force is known as Perumkulangarakavu. The King of Cochin invited one of the twins to Thripunithura to take charge of the Thantric rites of Thripunithura Poornathrayeesha Temple. The younger of the twins went to Thripunithura and settled there and his Mana came to be known as Thripunithura Puliyannur Illam. The elder of the twins settled in Karumaloor, near Paravoor and his Mana came to be known as Vezhamparambu Mana. Vezhamparabu Mana is highly famous for Thantric rites, Vasthu Sastra, architecture and astrology. The Thantric rites' right of almost all Temples in Paravoor region, barring few, is vested on Vezhamparambu Mana. The Mana has a number of feats to its credit. Bringing rain during drought through Yaga and entering into talks with evil spririts, including Yemen are few among them. The front region of the Mana is known as Manakpadi. The Mana is having few Temples, snake shrines, Temple ponds, centuries old giant trees etc. The Mana has a large library of Palm-leaf scriptures containing Thantric science, Ayurveda science and other ancient sciences and ancient literature and details of numerous art forms.

CHENDAMANGALAM - Kottayil Kovilakam is situated on the banks of the confluence of three Rivers. It is a small hilltop, where a Lord Krishna Temple and others spiritual places are exist depicting the cultural harmony of Kerala. It was the seat of Kshatriya chieftains of Villarvattom and is situated near the ancient Kunnathuthali Temple. On the riverside, a group of huge rocks known as 'Anapara' is the main highlight. The Kunnathuthali Temples were constructed 400 years ago.

Sree Venugopala Krishna Swami Devasthan - The Temple is dedicated to Sri Venugopalakrishna Swamy. The vigraha of Sri Venugopalakrishna Swamy is made of Shila stone. The Temple had been established in 1900 AD. In the Temple, there are Utsava vigrahas of Sri Venugopalakrishna Swamy along with Sri Garuda and Sri Hanuman. The Temple celebrates a six-day-long annual festival in the month of Vaisakh.

KALLIL TEMPLE AT KUNNATHUNADU TALUK - A 9th century Jain Temple shaped out of from a huge rock on a small hill in a picturesque surrounding. The visitor has to climb 120 steps to reach this rare historic Temple.

IRINGOLE FOREST TEMPLE AT RAYAMANGALAM - Iringole Kavu is a famous Temple in forest. Temple dedicated to Goddess Durga. This is one of the 108 Durga Temples in Kerala believed to have been consecrated by Lord Parasurama, the sixth avatar of Lord Vishnu. The Goddess is worshiped in three forms i.e. Devi Saraswati in the morning, Devi Vanadurga in the afternoon & Devi Bhadrakali in the evening.

SREEKRISHNA SWAMY TEMPLE AT CHELAMATTOM - Ghelamattam village, located on the banks of Periyar River, is blessed with three 'avatars' - Lord Krishna, Lord Narasimha and Lord Vamana. The first simple shrine with Lord Vamanamurthy as the presiding deity came into being on the north-east side of the present Temple complex; then came Lord Vishnu's Narasimha avatar, the household deity of Thottamattam Mana, followed by the holy arrival of Lord Krishna. As per legend, a ancient Brahmin Household, Veliyamkol Mana, held the key to the creation of this shrine: a self originated vigraha of Lord Shiva being worshipped as its family deity and that during one of the floods, a chest came floating near it. Veliyamkol Mana retrived the chest from the river: it contained the sacred ido! of Lord Krishna. The celestial sight the Patriarch and others around had, when the chest was opened, was beyond explanation. The elderly pious Brahmin carried the box to his Mana and worshipped it. After a very long time, he enshrined the vigraha ceremoniusly with all the attendant rituals in a temporary Sreekovil built on his compound. Ages passed. Later, the existing shrine was built at Chelamattam strictly according to precept and divine astrological predictions, re-enshrined the magnificent vigraha of Lord Krishna in the sanctum sanctorum on the right of the abode of Lord Nasimha under the same roof. The day on which the star Thiruvonam' falls in the Malayalam month of Kumbhom every year 'Arrattu' is held and valiya villakku is celebrated on preceding day with all pomp and show: the invoked vigraha is ascended on an elephant back, then taken ceremoniously in procession to the same place where the vigraha was temporarily installed and other rituals and Poojas are held uninterruptedly every year. Initially 9 measures of rice used to be cooked for offering to the God, of which very little was used as libation for the deity of Lord Shiva, the rest being offered to the Pullaya households conferring it as their rights. They preserve the cooked rice in powder form and it is still believed that it has amazing medicinal value for curing any decease that they may contract. The existing Sree Kovil of the Temple is believed to have been built by the then reigning Maharaja of Ambalapuzha. In deference to the wishes of the King of Travancore, Chelamattam Temple is recognized as one amongst the ten scheme Temples and that the hereditary priesthood (Tantri) is vested in the Nedumbilly Tharananallur household of Sree Padmanabha Temple at Thiruvananthapuram.

THIRU NAYATHODE SHIVA NARAYANA TEMPLE - The deity at this Temple is Lord Shiva and Lord Vishnu. This Temple is a protected monument by Archaeological Department, Kerala. Nearest Railway Station is Angamali.

KALADY - Kalady is the birth place of Adi Shankaracharya, the great Indian Philosopher & Theologian who lived in the 8th century.

Shri Krishna Temple - This Temple is known as the ancestral deity of Shankaracharya. It is mentioned as the kuladevata (ancestral deity) in verse 243 of Shankara's Prabodha Sudhakaram. The Temple is under Kalady Devasthanam. It is also the only surviving structure from the time of

Shankara. The worship in this Temple is also conducted by Namboothiris, unlike in the Shankaracharya Temple. The important event in this Temple is Kanakadhara Yanjam. Sree Sankara during pendancy of upanayanam went begging for alms around and reached door steps of a poor widowed lady who had nothing but a dried amla to offer. Moved by the condition of that lady and her broad mind to offer whatever is available to bala Bhikshu, Sankara instantly recited Kanakadhara stotram. The golden gooseberry rain fell in the garden of that old lady and the house got to be known as Swarnathu mana . The ancestral deity Temple of Sree Sankaracharya long back has started a Yagna during Sankara Jayanti season chanting Kanakadhara stotram by 32 Brahmins representing 32 years of life of that great guru.

Manickamangalam Temple - The Temple is dedicated to Bhagavathi, or the Goddess Durga. Shankara's father Sivaguru was the priest in this Temple. According to legend, one day he could not go by himself, so he sent little Shankara with a measure of milk as an offering to Devi. Shankara noticed that even after the offering, the measure of milk before Devi remained unchanged. He was sad and started to cry, so Devi took pity on the boy and drank the milk. References to the deity can be found in Soundaryalahari.

Mattoor Thiru Vellaman Thulli Siva Temple - According to legend, as Shankara's mother Aryamba got older, she could not walk to Vadakkunnathan Temple in Thrissur to worship. She still wanted to have darshan of the Lord. Lord Shiva appeared in a dream, and he suggested that Aryamba follow a dancing white deer that would appear before her house the next day. Lord Shiva promised the deer would lead her to an vigraha and disappear, saying she could worship the vigraha, and not walk the long distance to the Temple. This Shiva Temple was named Thiru Vella Man Thulli, or "dancing white deer."

Nayathodu Sankara Narayana Temple - The Temple is an example of Advaita in worship by Shankaracharya. According to legend, once Shankara prayed to Lord Vishnu in this Shiva Temple, Lord Vishnu also came to reside in same vigraha. To this day, after offerings are made to Lord Shiva, everything is removed and offerings are made to the same vigraha for Lord Vishnu.

Ramakrishna Advaita Ashram - The Ashram is a branch centre of Ramakrishna Math, headquartered at Belur, West Bengal. It has a spacious prayer hall and a shrine modeled on the Sri Ramakrishna Temple at Belur Math.

Sri Adi Sankara Keerthi Sthamba Mandapam - It is an eight-story memorial built by Kanchi Kamakoti Math. The entrance guarded by two elephant vigrahas, leads to the Paduka Mandapam.

Two silver knobs represent the padukas, or wooden sandals of the Teacher. The walls of the memorial feature framed relief paintings that tell the story of Adi Shankaracharya. Several large vigrahas of Ganapati, Adi Shankara, and others are also housed in this memorial. Adi Shankara's shrines in Kalady are open to all pilgrims irrespective of religion & caste. Visitors can review the life of Shankaracharya as they climb to the top. The famous Shankara Stupa has eight sides.

Shankara Temple - The Shrine, run by Sringeri Math, is situated on the northern bank of river Periyar. There are two major shrines in the Temple; one is dedicated to Shankara & other to Goddess Saradamba, the main deity of Sringeri. The samadhi of Shankara's mother is also located here. A small shrine to Vinayaka is the scene of evening prayers, chanted to the rhythmic ringing of cymbals. The worship is done by Tamil or Kannada Smartha Brahmins & not by Namboothiris.

THIRUMOOZHIKKULAM LAKSHMANA TEMPLE AT KURUMASSERY - The Temple is related to Ramayana Circuit. As per Sthala Puranam, during exile period, Lord Rama's brother Bharat comes to visit Lord Rama to bring him back to Ayodhya but Lakshmana misunderstood and think that Bharat came to kill Lord Rama. Later, as per Akashvani, Lakshmana realises his mistake & seeks forgiveness. When Bharat came & embraced Lord Rama and speak very softly, Thus, the name Thiru Moozhikkulam which means place of soft words. The Temple is one of the Nalambalam Temples worshiped during Karkidaka i.e. Ramayana month. The Temple is one of the 108 Divya Deshams. Here, Lord Prerumal is Sukthinathapperumal & Goddess is Maduraveni Thaayaar. It is believed that Maharishi Haritha done penance for Lord Mahavishnu at this place and Lord Mahavishnu appeared before him and gives advices which are called Thiru Mozhi, which means sacred words.

PAZHOOR - Pazhoor Perumthrikkovil is a Temple dedicated to Lord Shiva. It is Sandhara type Temple with cardinal doors on four sides. The plinth and the wall together are of granite stone work and the rest of timber and sheet roof in circular vimana. Dwarapalakas are made of wood. Main deity Lord Shiva is facing east. Square ardhamandapa contains beautiful wooden carvings on the ceiling. Pranala is a typical ornate Kerala type with standing Yaksha bearing at its tip. It has some of the notable examples of old workmanship in wood, illustrating various scenes from puranas and figures from Bhagavata Purana, Ramayana, and Mahabharata. The Temple can be dated to 12th century AD. There is a palace like traditional structure outside the Temple compound. Considering the structural and mural importance, the Temple was declared as protected monument by Kerala State Archaeology Department in 1994.

DISTRICT – IDUKKI (Railway Station – Teni)

S. No.	Temple	Address	Type
1	Sree Krishna Swami Temple	Thodupuzha - 685584	Krishna

SREE KRISHNA SWAMI TEMPLE AT THODUPUZHA - The Temple is located on the banks of Thodupuzhayar, a tributary of River Muvattupuzha. Lord Krishna presides there in the form of Navaneetha Krishna who holds butter in his right pam. The tantric rights of the Temple is held by the Aramallur Kavanattu Mana. The Poojas are conducted by two Mutts named as 'Padinjare Mutt' and 'Thuruthel Mutt'. The origin of the Temple is associated with many myths which date backs to the ancient era. Popular myths has it that once a wandering Brahmin who was on a pilgrimage to the various Temples reached here and got a divine vision of Lord Krishna. After getting the vision of Lord Krishna, he purified his body in the nearby river (Thodupuzhayar) and offered Nivedyam to the deity by lighting a lamp. This was on the day of Chothi in the Malayalam month of Meenam. This incident is commonly believed to be the prime reason for the Temple's origin. Later, the raja of Keezhmalanadu constructed a shrine for the deity and consecrated an vigraha. At present, the famous Chothioottu feast is conducted in the Temple. 'Nilapaduthara' or the holy platform is situated in front of the Temple where the Saint received the vigraha of deity. The vigraha is taken out of the sanctum sanctorum on the festival occasions to this platform and is taken back with fully decorated. The main offerings to the deity are owl & pigeon. Utsav Bali, a sacred ceremony is conducted on the ninth day of festivities accompanied by the presence of thousands of devotees. This Temple also have the largest 'Kalyana Mandapam' or wedding hall in central Travancore region named as 'Krishna Theertham'. The Temple has sub shrines of Goddess Bhagavathy, Lord Shiva, Ganapathi and Naga as subordinate deities.

DISTRICT – KANNUR (Railway Station – Thalassery/Kannapuram/Kannur)

S. No.	Temple	Address	Type
1	Sree Sundareswara Temple	Talap - 670002	Shiva
2	Shree Mookambika Temple	Pallikunnu - 670004	Mata
3	Shree Jagannath Temple	Thalassery - 670101	Jagannath
4	Sree Ramaswami Temple	Tiruvangad - 670103	Rama
5	Taliparamba Rajarajeswara Temple	Taliparamaba - 670141	Shiva
6	Sri Krishna Temple	Trichambaram – 670141	Krishna
7	Annapoorneshwari Temple	Cherukunnu - 670301	Mata
8	Sri Subrahmanya Swami Temple	Payyanur - 670307	Subrahmanya
9	Muthappan Temple	Anthoor, Parassinikadavu – 670563	Shiva
10	Sri Mahadevi Temple	Irukkur – 670593	Mata
11	Sri Mavilayikkavu Temple	Mavilayi – 670622	Ganpati, Mata
12	Sree Peralassery Temple	Mundalur - 670622	
13	Sree Thricherumanna Alias Kottiyoor Devaswom	P.O. Kottiyoor – 670651	Shakti Peetha, Shiva
14	Sree Mridanga Saileshwari Temple	Muzhakkunnu - 670673	Mata

SREE SUNDARESWARA TEMPLE AT TALAP - The Temple is dedicated to Lord Shiva. In 1916, it was built by Shree Narayana Guru - the famous Saint who devoted his life to uplift the downtrodden in Kerala. The interior of the walls are designed by Sri Chaithanyaall swami. This Temple is also fames as one of the largest Temples in Kannur. The eight-day annual festival of the Temple is celebrated in the Malayalam month of Meenam (March- April). On the last day the Arattu (Holy Bath) ritual is held and is followed by a procession of caparisoned elephants and fireworks, which mark the end of the festival. Many religious and cultural programs add colour to the festival.

SHREE MOOKAMBIKA TEMPLE AT PALLIKUNNU - The Temple is devoted to Goddess Mookambika. It is believed that the idea of establishing a Mookambika Devi Temple was of Adi Shankara.. As a result, around 1200 years ago, he himself installed an vigraha in this Temple. This Temple is of great importance as the presiding deity is considered as the manifestation of three Goddesses, Mahalakshmi, Shakti and Saraswati. The major attraction of this Temple is the Navratri festival, which is celebrated in the months of October and November. Janmashtami, popular as Krishna Jayanti, is also celebrated at this religious site. The Kanathoor Maha Vishnu Temple is another prominent attraction of Pallikunnu.

JAGANNATH TEMPLE AT THALASSERY – It is one of the best loved Temples in Malabar. Sree Narayana Guru consecrated the Temple in 1908. He was in the forefront of the fight against untouchability in Kerala. Construction of the Temple is in Kerala architectural style. The Sreekovil has no windows. Only the priests can enter the Sreekovil. A vigraha of Sree Narayana Guru was installed on the Temple premises in 1927. It was made in Italy and transported by ship to India.

SREE RAMASWAMI TEMPLE AT TIRUVANGAD - It is an important Temple. The Temple is generally known as the Brass Pagoda from the copper sheeting of its roof. A part of the Temple was damaged by Tipu Sultan's troops in 18th century but the Temple itself is believed to have been saved from destruction. The Temple contains some interesting sculptures and lithic records. The annual festival of Temple commences on Vishu day in Medam (April–May) and lasts for seven days. It is one of the five major shrines dedicated to Lord Sree Rama in Kerala. The Temple tank is known as Chira. The Temple is well maintained and has excellent wood carvings, terracotta art work, mural paintings carved on wooden planks in the ceilings are a repository of art treasure.

THE RAJARAJESHWARA TEMPLE AT TALIPARAMBA, KANNUR – It is one among 108 Shiva Temples in Kerala created by Lord Parasurama. The main deity is famous as Rajarajeswara Perumal. Rajarajeswara is one of the names of Lord Shiva. The old name of Taliparamba was 'Lakshmipura' as this place was considered as an abode of prosperity. This Temple has a prominent place amongst the numerous Shiva Temples in South India. If any problem is encountered in Temples of South India, the final solution is sought in this Temple through a prasna, a traditional method of astrological decision making. The prasna is conducted on a peedha (a raised platform) situated outside the Temple. It is regarded as one of the ancient Shakti Peethams. As per legend of Daksha Yagya & Sati's self-immolation, the head of Sati fell here, so this Temple is also popularly known as Rajarajeswari Temple. The Namaskara Mandapa (mukhamandapa) in front of the Sreekovil (sanctum sanctorum) is the place where Lord Sree Rama (on his way back to Ayodhya from Lanka after defeating Ravana) prostrated before Raja Rajeswara. As a respect to Sree Rama, no one is allowed into this namaskaramandapa and offer prayers, which is permitted in other Temples for Brahmins. The place is considered as most sacred for performing Koodiyattam and Chakyar Koothu. Whenever a new Koodiyattam is being directed, first it is usually performed at this Temple. However only the 'Maani' family of Chakyars solely possess the right of performing Koodiyattam here.

TRICHAMBARAM SREE KRISHNA TEMPLE – The Temple is dedicated to Lord Krishna. This is a famous & ancient Temple. It is believed that Bhagwan Parshurama did Prathishta of Lord Krishna here and Maharishi Shambara did tapasya here. Lord Krishna is sitting in Raudrabhavam here after Kansavadham. To pacify the Raudrabhavam of Lord Krishna, early morning at 3 AM, nivedyam is offered to Lord Krishna. All the balalilas of Lord Krishna & Balrama are shown here in a dance form and Shambara Muni and Bhagwan Parshurama witnessed all the Lord Krishna Nrityam alongwith Devaki & Vasudeva. Inside the Temple, Jala Durga can be seen & it is believed that Devi is yogamaya who has come here to stay with Lord. A famous Ilanji tree stands inside the Temple which does not bears fruits. Nrithyam, annual utsavam, done here. Eventhough Kerala is famous for Utsavam with elephants but this is a rare Temple were no elephants can go near it.

ANNAPOORNESHWARI TEMPLE AT CHERUKUNNU - The Temple is a famous Goddess Parvati Temple. The deity is worshipped as Annapurneshwari – the mother who vanquishes hunger. At this Temple, Lord Krishna is also there along with Goddess Sree Annapoorneswari. It is believed that Sree Annapoorneswari did visit the shrine which was under the sea centuries ago. The Temple was formally a Lord Vishnu/Krishna Temple dating back some 1500 years. The Temple after Amma's Prathishta (giving sacred power to the vigraha of Annapoorneshwari) was built by Avittam Thirunal Raja Raja Varma of Chirakkal Kovilakam. In mythology, it is said that the Goddess arrived from Kashi with two other Goddesses (Kalarivathikal Amma and Madai Kavail Amma) and a boatman in a golden ship and disembarked at Azhi Theeram, which is now known as Aayiram Thengu. The Punna Prathistha was done in 1994 in the month of Kumbham in the Malayalam calendar Pooyam Nakshtram, which now is observed as the Prathista Day every year. The main festivities in the Temple start from the Malayalam month of Medam Shankramam (April 15) and is celebrated in the following seven days. The other festivals that are celebrated in the Temple are Shivarathri, Navami, Ekadashi etc. The Temple is presently under the Malabar Devasom Board. A unique characteristic of this Temple is that it is built of one single type of rock and Sree Kovil of both Annapoorneshwari and Krishnan is of the same size as per Vasthu signifying that both the Goddess and the God are given equal importance. The entrance of the Temple is in front of Lord Krishnan's Sree Kovil and the reason there isn't a direct entrance to Annapoorneshwari's Sree Kovil is because during the olden days, it was believed that women from Brahmin families aren't supposed to be seen directly (Antharjanam). Hence there is a small window that is right in front of the Sree Kovil so that people can view the vigraha from outside. This Temple is one among the two Annapoorneshwari Temples in Kerala. It was built using polished stones and put together using avil and belam (a mixture of flattened rice and jaggery). Next to the Temple is the Temple pond or the Ambala Kolam.

SRI SUBRAHMANYA SWAMI TEMPLE AT PAYYANUR - The place is situated on the banks of the Perumba River. Payyannur derives its name from the renowned Sri Subrahmanya Swami Temple located here. Payyan is an appellation of Lord Subrahmanya and ooru means town or place. Thus, Payyannur means the land of Lord Subrahmanya. The earliest known mention of this town is in the Brahmanda Purana, when Garg Muni talks about this place to the Pandavas during their exile. 'Theyyam' and religious festivals (Kaliyattam) of various Temples attract people to Payyannur. Poorakkali and Kolkali are the major traditional dance ritual performances.

PARASSINIKADAVU MUTHAPPAN TEMPLE AT ANTHOOR – It is located on the banks of Valapattanam River. Principal deity of the Temple is Sree Muthappan, whose divinity is presented as a ritualistic theyyam enactment in two versions called Thiruvappana & Vellattam. According to the local tradition, the presiding deity is a manifestation of Lord Shiva in Nayattu (hunter) format. Rituals of the Temple is unique in that it does not follow the Satvic Brahminical form of worship, as in other Hindu Temples of Kerala. The main mode of worship is the ritual enactment of both the versions of Muthappan, through a traditional dance known as Muthappan Theyyam. Fish, meat & toddy are the customary offerings to Muthappan. Muthappan Thiruvoppana Mahothsavam is the major festival of the Temple celebrated for three days every year on 19, 20 & 21 of Kumbham.

Makreri Subramanya Temple - It is the only Temple in Kerala where the main thanthri is Lord Hanuman, who has installed the main deity & he still does all the Pujas. Hence the power of this Temple is unimaginable. The Temple Tank holds the rare distinction of being the only one in Kannur district to be sanctified by the presence of the holy river Kavery at the time of the Thula Sankramam and the eleven days following. Legend says that Lord Rama directed Shri Hanuman to bathe in a small pool of holy water before praying to the lord. Since the dimension of the pool were too small, Lord Hanuman struck his tail on the ground, thus creating a large body of water. The tank of Makreri Temple does not confirm to the dimension of other Temple ponds that are usually constructed on principles of vastu nor does it lie along a conventional direction. This fact is considered by devotees to lend support to the legend. Since the presence of Kaveri enhances the sanctity of the Makreri Temple pond during this period, it is an opportune ideal time for pilgrims to visit the Temple and bathe in the tank before praying to the Lord. By doing so, they will also be following the direction of Lord Rama.

MAMANIKKUNNU SRI MAHADEVI TEMPLE AT IRUKKUR - This Temple is situated on the eastern bank of Irikkur River. The Temple is dedicated to Lord Shiva and Shakti.

SRI MAVILAYIKKAVU TEMPLE AT MAVILAYI - The Temple is a well-known religious centre and an ancient Temple known for its unique rituals & cultural performances. Lord Ganapati & Goddess Bhagavati along with Lord Daivattar and Lord Vettakarumakan are worshipped here. Adiyulsavam (a mock fight festival) makes Mavilayikkavu distinct from the other Temples of Kerala. In this rare ritual, a group of performers, who are carried on the shoulders of men, hit each other. Adiyulsavam is observed annually during the Malayalam month of Medam & attracts hundreds of devotees and travellers. Mavilakkavu Theyyam, a ritual dance performed by the people of Peruvannan community, is another notable attraction of this Temple.

SREE PERALASSERY TEMPLE AT MUNDALUR - The Temple is one of the beautiful holy shrines of Kannur district. It is located on the bank of Anjarakandy river. This Temple is well – known for its stepped pool which is undoubtedly the magnificent structure. Lord Subramanya, the son of Lord Shiva, is the presiding deity of this Temple. Peralassery Subramania Temple also has a shrine for Serpent God has plenty of bronze and copper vigrahas of the snake.

SHAKTIPEETHAM - KOTTIYOOR & VADAKKESHWARAM TEMPLE AT KANNUR - Kottiyoor Temple is one of the oldest Hindu pilgrimage spot in the planet. The Temple is situated on the beautiful Sahya mountain range valley & is blessed with abundant natural beauty. It is also known as Dakshina Kashi. It is believed to be the place where the Daksha Yagya was conducted. There are two Temples - Akkare Kottiyur and Ikkare Kottiyur located on the opposite banks of Bavali River. Akkare Kottiyur is open during the Kottiyoor Vaisakha Mahotsavam only. As per calculations, the area needed for construction of a Temple was so vast that it would be impossible to construct an edifice of this magnitude. Hence, even today, the Temple exists in the form of several small Temples almost 72 numbers. The site of "Swayambhoo" has water surrounding, called 'Thiruvanchira'. A devotee standing east and facing west, while praying at the Manithara, the circular 'thara', seen to the left is 'Ammarakal Thara', the place of Sati's suicide. It is believed, Thiruvanchira is the blood scattered during Virabhadran's destruction of the Yaga. The shelter created for the Yaga has given

place to the thatched hutments seen today. Priests as well as Temple authorities stay in such huts. Moreover, Koothambalam, Kalavara, Ocher, Ullattumanushyar, Kudipathikal, Kanakkapilla, Aashari, Mooshari, Kollen, Kurichiyan have different sheds today. Places in this area are named reflecting the mental and physical conditions; Sati Devi went through on her passage to the "Yagashala". The place where she felt the pangs of separation from her beloved is "Manathana", when tears poured out, the place became "kanneer char", Feeling tired, she rested at "Aayothumchal". An ox provided for the tired Devi to ride on became "Kelakam". Noise emanating from 'Yagashala' made her stretch out to have a glimpse is now "Neendunokki". The place of taxation - "Chungakunnu". Where she walked slowly became "Mandhemcheri". The place where she fell down tired is "Murchilakadu". The sword which decapitated Dakshan, thrown on the ground is "Mutherikavu". Stone hearths used for boiling milk came to be known as "palukachiyamala". Anyway "Kottiyoor" remains as the place where Sati Devi, Lord Shiva & other holy men once came together. 'Ikkare Kottiyoor' is Nalukettu Temple complex where regular poojas happening. As per legend, hill tribes called Kurichyas were hunting deer in this forest area & he was sharpening his arrow on a stone, suddenly blood oozed out. This strange phenomenon confused the hill tribes & they reported this incident to nearby Padingitta Namboothiri's illam. The Namboothiri well-versed in tantric lore got an intuition that an vigraha is lying at a particular spot. Namboothiri told Kurichyas to inform four prominent Nair families in Manathana Village. Kurichyas reach Manathana & informed Kulangarayath, Aakkal, Karimbanakkal Chathoth & Thittayil families. All were went to the spot where the incident happen. Great surprise they found a bleeding stone in the forest. Ablutions with water, ghee & milk could not control the blood flow & finally tender coconut water stopped the blood. On consultation with astrologer, they come to know that it is a holy land, where Daksha conducted his Yaga & bleeding stone was a 'swayambu vigraha'. It is believed that Lord Shiva took form of 'swayambu' next to where Devi Sathi immolated herself in the 'yagagni'. The place where swayambhu vigraha was found is known as 'Akkare Kottyoor'.

SREE MRIDANGA SAILESHWARI TEMPLE AT MUZHAKKUNNU - The Temple is one of the 108 Durga Temple. It is believed that the Temple was established by Lord Parshurama. Goddess is the family deity of Kerala Varma Pazhassi Raja. Devi is present in three forms i.e. Kali, Lakshmi & Saraswati. Temple vigraham was stolen 3-4 times but because of power of Goddess, all the attempts were failed. As per police record, whenever thieves tried to steal, they lost there senses. It is believed that he Goddess will answer all the prayers of here devotees who pray to her with utmost devotion by lighting the ghee deepam.

DISTRICT – KASARGOD (Railway Station – Kasaragod/Kanhangad/Bekal Fort/Kumbla)

S. No.	Temple	Address	Type
1	Kammadam Bhagavathy Temple	Kasaragod - 670511	Mata
2	Mallikarjuna Temple	Kasaragod - 671123	Shiva
3	Srimad Anantheswara Vinayaka Temple	Madhur – 671124	Shiva, Ganesh
4	Group of Temples	Nileshwar - 671314	Shiva Temple
5	Sree Madiyan Koolom Kshethrapalaka Temple	Moolakandam – Madiyan Road, Manikoth, Kanhangad – 671316	Mata
6	Trikkannad Tryambakeshwara Temple	PO Bekal - 671318	Shiva
7	Sri Ananthapadmanabha Swamy Lake Temple	Ananthapura, P.O. Kannur – 671321	Vishnu
8	Muchilottu Bhagavathi Temple	Perne – 671321	Mata
9	Anandashram	Kanhangad - 671531	Swami
10	Sree Dharmasastha Temple	Panathur – 671532	Sastha
11	Edneer Mutt	Edneer - 671541	Mutt
12	Sree Mahalingeshwara Temple	Adoor – 671543	Shiva

KAMMADAM BHAGAVATHI TEMPLE AT KASARGOD - Kammatam Kavu is an evergreen forest with a perennial stream and is a centre of worship connected with Kammadam Bhagavathi Temple.

MALLIKARJUNA TEMPLE AT KASARGOD – It is one of the famous Temple in Kasargod District. The Temple festival and yakshagana are most attractive. Fringed by swaying coconut and palm trees, the beautiful Temple is dedicated to Lord Shiva and draws pilgrims with its splendid architecture and relaxing vibes. The Kumbala River flowing close by, adds to the picturesque beauty of the place. According to legend, the vigraha of Lord Shiva in the Temple was installed by Arjuna, one of the Pandavas from the epic Mahabharata. The Temple is also popular for hosting the annual Jathra Mahotsavam during the month of March. One of the major attractions here is the Yakshagana performance, which takes place every evening in the Temple premises. Another highlight of the Temple are the yearly Ganesh Chaturthi celebrations that invite thousands of pilgrims from all parts of the state.

SRIMAD ANANTHESWARA VINAYAKA TEMPLE AT MADHUR - The rich architecture, imposing structure of the Temple, with its turrets and gables and the copper plate roofing rises majestically against the beautiful land scape of hills paddy fields and gardens with the River Madhuvahini flowing leisurely in front of it. The Temple is a Shiva Temple with Srimad Anantheswara as its presiding deity but importance is given to the deity Maha Ganapathi. The Shivalingam of the Temple is said to have been found by a harijan woman, Madharu. The special festival of the Temple is Moodappa Seva, which is covering the large figure of Maha Ganapathi with appam made of ghee and rice. Namaskara Mandapam of the Temple has been decorated with beautiful figures of puranic heroes in wood. A closer examination of the wood carvings would disclose the various episodes of the Ramayana, beginning with the Seetha Swayamvaram. It is said that the Temple was attacked by Tippu Sultan of Mysore during his invasion and he felt thirsty and drunk the water from the Temple well, which changed his mind and left the Temple without damaging it. There is a mask on the Temple which is said to be made by Tippu with his sword.

NILESHWAR - Nileshwar is abbreviated form of Nilakanta Iswar. Formerly seat of Nileshwar Rajas who belonged to the Kolathiri family. In and around, there are several Kavus where nature, God and man commune serene silence. Major among them is Mannan Purathu Kavu, where the grand finale of the annual Temple festival of the region takes place. Porattu of Anjoottambalam Veerarkavu draws large crowds. Porattu is the satirical representation of everyday life presented in pageantry during the Poram.

SREE MADIYAN KOOLOM TEMPLE AT HOSDURG - The main deity of the Temple is Bhadrakali but there are also other deities like Kshetrapalak, Bhagavathi and Bhairava. A peculiarity of this Temple is that a Brahmin priest performs pooja only in the noon, while the morning and evening poojas are performed by a sect called Maniyanis. It is dates back as old as 500 years. Sri Madiyan Kulam is the headquarters of the 'Allada Swaroopam Mookatham Nadu'. The Temple famous for its century's old wooden carvings is also known for its epic poems which portrays unity of different religions and castes. The Temple consists of monuments built in traditional Kerala style architecture and is also famous for its sculptures and astonishing wooden carvings which depicts the ancient stories from Ramayana and other epics. Most of the carvings are found in Thekkini, western Gopuram and the Mandapa near the pond. The 'Thekkini Mandapam' has the etchings of Dakshayagam, Seethaswayamvaram and the Vanayathra of Lord Rama and Lakshmana. The western gopuram shows instances of Amruthamadhanam, Kaliyamardhanam and Ananthashayanam. The etchings showing the premier of churning ocean of "Palazhi" using Vasuki to make Amrut (Kshir Sagar) looks extraordinarily beautiful. The carvings also includes erotic wooden etchings similar to those of the world-famous Khajuraho Temple in Madhya Pradesh. A mural painting of the Narasimha avatar of Lord Vishnu is another attraction. The Temple houses two ponds. There is a small sculpture of a 'bowing' elephant near the entrance which is believed to be a curse to an elephant who was about to enter the Temple as elephants are not permitted inside the Temple premises. Similarly there is another sculpture of a snake in one of the ponds which is again believed to be a curse as legend has it that the snake was send to spew venom in the pond.

TRIKKANNAD TRYAMBAKESHWARA TEMPLE AT BEKAL FORT - A famous Temple on the sea shore near the Bekal Fort is dedicated to Lord Shiva. It is also known as Dakshina Kashi. As per legend, a ship of one of the Pandya King, who attacked the Trikkannad Temple, was converted into a rock by Lord Siva. Palakkunnu Bhagavathi Kshethram, near Trikkannad is famous for annual Bharani festival, which attracts thousands of devotees.

ANANTHAPURA LAKE TEMPLE – It is the only Lake Temple in Kerala. The Temple is in the centre of a rectangular Lake.It is the Moolasthanam (original seat) of Ananthapadmanabha Swami (Sri Padmanbha Swami Temple) Thiruvananthapuram. Local belief is that Ananthapadmanabha had settled down here originally. Here, in the Sreekovil, the sanctum sanctorum, of the Temple, Sri Anantha Padmanabha is depicted as seated on the divine serpent Anantha. On both the sides of the Lord are Bhoodevi, the Goddess of Earth and Sreedevi, the Goddess of Prosperity. Garuda and Hanuman stand in front of them praying with folded hands. Jaya and Vijaya, Lord Vishnu's attendants, stand in guard at the entrance. On the outer walls of the Sreekovil there are marvellous and ancient mural paintings on Puranic themes. On the north-East corner of the Lake, there is a big cave with a small pit with a perennial presence of water in it, which is considered as a sacred Theertham. It is believed to be the cave where boy Krishna disappeared. Near the south-west corner of the Lake, there is a shrine housing a very graceful vigraha of Sree Krishna believed to have been the same vigraha worshipped by Sri Vilvamangalathu Swamy. The vigraha of Sri Anantha Padmanabha Swamy and other vigrahas are neither metal nor stone but made of a rare combination of more than 108 materials called Kadu-Sarkara-Yogam. One can see from the ingredients used in the Katu-Sarkara-Yogam for the construction of the vigrahas that they are all medicinal. Just as the human body is protected with a natural medicinal coverage, the same concept is extended to the vigraha to which a living form is being bestowed. As such, it is of no surprise that vigrahas of this nature, though a speciality of Kerala, are so rare even in the land of their origin. A very unusual phenomenon of this Temple is the presence of a single crocodile in the Temple Lake, named 'Babia'. By tradition, the lake is inhabited by a single crocodile and in the memory of the very aged men the present crocodile happens to be the third one they have seen. When one crocodile dies another one invisibly appears in the lake and this continues to be an unexplained phenomenon. There is no river or pond nearby where crocodiles exist. The Crocodile is friendly and harmless to human being. Its presence in the lake around the Mahavishnu Temple reminds one of the well-known Gajendra Moksha Stories in the Bhagavatha Puranam.

PERNE - Out of the 28 Muchilottu Bhagavathi Temples, one Temple is located here in the north of Chandragiri near Ananthapuram. The mass marriage at the time of Pooram festival in the month of Meenam is a unique feature of this Temple.

ANANDASHRAM & NITYANANDASRAMAM AT KANHANGAD – Anandashramam was founded in 1939 by Swami Ramadas, a great Vaishnava saint of modern times. There is a hill to the east of the ashramam, to which the devotees retire for quiet meditation. The spot

at the highest point of the hill is so fascinating that the devotees, who go up the hill and sit silently, are blessed with deep peace and tranquillity. Nityanandasramam was founded by Swami Nityananda. Here, Swami Nityananda constructed 45 guhas (caves) in a mountain slope. There is a Temple built in 1963 after the style and design of the famous Somanatha Temple in Gujarat. A full size vigraha of Swami Nityananda in sitting posture made of panchaloha is one of the attractions of the ashramam.

SREE DHARMASASTHA TEMPLE AT PANATHUR – The Temple has many old stories. Many people from different places come to worship here. It is consecrated to Kshethrapalak and Bhagavathy. Eight day annual festival attracts large crowd from all over the district as well as from Coorg.

EDNEER MUTT - This Mutt belongs to the Sri Sankaracharya tradition, presently renowned as a seat of art and learning.

SREE MAHALINGESHWARA TEMPLE AT ADOOR – It is located in sylvan surroundings on the southern banks of the River Payaswini. It is an ancient Shiva Temple, which is believed to have been founded by Arjuna at the place where the Kiratha Yuddham battle between Arjuna and Lord Shiva took place. The adjacent forest not frequented by men is considered the abode of Lord Shiva and his divine consort. The stream below the valley is nature bounty. It contains a Sanskrit inscription in Kannada script which has been ascribed to the Western Chalukya King Kirthivarman-II (745 - 755 AD). Nearest Railway Station is Kayankulam.

DISTRICT – KOLLAM (Railway Station – Bhagavathipuram/Ochira/Aryankavu/Tenmalai)

S. No.	Temple	Address	Type
1	The Sastha Temple	Achencoil – 689696	Ayyappan (Vishnu)
2	Oachira Parabrahma Temple	Oachira – 690526	Brahma
3	Sree Venkatachalapathy Temple	Kollam – 691013	Vishnu
4	Aryankavu Shastha Temple	Aryankavu – 691309	Ayyappan (Shiva)
5	Kulathupuzha Sastha Temple	Kulathupuzha – 691310	Ayyappan (Vishnu)
6	Sree Mahaganapathi Temple	Kottarakara - 691506	Ganesh
7	Malamel Sankaranarayana Temple	Arackal – 691532	Shiva
8	Jatayu Juncion	Chadayamangalam – 691534	Jatayu
9	Major Sree Kottankulangara Devi Temple	Kottankulangara, Chavara – 691583	Mata
10	Mahadeva Temple	Thrikkadavoor - 691601	Shiva

THE SASTHA TEMPLE AT ACHENCOIL - It is situated amidst dense forest. It is one of the 108 Sasthalayas. It is also one among the famed Pancha Sastha Temples in Kerala. The Temple is located near the origin of the Achankovil River. The vigraha of Sastha is supposed to have been installed several centuries before the Christian era. Lord Ayyappa / Aiyanar presides there in the form of grihastha along with his two consorts Poorna & Pushkala and the vigraha faces east. It is believed to be installed by Lord Parashurama himself. The vigraha is known as Rudrakshasila. The right palm of the vigraha always keeps Chandanam (Sandalwood) and Theertham (sacred water) which is thought to have medicinal properties. The two important festivals of this Temple are Mandala Pooja (December-January) and the festival held at 'Revathi' (January-February). The two notable features of the festival are the Therotam (chariot festival) and Pushpabhishekam (offering of flowers). In no other Temple of South India, flowers are offered to the deity as lavishly as at Achencoil. The Temple is famed for curing poisonous Snake bites and thus Lord Ayyappa is often portrayed as a Mahavaidya (great physician).

OACHIRA PARABRAHMA TEMPLE – It is a very ancient Temple & is devoted to Parabrahman or Param Brahman or Ohmkaram. Ward & Conner, two British authorities entrusted to survey Travancore in the start of the 19th CE, mentioned their objective facts about Oachira in their report. In the report it was clarified that there was an extremely old and harmed pagoda on the eastern side of the Padanilam. It was also disclosed that there was a large reservoir at the centre of the vast ground on which the Temple stands, (which was now known as Kallukettuchira). There is an interesting legend about the origin of the Temple. There was a great Namboothiri devotee somewhere in the north. He had a servant to help in his pooja. It was the usual practice of the Namboothiri to sit in Pooja for a long time. One day his servant Unnikkoran Nair asked him what he was praying for. Namboothiri told him that he was worshiping for the Parabrahma. Then Unnikkoran Nair enquired how shape the Parabrahma was. Sarcastically the Namboothiri told him that the Parbrahama is like a "Madan Pothu". Thereafter, Unnikoran Nair also worshiped Parabrahma in the shape of "Madan Pothu". Parabrahma took the shape of "Madan Pothu" and blessed the innocent devotee.

SREE VENKATACHALAPATHY TEMPLE AT KOLLAM - With Sree Venkatachalapathy as the presiding deity, the Temple was built by Gowda Saraswat Brahmins who hailed from the state of Karnataka but had settled in Kerala. However, the Temple's architecture has similarity with the ones in Tamil Nadu & not Kerala. The deities in the Temple are placed on three steps. On either side of the principle deity, Sree Venkatachalapathy, are placed the vigrahas of Goddess Laxmi Devi & Goddess Bhumi Devi on the first step. The second step is graced with the Utsavmoorthy of Varadaraja with Laxmi Devi and Bhumi Devi on either sides. The third step has two samputas containing salagramas. Inside the Temple are smaller shrines dedicated to Lord Shiva, Lord Hanuman, Guru Swamy and Nagadevta. Built in 1822 AD, the Temple is located near the District Collectorate.

ARYANKAVU SHASTHA TEMPLE - The Temple is one among the five important Temples dedicated to Lord Ayyappa in Kerala. Lord Ayyappa is depicted here as a teenager. Lord Ayyappa is known as Tiru Aryan & therefore the place got the name Aryankavu. Just like in Sabarimala, women from the age 10 to 50 are not allowed inside the Temple. The rituals & pujas followed at the Temple is that of Tamil tradition. The sanctum sanctorum of the Temple has vigrahas of Devi, Shiva and Sastha. A young Ayyappa sits in the middle with Devi on the left side and Shiva on the right side. The festival at the Temple is celebrated during the concluding days of the Sabarimala Mandala Kalam. The most important festivals observed here include Pandiyan Mudippu, Trikkalyanam and Kumbhabhishekam.

KULATHUPUZHA SASTHA TEMPLE – The Temple is located in the reserve forest range of eastern Kollam on the banks of Kulathupuzha, a tributary of Kallada River. The presiding deity is Lord Ayyappa in the form of Bala Sastha. It is one among the 108 Sastha shrines in Kerala. The vigraha

here is believed to be installed by Lord Parashurama. The deity here is in a fierce mood as well as in auspicious mood. Lord Shiva, Yakshi, Vishnu, Ganapathi, Boothathan, Nagar and Karuppaswami are the other subordinate deities in the Temple. Legend says that the Temple was founded by Pandalam Raja but the vigraha of Sastha was founded by a Brahmin from Kottarakkara. The pond near to the Temple is another attraction. Devotees offer Meenoottuvazhipadu for healing the warts in the skin. All the devotees are so concerned about protecting the fishes in this pond, considering them as Lord Ayyappa's favourite ones. Fishing is also strictly prohibited here. The tantric rights of the Temple are held by Kokkalathumadom. Vishu Mahotsavam in the months of April & May is the important festival. The Tiruvutsavam is celebrated in the month of Medam from 5th to 14th.

SREE MAHAGANAPATHI TEMPLE AT KOTTARAKARA - The Temple is dedicated to Lord Shiva but Lord Ganesha is famous here. The original name of the Temple is Kizhakkekara Shiva Kshetram. Uniappam is a Nivedhyam which is offered to Lord Ganesha after opening Sri Kovil and is very popular.

MALAMEL SANKARANARAYANA TEMPLE AT ARACKAL - It is a famous rock Temple of Lord Shiva. The Temple has 5 doors and is considered to be divine and ancient because of the close proximity of Jatayupura (Chadayamangalam). It also has a cave at the extreme left of the Temple, into which a British Adventurer in the year 1946 tried in vain to venture, and which leads to the Kulathupuzha Forest. This cave is believed to be a haven for very venomous snakes. Temple festival is held on 3 December. Nearest Railway Station is Kollam.

JATAYU ADVENTURE CENTRE AT CHADAYAMANGALAM – It stands as a guardian to the hills and rocks by protecting them from mining. The destination is a masterpiece combination of artistry, mythology, technology, culture, adventure, leisure & wellness put together to give every visitor a spellbinding experience. The giant concrete vigraha of Jatayu is built on a mighty rock. The colossal vigraha is 200 ft long,150 ft wide & 70 ft making it the largest functional bird sculpture in the world with an enter into the Guinness Book of World Records. In the great epic Ramayana, Jatayu is characterized as a noble bird of divine origin. One day he happened to hear the plaintive cry of a lady. It was Devi Sitha lamenting for help while she has being abducted to Lanka by the demon king Ravana. Jatayu rushed to her rescue, stopped Ravana's chariot named Pushpaka Vimana & engaged in a battle with him. Eventually, Ravana took his powerful sword Chandrahasa, cut off the bird's left wing & went away with Devi Sitha. It is said that the injured Jatayu and his lost wing landed on top of a rock. In time, the rock got the name Jatayupara. This is where the monumental vigraha of Jatayu is now built. There is a pond near the rock which is said to be formed by the stroke of Jatayu's beak. It has water throughout the year and never goes dry. Legend also says that Lord Rama later came to Jatayupara and gave moksha to wounded & dying Jatayu. The good bird told the whole story & Lord Rama got the vital information about Devi Sitha. There is a mark of

footprint said to be that of Lord Rama. A Temple dedicated to Lord Rama is nearby. Jatayu is an embodiment of valour and chivalry. Risking his life, he tried his best to save sitha from her abductor. Hence the Jatayu sculpture uprights as a towering tribute to women's safety and honour. Jatayu also represents a bygone era when humans, animals, birds & other living forms cared for each other and fellow begins and lived peacefully on this Earth. A rain water reservoir is made on the hill top with a capacity to hold 1.5 million litres of water. Nearest Railway Station is Varkalasivagiri.

MAJOR SREE KOTTANKULANGARA DEVI TEMPLE – It is a ancient & holy centre where thousands of believers derive mental condolence & peace of mind to tide over the miseries of life. On the northwest corner, a small deep pond existed known as Bhoothakulam. People believed that this place was a comfortable shelter for poisonous snakes. On the eastern side, there was a huge extensive deep pond. During the days of rain, a stream originated from here & it would make the Kareelil Padom fertile & cultivable. One day, the cowboys got a coconut from this place. They found a stone on the southern part of Bhoothakulam. When they hit the coconut on the stone (with the intention of removing the husk), they all got alarmed & frightened as they found drops of blood dripping from the stone. They explained the wonderful phenomena to the elders. The astrologer suggested that the stone contained the supernatural powers of Vanadurga & poojas should be started immediately after constructing a Temple. It was a custom in ancient days that balikas used to prepare flower garlands, lit the pooja lamps in Kudumba Temples. Accepting this tradition, the cowboys wearing the dresses of women & girls, offered poojas in the Temple. The Temple features an unusual ritual where hundreds of sturdy men dress up as comely females. In this unique ritual called Chamaya Vilakku, the "damsels" come to the Temple at night in a long procession holding lighted lamps in their hands. The ritual is held during March end. The Temple which originated on the banks of the pond with Kottan as the first Naivedyam come to be known as Kottankulangara Temple. In order to commemorate the legend and origin of the Temple, the model of the ancient Temple is being constructed every year. Nearest Railway Station is Kollam.

MAHADEVA TEMPLE AT THRIKKADAVOOR - The Temple is the most famous Shiva Temple in Kollam district. In the Temple complex there are various antique brass articles which are weighing app. 2400 KGs. The Temple is under the administration of Travancore Devaswom Board.

DISTRICT – KOTTAYAM (Railway Station – Kottayam/Chingavanam/Changanaseri/Vaikom)

S. No.	Temple	Address	Type
1	Thirunakkara Mahadeva Temple	Thirunakara, Kottayam - 686001	Shiva
2	Surya Kalady Mana	Nattassery - 686006	Mana
3	Sree Karthyayani Devi Temple	Kumaranalloor - 686016	Mata
4	Vazhappally Maha Siva Temple	Changanacherry - 686101	Shiva
5	Santhana Gopala Swamy Temple	Changanacherry - 686101	Vishnu
6	Sree Maha Vishnu Temple	Thrickodithanam - 686105	Vishnu
7	Elankavu Bhagavathy Temple	Vaikom - 686141	Mata
8	Vaikom Mahadevar Temple	Vaikom - 686141	Shiva

S. No.	Temple	Address	Type
9	Sree Mahadeva Kshetram	Chirakadavu - 686519	Shiva
10	Panachickadu Devaswam	Kuzhimattom P.O. - 686533	Mata
11	Pazhaya Sreekanteswaram Temple	Puthenchantha - 686538	Shiva
12	Sree Kumaramangalam Subramanya Swami Mandir	Kumarakom - 686563	Murugan
13	Sree Mahadeva Temple	Kadappattoor - 686574	Shiva
14	Kondamarugu Mana	Ramapuram - 686576	Mana
15	Kaduthuruthy Thaliyil Temple	Kaduthuruthy - 686604	Shiva
16	Ettumanur Mahadeva Temple	Ettumanur - 686631	Shiva

THIRUNAKKARA MAHADEVAR TEMPLE AT KOTTAYAM – It is one of the 108 revered Shivalayas in central Kerala. The Temple is about 500 years old and was built by the Thekkumkoor Raja. It also preserves a number of unique sculptures and murals of various Hindu deities. This complex has a number of murals depicting the stories of Shiva and Dashavathara. A common belief is that the vigraha of Shiva here is installed by Sage Parashurama himself. No visit is complete without seeing its special Koothambalam, the special building in the Temple premises used for cultural purposes said to be right up there among the best in all of God's Own Country. The Thekkukkoor royal family considered the vigraha as their paradevatha (tutelary deity) in the form of "Thirunakkarathevar". There is an interesting story behind the Brahma Rakshas. One person called Moose was a great friend of the king. The king was not known for his beauty but his friend Moose was very handsome. The queen fell in love with this friend knowing which the king ordered his servants to kill Moose. Instead of killing him, the King's servants killed the junior priest of the Temple (keezhsanthi). The wife of the priest became a Brahma Rakshas and started seeking revenge. So the king built a Temple for her. For a long time afterwards, women do not prefer to enter this Temple. The first entrance to the Temple includes a small Temple for Lord Ganapathi. There is a Banyan Tree on steps which is considered sacred by the devotees. The Temple has shrines for various sub deities in different locations. The southeast entrance constitutes of the shrines of Lord Ayyappa and Ganesha. Naga pratishtas are also close to these shrines. The eastern section includes the shrines of Lord Subhramaniya & Durga and the northeast section has the installation of Brahmarakshas which is according to the myths the soul of a priest assassinated inside the Temple. The two storeyed square shaped Sreekovil of the Temple is very attractive & it is adorned by a golden Finial. The Sreekovil includes three separate rooms, one in the west is Garbhagriha which has the Shivalinga installed. An vigraha of Parvathi Devi made up of Panchaloha is also installed next to it.

SURYA KALADY MANA AT NATTASSERY - It is ancient as Bhagwan Parasuraman era. The ancestors of Mana were brought by Bhagwan Parasuraman. The history says that Bhagwan Parasuraman brought the Brahmins from outside to Kerala for entrusting them certain responsibilities. He entrusted them mainly the duties of Priesthood & Medical treatment. The Mana was entrusted with the responsibility of conducting Thantric rites. The Mana has produced a number of eminent personalities, some of them in literary works. The famous literary works – Ithihyamala , Kerala Sahitya Charitham & Surya Kalady which have found inroads to Magazines, Cinema, Television etc are the products of this Mana.

SREE KARTHYAYANI DEVI TEMPLE AT KUMARANALLOOR - The Temple is dedicated to Goddess Durga who is known as Kumaranalloor Devi Temple. The Temple is one of the most important Temples among the 108 Devi Temples in Kerala. It is believed that the Temple is more than 2400 years old. The architecture of the Temple is marvelous. The structure of the Temple is unique as nalambalam and sreekovil both of which have been built in the sreechakra style. This kind of architecture is rarely found in Temple architecture. The annual Trikarthika festival of the Temple is very famous.

VAZHAPPALLY MAHASHIVA TEMPLE AT CHANGANACHERRY - The Temple is believed to be constructed by the first Chera King of Kodungallur. The legends suggest that the installation of the vigraha of Lord Mahadevawas performed by Lord Parasurama himself. This Temple is one among the 108 Shiva Temples established by Lord Parasurama. It is one of the few Temples in Kerala where two nalambalams and two flag-masts are dedicated. The Temple, a Grama Kshetra, also contains some seventeenth century wood carvings (darusilpas) depicting figurines from epics. A Vattezhuttu inscription on the northern part of the base of the cultural shrine indicates that the repairs were completed in Kollam Era 840 (1665 AD). In the time of Pallibana Perumal, it was decided to convert the Neelamperoor Shiva Temple into a Buddhist Monastery. It is believed that the ten Brahmin families (later known as Pattiyillam Pottimar) came to Vazhappally by shaking the Shivalinga of the Temple of Neelamperoor and then merged with the existing Lord Shiva Temple in Vazhappally. The Shivalingam brought from Neelamperoor was first placed in the Devalokam at north part of Vazhappallygramam. Later, when they tried to shake the Shivalinga but was unable to do so, Parasurama appeared to the grieving Brahmin family and offered him the Shivalinga he had worshiped and advised him to build the Temple on the Ardhanariswara concept. He built a huge shrine for the Shivalinga and the Parvati vigraha. Dakshinamoorthy and Ganapathi were placed inside the sanctum sanctorum faces south. In the south-eastern corner of the Nambalam, there was a large Tidapalli built. Raja built the sub-shrine Temple for Sastha at the Kannimoola outside the Nambalam Temple.

SANTHANA GOPALA SWAMY TEMPLE AT CHANGANACHERRY - It is a rare Temple of Lord Maha Vishnu, who blesses the childless couples. The vigraham here is Vaikunthanathan sitting on a peetham carrying a baby in both hands. As per legend, after the Mahabharatha war, Arjuna became very proud of his power and Lord Krishna decided to teach Arjuna. There lived a brahmin & wife whose eight children died at birth. With disappointment, brahmin went to the pandavas and asked some solution. Arjuna promised to save the next child but he was not able to protect the child and he took a vow that he will end his life if could not protect the tenth child. Arjuna created protection using his divine weapons but the tenth child vanished immediately after birth. Arjuna decided to end his life, at that time, Lord Krishna came and took him to Vaikuntha. Arjuna saw there that all the ten children playing with Lord Mahavishnu & Goddess Mahalakshmi.

SREE MAHA VISHNU TEMPLE AT THRICKODITHANAM - The Temple is dedicated to Lord Vishnu and it is one among 108 Divya Deshams. Lord Mahavishnu is Atbudha Narayanan here. It is believed that the Prathishta of this Temple is done by Sahadeva, a pandava brother. The Chaturbahu Vigraham is made of Anjana Sila. At the entrance of the Temple, we can see Kuzhuvetti Kallu. It is a man flat on his back, held up on a stone pillar about 6 ft. height. King Rukmangatha of Suryavamsa got moksham here.

ELANKAVU BHAGAVATHY TEMPLE AT VAIKOM - The Temple is dedicated to Goddess Bhagavathy. Attuvala Mahotsavam is celebrated in Kerala when the Goddess of Kodungalloor arrives to visit her sister who is the Goddess of Elankavu. Water canoes carrying replica of the Temple is spectacular.

MAHADEVA TEMPLE AT VAIKOM - As per legends Vyaghrapada Maharshi got Lord Shiva darshan here so it was fittingly called Vyaghrapadapuram. Later, when Tamil spread, the word Vaiyaghra got transformed as Vaikom. Today, Vaikom is one of the most revered Shiva shrines in South India. The Temple along with Ettumanoor Siva Temple, Kaduthuruthy Thaliyil Mahadeva Temple is considered a powerful trisomy. The belief is that if a devotee worships at these three Temples before 'Uchapooja', all the wishes are fulfilled. Though Vaikkath Asthami is the better known festival at the Temple, it celebrates many other festivals, some of them unique to the Temple. The most important prasada of Vaikkathappan is Bhasma – Vibhoothi or Ashes. It is taken from the fire place of the big Kitchen where Sri Vaikkathappan is believed to do work in the disguise of a Brahmin. The legends proclaim this Bhasma as a holy remedy for fear, poison, wounds and even Hysteria. The belief of the miraculous power of the Bhasma is testified by the devotees in plenty. Four Gopuras or towers are built on all the four sides. The Temple faces the East. The pond in the northern side of the Temple compound is duly called 'Ganga Prapatha Theertha' or Valiyachira. The golden flag staff is really a pride of the Temple. Then we enter Balikalulpura (the place of the sacrificial stone) where Stambha Ganesh is seated at its north-east corner. Walking further we enter the Namaskara Mandapa. The story of Ramayana is sculptured on the inner roof. A huge Nandi made in a single stone together with a small one for Archana are in the east of this Mandapa. Passing through the stone laid inner way we reach the Sreekovil or The Holy of Holies of Shree Vaikkathappan – the Annadana Prabhu who fulfils every desire of His devotees. On the Peedhom, the most holy, famous and noble Shivalinga of Shree Vaikkathappan is consecrated. It is of about six ft high made of chaste black stone. The Linga is adorned with Chandrakala (crescent), three eyes, nose and four hands with Saivaabharanams (ornaments) in the form of 'anky' in pure gold. The outer walls of Sreekovil are decorated nicely with paintings of puranic stories and wooden sculptures. It is a very curious and peculiar fact that we are unable to obtain the Darsana of the Supreme Saiva Chaitanya from this Sreekovil without passing through six steps either from the Gopura or the Nada. It may be reminding us the Shad (six) vikaras (emotions) such as Kama, Krodha, Lobha, Moha, Madha and Mathsarya or the tantric chakras as per the tantric Kalpana. They are the Mooladhara Chakram, Swadhishtana Chakram, Manipuraka

Chakram, Anahatha Chakram, Visudhi Chakram and Jnana Chakram. In the Agni cone (south-east corner) outside the Sreekovil is the Vighneswara Prathishta on a Peedhom of stone, Maha Ganapathy in the South and Sakthy Ganapathy in the north are consecrated. The vigrahas are in panchaloha. The Mathrusila where the Belistones of the seven divine Mathas are kept is to the south of Sreekovil. In the Vayucone of the Sreekovil we would witness a centuries old Vilwa tree with two barks, still in a flourishing condition. The Ashtadikpalakas or Lords of the eight directions etc. are consecrated in the yard of the Sreekovil. Varuna - the Lord of water finds a special place in the west. In the Temple court of north we could see a very holy place called the 'Manya Sthana' where Vaikkathappan was seen eating Prathal dressed like a Brahmin, by Vilwamangalathu Swamiyar.

SREE MAHADEVA KSHETRAM AT CHIRAKADAVU - The Temple is dedicated to Lord Shiva. At this place, Lord Shiva is believed to be father of Sabrimala Ayyappa Swami, hence, devotees who travel to Sabrimala, comes here for worship of Lord Shiv also. Lord Shiva is Swayambhu here. Kulam is located in the eastern side of this Kshetram, thus, Temple is called Chirakkavadu. Balikkalu of this Temple is very big. The Velakali, a dance form, is conducted here by children between the age of five and twenty, who dressed up as warriors holding swords. Devotees, who face delay in marriage, prays here to remove all obstacles.

SARASWATI TEMPLE AT PANACHIKADU VILLAGE – It is known as Dakshina Mookambi. Even though many Sarawathi Temples perform pooja only during the 'Navarathri period, this Temple offers pooja throughout giving 'darshan' to the devotees. When we reach the precincts of the Temple, we see first a "Vishnu Temple" and south of the Vishnu shrine we can see the 'Saraswathy Temple' in a natural valley with the water dripping and flowing around the vigraha. The Temple does not have the traditional sanctum sanctorum and other pompous structures of the Temples elsewhere. The vigraha of 'brahmarakshasu' is also installed here. Even though there are yakshi shrines in other Temples as well, the power of the yakshi at this Temple seem to be super. In addition, there are vigraha of Shiva, Sastha, Ganapathi, Nagayakshi, Nagaraja and the like sub deities too here. The ghee enriched with Saraswatha Manthram is distributed to devotees from here. The intake of this ghee enriches the intelligence of children for intelligence and education this is considered very well. Thousands of literacy workers, artists, musicians etc. consider this Temple as their last resort for help.

PAZHAYA SREEKANTESWARAM TEMPLE AT PUTHENCHANTHA – It is one of the ancient Shiva Temples in Kerala. This Temple is the original abode of the Lord of Sreekanteswaram Mahadeva Temple. Lord Siva and Lord Krishna (Vishnu) are the principal deities in Old Sreekanteswaram. The Linga of Sreekanteswara is believed to have been installed by Sree Parashurama. According to devotees, the samadhi of Sage Kanwa is in the precincts of the Temple. Chettikulam, a pond nearby that was reclaimed decades ago, is referred to in Syanandura Purana Samuchaya and Anantapura Varnana as Kanvatirtha. The vigraha of Sri Krishna was installed later to reduce the ferocity of Shiva. The vigrahas of Lord Ganesha and Serpent gods also find place in the Temple. All the deities here face east. Mritunjaya Homam, Mrityunjaya Archana, Jaladhara, Pinvilakku and Kuvala mala samarpanam are the most popular offerings made to Lord Shiva. In the new Kovilvila Bhagavati Temple, the Guardian Deities of the Tharavad - Kalari Bhadrakali, Meru Sreechakram and Karanavar were duly installed by the Tantri Thrippunithura Puliyannoor Murali Narayanan Nambuthiripad on 21 March 2008. One-hooded Nagaraja, five-hooded Nagayakshi and Chitrakootam were installed by Amedamangalathu Vishnu Nambuthiri on the next day. Offering Neyvilakku for eleven consecutive days is the most important Vazhipadu in the Temple. Ayilyam in the month of Thulam is important for the Serpent gods. The Temple has in it grand mural paintings of Kalari Bhadrakali and Lalita Parameswari. According to Dr. M. G. Sasibhooshan, the mural of Lalita Parameswari is one of the largest of its kind.

SREE KUMARAMANGALAM SUBRAMANYA SWAMI MANDIR AT KUMARAKOM - The Temple is dedicated to Murugan Swamy. It is believed that this Temple is visible from space, as the 35 cm top bud part of the 80 cm tall dome of this Temple is made of the rare & costly metal Iridum. There have been many attempt to steal this precious dome but all have gone in vain.

SREE MAHADEVA TEMPLE AT KADAPPATTOOR - The Temple is dedicated to Lord Shiva where the Lord Shiva is worshipped in vigraha roopam. It is a famous Temple. As per Sthala Puranam, once there lived a Sage named Gauna Maharishi. He had a Kamandalu which was filled with water from the Saptha Nadhis. He was waiting there to worship Lord Rama who was coming that way on this way to Ayodhya but Gauna Maharishi could not worshipped Lord Rama as he was surrounded by Vanaras. In anger, he threw way his Kamandalu and the water which flowed down found the present Gauna Nadi. Later Lord Rama & Devi Sitha gave there darshan to Gauna Maharishi and suggested that Gauna Maharishi should continue his Tapasaya & give him a Lord Shiva Vigraham. Gauna Maharishi did Prathishta of Vigraham and named the place as Kadapetta Ooru which now changed as Kadappattor.

KONDAMARUGU MANA AT RAMAPURAM - As per legend, the ancient heads of Kondamarugu Mana and Changazhasseri Illam and the head Marar of Kuduk Tharavad (family) ventured out on a pilgrimage. When they reached Ambika Vanam of Kudajadri, the Namboodiri of Kondamarugu Illam prayed to Mookambika Devi for the welfare of his region. When the Namboodiri returned home he felt the presence of Mookambika Devi. The Mana constructed a Temple and installed the vigraha of Devi and started worshipping. Rakthachamundi, Rakteswari, Sreevidya, Bhairavan, Yakshi, Chathan and Serpent are sub-deites here. There is a Satrugna Swami shrine near the Temple. The Namboodiri of the Mana conduct Tantric rites in the presence of Porkala Devi. The number of people coming to this Mana for the solutions of their hurting problems is swelling day by day. All the visitors return home with pleasant mood.

KADUTHURUTHY THALIYIL MAHADEVA TEMPLE - It is believed that the consecration at Vaikom and Ettumanoor Temples was done at the same time as that of this Temple by the same person. There are also replicas of Vaikom & Ettumanoor Shiva vigrahas in the Temple, thus, it is believed that visit here is as good as a visiting all three noted Shiva Temples (Vaikom, Ettumanoor and Thaliyil Mahadeva) on the same day before noon. According to legend, the Shivalinga was installed here by a demon named 'Khara'. This demon (Khar-Dooshan demon duo) featured in the Ramayana worshiped Lord

Shiva at Chidambaram and obtained from him three Shivalingams. He travelled holding one Shivalingam in each hand and one in his mouth. Kadichiruthy Prathishitta later become Kaduthuruthy. The remaining two Shivalingas were installed at the Ettumanoor Mahadeva Temple and Vaikom Mahadeva Temple. The name Kaduthuruthy also believed to have emanated from this Temple and ethology has it that Kadichu (bite) Irutthy (make someone sit). The famous Sun Temple at Adityapuram, which is known to be the second Sun Temple in India. The Mahavishnu Temple at Devarthananam. The Kailasapuram Sreekrishna Temple and Mangattukavu Bhaghavathy Temple are in the area.

ETTUMANOOR MAHADEVA TEMPLE – It is an ancient Lord Shiva Temple in Kottayam. It has brought glory and fame to the place. Myths have it that the Pandavas and the Sage Vyasa had worshipped at this Temple. The name of the place has its origin from the word 'manoor', which means the land of deer. The present Temple building, with its gopuram and the fortress around it, was reconstructed in 717 ME (1542 AD). There are Dravidian mural paintings on the walls inside and outside of the main entrance. The fresco of Pradosha Nritham (Dance of Shiva) is one of the finest wall painting in India. There is a golden flag staff inside the Temple. On the top of it, is the vigraha of a bull surrounded by small bells and metal leaves of the Banyan Tree and in terms of architecture, this Temple stands out to be an ultimate testament for the Vishwakarma Sthapathis for their engineering skills. The Temple roofs are covered with copper sheets and it has 14 ornamental tops. Bhagavathi, Sastha, Dakshinamoorthy, Ganapathy and Yakshi are installed here as subordinate deities. There is a separate Temple for Lord Krishna. It is believed that the great philosopher, Adi Shankaracharya wrote 'Soundarya Lahari' while staying in the Temple. The vigrahattes are made of jackfruit tree and covered with nearly 13 KGs of gold plates. Ezhara Ponnana refers to the seven-and-a-half golden elephants which are kept in the Temple vault and taken out once in a year for darshan by the devotees. Ezhara Ponnana Darshan begins with the ceremonial procession carrying the eight golden vigrahattes of elephants and they are later kept at the Asthana Mndapam for the annual darshan by the devotees. Nearest Railway Station is Ettumanur.

DISTRICT – KOZHIKODE (Railway Station – Kozhikkode/Vadakara)

S. No.	Temple	Address	Type
1	Thali Maha Shiva Kshetram	Palayam, Kozhikode – 673002	Shiva
2	Nochipra Bhagavathy Kshetram Temple	West Hill, Kozhikode - 673005	Mata
3	Lokanarkavu Temple	Kavil Road, Villiappally, Vatakara – 673104	Mata

TALI SHIVA TEMPLE AT KOZHIKODE – It was built in the 14th century by the then reigning Zamorin, Swamy Thirumulpad, within his palace complex. The Temple is renowned for its annual cultural and intellectual event, Revathy Pattathanam. The intricate brass-relief on the walls of the sanctum sanctorum and elaborate brass carvings on the wooden roof of the Temple are sights to behold. The perfect example of the harmony achieved between wood and laterite, a remarkable feature of the Kerala style of architecture, the Temple is a veritable architectural marvel. The founding and prosperity of

Kozhikode city is closely linked with the sanctity of this ancient Temple. It is believed that the lingam in the sanctum of the Temple was installed towards the end of Dwaparayuga by Sri Parasurama. The posture in the sanctum is that of Umamaheswara.

NOCHIPRA BHAGAVATHY KSHETRAM TEMPLE AT WESTHILL - It is more than 900 years old Temple. The main deity is Bhuvaneshwari Amma, the divine mother. Bhuvanalswari meaning "Goddess of the Worlds" or "Queen of the Universe", where the worlds are the tri-bhuvana or three regions of bhuh (earth), bhuvah (atmosphere) and svah (heavens). In this most loved form, Bhuvaneshwari Amma becomes the provider and grants everything in abundance to her devotees and is capable of turning any situations per her wishes.

LOKANARKAVU TEMPLE AT MEMUNDA - Lokanarkavu is a short form of Lokamalayarkavu which means lokam (world) made of mala (mountain), aaru (river) and kavu (grove). The Temple dedicated to Goddess Durga has great historical importance as Thacholi Othenan, the legendary martial hero of Kerala, used to worship here every day. It is the official family Temple of the 500 Aryan Nagariks, who had migrated to Kerala and their successors. Pooram is the important festival here and it is conducted with great pomp & show. This is the only Temple where a peculiar folk dance called Poorakkali is presented during festivals. The dance resembles the martial art Kalarippayattu. Even today, all Kalaripayattu artists seek the blessings of the deity before their debut.

DISTRICT – MALAPPURAM (Railway Station – Ferok/Tirur/Tanur/Angadippuram)

S. No.	Temple	Address	Type
1	Elannummel Shiva Temple	Chelembra – 673636	Shiva
2	Sree Alathiyoor Hanumankavu	P.O. Allathiyur – 676102	Hanuman
3	Vellamassery Devaswom – Shri Garudan Kavu Kshetram	P.O. Allathiyur – 676102	Garuda
4	Sastha Temple	Chamravattom – 676102	Sastha
5	Trikandiyur Shiva Temple	Tirur – 676104	Shiva
6	Thriprangode Mahashiva Temple	Triprangode - 676108	Shiva
7	Thirunavaya Devaswom & Bharatappuzha	Thirunavaya P.O. – 676301	Vishnu, Triveni Sangam
8	Keraladheeswarapuram Sreekrishna Kshethram	Tirur – Kadalundi Road, Thanalur – 676307	Krishna
9	Vaidyaratnam P. S. Varier's Arya Vaidya Sala	Kottakkal P.O. - 676503	Vishnu, Shiva
10	Kadampuzha Devaswom	P.O. Kadampuzha – 676553	Mata
11	Sree Thirumandhamkunnu Bhagavathy Devaswam	Angadippuram – 679321	Mata, Shiva
12	Pulamanthole Mana	Pulamanthole - 679323	Mana
13	Vettakkorumakan Temple	Nilambur Kovilakam, Nilambur – 679329	Vettakkorumakan

ELANNUMMEL SHIVA TEMPLE AT CHELEMBRA, MALAPPURAM - The Temple is more than 2000 years old. The primary deity is Lord Shiva. It also contains a smaller Vishnu Temple in which the deity is represented as "Santhanagopalan". The legend is that Parasurama consecrated this Temple as one of several he founded in Kerala to promote the Sanathana Dharma. The Temple was previously supported by several "Manas" in the Chelembra.

SHRI ALATHIYOOR HANUMAN TEMPLE AT TIRUR – Lord Sri Rama is the presiding deity, however, the devotees popularly prefer to the Temple as the "Hanumankavu Temple" in a way it symbolizes the triumph of the supreme strength of bhakthi of Sri Hanuman as an ideal, which overshadows the presiding deity Lord Sri Rama. Here, Lord Sri Rama is visualized as the Maryada Purushothaman. Lord Sri Rama is seen entrusting Sri Hanuman the impossible task of locating the whereabouts of Seetha, who was abducted by Ravana. It is the task in which Lord Sri Rama seeks the assistance of his Bhaktha, Hanuman. All the Gods bestow Lord Hanuman with their enormous strength so that he succeeds in his mission. For Lord Hanuman, this is a very significant moment and hence, his pre-eminence at Alathiyoor. There is platform to commemorate Sri Hanuman's mighty leap to Lanka over the sea. There is a long granite stone at one end of the platform and symbolize the sea. Devotees come running and leap over the long stone. By doing this, auspicious result is expected especially for the better health and life of children.

SHRI GARUDAN KAVU KSHETHRAM AT ALLATHIYUR - The only Garuda Temple in India is known as Vellamassery Garudan Kavu Temple. Very near to it, there is a Mahavishnu Temple in Koormavathara form. This Garuda Temple is about 1800 years old. The vigrahas here have been shown their own special features. Sankara Narayana and Shiva prathist has facing the east. On the left of Lord Garuda, one can worship Veettekkaran and Kartha Veeryarjunan. Lord Vishnu and Sankara Narayanan have Namaskara Mandapa. Vishnu has a balippura on the south as well. At west one can pray Sastha, Bhagavathy, Ganapthy and Bhadra Kali. There is a gopuram at the west and a deepasthambham inside. The large and serene Temple pond on the south adds to the pride of this Temple. Worshipping here is mainly meant for easy recovery from diseases and for relief from serpent poisons. All Sundays are important here especially the 41 days of Mandalakalam. To the Hindus, Garuda is the Lord without beginning and without end.

CHAMRAVATTOM SASTHA TEMPLE - Believed to have been built by the legendary sculptor Perunthachan, the vigraha stands on the same level as the river, much below the sanctum sanctorum. Pilgrims heading for Sabarimala stop here en route.

TRIKANDIYUR SHIVA TEMPLE AT TIRUR – It is dedicated to Lord Shiva. The vigraha of this ancient Temple is believed to be installed by Lord Parasurama. The vibrant history, charming architecture and powerful deity all range among the attractions of this Temple. A few other Temples are there surrounding this Shiva shrine such as a

Krishna Temple, Ambalakulangare Temple and an Ayyapankavu. A major festival of the Temple is Vaavulsavam.

THRIPRANGODE MAHASHIVA TEMPLE - The Temple is dedicated to Lord Shiva. The Temple is one of the 108 Lord Shiva Temples in Kerala. Lord Shiva is Swayambhu here and is worshiped as Kalasamhara which means who destroyed Yama. As per Sthala Puranam, there was a Rishi named Mrikandu along with his wife Marudaviti. They were devotees of Lord Shiva. The couple was childless and they decided to worship Lord Shiva. Pleased by their devotion, Lord Shiva appeared before them and asked if they desired a son who live a long life or a son who would live until the age of sixteen years, the couple choose the latter. Thus, Markandeya was born. Markandeya learned Mrityunjaya Mantra and becomes a sage. When the age of sixteen years of Markandeya comes near, his parents become very sad and from them, Markandeya knew every thing. He went to Thinunavaya Navamukhunda Kshetram but a voice came and told to seeks shelter to Triprangode. Markandeya reached at this place & embraced Shivalingam holding tightly and prayed to Lord Shiva. Yama Deva came & threw his Kaala Pasham to take Markandeya but the Pasham surrounded Shivalingam too. Lord Shiva appeared from the Shivaligam & angered with Yama Deva's deed. Lord Shiva took his Trishul & destroyed Yama, but later revived him as requested by Devas. Thus, Markandeya granted wish that he will be always sixteen years old. Lord Shiva washed his Trishul at Kshetrakulam, which is considered very sacred. Devotees, who are suffering with various illness worshipped Lord Shiva here.

THIRUNAVAYA NAVA MUKUNDA TEMPLE – Dakshina Ganga - Bharathappuzha in Thirunavaya flows caressing the three Temples of Maha Vishnu on its North bank and Lord Brahma and Parama Shiva on its south bank. Hence, the Pithrukarmas performed at this 'Thrimoorthy Sangam' are considered as very sacred. The cultural uniqueness, tantric sanctity, religious harmony and diversity continue here through generations. The Nava Mukunda Temple was constructed about 5000 years back. Though it had undergone periodical renovations, the last and major renovation with the reconstruction of Sanctum Sanctorum was done about 1300 years back. The reconstruction had the typical ' Perumthachan Touch ' making the rays of the rising sun fall on the vigraha on every Medam First (in Utharaayana period) and on Kanni First (in Dakshinayana period). Besides the Navamukunda (Vishnu) which is the main deity of the Temple, there are two other deities in the Temple: Aadi Ganesa and Sree Mahalakshmi. There are five 'Yajna's which are sacred to the Hindus and one of them is Pithrutharpana (Oblation), the prayers for the souls of the departed and rituals involving offering of food and water to the departed. Lord Parasurama is believed to have come here to perform Tarpanam for the souls of the thousands of Kshatriyas he had killed.

TANUR KERALADEESHAPURAM TEMPLE – It is 3000-years odd old tile-roofed Temple. It was once visited in1546 by St Francis Xavier, the Apostle of the East who is resting in the Basilica of Bom Jesu in Old Goa. The deity in the Temple is Lord Krishna (Vishnu). Tipu Sultan's army ravaged vigraha was replaced recently.

LORD VISWAMBHARA TEMPLE AT ARYA VAIDYA SALA - Vaidyaratnam P.S. Varier consecrated a Temple for Lord Viswambhara in 1932. The beautiful and serene vigraha is carved in white marble. He personally anointed it and conducted daily pooja for the vigraha for an year before installing it at the sanctum sanctorum of the Temple. The four-armed Viswambhara is conceived as an incarnation of Lord Vishnu with the divine conch, discus, mace and lotus in the four arms. P.S. Varier also started an annual festival of the Temple in 1934. This seven-day annual festival has become famous for its pomp and cultural importance. Kathakali Artists and Musicians have been performing during the seven-day festivities. The Temple has become an abode of solace and consolation for a large number of patients visiting Arya Vaidya Sala. The fact that caste and creed were not barriers for entry to the Temple even at the time of its inception has been widely acknowledged.

KOTTAKKAL VENKATTATHEVAR TEMPLE - The Temple was famous for 64 mural paintings adorn the walls of the sanctum sanctorum of this Temple dedicated to Lord Siva and the Venkattathevar Utsavam in April.

KADAMPUZHA DEVI TEMPLE - The origin of the Temple is associated with the Mahabharata. However, the Temple was founded by Shree Shankaracharya. The origin of the name Kadampuzha is considered to have been formed from Kadan Ambu Eitha Uzha – meaning, The Place where Kiratha Shot the Arrow. Kadan is Kiratha, Ambu is Arrow, Eitha is Shot and Uzha is Place. Shree Adi Shankaracharya consecrate this place as a Temple and also constituted Lord Narasimha and Sudarshana Chakra in front of Devi and also decided to place Dharmashasta and Nagakanyaka on either sides of the Temple. He also stipulated the poojas and rituals that must be conducted at the Temple and these stipulations are followed till date. Devi is worshiped here in three forms. In the mornings she is worshiped as Vidya Durga (Saraswati) bestowing knowledge and excellence in career to all. In the afternoon she is worshiped as Vanadurga (Durga) in the Twaritha Devi form blessing the devotees with health, early marriage, and domestic harmony and in the evening as Aadi Durga (Mooladurga - Lakshmi) bestowing the devotees with wealth & overall prosperity. Here, the self-manifested divine presence is worshiped as a presence only. Unlike other Temples, Kadampuzha is unique in that there are no vigrahas for the Devi. To mark this place and for the common man's reference, a Thidambu or Arch is kept on top. Only during the "Poo Moodal" rite, the Thidumbu is removed & the hole exposed.

THIRUMANDHAMKUNNU BHAGAVTHY TEMPLE & ANGADIPPURAM TALI SREE MAHADEVA AT PERINTHALAMANNA – It is one of the ancient and famous Mahakshethras of Kerala. The King Mandhatha of Surya dynasty ruled the country for long period. He then gave away the kingdom to his successors and chose to meditate on Lord Shiva. Lord Shiva was pleased with his penance, gave him the most holy Shivalinga at Kailash, which used to be worshiped by Parvathy. Carrying the Shivalinga on head, Mandhatha started his downward journey from Kailash and reached the hill, now known as Thirumandhamkunnu. A spring with crystal clear water flowed along the northern slop of the hill. The surrounding of hill attracted the king. Feelings of vigraha on his head heavy he placed it on the ground. Immediately, the Shivalinga got stuck in to the earth. When Maa Parvathy turned up for worship the Shivalinga, it was not there. Parvathy, as Bhadrakali and a host of bhoothas to rush up to get back

the Shivalingam. The brightness emitted by the Shivalinga, installed by Mandnatha, was so great that it dazzled the eyes of Kali and bhoothas and they were unable to move up the hills. Expecting defeat in the strong fight, Mahamaya took her Viswaroopa and seeing this form, the ascetics fell down senseless. When mahamaya in this form reached the hilltop, Mandhatha was also helpless. He embraced the Shivalinga, she tried to capture it by force. In this struggle, the Shivalinga got split into two. In the "Jyothis" that arose from it "Thrimoorthis" (Brahma, Vishnu and Shiva) and Parvathy appeared on the spot. Parvathy told Mandhatha that separation from the Shivalinga is difficult for me, so I will enter into the Shivalinga and remain here forever. My daughter Kali is not different from me. Let her also be installed near me facing north and have all poojas and festival performed. This spot is the "Sreemoolasthanam". The Shivalinga here is still in split condition. The age old custom of "Attanga Yeru" on first of Thulam (The Malayalam month) on the new moon day before Pantheerady Pooja refers to the legendary fight between Mandhatha and Kali. Sree Parvathy appeared facing west. As ordered by Parvathy, Bhagavathy with Sapthamathrukkal, Veerabhadran and Ganapaty were installed facing north. This is called "Mathrusala". Pooram, Pattu and all such festivals intended for this goddess.

PULAMANTHOLE MANA - It is very famous for Ayurveda treatment based on Ashtavaida, a wing of Ayurveda science. Many of the patients come here as they tasted no success in the treatment elsewhere and return fully cured. It is widely known as a curable place for incurables. The Mana belongs to Mooss family. This family has its own Temple which is very famous – Pulamanthole Sree Rudra Dhanwanthari Temple and this Temple has a colourful history. The Maharaja of Travancore was inflicted by a severe stomach pain. The treatment given by many famed physicians gave no relief. As an ultimate source for cure, the King sent messengers to Pulamnthole Mana. When the message for treatment received, only a lady and his young son were in the Mana. Upanayanam was not yet done by the boy. The mother and son were upset as to what to do. The mother told the messengers that his son will come after completing 12 days Bhajana in their family Temple and advised the son to start the Bhajana. A Sanyasi appeared before the boy on the 12th day and gave 3 tablets and assured him that these tablets will cure the King. The monk further added that he should not accept any of the gifts offered by the King. Instead, request the King to allow to take the vigraha of Dhanwanthari lying in the Tamarapani River and install the same at the left side of the vigraha of Lord Shiva in their own Temple and build a shrine for it. The King was cured by the treatment of the boy. The pleased King agreed to the request of the boy and the vigraha was brought and installed. The Sanyasi was actually Lord Shiva who took the form of Sanyasi. Karnatic Music Emperor, Sri Chembai Vaidynatha Bhagawathar was once severelly hit by paralysis. He tried many physicians from many fields, but proved futile. As a last resort he approached Pulamanthole Mooss and he was cured.

VETTAKKORUMAKAN TEMPLE AT NILAMBUR - Vettakkorumakan is a Hindu deity worshipped in parts of North Kerala and North-Western Tamil Nadu. This deity is alternately referred as Kiratha-Sunu (son of Kirata) in Sanskrit. He is believed to be the son of Lord Shiva by his consort Parvathi, born when Lord Shiva assumed the form of a Kirata (hunter) to deliver a weapon known as Pashupathasthra to Arjuna. He is the family deity of the Rajas of Chirakkal, Nileshwar, Kottakkal, Nilambur Kovilakam, Kalathil Kartha's, Aluva, Amarambalam Kovilakam and Randulllam Vargam Nambiars. A special type of firecracker called "Kathina" was his favourite. During hunting, Vettakkorumakan, as a child,

killed many asuras but making free use of his bow and arrows and he also gave endless trouble to the Devas and Rishis. Unable to bear his mischief, they approached Mahavishnu who took the form of an old hunter and went to the boy. Mahavishnu displayed before the boy a golden churika (dagger-cum-sword) which was so beautiful that it attracted the boy who begged him to make a present of it. Mahavishnu agreed to provide the same on the condition that he would behave in a responsible manner by giving up his bow and started protecting the people instead of harming them. The boy accepted the condition and with the churika took leave of his parents from Kailasha and went to the land of Parasurama, Kerala. He crossed several mountains and forests and rivers and reached North Kerala where he first entered the Balussery Fort. Hence the importance of the Balussery Temple dedicated to Vettakkorumakan though the Lord later visited other places where He was revered and worshipped. Nearest Railway Station is Nilambur Road.

DISTRICT – PALAKKAD (Railway Station – Palakkad)

S. No.	Temple	Address	Type
1	Palakkad Fort	Palakkad - 678001	Hanuman
2	Sri Visalakshi Sametha Sri Viswanatha Swamy Temple	Kalpathi - 678003	Shiva, Mata
3	Kachamkurissi Maha Vishnu Kshetram	Kollengode - 678506	Vishnu
4	Mangottu Bhagavathi Temple	Athipotta - 678544	Mata
5	Panniyur Sri Varahamurthy Temple	Pattambi - 679303	Vishnu
6	Thiruvegapura Mahadeva Kshetram	Thiruvegapura - 679304	Shiva
7	Sri Rama Temple	Kottapadam - 679534	Rama
8	Vaidyamadom	Trithala - 679534	Mana

PALAKKAD FORT - The old fort situated in the very heart of Palakkad town is one of the best preserved in Kerala. It was built by Hyder Ali of Mysore in 1766 and later taken over and modified by the British in 1790. It is now preserved by Archaeological Survey of India. A Temple of Lord Hanuman is adjacent to the main entrance of the Fort. A museum of Archaeology is also functioning inside the Fort. The entire area is beautifully landscaped.

SRI VISALAKSHI SAMETHA SRI VISWANATHA SWAMY TEMPLE AT KALPATHI - Kalpathi Rathotsavam is an annual Temple festival is celebrated at the Sri Visalakshi Sametha Sri Viswanatha Swamy Temple, where the deities are Lord Shiva (Lord Viswanatha) and his consort Visalakshi, another name for Goddess Parvati. The annual ten-day chariot festival conducted here during the month of November is one of the most remarkable festivals of Kerala. Vedic recitals and cultural programmes are held in the Temple during the first four days of the festival. This is believed to be over 700 years old. On the last three days, thousands of devotees gather together to draw decorated Temple chariots through the streets. The ancient Temple nestles by the banks of the Kalpathy River, which is also known as the Nila River. The Temple dates back to 1425.

KACHAMKURISSI MAHA VISHNU KSHETRAM AT KOLLENGODE - The Temple is dedicated to Lord Vishnu. This is one among Maha Kshetrams in Palakkad. It is believed that the Prathishta was done by Kashyapa Muni and the place was called Kashyapa Kurissi and later came to be known as Kachamkurissi. It is believed that Kashyap Muni did Aswamedha Yagana here along with Muni Athri, Agasthya & Markandeya. The Yagya Kunda is called Yagna Tirtham and the waters are considered as sacred and will remove all doshas.

MANGOTTU BHAGAVATHI TEMPLE AT ATHIPOTTA - The Temple is dedicated to Goddess Bhagavathi. Goddess is known as Kshipraprasadi and she grants relief to those devotees who worship the Goddess with full faith & devotion. Mookken Chathen is guarding Devi here. As per legend, there was a weavier named Kuttan who was a devotee of the Goddess. During festivals, Kutan was so pleased by the vigraha of the Goddess and he requested her to come along with him. At that time, wind blew heavily and clothes of the vigraham flew away. Kuttan immediately decorated the Goddess with his cloths which stuck to the vigraham & returned to his village with his umbrella. The Goddess came with him in that umbrella and stayed at this place.

PANNIYUR SRI VARAHAMURTHY TEMPLE AT PATTAMBI - The Temple is dedicated to Lord Varaha, an incarnation of Lord Vishnu. This is believed to be the first Temple in Kerala, where Prathishta was done by Bhagwan Parshurama. As earth is saved by Lord Vishnu in Varaha Avatar, this Temple is famous to solve land related issues. Many devotees conduct Bhumi Pooja here, which is very special. They bring sand from around the Temple, which is used for pooja and then has to be returned to the same spot from where it was taken. It is also believed that Perumthachan, the legendry craftsman has abandoned his tools here.

THIRUVEGAPURA MAHADEVA KSHETRAM - The Temple is dedicated to Lord Shiva. The Temple is located on the banks of Thutha Puzha. The Temple is also known as Moonnumoorthy Temple. The place is known as Mahadev Kshetram but Lord Krishna & Shankaranarayanan are also worshiped here. As per Sthala Puranam the Shivalinga had been brought from Himalayas by Garuda Deva. Shivratri & Vaikkathashtami festivals are celebrated here with great pomp & fervor.

SRI RAMA TEMPLE AT KOTTAPADAM - The Temple is dedicated to Lord Rama. It is an ancient & famous Temple but the same was in ruined condition which was renovated recently by making it a new Temple.

VAIDYAMADOM AT TRITHALA - Vaidyamadom is a great Ashtavaidya family. This is the only family in Kerala, which belongs to Bharadwajeeya group. This family was brought over here by the renowned Mezhatole Agnihotri who is credited with conducting about 100 Soma Yagas. In Soma Yagas, the family is honoured as Sala Vaidya. Among Ashtavaidya families, Vaidyamadom has a crowning position. They are born Ashtavaidyars. Their family-name, Vaidyamadom, itself is born out of Vaidya. Madom denotes centre or abode. Where there are Yagas, the members of Vaidyamadom are there, as they have super knowledge in this specific and intricated field. They imparts knowledge of Vedas to the interested and many have come out from here as Vedic experts. Lord Dhakshinamoorthy (Lord Shiva in meditation) is the family deity of the Vaidyamadom. As per legend, a woman in the ancient ruling family was in delivery pains. The pain prolonged to an unusual length. The worried family tried out many Physicians in quick succession but for no avail. Incidentally, a member of Vaidyamadom happened to be there at that painful moment. He requested the King (the husband of the pain-eating pregnant lady) that he may please be permitted to try his hand. The King consented. He then plucked some herbal leaves from the Palace courtyard and made them paste by squeezing with fingers. He prepared two types of pastes and applied each on each side of a small wooden board. Then the attending Aya (mid-wife) was instructed to expose one side of the board to the vagina of the queen. Few minutes later, the queen delivered a male baby. Immediately on delivery, the Aya was directed to reverse the board and expose it to the vagina to forbid the womb and other internal organs coming out which may cause death. Nothing untoward happened. The excited King named the new born "Pareekshith". This incident alone amplifies the skill of Vaidyamadom in Ayurveda science. The present head of the family has wrapped the Vaidyasala in modern outfit.

DISTRICT – PATHANAMTHITTA (Railway Station – Sasthankotta/Tiruvalla/Mavelikara)

S. No.	Temple	Address	Type
1	Bhagavathy Temple	Mannadi – 686511	Mata
2	Sree Vallabha Temple	Tiruvalla - 689101	Vishnu
3	Valiyakoikal Temple	Pandalam – 689501	Ayyappan
4	Aranmula Parthasarathy Temple	Aranmula – 689533	Krishna
5	Kaviyoor Rock Cut Temple	Pathanamthitta – 689582	Shiva
6	Kadammanitta Devi Temple	Kadammanitta – 689649	Mata
7	Sabrimala Sree Dharma Sastha Temple	Sannidham – 689662	Ayyappan
8	Malayalappuzha Devi Temple	Malayalapuzha Thazgam - 689666	Mata
9	Mahalakshmi Temple	Kodumon – 691555	Mata

MANNADI - The ancient Bhagavathy Temple here has some exquisite stone sculptures. The annual festival is held in February/March. The Kerala Institute of Folklore and Folk Arts functions here.

THIRUVALLA - Sree Vallabha Temple is perhaps the only one in Kerala where Kathakali is performed as a ritual offering everyday.

Tharayil Kuzhikkat Mana - Bhagwan Parasuraman had taught Thantric skills to 12 Manas. Kuzhikkat Mana is one of them. It was originally in Malabar. The installation of the vigraha at Sree Vallabh Temple of Thiruvalla was done by this Mana. Following the installation by the elders in the Mana they settled in Thiruvalla. The installed vigrahas at Madaikavu Temple and 140 other Temples by one time head of the Mana, Brahmasree Maheswaran Bhatathiripad were razed by Tipu. Maheswaran Bhatathiripad was well-versed not only in Thantric rites but also in Astrology. 'Golamkettaka' was an instrument invented by him which helps study the movements of planets and make accurate predictions. In more than 800 shrines in and out of Kerala, the consecration ceremony has been carried out by members of the Mana. The Mana has their own shrine, where the deity is Bhadrakali. Yakshi is a sub-deity. Chathan is worshipped in the Nalukettu of the Mana. "Theeyattu" is the important offering in the Temple. For Yakshi, 'Vana Nivedyam' is the offering given.

PANDALAM - Sree Ayyappa, the presiding deity of Sabarimala, had his human sojourn here as the son of the Raja of Pandalam. As a holy town, Pandalam is perhaps second only to Sabarimala. The Temple is situated near the palace on the banks of River Achenkovil. It has been modelled on the Sabarimala shrine. Pilgrims usually stop here to worship before proceeding to Sabarimala. Three days prior to the Makaravilaku festival, the sacred ornaments of Sree Ayyappa are taken in a procession from Pandalam to Sabarimala.

ARANMULA PARTHASARATHY TEMPLE - Aranmula is famous for its Aranmula Kannadi (metal mirrors), the centuries' old Sree Krishna Temple, the unique ritualistic feast of `Vallasadya' and famed Aranmula Snake Boat Race 'Vallam Kali' etc. It is a global heritage site enlisted by the United Nations. It gets its name from the centuries-old Aranmula Parthasarathy Temple (dedicated to Sree Krishna) on the banks of the holy River Pamba, a virtual hotbed of devotees. The Temple is one of the major Temples in Kerala and has a great antiquity. It is one of the venerated 108 Vaishnava Temples in India and finds mention in Tamil classics. Main vigraha is of Lord Krishna, who is the charioteer of warrior Arjuna in Kurukshetra War. The Temple has fine murals from the 18thcentury. "Thanka Anki", the golden ornaments of Lord Ayyappa at Sabarimala is kept here. It is also the venue for the Aranmula Vallasadya, a ritual offering to the deity Lord Parthasarathy in which the oarsmen of the snake boats are offered a feast with over 70 dishes, it is probably one of the largest vegetarian feasts in India. Another ancient Temple, Pulikkunnumala Mahadeva Temple is just 4 KMs from Aranmula. The old Temple is traditionally said to be the worship place of the pandavas. Nearest Railway Station is Chengannur.

KAVIYOOR - The Mahadeva Temple, which was constructed in the early years of the 10thcentury, is one of the oldest of the Mahadeva Temples in Kerala. It is popularly known as the Rock Cut Cave Temple. The ancient Temple is carved on a massive rock and dedicated to Lord Shiva. The Temple is also having archaeological importance because of its close similarity to the Pallava style of architecture. The sculptures and carved rooms of the Temple are well preserved. The Archaeological Department preserves this Temple as a monument.

KADAMMANITTA DEVI TEMPLE – It is an ancient Temple in South Kerala. The main vigraha is Maha Bhairavi but it has separate shrines for Lord Shiva and Lord Krishna. There is also a shrine for Mala Deva, the initial protector of the goddess. It is believed that Kadammanitta Devi is very powerful and answers the prayers of devotees. Each devotee feels blessed after visiting this Temple. It is famous for the Padayani performance during the festival which conducts in the months of April or May.

SABARIMALA SREE DHARMA SASTHA TEMPLE – It is dedicated to Lord Ayyappa and is the most famous and prominent among all the Sastha Temples in Kerala. The Temple is situated on a hilltop (about 3000 feet above sea level) named Sabarimala, which is unique. The Temple is open to people belonging to all religions. Another unique aspect of this Temple is that it is not open throughout the year. It is open for worship only during the days of Mandalapooja, Makaravilakku, Vishu and also during the first day of every Malayalam month.It is said that the pilgrims have to observe celibacy for 41 days before going to Sabarimala.

King Rajashekara, the foster-father of Lord Ayyappa, belonged to Pandya dynasty, had one sorrow – he was childless and thus had no heir to inherit his throne. Both the hapless king and his queen prayed ceaselessly to Lord Shiva for a child. Determined to avenge her slain brother Mahishasur, Mahishi, secured a boon from Lord Brahma that no being except the offspring of Vishnu (Hari) & Shiva (Haran) could slay her. Lord Vishnu assumed the female persona of Mohini who helped the devas prize Amrit away from the asuras; it was decided that the male child born out of the union of Mohini and Lord Shiva would be placed under the care of Lord Shiva's childless devotee, King Rajashekhara of Pandalam. On one of his hunting trips to the forests near River Pampa, as King Rajashekara heard an infant's wails from the forest. Astounded, he followed the sounds and came upon a beautiful child furiously kicking its feet and arms. The king stood there, perplexed – he longed to take the child home to his palace. Whilst King Rajashekhara beheld the divine child, a sadhu appeared from nowhere and instructed him to take the infant to his palace. Also the mendicant assured him that the child would mitigate his dynasty's sufferings and that when the boy turned twelve, Rajashekhara would be aware of his divinity. As the child was wearing a gold chain, the sadhu directed the King to name him 'Manikandan' – one with a golden neck. Ecstatic, Rajashekhara took Manikandan home and narrated the happenings to his queen. They both felt that they had been blessed by Lord Shiva himself. When Manikandan turned twelve years old, he reminded his father that as he had accomplished the task for which he had created himself and he would return to Devaloka without fail. King Rajasekara told him that they wanted to construct a Temple in his memory and beseeched him to suggest a suitable place for the Temple. Manikandan aimed an arrow which fell at a place called sabari, where in Sri Rama's era, a Sanyasini called Sabari observed Dhavam. Lord Manikandan told the King to build the Temple in that place and then he disappeared.

Later, acting upon the advice of Saint Agasthya, King Rajasekara laid the foundation stone of the Temple at Sabarimala. Whilst they make their way up the steep slopes of Sabarimala, they adorn themselves with three-eyed coconut and foodstuff/Aantha Garland in their heads, as the Bhagwan did when he went to the forest to fetch tigress milk and bathed in River Pampa raising slogans of Saranam and climb the eighteen stairs. River Pampa is a holy River as River Ganga, Sabarimala is as holy as Kashi - Dharmasastha sent Parasuraman, who resurrected the land of Kerala from the bottom of the ocean to Sabarimala; it was he, who carved the figure of Lord Ayyappa and installed it on the day of Makarasankranthi. The deity of Nagarajav is placed adjacent to the Sreekovil (sanctum sanctorum) of Lord Ayyappa. Pilgrims after the Darshan of Lord Ayyappa and Kannimoola Ganapathi, make their darshan and give offerings to Nagarajav. Vavar (pronounced Vaa-var), also known as Vavaruswami. He was a Muslim saint who became a devotee of Lord Ayyappa. Malikapurathamma is the most important upadevatha in Sabarimala. As per Tantric view, pilgrims have to worship Malikappuram as 'Adiparasakthi'. The Temple of Karuppu Swami is located on the right side of the Pathinettam Padi or the eighteen holy steps. The Temple of Karuppu Swami also includes the murti of Karuppai Amma. The small shrine of Valiya Kadutha is located on the left side of holy steps. Valiya Kadutha is also an attendant of Lord Ayyappa. Mel Ganapathiprathishta is adjacent to the Sreekovil (sanctum sanctorum) of the Sannidhanam. Nearest Railway Sation is Kottayam.

MALAYALAPPUZHA DEVI TEMPLE AT MALAYALAPUZHA THAZGAM - The Temple is dedicated to Goddess Bhadrakali, who is known as Idathattil Bhagavathy. The vigraha of the Goddess had been made of Katu Sarkara Yogam & the vigraha is in Ugra Roopam here. It is believed that Goddess Bhadrakali had destroyed a demon named Darika. It is also believed that the Goddess blesses with all wishes of the devotees. Thiruvathira is very famous in the Temple and Vinayaka Chaturthi & Navarathri festivals are also celebrated here with great pomp & fervor.

KODUMON CHILANTHIYAMBALAM – It is also the birth place of Sree Shakthi Bhadra, author of Ascharya Chudamani. The water of the Chilanthikinar (well) in the premises of this Temple is believed to cure skin diseases. The Mahalakshmi of this Temple is worshipped by all people irrespective of caste and creed.

Pampa River - This is the main halting point on the way to Sabarimala. It is also known as Thriveni Sangamam – the meeting point of three Rivers.

DISTRICT – THIRUVANANTHAPURAM (Railway Station – Trivandrum)

S. No.	Temple	Address	Type
1	Attukal Bhagavathy Temple	Manacaud P. O., Thiruvananthapuram – 695009	Mata
2	Pazhavangadi Maha Ganapathy Temple	Pazhavangadi, Thiruvananthapuram – 695023	Ganesh
3	Sree Padmanabha Swamy Temple	Fort, Thiruvananthapuram – 695023	Vishnu
4	Sree Krishna Swami Temple	Neyyattinkara - 695121	Krishna
5	Maheswaram Sri Sivaparvathi Temple	Chenkal – 695132	Shiva-Parvathi
6	Sivagiri – Sree Narayana Dharma Sanghom Trust	Varkala – 695141	Shiva
7	Sarkara Devi Temple	Chirayinkeezhu - 695304	Mata

S. No.	Temple	Address	Type
8	Aazhimala Siva Temple	Pulinkudi -695501	Shiva
9	Vizhinjam Rock Cut Cave Temple	Vizhinjam – 695521	Shiva
10	Sree Kulathoor Kolathukara Shiva Temple	Kulathoor, Thiruvananthapuram – 695583	Shiva

ATTUKAL BHAGAVATHY TEMPLE AT MANACAUD – It is one of the ancient Temples of South India. It is popularly described as Sabarimala of the Women. The pilgrims from all over the country, who visit Sree Padmanabha Swamy Temple and worship the Lord, do not consider their visits complete without the visit to the shrine of the supreme Mother Attukalamma. Vishnumaya took the incarnation of Bhagavathy to annihilate the evil and protect the good in the world in the present Era namely Kaliyuga. The Pongala Mahotsavam is the most important festival of the Temple. On the ninth day of the festival the world famous Attukal Pongala Mahotsavam takes place. The Temple structure is a harmonious conglomeration of both Kerala and Tamil styles of architecture. The beautifully carved figures of Mahishasuramardini, Goddess Kali, Rajarajeswari, Sree Parvathy with Lord Paramasiva and various other depictions of the Goddess in and around the Temple are undoubtedly the work of a gifted artist. Equally well presented around the corridors surrounding the Temple are the depiction of various other Gods and the epic stories of the ten incarnations of Lord Vishnu viz., the "Dasavathara". On either side of the elegant front gopura - are the icons based on the story of Goddess Kannaki. On the southern Gopura, the puranic story of "Dakshayaga" is depicted in sculptures. There are two vigrahas of the Goddess in the sanctum sanctorum. The original vigraha is preserved in all its pristine beauty covered in ornamental gold embedded with installed stones. The second vigraha of the Goddess is installed besides the original one. Within the Temple corridors are also installed carvings and sculptures of Lord Ganesan, the serpent God and Lord Shiva. At the centre of the Sanctum within the Sreekovil, at a consecrated spot is installed the vigraha of the Goddess Attukal Bhagavathy emanating light and lustre to all.

GUINNESS WORLD RECORDS

CERTIFICATE

The largest annual gathering of women is achieved by 2.5 million women in an event organised by Attukal Bhagavathy Temple Trust in Kerala, India, on 10th March 2009.

GUINNESS WORLD RECORDS LTD

PAZHAVANGADI MAHA GANAPATHY TEMPLE AT THIRUVANANTHAPURAM - The main deity of the Temple is Sri Mahaganapathy (Ganesha). The main vigraha is installed in a seated posture with the right leg in a folded stance. Other deities worshiped at the Temple include Dharmasasta, Goddess Durga and Nagaraja. The Temple sculptures include 32 different forms of Lord Ganesha. As the vigraha was obtained by the will and blessings of the Lord from a river-bed, the vigraha is considered as self-revealed. A Bhajana-mandapam was opened on September 9, 1983. Laying the foundation stone of the imposing Mandapam with gopuram on the eastern side of the Temple was done on 31st December 1993. A reference Library with rare collections of religious books in Sanskrit, English and other languages was formally opened at the top floor of the Bhajana-mandapam on 9th March 2003. Three sides of sub-shrines of Lord Vettakkorumakan and Goddess Durga Bhagavati were covered with decorated brass sheets for safety and for ambience in August 2009.

SREE PADMANABHASWAMY TEMPLE AT THIRUVANANTHAPURAM – The Temple was built by the Travancore dynasty and it is certainly a spectacle to behold with its architectural beauty and the spiritual aura that it creates. A specialty of the Temple is its presiding deity Lord Vishnu. Here, Lord Vishnu is enshrined in the "Anantha Shayanam" posture, the eternal yogic sleep on the serpent Adisheshan. Sree Padmanabhaswamy is the tutelary deity of the royal family of Travancore. The Temple is noted for its architectural style, which is a mix of indigenous Kerala and Tamil Nadu styles.The Temple has references in Epics and Puranas. Srimad Bhagavatha says that Balarama visited this Temple, bathed in Padmatheertham and made several offerings. Nammalwar, 9th century poet and one among the 12 Vaishnavite saints of the Alvar tradition, has composed ten hymns in praise of Lord Padmanabha. One legend which finds a place in the old palm leaf records of the Temple, as also in the famous Grantha entitled "Ananthasayana Mahatmya", mentions that it was consecrated by a Tulu Brahmin hermit named Divakara Muni. On the 950th year of Kaliyuga, a reinstallation of the vigraha was done. It is also believed that the small Sree Krishna Swamy Temple located near the Western Swamiyar Madham has been built over the Samadhi of Vilvamangalathu Swamiyar. According to legend the Sree Narasimhaswamy and Sree Sastha shrines were established after the installation of the vigraha of Lord Sree Padmanabhaswamy. Divakara Muni was a great Vishnu Bhaktha. He reached a wooded area near the sea coast, caught a glimpse of the child disappearing into a huge 'Ilappa' tree. Immediately the tree fell into the ground and it assumed the form of Sree Maha Vishnu. The divine form had its head at 'Thiruvallam' (a place about 3 miles from East Fort at where the Temple of Sree Padmanabha Swamy is located) and its feet at 'Trippapur' (5 miles away towards the north). Overawed by the majesty and the size of the divine form, which manifested before him, the Sanyasi prayed to the Lord to condense Himself in size so that he could behold Him. There upon the vigraha of the Lord shrank to a size, three times the length of the Sanyasy's Yoga Dand. His prayers had been granted. He immediately offered a raw mango in a coconut shell (still this offering continues). The Lord ordained that poojas to Him should be conducted by Tulu Brahmins. In the year 1729, the great ruler Marthanda Varma became the king of Travancore, then he took the steps to renovate the Temple. In 1730, the vigraha was moved to 'Balalaya' prior to the renovation and reconstruction of the sanctum sanctorum. The old wooden vigraha was replaced by the one that we see today. Made of highly complex amalgam known as Katusarkarayogam, it contains 12008 Salagrams within it. The magnificent rectangular corridor built of solid stones protects the Deities during seeveli on rainy days. Similarly, the flag-staff in front of the main shrine was also erected at this time. The pole was then covered completely with gold sheets. Lakhshadeepam ceremony marks the 56-day Murajapam festival, a ritual held in every 6 years in the Temple provides a visual treat by lighting up 1 lakh oil lamps. Matras of Vedas are chanted in 7 session in last 8 days. Each round ends with Shiveli, a sacred procession.

SREE KRISHNA SWAMI TEMPLE AT NEYYATTINKARA - The Temple is dedicated to Lord Krishna. The Temple is also of great historic importance. The Temple enshrines Unnikannan in the form of (Navaneetha Krishna) as the presiding deity. Thrikkayyilvenna or Thrikkayyil Venna (butter) is a unique offering to Neyyattinkara Unnikannan – the deity of the Temple. World famous musicians, Sri. Neyyattinkara Mohanachandran and Neyyaattinkara Vasudevan used to perform concerts regularly in Temple festival. The Temple is built in traditional Kerala architecture and is decorated with beautiful artistic sculptures. The main gopuram displays a beautiful scene from Bhagavad Gita - Lord Krishna offering teaching to Arjuna. The sanctum sanctorum is built in the traditional Kerala style. Now the door to the Shri Kovil is painted with gold. There is a huge Gopuram in front of the Shri Kovil. Inside the main complex, there are the deities of Lord Ganesha & Dharmashashtha. Outside the main complex, Nagaraja is worshipped. The walls of the Sanctum are painted with various pictures, depicting the life of Shree Krishna and various other Gods. There is an elephant named "Neyyattinkara Kannan" in the Temple. Ashtami Rohini, Vishu, Navarathri, Mandalapooja are observed with great fervour in this Temple. The main festival of the Temple is its Annual Festival, which is during Meenam.

MAHESWARAM SRI SIVAPARVATHI TEMPLE AT CHENKAL – It is also known as "Dakshina Kailasam". It is the cradle of ancient Kerala culture. This Temple is built completely out of Krishna stone & wood in accordance with Vastu Shastra. Entire Rashichakra symbols are at Sreekovil entrance which symbolizes Sri Shivaparvathi is the controller of entire universe. vigraha for Sri Shivaparvathi is moulded in Panchaloham. There exist a three storied Raja Gopuram. Through east entrance Devotees can enter into Anakkottil. Pillars out of palm tree is one of the attractions of Anakkottil. Structure of Nandi is present on top of the kodimaram. Dvadasa (12) Jyothirlingam of Lord Shiva are installed inside the chuttambalam. There exist Lord Ganesha and Lord Kartikeya Temples inside the chuttambalam. 32 Forms of Lord Ganesha are installed and worshipped outside the chuttambalam. At North-West corner, there is Mahalingam having 111 ft height. Mahalingam at Maheswaram Temple is the world's highest Shivalingam. Mahalingam has plenty of unique peculiarities. One of the peculiarities is its style of construction. Devotees can enter into this Mahalingam. The construction of this Shivalingam is based on Shadadharam. Inside Mahalingam, 108 different Shivalingam and 64 forms of Lord Shiva can be seen.

SIVAGIRI AT VARKALA – It is popularly known as 'Dakshina Kashi'. It is a famous holy place from centuries ago. Sree Narayana Guru was attracted to this place not only because of its natural beauty and serene surroundings but was also due to its geographical nature of hill tops and valleys. In the beginning, he sat near a jack tree, later Guru made a temporary 'Parnasala' and stayed there. On its south side, there was a no man land hill, Guru managed to get it registered in his name and established his Ashram on the top of the hill and reside there. The place became known as Sivagiri from then onwards. Mahatama Gandhi came to Sivagiri on 12.03.1925 and stayed a day in the Ashram. Acharya Vinobabhave visited Sivagiri in 1925 and he proclaimed later that the Guru is an 'Avathar'. The vigraha of Maa Sarada, the goddess of wisdom and prosperity, was installed at Sivagiri in 1912. With the installation of Lord Shiva, the place justified its name "Sivagiri". After going flight of steps from the bottom of Sivagiri hill we can see the beautifully decorated Mahasamadhi Mandiram where the Great world Guru's eternal body rests. The art and architecture of the Prathima in white marble cannot be explained in the ordinary sense especially the Great Guru is looking in the distant horizon as the prathima is alive.

SARKARA DEVI TEMPLE AT CHIRAYINKEEZHU - The Temple is one of the most important Temples in South India. Tradition accords a remote antiquity to this Temple. Its main deity is Bhadrakali. The Temple assumed a significant status for many reasons and rose to historical importance mainly with the introduction of the famous Kaliyoot festival by Anizham Thirunal Marthanda Varma, the Travancore sovereign, in 1748. The Temple have some basic attachment with Nakramcode Devi Temple which located in Avanavanchery, Attingal. The Meenabharani festival is the second great annual festival in the Temple. This festival often falls on the occasion of the annual special pooja of Attavishesham.

JANARDHANASWAMI TEMPLE AT VARKALA - It is one of the major pilgrim spots in Kerala with a history of about 2,000 years. The Temple stands on a steep hill and has a beach road as an entrance. Though its religious significance is quite high, its architectural splendour also lures tourists its way. A high entrance arch with a tiled roof greets visitors from where they can admire the aesthetic glory of the Banyan Tree that stands as a sentinel in front of the Temple, with vigrahas of several serpent gods and goddesses installed nearby. The Temple also houses brightly painted vigrahas of Lord Hanuman, Lord Shiva and Garuda (a mythical bird), while the main shrine is dedicated to Lord Janardhana (an avatar of Lord Vishnu). With four arms carrying shanghu (the holy conch shell) chakra (wheel), gada (mace) and kumbham (pot) each, the vigraha is a striking sight.

AAZHIMALA SIVA TEMPLE AT PULINKUDI – Among the shores of Kerala, the Temple is blessed with its natural beauty. As the name suggests it is situated between the huge rocks and stands in the edge of the ocean. The scenario of the Temple is a fine example for its incomparable beauty. It is comprised of fantastic reminiscence's and story through the blessings of Lord Shiva. The original name of the Temple is Aaazhimala Pulinkudi Sree Mahadeva Temple. By the existence of Cheetahs in that area years ago was named as Pullikudi. Due to the course of time it changed into Pullingudi. 'Kudi' means home/Living space. This Ancient place was one of the hide out of Pandavas who were in disguise. Natural caves are found still in between the rocks. To quench Panchali's thirst, Bheemasena had to make a hole in the rock with his knee to fill the water is a reminder of ancient times. Recently a 58 ft. tall Murti of Gangadhareshwara has been unveiled for the devotees on 31st December, 2020.

VIZHINJAM ROCK CUT CAVE TEMPLE AT THIRUVANANTHAPURAM - It is one of the ancient rock - cut Temples in Kerala. This historic monument features 18th century rock cut sculptures which was left unnoticed for a long time. It is a small shrine with a central cell having an independent sculpture of seated Dakshinamurthi datable to 8th century. On the two sides of the cell are unfinished panel depicting sculptures of Tripurantaka and Shiva as Nataraja and Parvati standing close to him. Tripurantaka carrying a bow and arrow in two of his four hands. His left foot rests on Apasmara, the crown of hair elegantly carved as a high headdress and is highly ornate. It is interesting that different forms of Tripurantaka had developed at such an early date. This is a centrally protected monument under the control of ASI since 1965.

SREE KULATHOOR KOLATHUKARA SHIVA TEMPLE AT THIRUVANANTHAPURAM – The Temple was built at the request of Sri Narayana Guru in 1915.

DISTRICT – THRISSUR (Railway Station – Thrisur/Guruvayur/Irinjalakuda/Pudukad/Aluva)

S. No.	Temple	Address	Type
1	Sri Vadakkunnathan Temple	Kuruppam, Thrissur – 680001	Shiva, Vishnu, Rama
2	Punkunnam Sree Shiva Temple	Punkunnam – 680002	Shiva
3	Guruvayur Devaswom	Guruvayur – 680101	Krishna
4	Mammiyur Mahadeva Temple	Guruvayur – 680101	Shiva, Vishnu
5	Chowalloor Sivakshethram	Kandanassery - 680102	Shiva
6	Koodalmanikyam Devaswom	Irinjalakuda – 680121	Bharat
7	Choorakkottukavu Sri Durga Temple	Amalanagar - 680555	Mata
8	Peruvanam Mahadeva Temple	East Nata, Cherpu, Thrissur – 680561	Shiva
9	Arattupuzha Sree Satha Temple	P.O. Arattupuzha – 680562	Vasishta
10	Triprayar Sree Rama Temple	Triprayar P.O. – 680567	Rama
11	Sree Dhanwanthari Temple	Nelluvai P.O. – 680584	Dhanwanthari
12	Sree Kurumba Bhagavathi Temple	Kodungallur – 680664	Mata
13	Mahadeva Temple	Thiruvanchikulam – 680664	Shiva, Parvathi
14	Sri Payammal Temple	Poomangalam – 680688	Shatrughna
15	Nedumbilly Tharananallur Mana	Thanissery - 680701	Mana
16	Pampummekkatt Mana	Vadama - 680732	Mana

SRI VADAKKUNNATHAN TEMPLE AT THRISSUR – It is one of the oldest Temple in Kerala and an architectural marvel in wood and stone. The main deity of this Temple, Lord Shiva, is worshipped in the form of a huge lingam with thirteen cascading crescents of gold and three serpent hoods on top. It is said that the ghee offered here for centuries does not have any foul odour and it does not melt even during summer. In the outer Temple, there are shrines for Lord Krishna, Parashurama, Simhodara, Ayyappa, Vettekkaran (Shiva as a hunter), Serpent deities and Adi Shankara. Outside the main Temple, there are shrines for Lord Subrahmanya and Lord Ganapathi. Located on the

verandah of the Nalambalam is a large white bull Nandikeswara. The two-storied rectangular shrine of the Lord Rama facing west is located in the south. Between these two sanctums (srikovils) stands a third one, circular and double-storied in shape, which is dedicated to Shankaranarayana, the combined form of Shiva and Vishnu, facing west. There are mukhamandapams (halls) in front of all the three central shrines. The two important murals in the Temple, Vasukisayana and Nrithanatha (Nataraja), are worshipped regularly. Ganesha shrine is positioned facing the Temple kitchen. The offering of Appam (sweetened rice cake fried in ghee) to him is one of the most important offerings at the Temple. Propitiating him here is believed to be a path to prosperity and wealth. This Temple has monumental towers on all four sides. Mural paintings depicting various episodes from Mahabharata can be seen inside the Temple. There is a multi-shrine complex called as Nalambalam or Chuttamabalam in the centre with three main shrines dedicated to Lord Shiva as Vadakkunnathan, Shankaranarayana or Hari-Hara and Lord Rama. To the left of the entrance is the theatre hall called "Koothambalam". This Koothambalam is a tall and spacious structure which contains fine vignettes of wood carving and interesting bracket figures.

According to popular local lore, this is the first Temple built by Bhagwan Parasurama, the sixth avatara of Lord Vishnu. According to legend, Adi Shankara attained videhamukti ("freedom from embodiment") at this Temple. During the invasion of Tipu Sultan, this Temple was not attacked by Tipu's Army. According to historical accounts when Tipu Sultan was marching towards the Travancore lines, known locally as Nedumkotta, he had a short stay at Thrissur city from 14 to 29 December 1789. In order to feed his Army, he had borrowed cooking vessels from this Temple. Before leaving Thrissur city, he not only returned the vessels but presented the Temple with a large bronze lamp. Restoration of the stunning centuries-old murals, intricately carved wooden sculptures and exquisite wood work were done keeping in line with rituals and using the same methods and techniques that were used for the original construction. This has sent flutters in the international circuit by clinching the 'Award of Excellence' at the UNESCO Asia-Pacific Awards for Cultural Heritage Conservation. The Temple is also renowned across the world for its Pooram Festival where ceremoniously decorated elephants are paraded amidst much fanfare and which also involves a spectacular display of fireworks. The Temple, along with the mural paintings, has been declared as a National Monument by India under the AMASR Act.

PUNKUNNAM SHIVA TEMPLE AT THRISSUR - The Temple is a 1000 years old building, which reflects the Kerala style of architecture. This beautiful Temple showcases the glorious cultural heritage of Kerala, with an vigraha of Lord Shiva, the presiding deity of the city. With the main deity positioned in the central area of the Temple, the Temple offer a glimpse of other deities like Parvathy, Ganapathy, Sastha, Nagaraja, and Partha Sarathi (Lord Krishna as Charioteer to Arjuna). Its exquisite surroundings and conventional design, makes it one of the popular attractions in Thrissur, visited by more than one millions every year. A large number of pilgrim visit this Temple during the Sabarimala season, when the food is served and the Temple area is decorated in a grand style.

GURUVAYUR SRI KRISHNA TEMPLE - The historical importance of this Temple was connected with the legend behind this. In the great deluge of Dwaparayuga, Dwaraka was submerged & vigraha of Sri Mahavishnu worshiped by Devas in Devalokam & Lord Krishna at Dwaraka went afloat in the flood waters. Devaguru Brihaspathi & Lord Vayu with their insight came to know of this & were eager to consecrate somewhere. They went from place to place in search of a proper place in installing the vigraha and reached the holy Rudratheertha at Guruvayoor and sought the help of Lord Shiva, who was doing penance there. Lord Shiva instantly appreciating the noble purpose, readily moved away and requested them to consecrate the vigraha where he sat. Lord Shiva shifted his place to the other side of Rudratheertha. This greatness (Mahima) of Lord Shiva gave the name Mahimayoor which in course of time became Mammiyoor. The place where Devaguru Brihaspathi and Lord Vayu installed the vigraha came to be called Guruvayoor. It is for this reason that the worship at Guruvayoor becomes complete only with a visit to Mammiyoor. Guruvayoor is one of the 10 paradises in the world. The Temple is known as "Bhooloka Vaikunta", believed to be at least 5,000 years old. The Temple was built by Vishwakarma, the divine architect. Ulsavam (Festival) is conducted in the month of Kumbha (Feb-March) and lasts for 10 days. The Vrishchika Ekadasi (Suklapaksha) is called as Guruvayur Ekadasi. As a part of the Ekadasi fete, an 11-day Chembai music festival is organized, in which an incredible array of some 2000 Carnatic musicians give their best. The presiding deity in the Garbhagraha (central shrine) is Mahavishnu, worshipped according to the pooja routines laid down by Adi Sankaracharya & later written in to the Tantrasamuchaya by Chennas Narayanan Namboodiri (born in 1427). The Chennas Namboodiris are hereditary Tantri of Guruvayur Temple. The people at large, however, invoke the Lord as Unnikrishna or Balakrishna.

MAMMIYUR MAHADEVA TEMPLE AT GURUVAYUR - The ancient Temple is situated at a walkable distance to the famous Guruvayoor Sree Krishna Temple. The main deity is Lord Shiva in the form of Umamaheswara. Lord Vishnu is also given equal importance in a sanctum sanctorum near to that of Lord Shiva. It is one of the ancient Lord Shiva Temple in India which belongs to the group of 108 Sivalayas consecrated by Bhagwan Parasurama. It is believed that the place where Guru and Vayu consecrated the vigraha of Lord Krishna became Guruvayoor and the site that Lord Shiva chose for himself and his consort Sree Parvathy became Mahimayur, mahima evolving out of the status bestowed on Lord Shiva for voluntarily relinquishing his initial abode to accommodate Lord Krishna. This in course of time got colloquialised as Mammiyur. The Thanthri of Guruvayoor Sree Krishna Temple also holds the position of Thanthri in Mammiyoor Temple. Almost all of the poojas and rituals in this Temple are regulated in tune with the poojas and rituals of Guruvayoor Temple. The devotees who visit Sree Guruvayoor Temple for darshan pay pranams to Sree Mammiyoorappan. It is considered that any pilgrimage to Guruvayoor Temple is incomplete without having darshan here. This is about a hen that lived in the Mammiyoor Shiva Temple premises for about 10 years and finally absorbed in the Lord in 2015. This is the real but mysterious phenomenon occurred in the Temple.

CHOWALLOOR SIVAKSHETHRAM AT KANDANASSERY - The Temple is dedicated to Lord Shiva. Lord Shiva is said to have manifested himself on an umberella carried by one of his beloved devotees, a pious old Namboothiri from Chowalloor Mazhavannoor Mana (Illam of Namboothiri), who used to walk all the way to Thrissur to have daily darshan of the Lord. When the devotee became too old to walk and worship him regularly, the Lord is said to have accompanied him to his native home in Chowalloor. Later, a Temple was constructed at the very place, where the Lord appeared to the devotee and started regular pooja. As per local belief, the devotees have the good fortune to worship Lord Shiva family - a rare phenomenon (Lord Shiva, Sree Parvathy, Sree Ganesh, Sree Subrahmanian, Sree Ayyappa and Sree Anjaneya) which is not seen else where in Kerala. Navagraha Temple situates in the North East comer of the Temple complex. In the two tiered round Sreekovil, the Swayambhoo vigraha of Lord Shiva is seen facing west and that of his consort Sree Parvathy facing east affectionately showering blessings in all directions. The Sapthamathrukkal, precious black stone vigrahas symbolising the seven divine Mothers are also worshipped in the Temple in the form of Bimbas made of Krishnasila, yet another rare phenomenon. There is a 12 day long Thiruvathira Mahotsavam is organised annually.

KOODALMANIKYAM DEVASWOM AT IRINJALAKUDA - Koodalmanikyam is the Malayalam translation of the Sanskrit word Sangameswara. There is, however, another folklore about the name. One day the vigraha was found to give out uncommon brightness from its forehead, bearing unable to identify the source of the brightness, some brought a Quartz (Manikyam) in the possession of Raja of Kayamkulam for comparison. As they were comparing the brightness of the two, it is said that the stone brought from Kayamkulam mysteriously slipped from the hand and merged with the one on the vigraha. The merging of the two manikyams led to the name 'Koodalmanikyam'. Similar brightness is reported to have appeared on the vigraha once again much later in 1907. The eastern gateway (Gopuram) is an impressive structure in the typical Kerala style of architecture with tiled roof and white washed walls. Numerous carvings are embedded into the front wall of the gateway. The Temple is situated inside a well walled up ten-acre plot with attractive gateways on the East, South and West. The huge porches on the Eastern and Western approach ways to the inner Temple can accommodate not less than twenty-one elephants. The Sanctum Sanctorum is round shaped and is covered with copper plates. A six-foot Thaazhikakudam at the pinnacle adds to the beauty and majesty of the Temple complex. On the Southern courtyard is the well-known Koothambalam, the Natyagruha for Koothu and Koodiyattom. The Temple had also been an important centre of nourishment of the Temple Arts like Kathakali, Koothu, Koodiyattom and Thullal. Koothambalam stage had the rare fortune to witness historic stage shows by the maestros of Ammannoor Chakyar family.

CHOORAKKOTTUKAVU SRI DURGA TEMPLE AT AMALANAGAR - The Temple is dedicated to Goddess Durga. It is one of the ancient Temple in Thrissur district. The Temple has intricate carvings and it has been constructed in typical Keralite style & architecture.

PERUVANAM TEMPLE AT CHERPU - Some 10-15 Aswatha trees punctuate the Temple grounds with their wide spreading canopies. There are two Balikkals in front of the naalambalam coinciding with the axis of the two Shrikovils, that of Eratttayappan on the north and that of Maadathilappan on the south. There are two dvarapalakas on either side of the Shrikovil entry, standing on the coils of a snake. The vigraha consists of two lingas, contributing to the concept of Erattayappan, the lord in the double, signifying Ardhanareeswara to some and Shankaranarayana to others. Apart from the Shrikovil entry on the west, those in the south and east accommodate Dakshinamoorthy and Parvathy respectively. The southern side of the Shrikovil has Kirathamkatha engraved in wood, starting from Parvathi's shrine. Another woodwork which is worth mentioning is that of Garuda swallowing Jeemoothavahana and that of Dakshinamoorthy. A small Nandi is seen placed on the midlanding. The Temple complex is surrounded by a nalambalam which houses the shrines of Raktesvari and Manikantan in the north, Ganapathy and Pooru Maharshi both facing east on the north-west and south-west portions of the Valiambalam. There is a separate shrine of Lord Vishnu on the northern side of the naalambalam. It is believed that the two swayambhulingas represent Lord Shankara and Narayana, a pointer to the amalgamation of Shaivism and Vaishnavism. The Maadathilappan Shrine is one of the most outstanding Temple structures of Kerala. This type of tri-tala-vimana is known as Meru Mandhara Prasaada. On the three sides of the sanctum of Maadathilappan, above the ghanadvara portion, the upper tala displays wooden vigrahas of Lord Shiva and Sree Parvathy on the south side, Lord Brahma on the east and Lord Vishnu on Anantha on the north side. The Srikovil of Madathilappan is considered to be the tallest Srikovil in South India. As you enter from the east you are facing Sreeparvathy, the Goddess who is the consort of Irattayappan. It is the custom to start the worship with Irattayappan. There is a taboo all over Kerala in crossing the imaginary ray (Soma Rekha) emanating from Lord Shiva and going north. Hence, one does not make a complete perambulation in the inner courtyard of Lord Shiva Temples. Most devotees at the Peruvanam Temple go round the Bilva Tree to the north and return clockwise to the south side where there is a shrine of Ganapathy and Dakshinamoorthy. You, then, go back to the west and worship Irattayappan once again. Four Sastha Temples at Akmala, Kuthiran, Edathiruthy and Oozath are located on the boundaries of Peruvanam Gramam and Thiruvullakkavu Sastha Temple is located at the centre of the Gramam. Irattayappan is the 'Gramadhipathi' & Thiruvullakkavu Sastha is considered the 'Gramaraskhakan'.

Cherpu Bhagavathy Temple - After throwing his axe to claim Kerala from the seas, the sage

Parasurama built 108 Durgalayas across the length & breadth of the land. The Cherpu Bhagavathy Temple is considered to be the greatest of them all. The divine Mother presiding over the grand and gorgeous Temple set amidst the verdant greenery and the tranquil settings of Cherpu Padinjattumuri has been showering her benign blessings on her dear devotees for thousands of years. Bhagavathy, the divine consort of Lord Siva, acts as the host of the 2000 year old Peruvanam Pooram and is also a leading deity of the 1400 plus year old Deva Mela – the Arattupuzha Pooram. The Temple had been one of the main centres of Yajurveda for hundreds of years – the Othuttu at the Temple considered second only to the Murajapam at the Sree Padmanabhaswamy Temple in Thiruvananthapuram. In the Temple, Bhagavathy is in the form of Bhooma Devi, who is very calm in nature. Bhoomi Pooja is very special here and any issues relating to land are solved by praying here. Oil used here for lighting the Deepam in the Temple and for pooram festivals is coconut oil which is very rare and said to be auspicious. Devi is worshipped as Saraswati in the morning, Lakshmi in the noon & Parvathi in the evening to bless everyone with knowledge, wealth & health.

ARATTUPUZHA SREE SASTHA TEMPLE - The antiquity of this Temple dates back to 3000 years and the Temple hosts the most ancient and the world's second oldest festival "Devamela" (Festival when all gods and goddesses assemble) at Arattupuzha. The deity sits in a serene posture with an "Amrutha Kalasa" in his right hand resting on the right knee. It is believed that the deity is the embodiment of the divine potential of Guru Vasishta, the great master of Lord Rama. This is one of the rare Temples devoid of any other deities.

TRIPRAYAR SREE RAMA SWAMI TEMPLE – The Temple is situated on the bank of River Theevra. Theevra River is also called Purayar, hence, this place got the name Thirupurayar (sacred river) and later became Triprayar. It is one of the important Temple dedicated to Lord Rama. The deity Lord Rama is popularly known as Triprayarappan or Triprayar Thevar. The vigraha of Lord Rama was initially worshipped by Lord Krishna at Dwaraka. After the swargarohana of Lord Krishna, the vigraha was immersed in the sea. Later, some fisher men got the vigraha from the sea near Chettuva region of Kerala and the local ruler Vakkayil Kaimal constructed a Temple at Triprayar and installed the vigraha. It is said that when the vigraha of Lord Rama was discovered and was about to be consecrated, it was divinely ordained that a peacock would appear and mark the exact time for installation. Kaimal and his men waited for a long time for the peacock but it didn't appeared. Apparently the Tanthri (chief priest) installed the vigraha when a devotee bearing peacock feathers appeared. Soon after the installation the peacock appeared in front of the Sreekovil. It is said that the priests and Kaimal regretted their decision later and to make up for this deficiency the sacrificial stone or the valiyabalikkallu was installed at the spot marked by the peacock. Hence the balikkal is said to have the same importance as the deity itself. But this sacrificial stone showed a tendency to spin on its axis. It was Naranathu Bhranthan who fixed it at the spot by hammering a nail through it amidst the chanting of mantras. A mark of a nail can still be seen gives credence to this belief. In order to prevent any decline in the power of the vigraha on account of the change in its location Naranathu Bhranthan also arranged to install two goddesses on either side of the deity-Sree Devi on the right and Bhumi Devi on the left. The vigraha of Lord Rama (Triprayar Thevar) resembles the Chaturbhuja Vishnu form with four arms bearing a conch (Panchajanya), a disc (Sudarsana), a bow (Kodanda) and a garland respectively. There is also a lamp behind the vigraha which is kept burning all the time. Though there is no separate vigraha for Rama's best devotee Hanuman, it is believed that his presence is always there at the Namaskaramandapam (in front of the Sreekovil) of the Temple. There are two Ganapathyprathishtas inside the Nalambalam. Dakshinamoorthy is worshipped in the garbhagruha (near south door) of Sree Rama's Sreekovil. The vigraha of Dakshinamoorthy is in Shivalinga form adorned with Rudraksha garlands, crescent moon etc. Outside the nalambalam, there is an Ayyappa (Shastha) shrine. It is believed that the Shastha shrine is ancient than the Rama Temple. Thriprayar Thevar is the presiding deity of the Arattupuzha Pooram, one of the important festivals of central Kerala. Near the main Temple, there is a shrine of Gosala Krishna. The Temple is rich in wood carvings. The Sreekovil is circular in shape with a copper covered conical roof and is surmounted by a golden Thazhikakkudam. The circular sanctum has several sculptural representations of scenes from the Ramayana. Its walls are decorated with beautiful mural paintings. The namaskaramandapa, which is copper-plated, is profusely sculptured having 24 panels of wood carvings representing navagrahas.

SREE DHANWANTHARI TEMPLE AT NELLUVAI – It is known for its Oushada Prasada (prasada with Ayuvedic medicinal values). Known as Mukkudi, the offering is made every day under the guidance of Kuttancherry Manu Moos as he only knows the secret recipe of the prasada. Dhanwanthary Moorthy, known as the physician of gods (devas) is worshipped here. Lord Dhanwanthari is also referred to as the Lord of Ayurveda. It is believed that all type of diseases can be cured by worshipping Lord Dhanwanthari. In the western entrance of the Temple, there stands two Banyan Trees that look like offering namajapa to the Dhanvanthari Moorthi. The visitor can also see two big ponds on either side. There are Gopuras in the western and eastern entrances of the Temple. In the east-south entrance, the Sanctum Sanctorum of the Cheruthevar (Vishnu) is situated. Inside, there is an vigraha of Varaha Moorthi, stage that is made out of rock and one Vilakkumaadam inside the Chuttambalam with stone-paved courtyard. In the south-west, there are vigrahas of Lord Ayyappa, Ganapathi and Shiva facing towards the east. There is also a Lord Vishnu vigraha and Salagrama.

KODUNGALLUR BHAGAVATHY TEMPLE – It is a renowned Temple and is also known as Sree Kurumba Bhagavathi Temple. The Temple is dedicated to Goddess Bhadrakali. In Kerala, Goddess Bhadrakali is believed to be auspicious form of Kali. The Goddess is also well known as Kodungallooramma in this Temple. The vigraha of the Goddess Bhadrakali worshipped in this Temple has eight hands. One of the hands of the deity holds the severed head of Darikasura (a demon), while the other hands hold weapons and symbols such as sword, spear, discus, bow, pestle & Chelambu. The Temple follows a strict daily routine of rituals. It is said that after the formation of Kerala by Bhagwan Parasurama, he was troubled by a devil called Daruka. For assassination of the devil, Bhagwan Parasurama worshipped Lord Shiva for help. Then the Lord Shiva asked him to build a Temple and to consecrate the Shakti Devi as Bhagavathi. The Devi herself is considered to be Parashakthi. Consequently, Bhadrakali killed the devil Daruka. The Temple is surrounded by Banyan Trees. The Sreekovil of the Temple faces the north. The western hall of the inner Temple is the seat of Sapthamatrukas (Seven Mothers) who also faces the north. The vigrahas of Lord Ganapathi and Veerabhadra in the shrine face towards the east and the west, respectively. To the left of the Temple, there is a Samadhi of Vysoori. The vigraha of Kodungallooramma is 6 ft tall, built using wood of jackfruit tree. A Holy pond called Pushkarini is just 50 meters away from the Temple, where devotees take holy dip before entering the Temple. It is assumed that this pond came into existence when the goddess touched the land with her sword. Kodungallur Bharani is the major Temple festival of the Temple. The festival mainly begins with a ritual namely 'Kozhikkallu Moodal' that involves killing cocks and shedding their blood to make blood offering to the Goddess kali. This ritual is performed to please the mighty Goddess Kali and her devils with the offering of blood.

THIRUVANCHIKULAM MAHADEVA TEMPLE - It is more than 2000 years old. Out of the 274 Shaivite Thiruppathies in India, this Temple is the only one of its kind in Kerala. This is the only Thevaram Paadal Petra Shivasthalam in Kerala. It is constructed in the Kerala style of architecture.

Lord Shiva is worshipped as Mahadeva and his consort Parvathi as Umadevi. The Temple also has a healthy relationship with the Chidambaram Temple in Tamil Nadu. One of the main attractions of the Temple is a Namaskara Mandapam with 16 pillars that are constructed in front of the Sreekovil. The primary deity here has long been worshipped as the family god of the Cochin Royal Family. Other minor shrines dedicated to other Gods & Goddesses. Boasting a large collection of mural art, the Temple is a protected monument by the ASI.

SRI PAYAMMAL TEMPLE AT POOMANGALAM - This is one of the few Temples in India that is dedicated to Lord Shatrughna, youngest brother of Lord Rama. The Temple is the fourth Temple which devotees visit when they embark on the Nalambalam yatra or visit. Visiting Nalambalam is considered to be a sacred event during the Malayalam month of Karkidakam. The vigraha of Lord Shatrughna is housed in a squarish granite sanctum sanctorum. The original Panchaloha (Brass, Bronze, Copper, Gold and Silver) has been untraceable though efforts have been made to retrieve it from the Temple pond. The existing vigraha made of granite exudes a rare kind of divinity. A lamp is lighted behind the vigraha inside the Sreekovil. It is believed that this lamp or Pinvilakku is for Sruthakeerthi, the wife of Lord Shathrughna. Shathrughna is considered to be the reincarnation of the Sudarsana Chakra (disc) in the hands of Mahavishnu. Ganapathy is in the sub deity here.

NEDUMBILLY THARANANALLUR MANA AT THANISSERY - The Mana was built during the time of Aayillam Thirunal Maharaja. The structure of the Mana is a fine example of Kerala architecture with beautiful engravings on the wood. This Mana attracts many foreigners. It stands amidst village beauty. To study and make research on Thantric books and manuscripts on leaves, there is an institute called Sangama Grama Indological Research Centre. An uncommon traditional custom prevails here. Before the male-folks leave the Mana for religious rites, they seek the blessings from the elder women-folks. A teenaged boy once warranted to officiate senior members in their absence in a Temple festival. He left the Illam with a Granthom after obtaining his mother's blessings and he could perform the rites as vividly as elders do. The Granthom and the blessings gave him enough knowledge & power to perform the rites. It is after this incident the male-folks continued to obtain the blessings from elder female-folks.

PAMPUMMEKKATT MANA AT VADAMA - The Mana is famous for snake worship & for getting snake-related problems solved. The tradition is centuries old. The gate tower is embedded with snake vigrahas as a welcome posture. Normally, the Manas are Nalukettu but this Mana is Ettukettu – two Naluketts. There are five Kavus of snakes (& snake gods). The sanctum sanctorum of Nagaraja and Nagayakshi is in the Kizhakuni of a Nalukettu. There is no vigraha in the sanctum sanctorum. In its place, there is all time burning oil-lamp. The Prasadam given to the devotees is the oil from the lamp. The oil Prasadam has the power to cure the diseases caused due to the curse of snakes. Besides Noorum Palum, the other main offering to the serpent gods is Kadali Pazham. There is also a shrine of Bhadrakali. Vasiyedam Temple at Puthenchira, Sarangapani Sri Krishna Temple & Kunnathunadu Mahadeva Temple owned & managed by this Mana.

DISTRICT – WAYANAD (Railway Station – Vadakara)

S. No.	Temple	Address	Type
1	Valliyoorkavu Bhagavathy Temple	Arattuthara – 670645, Mananthavady	Mata
2	Sree Mahavishnu Temple	Thirunelli – 670646	Vishnu
3	Sita Lava-Kusha Temple	Pulpalli - 673579	Mata
4	Jain Temple	Sulthan Bathery - 673592	Jain

VALLIYOORKAVU BHAGAVATHY TEMPLE AT MANANTHAVADY – The Temple was built in 14th CE. It is dedicated to Goddess Bhagavathy, worshipped in three of principal forms of Goddess i.e. Vana Durga, Bhadrakali and Jala Durga. The Temple is famous for the annual 14-day festival. During the festival, the Temple premises witness the performance of traditional ritual arts like Kalamezhuthumpattum, Eedumkoorum and Sopananritham. The tribal dance performed by the tribe here using folk percussion instruments are another highlight of this festival.

THIRUNELLI TEMPLE AT WAYANAD – It is the only Temple in the world where the devotees can perform all the rituals related to one's life starting from birth to death & life after death. The rituals are performed on the banks of the stream Papanasini. People believe that Bhagwan Parasurama, the famous incarnation of Lord Vishnu visited Thirunelli & performed last rites of his father sage Jamadagni. He also took immersion in the Papanasini to wipe away sins committed owing to the annihilation of Kshatriyas. As per legend, when Lord Brahma was consecrating Lord Vishnu's vigraha, Garuda reached over the sky above the installation venue with the Amrit Kumbha. During Garuda's circling over, a drop of Amrit fell on the stream, which provided purifying power to the water in the stream. After that incident, the stream came to be called Papanasini. It is believed that here the prathishta of Lord Vishnu was performed by Lord Brahma. It is also known as "Sahyamala Kshetram" & "Kashi of the South". On the western side of the Temple is the Cave Temple Gunnika, dedicated to Lord Shiva. Thus Thirunelli becomes blessed by the unique presence of the trinity. Once Lord Brahma while traversing the world, he saw an vigraha of Lord Vishnu resting on an amla tree in the valley & thus the place came to be named Thirunelli. The Temple is also referred to as Amalaka Temple & Sidha Temple. The Temple is embellished in the Kongu-Chera styles of handiworks.

Thrissilery Shiva Temple - This stunning Temple of rather perfect architectural proportions is inextricably linked with the Vishnu Temple at Thirunelly. It is believed that the performance of ancestral rites at Thirunelly remain unfinished unless followed by offerings at this Temple. Within the premises there is also a shrine devoted to Jala Durga believed to have been installed by no less a personage than the legendary Sage Parasurama. There are many myths connected with the Temple tank here, which curiously enough never dries up!

SITA LAVA-KUSHA TEMPLE AT PULPALLI - This is the only known Temple dedicated to Lava and Kusha, the sons of Lord Rama. Local legends connect this region with many important episodes from the Ramayana. As the favoured shrine of the Pazhassi Raja, this Temple has traditionally permitted entry to devotees from all faiths.

SULTHAN BATHERY JAIN TEMPLE – This Temple is one of the most important amongst a series of ruins spread across the state of Kerala that testify to a period of a strong Jain presence in this region. It is believed to have been built in 13th century. Apart from this Temple, there are other significant Jain remnants in Wayanad. The Temples at Punchavayal and Puthenangadi are the best known of these. With their beautifully carved pillars now partly ruined and the area rather derelict, these sites exude a peculiar airomystery.

❖ ❖ ❖ ❖ ❖

LAKSHADWEEP

In 1956, the islands were constituted into a single territory and since then, have been directly administered by the Union Government through an Administrator. The Laccadives, Minicoy and Amindivi group of islands were renamed as Lakshadweep in 1973. India's smallest Union Territory, Lakshadweep is an archipelago consisting of 36 islands. It is known for its exotic and sun-kissed beaches and lush green landscape. The name Lakshadweep in Malayalam and Sanskrit means 'a hundred thousand islands'.

Capital City	Kavaratti
Total Population	64,429 (2011)
Official Language	Malayalam, Jeseri (Dweep Bhasha) and Mahal
Animal& Fish	Butterfly Fish
Bird	Noddy Tern
Tree & Flower	Bread Fruit
Airport	Agatti

S. No.	Temple	Address	Type
1	Sree Krishna Temple	Minicoy P.O. – 682559	Krishna

SREE KRISHNA TEMPLE AT MINICOY - The Temple is dedicated to Lord Krishna. There is regular Bhajans on every Thursdays. During Sabarimala season, there is special Pooja and Mahaprasadam distribution. Here, Sree Krishnan seems as Bala Gopalan who pours out love and grace, inspires devotees to solve the mystery and misery of life, ups and downs, sorrows and joys, through the acquisition of skills and knowledge, ever alert in attaining the ultimate destiny of life, which is self-actualization. Thousands of bhakts (devotees) and pilgrims visits the Temple every month.

❖ ❖ ❖ ❖ ❖

PUDUCHERRY

The territory of Puducherry comprises the former French establishment Puducherry, Karaikal, Mahe and Yanam, which lie scattered in South India. Puducherry, the capital of the territory was once the original headquarters of the French in India. It was under the French rule for 138 years and merged with the Indian Union on 1st November 1954.

Total Population	12,44,464 (2011)
Districts	04
Official Language	Tamil, Telugu, Malayalam, English and French
Motto	SatyamevaJayate
Anthem	Tamil Thai Valthu
Animal	Squirrel
Bird	Koel
Fish	Magur
Tree	Vilva Tree
Flower	Cannonball
Song	Invocation to Tamil Goddess (written by Bharathidasan)
Airport	Pondicherry

DISTRICT – KARAIKAL (Railway Station - Mayiladuturai J/Peralam/Karaikal)

S. No.	Temple	Address	Type
1	Sri Bhadrakali Mandir	Ambagarathur - 609601	Mata
2	Karaikal Ammaiyar Temple	Bharathiyar St., Karaikal - 609602	Mata
3	Sri Kailasanathar Temple	Bharathiyar St., Karaikal - 609602	Shiva
4	Sri Nithyakalyana Perumal Temple	Bharathiyar St., Karaikal - 609602	Vishnu
5	Sri Parvatheeswaraswamy Temple	Thiru Thelicherry, Karaikal -609602	Shiva
6	Sri Yazhmurinatheeswarar Temple	Dharmapuram - 609602	Shiva
7	Lord Darbaneswara Temple	Thirunallar - 609607	Shiva

SRI BHADRAKALI MANDIR AT AMBAGARATHUR - The Temple is dedicated to Goddess Kali which is a form of Goddess Parvathi. The Temple is old, ancient and famous. It has a alluring Rajagopura. As per legend, two devils called Ambaran and Amban were exceptionally remorseless and begun alarming the world. Whenever Lord Indra, Brahma and Vishnu went and grumbled about them to Lord Shiva, he sent Goddess Bhadrakali to slaughter them. Around then Ambaran appeared as a wild ox and battled with the Goddess. She removes his head utilizing her sword. devas asked the Goddess Kali to live in that place. The place was at first known as Ambara-harattur meaning triumph over Ambaran, which along these lines progressed toward becoming Ambagarathur.

KARAIKAL AMMAIYAR TEMPLE – It is dedicated to a celebrated woman Lord Shiva Saint 'Punithavathi' and subsequently elevated to the status of a Goddess. Karaikal Ammaiyar is the only woman out of the 63 Nayanmars. During the month of June and July (ie. Aani, a Tamil month – Full Moon Day), the Mangani Festival is celebrated. It is embedded with Sri Somanathar-cum-Karaikal Ammaiyar Temple, Sri Nithyakalyanaperumal Temple and Sri Kalilasanathar Temple. There are various other Temples such as Sri Yazhmurinatheeswarar Temple at Dharmapuram, Sri Parvatheeswaraswamy at Kovilpattu and Sri Thirumeniazhagarswamy Temple at Thiruvettakudi.

SRI KAILASANATHAR TEMPLE AT BHARATHIYAR ST., KARAIKAL - The Temple is dedicated to Lord Shiva. The Temple is situated opposite to Sri Karaikal Ammaiyar Temple. It is believed that the Temple is appx. 2000 years old. In the 8th CE, the Temple had been reconstructed by the Pallava Rulers. The Mangani festival is associated with this and Ammaiyar Temple as Lord Bikshatanamurthy is of this Temple and Ammaiyar is called as mother by Lord Shiva (who is not having father).

SRI NITHYAKALYANA PERUMAL TEMPLE AT KARAIKAL - The Temple is one of the three famous Temple in the port city of Karaikal. It is located nearby the Karaikal Ammayar Temple. The Temple tank of Chandra Theertham separates the two Temples. The Temple tank belongs to both the Temples. The Temple is a Vishnu Temple with the vigraha of Lord Vishnu in a lying posture named Nithyakalyana Perumal. In the praghara, there are many sanctums for the gods i.e. Chakkarathazhwar; Ranganayaghi Thayar; Narasimha avatar of Lord Vishnu; Hanuman; Avatars

of Lord Vishnu; Lord Krishna's Vishwaroopam; Lord Garuda; Aandal; Alamelu Thayaar. The festivals related to Lord Vishnu and his avatars are celebrated in a grand manner in this Temple. The Rama Navami, Vaikunda Ekadesi, Hanuman Jayanti and the entire month of Margazhi are celebrated here. During the Tamil month of Poorattadhi or Puratasi, many rituals take place in the Temple such as the Pavithra pradhistai, Kumba poojai, Poornahoothi, Chakarathazwar Aavahanam etc.

SRI PARVATHEESWARASWAMY TEMPLE AT THIRU THELICHERRY, KARAIKAL - The Moolavar of the Temple is Sri Parvatheeswarar, Sree Sameevaneswarar. The Ambal is Sri Swayamvara Thapaswini, Sri Shakti Nayaki, Sri Ampaduttakkannaal. The Theertham is Surya Theertham and Guha Theertham. The sacred Vriksham is Vilvam / Vanni tree. The Pathigam rendered by Saint Thirugnanasambanthar. The Temple is one of the 276 Devara Paadal Petra Shiva Sthalams and 50th Shiva Sthalam on the Southern bank of River Cauveri in Chozha Nadu. Lord Shiva in this Temple is a Swayambumurthi. This west facing Temple's main Rajagopuram has 5-tiers and it has 2 corridors.

SRI YAZHMURINATHEESWARAR TEMPLE AT DHARMAPURAM - The Temple is dedicated to Lord Shiva. The place is also known as Koilpatthu. Lord Shiva is called as Yazh Moori Nathar. His consort is known as Thenamirthavalli. It is one of the shrines of the 275 Paadal Petra Sthalams - Shiva Sthalams glorified in the early medieval Tevaram poems by Tamil Saivite Tirugnanasambandar.

LORD DARBANESWARA TEMPLE AT THIRUNALLAR - Lord Saturn is housed in this famous Temple. This Temple also has an 'Emerald Lingam'. This is the only Temple that is dedicated to Lord Saturn. When the planet Saturn transits between zodiac signs, literally millions throng this shrine. The legendary King Nala is said to have been relieved of his afflictions, which were due to the malefic influence of Saturn, after worship in this Temple. Of the numerous tanks Theertams, the Nala Theertam is the most important one. By bathing here, it is believed that one is washed off all kinds of misfortune and afflictions.

DISTRICT – MAHE (Railway Station – Mahe)

S. No.	Temple	Address	Type
1	Puthalam Temple	Mahe – 673310	Mata

PUTHALAM TEMPLE AT MAHE – It is an ancient Temple of Sree Bhagavathi. Every year, there is 'Thirayattam', a kind of ancient art with divinity and it can be seen during the month of March. The legend of the Temple relates the events that occurred during the conflict between the French and Indian armies.

DISTRICT – PUDUCHERRY (Railway Station – Puducherry/Villianur)

S. No.	Temple	Address	Type
1	Sri Kamakshi Amman Temple	Bharathi Street, Puducherry – 605001	Mata
2	Kanniga Parameswari Temple	Kamatchi Amman Kovil Street, Puducherry – 605001	Mata
3	Sri Varadaraja Temple	M.G. Road, Puducherry – 605001	Narasimha (Vishnu)
4	Sri Vedapureeswarar Temple	M.G. Road, Puducherry – 605001	Shiva
5	Arulmigu Manakula Vinayagar Devasthanam	Manakula Vinayagar Street, Puducherry – 605001	Ganesh
6	Sri Aurobindo Ashram	Rue de la Marine, Puducherry – 605002	Sri Aurobindo
7	Sri Vadukeeswarar Temple	TiruvandarKoil Post – 605102	Shiva
8	Sri Gokilambal Thirukameshwara Temple	Villianur – 605110	Shiva

KAMATCHIAMMAN KOIL AT BHARATI STREET - The Temple is different from most of the other Temples of South India. The singularity of the Temple lies in the unembellished form of the Temple structure. The Temple is devoted to Goddess Durga, who is representative deity of war. Although bereft of any ornamentation, the Temple never lacks the devotees and pilgrims who gather in large number every year to offer their prayers to the Goddess.

KANNIGA PARAMESWARI TEMPLE AT KAMATCHI AMMAN KOIL STREET - The Temple is dedicated to Goddess Shakti, who is the representative deity of power. Shakti is another form of the powerful Goddess Kali, who is one of the popular deities worshiped in Pondicherry. The Temple is unique in its architecture as it blends the style of the French with the traditional Deccan architecture of India. The interior ceiling of the sanctum is designed in the traditional style of the Tamil architecture and contains motifs on the granite pillars. The construction stands on monolithic pillars that represent the architecture of Europe. The walls of the Temple are arched and are ornamented and beautified with angels and heavenly creatures designed on them. These along with the stained glass panels are archetypes of French places of worship. Other than the main sanctum sanctorum, most of the Temple structure is designed in French architectural style.

SRI VARADARAJA TEMPLE AT M G ROAD – It is believed to be one of the oldest Temples in the town & is 800 years old. In the Temple, Lord Narasimha is placed behind Lord Venkatachalapathy, the principal deity. The architecture of the Temple is quite similar to the Vedhapureeshwarar Temple. Lord Vishnu as Varadaraja Perumal & Goddess Lakshmi as Thayar are worshiped in this Temple. It is believed that the vigraha currently placed in the Temple was found buried in earth. The 5 ft vigraha depicts Lord Vishnu standing tall. Legend has it that the Temple was originally built for Lord Rama, his wife Sita, his brother Lakshman & Lord Hanuman whose vigrahas were being brought via sea. This is

corroborated by the findings of these vigrahas in neighbouring Vaithikuppam - a fishing hamlet - back in 1902. The architecture reflects influence of the Dravidian style. It has a 'gopuram' decorated with bright colours & has number of beautifully carved pillars. One of the specialities of this Temple is that infants are given their first morsel of rice known as 'annaprasanam' in front of the deity so that the child may grow with the blessings of the deity. Saturdays are considered auspicious. The Temple wears a festive look during Deepavali, Pongal & Tamil New year days apart from other festivals.

SRI VEDAPUREESWARAR TEMPLE AT M G ROAD - This Temple is dedicated to Lord Shiva and also known as the Eashwaran Dharmaraj Koil. Lord Shiva is worshipped as Vedapureeswarar and his consort Parvathi as Tiripurasundari. Its 75 feet tall colourful 'gopuram' is adorned by vigrahas of gods and goddesses like most Temples in South India. The presiding deity is a 'Swayambu Linga'. It is said that the presiding deity was shifted to this Temple from the Mission Street's Samba Easwaran Temple 100 years ago. There is a special Temple for Lord Dakshinamurthy within this Temple on the southern side. Lord Muruga in this Temple is praised by Sri Ramalinga Swamigal in his hymns. An vigraha of Nandi faces the main shrine in the Maha Mandap. There are shrines of Vinayaga & Muruga before the Mahamandap and the sanctum is guarded by Dwarapalas. The shrine of Tiripurasundari is located in the second precinct. There also shrines of Lord Shani, Goddess Durga, Chandikeswara, Dakshninamurthy and Navagraha around the sanctum. The rectangular Temple Tank is located inside the Temple and has 35 steps to the basement. Devotees perform 'abhishekam' with water, milk, honey, ghee, fruit juice & other liquids. On auspicious days like - Kruthika, Sankatahara Chaturthi, Adi Kruthikai, Thai Kruthikai, Chitra Poornima, Adipooram & Pradosham days, the Temple is thronged by hundreds of devotees. Deepavali, Pongal & Tamil New Year are a few more of the important days.

ARULMIGU MANAKULA VINAYAGAR DEVASTHANAM AT MANAKULA VINAYAGAR STREET

– It is one of the famous ancient Temple in Puducherry. The main deity Manakula Vinayagar (Pranavamurthy) is facing east. The Temple is dedicated to Lord Ganesha. The monumental interiors of the Temple are decorated with forty incarnations and forms of Lord Ganesha, carved on the stone walls of the Temple. Presently, the Temple is built with outer mandapam, Raja gopuram, Kodikambam (18ft tall gold plated), front mandap, Mahamandap, Sanctum, other deity prahara etc. Inside the Temple, the presiding deity placed in Karuvarai area and the Vimanam above covered fully with gold plated. The presiding deity Moolavar in Sanctum blesses his devotees with four hands, the top two holding Angusam, Pasam and the right lower hand with abhayadana mudra and the left one varadhana mudra. On the north side of the sanctum, Komugi is kept for abhisheka water and a small Temple for Sandikeswarar. Sri Bala Vinayagar Temple and Sri Balasubramaniar Temple are below the silver vimana were found. Within the premises of the Temple lies the shrine devoted to Lord Murugan. Different kind of vahanas kept safely at vahana Mandap nearby the Temple.

SRI AUROBINDO ASHRAM AT RUE DE LA MARINE – It is one of the most well-known and wealthiest Ashrams in India. Devotees from India and all over the world flocking towards it for spiritual salvation. Its spiritual tenets represent a synthesis of yoga and modern science. The Ashram was set up in 1926 by Aurobindo Ghosh (Sri Aurobindo), one of India's greatest

philosopher, poets, who originally came to Pondy to escape persecution by the British. It was after arriving in Puducherry that he immersed into the spiritual realm and discovered the power of yoga. His philosophy was deeply rooted in yoga and his writings inspired a number of followers. One of them was a Parisian mystic, painter and musician called Mirra Alfassa, who was so inspired by his philosophy that she stayed on in Puducherry and was instrumental in establishment of the Ashram. After Sri Aurobindo's death in 1950, the running of the Ashram was entrusted to his chief disciple and companion, Mirra Alfassa, (known as 'The Mother'). The idea of Auroville or the 'City of Dawn' was conceived by The Mother. She died in 1973 at the age of 93. The main Ashram building is where the mortal remains of Aurobindo and the Mother are kept. Their 'Samadhi' or mausoleum, which is generally surrounded by supplicating devotees, is in the central courtyard under a frangipani tree and is covered daily with flowers.

SRI VADUKEESWARAR TEMPLE AT TIRUVANDAR KOIL - The legend associated with this Temple is of a demon called Mundasuran. After rigorous penance, he was blessed with a lot of powers by Lord Shiva. He also obtained the power that he could not be killed by other demons or devas. He started misusing his powers by harassing Lord Brahma and other celestial gods. They complained to Lord Shiva and sought his intervention. Lord Shiva directed Vaduka Bairavar, one of the eight Bairavars, to destroy the demon. After killing Mundasuran, it is believed that Vaduka Bairavar worshiped the Lord here to seek relief from the Brahmahathidosham (the sin accrued by the act of killing). Hence the Lord here is named "Sri Vadukeeswarar" and this place gets the name Vadukur. This is one of the 276 Devara Padal Petra Shiva Sthalams and 16th Shiva Sthalam in Nadu Naadu. Lord Shiva in this Temple is a Swayambhumurthi (self-manifested). The Lord of this Temple, Lord Vadukeeswarar is slightly leaning towards the left side. There is no flag post (Dwajasthambam) in this Temple. This east facing Temple's main tower is not tiered. In place of the Gopuram, there is a beautiful sculpture depicting Lord Shiva and Goddess Parvathy. This Temple is believed to have been built by the Chola King Paranthakan-I. It is constructed in a style that is similar to that of Tanjore Temple but it is much smaller in size. Currently, this Temple is under the control of the Archaeological Survey of India. Devotees believe that worshiping the Lord of this Temple would bless them with better job opportunities and promotions in works.

SRI GOKILAMBAL THIRUKAMESHWARA TEMPLE AT VILLIANUR – It is also referred as Villianur Temple. The presiding deity of the Temple is Lord Shiva in the form of a 'Shivalinga'. There are other Temples, which are devoted to Devi and Lord Murugan and they were constructed during the 12th century Chola period. This Temple has a little bit of French heritage attached to it, though not in its architecture, but in some of its traditions. The most popular festival being the Brahmotsavam, which is observed for ten days and devotees from all over India come here to receive the blessings of the Lord. The annual Temple Car Festival which is held between the months of May and June involves the pulling of a 15 meter tall chariot through the streets by a large crowd of devotees. Devotees believe that pulling this holy chariot will fulfil their wishes. Other devotees offer curds, buttermilk and 'sundal' to the multitude that follows the chariot. During French colonial rule, the Governor of Puducherry used to join this very procession and actively participate in the drawing of the chariot through the streets.

DISTRICT – YANAM (Railway Station – Kakinada)

S. No.	Temple	Address	Type
1	Shivam Bath	Ferry Road, Yanam – 533464	Shiva
2	Meesala Venkateswara Swamy Temple	Vishnalayam St., Yanam – 533464	Vishnu

SHIVAM BATH AT FERRY ROAD – It is located at the entrance of Godavari River Front. It is dedicated to Lord Shiva. A big Shivalingam installed here.

MEESALA VENKATESWARA SWAMY TEMPLE AT VISHNALAYAM STREET - This Temple is also known as "Venkanna Babu Temple", "Chaldikudu Venkanna Temple" & "Meesala Venkanna Temple". It has been very famous for performing Child Marriages in pre independence tenure. As the Yanam Region is under the control of French Rule, the people from the nearby State used to come this Temple for performing the Child Marriages. Daily, some thousands of Marriages were performed in this Temple. Hence, Yanam was also called as "Kalyana Puram". Due to dedicated efforts by the Social Reformer, Shri Raja Rama Mohan Roy, the "Sarada Act" (prevention of Child Marriages") was implemented by the then British Govt. in India. The speciality of Temple is Swamy vigraha is having big moustaches like the Lord Sathyanarayana Swamy of Annavaram. This Temple was built by kings of Rajamahendravaram, now called as "Rajahmundry" in 15th CE. Now, we can see sculptures of those period in this Temple.

The Venkanna Radham - The Venkanna Festival is celebrated in the month of March every year by the people of Yanam in a very grand manner for one month. Lord Venkateswara Kalyanam is the main day of the festival. Ponnavahanam, Radhayatra and Chakrateertham are the important events of the festival. The Ratham weight is around 15 Tonnes. It was built in 1950 by the then Committee. It was partially damaged to the heavy Cyclone in Nov, 1996. It was renovated in 1998. Govt. declares Holiday for all Govt. Offices on this special event.

TAMILNADU

Tamil Nadu was ruled by several dynasties like the Chalukyas, Cholas and Pandayas, which shape the region's cuisine, culture, and architecture. In the two centuries that followed, the imperial Cholas gained paramountcy over South India. Tamil Nadu was one of the first of British settlements in India. The State is the successor to the old Madras Presidency which in 1901 covered the bulk of the southern peninsula. The composite Madras State was later reorganised and the present Tamil Nadu was formed. Modern-day Tamil Nadu was formed in 1956 after the reorganisation of states on linguistic lines. The state is home to a number of historic buildings, multi-religious pilgrimage sites, hill stations and three World Heritage sites. Tamil Nadu is the most urbanised state in India and one of the most industrialised states. Tamil language is one of the longest-surviving classical languages in the world.

Capital City	Chennai
Total Population	7,21,38,958 Cr (2011)
Districts	38
Official Language	Tamil
Emblem	Tiruvilliputhur Andal Temple
Motto	Vaymaiye vellum (Truth alone triumphs)
Animal	Nilgiri Tahr
Bird	Emerald Dove
Butterfly	Tamil yeoman
Fish	Ayirai
Tree	Palmyrah
Flower	Kandhal
Fruit	Jackfruit
Sport	Kabaddi
Festival	Pongal
Song	Tamil Thai Valthu
Dance	Bharatnatyam
Airport	Chennai, Coimbatore, Madurai, Tiruchirapalli, Tuticorin

Note : The state shares a maritime border with Sri Lanka.

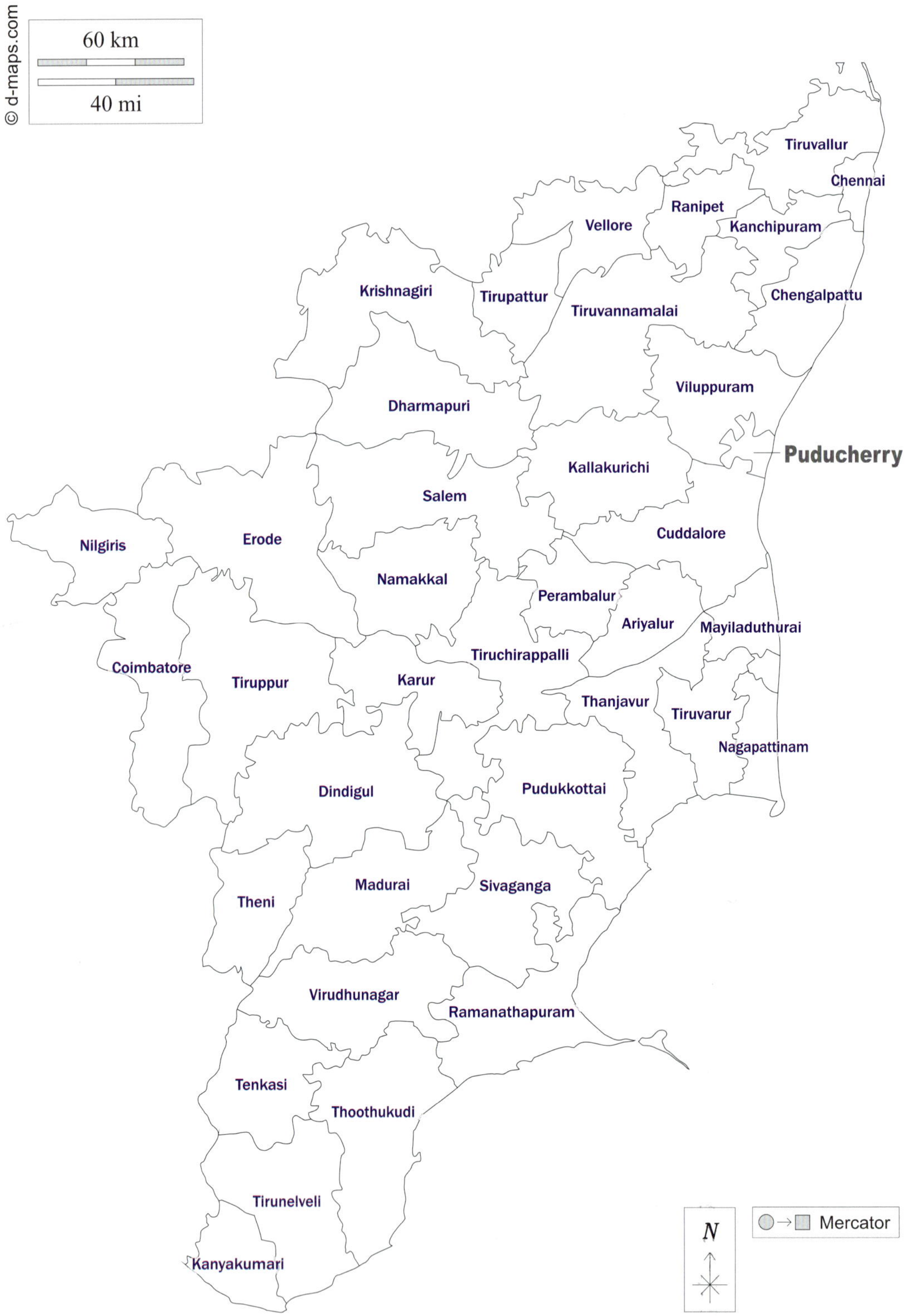
© d-maps.com
60 km
40 mi
Tiruvallur
Chennai
Ranipet
Vellore
Kanchipuram
Krishnagiri
Tirupattur
Tiruvannamalai
Chengalpattu
Viluppuram
Dharmapuri
Puducherry
Kallakurichi
Salem
Nilgiris
Erode
Cuddalore
Namakkal
Perambalur
Ariyalur
Mayiladuthurai
Tiruchirappalli
Coimbatore
Tiruppur
Karur
Thanjavur
Tiruvarur
Nagapattinam
Dindigul
Pudukkottai
Theni
Madurai
Sivaganga
Virudhunagar
Ramanathapuram
Tenkasi
Thoothukudi
Tirunelveli
Kanyakumari
N
Mercator

DISTRICT – ARIYALUR (Railway Station – Ariyalur)

S. No.	Temple	Address	Type
1	Buddha vigraha	Vikramangalam - 621701	Buddhist, Jain, Shiva
2	Shiva Temple	Govindaputhur - 621701	Shiva
3	Kondandaramaswamy Kovil	Ariyalur - 621704	Vishnu
4	Alanduraiyar Temple	Kilapaluvur - 621707	Shiva
5	Sundaresvarar Temple	Kilaiyur - 621707	Shiva
6	Shiva Temples	Sendurai - 621714	Shiva
7	Karkodeshwarar Thirukkoyil	Kamarasavalli - 621715	Rati, Shiva
8	Thirumazhapadi Vaidyanathaswami Temple	Thirumazhapadi - 621851	Shiva
9	Gangaikondacholisvarar Temple	Gangaikondacholapuram - 621901	Shiva

VIKRAMANGALAM - During the reign of Rajendra–I, this village came into existence. Inscriptions of Vikramachola, Kulothunga–II and Kulothunga–III indicate that this place was a sub capital for the Cholakings who resided in the royal palace and issued royal orders granting lands to many Temples in the Chola country. Beautiful Jain and Buddha sculptures of Chola period is also preserved in this village. The Lord Shiva Temple in this village is called Rajendra Cholisvaram and dates back to the period of Rajendra Chola–I (1012-1044).

GOVINDAPUTHUR – The village is located on the northern bank of the Kollidam River. The Lord Shiva Temple is called Ganga Jadadisvarar. Saint Appar and Sambandar, who lived during the period of Mahendravarma Pallava praised the Deity of the Temple in their Devaram hymns. From their songs we come to know that Parthan (Vijayan, son of King Pandu of Mahabharatha) worshipped Lord Shiva in this place and got a boon from the God. The celestial cow (Kamadhenu) also worshipped the God at this place by pouring its milk over the Shivalinga and hence place was called ko– karanda – puttur, and later became Govindaputtur. Inscriptions of Chola, Pandya and Vijanagar Kings are engraved on the walls of the Temple. The present Temple was built of stone in 980 AD during the period of Uttamachola (970-986) by his officer Ambalavan Paluvur Nakkan, who was a native of Kuvalalapuram (modern Kolar in Karnataka). The Temple is preserved with beautiful sculptures and bronzes of early Chola period. Inscriptions refer this place as Vijayamangalam, a Brahmadeya village in Sri Parantakachaturvedimangalam. A Devaram hymn of Saint Sambandar is engraved at the beginning of a record of Rajendra–III in this Temple.

KODANDARMASWAMY KOVIL AT ARIYALUR – It is dedicated to Lord Vishnu. Though the presiding deity in this Temple is Srinivasaperumal, it is popularly called as Kodandaramaswamy Kovil because of the existence of a shrine in which Lord Rama, Lakshmana and Sita are enshrined. The Temple faces the east. The main shrine is dedicated to Srinivasa Perumal and his two consorts Sridevi and Bhudevi. It has a garbhagriha, ardhamandapa and mahamandapa. The Kodandaramar shrine is a later addition, which is built of chalk stone and attached with the ardhamandapa of the main Temple by facing the south. Inside the shrine is installed the stone sculptures of Lord Rama, Lakshmana and Sita on a Pitha and bronze vigrahas of them are also in the

shrine. It is said that the vigrahas were found from the Kollidam River bank near Vikramangalam and brought here by a Chief of Ariyalur who built a shrine and installed the deities in it. In front of the main Temple is built a spacious mandapa called Dasavataramandapa wherein four rows of pillars with 10 pillars in each row are set up. In these pillars, the figures of the ten avatars of Lord Vishnu are carved out. At the entrance of the row, the sculptures of a Chief and his Queen are also carved out. A 6 storied Gopura (90 foot heigh) is built at the entrance. A shrine for Garuda is built in front of the Gopura. A tank called Kodanda Pushkarani is excavated in the southern side of the Temple. There are two inscriptions and one Copper plate in this Temple. The earliest record is dated to 1635 AD. A Copper plate charter is dated to 1729 AD. The above records show that this Temple came into existence during the period of Arasu Nilaiyitta Oppilada Malavarayar. The beautiful ornamental workmanship of the adhishtana, kumbapanchara in the sanctum, Dasavatara sculptures and the Gopura – all make this Temple as a beautiful centre of the architectural achievements of the Ariyalur Chief.

KILAPALUVUR - This place formed a part of the capital of the Paluvettaraiyar. It was called as Sirupaluvur, a Brahmadeya village in Kunra Kurram. Poems to the Alanduraiyar Temple here were sung by Thirugnanasambandar during the 7th century. It is said that the Sage Parasurama did penance in this place and got rid of his sins of having killed his Mother. This Temple was worshipped by the Malayali Brahmins during the period of Saint Sambandar. It was built of stone during the period Parantaka Chola–I and Uttama Chola.

MELAPALUVUR & KEEZHAIYUR - It was the capital of the Paluvettaraiyar Chiefs, who were from Kerala and ruled Ariyalur area as feudatories of the Chola Kings from Aditya-I to Rajendra Chola-I. The Sundaresvarar Temple in this place dates back to the period of Aditya Chola–I. Its name was Pagaividailsvaram. The eastern part of this village is called Kilaiyur which was called as Avani Kandarvapuram during the period of the Cholas. The Lord Shiva Temple at Kilaiyur was called Avani Gandarvalsvaram and built in 884 AD by Kumaran Kandan. This Temple is one of the finest stone Temples and one of the best preserved early Chola Temples offering different architectural styles with an array of beautiful and charming sculptures.

SENDURAI, SENNIVANAM AND SRIPURANDAN - Epigraphically evidences show that Lord Shiva Temples at Sendurai, Sennivanam and Sripurandan belong to the periods of Rajaraja-I (985-1014), Rajendra–I (1012-1044) and Kulothunga–III (1178-1218) respectively.

KAMARASAVALLI - The Soundaresvarar Temple with Goddess Valambal was built during the period of Sundra Chola in 962 AD. Local traditions say that it was the place where Rathi did penance and got back her husband Manmatha and hence the village name Kama-rathi-valli. A village called Alagiyamanavalam is located east of this village. It is held that it was named after the beautiful husband of Rathi i.e., Alagiyamanavalan (beautiful husband-manmathan.) A beautiful bronze vigraha of Rathi is also preserved in this Temple. Another story preserved in this Temple is that Karkotaka, the serpent King, got relieved of his curse by worshipping Lord Shiva in this village

and hence the God of the Temple is called as Karkodakalsvaram. A slab with figures depicting this lore is also preserved in this Temple. There are more than 40 inscriptions of Chola, Pandya and Hoysala periods in this Temple. Inscriptions mention this Temple name as Tirunallur Srikovil Mahadevar, Tirunallurparamesvarar and Tirukkarkotagalsvarattu Mahadevar. Inscriptions refer to this village as Kamadavallichaturvedi Mangalam, a Brahmadeya in Mirai Kurram. There are beautiful sculptures and bronzes of Chola period in this Temple.

THIRUMAZHAPADI VAIDYANATHASWAMI TEMPLE - The antiquity of this place goes back to the Sangam Period. It was an army camp of the valiant Malavar clan of the Sangam Age and hence called Malavar-padi and later as Thirumalapadi. The deity of the Temple was worshipped and sung by the Devaram Nayanmars viz. Appar, Sambandar and Sundarar. It was also visited by Ayyadigal Kadavarkon, who praised it in his hymns of Shetravenba. It is believed that the deity of this place appeared in the dream of Saint Sundarar and asked him to visit this place and praise him and hence the saint came to this Temple and sung peons in his famous Devaram hymns 'Ponnarmeniyane'. The Temple was built of stone during the period of Aditya–I (871-907). Rajaraja–I ordered for its rebuilding and was completed by his son Rajendra–I. The first and second gopuras of this Temple were built during the periods of the Pandyas and Cholas respectively. The famous festival celebrated in this Temple is the marriage for Nandi (nandikalyanam). It is a popular belief in this area that impediments in getting married will be overcome if they see the marriage festival of Nandi Devar.

GANGAIKONDA CHOLAPURAM – The Temple is known as Gangaikondacholisvarar Temple. It is the biggest Temple constructed during the reign of Rajendra–I in Ariyalur region. Following the conquest of the Gangetic plains in 1023 AD, Rajendra–I built a great city called Gangaikondacholapauram and a Lord Shiva Temple and a lake, Chola Gangam in commemoration of his victory. The gigantic stone Temple which he built in this place is rich repository of beautiful sculptures of middle Chola period. Many sculptures brought from Andhra, Karnataka and Bengal as war trophies are also preserved in the Temple and in the nearby villages. Chandesura Anugraha Murthy and Sarasvathy are the most beautiful sculptures of the Temple. At present, it is under the control of ASI and the HR&CE and UNESCO declared the Temple as one of the world heritage monument.

DISTRICT – CHENGALPATTU (Railway Station – Chengalpattu)

MAMALLAPURAM TEMPLES - Mamallapuram is also known by other names such as Mamallapattana and Mahabalipuram. Another name by which Mamallapuram has been known to mariners, at least since Marco Polo's time is "Seven Pagodas" alluding to the Seven Pagodas of Mamallapuram that stood on the shore, of which one, the Shore Temple, survives. It is an important place of classical Monuments in India, the monolithic and cave Temples. It is situated close to the sea and rich in artistic wealth. These monuments afford scope for not only the study ancient architecture and sculpture in the Tamil Region. The town has a collection of 7th and 8th century Hindu religious monuments that has been declared as a UNESCO World Heritage site. It is located on the Coromandel Coast of the Bay of Bengal. The site has 40 ancient monuments and Hindu Temples including Descent of the Ganges or Arjuna's Penance – one of the largest open-air rock relief in the world. The site includes several categories of monuments: ratha Temples with an architecture of monolith processional chariots built between 630 and 668 CE; the mandapaviharas with halls and stone roofs with narratives from the Mahabharata, Shaktism and Vaishnavism; rock reliefs particularly bas-reliefs of Shaivism, Shaktism and Vaishnavism; stone cut Temples particularly those dedicated to Lord Shiva that also reverentially display Vishnu and others, built between 695 & 722 CE; and archaeological excavations with inscriptions some dated to 6th century & earlier. The cave Temples & monolithic Temples were built during the Pallava Period. The site is managed by the ASI.

S. No.	Temple	Address	Type
1	Arjuna Penance	Mamallapuram – 603104	Mahabharat Circuit
2	Cave Temples	Mamallapuram – 603104	Varaha etc.
3	Pancha Rathas (Five Chariots)	Mamallapuram – 603104	Mahabharat Circuit
4	Arulmigu Sri Sthala Sayana Perumal Tirukovil Divya Desam	Mamallapuram – 603104	Vishnu
5	Shore Temple	Mamallapuram – 603104	Shiva, Vishnu
6	Arulmigu Thiripura Sundari Amman & Sri Veda Giriswarar Temple	Tirukalikundram – 603109	Shiva, Mata
7	Arulmigu Kandaswamy Temple	Thiruporur – 603110	Murugan
8	Sri Maha Prathyangira Peedam	Venpakkam Village - 603204	Mata
9	Adhiparasakthi Siddhar Peedam	Melmaruvathur - 603319	Mata

ARJUNA PENANCE AT MAMALLAPURAM - It is a huge rock in the canvas unfolding a scene of gods & demigods, birds, beasts & scenery. Some are of the opinion that it is in fact Bhagirath's penance to bring the celestial Ganges to the earth. A natural cleft in the rock has been cleverly carved into the turbulent River Ganges with serpent gods worshipping like devotees along the banks frozen in their prayer is a superb poetry in sculpture & a complicated magnificent piece of skillfully carved work, the largest bas-relief sculptures in the world. Arjuna is depicted here as sage doing penance in order to obtain the divine weapons from Lord Shiva. All the carvings are made out of a huge boulder. There is a natural cleft in the centre of the huge rock which is conceived as the sacred River Ganga descending to earth. Various divine figures have been carved on all the sides. This piece of work is a masterpiece of creation in expression, particularly the figures relating to the popular Panchatanthra stories. Bhagiratha's penance is one of the largest and the finest bas-relief sculpted on the face of two enormous adjacent rocks. The panel is divided by a natural crack

between the two rocks. Originally, the water fed from a collecting chamber above, flowed down the fissure. A figure of bearded sage with floating ribs, standing on his left foot, deeply absorbed in performing penance is believed to be Bhagiratha praying for the Ganga to descend to earth from the Himalayas. The figure of animals particularly, the two large elephants and scenes from the fables in the Panchatantra are remarkable & unpretentious.

CAVE TEMPLES AT MAMALLAPURAM – The rock-cut Temples are dating back to 7th century. These include the Varaha, Adi Varaha, Krishna, Mahishasuramardini (Durga), Ramanuja, Dharmaraja, Koneri, Kotikal, Panchapandava and others.

Krishna Temple - A stunningly beautiful bas-relief showing Krishna lifting the Govardhana mountain in order to protect the cows and the cowherds from the wrath of Indra, the god of rain, which is the highlight of this cave Temple.

Mahishasuramardini Cave – It is carved into three shrines bass relief of Somaskanda in the rear, Anantashayana Lord Vishnu canopied by Shesha, reclining on the serpent bed. Mahishasuramardhini is struck in bold relief in such an awe-inspiring way with the thrill of the beholder in the battlefield. This is another excellent bas-relief depicting Lord Vishnu sleeping on the coils of serpent king Adisesha and Goddess Durga fighting with demon king Mahishasura.

Trimurti Cave Temple - It is a triple-celled Temple, dedicated to the holy trinity of Hinduism, the three superpowers Lord Brahma, Lord Vishnu and Lord Shiva. Situated at the northern end of the Mamallapuram Hill, slightly away from Krishna's Butter Ball, one can visit this Cave Temple to witness the splendour of Pallava dynasty's architecture. Apart from the trinity, the backside of the rock cave is adorned with fine carvings of elephants. These caves are among the very few in India that can be categorised as complete excavations. The three shrines of the Cave Temple have been excavated on the western facade of a hill and there are different staircases to reach all the three shrines. The three shrines are also decorated with a set of intricately carved dvarpalas or gatekeepers.

Varaha Temple - Lord Vishnu is shown in the incarnation of Varaha (boar) and the Vamana as a dwarf. This is an exquisitely caved bas-relief. Varaha Cave illustrates the legend of rescuing the earth Bhoodevi by Lord Vishnu incarnated as a boar.

Aluvan Kuppam – It is located at a short distance of 4 KMs. The Tiger Cave is an excavated cave shrine with aureole of Lion heads. It was an open theatre where cultural programmes were held in the past on a beautiful monolithic stage. The modern open-air museum of sculptures reflects the cultural heritage of the Tamils from the Pre-Sangam days. The objects on display, shaped mostly from granite by

200 sculptures, include chains of stone, ornamental wheels and a host of other items. The themes here are many including those relating to historical and cultural events of the past, placing the contribution of the Tamils in proper perspective. Other structural Temples including the Olakkanesvara Temple and the lighthouse, along with rock-cut features such as the Draupadi's tank and Krishna's butterball. One can also see the old rock built lighthouse and the modern lighthouse side by side. There is a huge rock tub said to be the bathing tub of Draupathi. Krishna's butter ball a huge boulder with just a tip of it touching the rock giving the on-looker an impression that it may roll on him any moment.

Ganesha Ratha - This monolith Indian rock-cut architecture had been built during the reign of King Mahendravarman-I and his son Narasimhavarman-I. It was originally dedicated to Lord Shiva but in the 1880s, it is believed that villagers replaced the Shivalinga with an vigraha of Lord Ganesha & a permission had been sought from the then District Collector. The feature of the Ratha has 18 inscriptions in Grantha and Nagari scripts of the Sanskrit language, which are inscribed on its west portico.

PANCHA RATHAS (FIVE CHARIOTS) AT MAMALLAPURAM - Pandava Raths or monolithic shrines are five in number out of which four are carved out of a single rock, while the fifth is scooped from a small rock. These rock-cut Temples are the excellent examples of the Pallava art. These five monolithic pyramidal structures named after the Pandavas (Arjuna, Bhima, Yudhishtra, Nakula and Sahadeva) and Draupadi. The hut-like Draupadi Rath sports door-keepers, Durga with a worshipper cutting and offering is neck and the outer walls of Arjuna's rath have most lovely and graceful figures of gods and mortals carved by a skilful sculptor. Nakula-Sahadeva rath stands with a huge Monolithic elephant in front. Bhima's rath has two storeys and lion-based pillars. Dharmaraja's rath is the biggest and has 8 panels of exquisite sculptures. In addition, the Ganesha Ratha in the north side is also a beautiful piece of art. Pallava Kings attempted to move the Ganesha Rath but all the kings and there elephants are not able to move the boulder even by an inch.

ARULMIGU SRI STHALA SAYANA PERUMAL TIRUKOVIL DIVYA DESAM AT MAMALLAPURAM – It is also called as Thirukadalmallai Temple. It is dedicated to Lord Vishnu. It is built in a Dravidian style architecture. It is one of the 108 Vaishnavite Divya Desam. Presiding deities are Sthala Sayana Perumal and Nilamangai Thayar. It is the birth place of Boothathazhvar, the second of the 12 Alwars of Vaishnavism. Thirumangai Azhwar and Boothathazhvar sanctifies this Temple in the Nalayira Divyaprabandam through their hymns. Thirumangai Azhwar considers the reclining form of Vishnu special as it is the only place where Lord Vishnu reclines on the ground instead of the customary Adiseshan and Tiruparkadal [ocean of milk]. Shrine of Lord Narasimha and Adivaraha are located near the sea shore. Lord is known as "Valvendai Gnanapiran". The Ustavar [festival deity] is with a lotus bud in the hand, while the presiding deity displays the Gnana Mudra. The Festival Deity called 'Ulagu Uyya Nindra Piran" with his consorts; Valavendai Gnanapiran or Adivaraha and also Sri Rama from the Padavedu Temple take procession to the sea for the Theertha Vari [Divine Bathing] during the Masi Makam festival. Boothathazhvaravatara festival is also an important festival of this Temple.

SHORE TEMPLE AT MAMALLAPURAM - The stately shrine set elegantly on the edge of the sea is a long survivor among the seven magnificent Temples built over here. The construction originally started around the middle of the 7th CE & was later rebuilt during the reign of Narsimha Varma-II, also known as Rajasimha. It is one of the oldest Temples in South India and represents the first phase of structural Temples constructed in Dravidian style. This icon of the soaring aesthetic aspiration of the Pallavas has been listed among the World Heritage Sites of UNESCO and is one of the most visited monuments in Tamil Nadu. Originally, there were seven such Temples called as pagodas and only one has been spared. The Temple is built of cut stones rather than carved out of caves. It's style is characterized by a pyramidal kutina type tower that consist of stepped stories topped by a cupola & finial, a form quite different from the Northern India Shikhara. It has a vimana towering over 60 ft. built in basaltic rock. A prismatic Lingam is on the sanctum facing the sea & Lord Vishnu is seen reclining on the ground in his chamber in the rear. The Shore Temple is in fact complexes of three exquisitely carved shrines & are approached through a paved forecourt flanked by weathered perimeter walls supporting striking sculptures of numerous 'Nandi'. A Temple dedicated to Lord Vishnu is flanked by two Lord Shiva Temples, one facing the east & the other facing the west. Both the Lord Shiva Temples are crowned by soaring spires, while the Lord Vishnu Temple has none, as it may have crumbled with time.

ARULMIGU THIRIPURA SUNDARI AMMAN & SRI VEDA GIRISWARAR TEMPLE AT TIRUKALIKUNDRAM – It is an ancient Lord Shiva Temple with lofty tower. Nearby is a Hill called Vedagiri, 160m high, on the top of which also there is a small Lord Shiva Temple. It is said that two kites arrive regularly in noon to the summit of this hill to receive food from the hands of the Temple priest. At the south-east of the town is a spacious tank whose waters are said to have curative properties. Once in 12 years, a Shanka (conch) comes out of the tank according to the local tradition. A number of such conches obtained in the past are displayed at the Temple.

ARULMIGU KANDASWAMY TEMPLE AT THIRUPORUR – It is an ancient Temple dating back to the Pallava period and is one of 33 major Temples in Tamil Nadu dedicated to the worship of Lord Murugan. It is considered as the head of the places wherein Lord Muruga willingly lives. It is also known as Poriyur or Yuddhapuri or Samarapuri. It is said that after vanquishing Soorapadman at Tiruchendur, Skanda destroyed the rest of the demons here in aerial combat. As per Sthalapuranam, in ancient times, Lord Vishnu and his consort Lakshmi were subjected to the curse of Sage Kanva. Lord Shiva came to this place and liberated them from its effects. Therefore, the Temple is a very significant shrine dedicated to the worship of Lord Shiva as well as his son Lord Murugan. It is also believed that at this place Lord Murugan with his consorts Valli and Devayanai granted protection to devas and expounded the meaning of Pranava to Agastya Muni. The sanctum sanctorum of this Temple is situated on the eastern side wherein one can see the Palmyra Tree and the anthill under it wherein is Kanda Perumal with Valli and Devayanai on a small peetham. The murti in the anthill is covered with kavacham and other jewels but no abhishekam is performed for this deity. This Temple enshrines Skanda in several forms relating to legends from the Skanda Puranam. The foremost of these is the depiction of Skanda as a warrior, Samhara Subramanyar. The 24 pillared hall and the 30 pillared circular hall are other features of this Temple. There is a shrine to Vembadi Vinayakar under a Neem Tree. On the southern side of the Temple, there is Saravana Poigai and Valliyar Odai, the two sacred Teerthams. There is also another Teertham by name Pranavamritam. There is a glimpse of the exquisitely chiselled panchaloha vigrahas of Vighneswara, Somaskanda, Chandrasekara, Dwanishandeswara, Astra Deva, Brahma, Vishnu, Devendra, Nandi and Matruchandesa. The copper icon of Lord Muruga sitting on the lap of Lord Shiva is exquisite. The bas relief of upadesa to Agastya, Vallikalyana and Agni-ganta Subrahmanya have been chiselled very beautifully on the pillars of Sarvavaidya Mandapa. The yantra established by Chidambaram Swamigal can be found in the northeast of the Temple on a platform with kurma, ashtagaja, astnaga and ganas. In the outer mandapa is situated in the sannidhi of Teyvayanai. Skanda Sashti is celebrated in the month of Aippasi. Other festivals celebrated here include Margazhi Tiruvadirai and Navaratri.

SRI MAHA PRATHYANGIRA PEEDAM AT VENPAKKAM VILLAGE - Maha Pradyangira Devi with a thousand lion faces has two thousand arms, a large body, a dark complexion & a blue dress, wears a moon-head and carries weapons such as a scepter, a skull, an affection and a tamarugam. The Lord hangs his right leg, folds his left leg and stands like a lioness on a lion. Goddess is also known as Mahakali, Atharvana Bhadrakali & Ukra Pradyangira. Sarabhasakti appeared from Sarabari's forehead eye. "Bhadra" means blur. According to this, she is known as "Bhadrapriya" and "Bhadramoorthy". It is believed that worship of Goddess Maha Pradyangira, the Navagraharupini who rules over the Navagrahas, can solve the karmic sins committed by our forefathers, the karma committed by our ancestors, the incurable diseases, confusions and difficulties experienced in this life.

ADHIPARASAKTHI SIDDHAR PEEDAM AT MELMARUVATHUR - The Siddhar Peedam is being considered as the most Holy place for the past 2000 years. It is in this place, where 21 Siddhars, both men and women, attained Jeeva Samaadhi (leaving the mortal body, but living in astral plane). These 21 Siddhars belong to various religions. At Siddhar Peedam there is a Neem tree and

a huge Snake mound underneath it. One day, in 1960s, milk began to ooze out from the aforesaid Neem Tree. Wonderstruck by the miracle, people in the surrounding villages, thinking it to be a Divine Happening, drank the oozing milk. The milk was delicious though the sap of the Neem tree will always taste bitter. It served as a miracle-medicine for curing the various diseases of the village people. The people slowly started realizing the Divine Power and Grace of the tree. On 28.11.1966, there was a violent storm in Tamil Nadu. The Snake mound under the Neem tree was eroded in the heavy rain. The Neem tree also got uprooted due to the violent gusty winds. The Swayambu (Swayambu means "self-manifested" or that which is created by its own accord) emerged beneath the uprooted Neem tree. People then understood the revelation that it was because of the power of The Swayambu, the milk had high medicinal values, and the place became so sacred. The Sanctum Sanctorum of today's Siddhar Peedam is established in this very same place. The Swayambu is situated right in front of the Adhiparasakthi vigraha. Initially, The Swayambu alone was worshipped for many years. Thereafter, on 25.11.1977, the vigraha of Mother Adhiparasakthi was installed in Garbhagriha. Mother Adhiparasakthi instructed the unique form of this vigraha through Her Oracles. The vigraha is one metre tall, seated on a thousand-petal lotus seat, with her right leg folded and the left leg resting on the lotus petal. The thousand-petal lotus signifies & denotes meditation. She holds the bud of a lotus in her right hand & the fingers of Her left are folded in a way depicting the Chin Mudra. Her hair is plaited & knotted upwards like a crown.

DISTRICT – CHENNAI (Railway Station – MGR Chennai Ctl)

S. No.	Temple	Address	Type
1	Kalikambal Temple	Thambu Chetty Street, Chennai - 600001	Mata
2	Kandaswami Temple	Parry's Corner, Chennai - 600001	Murugan
3	Arulmigu Kapaleeswarar Temple	Mylapore, Chennai – 600004	Shiva
4	Arulmigu Madhava Perumal Temple	Mylapore, Chennai – 600004	Vishnu
5	Arulmigu Parthasarathyswamy Temple	Triplicane, Chennai – 600005	Vishnu
6	Gujarati Shwetambar Murtipujak Jain Mandir	Vepery, Chennai – 600007	Jain
7	Sri Aathi Mottai Amman Temple	Kosapet, Chennai - 600012	Mata
8	Sri Vaembu Aathi Muthumari Amman	Kosapet, Chennai - 600012	Mata
9	Valluvar Kottam	Nungambakkam High Road, Chennai – 600034	Saint Thiruvalluvar
10	Arulmigu Aadhi Vyadhi Hara Bhaktha Anjaneyar Temple	8th Street, Ram Nagar, Nanganallur, Chennai - 600061	Hanuman
11	Sri Prasanna Venkata Narasimha Swamy Temple	Kotturpuram, Chennai - 600085	
12	Shri Ashtalakshmi Temple	Elliots Beach, Besant Nagar, Chennai - 600090	Mata
13	Matsya Narayana Mandir	Uthandi - 600119	Varaha

KALIKAMBAL TEMPLE AT THAMBU CHETTY STREET - The Temple is dedicated to Goddess Kaligambal who is also known as Kamakshi and Lord Kamadeswarar. As per records, the Temple was originally located nearer to the sea shore and the same was relocated at this place in 1640 CE. It was then rebuilt in 1678. Chh. Shivaji Maharaj had worshiped in this Temple incognito on 3rd October 1667. It is believed that a fierce form of Goddess was held in worship earlier and that this form was replaced with the non-fierce form. Noted Tamil Poet Subramaniya Bharathi was a regular visitor of this Temple in the early 20th CE.

KANDASWAMI TEMPLE AT PARRY'S CORNER - The Temple is dedicated to Lord Murugan. It is also known as 'Mutthu Kumara Swami Devasthanam'. It is also famous as Kandha Kottam. It is believed that the original Temple was constructed by the Maari Chettiar in the 1670s. The present Temple was built with stone in the very early of 1800s. The Temple had seen various renovations. The Temple is located in a big complex. The Temple tank is known as 'Saravana Poigai' and the Sthala Viruksham is Magizham Tree. According to the stone inscriptions exist in the Temple, the vigraha of Lord Murugan had been discovered and brought from a tank bund near Thiruporur Shri Kandha Swami Temple. The vigraha of 'Shri Kandha Swami' is about two feet in height. Shri Deivanai and Shri Valli are on either side of the presiding deity. Next to the Temple tank, there is a shrine for Shri Kulakkarai Vinayagar with Siddhi and Buddhi as his consorts. There is a shrine nearby for Shri Kashi Vishwanadhar and Shri Kashi Vishalakshi. To the front of the Artha mandapam, there is a 'Dwaja Sthambam'. The Mukha Mandapam is where the vigrahas of Sarva Siddhi Vinayagar, Meenakshi Sundareswarar, Idumban, Ramalinga Swamigal and Pamban Swamigal are located. The Temple is associated with the life of the Saint Ramalinga Swamigal, who composed 'Deiva Mani Malai' here.

ARULMIGU KAPALEESWARAR TEMPLE AT MYLAPORE, CHENNAI - One of the sacred shrines in Tamil Nadu, it is an 8th century Pallava Temple. The Temple 'Gopuram' is made in the characteristic Dravidian style of architecture. Dedicated of Lord Shiva, this Temple has some beautiful sculptures among which the bronze vigrahas of 63 Saivaite Saints or the Nayanmars. They adorn the outer courtyard. There is a big tank on its West. The Temple & the tank are surrounded by broad streets on the four sides. In the courtyard under the old Punnai Tree is a small shrine depicting Goddess Parvathi in the form of a peacock worshipping Lord Shiva. The name of the Goddess is Arulmigu Karpagambal. It is from this legend that Mylapore derives its name, Mayil meaning peacock in Tamil & Oor meaning town. Mylapore is the hub of the Arubathumoovar Festival dedicated to the 63 Nayanmars held in March-April every year.

ARULMIGU MADHAVA PERUMAL TEMPLE AT MYLAPORE, CHENNAI - The Temple is the most famous Vishnu Temples of Mylapore and is dedicated to Lord Madhava, Lord Kesava and Lord Srinivasa. It is believed that this Temple is situated in the place where the Sage Bhrigu's asrama

existed. It is also the Avathara Sthalam of Peyaazhwar. It is also believed that Lord Vishnu directed Veda Vyasa here as the best place for liberation from Kali Dosham in Kali Yugam. The main Deity of this Temple, Lord Madhava, is in a seated posture with Goddesses Sridevi and Bhudevi by his side. He is also called Kalyana Madhava as he married Amritavalli Thayar here. In the mandapa in front of the principal sanctum is the shrine for Sri Peyaazhvar, while all the other Azhvars are worshipped in a sannidhi a little outside in the courtyard. The Peyaazhvar-avatara utsava is celebrated annually in the month of Aippasi. Next to the sanctum of this Azhvar is one for Sri Ramanuja, the pre-eminent Srivaishnava acharya. Many festivals like the Navaratri utsava and Tirukkalyana utsava during Panguni Uttiram are celebrated here. On all Fridays, the Oonjal utsava is conducted for those desirous of offspring.

ARULMIGU PARTHASARATHYSWAMY TEMPLE AT TRIPLICANE, CHENNAI - The Temple is one of the 108 Divya Desams. This Temple is dedicated to Parthasarathy, Lord Vishnu. It was built in the eighth century by the Pallavas and later renovated by the Vijayanagar rulers. It is said that for at least five thousand years, it has been a resting place for pilgrims who had come down from Tirupati to have a bath in the sea on the days of Solar and Lunar Eclipses & on other auspicious days. According to Brahmanda Puranam, the five Deities in the Temple are said to have been worshipped by the Saptah Rishis viz. Bhrigu, Manchi, Atri, Markandeya, Sumathi, Saptharoma and Jabali. There are five shrines for Lord Vishnu in his various forms. Parthasarathy - The main shrine is for Venkatakrishnan with Rukmini, Balaraman, Satyaki, Anirudha, Pradyumna - in a standing posture facing east. There are shrines for Ranganathar in a reclining posture with a separate sanctum for his consort Vedavalli, Rama along with Sita, Lakshmana, Bharata, Shatrugna & Hanuman, Varadarajan seated on the Garuda, Narasimhar in a seated posture. Apart from these, there is a separate shrine for Andal. The annual Brahmmotsavam is celebrated in the month of Chittirai. There is a beautiful glass palanquin. Vaikuntha Ekadasi celebrated in Margazhi is one of the important festivals. The float festival is held in Feb-Mar. The Utsavar is Parthasarathy. The vigraha of Lord Krishna bears the scars from Bheeshma's arrows.

GUJARATI SHWETAMBAR MURTIPUJAK JAIN MANDIR – It is credited with being one of the 1st Jain Temples in South India. Home to three beautifully carved gopurams & five doors, the Temple built completely in marble. The structure differs in construction from other buildings as the use of iron has been totally avoided. The vigraha that sits inside the premises is made of quartz. In the central hall, one can see extensive glass work due to which the hall glows with a spectrum of colours. It is believed that the architects, the stone carvers & the workers who were involved in the construction of the Temple were hired from Rajasthan. The deity worshipped in the Temple is Lord Parsvanatha, the 23rd Tirthankara.

SRI AATHI MOTTAI AMMAN TEMPLE AT KOSAPET - The Temple is dedicated to the Goddess, who is popularly known as Mariamman. Devotees visit the Temple with great devotion & they believe that the Goddess fulfills all their desires when they worship the Goddess with true heart. Sri Aathi Mottai Amman Jathirai is very famous festival in Kosapet area.

SRI VAEMBU AATHI MUTHUMARI AMMAN AT KOSAPET - The Temple is dedicated to Goddess Sri Vaembu Aathi Muthumari Amman. Sri Vaembu Aathi Muthumari Amman Aadi Thiruvizha & Sri Aathi Padavattamman Vilaku Poojai is celebrated with great pomp & fervor.

VALLUVAR KOTTAM AT NUNGAMBAKKAM HIGH ROAD, CHENNAI – It is one such historical monument which is dedicated to the well-known Intellectual Poet, Philosopher and Saint, Thiruvalluvar, who penned his well-known Thirukkural more than 2,000 years ago. All the 133 chapters of the Thirukkural comprise of 1330 verses. The construction of Valluvar Kottam was the finest way to pay homage to this great and renowned personality as well his tremendous collection of magnificent works. This is one of the significant sites located in Chennai and is visited by a large number of visitors, every year, from all over the world. In the cultural life of the Tamils, Saint Thiruvalluvar has great significance. The architectural pattern is like a Temple chariot (39 m high), inside which there is a huge stone effigy of the Saint Thiruvalluvar. A very unique feature is that it stands baseless, without the support of any pillar. The 1330 verses of the epic Thirukkural are engraved on the granite columns in the facade hall corridors, enclosing the vast auditorium of the Valluvar Kottam. The lion on the main gateway of the Kottam is very remarkable which decorated with attractive designs.

ARULMIGU AADHI VYADHI HARA BHAKTHA ANJANEYAR TEMPLE AT NANGANALLUR, CHENNAI – The main shrine houses 32 foot tall Viswaroopa Adhivyadhihara Sri Bhaktha Anjaneya Swamy inside a Temple Tower. Lord Anjaneya is facing west and the main entrance is on the West. The Temple is known for bestowing better health to the devotees. Lord Sri Rama, Sri Lakshmana and

Seetha with Sri Anjaneyar, Sri Vinayagar, Sri Ragavendra and Sri Krishna with his consorts Bhama and Rukmini are also indoctrinated here. The vigraha is believed to have special power and is considered a healer. On the North-West corner, a full-fledged Sannidhi for Lord Sri Rama has been built and here he has taken abode with Seetha and Lakshmana with Anjaneya in attendance. The Gods are facing east. Lord Rama's role as the protector and ruler is signified here as Lord Rama is seen carrying his bow, hence the name "Kothanda Rama" for the Lord here. On the South-West, a Sannidhi for Lord Krishna with Rukmani and Satya Bhama, all facing East has been built and a "thulam" (weighing balance) has been erected for offering "thulabaram" (offering made in different materials equivalent to the weight of the devotee).In the North-East part of the Temple, on a small platform, "Vinayaka" is housed facing east and to his left on a yet another platform 'Naga' has been installed.

SRI PRASANNA VENKATA NARASIMHA SWAMY TEMPLE AT KOTTURPURAM - The Temple is dedicated to Sri Prasanna Venkata Narasimha Swamy. The Goddess of the Temple is known as Alarmel Mangai. The tirtham of the Temple is Thamarai Pushkarini and Thala Virutcham is Shenbagam. The Temple is believed to be app. 1000 years old. It is believed that the original Temple had been dedicated to Lord Rama, Mata Sita & Lakshman. During renovations of the Temple about 700 years ago, the vigraha of Goddess Alarmel Mangai & Panchaloka vigrha of Lord Perumal found while digging a pit and these vigrahas had been consecrated in the Temple. Chithirai Brahmmotsavam, Navaratri, Narasimha Jayanti & Ram Navmi are major festivals which are celebrated in the Temple in addition to other various festivals which are also celebrated with great pomp & fervor.

SHRI ASHTALAKSHMI TEMPLE AT ELLIOTS BEACH, BESANT NAGAR - The Temple is dedicated to 8 forms of Goddess Lakshmi. The unique sanctorums are constructed in ashtanga vimana style which is a multi tier 8 parts complex with three floors. The speciality of the Temple is that the devotees can visit all the shrines without stepping over and of the sanctorums.

MATSYA NARAYANA MANDIR AT UTHANDI - The Temple is dedicated to Lord Varaha, who is an incarnation of Lord Vishnu. In the Birth Centenary Year of Gurudev Swami Chinmayanandaji, Chinmaya Tarangini was inaugurated by Pujya Guruji Swami Tejomayanandaji on 24th May, 2015.

DISTRICT – COIMBATORE (Railway Station – Coimbatore)

S. No.	Temple	Address	Type
1	Group of Temples	Coimbatore - 641001	Mata, Sai Baba
2	Jai Shri Shri Shri Jindatt Suri Jain Dadawadi	60, Robertson Road, R S Puram, Coimbatore - 641002	Jain
3	Sri Kamatchi Amman Temple	135, T.V. Samy Road, R.S. Puram Coimbatore - 641002	Mata
4	Shree Ashtamsa Varadha Anjaneyar Kovil	Peelamedu, Coimbatore - 641004	Hanuman
5	Arulmigu Patteeswarar Swamy Temple	Perur, Coimbatore – 641010	Shiva
6	Arulmigu Virundeeswar Temple	K. Vadamadurai Post, Coimbatore – 641017	Shiva
7	Sri Sharadhalayam	Race Course, Coimbatore - 641018	Mata
8	Arulmigu Echanari Vinayakar Temple	Eachanari – 641021	Ganesh
9	Sree Ayyappan Temple	Siddhapudur - 641044	Ayyappa
10	Munthi Vinayakar Koil	Puliakulam - 641045	Ganesh
11	Arulmigu Subramaniyaswamy Thirukoil	Maruthamalai - 641046	Murugan
12	Arulmigu Aranganatha Swamy Thirukoil	Karamadai - 641104	Vishnu
13	Sri Dharma Lingeswarar Temple	Marappalam, Madukkarai - 641105	Shiva
14	Sri Anuvavi Anjaneyar Nandhavanam	Periya Thadagam, Coimbatore – 641108	Hanuman
15	Isha Yoga Centre (Adiyogi)	Velliangiri Foothills, Ishana Vihar Post, Coimbatore – 641114	Shiva
16	Arulmigu Velliangiri Andavar Temple	Poondi, Coimbatore - 641114	
17	Arulmigu Vanabadrakaliamman Temple	Devikottam, Thekkampatti, Mettupalayam – 641305	Mata
18	Then-Thirumalai	Sirumugai Road Mettupalayam - 641305	Vishnu
19	Subramanyar Temple	Pollachi – 642001	Murugan
20	Arulmigu Masani Amman Temple	Anaimalai - 642104	Mata
21	Balaji Temple	Karumalai, Valparai - 642127	Vishnu

COIMBATORE TEMPLES –

Koniamman Temple – It is dedicated to Koniamman. She is the guardian deity of the city. Koyamma, the goddess worshiped by chieftain Koyan evolved into Koniamma and the name of the city Koyambuthur could have been derived from Kovaiamma. The Temple dates back to 16th century. An 84 foot gopuram, the tallest in the region was completed in 2011.

Sri Naga Sai Mandir – It is dedicated to Shirdi Sai Baba. In 1939, H.H.B.V. Narasimha Swamiji, Sri. C.Varadaraja Ayyah, Sri A.V. K. Chari started the Sai Movement in Coimbatore. The Temple was established in 1939. The place was opened for worship to everyone regardless of class, creed, caste or religion. Sai Bhajans were held regularly on Sundays and Thursdays. A marble vigraha of Shirdi Sai Baba was installed on 26th February 1961. The Temple holds a stick, which was used by Shirdi Sai Baba, brought from Shirdi. The Holy stick is used to bless all devotees who visit the shrine. The Mandir has a Golden Chariot (Thanga Ther) with a Golden vigraha of Sai Baba. The Sacred Dhuni flame has been brought from Bangalore Mandir which got the original Dhuni flame from Shirdi. The udi from the dhuni is given as prasadam to all the devotees. This udi has the power to cure all diseases.

Thandu Mariamman Temple – It is dedicated to Thandu Mariamman. According to mythology, the goddess is said to have cured the soldiers of the ruler of Kongu Nadu from chicken pox. The annual car festival celebrated in April, which is one of the important religious festivals in the region.

JAI SHRI SHRI SHRI JINDATT SURI JAIN DADAWADI AT R S PURAM - The Temple is dedicated to Shwetamber sect of Jainism. The Temple is big and beautiful and there are architectural carvings on the pillars and various sculptures have also been carved in the entire Temple.

SRI KAMATCHI AMMAN TEMPLE AT R.S. PURAM - The Temple is dedicated to Sri Kamatchi Amman. The Temple is ancient and famous.

SHREE ASHTAMSA VARADHA ANJANEYAR KOVIL AT PEELAMEDU - The Temple is dedicated to Lord Hanuman. The vigraha of the Lord Hanuman is made of Saligram stone. The eyes of the Lord is very graceful and they reflect the brightness of sun in the day time & gentleness of moon in the evening time and from whichever direction one have Darshan of the Lord, the eyes seems to be looking at you. The vigraha has eight unique and distinctive features. The tail of the Lord is fully visible facing north. There are different Alankaran each day which makes this Temple special.

ARULMIGU PATTEESWARAR SWAMY TEMPLE AT PERUR – It was built by King Karikala Cholan. The presiding deity is Lord Shiva & the 'Swayambu Lingam' is worshipped here. As per legend, the calf of Kamadhenu discovered a sacred Shivalinga. The foot print scar of divine cow Kamadenu is still visible on the head of Lord Patteeswarar. This sanctum is joint effort of Chola, Hoysala & Vijayanagara rulers. The greatest attraction of the Temple is the 'Kanaka Saba', which is adorned by a gold plated vigraha of Nataraja bestowing blessings upon the two Sages - Gowmuni & Pattimuni. The gopurams & pillars of the hall are exquisitely carved out sculptures highlighting Dravidian architecture. The Swami & Amman Temples were renovated in 18th CE & later on, the Mantap of 63

Saints was built. In the 20th CE, the Kalyana Mantapam & front Mantapam were built. The vimana of Mother Pachai Nayaki is square in shape. There is a shrine for Ambica Mother Manonmani. Lord Muruga is in between the shrines of Lord & Mother in the Somaskanda form. The shrine of Lord Varadaraja Perumal is outside the shrine of Mother Pachainayaki. Sri Anjaneya in the Temple is made of wood. There is a Tamarind Tree in the Temple, the seeds of which do not germinate if sown, indicating the truth that those pray to Lord Patteeswara will attain total salvation & will be freed from the cycle of births & deaths. The Cars have fine wooden carvings attract the cupidity of even foreigners. Even the small shrines surrounding the main Temple are very ancient. There is a Patti Vinayagar shrine. The Arasambalavanar Shrine, where Lord Shiva is believed to have his Tandav under a Peepul Tree. There are also vigrahas of Gajasamhara, Virabhadra, Bikshadana, Oordhva Tandava, Saraswati with Veena. The sacred trees associated with Temple are the palm & tamarind, called Irava Panai & Pirava Puli. The significance of Perur Temple in earlier days are unfolded in the poetic creations of Arunagiri Nather & Kachiappa Munivar. Pilgrims from all over visit this spot to pay homage to their ancestors. It is believed that the mortal remains turn into white stones after about 144 days. Lord Bhairava appears without his dog vahan as Gnana Bhairava.

ARULMIGU VIRUNDEESWAR TEMPLE AT K VADAMADURAI POST - As per Sthala Puranam, once Sundaramurthy Nayanar was travelling in this area. After having darshan at Avinashi, he came this side and he was very tired and hungry. He prayed to the Lord to come to his rescue. At that time, an elderly couple came that side and fed him sumptuous food mainly made with Drumstick leaves and fruits. When Sundarar's hunger was satisfied, to his surprise, he found that the couple were none other than Shri Parvathi and Parameswarar. As the Lord offered Virundhu (feast or food), He is called Virundeeswarar, who is the presiding deity of this Temple together with his consort Goddess Parvati, who is known as "Viswanayaki". It is one of the ancient Temples in the city which is more than 1300+ years old. The Lord Shiva is [Swayambumurthy] and there are actually two Lingams in the sanctorum- One Lingam [Swayambumurthy] at the back and a small Lingam in the front. The Temple is facing east. We usually see Lord Nataraja dancing with his long hair flying wide, the Lord dances here with his hair well dressed. Lord Shiva granted all powers to his vehicle Nandhi at this Temple, hence this Nandi is called "Adhikara Nandi". As per local people, the Adhikara Nandi concept in other Temples came into existence after this Temple. After several years, Maha-Kumbhabhishekam was held in the Temple on 11th July 2019. Every year on 17th of Panguni month, the Sun rays falls on Lord Virundeeswarar.

Sri Sharadalayam – The Temple is a branch of Dakshinamnaya Sri Sharada Peetham, Sringeri. Here, Sri Devi Sharadambal, Sri Adhi Shankar, Sri Bala Vinayakar, Sri Bala Murugar and Devi Chandika Parameswari are installed and worshipped.

ARULMIGU ECHANARI VINAYAKAR TEMPLE AT EACHANARI - Lord Vinayaga is a presiding deity of this Temple. The Moolavar of this Temple is actually made for the installation at Perur, Arulmighu Patteswarar Temple & since the cart carrying moolavar struck down at this place from Madurai and Eachanari become the blessed place of Lord Vinayaga. Hence, the Vinayagar in this place is called as "Eachanari Vinayagar", one of the famous Vinayaga of whole Tamil Nadu.

SREE AYYAPPAN TEMPLE AT SIDDHAPUDUR - The Temple is a well known and famous Temple and the devotees are much proud to honour the Temple as the Second Sabarimala. Devotees from the other states commence their Sabarimala Pilgirvigraha with the sacred garlanding and "Virtha" (procedural diet restrictions) and during their Yatra, they visit Sidhapudur Temple and stay on account of rest and then they continue the pilgrimage. This Temple has had a noble history of establishment since 1942. Around this location, the Temples for Lord Vinayaga, Goddess Durga, Lord Sri Muruga and Lord Sri Vishnu were also accommodated. During 1969, the first "Kumbabishekam" ceremony was conducted. In 1972, the "Dwajasthamba" was installed. From 1973, the traditional "Arattu Festival" meant for celebrating the festival in the Tank – water was also arranged. During 1988, His Holiness Kanchi Kamakoti Peedathipathi Sri Sri Jayendra Saraswathi Swamigal inaugurated the "Raja Gopuram". The doorways, kalasas, dhwajasthamba etc. have been converted into pure gold.

MUNTHI VINAYAKAR KOIL AT PULIAKULAM – The Temple is dedicated to Lord Ganesha. The most important feature is the vigraha of Lord Ganesha, which is 20 ft. height & 11 ft. width. It is the largest vigraha of the deity carved in stone. The vigraha of Lord Ganesha is an illustration of attentive work & mathematical calculation as well. The dedication of the sculptors can be seen in the majestic aura of the vigraha. The vigraha is seen sitting on a gigantic lotus flower with a pot of nectar on his trunk which circles to the right. This pot is also commonly referred to as the Amrut Kalash & symbolises blessings from Mahalakshmi. The vigraha has four hands, one that holds a piece of ivory to write the Mahabharata, one holding the Angusa, one holding a jackfruit & the fourth holding a whip. The serpent, Vasuki, can be seen wrapped around his hips and there is another lotus flower seen as an offering to Lord Ganesha on his right foot.

ARULMIGU SUBRAMANIYASWAMY THIRUKOIL AT MARUTHAMALAI, COIMBATORE – It is

800 years old Temple & the presiding deity is Lord Subramaniaswamy. The Temple is classified under Kunruthoradal, one of the six main abodes of the God. The flight of steps are interspersed with attractive mandapams. Near the foothill, there is a Temple for Pillayar known as the "Thaan Thondri Vinaayakar". There is a cave referred to as "Paambaatti Sitthar Kugai" dedicated to a Sitthar who lived here. The history of the Temple can be traced in Sage Kachyapar's Perur Puranam. The origin of the Temple is rooted in legendary antiquity & dates back to the age of Surapadama, the demon destroyed by Lord

Subramanya referred to in Skandapurnam. The inscriptions found in Thirumuruganathaswami Temple, Thirumurganpoondi places the origin of the Temple in the 12th CE. The Divine Cow Kamadhenu is reported to have grazed in the pastures of the hills of Marudhamalai. Perurpuranam lists the three neighbouring hills, Vellingiri, Nili & Marudhamalai as the very manifestations of Lord Shiva, Parvathi & Subramanya.

ARULMIGU ARANGANATHA SWAMY THIRUKOIL AT KARAMADAI – The main deity of the Temple incarnated three forms - as Lord Venkatesa Achudhan, as Lord Aranganadhar & as Lord Venkatesa Perumal. Sri Ranganayagi Thayaar of this Temple is also known as Pettathu Amman. The Temple is blessed with the presence of Mother Kodha Nachiyar. The Temple has streams of Holy water blessed by the merciful hands of providence. Behind the main deity is the presence of Brahma Theertham. The Holy Pond in the Temple has Theertham blessed by the miraculous hands of Lord Karuda. Along the route of the Temple's car procession are eight deities having eight streams of Holy water besides them, called the Ashta Theertham. For years together these Theertham have been satiating the spiritual search of the humble devotees of the Temple. The Temple is considered as one of the most significant place of worship with special Pandha, Thanneer & Kavaalapoojas done by holy devotees routinely all-round the year. This unique worship can be beheld conveniently only in this region.

SRI DHARMA LINGESWARAR TEMPLE AT MARAPPALAM, MADUKKARAI – It is a Lord Shiva Temple located on the top of a hill. Lord Dharmalingeswaraswamy, the Temple deity, is a Swayambumurthi (self-manifested). There are nearly 800 steps to reach the top of the Temple. The holy tree of the Temple is Vilwa.

SRI ANUVAVI ANJANEYAR NANDHAVANAM AT PERIYA THADAGAM, COIMBATORE – The divine location of Anuvavi Hills is situated in Periya Thadagam. Lord Hanuman blesses the devotees in a huge 45-ft form with Health, Wealth, Happiness, Courage and Prosperity. He is in "praying" form" where he discriminates duality and praises oneness. The worship of Sri Anuvavi Anjaneyar with total concentration & devotion, one experiences all the three states of dualism, non-dualism & conditional non-dualism. The core philosophy & concept of "Ekam Sat" is also perceived in the presence of Sri Anuvavi Anjaneyar. The legend & history relates to Anuvavi Hills states that when Lakshmana, the younger brother of Lord Rama fainted & went into an unconscious state, Lord Hanuman was assigned a protective role of bringing the Sanjeevani Mount from the Himalayan Mountains, the mighty aerial Hanuman flew all the way from the Indian, Srilankan Seas. On the way back Hanuman felt thirsty, as he flew over the Western Ghats & looked around for a Water resource devoutly praying to Lord Shiva who affectionately orders Lord Subrahmanya, to create a Waterfalls to quench Hanuman's thirst, & Lord Subrahmanya creates a Water source, a fountain on the Mountain & Sri Hanuman quenched his thirst heartily.

SRI ANUVAVI SUBRAMANIAR TEMPLE – It is an ancient Temple. The presiding deity is Lord Muruga. The vigraha is Swayambhumurthi. The vigraha is accompanied by his consorts, Valli and Deivanai. The vigraha is of standing posture. There is a Navagraha shrine in the Temple complex.

ISHA YOGA CENTRE (ADIYOGI) AT VELLIANGIRI FOOTHILLS - Over 15,000 years ago, predating all religion, Adiyogi, the first Yogi, transmitted the science of Yoga to his seven disciples, the Saptarishis. He expounded 112 ways through which human beings can transcend their limitations & reach their ultimate potential. Adiyogi's offerings are tools for individual transformation, as it is the only way to transform the world. On the auspicious night of Mahashivaratri, an iconic face of "Adiyogi – the Source of Yoga" was unveiled by the Hon'ble Prime Minister Shri Narendra Modi. Recognized as the world's largest bust sculpture by the Guinness World Records, the face of Adiyogi is 112 ft high, representing the 112 ways he offered for one to attain to wellbeing and one's ultimate nature. Installed near the Adiyogi is the Yogeshwar Linga, which was consecrated by Sadhguru, as manifestation of five of the major chakras in the human system. Adiyogi, with the presence of the Yogeshwar Linga, has become a living entity.

MAA LINGA BHAIRAVI AT VELLIANGIRI FOOTHILLS - As the darkest night, a pair of glowing eyes that penetrate deep into the recess of your heart, a gloriously sparkling Third Eye that perceives a dimension beyond the physical, graciously giving arms that bestow infinite Grace to all in need, a pure gold sari that reflects her grandeur – Linga Bhairavi is the most exuberant expression of the Divine Feminine, residing in a triangular-shaped abode at the Velliangiri Foothills. Unique in her manifestation in the form of a linga, the eight feet tall Devi was consecrated by Sadhguru as a powerful energy form with a solidified mercury core. The energy of Linga Bhairavi strengthens the three basic chakras in the human system; thus stabilizing one's body, mind and energy system. Various offerings are available in this space to allow devotees to benefit from Devi's abundant Grace. There are unique rituals that assist in every step that one takes in life, from birth to death and in-between. These rituals are designed to ensure that every life experience becomes a possibility to be touched by the Divine.

ARULMIGU VELLIANGIRI ANDAVAR TEMPLE AT POONDI, COIMBATORE - Mount Velliangiri is a part of Western Ghats containing natural herbs & all kinds of natural flora & fauna. On the top of the hill, under a natural cave, Lord Shiva is worshipped in the form of Swayambu Linga. This Linga is surrounded by adjoining four Lingas. So it is named as "Panchalingas". The experience which one enjoys here, he compared it with the "Sri Amarnath Yatra" in J&K. This place is also called as "Dakshina Kailash", in view of the natural place, on which it situates.

ARULMIGU VANABADRAKALIAMMAN TEMPLE AT DEVIKOTTAM, METTUPALAYAM – The Temple is situated on the banks of River Bhavani. River Bhavani's old name seems to be "Vani" and also called as "Poo Vani". Nellimalai with full of greens is located adjacent to the Temple along with Nellithurai Village. The deity "Devi Bhadrakali" of this Temple purifies her devotees and has been bestowing their wishes and prayers. Goddess Vanabadrakali Amman is a Swayambumurthi. Realizing their wishes, women use to put their mangal sutras in the hundi. They tie a stone in the sacred tree for child boon. Those starting a trade or beginning marriage proposals use to place white and red flowers in separate packets and seek the permission of the Goddess. If they get the flower of their choice, it means the permission is granted. Above all, the Temple is known for the sheep animal sacrifice. It is said that Aravalli, Sooravalli, Veeravalli along with their 7 Sisters ruled this area long back. They belonged to Reddy Community and were experts in witchcraft. They were very powerful and were not conquered by any other rulers in that region. Many of them died in the war against these Sisters and some of them were taken as prisoners. The Pandavas and Dhuriyodhanas belong to this Era and were ruling in their own areas. The vigrahas of Bheema and Pagasooran were installed in the Temple. Devotees who visit the Vanabadrakaliamman Temple used to offer prayers to these two also.

THEN THIRUMALAI AT METTUPALAYAM – It is located on a natural hill amidst sylvian surroundings at an elevation of about 1000 ft. The majestic looking Gopuram above the sanctum sanctorum and the Temple complex in white and grey add to the grandeur of the shrine against the backdrop of the greenish blue Nilgiri Mountains. In designing this Temple, care has been taken to maintain the dignity and divinity of the place while making it pleasing and attractive to the pilgrims and worshippers by preserving the greenery around. The tall and beautiful Coconut and Arecanut palms that form the natural boundary and the evergreen Mango & Banana plantations & flower gardens that hedge the long central pathway leading to the main Temple are a delight to the eye that would enrapture any visitor. Lord Sri Venkateswara Swamy Vari is in the main Temple. Sri Garudalwar sits facing the Lord. There is a separate Temple for Shri Adhivarahaswamy on the northern side of the Hill opposite to the pushkarani. Shri Varadarajaswamy Temple is on the south eastern corner of the main Temple. In a separate shrine, Sannadhis of Sri Sudarshana Azhwar, Sri Yoga Narasimhar, the four Vaishnavite savants Sri Ramanujar, Nammazhwar, Thirumangai Azhwar and Sri Vedanta Desikar are housed. A Vaigunta Dwaram is also built. Walk up the ascending garden path have Dharshan of Sri Anjaneya on the footsteps of the hill. By climbing about 33 steps you reach the main Temple which has a 45 ft. high Dwajasthambam. On north of the bottom layer of the hill is the Ranga Mandapam. A small lotus Pushkarni has also been built.

POLLACHI - It is popularly called the coconut city. Its geographical closeness to the UNESCO World Heritage Site of Western Ghats ensures that it has amazing climate throughout the year. The main attractions are the Subramanyar Temple, which invite hundreds of devotees every month. Konga Cholas built this Temple of 'Lord Shiva' & named it as 'Thiruvahatheswaramudayar' Temple 700 years ago. This Temple has a high architectural value. In due course, it came to be called 'Subramanyar Kovil' & 'Lord Subramanyar' is worshipped here. Pollachi has a pleasant climate throughout the year. The Jaggery Market in Pollachi is Asia's biggest Jaggery Market. It also boasts one of the largest jaggery markets in Asia and the largest cattle market in South India. Pollachi also outshines in the field of film industry. It is famous for shooting of South Indian films.

ARULMIGU MASANI AMMAN TEMPLE AT ANAIMALAI – It is a highly revered shrine and situated at the confluence of Aliyar River and the Uppar Stream. The Temple enshrines Goddess Arulmigu Masani Amman as the presiding deity. The deity is seen in a lying posture measuring 15 ft from head to foot. The deity is depicted with four hands; two placed on the ground and two raised above. Other deities worshipped include Neethi Kal (stone of justice) and Mahamuniappan. Legend has it that during Lord Rama wanderings in search of Mata Sita, he stayed here and made an vigraha of the Mother with the sand available in the crematorium and worshipped. When girls face some physical problems when they attain puberty, Mother helps them in such situations ensuring their health. Most noteworthy feature of the Temple is that it serves as a welfare government listening to the grievances of the public, as a clinical dispensary rectifying the physical ills of people and as a court of justice easing the suffering of men and women. Devotees also place their grievances in writing and tie it in the hands of Ambica. It is strongly believed that solution would knock the doors of the applicant within 90 days. Hundreds of devotees flock to the Temple, especially woman, during Tuesdays and Fridays. As there were huge numbers of elephants here, the place is called Anaimalai – Anai-Elephant. Pathitrupathu, Sangam literature mentions the place as Umbarkadu. The Prasad offered in the Temple is called Pachilam Marundu. Women consume this and tie a black thread in the hand for child boon and for relief from the effects of spells and witchcrafts. The annual Kundam Festival celebrated here is a major draw attended by thousands of devotees amid much pomp and splendour.

BALAJI TEMPLE AT KARUMALAI, VALPARAI - The chief deity worshipped here is Lord Balaji, who is also known by other names like Venkateswara or Vishnu. The vigraha of Lord Balaji placed in the Temple is made of gold. Devotees from all over the world drop in to worship Lord Balaji and Poojas are performed like the Tirupati Balaji Temple.

DISTRICT – CUDDALORE (Railway Station – Vridhachalam/Tirupadripulyur/Chidambaram)

S. No.	Temple	Address	Type
1	Pataleeswarar Temple	Tirupadiripuliyur – 607002	Shiva
2	Thiruvathigai Veerateeswarar Temple	Panruti - 607106	Shiva
3	Sutha Sanmarkka Sathya Gnana Sabhai	Vadalur – 607303	Saint Vallalar
4	Viruthageeswarar Temple	Virudhachalam – 607303	Shiva
5	Thiruvahindrapuram Devanatha Swamy Temple	Tiruvandipuram – 607401	Vishnu
6	Arulmigu Thillai Kali Temple	Chidambaram – 608001	Mata
7	Arulmigu Chidambaram Thillai Natarajar Temple	Chidambaram – 608001	Shiva
8	Amirthakadeshwarar Temple	Melakadambur - 608304	Shiva
9	Bhuvanagiri Sri Raghavendra Mutt	Bhuvanagiri, Chidambaram – 608601	Saint Raghavendra Swami
10	Sri Bhuvaraha Swamy Temple	Srimushnam – 608703	Varaha (Vishnu)

PATALEESWARAR TEMPLE AT TIRUPADIRIPULIYUR – The town is named after the Pathiri Tree and the Puliyur, a tiger-legged Saint who obtained absolution in the area. It is dedicated to Lord Shiva. It was constructed during the Pallava and Medieval Chola periods. The Shaivite Saint Appar is believed to have adopted Shaivism at this Temple. There is a belief that by worshiping the God here single time is equal to 16 times worshiping the Lord Shiva in Kashi, 8 times in Thiruvannamalai and 3 times in Chidambaram.

THIRUVATHIGAI VEERATEESWARAR TEMPLE AT PANRUTI - The Temple is one of the biggest Shaivite Temples in Tamil Nadu. The Temple is dedicated to Lord Shiva. Here, Lord Shiva in Lingam Form is worshipped in Veerattaaneswarar and his concert Goddess Parvati is depicted as Thiripurasundari. Lord Shiva is Swayumbumurthi, large in size and having 16 stripes. Thiruvathigai is one of the eight Temples in Tamil Nadu, where the Lord Shiva is seen in his fierce form as the destroyer of evil. On the vimana, above the sanctum, one can see the sculpture of Tripura Samhara Murthy with twelve hands. This 'paadal petra sthalam' is mentioned in the Tamil Shaivite holy book Tevaram in 7th CE AD.

SUTHA SANMARKKA SATHYA GNANA SABHAI AT VADALUR - Arutprakasa Vallalar Chidambaram Ramalingam (5 October 1823 – 30 January 1874 [Attained Immortality]), whose pre-monastic name was Ramalingam, is commonly known in India and across the world as Vallalar. He was one of the most famous Tamil Saints and also one of the greatest Tamil poets of the 19th century and belongs to a line of Tamil Saints known as "gnanasiddhars" (gnana means higher wisdom). The Samarasa Suddha Sanmarga Sathiya Sangam was spread and passed on by him not only in theory but mainly in practice by his own way of living which by itself is an inspiration for his followers. Through the notion of Suddha Sanmarga Sangam, the Saint endeavoured to eliminate the caste system. According to Suddha Sanmarga, the prime aspects of human life should be love, connected with charity and divine practice leading to achievement of pure knowledge. Ramalinga Swami advocated the concept of worshipping the flame of lighted lamp as a symbol of the eternal Power.

VIRUTHAGEESWARAR TEMPLE AT VIRUDHACHALAM – In the remotest past, when Lord Brahma thought of creating the earth, he created water. Lord Vishnu happened to cut down the evil Madhukaidavas. The cut pieces of the bodies floated on water created by Lord Brahma. On seeing that Lord Brahma prayed to Lord Shiva to create the earth out of the hardened compound from the water and the flesh of the bodies. Lord Shiva appeared as a mountain. Lord Brahma who did not know this, created many different mountains. As they did not have space to exist, he was sorrowful. The Pranava God appeared and conveyed Lord Brahma the truth through gestures. Lord Brahma worshipped Lord Shiva who was the form of mountain. Lord Shiva created the earth combining the flesh and the water compounded in a hardened form. He called it medhini. He gave space for the mountains of Lord Brahma. Hence the mountain of Lord Shiva was named

Pazhamalai (Old Mountain). According to him, that Pazhamalai would be hard pressed on the earth appearing as Shivalinga. Those who worshipped it would get all they wished for. Thus, the oldest of all mountains is invisible, but the top layer of it is said to appear in the river-bed of Cuddalore at Vayalur, about four km north of Virudhachalam. Number five has a significance in this Temple. Murthis are five – Lords Vinayaka, Muruga, Shiva, Shakthi and Chandikeswara. Lord is praised by five names – Virudhagireeshwarar, Pazhamalai Nathar, Vruddhachaleswarar, Mudhu Kundreeswarar and Vruddhagiri. There are five Vinayakas in the Temple – Aazhathu Vinayakar, Mattru Uraitha Vinayaka, Muppillayar, Dasabhuja Ganapathy and Vallabha Ganapathi. Five Rishis had the darshan of Lord – Romesa, Vibasiddhu, Kumaradeva, Nada Sharma and Anavardhini. There five towers in the Temple at east, west, south, north and Kandarathithan (a Chola king) gopuram. There are five prakaras – called Thiruchutru in Tamil, they are Kailaya, Vanniyadi, 63 Nayanmar Chuttru and Panchavarna Chuttru. There are five Kodimarams - flag post with five Nandhis – Indra Nandhi, Vedha Nandhi, Athma Nandhi, Maalvidai Nandhi and Dharma Nandhi. There are five inner Mandaps – Artha, Idaikazhi, Thapana, Maha and Isai Mandapams. Outer Mandapams are 20 pillar mandapam, Deeparadhana, 100 pillar mandapam, Vipachithu and Chitramandapam. Five-time puja is followed in the Temple - Thiruvanandal, Kalasanthi, Uchi Kala, Sayaraksha and Arthajama at scheduled times from early morning till night. The Temple has five cars-Raths for Lords Vinayaka, Muruga, Pazhamalai Nathar, Mother Periyanayagi and Sri Chandikeswara. The place has five names – Tirumudhu Kundram, Vruddha Kasi, Virudhachalam, Nerkuppai and Mudhugiri.

DEVANATHA SWAMY TEMPLE AT TIRUVANDIPURAM – It is dedicated to Lord Vishnu. Constructed in the Dravidian style of architecture, the Temple is glorified in the Divya Prabandha, the early medieval Tamil canon of the Azhwar Saints from the 6th–9th centuries. It is one of the 108 Divyadesam dedicated to Lord Vishnu, who is worshipped as Devanathaswamy and his consort Lakshmi as Hemabhujavalli. The Temple in its current form is believed to have been built during the Medieval Cholas, with later expansion from Pandyas, Hoysala and Vijayanagara Empire. The Epigraphical Department has found more than 50 inscriptions in the Temple belonging to the Medieval Chola period. A Temple tower was erected during the reign of Koperunjinga, while the procedures of worship were accorded similar to other Temples during the reign of Maravarman Sundara Pandyan. The descendants of Ramanuja were given special provisions for worship during the period of Vijayanara Empire.

ARULMIGU THILLAI KALI TEMPLE AT CHIDAMBARAM - It was built by Chola King Kopperunjingan who ruled between 1229 and 1278. Legend says that Goddess Kali moved here after losing to Lord Shiva in the celestial dance contest. It was an argument that who is superior, either 'Shivam' (Lord Shiva) or Shakthi (Parvathi). In order to resolve thus, they performed a dance program at Chidambaram in front of Lord Vishnu, Lord Brahma and other deities. While they were playing dance, Lord Shiva was about to be defeated but knowing fully well, Lord Shiva played "Oorthuva Taandava" i.e. raising one leg above his head. This "Oorthuva Taandava" is one of the posture in the dance. It could not be played by the women folk due to their modesty and shyness. In this Goddess Parvathi could not play equally well to this posture and agreed her defeat. She had to go outside the borders of the town in order to contain her haughtiness and to teach a lesson that Shivam and Shakthi are both equally important in our life.

'Thillai Kali' is a deity in anger. This anger was pacified by Lord Brahma by chanting Veda and also praising her. Because of the penance of Lord Brahma, 'Kali' became cool. So that Goddess 'Thillai Amman' in this Temple seems with four faces.

ARULMIGU CHIDAMBARAM THILLAI NATARAJAR TEMPLE - This Temple is dedicated to Lord Shiva. The Temple has a deep mythical connection. When the name of the town was Thillai, a Lord Shiva shrine used to be there. Among the "Pancha Bootha" Temples, Chidambaram denotes the Skies. Kalahasthi denotes Wind. Kanchi Ekambareswar denotes land. All these 3 Temples are located in a straight line at 79 degrees 41 minutes Longitude. This can be verified. An amazing fact & astronomical miracle! The architecture of the Temple represents the link between arts and spirituality. The Temple was constructed during the 10th century, when Chidambaram used to be the capital of the Chola dynasty. The Cholas considered Lord Shiva as Nataraj as their family deity. Although Lord Shiva is the main deity of the Temple, it also represents major themes from Vaishnavism, Shaktism and others with all due reverence. The most unique characteristic of the Nataraj Temple is the bejewelled vigraha of Nataraj. The Temple has five main Halls or Sabhas namely the Kanaka Sabha, the Cit Sabha, Nritta Sabha, Deva Sabha and Raja Sabha. Nataraj happens to be one of the most momentous forms of Lord Shiva. Chidambaram Temple is based on the Human having 9 Entrances denoting 9 Entrances or Openings of the body.

Temple roof is made of 21600 gold sheets which denotes the 21600 breaths taken by a human being every day. Kalasas on the Golden Roof represent the 9 types of Sakthi or Energies. The 6 pillars at the Artha Mantapa represent the 6 types of Sashtras. The dance of Lord Nataraja is described as Cosmic Dance by Western Scientists. Now R & D, Western scientists have proved that at Lord Nataraja's big toe is the Centre Point of World's Magnetic Equator. Ancient Tamil Scholar Thirumoolar has proved this Five thousand years ago! His treatise ThiruMandiram is a wonderful scientific guide for the whole world. A couple of annual festivals and traditions that are celebrated with utmost grandeur and pomp are Aani Tirumanjanam and Margazhi Tiruvaadirai.

AMIRTHAKADESHWARAR TEMPLE AT MELAKADAMBUR - This Temple and village has around 1400 years old history and its figures in Devaram sung by both Aappar and Sambandhar. Lord Ardhanarishwara is a 12th CE Chola architecture by Kulothunga Chola-I. This is one of the Paadal Petra Sthalam. As per Sthala Puranam, Devas after Palazhi Mathanam began to consume it without worshipping Lord Vinayaka who angrily took away the pot to teach them a lesson. When he passed through this place, a drop of nectar fell on the earth and it became a Swayambhu Linga. The Temple structure is like of Chariot. One of the wheels is stuck to earth as Lord Vigneshwara pressed it to earth.

BHUVANAGIRI SRI RAGHAVENDRA MUTT – It is the birthplace of the Saint of South India, Raghavendra Swami. The town is also close to the birthplace of Saint Ramalinga Adigalar (town Maruthur). The word Bhuvanagiri is a combination of two Tamilized-Sanskrit words – Bhuvanam (means World) and Giri (means Mountain or Unmovable). Hence, the name Bhuvanagiri can mean "the place (world) that does not move". Bhuvanagiri is internally referred to by the local population as "Mel Bhuvanagiri" (Western Segment) and "Kezh Bhuvanagiri" (Eastern Segment).

SRI BHUVARAHA SWAMY TEMPLE AT SRIMUSHNAM – Constructed in the Dravidian style of architecture, the Temple is dedicated to Varaha, the boar-avatar of Lord Vishnu and his consort Lakshmi as Ambujavalli Thayar. The Temple had contributions from Medieval Cholas of the 10th century with later expansions by Thanjavur Nayak King Achuthappa Nayak. A granite wall surrounds the Temple enclosing all the shrines and the Temple tanks. There is a seven-tiered rajagopuram, the Temple's gateway tower. Six daily rituals and three yearly festivals are held at the Temple, of which the Chariot festival, celebrated during the Tamil month of Vaikasi (April–May), being the most prominent. The festival also symbolises Hindu-Muslim unity in the region – the flag of the chariot is provided by Muslims; they take offerings from the Temple and present to Allah in the mosques.

DISTRICT – DHARMAPURI (Railway Station – Dharmapuri)

S. No.	Temple	Address	Type
1	Dharmapuri Fort Temple	Dharmapuri – 636701	Shiva, Mata
2	Shri Kalabhairavar Temple	Dharmapuri – 636705	Bhairav
3	Chenraya Perumal Temple	Adhiyaman Kottai – 636807	Vishnu
4	Shri Theerthagirishwarar Temple	Theerthamalai – 636906	Shiva

DHARMAPURI FORT TEMPLE - This Temple is dedicated to Lord Mallikarjuneswarar and Goddess Kamatchi Ambal. It belongs to the period of Cholas. It is told that it is the Temple where Adhiyaman, the King of Thagadur used to visit and worship the deity here. This Temple attached very great importance to feminine, so the Lord himself has given superiority to the Goddess Sakthi; Lord Mallikarjuneswarar has been seated lower than Ambigai. Hanging sculptured pillar in the Temple is its special feature.

SHRI KALABHAIRAVAR TEMPLE AT DHARMAPURI - Devotees come here and worship in this Temple during the special and festival seasons from various places. The special poojas are being organised in Sundays and Poornima days.

CHENRAYA PERUMAL TEMPLE AT ADHIYAMAN - The capital of Adhiyamans, ancient rulers of Thakadoor, was Adhiyamankottam. The ruins of the roughly oval shaped fort is still there. The Chenraya Perumal Temple is the biggest of the lot which is held as a protected monument and which is believed to have been constructed both by the King Krishna Deva Raya and Hoysala Kings.

SHRI THEERTHAGIRISHWARAR TEMPLE AT THEERTHAMALAI – It is an important sacred place. The Temple is located at the top of a hillock. Chola and Vijayanagara Kings have donated liberally to this Temple. A lot of devotees throng the Temple during the Mahashivarathiri. Theerthamalai is declared as an important tourist spot in Dharmapuri District.

DISTRICT – DINDIGUL (Railway Station – Dindigul/Metupalaiyam)

S. No.	Temple	Address	Type
1	Arulmigu Nanmai Tharum Vinayagar Temple	Begumpur, Dindigul - 624001	Ganesh
2	Sri Anjali Varadha Anjaneyar Temple	Chinnalapatti - 624301	Hanuman
3	Agasthyar Puram	Sirumalai – 624304	Saint Agastya, Shiva
4	Arulmigu Dhandayuthapani Temple	Giri Veethi, Palani – 624601	Murugan
5	Arulmigu Soundarajaperumal Temple	Thadicombu – 624709	Vishnu
6	Shri Bhaktha Anjaneyar Temple	Vedasandur – 624710	Hanuman

ARULMIGU NANMAI THARUM VINAYAGAR TEMPLE AT BEGUMPUR - The Temple is dedicated to Lord Ganesha. The Temple is one of the Panchaloka Ganesha Temple. The Tirtham is Gopala Samudra on the shore of which Dindigul is located. The vigraha of Lord Ganesha is 16 ft. and it is Gajamukha and known as Raja Ganapathi. There are 107 vigrahas of Lord Ganesha in the front hall and also vigraha of Annamalai, Unnamali Amman & Srinivasaperumal. Ganesh Chaturthi is a major festival in addition to other festivals which are celebrated with great pomp & fervor.

SRI ANJALI VARADHA ANJANEYAR TEMPLE AT CHINNALAPATTI - The Temple is belived to be more than 5000 years old. The Temple is dedicated to Lord Hanuman. The Temple is also called Viswarupa Anjaneyar since the Murthy is 16 feet tall. The uniqueness of the vigraha is that it is made up of Saligrama stone. The Lord Hanuman stands with his hands folded with his mace (gadha)

resting on his legs. The vigraha is so huge and installed in such a way that the people could have darshan from a distance. The eyes of the Lord are polished well like black marbles and give an impression that He is looking at you from all angles. The Lord Hanuman is adorned with Vada, Jelebi, butter, fruits, flowers etc. Of the above, the most popular one is Vada Mala consisting of either 108 or 1008 vadas, based on the desire of the devotee. The Lord is decorated in Green when He is presented as Maruthi. Occasionally, He is also presented as a king in the Rajalankara. The place is very familiar due to the well known sarees.

SIRUMALAI – There are many high hills in the area. It is a dense forest region with a moderate climate throughout the year. With an altitude of 1600 metres above sea level, it contains diversified flora and fauna. The hill has 18 hairpin bends.

Agastya Puram – It is located in Sirumalai Hills named after the prominent Agastya Siddhar. It is a holy place where siddhas (monks) have lived since ancient days. The area is surrounded with medicinal herbs and plants. In the tip of the hill, there is historic Shivalingam, which dates back at least 500 years.

Sanjeevani Hills - The hill became famous when Lord Hanuman had to search for a certain herb and not finding it, he had to take the entire hill with him to cure Laxman. On his way back from Sri Lanka with the hill, a piece fell down here and it came to be known as Sanjeevani Hills.

Vellimalai Murugan Temple - The famous Lord Murugan Temple is located in the mountain which is away from 45 minutes climbing over the valley. This Temple is renowned throughout the neighbouring villages and towns.

ARULMIGU DHANDAYUTHAPANI TEMPLE AT PALANI – It is one of the Six Abodes of Lord Murugan. Sage Narada once visited the celestial court of Lord Shiva at Mount Kailash to present him a fruit, the gyana-palam (literally, the fruit of knowledge) that held in it the elixir of wisdom. Upon Lord Shiva expressing his intention of dividing the fruit between his two sons, Lord Ganesha and Murugan, the Sage counselled against cutting it. He decided to award it to whichever of his two sons first circled the world thrice. Accepting the challenge, Lord Karthikeya started his journey around the globe on his mount peacock. However, Lord Ganesha, who surmised that the world was no more than his parents Lord Shiva and Shakti combined, circumambulated them. Pleased with their son's discernment, Lord Shiva awarded the fruit to Lord Ganesha. When Lord Kartikeya returned, he was furious to learn that his efforts had been in vain. He left Kailash and took up his abode in Palani hills in South India. The vigraha of the Lord Muruga in Palani was created and consecrated by Sage Bogar, one of aaseevaham's (Ancient Tamil Culture) eighteen great siddhas out of an amalgam of nine poisons or navapashanam. The legend also holds that, the sculptor had to work very rapidly to complete its features but that he spent so much time in creating the face, he did not have time to bestow but a rough grace upon the rest of the body,

thus explaining the contrast between the artistic perfection of the face and the slightly less accomplished work upon the body. A shrine to sage Bhogar exists in the southwestern corridor of the Temple, which, by legend, is said to be connected by a subterranean tunnel to a cave in the heart of the hill, where sage Bhogar continues to meditate & maintain his vigil, with eight vigrahas of Lord Muruga. One of the main traditions of the Temple is the tonsuring of devotees, who vow to discard their hair in imitation of the Lord of Palani. Another is the anointing of the head of the presiding deity's vigraha with sandalwood paste at night, prior to the Temple being closed for the day. The paste, upon being allowed to stay overnight, is said to acquire medicinal properties, is much sought & distributed to devotees, as rakkalachandanam.

ARULMIGU SOUNDARAJA PERUMAL TEMPLE AT THADICOMBU - The main deity of the Temple is Lord Alagar. The main festival of the Temple is celebrated during the Tamil month of Chitrai, which falls in April and May. During this festival, the deity is offered regular prayer for 12 days. Those having prayer commitments to Madurai Azhagar can offer the same in this Temple. Those weak in education, suffering from lack of memory pray to Lord Hayagriva and Mother Saraswathi gracing from their shrines in the Prakara. On Tiruvonam star day, they perform special pujas to Lord Hayagriva with honey, coconut and a nivedhana made of jaggery powder and ghee and cardamom garlands. There is a separate shrine for Lord Dhanvanthari. On new moon days, abhishek is performed with oil and herbal paste known as Lehiyam. Chakarathalwar graces with deities attributed to Gayatri Mantra. Lord Narasimha graces with Ashtalakshmis. There are also shrines for Vishwaksenar, Twin Vinayaka, 10 incarnation forms of Lord Vishnu, Lakshmi Narasimha, Venugopala, Anjaneya and Swarna Bhairava. Arulmighu Soundaraja Perumal is found in the sleeping posture in this Temple and it is said that this place was previously known as Thaalamaapuri. Though it is a Vaishnava Temple, the sthalavriksha is the vilva tree. The Swarna Aakarsha Bairavar here is believed to solve people's economic problems. The sculptures in this Temple speak of the artistic skill of the builders and it is surprising to see even minute details like the nail tip, muscles, nerves and eyelashes sculpted with such finesse. Lord Soundararaja Perumal graces from sanctum sanctorum with His consorts Sridevi and Bhudevi in a standing form. As it is believed that Lord Kallazhagar of Madurai has connections with this place also, a festival of the Lord visiting the Kudaganaru River is celebrated as in Madurai in Vaigai River. The festival represents the grace of the Lord to Sage Mandukya. On each Tiruvonam star day, a deep is lit at the feet of the Lord. The procession deity would be following the lamp taken before Him. It is believed that those fortunate to have this darshan would be relieved of their sins.

SHRI BHAKTHA ANJANEYAR TEMPLE AT VEDASANDUR - Earlier, the Temple was called as a Tulasi Garden. Inside the shrine, Shri Bhaktha Anjaneyar is installed with a big Gada on his left hand with a graceful look. Moreover, a tall sculpture of Shri Bhaktha Anjaneyar with a height of about 51 foot has been installed above the shrine which resembles like a Tomb on the Temple. This peculiar attraction remains unique in the whole south of Tamil Nadu. Another Temple made of crystal stone is constructed inside the campus of sacred corner (Kanni Moolai) where Lord Shri Jeya Vera Anjaneyar is installed. It is

said that Lord stays in the sacred Corner. Every month on special days like full-moon day, Amavasya, Ekadashi, Jenma Nakshatra etc. special Puja's will be conducted without any interruption and on every Saturday after Puja Prasadam (Sacred food) is distributed. People from various places visit this Temple to have a glimpse of Shri Bhaktha Anjaneyar.

DISTRICT – ERODE (Railway Station – Erode)

S. No.	Temple	Address	Type
1	Arulmigu Arudra Kabaliswarar Temple	Eswaran Koil Street, Erode – 638001	Shiva
2	Arulmigu Velayutha Swamy Temple	Thindamalai, Erode – 638012	Murugan
3	Murugan Temple	Chennaimalai – 638051	
4	Kodumudi Temple	Kodumudi – 638151	Trinity
5	Sri Arulmigu Sangameswarar Temple	Bhavani Kudal, Bhavani – 638301	Sangam, Shiva
6	Arulmigu Bannari Mariamman Temple	Bannari, Sathyamangalam – 638401	Mata
7	Adhi Narayana Perumal Kovil	Ammapalyam – 638451	Vishnu
8	Amarapaneshwara Temple	Pariyur – 638452	Shiva
9	Arulmigu Kondathu Kaliamman Temple	Pariyur, Gobichettipalayam – 638476	Mata
10	Arulmigu Subramanyaswamy Thirukkkoil	Panchaimalai, Modachur, Gobichettipalayam – 638476	Murugan
11	Shri Nattatreeshwarar Temple	Kangayam – 638701	Shiva

ARULMIGU ARUDRA KABALISWARAR TEMPLE AT ESWARAN KOIL STREET - The main deity of the Temple is Lord Thondeswara. The main tower (Rajagopuram) is an outstanding example of architectural beauty. There are 108 Lingas carved on the Presiding Lord of the Temple, hence, it is a miracle and there are very pleasing darshan to the devotees. Another miracle is scientific based rays of Sun fall on the Lord on 25, 26 and 27th Masi month (February-March). Sun God graces in the front hall (Mandap) with his consorts. Lord Kanni Vinayaka graces in the Southwest corner, while the holy tree Vanni is at the west. The Temple has Pollapillayar with 63 Nayanmars in a sitting position. Lord Dakshinamurthy is near the Nayanmars. After passing through the Saptha Kannikas (Seven maidens) on the west, devotees can have the darshan of the paintings of Five Shivalingas representing five philosophies. It is believed that Sage Durvasa had installed Lord Shiva in a lying form (Pallikonda Kolam) in the Temple. The Lord is also praised in the names of Thondeeswarar, Cheddeswarar, Chozheeswarar and Arudra Kabaleeswarar. Epigraphy mentions the Temple as Thondeeswaram and the Lord as Thondeeswarar, Thondeeswaram Udaya Mahadeva, Thondeeswaram Udaya Thambiranar, Thondeeswaram Udaya Pidarar, Nayanar, Thondargal Nayanar, etc. Majority of the devotees are from the weaving community praying for development of the industry besides general public praying for removal of obstacles in marriage alliances, for child boon and progress in education. A poor weaver Thandavan living with his family in the area used to worship Lord Arudra Kabaleeswarar before proceeding to work. The Lord, with the intention of making the weaver's devotion to him known to all, went to his house when the weaver was absent. His wife alone was in the house. The Lord told her that he was suffering from biting cold and begged for a piece of cloth for cover. The woman told the Lord that she too had only one piece and promised what she could do for him and asked his address. She was told that he would be outside the Arudra Temple and left. Sooner Thandavan returned after work, his wife told him what happened during his absence. The weaver rushed to his boss seeking a piece of cloth on credit promising to pay the price in instalments and got the cloth. He took the cloth to the old man in the Temple, gave it to him.

When the Temple priest opened the sanctum sanctorum the next morning, he was surprised to see a new piece of cloth on the Lord and the Parivattam was absent. He informed the matter to all in the place. All gathered there including the weaver boss who said that he gave it to Thandavan. Thandavan narrated what happened. None believed the poor man, tied him in a pillar and began to beat him. Lord Shiva possessed on the son of the village head and shouted. "Despite one's own difficulties, he/she should not hesitate to help those poorer than them. To establish this Dharam, I acted through Thandavan" and explained what happened. Devotees began to throng the Temple to have the grace of Lord Arudra Kabaleeswarar.

ARULMIGU VELAYUTHA SWAMY TEMPLE AT THINDALMALAI - People strongly believe that there is abundance of prosperity in Erode because Lord Thindal Muruga is facing towards Erode. The Deepa Sthamba (Lamp post) in the Tindalmalai Murugan Temple has a different design compared to other South Indian Temples. Lord Vinayaka, the first while entering the Temple graces under a Bodhi Tree with Nagars while Siddhi Vinayaka graces with two Nagars. Nagar is an vigraha designed with two twisting snakes. Lord Muruga in the Temple is endearingly called Kuzhandai Velayuthaswami and Kumara Velayuthaswami. Idumban in the Temple enjoys a special reputation. The art of Vinayagar, Subramaniyar, Valli Theyvanai, Mayilvakanam, Sivan, Parvathi, Saraswathi, Laxmi is decorated in beautiful arch. Thannasi Cave is located northwest side from the Velayuthaswamy Temple. Theertha Sunai is located northeast side from the Thindalmalai.

CHENNIMALAI - This place has an ancient Temple of Lord Subramaniya Swamy. This Temple is on a small mountain which has 1320 steps and 4 KMs route for vehicles. The sculptures Valli and Deivanai are more artistic. Thaipusam, Panguni Uthiram, Surasamharam and Karthigai Deepam festivals are being celebrated here.

KODUMUDI - The special feature of this town is the Temple of Lord Shiva called Muchukundeswarar, Lord Vishnu called as Veera Narayan Perumal and Lord Brahma as Trinity installed in the same Temple complex. It is one of the important Temple of the District. 10 day Chithirai Utsavam [April-May] and Panguni Uthiram [Mar–Apr] are the most important festivals of the Temple.

SRI ARULMIGU SANGAMESWARAR TEMPLE AT BHAVANI KUDAL - Confluence of three Rivers - Cauvery, Bhavani and invisible Amudha at this pilgrimage place and termed as Mukkoodal. This is also called as the Triveni of the South. The Temple is an ancient Temple. This is one of the 276 Devara Padal Petra Shiva Sthalam and 3rd Sthalam in Kongu Nadu. Lord Shiva in this Temple is a Swayambhumurthi (self-manifested). The town, the Goddess of this Temple and the nearby River all have the same name - Bhavani. Bhavani is mentioned in the Hymns as Thiru Nana whereas it is now called Kooduthurai by the locals. The Temple is situated at the foothill of Padma Giri and is surrounded by four hills - Naga Giri, Veda Giri, Mangala Giri and Sanga Giri. The Temple has a beautiful five-tiered main tower (Rajagopuram) with two corridors. The Temple having been built by the first Pallava King, Mahendra Verman. It is also said that a British dignitary by the name of

William Garo donated a swing / cradle (Oonjal) made of ivory after he miraculously escaped from the collapse of his Rest house in the year 1802. He felt that he was saved by the Goddess herself and became an ardent devotee after this incident. His signature can be seen on the frame of the cradle. The legend is that Kuber, the Lord of wealth was visiting various Shiva Temples when he saw an Ilandhai Tree on the banks of Cauvery. He was astonished to see that a deer, a tiger, a cow, an elephant, a snake and a rat were drinking water without any sign of enmity. He felt that the peace and prosperity of this place could be due to the worship and penance performed by the holy men (Gandharvas) who inhabited this place. It is believed that Kuber heard a voice from the sky saying that this was the place where the Vedas had originated and that he would find a Shivalingam beneath the Ilandhai Tree. He was also advised to worship the Shivalingam to seek the Lord's blessings. Kuber worshiped the Lord and was blessed with a darshan. The Tree is still there and bears a lot of fruits. Another legend associated with this place is that Sage Vishwamitra is said to have installed another Lingam on the banks of River and worshipped it by chanting the Gayathri Mantram. Hence this Lingam is called "Gayathri Lingam". At the entrance, shrines of Kottai Vinayagar on the left and Kottai Anjaneyar on the right can be seen. Inside the main tower, shrines of Raja Ganapathi and Lord Muthukumaraswamy (Murugan) are present. Shrines of Lord Vinayakar, Lord Murugan and his consorts, Goddess Gajalakshmi, 63 Nayanmars, Jurahareshwarar (in dancing posture), "Pancha Bhootha" Lingams, Kashi Viswanathar, Goddess Visalakshi, Amirthalingam, and Jeshtadevi can be seen in the corridors. Separate shrines for Lord Adhikesava Perumal, Goddess Soundaranayaki and Yoga Narasimhar are also present in this Temple. Bhavani is a famous Sthalam for performing rituals to satiate one's ancestors. Here Parikarams are also conducted for all dhoshams, including Nagadhosham. During Adi Perukku day, large number of devotees can be seen taking a dip at the junction of Rivers Cauvery and Bhavani. Daily Komadha Pooja (Cow pooja) is performed in this Temple for the welfare of the populace. Saint Arunagirinathar in his Thirupugazh praised lord Murugan of this Temple. Lord Dakshinamoorthy's shrine is beautifully architected with intricate reliefs and iconographical sculptures. The procession vigrahas of all the 63 Nayanmars are beautifully arranged on a few steps (displayed like a "Navratri Golu"). Surprisingly, Thirumuruga Kripananda Vaariyaar also finds his place as the 64th Nayanmar. There are two identical stone vigrahas in front of the Ambal shrine. When water or milk is poured on them, it looks as if one of the vigrahas is smiling while the other is shedding a tear. This exemplifies the artistic excellence of the era. It is believed that those who take a dip at the confluence spot of Rivers Cauvery and Bhavani during the Solar and Lunar Eclipse can attain moksham (salvation). It is also believed that worshiping the Amirtha Lingam in this Temple can grant the boon of childbirth to couples.

ARULMIGU BANNARI MARIAMMAN TEMPLE AT BANNARI - Around 300 years ago, the Dana Nayakkan or Dhandanyakkan Forest is now called as "Bannari". This name Bannari for this great historical place originated because of the great Temple "Bannari Amman Temple". In ancient days, Tamil Nadu consisted of five division known as Chera Nadu, Chozha Nadu, Pandiya Nadu, Thondai Nadu and Kongu Nadu. Kongu Nadu was situated on the western side of Tamil Nadu. The Temple facing south and it is surrounding by thick forests with verdant vegetation on the southern, northern and western directions. The Artha Mantapa, Maha Mantapa and Shobana Mantapa enhance the

beauty of the Temple. Separate shrines for such Gods as Vinayaka, Bommairayan, Madeswara Sarugu Mariamman and Muniyappa are found in and around the Temple. The Bommarayan Temple is in Arthamandapam facing west side and the Ganesh Temple is in front mandapam facing east. God Matheshwaran is placed on a slab which is on the southern side of the Goddess Temple. Near the Temple pond, a small Temple facing west is constructed for Sarugu Mariamman is placed. On the west side of the Temple pond a big pit is present. To the left side of the way to the Temple pond, God Vandi Muniappar is placed on a slab.

ADHI NARAYANA PERUMAL KOVIL AT AMMAPALYAM – It is dedicated to Lord Vishnu and the chief deity of the Temple is Adhi Narayana Perumal. He is seen along with his companions Sri Devi and Bhu Devi. The specialty of the Temple is that there is a separate shrine dedicated to Lord Hanuman. The vigrahas of Sanjeevi Anjaneyar, Veera Anjaneyar and Alwars are seen inside the main Temple complex. Garuda Alwar is seen in front of the main sanctum. The main Gopuram of the Temple depicts the scene of narration of Bhagavad Gita, the holy book of Hindus. Vaikunta Ekadashi and other festivals of Vishnu are celebrated here.

AMARAPANESHWARA TEMPLE AT PARIYUR – It is dedicated to Lord Shiva and his consort Soundaranayaki Amman. The Temple itself is built completely of white marble and there are separate shrines dedicated to Lord Karthikeya with his wives Deivayanai and Valli, Ganesha known as Anukkai Vinayakar, and Nandhi, the vehicle of Lord Shiva. There are also shrines dedicated to Navagraha, Bhairava, Nayanmars and other Hindu Gods. Maha Shivaratri and Pradhosam is celebrated with much grandeur apart from other festivals of Lord Shiva and Murugan.

ARULMIGU KONDATHU KALIAMMAN TEMPLE AT PARIYUR – It is one of the famous and ancient Temple. The no. of deities are installed here Kondhathu Kaliyamman, Amaravidanga Peruman, Adhinarayanaperumal, Angalamman etc. Two shrines are dedicated to Lord Shiva and one shrine is dedicated to Lord Vishnu. The Temple has many cultural work. There are Vanni Vinayagar; Varasitthi Vinayagar; Sapthakannier Temple; Ponkaliyamman and Vinayagar. It is believed that who pray the Muniyappa Swamy, those are all get rid of problem like pilli, sooniyam, evil etc. The Temple have 28 stone pillar each and every pillar have different arts.

ARULMIGU SUBRAMANYASWAMY THIRUKKKOIL AT PANCHAIMALAI – Once upon a time, Saint Dhurvasar reached Kunnathur. He worshipped at Lord Shiva Temple at Kunnathur. Then he found out that a place called Modachur on the outskirts of present Gobi town is a good place to perform his routine worship of Lord Shiva. While worshipping, he wanted to have Darshan of Lord Subramanya. Not finding a Temple, he went into penance to find out the best place for the worship. He found through his penance that there is a Lord Subramanya Temple on a small hill near Modachur and the main deity faced west. The Saint reached the hill to find Lord Subramanya and continued his worship. He also learnt the similarities between the Temple and Palani where the Lord

is facing west as Dhandapani. All these events were forgotten as time proceeded. Around 1954, a landlord named P. K. Kuppuswamy Gounder visited the Temple. The life turned around for him that moment as he decided to renovate the Temple. This was after he felt that the Lord is not taken care by anybody. He understood the need for regular pooja and the care that the Temple craves. Starting then, the renovation moved into a fast pace. First Swarnabandhana Maha Kumbabishekam was performed in 1980 led by Thiru. P. K. Eswaran as renovation committee head. Since then, scores of people have joined the renovation committee and lot of work has happened in the Temple. The latest and second Swarnabandhana Kumbabishekam was performed around June 2006. It is uncommon to find Swarnabandhanam being done for the deities. You can really count the number of Temples where Swarnabandhanam (Gold plating the base of Vigraha where it stands) has been performed for deities in Tamilnadu and elsewhere. It should be noted that a large wooden chariot runs around Pachaimalai for every Panguni Uthiram during the Chariot (Ther) Festival. It is the largest wooden chariot in this area after Avinashi Ther. A golden chariot is available for Lord Murugan to play around his abode. The beauty of Dhandapani in golden chariot should be seen and as it is unexplainable. Arulmigu Dhandapani goes to golden chariot in his mount 'golden peacock' with complete golden attire. This cannot be seen even in Palani and Thiruchendur. Now, there is seven period regular poojai performed with two period of Abishekam daily. The night time Ardha Jaama Poojai is performed in comparison with Palani.

SHRI NATTATREESHWARAR TEMPLE AT KANGAYAM – It is dedicated to Lord Shiva located on Hillock Island inside the River Kaveri. To get rid of any kind of Dosham', Sage Agasthiar made a Lingam out of sand, placed it on the hillock in the middle of the River Cauvery, garlanded the Lingam with his Rudhratcha Malai and sat in deep meditation. It was believed that meditation would be disturbed at the dawn of the New Year. On the first day of "Chithirai" – Tamil New year day – Sage Agasthiar was disturbed from his meditation and he tried to remove his Rudhratcha Malai from the Lingam. Then he heard the holy voice of Lord Shiva asking him not to disturb the present setup and telling him that he went there not only to bless him alone but also his devotees and whoever goes there and worships him. Thus, Lord Shiva established himself in the Temple. Later Sage Agasthiar went to the south and finished his assigned work. He prepared an herbal tablet. On consuming the tablet he could present himself in any place he wanted to go. Using such power he came again to the hillock where he was welcomed and blessed by none other than Lord Muruga. About 1000 years ago, Chola Kings constructed the Temple and named the deity as Agastheeswarar. The Athee Tree located inside the Temple is believed to be 3000 years old. Devotees throng this Temple in thousands on Tamil New Year day and offer prayers to Him to get His blessings.

DISTRICT – KALLAKURICHI (Railway Station - Chinna Salem)

S. No.	Temple	Address	Type
1	Ulagalanda Perumal Temple	Thirukkoilur - 605757	Vishnu
2	Sri Veeratteswarar Koil	Thirukkoilur – 605757	Shiva
3	Sri Aadhi Thiruvarangam Perumal Temple	Kallakurichi – 605802	Vishnu
4	Jain Temples	Thirunarungondai – 606107	Jain

THIRUKKOILUR ULAGALANDA PERUMAL TEMPLE - The presiding deities of the Lord Vishnu Temple are Ulagalanda Perumal (Thiruvikrama Swami) and Pushpavallithayar. Kabilar Kundru is also picnic spot, which is situated in the middle of the River Pennayar. Kabilar was Saint here and his last resting place is maintained by the state Archaeological Department.

SRI VEERATTESWARAR KOIL AT THIRUKKOILUR – This Temple is one of the eight Veeratta Temples. Saints Sambandar, Appar and Sundarar had sung the praise of the Lord in their Thevaram hymns. Addressing the ignorant struggling for enlightment, Saint Gnana Sambandar advises them saying "If you wish to know what is eternal & avoid letting your legs into mud & struggle to pick it up, think of the one with Ganga on His turf gracing at Veerattanam. It so happened that the world became dark when Mother Parvathi covered the eyes of Lord Shiva which are but Sun & Moon in a play. The darkness took the form of a demon. Andhaka means darkness & also ignorance. Life becomes dark due to ignorance. Lord Shiva struck the Andhaka-darkness giant on his head with a club in his Hand. The head of the demon began to bleed. Every drop of blood that fell on earth grew into a demon & war continued. Mother Parvathi prevented the blood from falling down by collecting it in a bowl. The blood that fell down became 8 vertical & 8 horizontal lines crosswise & made 64 squares. With His power, Lord Shiva created 64 Bhairavas for each square & prevented further production of demons and blessed the Devas in the celestial world. This later came to known as Vasthu Shanti Puja for Bhairavas. This also personifies the destruction of ignorance leading to enlightenment. The main deity is Veeratteswarar & Utshavaris Anthakashuvath Moorthy. The Ambal is Periya Nayagi, Shivanathavalli & the Holy Tree is Sarakkontrai. The Holy Water is Thenpennai and the historical name was Anthakapuram, Thirukkaivelur.

SRI AADHI THIRUVARANGAM PERUMAL TEMPLE – It is one of the 108 Divya Desams Sthals. It was established on the 1st incarnation of Lord Vishnu, hence, it is more popular and ancient. A demon called Somugan, who belonged to the asura pedigree obtained immortality and many boons by performing rigorous penance. He vanquished the earth and the heaven and made the sages and devas his slaves and ordered them to obey him. He imprisoned Lord Brahma and seized the Veda Mandras from him. Lord Brahma, Devas and the Sages went to Sri Narayanan (Vishnu) and prayed him to protect them by quelling Somugan. Sri Narayan went to fight Somugan. A terrific war broke out between them. Somugan exhausted all his magical tricks and became tired. He feared that Sri Narayan would killed him, if he stayed there anymore. He went inside sea and hide themself. Sri Narayan quelled with Somugan by taking the incarnation of 'Mathsya' and retrieved the Vedas. The Devas and the Sagas became elated and worshipped Sri Narayanan at Utharangam. The main deity is Ranganatha Swamy (Lord Vishnu) and the Ambalis Rangavalli Thayar. The Holy Water is Chandra Pushkarani, Thenpennai River. Various festivals such as Saturday of Purarttasi, Pournami and Vaikunda Ekadasi are celebrated here.

THIRUNARUNGONDAI - Hillock at the village contains a Jain Cave and two Temples, which are dedicated to Lord Parsvanatha and Chandraprabhu. Cave served as the monastery of the monks of Virasangha in the 8th– 9^{th}century. Rich collection of bronze vigrahas are found in the Temple. Annual festival (Jan-Feb) celebrated on a grand scale and attended by Jains from all over Tamil Nadu.

DISTRICT – KANCHEEPURAM (Railway Station – Kanchipuram/MGR Chennai Ctl/Arakkonam)

SAPTAPURI - Kanchipuram is a land of thousand Temples. The district is a spectacular site of Temples and the district headquarters is also known as the Temple city. The Temples of Kanchipuram district reflect the glorious traditions of South India. Sriperumpudur is another place of tourist interest in the district. It is the birth place of Saint Ramanuja, the father of Visishtadvaida philosophy of Vaishnavism and hence, an important pilgrim centre for the Vaishnavites. Kamakodi Peetham and Kammakshi Amman Temple are closely associated with the life of Shankaracharya. The Kamakoti Peetham is enshrined in the Sri Chakra just in front of Sri Devi and all pujas and sacrifices are offered to the Sri Chakra. Sri Ekambareswara Temple is the most famous Lord Shiva Temple. Kailasanatha Temple was constructed by the Pallava Dynasty during the first quarter of the 8th Century. The Temple is built of red sandstone and has innumerable carvings of Pallava art, of which the Urdhva Thandava dance of Shiva and the laughing face of Parvati are worth seeing. Another famous Temple of this district is the Sri Ulagalandar Temple. The Temple was constructed in the Chola period. Some of the other Temples of this district are Sri Vardaraja Perumal Temple, Vaikuntha Perumal Temple, Sri Vijayaraghava Perumal Temple, Sri Subramaniya Swami Temple, Jain Temples and Kumarakottam Temple etc. Apart from the Temples, some of the other major attractions are Muttukkadu (a large lake), Bird Sanctuary at Vedantangal, Sadras, Anna Memorial, etc. In Vaishnavism Hindu theology, Kanchipuram is one of the seven Tirtha (pilgrimage) sites for spiritual release. Of the 108 Holy Temples of Lord Vishnu, 15 are located in Kanchipuram. The city is particularly important to Sri Vaishnavism but is also a holy pilgrimage site in Shaivism. The city is most famous for its silk production and old Temples. The city is located on the banks of Palar River. The city also attracts tourist and foreigners in plenty due to its rich culture and heritage. There are many eminent scholars like C.N. Annadurai who were born in this city.

S. No.	Temple	Address	Type
1	Arulmigu Subramanya Swami Temple	Kunnathur - 600069	Murugan
2	Srinivasa Perumal Temple	Semmancheri – 600119	Vishnu
3	Sri Perumal Temple	Tiruneermalai - 600132	Vishnu
4	Ramanuja Swamy Temple	Sriperumbudur – 602105	Saint Ramanuja
5	Dakshinakshetra	Kannathur Reddykuppam, Post Kovalam, Chennai – 603112	Jagannath (Vishnu)
6	Nityakalyana Perumal Temple	Thiruvidanthai – 603112	Varaha (Vishnu)
7	Sri Veerapathiradhasapuja Anjaneyar Temple	Ananthamangalam - 603307	Hanuman

S. No.	Temple	Address	Type
8	Sri Sundara Varadararaja Perumal Temple	Uthiramerur – 603406	Vishnu
9	Sri Ashtabuja Perumal Temple	Gandhi Road, Ennaikaran, Kancheepuram – 631501	Vishnu
10	Arulmigu Devaraja Swamy Temple	Kancheepuram – 631501	Vishnu
11	Arulmigu Ekambaranathar Temple	Kanchipuram – 631502	Shiva
12	Sri Jurahareswarar Temple	Kanchipuram - 631502	Shiva
13	Kailasanathar Temple	Kanchipuram – 631502	Shiva
14	Kanchi Kamakoti Peetam	Kanchipuram – 631502	Adi Shankaracharya
15	Kanchi Kamakshi Ambal Devasthanam	Kamakshi Amman Sannathi Street, Kanchipuram – 631502	Shakti Peetha
16	Sri Perarulaalan Perumal Temple	Kanchipuram – 631502	Vishnu
17	Jeenaswamy Trilokyanathar Temple	Thiruparuthikundram – 631502	Jain
18	Sri Ulagalanda Perumal Temple	Kamakshi Amman Sannidhi Street, Periya, Kanchipuram – 631502	Vishnu
19	Sri Vaikuntha Perumal Temple	Kanchipuram – 631502	Vishnu
20	Vallakottai Subramaniya Swami Temple	Vallakottai - 631604	Murugan

ARULMIGU SUBRAMANYA SWAMI TEMPLE AT KUNNATHUR - The Temple is dedicated to Lord Murugan & this is the only Temple where Lord Muruga is facing north. Garbhagraiham of this Temple is very unique. Lord Murugar is worshiped here with Valli and Deivanai taai but we can see only Lord Murugar if standing straight to sannidhi. It is believed that Lord Subrahmanya did partisthta of a Shiva Lingam in the foot of the hill which is known as Kandhaleeswarar.

SRINIVASA PERUMAL TEMPLE AT SEMMANCHERI - The Archaeological Department confirms that the present structure could be around 500 years old but locals call it a 1500 years old Temple. It is said that a Pallava King who lost his eye sight got back his vision on worshipping Srinivasa Perumal here. Even now, people believe that anyone with eye problems get it cured by worshipping the Perumal here. This is also said to be a Prahtanasthalam for the unmarried and childless couples.

SRI PERUMAL TEMPLE AT TIRUNEERMALAI - The Temple is old and famous. The Temple is dedicated to Lord Vishnu.

SRIPERUMBUDUR - Famous for the Ramanuja Swamy Temple, which is also known as the Adikesava Temple, Sriperumbudur lies on the outskirts of Kanchipuram. This must-visit Temple has three vigrahas of Saint Ramanuja that were made during the Saint's lifetime in Srirangam, his birthplace of Sriperumbudur and Melkote, in the neighbouring state of Karnataka. In front of the shrine of Sri Ramanuja lies a resplendent golden mandap, which was built by the erstwhile Maharaja of Mysore. Four kalasas, representing the four Vedas, have been built on this mandap. There are several vigrahas that sit on the mandap, under the kalasas, which is why the mandap looks like a Temple itself. On the day of Vaikunda Ekadasi, which typically falls between the months of December and January, both the Saint and Lord Vishnu, to whom the Temple is dedicated, are worshipped. On this occasion, the belled doors of the Temple are opened so devotees can have the Lord's darshan. Other festivals, such as Masi Pooram in February-March and Panguni Uthiram in March-April are celebrated with much pomp and show.

DAKSHINAKSHETRA AT KANATHUR REDDYKUPPAM – The Temple is unique in many respects. The lofty granite shrine in Odiyan architectural style and dedicated to Lord Jagannath along with six other shrines (Ganesh, Shiva, Lakshmi, Vimala, Navagraha and Yajna Nursingha) overlooks the sea in awe-inspiring splendour. A marble floored meditation hall and an open Yajnamandap are added advantages. A unique union of three auspicious trees (Neem, Banyan and Peepal) standing in the middle of Vahana-mandap next to the Vinayaka Shrine is believed to have divine sanction as Kalpataru.

NITYAKALYANA PERUMAL TEMPLE AT THIRUVIDANTHAI – The history of this Temple dates back more than 2000 years. It is near the Bay of Bengal seashore. The beautiful deity here is Varaha Perumal, otherwise called Nitya Kalyana Perumal. The Temple was built by Pallavas. A large Temple tank is in front of the Temple, known as the Kalyana Theertham. There is a separate shrine for Komalavalli Nachiyar. Perumal appears majestically in his standing form on Adisesha facing east and his consort on his left thigh. The Vimana above the sanctum sanctorum is called Kalyana Vimanam. There is also separate shrine for Andal. The Temple follows Thenkalai Sampradayam. Sage Markandeya and King Mahabali visited this holy place. The deity is believed to bestow marital bliss to the unmarried devotees who worship him. Those who want to get married offer two garlands. After Puja, the priest gives back one of the garlands. The person wears that garland and does Pradakshinam around the Temple. Later they bring the Garland home. This pooja blesses one to have early and happy married life. After marriage as a thanksgiving gesture, the couple revisit the Temple and offer flower garlands to the Lord. They carefully bring the old garlands from home and offer them to the divine tree in this Temple, which is a Punnai Tree (Calophylluminophyllum). People without children also worship here and it is believed that the couple will be blessed by a child at the earliest.

SRI VEERAPATHIRADHASAPUJA ANJANEYAR TEMPLE AT ANANTHAMANGALAM - The Temple is dedicated to Lord Hanuman. Lord Hanuman has ten hands & three eyes and each hand holds special weapon of each God & Goddess, hence, known as Trinethra Dasabuja Anjaneyar. As per legend, after Lanka war, all asuras were killed but two of them i.e. Raktha Bindu & Raktha Rakkadhan have survived. Lord Rama instructed Lord Hanuman to killed these two asuras and he gave his bow & arrow to Lord Hanuman and other God & Goddess also gave their weapons such as Conch & Discus, Trident, Vajrayutha, Whip & butter ball, Axe & deer and Lord Shiva also gave third eye & wings by Garuda. Lord Hanuman killed the two asuras by dragging them out of water. On his way back Lord rested at this place.

SRI SUNDARA VARADARARAJA PERUMAL TEMPLE AT UTHIRAMERUR – This Temple is about 1200 years old built by Nandhi Varma with the help of Paramesa Vathan, an extremely skilled Vasthu Sasthra expert. This Temple has numerous inscriptions about Chola and Vijayangaram regime. The rituals in this Temple are performed as per Krishna Yajuveda Vaikasana Agamam. Lord Vishnu is generally seen in either of the 3 forms, Nindraan (Standing), Irundhaan (Sitting) or Kidandhaan (Reclining). This is one of the few tempstandingles where you can have dharshan of Maha Vishnu in all this 3 forms. The sanctum also houses the vigrahas of Sridevi and Bhudevi on either sides of Sundaravarada. There are smaller shrines of Lakshmi Narasimha, Rama, Andal, Arjuna, Krishna, Yoga Narasimha and Manavala Mamunigal. Another set of steps leads to the top floor leading to the sanctum of Ananda Padmanabha in reclining posture in his serpent bed of Adisesha. The vigrahas of Bhudevi and Sage Markendeya are seen in the sanctum. The roof of the sanctum is called Padma Kosthta Ashtanga Vimana, which has sculptural depiction of the nine different forms of Lord Vishnu. The Temple tank, called Vairameghatataka, located to the west of the Temple, is mentioned in a lot of inscriptions.

SRI ASHTABUJA PERUMAL TEMPLE AT KANCHEEPURAM - This Temple was built by Thondaiman Chakravarthy, who is popularly named as Vayiramoghan. The Temple is one of the 108 Divyadesams of Perumal. A separate Mangalasasanam (hymns) is addressed to Goddess by Azhwar only in this Temple. Deviating from the normal posture with four arms, Lord Vishnu is in standing posture with 8 arms called as Ashtabuja Perumal. He holds Chakaram, Sword, a Flower and an Arrow on the right hands and Sangu, Bow, Kedayam and Gadha on the left. He is seen having Mahalakshmi in his chest and sported with a garland made of Saligrama. This Temple with a single prakaram has a 3 tiered rajagopuram in its northern entrance and the Temple tank is Gajendra Pushkarini. There are

shrines to Alwars, Chakra, Sarabeswara, Bhuvaraahar, Aandal, Peyalwar and Hanuman. There is a separate shrine for Pushpakavalli Thayar, the consort of Perumal. There is a four pillared hall named Friday Mandapam in front of the shrine. It is customary to worship Thayar before proceeding to the worship of Perumal. There is a shrine for Varaha Perumal in the complex, who is sported in seated posture under the hoods of two serpents. As per Hindu legend, once there was an argument between Goddess Saraswathi, the consort of Lord Brahma and Lakshmi on superiority. They went to Indra, the King of celestial deities. Indra judged Lakshmi as superior and not satisfied with his argument, Goddess Saraswathi went to her husband, Lord Brahma. He also chose Lakshmi to be the superior one. Goddess Saraswathi was unhappy with the decision and decided to stay away from Lord Brahma. Lord Brahma did a severe penance praying to Lord Vishnu and did an Aswametha Yagna. Goddess Saraswathi was still angry that the yagna, which usually is done along with consorts was done alone by Lord Brahma. She tried to disrupt the penance in various ways but Lord Vishnu interfered in all her attempts. After all the demons were killed by Lord Vishnu, who were sent by Goddess Saraswati to destroy the yagna (penance), she finally sent a ferocious Sarpam (snake). Lord Vishnu took the form of Ashtabhuja Perumal holding eight different weapons to kill the snake. The snake is found on the Vaayu end of the yaagasala as "Sarabeswaran" in this Temple. The Boodha Ganas of Lord Siva, cursed by Lord Shiva himself for their mistake, prayed to Lord Vishnu on the bank of Anantha Saras Theertham at Sriperumbudur, to get relieved of the curse. Lord Vishnu appeared before them and blessed them. As an act of Gratitude, Bhooda Ganams constructed this Temple for Lord Vishnu. Hence this is also called as Bhoodhapuri.

Metraleeswarar Temple at Piaaiyarpalayam - The Temple is dedicated to Lord Shiva. The Temple is one among the Paadal Petra Sthalamas. There are two Sanctum Sanctorums which are of Lord Shiva as Metraleeswarar, Odha Urugeeswarar and Goddess Parvati as Metrali Nayagi. Lord Shiva is Swayambhu here as Paramshiva & Goddess Parvati as Parasakthi here. It is believed that Lord Vishnu did penance at this place and Sambandar visited here and praised Lord Shiva without knowing that Lord Vishnu is here. Lord Vishnu attained the Shivalinga form after hearing the Sambandar.

Swami Ramanujar Avathara Sthalam / Than Ugarndha Thirumeni Sthalam - On a Thursday, in the Tamil Month of Chitrai, on Arudra [Thiruvadirai] Star, Sukla Pakshapanchami, in the year 1017, Sri Ramanujar was born to the vaishnavite couple Asuri Keshavachar and Kandhimathi. He is also called as Bhashyakar, Emperumanar, Elayai Alwan, Yathirajar, Udayavar. During the 10 day Chitirai Festival or Brahmotsavam, Sri Ramnujachariar graces from the mandapam where he was born. On His Janma Star [birth star] day, he is placed in a cradle as a child and fed with milk in a conch. Parivattam [Holy Turban] from 36 Divya Desams is offered to Sri Ramanuja as a mark of respect and devotion during this festival. Before attaining the Vaikunta Prapthi [the lotus feet of the Lord], Sri Ramuja hugged the Archa Vigraham brought by his Disciple Mudhalianandan's son Kanthadai Annan, believed to have transferred all his powers and instructed the disciple that same to be installed in the Temple. The Vigraham was consecrated in a separate Shrine at Sri Perumbudur and it is also called as the Than Ugarndha Thirumeni. It is a Pancha Ulogam [Five Metal] Vigraha that is still existing and worshipped by thousands of devotees regularly. The Temple does not have a swargavasal [Paramapada Entry] since it is believed that, praying to Swami Ramanuja itself is a way to reach vaikuntam. On the Vaikunda Ekadasi day, Lord and Acharya grace together in the Boodhakal Mandapam. As a formality, only the belled doors of the shrine are opened on the occasion. Eravadai Theertham is the special prasadam to the devotees. After Abishekam to Ramanujar, the vasthram worn by Ramunja Vigraham is squeezed & water collected from that is distributed as special prasadam to the devotees. It is believed that it cures all types of diseases and extends harmony in the family life. A dip in the Anantha Sarasu gives relief from ill effects of Rahu-Kethu Dosham & also relief to devotees with Kaala Sarpa Dosham.

SRI VARADARAJA PERUMAL TEMPLE AT KANCHIPURAM - The Temple is dedicated to Athivaradaraja, an incarnation of Lord Vishnu. There is a huge Vigraha of Lord made out from the wood of Athi (Fig) Tree and preserved in an underground chamber of Temple tank known as Ananta Tirtham and the same is brought out once in every forty years. The Vigraha is worshipped for 48 days and allowed for darshan after which it is again immersed in the Temple tank. It is believed that heavy downpour occurs after the Vigraha immersed to fill the tank. The Temple is one of the Divya Desams, the 108 Temples of Lord Vishnu believed to have been visited by the 12 poet saints, or Alwars. One of the greatest Hindu scholars of Vaishnava Vishishtadvaita philosophy, Ramanuja is believed to have resided in this Temple. The Temple along with Ekambareswarar Temple & Kamakshi Amman Temple in Kanchipuram is popularly known as Mumurtivasam (abode of trio), while Srirangam is referred to as: 'Koil' (meaning: "Temple") and Tirupati as: 'Malai' (Meaning: "hill"). Among the Divya Desams, Kanchipuram Varadaraja Perumal Temple is known as: 'Perumal Koil'. This is one of the most sacred places for Vaishnavites. This has become a centre of attraction with exquisite carvings and delicate works of art. The Tiruppanies done by Alam Kheer Basha of Delhi during 1645 was inscribed on the walls of Temple. The Temple has 19 vimanams & around 400 pillared hall. It has a similar marriage hall, commemorating the celestial wedding of Lord Vishnu with Goddess Lakshmi. The Brahmotsavam during (May/June) is main festival of the Temple.

ARULMIGU EKAMBARANATHAR TEMPLE AT KANCHEEPURAM – The Temple is dedicated to Lord Shiva. It is one of the largest Temples in Kancheepuram. The origin of this Temple goes back to the time of the Pallavas and the Chola rulers extended it later. The great ruler of the Vijaynagar Empire, Krishnadevaraya, built its 59 meter high Gopuram and massive outer walls in the early 16th century. The highlight of this Temple is its thousand-pillared mandapam (hall). It is one of the five major Lord Shiva Temples of Pancha Bootha Sthalams (each representing a natural element) representing the element – Earth. Reaching a height of 59 metres, the Temple's Raja Gopuram (the entrance tower to the Temple) is one of the tallest in south India. The Temple's inner walls are decorated with an array of 1008 Sivalingams. No separate shrine for Parvati exists here. There is a small shrine for Lord Vishnu named Thiru Nilaaththingal Thundathan. Here, the Lord Vishnu is prayed as Vamana Murthy. The sthala-virutcham is a 3,500 year old Mango Tree in the outer court, which is revered as most sacred and it is believed that if it is worshipped by childless couple, they will be blessed with a child. As per legend, once Parvati was doing tapas under the Temple's ancient Mango Tree. In order to test her devotion Lord Shiva sent fire on her. Goddess Parvati prayed to her brother, Lord Vishnu for help. In order to save her, he took the Moon from Lord Shiva's head and showed the rays which then cooled down the tree as well as

Parvati. After that, Lord Shiva again sent the River Ganga to disrupt Parvati's tapas. Parvati Devi prayed to Ganga and convinced her that both of them were sisters and so should not harm her and so Ganga did not disturb her penance after that. Then Parvati made a Shivalinga out of sand and got united with Lord Shiva. According to another legend, it is believed that Parvati worshipped Lord Shiva in the form of a Prithivi Lingam (or a Lingam improvised out of sand), under a Mango Tree. Legend has it that the neighboring Vegavati River overflowed and threatened to engulf the Shivalingam and that Parvati or Kamakshi embraced the Lingam. Shiva touched by the gesture materialized in person and married her. In this context, he is referred to as Tazhuva Kuzhainthaar ("He who melted in her embrace") in Tamil.

SRI JURAHARESWARAR TEMPLE AT KANCHIPURAM - The Temple is dedicated to Lord Shiva. The Temple belongs to 8th CE and the same was built by Pallava King Narasimhavarman - II. As per legend, a demon Juraha was killed by Lord Shiva here, hence, the Temple got the name Jurahareshwarar. There is a Shivalingam and Vigrahas of Kubera, Ganesha, Subrahmanaya, Karthikeya and others established in the Temple. The Temple tank is called Vepperi Kulam. The Temple is famous for its splendid Vimana and Nandi. The Temple is a protected monument & is maintained by Archeological Survey of India.

KAILASANATHAR TEMPLE AT KANCHEEPURAM – The Temple is dedicated to Lord Shiva. It is the oldest Temple of Kanchi. It reflects the freshness and simplicity of the early Dravidian style of Temple architecture and was built by the Pallava King Rayasimha. It can also be described as the worthy successor of the rock Temples at Mahabalipuram, which were also built by the Pallava rulers. The bases of the pillars in the Temples at Mahabalipuram have seated lions while at Kanchipuram; the confident grimacing lions stand on their hind legs, as if ready to pounce on anyone trying to harm the Temple. This Temple was constructed in the late seventh century and Rayasimha's son added the front portion later. The eighth century remains of murals within the Temple are an indication of the magnificence of the original Temple. There are 240 or so panels engraved into the Temple walls that display Nagara and Pallava Grantha scripts; incidentally, some of the earliest works of calligraphy are also found at this Temple. It holds one of the earliest sculptures of Jyeshta Lakshmi (Moodevi) and Vaali as well. There are 60 smaller shrines within this Temple dedicated to Lord Shiva, Goddess Parvati (Lord Shiva's consort) and their sons Ganesh and Murugan. The Shivalingam in this Temple is 10 foot high. It is famous for its magnificient Vimana, the gopuram over the sanctum sanctorum. Lord Shiva's vehicle, Nandi (bull god), is also worshipped here. It speaks volumes of architectural beauty that flourished in the reign of Pallava king. The foundation of the Temple is laid on granite tones while the superstructure is carved out of sandstone. Currently the Temple is well maintained by the Archaeological Survey of India.

KANCHI KAMAKOTI PEETAM - It is believed to be established by Adi Sankara himself as Moolamnaya Sarvajana Peetam. Kanchi Mahaswami Sri Chandrasekarendhra Saraswathy Swamigal, the 68th pontiff of this Mutt lived for 100 years and his Brindavanam is located inside the Mutt's premises. Sree Jayendra Saraswati Swamigal and Sankara Vijayendra Swamigal are the 69th and 70th pontiffs of this Mutt respectively. It was established in the year 482 BC and has the distinction of an unbroken line of 70 Acharyas (spiritual leaders). From available biographical

information, it is learnt that Shankaracharya placed one of the five Sphatika Lingas got at Kailash and kept the Yoga Linga for his own personal worship and that of his successors at Kanchi. It may be noted that the name of Sri Shankaracharya is found only in the official seal of Kanchi Kamakoti Matha. Bhagavatpada Sankara got Kanchi city remodeled and also caused the reconstruction of the three principal Temples of Kanchi viz. the Temples of Sri Ekamranatha, Devi Kamakshi and Sri Varadaraja with the assistance of Rajasena, Ruler of Kanchi. Sankara consecrated the Srichakra before Devi Kamakshi and thereby secured her bounteous grace for devotees having her darshan. This 120 foot Vigraha in Enathur, near Kanchipuram, is the largest Vigraha of Sri Adi Shankara in the world. This Vigraha was inaugurated in the benign presence of Their Holinesses Pujyasri Jayendra Saraswathi Shankaracharya Swamiji and Pujyasri Sankara Vijayendra Saraswathi Shankaracharya Swamiji by the King of Nepal. Right behind the Vigraha is an International Library that contains a large and rare collection of historic manuscripts, collected from various parts of the country during the Vijaya Yatras performed by Their Holinesses to various parts of the country. Efforts are being made to preserve the manuscripts in their original form, as also in electronic form through digitization.

MAHASHAKTIPEETHAM – SRI KANCHI KAMAKSHI AMBAL DEVASTHANAM - The impressive Temple is dedicated to Goddess Parvati in the form of Kamakshi or the Goddess of Love. It is a 12thcentury Temple in the heart of the town. "Ka" means Goddess Saraswathi (God of Education), "Ma" means Goddess Lakshmi (God of Wealth), "Akshi" means Eye. The name in full refers Kamakshi with Goddess Saraswati and Goddess Lakshmi as her both eyes. It is an important Sakthi Sthalam called as the "Nabisthana Ottiyana Peetam". The Goddess Kamakshi prevails in the form of Shakti. There are 51 Shakti Peethas across the country. The Temple also has a golden Gopuram on the Sanctorum of Goddess Kamakshi deity. The Temple sanctorum consists of a deity "Adivaraha Perumal" which is one of the 108 Vaishnaivaite deity worship Temple and it can be reached by passing through a large mandapam (hall) with ornate pillars. Kanchi is also called as Satyavrita Kshetra. The Goddess worshipped Lord Shiva by creating a mud Vigraha in Kanchi. At that moment, Lord Shiva incarnated as Kamba River with high tides to test the worship of the Goddess, the Goddess grasped the Vigraha closely with her two hands from eroding in the tides. This prevented the Vigraha from getting eroded in the floods. The Goddess also performed Pooja by sitting in a needle tip surrounded by "Panchakagni" (surrounded by 5 fires) to free herself from the interest of livelihood. The Lord Shiva became happy, gestured before her and married the Goddess. Though there are many Lord Shiva Temples in the city but the only Temple to have the sanctorum of the Goddess is 'Sri Kamakshi Amman Temple'. There are also eight other Shakti Goddesses surrounding the Temple. The place where Goddess resides is "Gayatri Mandapam". The Goddess lives in Temple in 3 forms. They are Sri Kamakshi, Sri Bilahasam and Sri Chakram. The Goddess is in a sitting posture of "Padmasana". The Goddess contains Pasa, Angusa, Pushpabana and Sugarcane in her forehands. The Goddess Mahalakshmi was given curse by the Lord Vishnu to incarnate as Aarupam form. The Goddess Mahalakshmi comes to Kanchipuram and performs the

worship chanting in the name of Lord Vishnu to free her from this Aarupam. After long prayers, the Goddess is freed from her Aarupam and given a Rupam by the Lord Vishnu. There exists a belief that Goddess Kamakshi's kumkum has to be offered to the Vigraha of Aarupa Lakshmi within the sanctorum where by the Goddess Lakshmi will fulfil your needs on the prayer. The history reveals that King Dasaratha performed "Putra Kameshi Yagam" in the Temple for the birth of a child to his kingdom. The King performed pooja to the "Nabisthanam" of the Goddess in the Temple. The King Dasaratha within a few months received a child. The King Dasasratha belongs to the "Ekshuvagu Vamsam" whom the prime deity is Goddess Kamakshi. The extract of this story is visible in "Markendeya Puranam". The faith is if prayed truly the goddess provides child for the childless couples. The Saint Adisankara born at Kaladi in Kerala travelled across all the parts of the country. When he visited Kanchipuram he felt the Goddess is in a ferocious mode that the entire sanctorum was very hot. So to personify her and accomplish to her to normal state, the Saint sung songs in the praise of Goddess named "Soundarya Lahari" then he established a Sri Chakra in front of her Vigraha to keep her cool and personified. This Srichakram is visible to all of us and all the poojas are done to srichakram too. The Temple was visited by a dumb devotee named "Mookan". The devotee begged the Goddess to free him from this dumbness so that he can perform poems on the praise of the Goddess. The Goddess suddenly provides him grace by freeing him from dumbness & giving him intellectuality in creating poetry. He was very happy with the Goddess that he wrote a poetry named "Mookapanchashati" in which he praises about the grace of the Goddess with her beauty. The special occasions for Goddess Kamakshi are Navratri, Bhramotsavam & Pournami (Full Moon Day).

KANCHIPURAM MONASTERY – It is the largest centre for Buddhism in Kanchipuram and the earliest literary record of the region speaks of a local king commissioning the Monastery in 2nd century. Other evidence points to the site being active till 14th century. Today, it is a peaceful place that allows visitors a glimpse of the history of the town while enjoying a few moments of quiet and serenity. Many famous Buddhist Monks once lived in the ancient city of Kanchipuram, which was an important Buddhist centre. Some of these centres are still present in the city. Sumati, Buddhaghosha, Jotipala, Acharya Dharmapala, Aniruddha, Deepankara Tero, Ananda Tero, Saddhamma Jotipala were some of the noted Buddhist monks who made Kanchipuram their home.

Kumarakottam Temple - The Temple is dedicated to Lord Murugan. The Temple is also known as Subramaniya Swami Temple. It is an ancient Temple, which was rebuilt in 1915 CE. Saint Arunagirinadhar has sung hymns in praise of Lord Murugan who is icon of this Temple. As per Tamil version of Skanda Purana, Lord Murugan had imprisoned the Brahma Dev here for the latter's ignorance of Om. Lord Shiva ordered Lord Murugan to release Brahma Dev. When Lord Murugan realized his mistake in not obeying his father's instruction, he did penance before a Shivalinga. Which subsequently was worshipped by the name of Devasenapathisar. The Temple has Shikhara above the main sanctum, which is built in granite and is in the shape of a dome called the chakra vimanam. It is a Chola period structure. The corbels and the pilasters with epigraphs decorate the walls of the Temple. The Temple has two prakarams and various other deities are also installed in subshrines around it. The vigraha of Lord Murugan is uniquely depicted as Brahma-Shasta holding a water pot and prayer beads of Rudraksha. The Shivalinga worshipped by Lord Murugan is deified in a separate shrine.

SRI PERARULAALAN PERUMAL TEMPLE AT KANCHIPURAM - The Temple is dedicated to Lord Vishnu. The Lord Subhodhayam with Goddess Sri Perundevi Thayaar Samaetha Sri Peruralan Perumal has been consecrated in the Temple. The Temple has large gopuram and built with Dravidian Style of Architecture.

JEENASWAMY TRILOKYANATHAR TEMPLE AT THIRUPARUTHIKUNDRAM - The Temple is a standing example for the existence of Jainism in Kanchipuram in ancient period. Built in 9th century by Pallavas, there are two Jain Temples termed as Trilokyanatha Temple and Chandra Prabha Temple. The suburb where these twin Temples are located is called as "Jaina Kanchi". Pilgrims can see beautiful paintings on the ceilings of the Temple. The main deity of Lord Mahaveerar was made up of bright pink stone. Temple built out of yellow stone has inscriptions which belong to 9th century. Currently the Temple is under the control of Tamilnadu Archeological Department.

SRI ULAGALANDA PERUMAL TEMPLE AT KANCHEEPURAM - Ulagalandha Perumal is the fifth incarnation of Lord Vishnu (known as Vamana Avataar). This talks about the divine happening of measuring the entire universe in one step by Lord Vishnu in the form of a Brahman, as a gift from King Mahabali. This Temple was built by Jayam Konda Cholan. This architecturally beautiful Temple has a unique feature of having four Divya Desams in the same complex. 1. Thiru Ooragam 2. Tirukkaragam 3. Thiruneeragam 4. Thirukkarvanam. This is a unique feature which can't be seen anywhere. It is a great benediction to Kanchi to have 4 "Divya Desams" in a single Temple. The Temple has three tiered rajagopuram (main towers) with seven kalasas. Constructed in the Dravidian style of architecture, the Temple is glorified in the Divya Prabandha, the early medieval Tamil canon of the Azhwar Saints from the $6^{th} - 9^{th}$ centuries. It is one of the 108 Divyadesam dedicated to Lord Vishnu, who is worshipped as Ulagalantha Perumal and his consort Lakshmi as Amudavalli. The Temple is believed to have been built by Pallavas, with later contributions from Medieval Cholas, Vijayanagar kings and Madurai Nayaks.

Tiruooragam - The central shrine of Temple is most commonly referred as Peragam, while the smaller shrine where the vigraha of the snake god Adisesha is houses called Tiruoorgam. As per traidition, Mahabali at the foot of Vamana could not view the Viswaroopam and requested to have a smaller form. Vishnu obliged and appeared as a snake in a smaller shrine. The shrine is frequented by childless couple praying for offspring.

Tirukkaragam - The shrine is located on the third precinct of the Temple. As per Hindu legend, Sage Garga performed his penance at this Temple and obtained knowledge. The place thus derived its name Garagaham, which later became Kaaragam. The presiding deity of the shrine is Karunakara Perumal facing north and seated on Adisesha and his consort Padmamani Nachiar. The Temple tank associated with it is called Agraya Tirtha and the vimana is called Vamana Vimanam or Ramaya Vimanam.

Tirukkarvanam - The shrine is located in the second precinct. The presiding deity is called Kalvar and faces north, while his consort is Kamalvalli Thayar. Gauri Tatakam and Taratara Tatakam are the Temple tanks associated with the Temple and the vimana is called Puskala Vimana.

Tiruneerakam - The Temple has no presiding deity but just a festive vigraha probably brought from other shrine. The vigrahas of the festival deity, Jagadiswara, facing East and having four arms, is housed in a hall in the second precinct. The water body associated with the Temple is Akrura Tirthamand the vimana is Jagadiswara Vimanam. As per Pillai Perumal Aiyangar in his Nurrettrutiruppatiyantati, Vishnu revealed himself to a sage in the form of a child in a banyan leaf.

SRI VAIKUNTHA PERUMAL TEMPLE AT KANCHEEPURAM - The Temple is also dedicated to Lord Vishnu and was built shortly after the construction of the Kailashnathar Temple. The covered passages inside the outer walls of this Temple are supported by lion pillars, which are representative of the first phase in the architectural evolution of the grand thousand pillared mandaps built later within numerous South Indian Temples. The sculptures within the Temple depict the history of the Temple with explanatory details in an eighth century script. The main shrine is dedicated to Lord Vishnu on three different levels and contains the vigrahas of Lord Vishnu in standing, sitting and reclining postures. It consists of three tiers. On the first tier, Moolavar Vaikunda Perumal graces in his sitting posture facing west. On the second tier, Araganadha Perumal places his head towards north and showers his grace in his reclining posture. On the third tier, Paramapadanadhar graces in his standing posture. It is one among the 108 Divyadesams dedicated to Lord Vishnu, who is worshipped as Vaikunthanathan (Lord Paramapadanathan) and his consort Lakshmi as Vaikundavalli. It was built by Pallava King Nandivarman in the 8th century. The Temple tank is called Airammadha Theertham and the Vimanam is known as Mukunda Vimanam. This Temple presently is under the care of Archaeology Department, Govt. of India.

VALLAKOTTAI SUBRAMANIYASWAMI TEMPLE - The Temple is dedicated to Lord Murugan. The Temple is believed to be built in 9th CE. The Temple had been constructed in typical Dravidian style of architecture. The Temple has a five tiered rajagopuram and pillared porch. The sanctum faces East & the vigraha of Lord Murugan is 7 ft tall in standing posture. There are twin vigrahas of peacock, the divine bird of Lord Muruga. As per legend, there was a demon by the name Vallan, who was troubling the Devas. The Devas sought the help of Lord Murugan who eventually waged a war & slayed the demon at this place. Lord Murugan established the place as Vallan Kottai, which literally means the "Fort of Vallan". Indra Dev requested Guru Brihaspathi to suggest a place for him to worship Lord Murugan, who suggested him to visit Vallakottai. Indra Dev came to Vallakottai & pierced the earth with Vajrayudha to create a tank to extract water. He performed ablution to vigraha of Lord Murugan at this place & attained his needs. Since Indra Dev created the tank with his Vajrayudha, the Temple tank is named as Vajra Theertha. Five daily rituals & many yearly festivals are held at the Temple. The Adi Pooram festival is the most prominent festival.

DISTRICT – KANNIYAKUMARI (Railway Station – Kanyakumari/Nagercoil/Kulitthurai)

S. No.	Temple	Address	Type
1	Chitharal Rock Jain Temple (Malaikovil)	Vellamcode – 629151	Jain
2	Arulmigu Kumaraswamy Thirukkoil	Velimalai – 629164	Murugan
3	Arulmigu Aadhikesava Perumal Temple	Thiruvattur – 629177	Vishnu
4	Mandaikadu Bhagavathi Temple	Mondaikad - 629252	Mata
5	Ayya Vaikundar Temple	Swamitopur, Thamaraikulam – 629701	Saint Ayya Vaikundar
6	Arulmigu Bhagavathyamman Thirukkoil	Kanniyakumari – 629702	Shakti Peetha
7	Bharat Mata Mandir	Vivekanandapuram, Kanniyakumari - 629702	Shiva, Hanuman
8	Shri Guganatheeswarar Temple	Kanniyakumari – 629702	Shiva
9	Tirupati Tirumala Devasthanam	Kanniyakumari - 629702	Vishnu
10	Arulmigu Nagaraja Temple	Nagercoil – 629702	Nagnath
11	Triveni Sangam	Kanniyakumari - 629702	Sangam
12	Lord Jagannath Temple	Kanniyakumari - 629704	Jagannath
13	Arulmigu Thanumalayan Thirukkoil	Suchindram – 629704	Shakti Peetha, Trinity

CHITHARAL ROCK JAIN TEMPLE (MALAIKOVIL) AT VELLAMCODE – It is famous for Rock-cut Temple. Hillock at Chitharal has a cave containing Rock-cut sculptures of Thirthankaras & attendant deities carved inside & outside dating back to 9th century. Among the rock-cut relief sculptures is a figure of the Goddess Dharmadevi. King Mahendra Varman-I was responsible for the Jainism influence in this region. It was converted into Bhagavathy Temple in the 13th CE. The Jain vigrahas have been preserved by the ASI, Govt. of India.

ARULMIGU KUMARASWAMY THIRUKKOIL AT VELIMALAI - It is believed that this Temple was built before 3000 years back. The Vigraha of Lord Muruga found here is around 8' 6". The Vigraha of Goddess Valliamman is of 6' 8" found on the left side of Lord Muruga. Goddess Valli's marriage is celebrated here. The mountain Velimalai is found here and it is believed that hunters of Goddess is still staying here. Lord Murugan is in old man form, Valli bathe pond and Lord Ganapathy in the form of Kalyana Vinayaga are the famous places nearby this Temple. Every year, during the Tamil month Panguni on Anusha Star, the Thirukalyanam function is celebrated. As Lord Murugan stayed here as Vengai Tree to marry Valli, this Tree became the holy tree of this Temple. To marry Valli, it is said that Lord Muruga killed lots of hunters. The natural springs on the hill are said to be associated with Valli. This rock cut hill Temple is built on top of a small hill accessed through a flight of 300 steps. Much of the Temple is within a cave. The Cave Temple is in three levels successively increasing in elevation. There are also shrines of Kashi Viswanathar here. The construction in this Temple is attributed to the Pallava rulers and to the Madurai Nayak rulers. Many wish that this Temple should be the seventh Padai Veedu (army camp) of Lord Muruga along with six in Tamilnadu. This was earlier in Kerala. Gruel offered in the Temple is considered as an effective cure for many diseases.

ARULMIGU AADHIKESAVA PERUMAL TEMPLE AT THIRUVATTUR – It is one of the 108 Divya Desams. The Temple is a picturesque setting surrounded on three sides by Rivers namely Kothai, Pahrali and Thamirabarani. Due to an error in the conduct of a yajna by Lord Brahma, two demons appeared from the fire – Kesan & Kesi. They caused troubles to Sages & Devas. The Sages & Devas came to Lord Vishnu for protection. Lord killed Kesan & used Kesi as a pillow for his bed. The demon's wife, to avenge the Lord, called Rivers Ganga and Tambiraparani to help her. They came in spate to wash off the Lord. Mother Earth raised the ground level where Perumal was reclining. Both Rivers went around the Lord, prayed to him & continued to flow round as two garlands. This event is mentioned in Nammalvar's Mangalasasanam hymn. As Lord Perumal destroyed demon Kesan, he is named Kesava Perumal. Kesi tried his best to escape from the Lord with his 12 hands. Lord put 12 Rudrakshas in his hand & foiled his escape bid. 12 Lord Shiva Temples came into being through these Rudrakshas around Tiruvattaru. During Shivaratri, devotees run to cover all the 12 Lord Shiva Temples and end the prayer with Lord Shiva at the feet of Adikesava Perumal. The practice continues even today. The Temple was built during Cholas, Vetanattu Kings, Thiruvathangur Kings period. There are 224 pillars decorated with lamping girl icon around the mandapam. This lamping girl icon is known as Deepalakshmi. The Temple has got Sribali Mandapam. The wood sculptures, single-stone mandapam, Udayamarthanda Namaskara Mandapam & Sastha Temple front elevation are depicted with puranic stories. The main Vigraha is 22 ft. length. The Lord Perumal made up of pepper and sugar found slept upon Snake is 16008 ft. in length. People throng the Temple and offer Neikathali variety of banana fruits. Devotees offer Tulasi water, Milk porridge to the Lord & also offer the traditional nivedhanas. Once in a year, the priests from Thiruvananthapuram come to this Temple and perform pushpanjali.

ARULMIGU BHAGAVATHYAMMAN THIRUKKOIL AT MANDAIKADU - This Temple was built in Kerala tradition in very simple style. Holy Trees for this Temple are Bo Tree & Neem. Pujas is performed four times daily. The Temple is known as a Sabarimala for Women. The 15 ft. tall anthill is the Bhagavathi Amman. Women visit the Temple with the Irumudi (a bundle containing puja items for the Goddess) as men go to Sabarimala. The Goddess Vigraha is made up of sand hill. It is believed that this Vigraha is increasing in size by every year. His Holiness Sri Sankaracharya was performing Srichakra Puja with his Kerala disciples here. One day the Chakra did not turn back after the puja was over as usual. The Acharya stayed here itself and attained Samadhi. It is on this spot where the Srichakra existed, the anthill began to grow. Children playing this side and hitting the anthill were injured. Marthanda Varma, the king of Kerala came to know of these developments and built a Temple and performed pujas regularly. Every year people is celebrating the festival "Kodai Vizha" during the month of Masi. Keralites undergo 41 days fasting & reach this Temple by walk. On the last Tuesday of Masi, Kodai Vizha is celebrated.

AYYA VAIKUNDAR TEMPLE AT SWAMITOPUR - This is the birth place of Ayya Vaikundar. After the enlightenment at Thiruchenthur on 3rd March, 1833 at the age of 24, Ayya Vaikundar returned to this place where he started his social reformation. This can be considered as the first pathi. On Sundays, large number of people comes here for Uchipadippu. Car festivals are conducted thrice a year. During Car Festival, Vaikunta Jyothi is lighted on a hill top called Vaikuntamalai.

SHAKTIPEETHAM - ARULMIGU BHAGAVATHYAMMAN THIRUKKOIL AT KANYAKUMARI -

The legend of this Temple is as romantic as the place itself. Dedicated to the virgin Goddess Kanniyakumari, Parvati who stands guard over the country, the Temple is built at the spot where the Goddess is believed to have waited for her consort Lord Shiva to come and claim her hand in marriage. At one time the shifting sands at the shores of Kanniyakumari were believed to be multi-hued as a result of the coloured rice that was sprinkled by the approving gods over the couple at their wedding. Equally fascinating is the story about the diamond nose stud worn by the Goddess, believed to have led many a ship to be shipwrecked on the treacherous rocks near the shore. So bright was the threat of the reflected light from the nose-stud to the unsuspecting ships that the door on the side facing the sea had to be closed for ensuring the safety of the ocean liners. Kanniyakumari derives its name from Goddess Kanniyakumari Amman, the presiding deity of the area. Goddess Kanniyakumari has the legendary account that once Banusura, the demon king got supremacy over Devas and meted out cruel punishment to them. The Devas performed a Yagna pleading to annihilate the evils. Goddess Parasakthi came to Kumari in the form of a virgin girl and began her penance. Meanwhile Lord Shiva fell in love with her and arrangements for the marriage were made in the midnight a particular day. Now the Devine Sage Narada realised that their marriage would destroy the chances of annihilating Banusura because he could be killed only by a virgin. When Lord Shiva was on his way to Kanniyakumari from Suchindrum, Sage Narada assumed the form of a cock and crowed falsely heralding the break of dawn. Thinking that the auspicious time for the marriage was past, Lord Shiva returned disappointed. The Goddess too decided to remain virgin after that. Then, when Banusura attempted to win the Goddess by force, she killed him with her Chakragudha and relieved the sufferings of Devas. Then she resumed her penance and remained virgin. The Temple is located at the confluence of three seas of India's South Corner. Though the Temple is on the sea shore, the water in the well in the Temple is sweet and not salty. This Temple was constructed before 3000 years by Lord Parasuram and then renovated by one of the kings of Pandya Dynasty. People use to light lamps in the Temple and offer new saris to the Goddess besides usual abhishek and archanas. People bathe in the sea and offer Tarpan to the departed ancestors for their salvation.

Vivekananda Memorial - There are two great rocks in the eastern direction in the sea. The bigger one measures about 3 acres & is 55 foot above the sea. There is also a symbol on this rock in the shape of a foot which devotees believe to be that of the Goddess. In 1892, Swami Vivekananda visited Kanyakumari, spent his time on the rock in deep meditation. A Mandap is constructed on this rock in his memory.

Bharat Mata Mandir at Vivekanandapuram - The Temple is also known as Ramayana

Darshanam. The Temple is dedicated to Bharat Mata. A 12 ft. tall vigraha of Bharat Mata had been consecrated in the Temple which is made of brass metal. There are vigrahas of Swami Vivekananda & Devi Kanyakumari, Bhagwan Vishnu & Nataraja, which are made of fibre glass. The whole complex is situated in a beautifully manicured lush green lawn overseen by a majestic fiber glass. The vigraha of Gangadhara Shiva supported by four gold-copper tinted elephants is one of the beautiful vigrahas existed in the Temple. The place is having 108 panels which depicts important episodes from Ramayana & is also having a 27 ft. tall vigraha of Lord Hanuman.

Thiruvalluvar Vigraha - On the other rock, the Vigraha of Saint Thiruvalluvar is installed representing the minute skills in sculpture. The tallest Vigraha of 133 ft is very beautifully designed and stands so majestically as if conversing with tides. The entire monument depicts the 3 sections of Thirukkural, namely virtue (38 chapters), wealth (70 chapters) and love (25 chapters).The Vigraha, with its slight bend around the waist is reminiscent of a dancing pose of the Hindu deities like Nataraja. The Vigraha weighs 7,000 tons.

SHRI GUGANATHEESWARAR TEMPLE AT KANYAKUMARI – It is a 1000 year old Temple and is said to have been built by the King Raja Raja Chola. The architectural style of the Cholas is quiet apparent in this Temple. There are 16 inscriptions found in this Temple that date back to the years 1038 AD, 1044 AD, 1045 AD.

TIRUPATI TIRUMALA DEVASTHANAM AT KANYAKUMARI - Tirupati Tirumala Devasthanam has established a replica of Tirupati Balaji Temple in Kanyakumari. It was established in January, 2019. It is a huge complex & located close to the shore. Thousands of devotees from Tamil Nadu, Andhra Pradesh and Kerala took part in the consecration ceremony. The construction of the Temple began in July 2013 to benefit devotees coming from far and wide to Kanyakumari. All the special occasions observed in Tirupati are also observed at this Temple on the respective days.

ARULMIGU NAGARAJA TEMPLE AT NAGERCOIL – It is one of the Temples of associated and unassociated Temples of Suseendram. It is said that the place "Nagercoil" is named because of Nagaraja (five headed) Temple. The greenish area, the arduous coconut tree and flowered gardens surrounded by this Temple attracts everyone's heart. It is believed that the Naga Flower in this garden is worshiped as the symbol of Nagaraja vigraha. It is also believed that the snakes around this place is protecting the Temple and the garden. This is a proven one in World's Religious encyclopedia that even though lots of snakes are found, no one is died because of snake-biting and this is the specialty of this Temple. Apart from Nagaraja, Lord Shiva in the form of Vaayu, Lord Thirumal in the form of happiness are also found. The penance posture of Parchuva Nathar and Mahaveer of Jainism are depicted in the pillars of this Temple. The front elevation remains us the strain of Nepal's Buddhist religion. The Temple is found as the assembled principle of Saivam, Vaishnavam, Jainism and Buddhism. The ceiling covered by thatch is one of the specialties of the Temple. The pace where the seated posture of Nagaraja found is always wet and the sand taken from here is considered to be the main Prasadham. This sand is found in black colour for six months and in white colour for remaining six months. Though moving through dust, it does not touch the Naga body. Nagas-snakes are not affected by any object on which they move or live around. Presiding deity Nagaraja graces from the sanctum sanctorum with five heads. As Chandi and Mundi are the Dwarapalakas in Lord Shiva Temples and Jayan and Vijayan in Lord Vishnu Temples, a male snake Darnendran by name and female snake named Padmavathi are the dwarapalakas (securities) in this Temple. It is believed that snakes are here as securities of the Temple. Lords Ananthakrishna and Kasi Viswanatha shrines are right of Nagaraja shrine. After puja to Nagaraja, pujas are performed in these shrines. However, the last puja of the day-Arthajama puja - is dedicated to Lord Ananthakrishna. Though Nagaraja is the presiding deity of the Temple, Kodimaram-flag post is for Lord Ananthakrishna only. Thai Brahmmotsavam is also dedicated to Perumal only with car festival on Thai Poosam day. Aarattu and Krishna Jayanthi too are celebrated for Lord Ananthakrishna. It is also noteworthy that a tortoise occupies the place of Garuda in the flag post against tradition. Garuda and snakes are natural enemies. The Temple has a shrine for Mother Durga. As the Vigraha was found in the sacred spring here, she is praised as Theertha Durga. People facing adverse aspects of Rahu and/or Rahu-Kethu planets worship here during the Rahukalam time on Tuesdays – between 3.00 PM and 4.30 PM. Keralites call aged women as Ammachi as a mark of respect. Mother Durga here is addressed respectfully as Ammachi Durga.

TRIVENI SANGAM AT KANNIYAKUMARI - It is one of the holiest places in the world, where one can see confluence of three Seas i.e. Indian Ocean, Arabian Sea & Bay of Bengal. At this place, devotees gathers to witness Sunrise & Sunset. It is believed that it is the only place in the world of such importance.

LORD JAGANNATH TEMPLE AT KANYAKUMARI - The Temple is dedicated to Lord Jagannath. The Temple is an example of fine Kalinga architecture with Dravidian style.

Marundhuvazh Malai - It is also known as the Marundhu Vazhum Malai/Maruthwamalai ("the abode of medicinal herbs"). People living in southern Kerala call it Maruthuva Mala. According to tradition, the Maruthuva Malai is a fragment of the Sanjeevi Mountain, a piece of which fell down here, and it was carried by Hanuman from Mahendragiri to Lanka for healing the fatal wounds of Lakshmana, the brother of Rama, the epic hero. It stretches for more than a km, reaching a height of 800 feet at the highest point. From the highest point of the hill, one can see the 'V' section of the Indian subcontinent . The three Sea (Bay of Bengal, Indian Ocean and Arabian sea) with different shades of blue and coconut trees with different shades of green are visible from this hill.

SHAKTIPEETHAM - ARULMIGU THANUMALAYAN THIRUKKOIL AT SUCHINDRAM - The Thanumalayan Temple, also called Sthanumalayan Temple, is an important Temple located on the bank of the River Pazhayar. Suchindrum means the place where Indra attained 'Suchi' i.e. purification. Although well known to local devotees as a Lord Brahma Temple, Suchindram (Susindram) is seldom included on the short lists of Lord Brahma Temples in India, most likely because the presiding deities here are Trimurti and the Temple is dedicated to Lord Shiva

Sthanunatha. As usual, there are a number of different historical and place names for this Temple, including Suchindram Thanumalaya Temple, Sri Sthanumalaya Perumal Swamy Temple and Arulmigu Thanumalayar Temple. The Temple may will be considered as one of the store houses of the richest specimens of Dravidian style of Art, Architecture and Sculpture in stone. The Gopuram itself is a gigantic structure depicting mythological stories from Indian scriptures. The moment one enters the Temple through the Gopuram, which is 134 foot high, one comes across the hollow trunk of a tree estimated to be over 2500 years old. The trunk has been plated to preserve it from decay. In that hollow, there are 3 Lingams having 16 moons (Chandrakala) one over the other under the canopy of the serpent Naga and these 3 lingams represents Lord Brahma, Vishnu and Maheswara, the Trinity of Indian scriptures and the vigraha of Anasuya who turned them into babies is at its centre. A small artistic shrine has been made in front of it. By its side, the white Bull Nandi of Lord Shiva is installed looking towards the sanctum. Suchindrum known as Gnanaranya, is well known for its sculptural wealth. It is believed that the Trinity appeared here at the request of a Sage Atri and his wife Anusaya. vigrahas of Vigneswari (a feminine form of Vinayaka), Goddess Aram Valartha Nayaki, Indra Vinayaka, Kala Bhairava and Saakahi Ganapathy are also enshrined. Inscriptions of 9thcentury are found in this Temple. On the eastern corridor is the shrine of Guru Dakshinamurthi next to Konnayadi. The Navagrahas are engraved on the ceiling. On the outer prakaram, there are separate shrines for Cheravasal Sastha, Lord Rama and Lord Muruga. There is an imposing monolithic vigraha of Lord Anjaneya opposite to Lord Rama's Shrine. It is about 5.5 m high and is said to represent the Viswarupa of Hanuman as shown to Mata Sita at Ashoka Vana in Lanka. On the northern corridor, there are four musical pillars cut out of single granite blocks.

DISTRICT – KARUR (Railway Station – Karur)

S. No.	Temple	Address	Type
1	Arulmigu Kalyana Pasupatheswarar Temple	Karur – 639001	Shiva
2	Arulmigu Mariamman Temple	Karur – 639001	Mata
3	Arulmigu Sadasiva Brahmendra Adhistanam	Nerur – 639004	Shiva
4	Arulmigu Kalyana Venkataramana Swamy Temple	Thanthonimalai - 639005	Vishnu
5	Arulmigu Balasubramanian Temple	Vennamalai – 639006	Murugan
6	Arulmigu Kadambaneswarar Temple	Kulittalai - 639104	Shiva
7	Arulmigu Agatheeswarar Temple	Thirumukkudalur - 639114	Sage Agastya
8	Arulmigu Balasubramanian Swami Temple	Velayuthampalayam - 639117	Murugan
9	Arulmigu Rathinagreeswarar Temple	Sivayam – 639120	Shiva

ARULMIGU KALYANA PASUPATHESWARAR TEMPLE AT KARUR – It was the capital of early Chera Kings of Sangam age. The Temple is the land mark of the Karur City. Group of sculptures representing Pasupatheeswarar Lingam, milk oozing cow and a Rangamatha are adding more attraction to the Temple. The Shivalinga is Swayambhu. The Rajagopuram of the Temple is 120 ft. high & it has 7 tiers and 2 corridors which are believed to be constructed during Chola period.

ARULMIGU MARIAMMAN TEMPLE AT KARUR – The famous Temple is dedicated to Sri Mariamman. All groups of people irrespective of caste, creed participated in Kumbum Festival celebrated during the month of the May every year. The sacred water is brought by every devotees from the River Amaravathi to this famous Temple to worship is one of the glorious event.

NERUR - Arulmigu Sadasiva Brahmendra Adhishtanam and Arulmigu Kashi Vishwanatha Temple are located at the Village. This Jeeva Samadhi is located in an Oasis of Cauvery River bank. Here Cauvery River running towards south is a very special feature. It is a wonderful place where not only people from Tamil Nadu pay a visit but devotees from various other states are also visiting.

ARULMIGU KALYANA VENKATARAMANA SWAMY TEMPLE AT THANTHONIMALAI – The Temple is dedicated to Lord Kalyana Venkataramana Swamy at a raised portion of a hillock. This Temple is also known as Then Thirupathi (South Thirupathi).

ARULMIGU BALASUBRAMANIAN TEMPLE AT VENNAMALAI - This place is famous for the Temple dedicated to Lord Murugan. The Hindu exponents like Arunagirinathar and Avaiyar sang their Hymns to praise this Lord.

ARULMIGU KADAMBANESWARAR TEMPLE AT KULITTALAI – The Temple is dedicated to Lord Kadambaneswarar. Thaipoosam is a festival celebrated every year in a grand manner during the Tamil Month of Thai (January) here.

SELLANDIAMMAN TEMPLE AT THIRUKKAMPULIYUR – It is one of the main attractions of this village and a most sacred pilgrimage site for Hindus of its surrounded villages. The Goddess in this Temple is called as Sellandiamman. It is situated on the bank of the River Cauvery.

ARULMIGU AGATHEESWARAR TEMPLE AT THIRUMUKKUDALUR - The River Cauvery, Amaravathi and Manimuthharu are confluence in this place. This Temple was built by Rajendra Chola-I of Chola Dynasty. People believed that Agasthiya Munivar worshipped the Lord Shiva in this Temple.

ARULMIGU BALASUBRAMANIAN SWAMI TEMPLE AT VELAYUTHAMPALAYAM – The Temple is dedicated to Lord Subramania on a small hill. It is famous for its sculptures. This is situated on the banks of River Cauvery.

ARULMIGU RATHINAGREESWARAR TEMPLE AT SIVAYAM – The Temple is dedicated to Arulmigu Rathinagreeswarar. Every year Brahmotsavam Festival of 15 days, Chithirai Festival, Thaipoosam Festival, Karthigai Festival, Panguni Uthiram Festival and Teppam Festival are celebrated here in grand manner.

DISTRICT – KRISHNAGIRI (Railway Station – Hosur / Dharmapuri)

S. No.	Temple	Address	Type
1	Sri Kattu Veera Anjaneya Temple	Krishnagiri - 635001	Hanuman
2	Pettaraya Swamy Temple	Denkanikottai - 635107	Vishnu
3	Shree Parshwa Padmavathi Shakti Peetha Tirth Dham	Sadanapalli - 635108	Jain
4	Arulmigu Chandrasoodeswarar Temple	Hosur – 635109	Shiva
5	Maa Pratyangira Kalika Alayam	Moranapalli, Hosur – 635109	Mata
6	Hanuman Theertham	Hanumantheertham - 636902	Hanuman

SRI KATTU VEERA ANJANEYA TEMPLE AT KRISHNAGIRI – The Temple is said to be 2500 years old and Lord Anjaneya here ensures that one wish which one pray with full devotion is said to come true within 3 months. There is a very good procedure to handover the wish to the Lord. There is one natural rock formation Nandi which one cannot miss and shows the presence of Lord Shiva too here.

PETTARAYA SWAMY TEMPLE AT DENKANIKOTTAI - It is 14th century Temple and the main deity is Lord Vishnu. Car festival is the main attraction of the Temple in the month of Mar-Apr every year. The Temple is one among the 108 Divya Desam.

SHREE PARSHWA PADMAVATHI SHAKTI PEETHA TIRTH DHAM AT SADANAPALLI - Jain dharma consists of 24 Theerthankaras. In these 24 Theerthankaras, the 23rd Theerthankara is considered to be Swami Parshwanath Bhagwan. As per local belief, the Shaktipeetha is the world's highest (365 ft height) Jain Temple adorning vigrahas of the Tirthankar Arihanta Paramatmans.

ARULMIGU CHANDRASOODESWARAR TEMPLE AT HOSUR – The Temple is located on a Hillock. The presiding deity is Lord Shiva in the form of Arulmigu Maragathambal Samadha. Devotees from Tamilnadu, Karnataka, Andhra Pradesh are visiting this Temple. Stone inscription of 11^{th}century pertain to Chola period exist in the Temple. Car Festival of the Temple is very famous.

MAA PRATYANGIRA KALIKA ALAYAM AT MORANAPALLI – The Temple has the biggest Pratyangira Vigraha and it is installed on the rajagopuram on the Temple. The Temple currently still being constructed. The Temple has many people in the weekends and on weekdays. The Temple worships Pratyangira, Sarabeswara, Narasimha, and Mariamman. Inside the Temple, there is a long waiting until you get inside the Temple. The Temple then has Simha's mouth open wide where the people worship. People worship Pratyangira by putting garlands and setting Vilakku (ghee lamp) under Pratyangira's feet.

HANUMAN THIRTHAM - This place is situated on the bank of Pennaiyar River and traditionally associated with Theerthamalai. It is believed that Lord Hanuman, who was instructed by Lord Rama, to get the water from the Ganges for his penance at Tirthamalai which he could not do it in time. So Lord Rama was said to have done it with Asthrapryogam and got it. Disappointed at this, Lord Hanuman was said to have thrown down the vessel in which he brought the holy water and this spilled water is believed to be the 'Hanumantirtham'. The water is considered sacred.

DISTRICT – MADURAI (Railway Station – Madurai)

S. No.	Temple	Address	Type
1	Arulmigu Koodalazhagar Temple	Periyar, Madurai – 625001	Vishnu
2	Arulmigu Meenakshi Sundareswarar Temple	Madurai – 625001	Mata, Shiva
3	Arulmigu Mariamman Teppakulam	Vandiyur, Madurai – 625001	Sarovar, Ganesh
4	Sri Prasanna Venkatesa Perumal Temple	S Krishnan Koil Street, Madurai - 625001	Vishnu
5	Arulmigu Subramanya Swamy Temple	Thiruparankundram – 625005	Murugan
6	Samanar Hills	Kilakuyilkudi - 625019	Jain
7	Arulmigu Kallazhagar Temple	Alagar Kovil, Melur Taluk – 625301	Vishnu
8	Arulmigu Subramanian Swamy Temple	Solaimalai, Alagarakoil – 625301	Murugan

ARULMIGU KOODALAZHAGAR TEMPLE AT PERIYAR, MADURAI – This Temple is dedicated to Lord Vishnu and one of the 108 Divya Desams. Koodal is another name for Madurai and Azhaghar means the beautiful, hence, he is called Koodal Azhagar. Koodal Azhagar is installed in three postures: in sitting posture as Koodal Azhagar, in standing posture as Sri Surya Narayanan and Sri Ranganatha in reclining posture in three separate Sanctum Sanctorums, one above the other. The shadows of Ashtanga Vimanam (tower) do not fall on the ground. Lord Azhagar is taken on procession for a dip in the Vaigai River on the Chitra Paurnami Day [Full Moon Day – Apr-May], which is the most colourful festival that brings the entire Madurai Town to standstill. A 10 day Float Festival is celebrated in the month of Masi [Feb-Mar] on the Masi Magam [star] day.

ARULMIGU MEENAKSHI SUNDARESWARAR TEMPLE AT MADURAI - The Meenakshi Temple is the elegant twin Temple of Sundareswarar and Meenakshi and the life of Madurai City revolves around this Temple. The Goddess Meenakshi is the principal deity of the Temple, unlike most Lord Shiva Temples in South India where Lord Shiva is the principal deity. Lord Shiva in his incarnation as Sundareswarar and his fish-eyed spouse, Goddess Meenakshi are enshrined in this twin Temple. There are five massive gateways enclosing these two shrines. Even a casual visitor is fascinated by the many paintings and sculptures. The construction process of the Temple began 2000 years ago. Contributions from different rulers and special contribution from Thirumalai Naicker made this complex to extend by leaps and bounds. 4 Nine tier Gopurams, 1 Seven tier Chittirai Gopuram, 5 Five Tier Gopurams, 2 Three Tier Gopurams and 2 Golden Gopurams are the majestic towers of the Temple. Because Golden Lotus for Indira's Puja blossomed in the tank inside the Temple, it is called as Golden Lotus Tank [Pon Thamarai Kulam]. The Hall of Thousand Pillar of the Thirumalai Naicker period is called as Ayiramkaal Mandapam in Tamil. The architectural excellence of this hall is that the pillars viewed from any angle will be on a straight line. The musical pillars carved out of stone decorate the corridors of the outer courts. The Goddess shrine has the green stone vigraha of Goddess Meenakshi standing in bent-leg posture. Her raised hand holds a lotus, on which sits a green parrot. Her left hand hangs by her side. This vigraha is set in a square garbhagriha (central sanctum). A copy of this vigraha has been made from metal and is kept in the Temple complex. The metal version is used for a festive procession. A distinct feature of Goddess Meenakshi in terms of iconography is the presence of parrot in her right hand. The parrot is generally associated with the Vaishnava Azhwar Saint Andal. The Sundareswarar shrine has a stone Linga in its square plan sanctum, and this anicon is shaded under a stone cobra hood. In the northeast corner is another stone vigraha of his consort. None of these travel during a festive procession. Rather, Sundareswarar is represented in the form of anthropomorphic

Somaskanda vigraha. There is another metal symbolic vigraha of Lord Shiva called the Cokkar, which is merely a pair of embossed feet on a metal stool. This symbol is kept near Sundareswarar sanctum all day, then carried in a palaki daily to Meenakshi's chamber every evening so that the two can symbolically spend the night together. In the morning, the Temple volunteers wake the divine couple and the symbolic Cokkar vigraha is carried back to the Sundareswarar sanctum. The Temple has other shrines, such as Lord Murugan in the northwest corner of the second courtyard. A tall monolithic Ganesha sculpture with a large rice ball, locally called the Mukuruny Vinayakar. According to a legend found in the Tamil text Tiruvilaiyatarpuranam, King Malayadwaja Pandya and his wife Kanchanamalai performed a Yajna seeking a son for succession. Instead a daughter is born out of the fire who is already 3 year old and has three breasts. Lord Shiva intervenes and says that the parents should treat her like a son and when she meets her husband, she will lose the third breast. They follow the advice. The girl grows up, the king crowns her as the successor and when she meets Lord Shiva, his words come true, she takes her true form of Meenakshi. The marriage of Goddess Meenakshi and Lord Shiva was the biggest event, with all gods, goddesses and living beings gathered. Lord Vishnu is believed to be the brother of Goddess Meenakshi. Lord Vishnu gives her away to Lord Shiva at the wedding.

ARULMIGU MARIAMMAN TEPPAKULAM AT VANDIYUR, MADURAI – It is a beautiful square tank spread over a huge area. The tank is the scene of the colourful float festival held in January/February to celebrate the birth anniversary of King Thirumalai Nayak, who built this tank. The deities of Meenakshi and Sundareswarar are placed in a float, called "Teppam", decorated with flowers and illuminated with hundreds of lights. This float is taken around the tank to the sound of traditional music. On the Northern side of the tank, a Temple is dedicated to Mariamman, a famous village deity of Tamil Nadu. Built in 1645 AD during the rule of Thirumalai Nayak, this Temple pond is surrounded by granite steps on all the four sides while in the middle a Vigneshwara Temple is located, which is dedicated to Lord Ganesha. There is a legend behind Vandiyur Mariamman Teppakulam. According to the legend, to build Thirumalai Nayakkar Mahal sand was dug out of this tank to get the soil for creating bricks. Owing to this the palace is considered to be a blessed one. During the digging process, an Vigraha of Lord Ganesh was unearthed. The same Vigraha has been enshrined in the Temple.

SRI PRASANNA VENKATESA PERUMAL TEMPLE AT MADURAI – The Temple is dedicated to Lord Vishnu. It is an ancient and famous Temple. Lord Vigraha is a Swayambhumurthy. Lord, as a replica in Tirupati, graces from the sanctum sanctorum. There is a shrine of Lord Krishna at the front mandapam appearing in a Nardana-dancing posture. Lord Vaishnava Vignesha shrine is at the entrance of the Temple, having two tusks. Garuda is seen in a worshipping form. There is a separate shrine for Lord Lakshmi Hayagriva. There is a shrine for Mother Andal. There are shrines for Anjali

Anjaneya, Azhwars Saints and Sudharsana, Lord Perumal in reclining form, Panduranga with mother Raghumayi, Rama, Narasimha and mother Natana Gopala Nayaki. Theertham is Sarva Abishta Theertham. Devotees offer flake porridge, butter and dry ginger as Nivedhana and offer Tulsi garlands seeking boon of wise children. Recently, 108 veena artists performed 'Mahishasura Mardini Strotam' at the same time at the Temple.

ARULMIGU SUBRAMANYA SWAMY TEMPLE AT THIRUPARANKUNDRAM – Cave shrines are calculated as 8th century creation of the Pandiyans and the Temple of the later Nayaks. One of the Six Special Abodes of Lord Murugan dedicated to Lord Subrahmanya is located here. The Sanctum Sanctorum is carved out of a single rock and the Temple is believed to be in existence for many centuries. The walls and the pillars are carved with sculptures that still fascinates the visitors. The importance of this Temple is that the marriage of Lord Subrahmanya with Devayanai, the daughter of Indra, was celebrated here.

SAMANAR HILLS AT KILAKUYILKUDI - It is also known as Samanar Malai. It is a hill rock complex. The hill has been declared as a protected monument by the Archaeological Survey of India. Samanar means 'Jain' in Tamil and Malai means 'hill'. This hill has caves where Tamil Jain (Samanar) monks lived. The hill was also known as Thiruvuruvagam. The hill has several Tamil-Brahmi inscriptions, a number of stone beds and many sculptures, which shows authority for Jainism in the ancient times. The hill contains two famous sculptures, Settipodavu and Pechipallam, which show vigrahas of Tirthankaras made by Jain monks in the 9th CE. The Settipodavu contains the vigraha of Bhagwan Mahavira. The Pechipallam contains eight sculptures, including Bhagwan Bahubali and Mahavira. Archaeologists have also found more than 2200-year-old Jain Tamil-Brahmi inscriptions and Vatteluttu writings. The inscriptions reveal that hundreds of Jain monks took sallekhana ('fast unto death') there. The findings through the Tamil inscriptions show that there was a Jain monastery at the top of the hill known as Maadevi Perumpalli. In the foothills, there is a Karuppanasamy Temple and lotus pond. Some vigrahas made by Jain monks are in Karuppanasamy Temple.

ARULMIGU KALLAZHAGAR TEMPLE AT MELUR TALUK – It is a Lord Vishnu Temple on a picturesque wooded Hill. Here Lord Vishnu presides as Goddess Meenakshi's brother 'Azhgar'. During the Chitrai festival in April/May, when the celestial marriage of Goddess Meenakshi to Lord Sundareswarar is celebrated, Azhagar travels to Madurai. A gold processional icon called the Sundararajar is carried by devotees in procession from Azhagar Kovil to Madurai for wedding ritual. Palamudhirsolai, one of the six abodes of Lord Subramanya is on the same hill. A natural spring called Nuburagangai where pilgrim bath is located here. It is famous for its ancient Vaishnavite Temple and

the beauty of exquisite sculptures in the hall and other 'mandapams' of the Temple. The Alwars have sung in praise of the deity of the place and the hills. In addition, Nakkirar, the Tamil poet has composed several popular poems about this deity. As the place itself suggests, the Temple is dedicated to Alagar who is popularly known as Sundararajar. It is said that Alagar Kovil attracted pilgrims even in the early days of the Sangam age. The Temple is built on an extensive area in a very picturesque spot, surrounded by the ruins of a historic fort. The impressive main tower at the entrance, believed to have been built by the Pandyan Kings, has some beautiful sculptures depicting scenes from the epics. According to historical records, Malayadhwaja Pandyan, son of Kulasekhara Pandyan, who is said to have established the Pandyan kingdom, appears to be the earliest known monarch who patronised this Temple. Jatavarman Sundara Pandyan, who reigned during the period 1251-1270 AD beautified the 'vimana' of the 'sanctum sanctorum' with gold plates. Later, during the reign of the Vijayanagar, King Krishnadeva Raya, the Temple was endowed with revenues from two villages for conducting regular festivals. Azhagar Kovil Dosai is the special kind of Dosa that is prepared with black urad dal & ghee, spiced with black pepper and this Dosa is offered to the Lord and then distributed to the devotees as Prasadam.

ARULMIGU SUBRAMANIAN SWAMY TEMPLE AT SOLAIMALAI - This is the only one among Lord Murugan's Aru Padai Veedu Temples, where he graces the devotees with his consorts Valli and Deivayanai. The wedding festival is celebrated along with Skanda Sashti festival. Pazhamudircholai is a Temple located atop a hillock covered with dense forests. Divine Poet Avvaiyar, while relaxing under the Naval Tree, encountered Lord Murugan in the form of Shepherd Boy on that tree, who played a prank with her to make her realize that materialism should be removed from the mind to visualize the truth and seek God. It is also said that the actual Temple was Azhagar Kovil relocated as Pazhamuthirsolai by the then ruler of Madurai – Thirumalai Naicker of the Nayaks dynasty. Lord Vithaga Vinayaka is on the right side. People take bath in the Noopura Ganga and worship the Guardian Deity Sri Rakkayi Amman. Usually the Naval Trees yield fruits in July-September months, the tree here yields fruits in Aipasi (October-November) when Lord Muruga's Skanda Sashti festival takes place.

DISTRICT – MAYILADUTHURAI (Railway Station – Mayiladuturai)

S. No.	Temple	Address	Type
1	Arulmigu Mayuranathar Temple	Mayiladuthurai – 609001	Shiva
2	Arulmigu Mullaivananathar Temple	Thirumullaivasal – 609113	Shiva
3	Vaitheeswaran Kovil	Vaithiswarankoil – 609117	Shiva
4	Sri Abhirami Amirthakadeswarar Temple	Sannathi St., Thirukadaiyur – 609311	Shiva

ARULMIGU MAYURANATHAR TEMPLE AT MAYILADUTHURAI – The main icon is a Lingam and the presiding deity is called Mayuranathar. According to the Hindu mythology, Annai Parasakthi danced in the form of a peacock, hence the place is called Mayiladuthurai. Devotees after worshipping Mayuranathar can travel from here to all the places of Navagrahas and other important Temples. The festival of Holy bath in the River Cauvery, known as Kadai Muzhukku, is celebrated in the month of Ippasi. It is one of the shrines of the 275 Paadal Petra Sthalams - Shiva Sthalams glorified in the early medieval Tevaram poems by Tamil Saivite Nayanar Tirugnanasambandar. There are three smaller shrines to the God Ganesha & another to Lord Shiva as Nataraja. One of the sculptures in the Temple represent Lord Shiva embracing Goddess Parvathi. It is believed that Lord Brahma, Lakshmi, Sage Agastya, Manmatha, birds & animals worshipped Mayuranathar. The Vigraha of Maa Durga is expertly sculpted & differs from those in other Temples. On the Temple walls, there is the sculpture of a devotee trying to sever his head as an offering to the God.

ARULMIGU MULLAIVANANATHAR TEMPLE AT THIRUMULLAIVASAL – It is an ancient Temple. It is dedicated to Lord Shiva. The presiding deity of this Temple is Arulmigu Mullaivananathar and his consort is known as Ani Konda Kothai Ammai. The Temple was constructed by the Chola King Killivalavan. It is one of the shrines of the 275 Paadal Petra Sthalams - Shiva Sthalams glorified in the early medieval Tevaram poems by Tamil Saivite Nayanar Tirugnanasambandar.

VAITHEESWARAN KOVIL – It is also known as Pullirukkuvelur. The Temple is dedicated to Lord Shiva, who is worshipped as Vaidyanathar or Vaitheeswaran meaning the "God of healing" and it is believed that prayers to Vaitheeswaran can cure diseases. Vaitheeswaran is a Tamil derivative from vaidya (Doctor) & Ishvara (God/Master). The presiding deity is Sri Vaidyanathan, facing towards west. It is one of the Navagraha (nine planets) Temples and is associated with the planet Mars (Angaraka). The village is also known for palm leaf astrology called Naadi astrology in Tamil. The holy waters of the Siddhatirtham tank within the Temple complex contains nectar and a holy dip is believed to cure all diseases. The Temple is revered by the Tevaram hymns of 7thcentury Saiva Nayanars & is also classified as a Paadal Petra Sthalam. During the Ramayana period, Lord Rama, Lakshmana & Saptarishi have worshipped the deity in this place. There is a pond at this Temple called Jatayukundam (pot of Jatayu having holy ash of Vibhuti). One of the nine planets, Angaraka (Mars), suffered from leprosy & was cured by Vaidhyanathaswamy. Parvati, the consort of Lord Shiva, asked her son, Subramanya to appear with one face from his regular appearance of six faces. When he did so, she was pleased & presented him with vel (a weapon) to slay the demons. Subramanya overcame the asura Surapadman (a demon) & in the war, his army was severely injured. Lord Shiva came out as the healer Vaitheeswaran and cured the wounds. As per another legend, Lord Shiva came as Vaidya & cured the leprosy of a staunch devotee named Angahara. Jatya, Rig Veda, Muruga & Surya were all believed to have worshipped Lord Shiva here. Lord Murugan obtained a trident at this place and is called Selvamuthu Kumaran. As per local legend, Lord Shiva was doing penance at Mount Meru when a drop of water fell from his forehead which turned into a beautiful child. Bhoomidevi brought up the child, who went on to become a staunch devotee of Lord Shiva. Pleased by the devotion, Lord Shiva turned him to a planet. Based on his colour, Angaraka (Mars) is usually clad with red coloured cloth. Vaitheeswaran is believed to preside over Angarakan in the Temple. The Temple has a five-tiered gopuram (Temple tower), two inner gopurams and large precincts. The central shrine is that of Vaitheeswaran present as Lingam in the inner most sanctum. The first precinct around the sanctum has the metal vigraha of Subramanya, worhsipped here as Muthukumara Swamy. The other metal vigrahas in the sanctum are of Nataraja, Somaskanda, Angaraka & stone sculptures of Durga, Dakshinamoorthy, Surya (Sun god), Jatayu, Vedas, Sampati. The shrine of Thaiyalnayaki in the second precinct facing south houses the vigraha of Thiyalnayagi sported in standing posture with the medicinal oil to cure the diseases. The large precinct also has a small shrine of Dhanvantari and shrine of Angaraka in stone sculpture. The southern gateway from this precinct leads to the Temple tank and directly faces the Thaiyalnayaki shrine. The Sthala Vriksha (Temple tree) is margosa (Azadirachtaindica, neem tree), believed to possess medicinal properties. The eastern gateway also has the shrine of Adi (original) Temple that has a smaller replica of the main shrines. There is a fine metal vigraha of Gangavisarjanar inside the Temple. The shrine of Angaragan (Mars) is present near the Eastern gateway in the third precinct. Nearest Railway Station is Vithisvarankol.

SRI AMIRTHA KADESWARAR TEMPLE AT TIRUKADAYUR - It is dedicated to Lord Shiva in his manifestation as "Destroyer of Death" & his wife Goddess Parvati as Abhirami. The famous Amritaghateswarar – Abirami Temple is associated with the legends of Markandeya and Abirami Pattar, which is a replica. The original Temple, Thirukkadaiyur Mayanam is now called Thirumeignanam. This is one of the holy places of Shaivism today. Markandeya grew up to be an ardent devotee of Lord Shiva. The destined time came, when Yama (the lord of death) tried to snatch the life of the boy. Markandeya went to the Temple and clutched at the Shivalingam in a bid to escape death. Pleased by the boy's belief, Lord Shiva rescued him from death. It is one of the most important seats of Sakthi. Saint Abirami Bhattar composed the divine songs of Abirami Anthathi. The Temple, in line with the Temple architecture of the Chola dynasty, occupies a very vast area of 11 acres with five courtyards, several imposing Temple towers, large & spacious mandapas. There are three Temple Tanks known as 'Amrita Pushkarini', 'Kaala Theertham' & 'Maarkandeya Theertham'. There is a separate shrine dedicated to Abhirami. The Temple also maintains a separate shrine for Markandeya worshipping Kalasamhara Murti. Although Thirukadaiyur is a Shaiva Temple, it contains an old Vaishnava Temple. Shastiapthapoorthi (60th birthday), Bhimaradha Shanthi (70th birthday), 80th birthday (sadabishegam) and other Ayul Shanthi fire worships are very famous here.

DISTRICT – NAGAPATTINAM (Railway Station – Nagappattinam/Mayiladuturai/Sirkazhi)

S. No.	Temple	Address	Type
1	Arulmigu Nagannathaswamy Temple & Arulmigu Kethu Sthalam	Keezhaperumpallam – 609105	Nagnath, Ketu
2	Arulmigu Sattanatha Swami Temple	Sirkali – 609110	Shiva
3	Arulmigu Swetharanya Swami Temple	Thiruvengadu – 609114	Shiva
4	Sri Arul Somanathaswamy Temple	Nidur - 609203	Shiva
5	Arulmigu Rajagopalaswamy Temple	Ananthamangalam – 609307	Hanuman
6	Veerateeswarar Temple	Valuvur - 609401	Shiva
7	Sowriraja Perumal Temple	Thirukkannapuram – 609704	Vishnu
8	Shri Kayahorana Swami Neelayathatchi Amman Temple	Nagapattinam – 611001	Shiva

S. No.	Temple	Address	Type
9	Sri Nellukkadai Mariamman Kovil	Melakottaivasal - 611003	Mata
10	Sri Soundararaja Perumal Temple	Nagapattinam – 611003	Vishnu
11	Loganatha Perumal Temple	Sikkal – 611108	Vishnu
12	Singaravelavar Subrahmanya Temple	Sikkal – 611108	Murugan
13	Uma Maheshwara Temple	Konerirajapuram - 612201	Shiva
14	Sri Tazuvikuzandheswarar Temple	Thiruvalangadu – 631210	Shiva
15	Vadaranyeswarar Swamy Temple	Thiruvalangadu – 631210	Shiva

ARULMIGU NAGANNATHASWAMY TEMPLE AND ARULMIGU KETHU STHALAM AT KEEZHAPERUMPALLAM – This Temple is the seat of the Ninth Navagraha, Sri Kethu. During the churning of the milk ocean, Vasuki, the serpent used as the rope for the purpose got exhausted and split its venom. Devas ran to Lord Shiva for the protection from the impact of the spreading poison. Lord swallowed the poison & protected the world. Vasuki felt that it had caused Lord Shiva to swallow its poison & performed penance seeking Lord's pardon. Lord gave darshan to Vasuki and admired its sense of sacrifice. Vasuki begged Lord Shiva to stay in the place. Lord obliged Vasuki & stayed here named after the serpent - Naganathar. The Naganathar are believed to be the transmitters of Universal, quintessential energy & power. The Naganathar are closely associated with the fixed stars in the Zodiac. In this Temple, Lord Kethu is present in the form of human body and serpent head. Though Lord Shiva is present here as the presiding deity, Lord Kethu is worshipped first and then only the devotees visit the sanctum to get blessings from Lord Naganathaswamy & Sri Soundharyanayagi. Lord Kethu is specially offered with offerings like Lilly flowers, horse gram (Kollu) & multi coloured cloths.

ARULMIGU SATTANATHA SWAMI TEMPLE AT SIRKALI – The Temple has many wonderful architectural & sculptural features. Three different forms of Lord Shiva are worshipped here, the Shivalingam (Bhrammapureeswarar), a colossal vigraha of Uma Maheswarar (Toniappar) at the medium level & Bhairavar (Sattanathar) at the upper level. The Temple is associated with the legend of child Sambandar who is believed to have been fed by Goddess Parvathi on the banks of the Temple tank. The child later went on to compose Tevaram, a Saiva canonical literature & became one of the most revered Saiva poets in South India. This Temple has been glorified in the divine songs of Thevaram. Every year in the Tamil month of Chithirai, Thirumulaippal festival is celebrated in a grand manner.

ARULMIGU SWETHARANYA SWAMI TEMPLE AT THIRUVENGADU - Another Navagraha Budhan is situated inside the Temple of Arulmigu Swetharanya Swami. Lord Shiva is worshiped as Swetharanyeswarar & is represented by the Lingam. His consort Parvati is depicted as Brahmavidyambigai. It is said that Agora Murthi was one of the furious incarnation of Lord Shiva. The presiding deity is revered in the 7th century Tamil Saiva canonical work, the Tevaram, written by Tamil saint poets known as the Nayanars & classified as

Paadal Petra Sthalam. It is significant as one of the Temples associated with the nine planet elements, the Navagraha Stalas & specifically Budha. Devotees from all over India and abroad come to worship Budhan every day. The Temple has a number of shrines, with those of Swetharanyesarar, Aghora & that of Nataraja, being the most prominent. All the shrines & three Temple Tanks of Temple are enclosed in concentric rectangular granite walls.

SRI ARUL SOMANATHASWAMY TEMPLE AT NIDUR - The Temple is more than 1000 years old. The Temple is dedicated to Lord Shiva who is known as Somanathaswamy. The amman is Veyurutholi Ammai. There are 9 Theerthas in the Temple. Siddhivinayaka graces the devotees from the shrine. There are shrines of Lord Sivalokanathar, Kailasanathar, Kasiviswanatha, Ananda Thandavamurthy, Muruga and Saptha Kannikas. Lord Nataraja is in sudha form. The vimana in the sanctum sanctorum is of irudala design. Those facing delays in wedding, concerned with the welfare of children, seeking pardon for wrong doing prays the Lord here for solution.

ARULMIGU RAJAGOPALASWAMY TEMPLE AT ANANTHAMANGALAM - People from all over Tamilnadu visit the Temple of Lord Anjaneyar for his grace. Lord Anjaneya Temple is facing towards east. The divine Vigraha of Lord Anjaneya is unique with its three eyes and ten hands. He holds the Conch, a Chakra, a Soolam, a Kabalam, a Madhatchagam, Pasamankusam, a Bow, an Arrow, a Sattai, a Navaneetham and two feathers in each of his hands. Special worship of Lord Anjaneya is held on Saturdays and on the days of Amavasya.

VEERATEESWARAR TEMPLE AT VALUVUR - The Temple is also called Vazhuvur Veerateeswarar Temple. The presiding deity is Lord Shiva in the form of Veerateswarar & his consort is known as Bala Gujambigai. The village is mentioned in the 7th CE Tamil Saiva canonical work, the Tevaram, written by Tamil saint poets known as the nayanars & classified as Vaippu Sthalam. As per legend, Lord Shiva is believed to have destroyed eight different demons & Veeratanam Temples are built signifying each of his victories. The Temple is one of the 8 Temples where Lord Shiva is believed to have punished the elephant taking the form of Gajasamhara. The present masonry structure was built during the Chola dynasty during 9th CE, while later expansions are attributed to Thanjavur Nayaks.

SOWRIRAJA PERUMAL TEMPLE AT THIRUKKANNAPURAM – The Temple is revered in Nalayira Divya Prabandham, the 7th – 9th CE Vaishnava canon, by Periyazhvar, Andal, Kulasekaraazhvaar, Nammazhwar and Thirumangai Azhwar. The Temple is classified as a 108 Divyadesam. The Temple is also mentioned in 108 Tirupathi Anthathi by Divya Kavi Pillai Perumal Aiyangar. A work by T. S. Rajagopalan on Tirukannapuram glorifies the features of the Temple. This Temple is one of the Panchakanna (Krishnaranya) Kshetrams and considered the foremost among the five Temples. Sage Kanva is believed to have worshiped the presiding deity. Tirukannapuram is one among the eight Temples including

Tirupathi, Srirangam, Srimushnam, Naguneri, Saligram, Pushkar and Padarikashram that are considered the eight holy centres of salvation in Vaishanava mythology. They are believed to stand for Ashtatshara (eight lettered) spell of "Om Namo Narayana" with each centre representing a letter each. The Temple is the place where Lord Vishnu is believed to have represented himself in all the eight forms, the combination of the all the eight Temples. The Temple is also called Bhoologa Vaikundam. A granite wall surrounds the Temple enclosing all its shrines and three of its seven bodies of water. The Temple has a seven-tiered rajagopuram, the Temple's gateway tower and a huge Temple tank in front of it. The Temple is believed to have been built by the Cholas with later additions from the Thanjavur Nayaks. The vigraha of the presiding deity, Neela Meghar, is housed in the sanctum, which is approached through the gateways and the Mahamandapa. The sanctum also houses the vigraha of Sridevi and Bhoodevi on either side of Neelameghar, Dandaka Maharishi and Garuda. The metal vigraha of the festival deity, Sowriraja Perumal, is also housed in the sanctum, with four consorts namely Sridevi, Bhudevi, Padmini and Andal. There are also metal vigrahas of Santhana Krishnar and Chakrathaazhwar. There are separate shrines for Senai Mudaliar (the general of Lord Vishnu's forces), Nardhana Krishna, the twelve Azhwars, Rama, Consort of presiding deity and Thaylapura Nayagi. There are four Temple tanks associated with the Temple, with the largest, Nityapushkarani, located opposite the Temple. Ksheerapati Pushkarani, Bhootavadan and Muthakaram are other three tanks of the Temple.

SHRI KAYAHORANA SWAMI NEELAYATHATCHI AMMAN TEMPLE AT NAGAPATTINAM – The Temple is dedicated to Lord Shiva, who is worshipped as Kayarohana. His consort Goddess Parvathi is worshipped here in the form of Neelayathakshi. The Temple was built in the 6th century by the Lakolisa cult (one of the oldest sects of Shaivism) which has its origin in Gujarat. The only other Temple built by this cult in Tamil Nadu is at Kanchipuram. The Temple houses the Vigraha of Thyagaraja, a renowned composer of Carnatic music. The uniqueness of this Vigraha is that it is made of lapis lazuli (a deep blue metamorphic rock). The Temple is one of the 275 Paadal Petra Sthalams. The Temple has been rebuilt by the Pallavas and Cholas. Kayarohana Swamy Temple is one of the Temples that depicts the dance styles regarded as Saptha Vidangam or seven dance moves. The Temple falls under the category of Adhividangar Temple, known for Vilathithaanam dance pose (meaning dancing like waves of sea). The Temple is a Shakti Peetam and has been greatly praised by the revered Saints Sambandar, Appar and Sundarar in their Thevaram hymns.

SRI NELLUKKADAI MARIAMMAN KOVIL AT MELAKOTTAIVASAL – It is one of the most famous Temples of Tamil Nadu. Built by a rice trader, the Temple was built as per the wishes of the Goddess who had appeared in his dreams. The Temple is believed to have mystical powers. Devotees throng to this place every year during Thiruvizha to offer their prayers.

SRI SOUNDARARAJA PERUMAL TEMPLE AT NAGAPATTINAM - Constructed in Dravidian style of architecture, the Temple is glorified in the Divya Prabandha, the early medieval Tamil canon of the Azhwar saints from the 6th–9th centuries AD. It is counted as one among the 108 Divya Desams dedicated to Lord Vishnu. Lord Vishnu is worshiped as Soundararaja Perumal and his consort Lakshmi as Soundaravalli. The Temple is believed to have been built by the Medieval Cholas of the late 8th century AD, with later contributions at different times from Thanjavur Nayaks. The Temple has two inscriptions dating from the Chola period. The Temple has a five-tiered rajagopuram (gateway tower) within a granite wall. The complex contains all the shrines and water bodies associated with it. The Temple observes six daily rituals and three yearly festivals. The chariot festival, celebrated during the Tamil month of Chittirai (March–April), is the most prominent festival of the Temple. The main entrance of the Temple faces the East and, at the entrance of the Temple, there is a four pillared open hall. A rare vigraha of Lord Narasimha with eight hands, one blessing Prahlada, another showing Abhaya Mudra and the others involved in the killing of the demon, Hiranyakashipu, is present in the Temple. There is a four-pillared hall in front of the shrine of Soundarvalli shrine that has beautiful architectural carvings. The hall has the vigrahas of the architects who designed it. The Nayaka hall is built like a chariot with wheels outside it. The hall which has entrance to the Temple has two eight foot sculptures of the guardian deities Sumba and Nigumba.

LOGANATHA PERUMAL TEMPLE AT SIKKAL – The Temple is dedicated to Lord Vishnu. Constructed in the Dravidian style of architecture, the Temple is glorified in the Divya Prabandha, the early medieval Tamil canon of the Azhwar Saints from 6th – 9th centuries. It is one of the 108 Divyadesam dedicated to Lord Vishnu, who is worshiped as Loganatha Perumal and his consort Lakshmi as Loganayagi. The Temple is believed to have been built by the Medieval Cholas of the late 8th century with later contributions from Vijayanagar Kings and Madurai Nayaks. A granite wall surrounds the Temple enclosing all its shrines and its bodies of water. The Temple has a five-tiered rajagopuram, the Temple's gateway tower. Loganatha Temple is believed to have appeared to Lord Brahma, Sages Gautama, Uprivasu, Vashista, Bhrighu and Madarar. Six daily rituals & four yearly festivals are held at the Temple, of which the Panguni Brahmostavam, celebrated during the Tamil month of Panguni (April–May), is the most prominent. As per Hindu legend, Sage Gautama is believed to have worshiped the deity here. The Temple tank is right outside the Temple. The prime deity, Loganathar has an imposing vigraha, which is housed in the sanctum. The sanctum is approached from the gateway tower through a flag staff located axial to the entrance and the sanctum. The sanctum is approached through two pillared halls named Mukha Mandapa and Ardhamandapa. The shrine of Loganayagi & other deities are located around the sanctum in the first and second precinct. This Temple is one of the Panchakanna (Krishnaranya) Kshetrams.

SINGARAVELAVAR SUBRAHMANYA TEMPLE AT SIKKAL - A beautiful Lord Muragan Temple, dedicated to Lord Singaravelan, is housed in a large complex. The pillars of this Temple are adorned with intricate and exquisite carvings. The beautiful paintings of a bygone era are amazing in colour and portrayal. Beside this Temple, it has the shrine of Lord Shiva, Vishnu and Hanuman. It is a rare combination indeed. It is believed that worship in this Temple removes all the hurdles of the devotees. Actually, this is a Shaiva Temple with Lord Shiva bearing the name Sri Navaneetheswara but the main deity is Lord Subrahmanya, called Singaravelavar. Sage Vasishta made a Shivalinga out of butter, which was obtained from the milk of a divine cow Kamadhenu for worship. After puja, the Shivalinga could not be shifted and got stuck and hence the name Sikkal in Tamil for this place. This Temple was worshipped by Sages Vasishta, Viswamitra, wish-granting cow Kamadenu and Emperor Muchukunda of Deva Loka. Saints Sambandhar and Arunagirinathar have sung in praise of the Lord Sikkal Singaravelavar. The name of the Goddess in the standing posture here is

Velnedunganni. Lord Ganapati, Mahalakshmi, Nataraja, the sixty three Nayanmars, Bhairava, Surya and Chandra are also having sannadhis at the respective places as per agamic standards. The Sthalavriksha (sacred tree) here is jasmine. There are three holy tanks for this Temple namely Ksheera (ie. milk), Gaya and Lakshmi Tanks. During the Tamil month of Arpasi, Skanda Shashti is celebrated in a grand manner for the main ruling deity, Singaravelavar. Tradition tells us that the Lord received the Vel at Sikkal and killed Surapadman at Tiruchendur the next day. During Skanda Shashti, Lord Singaravelavar will receive the Vel one day prior to Surasamharam from his mother to destroy the demon Surapadman. After receiving the Vel even today, one will find Lord Muruga's face perspiring, which is a miracle. The Singaravelavar is in the form of utsavamurti with his consorts Valli and Devayanai, showering his divine grace. The Ksheera Pushkarini (Paal Kulam) tank is located behind the Temple. Legend also has it that Lord Vishnu sought the blessings of Lord Shiva before venturing out to the court of the demon King Mahabali and there is a Kola Vaamana Perumaal shrine adjacent to the Temple. The seven-tiered rajagopuram that adorns the entrance to this Temple is about 80 foot in height. The Kartikai Mandapam in the forefront exhibits a number of paintings depicting legends related to Lord Subramanya. This Temple is one of the important Lord Murugan Temple in Tamilnadu and in particular one of the noted Temples in Nagapattinam.

UMA MAHESHWARA TEMPLE AT KONERIRAJAPURAM - The Temple is known for a huge 9.5 ft. bronze vigraha of Lord Natarajaswami with his consort Goddess Sivagami Sundari. The Temple was initially built by Queen Sembian Mahadevi of Cholas and later the Temple was renovated by Vijayanagara rulers.

THIRUVALANGADU –

Sri Tazuvikuzandheswarar Temple – The Temple is another big Temple.

Sri Vadaranyeswarar Swamy Temple – It was built by the Cholas during the 12th century. The inscriptions evidence available is said that it was built in 5th century. It is regarded as a sacred Shivaite Temple. In the Temple, there is one of the 5 majestic cosmic dance halls (panchasabhai) of Lord Shiva, known as "Ratna Sabai". This is one of the 44 Paadalpetrasthalams where all the "Moovars" have rendered their pathigams. This is one of the 276 Devara Paadal Petra Shiva Sthalams and 15th Shiva Sthalam in Thondai Nadu. Lord Shiva in this Temple is a Swayambhumurthi (self-manifested). This Temple is considered to be a place where one can attain salvation. This Temple has three corridors and its main tower (Rajagopuram) has 5-tiers. The Natarajar Vigraha can be seen with its left leg almost touching the left ear. The Vigraha of Goddess Sivakama Sundari can be seen with her face reflecting her astonishment. This Temple has a beautiful 100-pillars hall where Lord Natarajar's abishekam is performed. In Lord Natarajar's shrine, there are two Shivalingams - one made of Spadigam (crystal) and the other one made of Maragatham (emerald). It is believed that Lord Murugan, Goddess Lakshmi and Saint Thirumular have worshiped Lord Shiva in this Temple. Two demons Sumba and Nisumba chose this banyan jungle for their stay and began harassing the Devas. The Devas appealed to Mother Parvathi for protection. Mother Parvathi created a furious Kali and destroyed the demons. Kali consumed the blood of the demons and their army and grew more furious. At the request of Sage Munjikesa Karkodaka, Lord Shiva reached the place. Kali challenged the Lord for a dance and said that she would give her right in the place to the Lord, if he won. The dance began. Lord dropped his ear ring on the ground, picked it by the toe of his left leg and fixed it back on his ear in the dance. Kali accepted her defeat. Lord Shiva said that he alone was equal to her and said further that those coming to worship Him here, should worship her first to reap the full benefit of the worship. Since then, Kali has her own Temple to grace the devotees. It is in this Temple that Lord addressed the Great Shiva devotee Karaikkal Ammeiyar as "Ammaye". Ammeiyar enjoyed the dance performance of the Lord standing upside down. Ammeiyar reached this Temple by head as she thought walking by feet to Lords shrine was a sin. She reached the state of bliss here. Karaikkal Ammaiar also rendered her "Mootha Thirupathigam" about Lord Shiva here. This is a Parihara Sthalam for Bharani Nakshathiram (star). Those who are born during the period of Bharani Nakshathiram can perform special poojas here. This is an important place for Mantheeswarar Pariharam and poojas can be performed on Saturdays. Mantheeswarar Pariharam is performed for removal of obstacles in marriage proposals, to help married couples get the blessing of child birth and to seek relief from debts. Since Mantheeswarar is the son of Lord Shani (Saturn), poojas related to Shanidoshams can also be performed here. Also, those aspiring for mastery in the art of dance can pray to Lord Vadaranyeswarar here and seek his blessings.

DISTRICT – NAMAKKAL (Railway Station – Namakkal)

S. No.	Temple	Address	Type
1	Namakkal Fort	Namakkal – 637001	Rama, Hanuman, Trinity
2	Arulmigu Narasimha Swamy Temple	Namakkal – 637001	Narasimha (Vishnu), Mata
3	Arulmigu Anjaneyar Temple	Namakkal – 637002	Hanuman
4	Arulmigu Arthanareeswarar Temple	Tiruchengode – 637211	Shiva-Parvati
5	Kollimalai Hills	Kolli Hills - 637411	Shiva

NAMAKKAL FORT- It lies at the foot of the single rock Hillock. On top of this hillock [also known as Saligramam], is a Rock Fort. This rock fort is the special attraction of the town. There is a legend in mythology about this hillock, which is connected to Lord Hanuman during Ramanaya period. The Cave Temple houses the shrines of Lord Ranganathar and Lord Lakshmi Narasimhan. The caves were constructed by Adhiyaman rulers who ruled over Kongu Region during the 7th century. The Temple have been declared a monument by the HR&CE department of Government. As per the legend, Goddess Mahalakshmi was on a penance to subdue the anger of Lord Narasimha after his Hiranyakashyap sanhar. Lord Anjaneya on his way back to Sethu was returning with a rare Saligramam of Lord Narasimha and Lord Ranganathar. He halted at this place for prayers and requested Mahalakshmi to guard the saligramam till he completed his prayers. Because he was late, Mahalakshmi leaves the Saligramam near Anjaneya and left. Since it was put down, Sri Ranganathar and Sri Lakshmi Narasimhar was installed at the same site. Hence the Cave Temple houses both the deities in separate shrines. Lord Narasimha is seated facing west with right leg on the ground and left leg placed on the right thigh. The 'Vajra Naka' with which Lord Narasimha performed the Hiranya Sanhar can be seen. Janakan and Sanadhan on the left and right side of Lord respectively are believed to be describing the concept of "Lokashama" [pardon] in his hears. This is a special Temple with both Lord Shiva and Brahma are in the same shrine with a plea to subdue the anger mood of Lord Narasimha. Because of this rare appearance, it is called as Tirumurthi Sthalam and one can worship Lord Brahma, Vishnu and Shiva here in one place. Since he is with joined by Sri Devi after the penance, he is called as Lakshmi Narasimha. Sri Ranganathan Temple is very near from the Lord Anjaneya's shrine. The darshan of Sri Ranganatha, a 10 foot Vigraha, will be in three parts as found in the Ananda Padmanaba Swamy Temple of Trivandrum. Lord Ranganatha is seen holding Conch, Chakra, bow-arrow, mace and Sword.

ARULMIGU NARASIMHA SWAMY TEMPLE AT NAMAKKAL – The Temple is dedicated to the Goddess Namagiri Amman. It is situated within the Temple complex of Narasimha Swamy Kovil. According to the legends, Namagiri Amman (or Namagiri Lakshmi) appeared in the Kamalalayam and performed penance which pleased Narasimha Swamy. The Amman is reputed for granting prayers for marriages and children. The Temple is located facing the Narasimha Swamy Kovil and contains a holy water spring known as the Narasimha Theertham. The sculptural works of the Temple exhibit influence of the Pallava and Chalukya art. The Lord is generally known as Sri Lakshmi Narasimha, Mother Sri Lakshmi is on his lap. In this Temple, Sri Mahalakshmi has her place on the chest of the Lord. Sri Namagiri Thayar (Mother Lakshmi) has her shrine here facing east. It is believed that the devotee would become a pundit in mathematics if he/she worships Mahalakshmi. There is a separate Temple for Bhakta Anjaneya who brought the Anjaneya Salagrama. The colossal stone Vigraha 18' high of Visvarupa Anjaneya, popularly known as Hanumantharaya Swamy, with a japamala in hand and a sword in the waist. While Sri Anjaneya was bathing in River Kandaki in Nepal, He got a stone named Salagrama in the shape of Lord Vishnu. Here, Sri Mahalakshmi's prayer made Sri Narasimha calm, then he blessed Sri Mahalakshmi and gave her so many Varams. From that time, the name to Mahalakshmi was spread as Sri Namagiri Lakshmi. The Sanctum Sanctorum and Ardhamandapam are in the cave. Sri Narasimhaswamy is sitting with the Sages Sanaka, Sanandana, Soorya, Chandra and Chamaram and in the last Lord Shiva and Brahma are praying. We can see Ardhamandapam walls with very beautiful sculptures of the Mahavishnu's Avatharams! Abhaya Narsimha is also here. In the next wall, we can see Sri Ugra Narasimha tearing the Hiranya's chest by nails. On the other side wall Sri Vaamanamoorthy is getting danam by Mahabalya Chakravarty. Sukrachari is punished by Garuda for disturbing the Danam. Jambavan is drumming in the sky. In the same wall Sri Mahavishnu as Threvikrama is measuring the earth and sky. In the next wall, Sri Varaha Moorthy is bearing the four Vedas all power heads on the nose and holding Sri Bhoomadevi by two hands. Sri Namagiri Amman's lotus eyes are merciful. She is sitting on the lotus, face is lotus, mouth is lotus, hands are lotus, feet are lotus and her birth place is lotus. She is also holding the lotus. The glories of Goddess Sri Namagiri Thayar is spread in all over India up to Himalayas and Cape Chomarin. The devotees who visit Namakkal first; they heartly worship Namagiri Thayar and apply their application about

diseases, want of child and other wanting. In time their wants are fulfilled by Sri Namagiri Ammal's mercy. They are offering Kanikies, Sarees and Jewels etc. The Dasara festival is performed for ten days. The Car festival is celebrated for 15 days to Sri Narasimha, Sri Ranganatha, and Sri Hanuman in the star of Panguni Hastham in every year. The Hanumanth Jayanthi is celebrated by devotees during the New Moon day of Margazhi month.

ARULMIGU ANJANEYAR TEMPLE AT NAMAKKAL – The famous Temple is almost 1500 years old. Lord Anjaneya with a Japamala in hand and a sword in the waist is in the form of a life size 18 foot tall Vigraha, carved out of a single rock. The special feature of this Temple is the Lord Anjaneya on constant guard and worship and has his sight fixed exactly on the divine feet of Lord Narasimha at the hillock. The Anjaneya shrine is without a roof, open to the sky. Lakhs of people visit this Anjenayar throughout the year from different parts of the country. There is also a shrine of another Anjaneya Vigraha on the banks of the Temple tank called Kamalayam. It is constructed in the Dravidian style of architecture. The legend of the Temple is associated with Lord Narasimha, an avatar of Lord Vishnu appearing for Hanuman and Lakshmi. The Agamam is followed by "Sri Vaikhanasam". The Temple has a pillared hall leading to the sanctum. In Threthayuga, during the Ramayana period, Sri Hanuman lifted the Sanjeevi Mountain from the Himalayas to get medical herbs. He then took the mountain back and replaced it in its original place. When he returned, he brought a salagramam. During his journey, as the sun rose, he went down to the earth and performed the ritual of santhayavanthanam after placing the salagramam near Sri Mahalakshmi's tapavanam. After performing the pooja, Hanuman tried to lift the salagramam but was unable to move it as easily as before. Suddenly, the salagramam grew larger and Lord Hanuman heard an oracle saying, "Lord Narasimha wishes to stay here and he wants Lord Hanuman to save Sri Ramachandramurthy first of all." Thus, Sri Hanuman completed his task and came to Namakkal Sthalam on the western side of the rock, where he stands in open air and worships Lord Narasimha Swamy.

ARULMIGU ARTHANAREESWARAR TEMPLE AT TIRUCHENGODE - It is one of the seven Shivasthalams in Kongunadu. The Temple is located on a hill. The presiding deity is depicted as half-male and half-female, vertically to represent Lord Shiva and Goddess Parvati worshipped as one form. It is considered one of the oldest Temples in this region.

KOLLIMALAI HILLS - The Hills are situated on Eastern Ghats at an altitude of 1200 meters above sea level. The Kollimalai Hills are known for medicinal herbs and plants that grow in abundance on the hill slopes. The Arapaleswarar Temple, the Horticulture Farm, the Herbal Farm, Agaya Gangai Waterfalls, Boat house, Peryaswamy Temple, Ettukai Amman Temple, Pineapple farms, View Point and Telescope House are the places to visit for the interested tourist. Attukalkilangu soup and raw was selling in this hills. This is good medicine for knee pain. The Valvil Ori festival is organised here every year during the month of August.

DISTRICT – PERAMBALUR (Railway Station – Ariyalur)

S. No.	Temple	Address	Type
1	Arulmigu Ekampareshwarar and Thandayudhapani Temple	Chettikulam - 621104	Shiva, Murugan

S. No.	Temple	Address	Type
2	Arulmigu Siruvachur Mathura Kaliaman Temple	Siruvachur - 621113	Mata
3	Valeeswarar Temple	Valikandapuram – 621115	Shiva

ARULMIGU EKAMPARESHWARAR AND THANDAYUDHAPANI TEMPLE AT CHETTIKULAM - In the earlier days, this place was surrounded by a canopy of Kadamba Trees. The Chola King was ruling, having Uraiyur as capital. At that time, a Trader from his region, went towards Northern side, from Uraiyur, to trade. When he reached Kadambavanam, it was dusk and dark. So, he decided to stop his journey and rest there. He climbed up and sat on a Banyan Tree. A flash of light appeared suddenly like a fire in the midnight, which was in the form of Shivalinga amid the Lords and Saints, worshipping, then it disappeared. This wonderful scene was witnessed by the trader. Out of astonishment, the trader returned back to his native place Uraiyur and described that spiritual scene to the great King Parandaha Cholan. The Chola and Pandian Kings along with the trader and soldiers reached Kadambavanam. They searched for the Shivalinga in all directions. At that time, an old man with a sugar cane in his hand revealed them the place of Linga and disappeared. The Kings were astonished to see, at a distance, a small hill on which Lord Muruga stands as Thandayuthapani with a sugar cane. Both the Kings were almost immersed in Bhakthi and Kulasekara Pandian constructed both the Ekambareswarar and Thandayudhapani Temple at a time. Towards the East is the Ekambareswarar Temple and Arulmigu Thandayuthapani on the hill faces his father towards west is a unique feature. On 19,20,21 dates of Panguni month, the sun's rays fall on Shivalinga in the dawn and gradually works, falls on Kamatchi Amman. On 19,20,21 dates of Maasi month, the sun's rays fall on Lord Thandayuthapani in the dusk. Thaipoosam Festival celebrated in Ekambareswarar Temple is of great unique. Panguni Festival celebrated in the hill of Lord Thandayuthapani is also of great unique and the Lord will come down the hill and will give his darshan to the devotees. Devotees in wanton of child will have to fast on Shasti days, praying and they have to tie a cradle on the Vilva Tree. After getting fulfilled their prayer, the devotee has to bring his child in sugar cane cradle to the hill. In Arulmigu Ekambareswarar Temple, there is a Temple separately for Kuberan opposite to Ambal Temple. Here Kuberan's darshan is with Chitralekha sitting on Lotus. Here, green colour Kumkum is given as Prasad. This is one of the unique qualities of this Temple. Besides that, for 12 Zodiac symbols are present in 'OM' shape in all the Temple pillars. Offering Green dhoti is also a special one. On Kuberan's birth star 'Poorattadhi' Kubera Homam and special prayers will be performed in a grand manner every month. There is a holy pond called Panchanadi Theertha Pond.

ARULMIGU MATHURA KALIAMMAN TEMPLE AT SIRUVACHUR – The renowned Temple has an antiquity dating back to 1000 years. According to tradition, Chelliamman was the local deity of Siruvachur. An evil magician through his intense devotion to the deity won her favour. Pleased with his devotion, Chelliamman granted him any boon he wished. The cruel sorcerer wished that the deity should be his servant and do his bidding at all times. Bound by the power of her own boon, Chelliamman had no other option but to obey all his evil commands. At this time, Kannagi the embodiment of virtue and chastity happened to visit Siruvachur. Kannagi was the devoted wife of Kovalan, a merchant. The happy couple led a blissful life till Kovalan in the course of his travels met Madhavi a beautiful danseuse. Enamoured by her grace, Kovalan started living with her and spent all his wealth on her. This went on for over a year during which he had a daughter Manimegalai through her. When his resources were exhausted, Kovalan realized his folly and returned to his

devoted wife Kannagi. The couple went to Madurai to eke out their livelihood. Kovalan, hard pressed for money, tried to sell one of the precious anklets of his wife. The anklets resembled those of the queen of Madurai and so Kovalan was charged with theft and swiftly beheaded by the king without even a trial. On hearing this, Kannagi seething with anger rushed to the king's court and accused him of taking an innocent man's life by his hasty and unjust ruling. With fuming rage, she took out the other anklet and threw it down. All at once, by the power of her chastity the entire city of Madurai went up in flames. After this, Kannagi left Madurai and traveling towards north arrived at Siruvachur. There she rested for the night at the deserted Temple. Something strange happened. The deity of the Temple Chelliamman came out of the sanctum and requested Kannagi not to stay there as she could be killed by the cruel magician. Chelliamman narrated to Kannagi her sorry tale. Kannagi was very much moved and offered to help Chelliamman rid herself of the evil. Kannagi entered the sanctum with Chelliamman and lay there waiting. In the middle of the night the magician came and ordered Chelliamman to come out. Kannagi immediately invoked the blessings of her family deity Kali. Goddess Kali bestowed her powers on Kannagi who then leapt out of the sanctum, fought the magician, vanquished and beheaded him. Chelliamman was thus rid of her bondage. Filled with gratitude Chelliamman prayed to Kannagi to stay at the Temple permanently to bless and protect all devotees who seek her refuge. Chelliamman said that she would retreat and stay at the nearby Periyasami hills. Kannagi willingly consented but on condition that she would stay at the Temple only on Mondays and Fridays and with Chelliamman on all other days. Since Kannagi came from Madurai and had invoked the blessings of Goddess Kali to slay the magician, she was worshiped as Mathura Kaliamman when she took the seat at Siruvachur Temple. Thousands of devotees visit the Temple on Mondays and Fridays to seek the blessings of Mathura Kaliamman. During Puja, Aarthi is first lifted towards Periyasami hills to offer prayers to Chelliamman and then it is offered to Mathura Kaliamman. In accordance with the magician's dying wish, his samadhi is located in front of the sanctum. Devotees stamp over the samadhi while entering the sanctum as wished for by the magician. The priests at the Temple are said to be the descendants of the magician but entirely free of his evil proclivities by the divine grace of the deity. It is said that the deity at the Temple was originally consecrated by Adi Sankara. The revered Saint Sri Sadasiva Brahmendral has installed a powerful Srichakram in this Temple. The deity is also the Kuladeivam of Kanchi Mahaswami, Shri Chandrasekharendra Saraswathi. The Chithirai Festival and other Festivals are celebrated with great pomp and fervour.

VALEESWARAR TEMPLE AT VALIKANDAPURAM - The Temple is dedicated to Lord Shiva. The presiding deity is called as Valeeswarar / Brahmapureeswarar and Amman is called as Valambigai / Bhrihannayaki. The Temple is located on the eastern banks of Koneri River. The Temple was built by the Cholas before the construction of Tanjore Brihadeeswarar Temple. The Temple has about 130 stone inscriptions including one from the Chola period. Krishnadevaraya has contributed to the development of this Temple. Lot of inscriptions in this Temple refers to donations of lamps to this Temple by the merchants. The Temple is having a imposing seven tiered Rajagopuram.

DISTRICT – PUDUKKOTTAI (Railway Station – Pudukkottai/Tiruchchirapali/Keeranur)

S. No.	Temple	Address	Type
1	Sri Athmanathar Temple	Avudayarkoil - 614618	Shiva
2	Meinindranaadha Swami Temple	Keeramangalam – 614624	Shiva
3	Muvar Koil & Mujukundeeswarer Temple	Kodumbalur – 621316	Shiva
4	Lord Subramania Temple	Viralimalai - 621316	Subramania
5	Kokaraneeswarer Temple	Tirugokarnam - 622002	Shiva
6	Group of Temples	Narthamalai - 622101	Shiva, Mata
7	Cave Temple	Chithannavasal – 622101	Jain
8	Sri Shikanathar Temple	Kudumianmalai - 622104	Shiva
9	Lord Shiva & Murugan Temples	Kunnandarkoil - 622502	Shiva, Murugan
10	Lord Shiva & Vishnu Temple	Malayadipatti - 622502	Shiva, Vishnu
11	Thirumayam Fort	Tirumayam – 622507	Shiva, Vishnu

SRI ATHMANATHAR TEMPLE AT AVUDAYARKOIL - The Temple is dedicated Athmanatha Swamy. It contain life-size sculptures. The roof is made up of copper plate similar to that of the Nataraja Temple at Chidambaram, which is having golden plates. The Temple is noted for its granite roof work. The Saint Manickavasaga had been given high focus in this Temple. It has been under the control of Thiruvadu Thurai Atheeyenam.

MEININDRANAADHA SWAMI TEMPLE AT KEERAMANGALAM – There is an 81 foot Vigraha of Meinindranaadha Swami (Lord Shiva) & 7.25 foot Vigraha of the Chief Poet "Nakkeerar".

MUVAR KOIL & MUJUKUNDEESWARER TEMPLE AT KODUMBALUR – The name Kodumbaloor has been mentioned in the Tamil epic Silapathigaram. The architectural structure existed here are the forerunner for Dravidiyan style of architecture. The remaining structures of Muvarkoil and Mujukundeeswarer Temple attracts many tourist to this place. It is under the control of Archaeological survey India.

LORD SUBRAMANIA TEMPLE AT VIRALIMALAI - A small Temple dedicated to Lord Subramania is situated on the top of a hillock. An inscription of this Temple mention that the original Temple has been built by a King Azhakiya Manavalan. Later on, the additions were made in this Temple by the Chola dynasty. Some other inscriptions told that the renovations of the Temple were made by Adhithiya Chola. Other additions like pragaram & mandapas were made by Nayaks & Marungapuri dynasty, the Navarathiri Mandapam constructed by Pudukkottai Emperors. Green plantations, roaming of peacocks are the adding attractions of this Temple. Lord Subramanya with his consort Theyvanai have fulfil the wishes of the devotees. Chithirai Paurnami, Vaigasi Visagam, Teppa Thiruvizha, Kandasasti and Panguni Uttiram are the important festivals celebrated here. During the days, dramas were performed from the Viralimalai Kuravanchi wrote by Muthu palani Kavirayar.

KOKARANEESWARER TEMPLE AT THIRUGOKARNAM - A rock cut Cave Temple was built by Mahendravarma of Pallava dynasty. Lord Shiva (Kokaraneeswarer) and Goddess Sakthi (Pragadambal) are the main deity of this Temple. The later additions were made by Pandyas, Cholas and Thondaman Dynasty and become a great structure of Temple. Many festivals and dance programmes were frequently performed here in ancient days. Drama, dance and music flourished to its peak during the Thondaman dynasty. Chithirai Festival, Adi Pooram and Navarathiri Vizha are the important festival celebrated here.

NARTHAMALAI – It is Headquarters for the Chieftain of Mutharaiyar. The earliest structural stone Temple circular in shape, Vijayalaya Choleeswaram Cave Temple and Kadambarmalai Temple are the main attractions of Narthamalai. Now-a-days, the Narthmalai Muthu Mariamman Temple also attract many tourists to this place. The Mullaipari procession is an attracting event of this Temple.

CHITHANNAVASAL - In ancient days, the Jain Monks used to live in cave and hillocks so as to perform their ascetic life. They polished the hill for the purpose of poojas and penance in the open shelter. The rare Brahmi Tamil script inscriptions are found near the beds. The Jain Beds are collectively known as Ezhadipattam. A second century Jain Temple consisted of Lord Mahavir Vigraha on both sides of wall, which is considered as a 'Meditation Hall' or Arivar Temple. The ceiling of the Temple are full of fresco herbal painting dates back to Mahendravarma of Pallava dynasty. Paintings of a royal couple and a lotus tank with marine creatures are notable. These paintings are considered to be the next of Ajantha cave Paintings at Aurangabad. The Cave Temples are under the control of Archaeological survey of India.

Jambunatha Cave - Jambunatha Cave or Navach-chunai, in the style of late Pandya Temples of 13th century is a tarn located between Ezadippattam and Arivar Kovil caves. It is on the eastern slope on the central part of the hills. This is a small rock-cut Temple which is submerged in a small lake (tarn). An old Jambu Tree (Syzygium Jambolanum) is seen near the lake, which gives its name to the Cave. It has a Lord Shiva Temple with a Shivalingam in the centre, which is worshiped by baling out water from the lake.

SRI SHIKANATHAR TEMPLE AT KUDUMIANMALAI - The Cave Temples situated here are the testimony for the ancient art and culture. There is Lord Shiva Temple on a hilllock dedicated to Sikkanatheeswarer and life size sculpture were surrounded by this Temple. There are more than 100 inscriptions with a highlight of an inscription expressing the grammatical notes of Carnatic music.

KUNNANDARKOIL – It is also called as Thirukundrakudi in the inscriptions available in this Temple. A Lord Shiva Temple (Cave Temple) has been constructed during the period of Nandhivarma of Pallava dynasty (775 AD). Lord Muruga Temple is also exist on the top of a small hill. There is mandapa in the shape of a chariot with horses attract many tourists in this spot.

MALAIYADIPATTY – There is a Lord Shiva Temple together with Lord Vishnu Temple. During 730 AD Nandhivarma of Pallava dynasty carved the Lord Shiva Temple (Vakeeswarar) from the Hilllock. The Lord Vishnu Temple is constructed later than the Lord Shiva Temple and Lord Narasimha Vigraha, Thirumal, Ananatashayana and Adhishesha Vigraha are the attractive vigrahas situated in this Lord Vishnu Temple. Some of the paintings depicting the ten incarnation of Thirumal have been beautifully painted on the walls of Thirumal Cave Temple.

THIRUMAYAM FORT – It was built by Sethupathy Vijaya Ragunatha Thevar of Ramanathapuram in 1687 AD. The actual Fort is two times greater than the Fort, as we see today. The main entrance of the Fort is situated one KM away from the present structure. A rock cut Lord Shiva Temple and a Lord Vishnu Temple with different vigrahas, Darbar Hall, some inscriptions and pillared corridor were situated at the foot of the hillock adjacent to the Fort. It is under the control of the Archaeological Survey of India. Nearest Railway Station is Tirumayam.

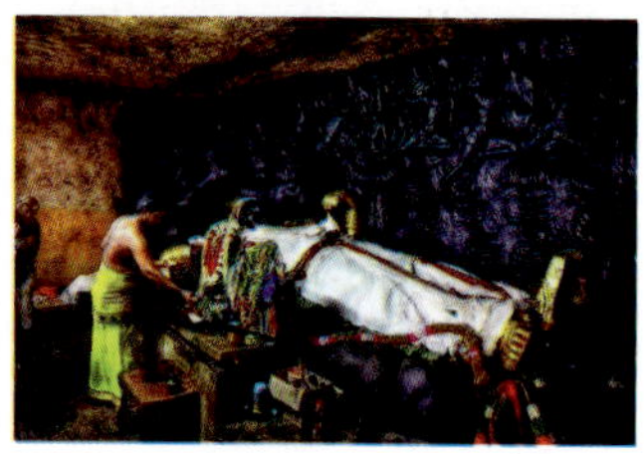

DISTRICT – RAMANATHAPURAM (Railway Station – Rameswaram)

RAMESWARAM – It is a small Island and major Pilgrim centre in the Gulf of Mannar. It is connected to the mainland by Pamban Bridge. On his return from Ceylon after Ravana Yudhdham (war) in Lanka, Lord Sri Rama offered his repentance prayer to Lord Shiva to absolve his sins that he had committed by slaying Ravana. Every day, this island receives thousands of pilgrims from all parts of the Indian subcontinent to get absolved of their sins and also perform rituals for their ancestors. This is at par with Varanasi or Benares in sanctity of the North India.

S. No.	Temple	Address	Type
1	Devipattinam	Rameswaram – 623514	Ramayana Circuit
2	Dhanushkodi	Pamban Island – 623521	Ramayana Circuit
3	Agni Theertham	Rameswaram – 623526	Ramayana Circuit

S. No.	Temple	Address	Type
4	Gandhamana Tirtham	Kendhamana Paruvatham – 623526	Ramayana Circuit
5	Panchamugi Hanuman Temple	Kendhamana Paruvatham – 623526	Hanuman
6	Sakshī Hanuman Temple	Kendhamana Paruvatham – 623526	Hanuman
7	Jada Theertham	Rameswaram – 623526	Ramayana Circuit
8	Kothandaramar Temple	Rameswaram – 623526	Ramayana Circuit
9	Shri Nambunayaki Amman Temple	Rameswaram – 623526	Mata
10	Arulmigu Ramanathaswamy Temple	Rameswaram – 623526	Dham, Jyotirlinga
11	Sugriva Tirtham	Madurai-Rameswaram Road, Rameswaram – 623526	Ramayana Circuit
12	Villondi Theertam	Rameswaram - 623529	Ramayana Circuit
13	Sri Bhadrakali Amman Temple	Ramanathapuram – 623530	Mata
14	Adi Jagannatha Temple	Thiruppullani - 623532	Vishnu
15	Arulmigu Mangalswari Samadha Mangalnadhar Temple	Uthirakosamangai – 623533	Shiva
16	Chenchudanathar Karunakadakshi Amman Temple	Near Sayalkudi, Kadaladi Taluk – 623703	Shiva, Mata

DEVIPATTINAM – The word Devipattinam is a Tamil name (Devi = Goddess Devi, pattinam = city or abode) which literally means the abode of the Goddess Devi/Parvathi. It is a coastal village and also known as Navashabashanam. It is believed that Lord Rama worshiped Navagraha (the 9 planets) here to worship before commencing the war with the demon King Ravana, who kidnapped Rama's wife Mata Sita. The Temple is dedicated to Devi, who is said to have killed the demon Mahishasura at this spot. Hindus perform religious rites for their forefathers here. It is believed by the pilgrims that by took bath in this sea and worship the 9 planets, all our karma related problems and Navagrahadhoshams (astrological predictions about one's misfortunes based on the planetary disorders in one's astrology chart) will be rectified.

DHANUSHKODI - It is the southernmost tip of the Pamban Island. Danushkodi was completely washed away in the 1964 cyclone but the Kothandaramasamy Temple here remains intact. A popular belief is that, it is where Vibhishana, brother of King Ravana surrendered before Lord Rama. Dhanushkodi has a fine beach, where sea surfing is possible. One of the smallest towns in the world, with a length of just 50 yards, Dhanushkodi is the land border between Sri Lanka and India. It is around 15 KMs away from Sri Lanka. It is surrounded by Bay of Bengal on one side and Indian Ocean on other side. According to legends of Ramayana, Dhanuskodi is the place where Lord Rama, Lakshman along with Hanuman and the Vanar Sena had built a bridge to Lanka so as to rescue Goddess Sita who was in the captivity of demon Ravana. This bridge is known as Ram Setu. The Ram Setu is an icon of sacrifice, devotion and perfectly illustrates the true culture and history of India. It is believed that the Ram Setu was in existence 7000 yrs. ago. It was created with lime floating stones and it was 30 KMs long and 3 KMs wide. Later, after winning the war, Lord Rama had crowned Vibhishana, brother of

Ravana, as the King of Lanka. Vibhishana later asked Lord Rama to destroy the Ram Setu. Upon his request, Lord Rama broke the bridge with an end of his bow. This is the reason why the place has been named as Dhanushkodi, which means 'end of the bow'.

SETHUKARAI - A place of immense religious significance, Sethukarai or the Sethu Coast is where Lord Rama is believed to have constructed the popular Rama Sethu (bridge) to reach Sri Lanka to rescue Goddess Sita from the clutches of Ravana. Ruins of a bridge are still visible there. Tourists can visit the Adi Sethu for a sacred bath. This is the point where Lord Rama is said to have taken a bath before leaving for Sri Lanka. A small Temple dedicated to Lord Hanuman is a popular attraction in Sethukarai and draws scores of pilgrims every day. The Temple is also referred to as the Sethu Bandhana Anjaneya Temple and is situated right on the seashore.

AGNITHEERTHAM – It has been mentioned in sacred Hindu texts such as Skanda Purana, Narada Purana and Sethu Purana. Sri Ramanathasamy Temple faces the Theertham on the eastern side. The sea is very calm and peaceful. Since it is considered sacred, it is called Agni Theertham because agni is considered to be purified element. Poojas and Rituals are performed to please the ancestors in this shore area. According to the legend, after killing demon Ravana, who also a half brahmin and an ardent devotee of Lord Shiva, Lord Rama had prayed to Lord Shiva to recompense his sins of killing a brahmin. He had bathed in the waters of Agnitheertham. This is the reason why bathing in holy Agnitheertham is said to atone past sins of the devotees. According to some belief, childless couples, if bathe in its water and offer prayers to Lord Shiva, are blessed with children. Many devotees come here to pray for children.

GANDHAMANA TIRTHAM – It is also known as Gandamadana Parvatham, which is a hillock and is the highest point in the island. It is also known as Rama Theertham. From here one can see the imprint of Lord Rama's feet on a chakra. The entire island of Rameswaram is visible from this point. The view of sunset and sunrise is especially captivating here. There are other shrines too which are located nearby such as Satchi Hanuman Temple and Sukreevar Teertham. It is also located close to another popular shrine Dhanushkodi Temple. It has many legends associated to it. According to a legend, Lord Rama had met Vibhishana, brother of demon Ravana at this place. The Temple also has an vigraha of Vibhishana. As per another legend, it is the first place where Lord Rama has rested after his extensive search for Goddess Sita when she was captured by demon Ravana. It is believed that Lord had waited here for a while looking at the vast expanse of Ocean between the places where he was standing and Lanka where Goddess was kept in confinement.

PANCHAMUGI HANUMAN TEMPLE - The deity Lord Hanuman is drawn with vermillion. Vigraha of Lord Ram, Sita and Hanuman brought from Dhanushkodi during the 1964 cyclone are placed there. The floating stone used to build the Sethu Bandhanam or the bridge between India and Lanka too can be found in this Temple. It is said that Lord had revealed his five faces here, hence the Vigraha of Lord Hanuman is depicted with five faces along with faces of Lord Narasimha, Lord Adivaraha, Lord Garuda & Lord Hayagriva on the sides.

SATCHI HANUMAN TEMPLE - This Temple is the place where Lord Hanuman delivered the good news of finding Mata Sita with Choodamani, a jewel that belonged to Mata Sita, as Satchi [evidence] to Lord Rama. Hence, it is called Satchi Hanuman Temple. It is also believed that Lord Rama cried in happiness on having realized that his wife was still alive. Lord Rama also acknowledged Lord Hanuman as his true 'bhakt' or follower, who went through a lot of hardships to bring him the news of Mata Sita. Devotees of both Lord Rama and Hanuman visit the Temple every year.

JADA THEERTHAM - It is believed that Lord Rama on his return from Lanka after Ravana Vadham washed his Jada [hair] in this Theertham to purify him before proceeding to worship Ramalingeswarar. There is one more legend associated with Jada Theertham. According to it, it is at this place the bird Jatayu, an ardent devotee, had given up his life after his wings were cut by demon Ravana. There is a Temple near Jada Theertham, Kaveri Theertham which is dedicated to Lord Kapardis Vara. Built near a huge peepal tree, this Temple captivates visitors with its architectural beauty as well. Although the structure is small in size, the Temple presents alluring craftsmanship and its lattice work is especially attractive. According to legend, Lord Rama, Goddess Sita and Lakshmana had rested under the same peepal tree when they were on vanvas (Exile) from their kingdom Ayodhya.

KOTHANDARAMASWAMY TEMPLE - This Temple is situated on the island surrounded with sparkling waters of Bay of Bengal on one side and majestic Gulf of Munnar on another side. The Temple is believed to be more than 1000 years old. The Temple has the deities of Lord Rama, Lakshmana, Sita, Hanuman and Vibhishana. It is believed that Lord Rama performed the "Pattabhishekam" (ascension to king of Lanka) of Vibhishana at this place. The story is depicted in painting across the walls inside the shrine. According to one more legend associated with the Temple, there is place near the Temple named as Nandavanam where lord Rama is believed to have stayed with Sage Bhringi at his ashram for a few days. There is also a Temple tank, which has been named after Sage Bhringi.

SHRI NAMBUNAYAKI AMMAN TEMPLE – The Temple is greatly venerated by the people of the district. As there are majority of people having 'Nambu' in their names (like Nambu Rajan, Nambu Lakshmi, Nambu etc.) in Rameswaram, the name “Nambu” is so common and famous word around Rameswaram Island. She is considered as the protecting Goddess of the south direction. Those who don't have children pray the deity and tie a small cradle with baby Doll in the tree in this Temple and worship her. Many children in the Rameswaram Island took birth after praying the Goddessi, hence, the name Nambu is majority in Rameswaram. People who are awaiting for marriage, those who have problems in their marriage or with their marriage and those who have troubles in their life worship and pray and perform fasting to remove their problems and troubles. Those who suffering from depressed mind or having mental illusions stay in this Temple and take a bath in the Theertham for cure. It is believed that Theertham in this Temple possess medicinal properties. Turmeric is provided as prashadham in this Temple. Long ago, there were two Sages named Dakshina Duruvan and Paschima Duruvan performed intense penance near the Temple and by pleased by their deep worship, Mother Parvadhavardini appeared before them and graced them. Since then, the Sages continued to stay in the place and began treating those suffering from diseases. It is still believed that the Rishis are helping people those who asking for the cure to the Goddess.

SRI RAMANATHASWAMY TEMPLE – It is located near the sea on the eastern side of the island. The primary deity of the Temple is Sri Ramanathaswamy (Lord Shiva) in the form of Lingam. There are two Lingams inside the sanctum - one built by Lord Rama from sand residing as the main deity, Ramalingam and the one brought by Lord Hanuman from Kailash called Vishwalingam. Lord Rama instructed that the Vishwalingam should be worshipped first since it was brought by Lord Hanuman - the tradition continues even today. It is well known for its architectural beauty of magnificent Prakaras or corridors with massive sculptured pillars on either side. 197 mts corridor East to West believed to be the longest in the world and another corridor of 133mts wide from South to North. Special pooja is performed every day to the Sphatikalingam [crystal lingam] installed by Adi Sankara in this Temple. The Holy abode of Lord Shri Ram (addressed so with all respect & humility) is a virtual paradise for the devout. No Hindu's journey is complete without a pilgrimage to both Varanasi and Rameswaram for the culmination of his quest for salvation and is hallowed by the epic 'Ramayana'. Lord Rama is believed to have sanctified this place by worshipping and glorifying Lord Shiva and hence marks the confluence of Shaivism and Vaishnavism and is thus revered by both Shaivites and Vaishnavites alike and thus there is a strong belief that bathing in the 22 'Theerthams' or natural springs is a step forward in enlightenment. The number 22 indicates the 22 arrows in Rama's quiver. There are sixty-four Tīrthas (holy water bodies) in and around the island. According to Skanda Purana, twenty-four of them are important. Bathing in these Tīrthas is a major aspect of the pilgrimage to Rameswaram and is considered equivalent to penance. The first and major one is called Agni Theertham, the sea (Bay of Bengal). It is said that Swamy Vivekananda offered prayers at this Temple in 1897. The Temple is one of the holiest Hindu Char Dham (four divine sites) sites comprising Badrinath, Puri, Dwarka and Rameshwaram. The journey across the four cardinal points in India is considered sacred by Hindus who aspire to visit these Temples once in their lifetime. It is also one of the twelve Jyotirlinga Temples, where Lord Shiva is worshipped in the form of a Jyotirlingam. It is one of the 274 Paadal Petra Sthalams, where the three of the most revered Nayanars (Saivite Saints), Appar, Sundarar and Tirugnana Sambandar, have glorified the Temple with their songs. There are separate shrines for Ramanathaswamy and his consort Goddess Parvathavardhini separated by a corridor. There are separate shrines for the Goddess Vishalakshi, the utsava vigrahas, Sayanagriha, Lord Vishnu and Ganesha. There are various halls inside the Temple, namely Anuppu Mandapam, Sukravara Mandapam, Setupati Mandapam, Kalyana Mandapam and Nandi Mandapam. The Temple and the island of Rameswaram have acquired this name because Lord Rama worshipped Lord Shiva here on return from Sri Lanka. According to legend, after killing Ravana Lord Rama returned with his consort Goddess Seetha to India first

stepping on the shores of Rameswaram. To expiate the "dosha" of killing a brahmin, Lord Rama wanted to offer worship to Lord Shiva. Since there was no shrine in the island had despatched Sri Hauman to Kailash to bring an Vigraha of Lord Shiva.

SUGRIVA TIRTHAM - Sugreeva is the younger brother of Bali, the monkey king. During Ramayana epic, Sugreeva helped Lord Rama in his fight with demon King Ravana. There is also a famous lotus pond on the way to Ramar Padham near this Temple. This pond is known as Sita Kund as it was dedicated to Goddess Sita, wife of Lord Rama.

VILLONDI THEERTHAM AT RAMESWARAM - It is one of the 64 Teerthas in Rameswaram. It is also one of the beaches. As per legend, while returning back to Ayodhya from Lanka, Devi Sita felt thirsty. Lord Rama took his arrow and shot it into the sea and the place, where the arrow pierced the sea, a spring emerged. The word 'Villondi' means the place pierced by arrow and "Theertham' means sacred water. The place has pure fresh water in the midst of salty water everywhere.

SRI BHADRAKALI AMMAN TEMPLE - Its captivating architecture also attracts people along with its religious significance. This Temple is one of the unique Temples in Tamilnadu. Here, Goddess Kali is worshipped as one of the 10 Mahavidya that is a form of Adi Parashakti. The Vigraha of the main deity has been made from gold. The tower at the Temple, which is studded with gold, also mesmerizes visitors. This Temple has seen many changes and additions to its structure, owing to various dynasties that ruled over this area, leaving their mark on the Temple. Its structure & historical background makes it an interesting place to visit for architecture & history explorers.

ADI JAGANNATHA TEMPLE AT THIRUPPULLANI – The Temple is dedicated to Lord Vishnu. It is believed that Lord Rama used grass ('pul' in Tamil as a pillow (thalaiannai in Tamil) to sleep and hence the village attained the name Thiruppullani. Constructed in the Dravidian style of architecture, the Temple is glorified in the Divya Prabandha, the early medieval Tamil canon of the Azhwar Saints from the 6th–9th centuries. It is one of the 108 Divyadesam dedicated to Lord Vishnu, who is worshipped as Adi Jagannatha and his consort Lakshmi as Padmasini. The Temple is believed to have been built during the late 8th century. As per Hindu legend, Lord Rama is believed to have done penance to worship the god of ocean to seek way to Lanka in grass, giving the name Dharbasayanam to the place. The Temple has a five-tiered Rajagopuram (gateway tower) facing east. The shrine houses the vigraha of Adi Jagannatha, Bhudevi and Sri Devi in sitting posture. The consort of Adi Jagannatha is Padmasini, housed in a separate shrine. There is a shrine for Dharbasayana Ramar in a reclining posture. There is a metal vigraha of Lord Krishna from the 13th century Pandya period. The vigraha depicts Lord Krishna dancing in a snake, a rare historical depiction of Krishna in a metal vigraha.

ARULMIGU MANGALSWARI SAMADHA MANGALNADHAR TEMPLE AT UTHIRAKOSAMANGAI - There is an ancient Lord Shiva Temple considered to be 3000 years old, the oldest in the world. The presiding deity is carved in Emerald. A hall of Saharastralingam has thousand lingams enshrined in it. The Temple is considered sacred along the lines of Ramanathapuram, Sethu Madhava Theertham and Lakshmana Theertham. The Temple has numerous shrines such as Mangalanathar, Mangalambigai and Natarajar being the most prominent. The Temple houses a 6 ft tall emerald Vigraha, being the one of its kind. The granite

vigrahas of the deities Lord Ganesha, Murugan, Nandi and Navagraha are located in the hall leading to the sanctum. The first precinct or the walls around the sanctum of Erumbeeswarar has vigrahas of Thenmugaparaman (Dakshinamurthy - Lord Shiva as the Teacher), Durga (warrior-goddess) & Chandikeswarar (a saint and devotee of Lord Shiva). Annual Arudhra festival in December attracts a large number of devotees. As per Hindu legend, once hundreds of Rishis (ascetics) performed penance worshipping Lord Shiva, who told the Rishis that he would appear in the form of a fireball to acknowledge the penance of Mandodari, the wife of King Ravana in Sri Lanka. Lord Shiva appeared in the form of a small child in Ravana's palace. Ravana lifted the beautiful child and there was a small wound out of it. Simultaneously, there was a fireball out of the Agni Theertham (Temple tank), which the Rishis felt were on account of Lord Shiva attacking Ravana. Out of thousand, 999 killed themselves by falling in the fire, while one of them remained to save the vedic books. Lord Shiva was pleased by the Rishi & appeared as Sahastralingam (thousand lingams) for the 999 & one more for himself in the Temple. The single Rishi was believed to have emerged later as Manickavasgar in his later birth.

CHENCHUDANATHAR KARUNAKADAKSHI AMMAN TEMPLE AT KADALADI TALUK – It is an ancient Temple, which is more than 2000 years old. The Temple is dedicated to Lord Shiva and Goddess Karuna Kadakshi. It was built by red granite. It is an awe inspiring structure is an iconic example of ancient building techniques and stunning craftsmanship. There was renovation of Temple by Pandya Kings of Madurai in 800 AD and the rock cut carvings on the Temple walls reveals details of the renovation.

DISTRICT – RANIPET (Railway Station – Walajah Road Jn)

S. No.	Temple	Address	Type
1	Nemili Sri Bala Peetam	Chatram Street, Nemili – 631051	Mata
2	Sri Manikandeswarar Temple	Tirumalpur – 631051	Shiva
3	Sholingur Group of Temples and Theerthams	Sholingur – 631102	Narasimha (Vishnu) Brahma, Mata, Hanuman
4	Jalantheeswarar Temple	Takkolam – 631151	Shiva
5	Kanchanagiri Hills	Kanchanagiri Hills – 632405	Shiva
6	Mahendra Vishnukiraham Rock Carvings	Mahendravadi – 632502	
7	Group of Temples	Kalavai – 632506	Mata, Shiva, Vishnu, Muruga
8	Group of Temples	Walajapet – 632513	Dhanvantri, Vishnu, Shiva

NEMILI –

BALA THIRIPURA SUNDARI KOVIL - Nemili Sri Bala is a small and young Goddess but considered as powerful as the Sun by her devotees. Sri Bala Peetam is not a Temple but a small house where Sri Bala Vigraha decided to reside. About a hundred years ago, the Goddess appeared in Shri Subramanialyer's dream, asking him to come and fetch her from the River Kushasthalai. For about three days, Shri Subramanialyer searched the backyard of his home and the river banks but in vain. The next day, he got hold of the three-inch bronze Vigraha in the river, which he consecrated and placed in the centre of his house, which is now currently the Bala Peetam. The prime deity of this Temple is Raja Rajeswari, the family deity of the pundits over there. The deity Bala Thiripura Sundari has supposedly come on earth as a child goddess. The devotees are expected to wish and pray, without offering something in return as a bribe. It is believed that she is upset by the bargaining attitude of devotees. The prayers to the Goddess should not be accompanied by a promise to be fulfilled on attainment of the wish. Sri Kanchi Paramacharya performed pooja here in 1945 along with his religious group for three full days. It was Thirumuruga Kripananda Variyar, who told the following quotes "I see in this great peetam, the collection of all our Gods on earth".

SRI MANIKANDESWARAR TEMPLE AT TIRUMALPUR - The Temple is dedicated to Lord Shiva. The Temple is also classified as a Paadal Petra Sthalam. Lord Vishnu, also called Tirumal, is believed to have worshipped Lord Shiva in this Temple and, hence, the name Thirumalpur. The Temple has a four-tiered Rajagopuram. The Temple has set of inscriptions from Chola period of Rajaraja Chola-I. Appar, the 7th century Saint Poet glorified the deity in Tevaram in one verse. The Temple is also referred as Hari-Chakrapuram. The Nandi is in standing portion in this Temple unlike other Shiva Temple, where Nandi is in sitting posture. The Temple tree is Vilvam. Some of the local tradition indicates Tirumalpur as the place where Lord Vishnu asked Mahabali Chakravarthy to give him land of the extent measured by three steps of Lord Vishnu.

SHOLINGUR GROUP OF TEMPLES/THEERTHAMS -

LORD AADHIKESAVA PERUMAL SHRINE - Behind Bhakthositha Swamy is the shrine of Lord Aadhikesava Perumal. Lord is seen in standing posture with Nachimars. We can also see the Andal Shrine nearby. Copper vigrahas of Alwars and Achariyars are available in the shrine. Some of them are Nathamunigal, Aalavandar, Mudaliandan, Thirukkachi Nambi, Ramanujar. Embar, Koorathalvar, Manavala Mamuni, Erumbilappan and Dhottachar Swamy.

ARULMIGU BHAKTHOSITHA SWAMY TEMPLE - This Temple with rectangular shape is at the centre of Sholinghur. Raja Gopuram is facing east with 5 Storey and 7 Kalasams. Height is 90 foot. 2 four pillared Mandapams are in front of the Temple. 2 four pillared Mandapams are in front of the Temple. The Temple has only one Prakaram (Corridor). Ranga Madapam looks beautiful with vigrahas. This was constructed during 19th century. Besides Andal Shrine, this corridor consist the shrines of Nammalvar, Ramanujar, Manavala Mamunigal and Dhottachar. Opposite to main entrance is Palipeetam at the inner side of the Temple. The Vigraha of Perumal's sacred feet is built on a dais. Important festivals such as Garuda Vahana Urchavam are also conducted here. In the shrine of Bhathositha Swamy, the Procession deity is seen in standing postures with Sridevi and Boothevi.

BIG HILL TEMPLE - The stone hill, which is the abode of Lord Yoga Narasimha Swami, is of 750 foot height with 1305 steps. Lord Narasimha with Sangu Chakram, Salakirama Haram, Yoga Peetam, koraiteeth, long nails and strong hair give darshan to the people as Santhamurthi.

BRAHMMA THEERTHAM - The Sthala Theertham named as Brahma Theertham or Thakkankulam is a boon to the devotees who throng from several places and they have a sacred dip in the Tank before climbing the Hills. It is found en-route to hills. It is told that 108 Theerthams are available in

Kadighachalam. The most important one among all these Theerthams is Brahmma Theertham alias Thakkan Kulam (Temple Tank). The tank has 25 steps. Sri Varadaraja Swamy Temple is on the banks of this Tank. Float Festival and Theerthavari to Perumal is celebrated here. We can see a big Pali Peetam and flag mast at the northern side. We worship Amrithavalli Thayar shrine first and there more on to Perumal shrine. Goddess Amrithavalli is facing east. After offering prayers to Goddess, we can see 2 Thuvarabalagar guarding the Lord. After worshipping them, we can enter Lord Narasimhars Shrine through a front hall. Garudalval is standing in front of Perumal. There is a small window at the backside of Garudalvar. It is told that the eyes of Yoga Anjaneya in Small Hill are fixed at the feet of Yoga Narasimhar. The shrine of Arulmigu Yoga Narasimha Swamy consists Hemakodivimanam with a kalasam. Also vimanam with one kalasam is on the shrine of the Goddess Amirthavalli.

HANUMATH THEERTHAM - Adjacent to Lord Anjeneya Shrine is a big Tank called in so many names such as Rama Theertham, Hanumath Theertham, and Chakra Theertham etc. There is a Mandapam with Lord Rama shrine at the eastern side of the tank. Next to this, is Lord Aranganathars Shrine. Three Vimanams are available on the shrines of Lord Anjeneya, Lord Aranganathar and Lord Rama.

NARASIMMAR TEMPLE - Sholinghur or Chola Simhapuram is anciently known as Thirukadigai. The name Kadigachalam came as the Lord gave darshan to the Saptharishi to a kadigai time and gave mukthi. He also gave darshan to Prahalada by changing his figure of Terror and in the yoga stage. It is known from the inscription that the Temple is an ancient one. The Temple is in the midst of the Town with a Tank and Car Mandapam. Lord Anjeneya who is in the yoga stage helped Indrathymna Maharaja in killing the Arakkan Nikumban and saved his country. It was held on Sunday and hence every Sunday is important for Siriya Thiruvadi. People take a bath in the Chakra Theertham of the small hill and worship the Lord. People believe that Lord come and fulfil the wishes of the devotees in their dreams. Swamy Dhottachar used to worship Lord Varadaraja Perumal of Kanchi on the third day of Brahmotchavam every year. Once he was not able to visit Kanchi and thus missed the Seva. The worried Dhottachar offered prayers to Lord Varadharajar sitting on the banks of Brahma Theertham at Sholinghur. Lord Varadarajar of Kanchi pleased by the prayers of Swamy Dhottachar, appeared before him on Garuda Vahanam (Mount). This incident resulted in a ritual called Dhottachar Seva performed on the third day of Brahmmotchavam at Kanchi Varadarajar Temple even now.

Perunkanchi - The Status of Seven Mothers are one among the monuments being preserved by the Archaeological Department. The statues sculptured here belongs to the Pallava Kings of 8th century. These statues serve as the best example fiction of the Pallava's art of sculpture. The Seven mothers are: Brahmi, Chamunda, Indrani, Kaumari, Maheshwari, Vaishnavi, Varahi. The statues of Lord Vinyagar and Veerabhadrar located here is even more noteworthy.

SMALL HILL TEMPLE - The Lord is praised by Thirumangai Alvar, Peyalvar and Nammalvar. They praise him as Ilangkumaran and Akkarakani.

STHAVA VRIKSHA (HOLY TEMPLE TREE) - No Sthala Vriksha is at the Big Hill. In Town Temple, there was a Parijatha Tree sometime back. There is a Temple Tree (Ashoka Tree) at Small Hill adjoining to the tank.

TOWN TEMPLE - The Adikesava Perumal Sannadhi of the Town Temple is also a sacred one. People pray for rain by a 1008 pot abishegam. It is a known fact that even today it is observed that such abishegam bring rain to this place. There is no exit place for the water and it is immersed in the feet of the Lord. This is a great wonder which is observed by all.

YOGA ANJENEYAR - It is a pleasant sight to see the Lord in the Yoga form with Sanguchakram. This form is the unique one in the Bharatha Kandam. It is situated on a hill with 406 steps. Pandava Theertham is at the foot of this hill. There are two mandapams in between foot hill & the entrance of Raja Gopuram. This gopuram is facing north with 3 Storeys & 5 Kalasams. Yoga Anjeneyar Shrine is at right side. We can see from here, the flag staff of Big Hill Temple at the Western side. The Lord is doing penance by looking at the feet of Yoga Narasimhar.

JALANTHEESWARAR TEMPLE AT TAKKOLAM - The Temple is also called Thiruvooral. The Temple is dedicated to Lord Shiva. Lord Shiva is worshipped as Jalantheeswarar and is represented by the Lingam. His consort Goddess Parvati is depicted as Giriraja Kannikambal. The vigraha of Lingam is made of sand and sacred ablution is performed only on the Aavudayar. The shrine of the consort of Lord Shiva facing west is located in the Mahamandapam leading to the sanctum. The central shrine is approached through the flagstaff and Mahamandapam. The central shrine has entrance towards South and can be approached circumbulating the shrine. The Temple tank has natural spring, which fills through Nandi's shrine. Since water comes out of Nandi's mouth, it called Pokkeswarar Temple. The shrines of Lord Vinayaka, Murugan, Navagraha, Chandikesa and Durga are located around the precinct of the main shrine. The Temple has specimen of Thyagaraja, which is classified as Pre-Rajasimha style of Pallavas. Lord Shiva is sported in seated posture holding a rosary and an axe in the back left and right hands. Skanda is seen in standing posture between Lord Shiva and Goddess Uma. The model in the Temple is seen similar to the one at Thyagaraja Temple, Tiruvarur. The Temple has Koshta Murthi (Lord Vishnu) in place of Lingothbhava on the wall around the sanctum. There are sculptures of Goddess Durga and Koshta Murthi of Lord Brahma is also found seated. The presiding deity is revered in 7th century Tamil Saiva canonical work, the Tevaram, written by Tamil Saint Poets known as the Nayanars and classified as Paadal Petra Sthalam. The Temple complex entered through a three tiered Gopuram. The Temple has a number of shrines, with those of Jalantheeswarar and his consort Giriraja Kannikambal, being the most prominent. All the shrines of the Temple are enclosed in large concentric rectangular granite walls. The Temple has four daily rituals at various times and four yearly festivals on its calendar. The Brahmotsavam festival is celebrated during the month of the Chittirai (April - May) is the most prominent festival. The original complex is believed to have been built by Pallavas, with later expansion from Cholas, while the present masonry structure was built during the Nayak in 16th century.

KANCHANAGIRI HILLS - It is surrounded by a range of mountains and in the middle, there is a plain land and also a big Pond in the centre. The place is famous for small Lord Shiva Temples on a plateau surrounded by Hills. There are many swayambhu Lingams and it is believed that they all were Siddhas living there thousands of years ago. There are Banyan Trees, which are more than 1000 years old. There is also a perennial rivulet. There are 1008 Lingams and even today, devotees come here for worship.

MAHENDRAVADI - Mahendra Vishnukiraham rock carvings is one of the notable historic monument. This monument is preserved by the Archaeological Survey of India. It is a very ancient rock Temple of Tamilnadu. These rock carvings were built during the period of King Mahendravarman from 600-630 AD. The Grantha script inscription of Mahendra Varman period ensure that Mahendra Vishnukiraham is named after the King Mahendra Varman. The carvings are done in a monolithic stone in an open space, which is one of the special features of the monument with a couple of full pillars and one half pillar and the Temple is constructed that attracts the visitors. Podhigai is carved in the pillars, which look very simple.

KALAVAI –

ANGALAPARAMESHWARI AMMAN TEMPLE - It is 19th century Temple and very famous in entire south India and other states like Andhra Pradesh, Karnataka and Kerala. Peoples are regularly visiting the Temple for recovery of black magic effects. The Goddess is seated in the sanctum with four arms holding Udukka, and Trisula in the rear arms and sword and varada pose in the front arms but what is significant is that an vigraha of the Goddess, over five meters in length, is portrayed in stucco, brightly coloured, with multiple arms wielding weapons, lying face up on the ground in the front mandapa. She is portrayed as if in a Shadkona (six sided) sacrificial pit. The vigraha is awe inspiring and clothed and decorated with garlands. It attracts tens of thousands of devotees on the Mahasivarathiri day for the Masana Kollai festival when the Goddess is taken in procession to the cemetery.

KAMALAKKANI AMMAN TEMPLE – The Temple is dedicated to Goddess Kamalak-kanni which also attracts large number of devotees. This is almost identical with the Angala Parameswari Temple with a sanctum inside and a huge stucco figure of the Goddess in lying position with multiple hands in the front mandapa. This is considered Goddess Mahalakshmi. This Temple was built in 1979 by Swami Sacchidananda who settled here after several years of wanderings in Northern part of India including the Himalayas and other places as a mendicant. This Sanyasin who remains in the Temple premises observes complete silence and does not speak to any for the past sixteen years. He communicates through gestures and also written messages. He is a noble personality, venerated and held in high esteem by the devotees and village people.

KARIVARADHARAJA PERUMAL TEMPLE - The Lord Vishnu Temple is in existence from the 13th century but seems to have been rebuilt in the Vijayanagara times in the 16th century. The moolavar looks like Tirumala Balaji.

SANKARA MATHAM - The town is historically significant for the Sankara Matham and houses the Adhistanams (place where the mortal remains of a saint are interred) of the 66th and 67th pontiffs of Sri Kanchi Kamakoti Peetam - Sri Chandrasekarendra Sarswathi-VII & Sri Mahadevendra Saraswathi - V. The 68th Pontiff Sri Chandrasekharendra Saraswati Swamiji was initiated into ascetic order and ordained as the 68th Acharya of the Kanchi Kamakoti Math in Kalavai. Kalavai sprang into worldwide prominence with the association of Sri Chandrasekarendra Sarasvatiswamigal, the Mahaswamigal of Kanchi Kamakoti Pitha. Two of his predecessors on the Pitha attained samadhi merged with (Para-brahmam) in the village and the Brindavan Temples are enshrined. Providence brought young Swaminathan (the pre sanyasa name of Mahaswamigal) to Kalavai when he was hardly 13 years of age and was ordained as the Head of the Kanchi Mutt under the diksha name Chandrasekarendr Sarasvathi in 1907. The Acarya started his march of peace and spirituality from this village and ever since this village is a place of pilgrimage not only for the devout but all sections of people.

SUBRAMANYA SWAMY TEMPLE – The beautiful bronze vigraha of Lord Subramanya belongs to 16th century. The Temple is in a neat surrounding with a good tank and enclosure. The Temple includes a sub-shrine for Lakshmi-Narayana and another for Shiva Akhilandeswari with Goddess Meenakshi. The Temple attained popularity with the Mahaswamigal presenting a yantra for consecration in the Temple in the year 1978.

THIRUKKARAESVARA TEMPLE - The Temple was built by one Thirukkarai and hence the name Thirukkaraesvara (on analogy with Rajarajeshvara).

THIRUKKARISANADHAR TEMPLE (KOTTAI KOIL) – There is a 7th century Shivalinga with sixteen facets on its cylindrical part. There is also a Natarajar Vigraha which look alike the same as Chidambaram Natarajar. This Temple's Moolavar Linga and that karuvarai campus having so many inscription (kalvattu) which are inscribed by ancient kings.

WALAJAPET –

SRI DANVANTRI AROGYA PEEDAM – This is the first universal Peedam with Lord Danvantri, referred to as the Aadhi Vaidhyar ("The first Doctor"), who is the main deity. The Sanctum Sanctorum has been energised by mantras written by common people irrespective of caste and creed. Mantras poured in and the count of mantras received stood at 54 crores!!! The celebration of 5 celestial weddings (Siddhi Buddhi Ganapathy, Valli Devasena Murugar, Meenakshi Sundareswarar, Seetha Ramar, Arogya Lakshmi Danvantri) on the same platform is unique and has not been attempted before. The homamagni (fire) here for global welfare has been burning, 24 hours a day since 2004. Here, the Gayatri Devi (5-head Goddess) representing the Vedas and Maha Meru are installed together. It is the one & only centre, where a wheel of life ('Kaala Chakram') has been built consisting of plants for 27 stars, 12 star-signs, 9 planets which represents the astronomy & astrological science, circumambulating which we include the entire humanity of the world. Lord Muneeswara is situated in an herbal garden consisting of 108 varieties of herbs. Shirdi Baba can be seen two sides - Golden Baba facing the west represents value and Marble Baba facing the east represents material. Lord Danvantri and Vinayaka sculpted on a single stone. Rahu and Kethu as a single identity sculpted on a single stone. Mahishasuramardhini with a smile and the Mahishi in full form can be seen. 468 siddhars in the form of Lingams are also exist. Sanjeevi Anjaneyar, the restorer of life in our epic Ramayana, positioned in an open space, as he is the son of Vayu (Wind) with nine different types of Anjaneyar in the nine steps (Nine steps representing Nine Planets) as he is the Nava Vyaakarna Pandithar. Kulandhai Anandha Swamigal with his disciple Seshadri Swamigal in the base of the pedestal with sun and moon on both sides and with Divine Mother Meenakshi Ammal embossed on his chest. Shri Raghavendra with Kamadhenu (the cow that gives everything) are also installed. Bala Murugar - with his foster mothers called 'Karthigai Pengal' (celebrated as the six stars) holding children play items (Sun, Moon, Peacock, Spade, Lotus, Milk bowl) is depicted at the base of the pedestal; Pattabhisheka Ramar, 14 vigrahas sculpted in single stone, showing the power and administration plays a role in keeping people healthy; (a very contemporary idea); Maraghadha Lingam on a Nandhi pedestal is also here; Vasavi Kannika Parameswari, the ruling deity of a specific community in a peedam is also installed; Danvantrilikhita mantras below all the vigrahas are also installed. Nava Kannigaigal, without a face, under a sacred tree (Athi Maram) are here depicting different attributes. 6-foot circled Vaasthu Purushar Vigraha facing the sky with Ashtadhik Balakas (Deities guarding the eight directions of this universe) in the form of Sivalingams are also installed here.

SRI KASI VISWANATHAR TEMPLE – The Temple is believed to be more than 500 years old. The Temple has 5 tier gopuram. The presiding deity is Kasi Viswanathar and the mother is called Vishalakshi. Shrines of Navagrahas, Nalwar, Ganesha, Dakshinamurthy, Lord Vishnu, Brahma, Durga, Chandikeswara, Naganathar and Muruga with consorts can be found in the Temple. Kala Bhairavar and Shani are opposite to each other in the Temple and this is a Shani Dosha Nivarthi Sthal.

SRI SRINIVASA PERUMAL TEMPLE – It is one of the ancient Temples of Tamilnadu. The main deity of the Temple is Sridevi Bhoodevi Sametha Srinivasa Perumal. Other deities in the Temple are Sri Padmavathi Thayar and Sri Aandal and Sri Ranganathar and Sri Sudharsanar. The architectural features are of Vijayanagara style. Festivals like Navarathri Bramotsavam, Thiruvona Nakshatram Abishegam, Thirukalyana Utsavam, Purattasi Sani, Margazhi Month Thiruppavai are celebrated here.

DISTRICT – SALEM (Railway Station – Salem)

S. No.	Temple	Address	Type
1	Arulmigu Alagirinatha Swamy Temple	Kottai, Salem – 636001	Vishnu
2	Arulmigu Sri Suguvaneswarar Temple	Salem – 636001	Ganesh
3	Kottai Mariamman Temple	Fort, Salem – 636001	Mata
4	Appa Paithiyam Swamy Temple	Suramangalam, Salem - 636005	Saint Appa Paithiyam
5	Karapuranathar Temple	Uthamasolapuram – 636010	Shiva
6	Kumaragiri Murugan Temple	Salem – 636015	Murugan
7	Sri Kameswara & Karivarada Perumal Temple	Aragalur - 636101	Shiva, Vishnu
8	Kodandapani Kovil	Ayodhiyapattinam - 636103	Vishnu
9	Sri Thanthondreeswarar Temple	Belur – 636104	Shiva
10	Sri Skandhashramam Temple	Odayapatti - 636140	Saint Gnanaskandar

S. No.	Temple	Address	Type
11	Sri Sathya Narayana Sithar Peedam	Seelanaickenpatti - 636201	Satyanarain
12	Lingam Temple	Ariyanur - 636308	Shiva
13	Arulmigu Badrakaliamman Temple	Mecheri – 636453	Mata
14	Kailasanathar Kovil	Tharamangalam - 636502	Shiva
15	Group of Temples	Yercaud - 636601	Vishnu, Rama, Mata
16	Mata Temple	Idappadi - 637101	Mata
17	Sankari Fort	Sankari Taluka – 637301	Vishnu
18	Siddhar Temple	Edanganasalai – 637502	Kalangi Siddhar
19	Sundhara Kandaswamy Kovil	Salem – 637503	Murugan

ARULMIGU ALAGIRINATHAR SWAMY TEMPLE AT SALEM – It is popularly known as "Kottai Perumal Koil". The place also contains Temple dedicated to Azhagiri Perumal and Mariamman. It is an ancient Temple. It is believed to have 5 praharams. It was called as Sri Sundararaja Perumal Temple. A pillar with mandapam bearing Lord Krishna vigraha is there. It is surrounded by compound walls on four sides and its location is just west to the River bank of Manimutharu River. The monuments and inscriptions inside the Temple walls shows that the Temple was renovated by the Nayakars.

ARULMIGU SRI SUGUVANESWARAR TEMPLE AT SALEM - There are so many historical monuments & Vigraha in the Temple. Moolavar of this Temple is Arulmigu Sugavaneshwarar. The name of the God underlying because parrot get a wishes from this God. Other names of Amman in this Temple is Sornambigai, Maragathavalli, Patchivalli. Vinayagaralies Valampuri Vinayagar (Irattai Vinayagar). These gods are "Mummoorthigal" of this Temple. The 500-years-old Lord Shiva Temple, which carries the historical traces of the rulers of Cheras, Chozhas and Pandias of the yonder past and the Mysore dynasty with its imposing towers. The Temple garden contains many varieties of flowers and tall coconut & 'Vilwa' trees in hundreds.

KOTTAI MARIAMMAN TEMPLE AT FORT - This Temple was built during the periods of Chera Kings belongs to Cheranadu. The Goddess is known as Malaimari.

APPA PAITHIYAM SWAMY TEMPLE AT SALEM - Appa Paithiyam Swami was born in the zamindar family of Karur Fort in the year 1859. A Temple has been built on his Samadhi. Several thousands of devotees throng the Temple during the birthday of Swami and his Guru pooja on the day of Ashwini in the Tamil month of Thai.

KARAPURANATHAR TEMPLE AT UTHAMACHOLAPURAM – It is an ancient Temple. The main deity is Lord Shiva in Lingasorubam. The Temple is located near the west bank of Thirumanimutharu River. The Lingam is swayambhu. The meaning of Karapuranathar Karai-River bank, Puram-place, Nather-Lord. The Temple was built in 9th century.

KUMARAGIRI MURUGAN TEMPLE – The Temple is dedicated to Lord Muruga. It is located at Kumaragiri Hills. It is also known as Sri Dhandayuthapani Temple.

ARAGALUR - Aragalur has two imposing Temples. One is dedicated to Sri Kameswara and the other to Karivarada Perumal. There is a big Lord Buddha Vigraha at Thiyaganur village on the periphery of the village.

KODANDAPANI AYODHIYAPATTINAM KOVIL - The town is supposed to have been named after Ayodhya, the birth place of Lord Rama. It contains a beautiful Lord Vishnu Temple dedicated to Kothandaramar. There are beautiful musical pillars and marvelous sculptures in the Temple. As per Sthala Purana, it is believed that Lord Rama along with Sitamata & Lakshman with Vanara Sena were passing through this place while returning to Ayodhya from Lanka. Due to a hill, they took shelter in the night. As coronation ceremony time in Ayodhya was near, it is believed that coronation ceremony also took place here. There is also a separate sannidhi of Lord Anjenaya, on which sunrays falls for some time. It is also believed that the devotees who could not visit Ayodhya to get the darshan of Lord Rama, they worship here. Ramnavmi festival is major festival which is celebrated here with great pomp & fervor. Those who face obstacles in marriage, they worship here.

SRI THANTHONDREESWARAR TEMPLE AT BELUR – The Temple is also known as Sri Thanthondrieswarar Temple. The variety of sculptures are famous here. The Temple was built by the Cholas Kingdom in the 12th CE. The main deity is Lord Thanthondreeswarar (Lord Shiva) & the female deity is Goddess Dharmasamvarthini. The Temple is located on the banks of Vasishta Nadi (Vasishta River). The Temple has a serene atmosphere and is surrounded by beautiful hillocks. The Rajagopuram is about 97 ft. tall having 7 floors. Consecration ceremony (Kumbabishekam) for the new Rajagopuram was performed on 24th February 2002. Brahmandapurana is one of the 18 puranas in Sanskrit and is written by the great Saint, Vedha Vyasa. In 130th chapter of this purana, Sudamuni narrated the glory of Lord and this Temple to his disciples & other Saints. The Temple is constructed in such a way that every year, in the first week of Tamil month (Chithirai), the sunlight falls on the main deity in early morning. A structure of a mythical lion, "Yazhi" is made out of a single stone with a rolling ball inside its mouth, which is carved on two pillars. A structure of Lord Shiva riding a vedhic horse is carved on two other pillars made out of a single stone.

SRI SKANDHASHRAMAM TEMPLE AT UDAIYAPATTI - This Temple was constructed by Santhanandha Brahmendhra Saraswathi & Adhya-vadhutha Swami. It is situated on the extreme northern end of the Jarugu hill on the banks of Kannimar Odai.

SRI SATHYA NARAYANA SITHAR PEEDAM AT OOTHUMALAI – The Temple has special features as the presiding deity is Sri Sathya Narayana, which is present on the hills and similar type of Temple is not found anywhere in Tamilnadu.

LINGAM (1008) TEMPLE AT ARIYANUR - This Temple is controlled by Vinayaga Mission. This Temple contains 1008 Lingam with Nandi in the 'Moolasthanam'.

ARULMIGU BADRAKALIAMMAN TEMPLE AT MECHERI - The Temple is facing north. It is a holy site. Rajagopuram is the Temple's main entrance.

KAILASANATHAR KOVIL AT THARAMANGALAM - There are Vigraha of Rathi and Manmadhan. A Shivalingam has also been consecrated for the welfare of the devotees. This Lingam is called Paathala Lingam. It is believed that if the childless people worship here, they will get child, unmarried people will be married.

YERCAUD –

SRI RAJA RAJESWARI TEMPLE - This is said to be the Goddess of all gods in the Hindu Pantheon and by praying to her one can attain wealth and prosperity and be elevated to higher levels of spirituality.

PAGODA POINT – There is a Lord Rama Temple.

SHEVARAYAN TEMPLE – It is a Cave Temple. The presiding deity is Lord Perumal. This Temple is located on the flat top of the Shevaroy Hills and is nestled in a narrow cave. It is dedicated to Lord Shervaroyan and Goddess Kaveri, who are worshipped with much reverence by the locals. A common lore says that the Cave Temple is over 2,000 years old and touches River Cauvery in the state of Karnataka, around 480 km away. There is a wishing Well near the Temple in which, locals say, if you throw at least one stone from the

three picked near the Temple, with your back to the Well, success is achieved in whatever you plan to do. In the month of May, there is an annual festival organised that is celebrated with gusto by the tribal people of this region.

MATA TEMPLE AT IDAPPADI – It is a famous Temple dedicated to Goddess & also believed to be a Shakti Peedam.

SANKARI FORT – The Fort is a historical Fort, which is maintained by the Archaeological Survey of India. It was built in 15th century by the Vijayanagar Empire. The Fort has 2 Varadhraja Perumal Temples.

SIDDHAR TEMPLE AT KANJAMALAI - Kalangi Siddhar is one among the eighteen Tamil Siddhas. There is one Temple dedicated to him

SUNDHARA KANDASWAMY KOVIL – The Temple is one of the seven richest Temples in the District.

DISTRICT – SIVAGANGA (Railway Station – Sivaganga/Karaikkudi/Manamadurai)

S. No.	Temple	Address	Type
1	Ariyakudi Tiruvengadamudayan Temple	Ariyakudi – 630202	Vishnu
2	Sri Dhakshinamoorthi Temple & Aalamaram	Pattamangalam – 630204	Gurusthalam
3	Arulmigu Shanmuganathan Temple	Kundrakudi – 630206	Murugan
4	Karpaga Vinayagar Temple	Pillaiyarpatti – 630207	Ganesh
5	Sri Sowmiya Narayana Perumal Koil	Thirukoshtiyur – 630210	Vishnu
6	Arulmigu Swarna Moortheeswarar Temple	Kandadevi – 630314	Shiva
7	Sri Swarna Kaleeswarar Kovil	Kalayarkoil – 630551	Shiva
8	Sri Maha Ukra Prathiyangira Devi Temple	Silathagudi - 630553	Mata
9	Arulmikkuttiyar Kaliyamman Temple	Ariyakurichi, Vittaneri – 630556	Mata
10	Sri Kannudayanayaki Temple	Nattarasankottai – 630556	Mata
11	Sri Badrakali Amman Temple	Madapuram, Tiruppuvanam – 630611	Mata
12	Arulmigu Muthumariamman Thirukovil	Thayamangalam – 630709	Mata

ARIYAKUDI TIRUVENGADAMUDAYAN TEMPLE - A marvellous Temple of 17th century for Lord Srinivasa. Thiruvenkadamudaiyan means The Lord who has Thiruppathy Thirumala as his abode. This place of worship fondly called the Southern Thiruppathy. It is said to be built 400 years ago by a Shaivite devotee under the command and guidance of the Lord Himself. A Shaivaite by name Sevugan Chettiar was an ardent devotee of Lord Ventakateswara of Thiruppathy Thirumala. He used to keep a kalasam, a metal pot, at his home in Ariaykkudi to collect donations from the public

for Lord Ventakateswara. He carried this kalasam every year and travelled on foot to Thirumala to pay this and worship the Lord. He did not stop this worship even in his old age. The story goes that in one such journey, he almost reached a hilltop but could not mount it due to his old age. He fainted and fell down. Then Lord Venkateswara appeared in his dream and told him to build a Temple for Him in his own village and continue his worship. The Lord in dream showed the exact spot and place for His own abode and in this very spot showed by Him the Temple stands today majestically in Ariyakkudi. The Nagarathar devotee collected huge sum and erected the Temple and conducted the sacred consecration. The Temple has two separate towers one called Rajagopuram and the other called Rishigopuram. Besides this, there are six small towers also for various Gods and Goddesses. The Temple has various deities installed from the very inception. Alarmel Mangai Thayar (The Divine Mother Alamelu), Karudazhvar (the sacred bird - Vishnu's flight career) Andal (the pious woman of Srivilliputhur), Ramanujar (The sacred saint). The ten avatars (birth incarnations) are inscribed in ten pillars of a mantap. Sorgavasal, the sacred gate leading to swarga, the heaven, is beautifully built with exquisite wooden carving roof. The Garuda in a corner on the northern outer ring wall in a ready-to-fly mood is known for His ready redressal of faithful prayers. He is aptly called moolai Garudan. As history goes, the utsavmoorthy taken on procession and the sadari, the brass sacred feet, used to bless the devotees by placing it on their head, were donated by the Thirumala Temple of Thiruppathy.

SRI DHAKSHINAMOORTHI TEMPLE & AALAMARAM AT PATTAMANGALAM - The sculptures of ancient people and damaged vigrahas of 9th century are seen 1 km west. This is the only Temple in India where Lord Dakshinamoorthy graces his devotees by facing west. This Temple is one of the Guru Sthalam (the Temple dedicated to Lord Dakshinamoorthy). The main deity of this Temple is Lord Shiva and he is known by the name Sundareshwarar. The Goddess of the Temple is Meenakshi Amman. People who are willing to pursue their higher studies without any hindrance visit this Temple and pray to Lord Dakshinamoorthy by circumambulating the shrine of Lord Dakshinamoorthy and the Banyan Tree for 108 times. Moreover, in this Temple, one can see Lord Muruga in the inner space behind Shivalinga and he graces in the form of Lord Shanmuganatha with 5 heads accompanied with his consorts Valli and Deivanai. Navarathiri Thiruvizha and Panguni Uthiram Thiruvizha are celebrated every year. People visit the Temple regularly to seek blessings of the God for their happy married life and to be blessed with children.

ARULMIGU SHANMUGANATHAN TEMPLE AT KUNDRAKUDI – Kundram means hillock and Kudi means village. Hence this village is called Kundrakudi. This Temple is an abode of Lord Murugan called "Shanmuga" with six faces and 12 hands. On the western side of the hill are three excavated shrines at the ground level. Later structures have been added to these shrines. All these caves are dedicated to Lord Shiva. The Temple had been constructed in Dravidian style of architecture. There are a number of old inscriptions in this region which attracts research minded historians. The Temple is stunning with four Teppakulams on all the four sides of it. The carvings of

9th, 10th and 12th century are seen here. The Temple has a five-tiered gateway tower, the gopuram in the hill, leading to a pillared hall and the sanctum. There are various sculpted vigrahas of Lord Vishnu, Durga, Lingodbhava, Harihara. Devotees get married in the Temple and worship for cure from diseases. Kundrakudi Adigalar a famous Tamil Saint lived here and served the religion and the society. He attained Samadhi here. The Temple is praised in the Tirupugazh hymns of Saint Arunagirinadhar. The springs of the Temple are Saravana Poigai, Thenaru and Mayil Theertham. The special feature of the Temple is that Valli, Deivanai and Lord Muruga grace darshan individually sitting on a peacock. The rock-cut caves are maintained as a protected monument by the Archaeological Survey of India.

KARPAGA VINAYAGAR TEMPLE AT PILLAYARPATTI - It is one of the oldest Cave Temples (Rock Cut) of Tamilnadu. Karpaka Vinayakar or Desi Vinayaka Pillaiyar is the presiding deity here and he is portrayed with two arms and a trunk curled towards his right in the valampuri mode. Also, he is seen seated without Angusapasam, with his legs folded and stomach not touching the Asanam in the form of "Artha Padma" Asanam. This 6 foot tall mammoth vigraha of Lord Ganesha is a bas relief in an excavated cave off of a hill in the precincts of the Temple. When we draw a line from the broken left tusk, starting upward, then turning left towards right ear and after passing through the bended left tusk up to the tip of trunk, Tamil alphabet "O" appears. The Lingam in the hand indicates the alphabet "M". Together they form "OM". This is confirmed by the Lord here "Valamburi Pillayar". As Vinayagar satisfies the wishes of his devotees like Karpagam Tree, he is also known "Karpaga Vinayagar". The deity of this Temple is known as "Marudeeswarar" as Marudha Tree (in Sanskrit Arjuna Virutcha, the Botanical name is Termanalia Arjuna) worship is followed in this Temple which indicates that this Temple in an ancient Temple. The sculpture of Pasupatheeswarar, "A cow worshipping Lord Shiva by offering his milk" is the special feature of this Temple. Also Kuberan, the Lord of wealth had worshipped at this Temple. A sculpture of five headed snake wearing a Lingam on its neck is found here. The five head of the snake indicate the five senses while the Lingam indicates God. Also adding to the spirituality Goddess Laxmi, Saraswathi and Durga are found together at the same sport. Unlike other places the three Lingams Thiruveesar, Marudheesar and Senchadeswarar and the three Goddess Sivagami Amman, Vadamalar Mangaiamman and Soundara Nayaga Amman all appear together at the same place and bless the devotees. It is believed that by worshipping Kathyayini Amman at this Temple, women get relived from sevvaidosham which prevent them from getting married. "Sabda Madhar" whom importance due to changing time are provided with a separate sannidhi known as Shakthi Sannidhi at this Temple.

SRI SOWMIYA NARAYANA PERUMAL KOIL AT THIRUKOSHTIYUR - The Temple is a famous vaishnavaite pilgrim place. "Thiru" means "sacred", "Koshty" means "assembly" and "Ur" means "place" (i.e. Place of sacred assembly). All the Gods are supposed to have assembled here and discussed how to kill the demon Iranyan. Presiding deity (Moolavar) is Lord Uragamellanaiyan, Moolavar is in Bhunjanga Sayana. Uthsavar is known as Sowmiya Narayan and he is in Ninra Thirukolam. Thayaris known as Thirumamagal Thayar and she is in separate Sannidhi. Among the 108 Thiruppathis of Lord Vishnu, this

type of Ashtanga Vimanam is there in few Temples only. Sri Ramanujar climbed the Vimana of this Temple, called all the people and chanted the Narayana mantra from here. This is the 95th of the 108

Divya Desams. It is believed that if we pray in this Temple, any obstacles to the marriage will be removed. Prayers can be offered here for material prosperity of the family. As soon as you enter, a compact Rajagopuram welcomes you. The first Sannidhi is of our Emperumanar small compact Vigraham of Moola and Uthsava Moorthy is there, then next to him is his Guru Thirukoshtiyur Nambhigal Sannidhi. Here Sannidhi is divided into three parts, it is Garbhagruham, then Arthamantapam, Munmatapam which is a Kannadi (Glass room) arai, Uthsavamoorthy is in Kannadiarai, he is in Gyana Mudrai. His Aradhanimoorthy Anjaneyar, Lakshmana, Sita Sametha Sri Ramachandra Moorthy, then Bhavishyath Acharya Moorthy (It is the Moorthy in which Emperumanar is seated at the feet of Namalwar). This moorthy was worshipped by Srimath Nathamuni and Yamuna Muni. Kalyana Mandapam is full of sculptures. A Lord Shivan Sannidhi is there. In the first Sannidhi, there is Rukmini Sathayabhama Sahitha Nardhana Krishna. There is Thirunamam of Moolavar which is Uragamellanaiyan. He is also known as Pannaga Mrithu Sayi. Sri and Bhoo Devi are sitting near the legs. He is resting on Ananthan. Near his head is Kadambha Maharishi, near feet is Indira, Madhu Kaibadar, Purvasu Chakravarthi and then Brahma, Gayathri, Savithri Suryan, Chandran Garudan, Naradhar etc. are there. There is a giant Narasimhar doing Yudham with Hiranyakashipu, then you will find one more Vigraha of Narasimhar keeping Hiranyakashipu in his lap tearing him. Narasimhar is giving darshan in Ashta Bhujam.

ARULMIGU SWARNA MOORTHEESWARAR TEMPLE AT KANDADEVI - The Temple is dedicated to Lord Shiva and called as Arulmigu Swarna Moortheeswarar alias Siragilinathar. The Amman is called as Periya Nayaki Amman. This is a 350 years old Temple. The Temple is maintained by Sivaganga Raja. This Temple is associated with Ramayana - the kidnaping of Mata Sita by Ravana. Jatayu died in the hands of Lord Rama after narrating the kidnaping of Mata Sita by Ravana. Lord Rama installed a Shivalinga and named "Siragilinathar" meaning the Lord without feathers. It is here that Lord Hanuman said "Kanden Deviyai" to Lord Rama after finding Mata Sita at Lanka and hence this place is called as Kandadevi. Behind the Temple, there is a big tank called the Jatayu Theertham. It is said that the Temple tank has never dried up even during drought or intense summer seasons. The Aani Urchavam is very famous festival for this Temple, which is celebrated every year, during the month of June by the people of 75 Villages.

SRI SWARNA KALEESWARAR KOVIL AT KALAYARKOIL – The place was called as Kaanapair during Sangam period. This Temple is also called as Sorna Kaleeswara Temple. It is one of the shrines of the 275 Paadal Petra Sthalams. There are three shrines in this Temple associated with the three functions of creation, preservation and completion. The shrine is regarded as 10th of the Tevara Stalams in the Pandya region of Tamilnadu. A lofty 150 ft Rajagopuram and a grand tank (Teppakkulam) named Aanai Madu are two special features of this Temple. Airavatam, the elephant of Indra, is said to have created this tank. The vigrahas of three Maruthu Brothers are also found in this Temple. Saint Gnana Sambhandar, Simdarar, Appar and Arunagirinathar have visited this Temple and have sung hymns in praise of the Lord. Samadhi of Marudhu brothers is opposite to the old entrance on the eastern side.

SRI MAHA UKRA PRATHIYANGIRA DEVI TEMPLE AT SILATHAGUDI - The Temple is dedicated to Goddess Maha Ukra Prathiyangira Devi. The Temple has a special feature i.e. the vigrha of Maha Sadashiva, which is one of the 64 forms of Lord Shiva. This form is considered the highest form. In this form, Lord Shiva is depicted with 25 faces, 75 eyes & 50 hands. Navratri & Shivratri are major festivals here which are celebrated with great fervor.

ARULMIKKUTTIYAR KALIYAMMAN TEMPLE AT ARIYAKURICHI - Generally, Kali Amman is either east or north but the Temple is cut to the west by Kaliyamman with 8 arms i.e. Kaliyamman is on the south-facing side, just south of Ayyanar. The paintings on the walls & ceiling of the Temple depict the fame and eminence of deity Kalidevi. The history reads that Maruthu Pandian brothers worshipped this deity with their battlefield coins. War weapons and coins were manufactured here during the reign of the Sivagangai rulers. Judge Ambika sits on the right leg and sits down with eight hands on her feet. Victims of murder, robbery, rape, betrayal, vandalism, disgrace and wrongdoing get justice for themselves. It is hoped that all these injustices will be exposed and punished. It is also customary to say, "Anyone who fails in the villages around the area will be punished" for punishing them. Devotees call her the "Judge" because she is the judge of justice and resolves the problems of the people. She has special poojas on full moon, Tuesday and Friday. In the Temple, Ayyanar is in the opposite direction of Ambikkai. He is wearing a penalty on the right. Here Kali sits on her right leg and hangs her left leg. The knife, shield, bow, arrow & other weapons she possesses will make us fearful when viewed from a far. Opposite the shrine of Kali are Anjaneyar, Meenakshi Sundareswarar, Solaimalai, Vishnu, Karuppasamy, Veerappasamy, Muniyapasamy, Pachiamman, Sulattukali & Bhairavar. The most fascinating among the devotees is Sulatakkali.

SRI KANNUDAYANAYAKI TEMPLE AT NATTARASANKOTTAI – Nattarasankottai is an ancient

village and it is believed that the Nagarathar community migrated to this place in Pandian Kingdom. The Temple was constructed in 18th century by Nagarathars. The Temple is also efficiently managed by them. The deity, Kannathal alias Kannudaya Nayaki Amman is famous for her powers in giving the boon of eye sight to the devotees with eye defects and other ailments. There is a big pond at the front of the Temple. Goddess Kannathal at this Temple is a Swayambumurthi (self-emerged). The Amman is seen in a standing posture with eight hands and has an "udukkai" and "muvizhaisoolam" in her hands. Her left leg stamps the Asura by name Mahishan. The Temple is famous for its architectural beauty and golden kumbhams over the Temple tower. A Lord Shiva Temple and a Vishnu Temple are also popular here. Vaikasi Visakam festival is celebrated for 10 days in this Temple. The famous poet Kamber, who wrote Ramayanam in Tamil, spent his last days in Nattarasankottai and his tomb is located here.

SRI BADRAKALI AMMAN TEMPLE AT MADAPURAM - The Temple holds immense reverence in the hearts of Tamilnadu people. Even uttering the name of this Goddess will cast a chill down the spine of devotees. Madapuram Kaliamman stands only for justice, she can bring tremendous change in our life, if we pray to her with complete devotion. This Goddess stands in an open space on a stone pedestal under the shelter of a magnificent horse. The horse is about 30 foot high with bulging eyes and fierce look and on either side of Kali stands the Demons. To depict her anger, fury and outrage, her head is adorned with a crown of flame and her eyes glare with intolerable rage. The very sight of her will shook anyone from head to toe and shows that she is the destroyer of evil and an instant warrior of the poor and needy. Near the Kali Shrine is the Adaikalam Katha Ayyanar sanctum, this Ayyanar is named like this because it's a legend that he is the one who gave shelter to Maa Kali and even gave one of his horses to shield her from rough weather. Usually Ayyanar (custodian god) is found riding on a horse but in this Temple, he is found in standing posture, which is a significant one. People first pay tribute to Ayyanar to bless their house and keep them sheltered all their life time and then proceed to Maa Kali seeking justice for their loss or pain. The main tower (Rajagopuram) has five tiers and the Goddess is found in the open space. Inside the Temple, there is a Vinayaka shrine, who is worshipped first before going in. It's a custom that people seeking justice come here along with the prosecutor and take oath before Bathrakali Amman that what they are saying is truth. After taking the oath, they will return to their place. It is a belief that within 30 days, the false oath taker will be punished and sometimes the culprit can't even cross the boundary of the village. Later the offender surrenders before the God and gives back the victim whatever they lost because of him. The people affected by black magic, evil spirits and ill luck, come here do certain poojas and pray whole heartedly to get released from all evil spirits. Poor people who are affected by their rich masters, come here in wet clothes and stand before the Kali's pedestal and pour out all their worries. Later, they cut a coin in a black stone (Pattyakal) that's installed before Kali and ask to punish their greedy unfaithful master or partners. A bag full of cut coins can be found in the Temple.

ARULMIGU MUTHUMARIAMMAN THIRUKOVIL AT THAYAMANGALAM – The town takes its name from the Goddess 'Thai', which means mother. Thayamangalam Kovil is a powerful Temple and the primary God Muthumari Amman resolves all the problems of people who pray to her. The black stone Vigraha of the Goddess and the Temple was built in the year 1914. A big Theppakulam is located near the Temple. It is believed that the Goddess appeared to a childless man named Muthu Chettiyar and instructed him to make a deity and worship her. The successors of Muthu Chettiyar are maintaining the Temple for the past seven generations. Kappu Kattudhal is tying a sacred rope around one's wrist, which may be called an announcing or inauguration of the Temple Festival. Till the conclusion of the festival, the residents should not leave the village. Procession with milk pots, Theerthvari, Pookuzhi or Fire Pit Festival are the rituals during "Thiruvizha" Navarathri is celebrated in September-October.

DISTRICT – TENKASI (Railway Station – Tenkasi)

S. No.	Temple	Address	Type
1	Arulmigu Paramakalyani & Sivasailanatha Swamy Thirukkoil	Sivasailam – 627412	Shiva
2	Group of Temples	Kadayam – 627415	Shiva, Mata
3	Arulmigu Sankara Narayana Swamy Temple	Sankarankovil – 627756	Shiva
4	Sri Balasubramania Swamy Temple	Sivagiri – 627757	Murugan
5	Arulmigu Cinthamaninadha Swamy Thirukkoil	Vasudevanallur – 627758	Shiva
6	Arulmigu Courtralanathar Swamy Temple	Courtrallam – 627802	Shiva
7	Thiruvilanji Kumaran Koil	Ilanji – 627805	Murugan
8	Arulmigu Narasingaperumal Thirukkoil	Kilapavur – 627806	Narasimha
9	Arulmigu Thirumalaikumaraswamy Thirukkoil	Panpuli – 627807	Murugan
10	Arulmigu Kasi Viswanathar Temple	Tenkasi – 627811	Shiva
11	Arulmigu Kailasanathaswamy Thirukkoil	Virasigamani – 627862	Ganesh

ARULMIGU PARAMAKALYANI & SIVASAILANATHA SWAMY THIRUKKOIL AT SIVASAILAM – The Temple is dedicated to Lord Shiva. The Temple is west facing, an unusual, rare phenomenon. The Shivalinga with hair in the backside is also an unusual phenomenon, which can be seen from all the four directions. There is a four handed Goddess vigraha. Gorgeous Nandhi believed to be sculpted by Mayan the Chief sculptor of Heaven attracts all.

GROUP OF TEMPLES AT KADAYAM - Kadayam was historically known as Kadayan Patti, which literally means the "Village of Kadayans" (a specific Hindu caste). Kadayam is known for its ancient Temples scattered across the length and breadth of the village.

Arulmigu Vilvavananatha Swamy Thirukkoil at Kadayam - The Temple is located amidst the lushly green paddy field at the serene foothills of Western Ghats. The famous verse of Mahakavi Subramaniya Bharathi, "Kaani Nilam Vendum Parasakthi" took birth here at this Temple.

Nithya Kalyani Amman Temple at Kadayam - A local legend says that its people were originally living around the Kalyani Amman Temple; however, the Temple Goddess could not tolerate the noise created by the inhabitants, so she pulled out a Kadagam (a bracelet in ancient Tamil) and threw it outside. She instructed the people to go and reside around the spot where the bracelet fell, thus making the new area known as Kadagam which later became Kadayam.

A Shastha (Thala Malayan) Temple lies on the banks of the Ramanadhi River (a tributary of the Thamirabarani River) as well as a Sri Pathrakali Amman Temple and Sri Muppudathiamman Temple in Kilakadayam. The former is dedicated to the 18 Patti (Village) people, who celebrate the 8-days festival.

ARULMIGU SANKARA NARAYANA SWAMY TEMPLE AT SANKARANKOVIL – Lord Sri Sankaranarayana is the main deity in the Temple. Lord Vinayaka is Anugnai Vinayaka. The Temple has a 9 tier Rajagopuram of 125 foot height. The ant-hill sand is offered as Prasad which the sick consume along with water for cure. Devotees facing problems due to the presence of poisonous creatures in their houses as lizards, scorpions and snakes offer silver pieces embossed with the vigrahas of such creatures for solution. One time Goddess Umadevi requested Lord Shiva to remove the difference among the devotees, who is the powerful god, whether Lord Shiva or Hari. Then the Lord Shiva appeared as Sankaranarayanar. In the 11th century, King Ukkirapandia ruled over Ukkirankottai. He used to go over to Madurai for darshan of Lord Arulmigu Somasundarar.

One day, when he was proceeding to Madurai for worship, the elephant tusked the earth on the way and plunged into a pit. At that time, Manikireevan, the watchman of Punnai forest came there and told the king "Oh king! Here is an anti-hill in the midst of Punnai forest. When the anti-hill was demolished there appeared a tail less cobra. Its' might is unexplainable. It belongs to the God. On hearing this, the King rushed to the Punnai forest and saw the Shivalingam by the side of the ant- hill. Then he had a bath in the Nagasunai (holy tank) and worshipped the God. Later on, according to history, the King destroyed the forest in the vicinity of the ant – hill and constructed this Temple with Mandapams, Gopuram (Tower) and Compound walls. In the 12th century, King Seevalaramapandian constructed the Rajagopuram (big tower) and front Mandapam. This Temple has three important sannadhis with in its premises. There is a Nagasunai (holy tank) inside the Temple premises, which was said to have been dug by serpent kings named Paduman and Sangan. People who take a bath in this holy tank, adore ant-hill earth on their body and offer holy prayers to the presiding deities of this Temple have a permanent relief from all sorts of dreadful diseases. Tree for the Temple is Punnai (Calophylluminophyllum) Tree. Once upon a time this area covered by these trees. It is believed that if the people wear the puttumann (Anti hill soil), found in Amman Sannathi, daily with belief, it will cure cancer, skin diseases and all other incurable disease. The soil is giving miraculous results, if it is worn with belief.

SRI BALASUBRAMANIA SWAMY TEMPLE AT SIVAGIRI – It is an ancient Temple, which is more than 500 years old. It is located on a small Hill. The Padamandapa of the Temple is at the place where the Lord gave darshan to Sage Agasthya. There is also a Shivalinga installed. Lord Muruga is praised as Navagraha Muruga in the Temple. Lord Vinayaka is known as Anugnai Vinayaka. Those facing adverse planetary aspects, to children in particular and those suffering from paralysis can pray here for relief. There are various festivals celebrated.

ARULMIGU CINTHAMANINADHA SWAMY THIRUKKOIL AT VASUDEVANALLUR - Its antiquity dates back to 14th Century A.D. It is dedicated to Ardhanareeswarar, whose symbol is not a Lingam but an vigraha, parted the vigraha with his consort. This is a rare phenomenon witnessed here, other than Thiruchengodu in Namakkal district.

ARULMIGU COURTRALANATHAR SWAMY TEMPLE AT COURTRALLAM – The Temple is famous for one of its Pancha-Sabha known as Chitra - Sabha. The Temple is dedicated to Sri Thiru Courtrallanathar, Thirukootachalapathi and Kuzhalvoimozhi Amman (Devi whose voice is as sweet as the music of the flute). Jack tree is the Sthala Vruksha. Saint Tirugnanasambander of 7th century glorifies the Lord of Kutralam in 2 pathihams one of which relates to the Sthala Vruksha. Other Saints Tirunavkarasar Manickavachagar Pattinathar have poured their feelings of spiritual ecstasy in soul – stirring lyrics. At Kutralam, a Vaishnava Temple which transformed into a Lord Shiva one, Lord Vishnu changing into Shivalingam, the conch in his hand, expanding as the Temple and the chakra rising as the siharam. The Temple is therefore conch – shaped – a peculiarity unlike other Temples that are either squares of rectangles in shape. The Sthalapurana describes this story in interesting detail. Three major festival of ten days each are celebrated in a year; Vishu festival (April) Aipasi Vishu festival (October) Arudra (Erato) Festival (Dec – Jan). A special feature of this Temple is that during Arudra festival, Thandava Deeparedhana representing the cosmic Dance of the Supreme being is offered daily to God Nataraja both morning

and evening in the Temple and specially on the Arudra – day and during the other two festivals this offering and picturesque festival days. Kuzhalvoimozhi Amman is the consort of Lord Courtralanatha Swami. Her shrine is on the southern side of Lord Shiva's shrine. The peedams of Annavi Pillai and the other deities are seen in front of this shrine. Along the periphery of this shrine are seen vigrahas of Kailasanathar on the southern side and Sri Durga on the northern side. Along the outer periphery are seen vigrahas of the Gods, Goddesses and Saints such as Kurumbalanathar, sixty three Nayanmars, Nannagara Perumal, Sailappar, Vallabha Vinayagar, Papanasar, Ulagamman, Nellaippar, Gandhimathi Amman, Manakkola Nathar, Narumbunathar, Sankaralinganathar, Palvannanathar, Oppanai Amman, Chockalingar, Meenakshi, Sastha, Madunatheswarar, Aram Valarthanayaki Amman, Agasthiar, Vasugi, Pancha Darshana, Sahastralingam (1000 Lingam), Kasiviswanathar, Visalakshi, Sivalaya Muni, Bairava, Yagashala, Navagraha (a shrine of nine planets). Hence, worship at this Temple is equivalent to worshipping at all important Shaivite Temples. At both sides of Lord Kutralanathar Sannathi's mahamandapams, one can find Anukkai Vinayagar towards south side and Lord Nataraja towards north side. In the Swamy Sannathi, Lord Dakshinamoorthi and opposite to it Brahmi, Maheshwari, Gowmari, Vaishnavi, Varahi, Indrani, Samundi are the Saptakanniga's found along with Mahalakshmi, Ayyanar, Marayanar and Narasimma. Lord Brahma are also installed inside the Temple. In the west, one can find Sannathi of Thandeer Vaanmiganathar Sambukeswarar Annamalainathar, Thirukaalathiyappar, Thirumoolanathar and Ramalingar. In the north western corner, Lord Subramaniyanar is found along with Valli and Deivanai. Moreover, in the north side of the Swami, Lord Saneeswaran is found in a separate Sannathi in the standing posture. Then one can find the Chandikeswarar Sannathi also. In the south of the mandapam, Lord Vinayagar and in the north Lord Arulmigu Nayanar's Sannithi are found.

Courtallam Falls - It is situated at the Western Ghats. The famous waterfalls on rocks and tiny droplets are sprinkled in the air. The water falls of Courtallam have medicinal value as they run through forest and herbs before their decent. The Courtallam is called as 'Spa' of South India. There are seven different falls of Courtallam, which are known as Peraruvi, Citharuvi, Iyentharuvi, Puliyaruvi, Palaiya Courtallam, Senbakadavi, Theanaruvi. The Peraruvi is the main and biggest falls and is about 60 m high. In Chitraruvi, which is known as the small falls, the flow is thin. At Shenbagadevi falls, the water flows through Shenbaga (Michaela Champak) Trees. There is also a Temple there dedicated to Shenbagadevi Amman. The Thenaruvi, known as Honey Falls, is 40 m high and cascading between two large stones. Aintharuvi, known as Five Falls, wherein five separate cascades of water form this waterfall. From the orchard above flows Pazhathotta Aruvi, the 'VIP falls'. Only VIP's are allowed in Pazhathotta Aruvi.

THIRUVILANJI KUMARAN KOIL AT ILANJI - It is a beautiful Temple of Lord Murugan overlooking the fields and farms is the main Temple of Ilanji. The Lord is Valli Devasena Sametha Arulmigu Ilanjikumarar Iruvaluka Nayagar. The Goddess is Arultharum Iruvulaga Eeserkiniyal. The Theertham is Chithra Nadhi. The Sthalavriksham is Magizha Maram. The Agamam is Maguda Agamum. Arunagirinathar has sung about the Thiruilanjikumarar, who is in Ilanji, which is full of Rivers and Lotus in his Thirupogal. In addition, the town boasts of other Temples including Keela Koil, Pillayar Koil, Perumal Koil, Sri Krishnan Koil, Sitrattu Veerimman Koil (also known as Sithai Amman Koil) and Kali Amman Kovil Temple.

ARULMIGU NARASINGAPERUMAL THIRUKKOIL AT KEEZHAPAVOOR - The history of this Temple dates back to 10th Century A.D., which was the imperial Chola reign. The presiding deity of the Temple poses with 16 hands, performing destruction of Hiranyakashyap.

ARULMIGU THIRUMALAIKUMARASWAMY THIRUKKOIL AT PANPULI - The Temple is dedicated to Lord Muruga. The Theertham is Poonjunai. The Sthalaviruksham is Tamarind Tree. The Agamam is Karana Agamam. The Temple has 605 steps. It is believed that Kaviaramalai, a place ruled by feudal ruler of Sangam Age, Aiy Andiran is this place. Saint Arunagirinadhar praised this shrine in his hymns. The place is surrounded by Western Ghats and with road approach atop the hillock. The Hill is in the form of OHM and about 400 ft from Landmark. There is a pure water tank on the top of the Hill. It was formed with the divine power of Sage Agasthiyar. It is said that daily a lotus flower would blossom in this tank. Indras and Sapthkanniyars plucked and placed it at the foot of Thirumalai Murugan and worshipped daily. It is a boon and sacred water.

ARULMIGU KASI VISWANATHAR TEMPLE AT TENKASI - Lord Shiva graces in the Temple as a Swayambhumurthi. Worshipping the Lord in this Temple is as equal to worshipping the Lord in Kashi – Varanasi. Presiding deity, Lord Kasi Viswanatha is visible to the devotee even from a distance of one KM. While Mother Durga faces south in almost all the Temples, She faces west in this Temple. About 700 years ago, King Parakrama Pandiya was taking up a pilgrimage to Kashi as and when he desired to worship Lord Viswanatha. The Lord appeared in his dream that he could build a Temple here itself to avoid a long journey to the north. He advised the King to follow the movement of ant's row and build the Temple where it ended. The ant-line ended on the banks Chitraru River dense with Shenbaga trees. He found a Swayambhulinga, near an anthill and built the Temple as directed by the Lord. The Temple is noted for the three importance of Swayambhumurthy (the deity), Thalam (holiness of the place) and Theertham, the holy water attributed to the Temple. The beauty of the sculptures of the Temple is widely known the world over. The twin sculptures – the Veerabadras, Thandavamurthis, two Tamil Mothers, Rathi and Manmatha (the cupid and his beautiful wife Rathi), single sculptures as Lord Vishnu and Kali Devi are noted for their exquisite beauty.

ARULMIGU KAILASANATHASWAMY THIRUKKOIL AT VIRASIGAMANI - This is a rock cut Temple ascribed to Sixth Century A.D, when the Temple architecture reached a new dimension of evolution, to excavate rocks to build Temples. The vigraha of Lord Vinayaka carved in the rock here is considered to be the primitive one among the Vinayaka vigrahas available in Tamilnadu.

DISTRICT – THANJAVUR (Railway Station – Kumbakonam/Thanjavur/Darasuram)

THANJAVUR - Historically speaking, the Temples of Thanjavur are not as old or ancient as the Temples of 108 Divya Desams or the 274 Saivaite Temples established and glorified by Alwars and Nayanmars respectively between 7th and 9th century. They are majestic monuments of the past glory of the Chola Regime and famous for its excellent Architecture and Sculptural work. Thanjavur and the adjoining areas of Kumbakonam and Nagapattinam boasts of hundreds of important and ancient Temples. Cholas, Pandiyas, Nayaks and the Marathas have contributed their might for making these areas to be called as Treasure House of Temples.

S. No.	Temple	Address	Type
1	Arulmigu Chakrapani Swami Temple	Kumbakonam – 612001	Vishnu
2	Kambatta Viswanathar Swamy	Kumbakonam – 612001	Shiva
3	Mottai Gopura Vasal Athi Kumbeshvarar Temple	Kumbakonam – 612001	Shiva
4	Nageswaran Temple	Kumbakonam – 612001	Nagnath
5	Ramasamy Koil	Kumbakonam – 612001	Rama
6	Sarangapani Temple	Anna Nagar, Kumbakonam – 612001	Vishnu
7	Someswara Temple	Anna Nagar, Kumbakonam – 612001	Shiva
8	Sri Prananatheswarar Temple	Tirumangalakudi - 612102	Shiva
9	Sri Kampaheswarar Temple	Tirupuvanam - 612103	Shiva
10	Shankara Mutt	Tiruvidaimarudur - 612104	Shiva
11	Sri Naganatha Swami Temple	Thirunageswaram – 612204	Shiva
12	Arulmigu Oppliyappan Temple	Thirunageswaram – 612204	Vishnu
13	Sri Kabartheeshwara Mandir	Tiruvalanjuli - 612302	Ganesha
14	Arulmigu Swaminatha Swami Temple	Thirumanjana Veedhi, Swamimalai, Thanjavur – 612302	Murugan
15	Sri Satchinadeswarar Temple	Tirupirambiyam - 612303	
16	Chandramouleesvarar Temple	Thazhamangai - 612405	
17	Shri Airavatesvara Temple	Darasuram, Kumbakonam – 612702	Shiva
18	Thenupuriswarar Temple	Patteeswaram – 612703	Shiva
19	Arulmigu Peruvudaiyar Temple	Gangaikonda Cholapuram – 612901	Shiva
20	Arulmigu Pragadeeswarar (Periya Koil) Temple	Thanjavur – 613001	Shiva
21	Neelamega Perumal Temple	Thanjavur - 613002	Vishnu
22	Panchanatheeswar Temple	Thiruvaiyaru - 613204	Shiva
23	Punnainallur Sree Maha Mariamman Temple	Mariammancoil – 613501	Mata
24	Gajendra Varadha Perumal Temple	Kabistalam – 614203	Vishnu
25	Kalyansundaresar Temple	Nallur - 614207	Shiva
26	Sri Mullaivananatharswamy & Garbarakshambigai Amman Temple	Tirukkarugavur - 614302	Shiva, Mata

ARULMIGU CHAKRAPANI SWAMI TEMPLE AT KUMBAKONAM – The Temple is the solitary Temple complex for Sri Chakrapani. Chakrapani otherwise called as Sakarathazhvar is located on the southern Bank of River Cauvery. It is believed that Lord Vishnu appeared in the form of Sudharsana Chakra to put down the arrogance of Lord Surya. It is said that the Chakrapani has the third eye like Lord Shiva. The second biggest Vaishnavite Temple of Kumbakonam. Agampara Vinayakar, Panchamuka Anjaneyar and Thayar Vijayavalli are enshrined here in this complex. Utharayanam [Thai – Aani] and Dakshinayanam [Aadi – Panguni] have two different entrances to worship Sarangapani in the Sanctum Santorum. They are called as Dakshinayana Vayil [gate] and Utharayana Vayil (gate). The outer court adjoining the Sanctum Sanctorum has been designed like a balcony.

KAMBATTA VISWANATHAR SWAMY AT KUMBAKONAM - Pettai Adhi Kambatta Viswanathar enshrines the presiding deities of Kambatta Viswanathar and Anandha Nidhiambigai. It is located on the south of Adi Kumbeswarar Temple. It is called as Malathi Vanam also. This Temple is also called as Kambatta Viswanadhari because the coin minting was done here during the Nayaka Period. It is believed the famous saint 'Thoomakethu' found this Temple.

MOTTAI GOPURA VASAL ATHI KUMBESHVARAR TEMPLE AT KUMBAKONAM – It is one among the important Temples dedicated to Lord Shiva. It is a padalpetrasthalam. This Temple complex has four gateways on all four sides, the tallest being the 11 stage, tall tower on the eastern side. Apart from the presiding deities of Kumbeswarar and Mangalambigai Amman, many shrines are located in this prominent Temple complex. The sixteen-pillared hall built during the Vijayanagar period has all the 27 stars and 12 zodiac signs carved in a single stone. Masi Magam festival is the important festival of the Temple. 9th century Chola dynasty and the Thanjavur Nayaks made remarkable contribution to the development of Temple.

MAHAMAHAM TANK AT KUMBAKONAM - It is a huge Temple Tank. It is considered to be the foremost & one of the largest Temple Tanks in Tamil Nadu. The Masimaham festival held in the tank has 100,000 visitors & the 12 year Mahamaham Festival has close to 2 million visitors. In the northern bank mandapa, there is an inscription of Tulapurshadana, a practice of weighing oneself against gold. As per legend, after the end of each era, the whole world immerses in a deluge on account of the wrath of Lord Shiva for the sins committed by humans on earth. Lord Brahma recreated the world during the start of Kalyuga. Lord Shiva declared that after the end of previous era, a divine pot would reach a holy spot. As the divine pot reached Kumbakonam, Lord Shiva, in the form of a hunter, broke the pot with an arrow. The pot broke into many parts & scattered around, which became the cause for so many Temples in the town. Lord Brahma prayed to Lord Shiva to allow pilgrims to visit the tank during the sacred occasion. Lord Shiva acceded to the demand and is believed to arrive along with Lord Vishnu and other celestial deities at the centre of the Tank. Astronomically, when the planet Jupiter passes over Leo on the day of the festival, it is believed to bring all water bodies together and enrich the Tank with minerals. Similarly, a lake in Kotihar in Jammu and Kashmir gets full supply of water the same day, which otherwise remains empty during the other 11 years. Since Lord Brahma reconstructed the world after the last deluge, there is a Temple dedicated to him in Kumbakonam, though he is cursed not to have any Temple for him anywhere else. The Tank is surrounded by sixteen small Mandapams (shrines) and has 21 Wells inside the Tank. The names of the Wells carry the name of Lord Shiva or that of Rivers of India. At the centre of all these exists the Sixty-six crore theertham, believed to be the most sacred of all.

NAGESWARAN TEMPLE AT KUMBAKONAM – It was built by Aditya Chola during 9th century. This Temple has Pralayakala Rudra Sannidhi. Adisesha & Surya had worshipped Sri Nageswara here. It is also a Rahu Parihara Sthalam. The Temple is incarnated by the hymns of Thevaram & is classified as Paadal Petra Sthalam. A legend has it that the mythological serpents Adiseshan, Dakshan & Kaarkotakan worshiped Lord Shiva here. The orientation is structured in such a way that it allows sunlight inside the Temple right on the sanctum sanctorum only during the Tamil month of Chithirai

(April/May). It is also called Surya Kottam or Keezha Kottam. It is said that Sanctum Sanctorum of both Nageswaran Temple & the Sarangapani Temple are similar in the form of a chariot. The Temple consists of three Gopurams. There is a local belief that visiting Nageswaran Temple, Tirunageswaram & Thirupampuram in the morning, afternoon & evening has significant meaning for Rahu Dosha Pariharam. During the time when Adisesha was feeling under the weight of the earth, he did penance at Kuvivanam. Sri Parvathy appeared & blessed him at this place to get strength. The water body in the Temple is called Naga Theertham. The Devi shrine is an independent structure situated in the outer prakaram detached from the axial unit, though it faces south, a feature common to Shaiva Dev in shrines. The complex of Nataraja shrine is in the form of a chariot on wheel drawn by horses. The Temple had been a centre of learning as seen from the inscriptions in the Temple. The inscriptions indicate specific subjects like Purvamimansa styled as Pravahakarma.

RAMASAMY KOIL AT VALAYAPETTAI AGRAHARAM, KUMBAKONAM – It was built in 16th century by King Achutha Nayak of Thanjavur. The Temple has a 3-tiered gopuram. Shrine of Lord Sri Rama with Vyakara Mudra seated with Mata Sita has been installed in the Sanctum Sanctorum. Lakshmana, Bharatha and Shatruguna is in standing posture next to Lord Rama and Hanuman kneeling down holding the Manuscripts. The outer court has pillars sculpted with finesse, various sequences of Ramayana and each pillar is carved out of a single rock. Paintings of Pattabishekam [coronation] of Vibhishnan and Sugriva; Lord Hanuman playing the Veena, Agalya getting relieved of the curse too are found in the Temple. The Temple is a typical Nayak style of Temples. One can read the Chitra Ramayana On the walls of the Sanctum Sanctorum while going around the Sanctum Sanctorum.

Papanasam Sri Ramalingaswami 108 Shiva Mandir - The Temple is dedicated to Lord Shiva. It is believed that the Temple had been built by Lord Rama himself. Lord Rama had consecrated 107 Shivalingas and 1 Shivalinga had been brought from Kashi by Lord Anjaneya. The main Shivalinga had been known as Ramalingaswami & the Shivalinga brought from Kashi by Lord Anjaneya is known as Hanumanthalinga. It is believed that by worshiping Lord Shiva here would remove all sins of the devotees.

SARANGAPANI TEMPLE AT ANNA NAGAR, KUMBAKONAM – The Temple is dedicated to Lord Sarangapani / Aravamuthan and Goddess Nacciyar Komala Valli. It is one of the 108 Divya Desam glorified by the Alwars of Vaishnavite Sect and also classified as one of the Pancharanga Kshetram on the banks of River Cauvery. Medieval Cholas, Vijayanagar and Madurai Nayaks have developed this Temple during their reign. Lord Sarangapani is in reclining position called as Udhana Sayana. 175 foot tall, 11 tier Raja Gopuram or the tower is the highlight of the Temple. The Temple Tank called as Potramarai Kulam is located on the western side. Sanctum Sanctorum is made up with 12 columns, shaped like a chariot. Lord Sarangapani believed to have appeared and blessed Saint Hemarishi here. Chariot Festival is the most colourful festival of the Temple in the month of Chithirai [Apr-May]. The chariot is said to be weighing 300 tons.

SOMESWARA TEMPLE AT ANNA NAGAR, KUMBAKONAM – The Temple faces the North and there is a big tower or gupuram on the eastern side. The architectural style and element of this Temple resembles the Dravidian architecture of 13th century of the Chola regime. Aravamuthar and Thenar Mozhi Thayar are the other deities enshrined in this Temple complex.

SRI PRANANATHESWARAR TEMPLE AT TIRUMANGALAKUDI - The Temple is dedicated to Lord Shiva. The Temple is believed to be more than 1000 years old. Lord Shiva is known as Prananatheswarar and the Goddess is known as Mangalambikai. There are Mangala Tirtham, Surya & Chandra Tirthams which makes this Temple special being 3 Tirthams in one Temple. The glory of the Temple is praised in the hymns of Saint Tirugnana Sambandar. It is 38th Shiva Temple on the northern bank of River Cauvery which are mentioned in the Thevaram hymns. 10 days Panguni Uthiram Brahmmotsavam with wedding festival on the 2nd day is important event of the Temple.

SRI KAMPAHESWARAR TEMPLE AT TIRUPUVANAM - The Temple is dedicated to Lord Shiva. Lord Shiva is worshiped as "Kampahareswarar" as he removed the quaking (Skt. Kampa) of a king who was being haunted by a Brahmarakshasa. It was built by Kulothunga Chola - III & is considered the last of the four masterpieces built during the Medieval Chola era. The Temple has a shrine for Sharabha, a depiction of Lord Shiva, a part-lion and part-bird beast, who, according to Sanskrit literature, is eight-legged & more powerful than a lion or an elephant, possessing the ability to clear a valley in one jump. It is one of the shrines of the Vaippu Sthalams sung by Tamil Saivite Nayanar Appar. The Temple follows the Tamilian style of architecture. An unusual feature of the Temple is that the vimana is extremely high unlike other Dravidian-style South Indian Temples. There is a separate shrine for Sarabeswarar & a metal icon of the same deity within the sanctum. Yali, a mythical creature with the face of a lion, which is otherwise considered a symbol of Nayak architecture has its earliest representation in Chola art in the Temple. The Temple is approached through a five-tiered pyramidal rajagopuram, the original structure. The vimana, the shrine over the sanctum is axial and of same height of that of the gopuram. Lord Narasimha is shown with eight arms, flaying and struggling under Sharbeshwaramurti's feet. The shrine has sculptures of Sridevi & Bhudevi, the consorts of Lord Vishnu.

SHANKARA MUTT AT TIRUVIDAIMARUDUR - The Temple in the Mutt is dedicated to Lord Shiva and the Temple has a very unique Shivalinga with a hand appeared in it. It was blessed by Adi Shankracharya and it is believed that the hand in the Shivalinga appeared to give acceptance to the Advaita concept of Adi Shankracharya by saying Satyam Advaitam.

Thiruvidaimaruthur Temple - The Temple is dedicated to Lord Shiva. It is one of the three Shiva Temples in India which adopt Maruda Tree as their Sthala Vriksham. Hence it is called as Idai Marudur. The other two Shiva Temples are Thalai Marudur in Sriselem & Kadai Marudur in Ambasamudram. The Shivalinga is Swayambhu & it is known as Mahalingam. The Lord Shiva is existed with his consort Goddess Brihatasundaragujambigai. Chakra Mahameru is also installed in this shrine. The Temple has imposing Gopuram which is one of the Panchalinga Kshetrams as there are five Shivalingas, four of which are in the four cardinal directions and fifth one as Mahalingaswamy at the centre.

SRI NAGANATHA SWAMI TEMPLE AT THIRUNAGESWARAM - There are 4 gateways with gopuram in the big & high compound walls of the Temple. On the eastern gateway, one can find Vinayaga Temple, Balibeedam, Nandeeswarar Mandapam & Dhwajasthambam. There are artistic features on its eastern wall. This Temple is considered most sanctified by its presiding deity location & sacred water & most benevolent because Shaiva Saints, Thirugnana Sambanda Swamigal, Thirunavukkarasu Swamigal & Thiru Sundaramoorthy Swamigal have sung in praise of Lord Shiva here besides being the most worshipful place of legendary fame Shaiva Saint, Sri Sekkizar Swamigal who brought out the sacred Shaiva text 'Peria Puranam'. This place is one of the 127 worthy places of divine worship spread over the southern bank of River Cauvery. Among the nine worship places, for the nine planets, Thirunageswaram is the place where Rahu Bhagvan is obviously active to bestow his grace. Here, Rahu Bhagvan can be seen with his two consorts Nagavalli & Nagakanni together and prayers for fulfilment of desires at this shrine are favourably answered with success. This Temple is one where Lord Shiva was worshipped by Rahu Bhagvan and got relived of a curse. In this Temple only we can see the Rahu Bhagvan with human face, whereas at all other places, we can see the Rahu with Serpent Face. As per Astrological system, by doing Milk abhisekam here for Rahu during Rahukalam, the delay in getting married; childlessness, troublesome married life, ill-effects of Kalasarpa Dosha, Kalasthra Dosha, Sarpa Dosha are all cured. The milk while being over poured over the Vigraha, turns blue even today and it is really to be seen and to be believed. At Shenbagaraniyam, under the Shenbagam Tree, Lord Shiva known as Shenbagarane Eswara was gracefully giving bless to devotees. It is here that Nandi worshipped the Lord & attained the status as Nandeesan, so too Vinayaga, the status of Head of Ganas. Sages

Gowthama, Vashishta, Parasarar & Kings Nala, Pandavas and Bageerathan obtained relief after worshipping Sri Naganatha Swami here. Kings of Snakes Aadisesha, Thakshagan & Karkotagan worshipped the Lord here & got blessed.

ARULMIGU OPPLIYAPPAN TEMPLE AT THIRUNAGESWARAM – Lord Vishnu-Perumal came to Sage Markandeya on a Panguni (March-April) Tiruvonam star day seeking his daughter's hand in marriage. The wedding took place on Aipasi (Oct.-Nov.) Tiruvonam Star day. Remembering this event, on Tiruvonam Star day each month, special pujas are performed with agandadeepa (big deepa) & long deepa – vaaldeepa lighting. It is believed that Mother Mahalakshmi graces devotees from these lamps. This darshan is considered a lucky one by the devotees. On Aavani Tiruvonam star day, Perumal grants darshan – Udaya Garuda Sevai. Then, he bathes in the Nattaru River praised as Dakshina Ganga. Special pujas are performed after this event. Once Sage Narada prayed to Lord Brahma to enlighten him on the history and greatness of the holy Markandeyakshetra that will also be for the benefit of humanity. On hearing this, Lord Brahma gladly started narrating the greatness of Tiruvinnagar and its presiding deity, whose glory cannot be described even by Adisesha with his 1000 tongues. Once Tulasidevi, who was born along with nectar (amrita) while churning the milky-ocean, begged Lord Narayana that she also be adorned by him on his chest like Mahalakshmi. Thereupon, the Lord said that Lakshmi did very severe penance to gain a place on his chest. The Lord further said that Lakshmi would appear as Bhoomidevi at a holy place near Kumbakonam to the south of River Kaveri and would be brought up by Sage Markandeya as his daughter. Tulasi should go there earlier and be in the form of lovely Tulasi plant at the Sage's hermitage. Then Lakshmi would appear under the Tulasi plant as Bhoomidevi. Later on Lord Narayana would come and marry Bhoomidevi and live there forever. Then the glory of Tulasi will become known to all. The Lord further said that those who worship him with petals of Tulasi shall attain all prosperity in the world and also the benefit of performing 'Asvamedhayaga'. All those who reside in this holy place will attain Sri Vaikunta at the end of their lives. From then onwards, Tulasi lived in this holy place, which therefore came to be known as Tulasi Vana (Tulasi forest).There are various holy tanks in the Temple complex. Devotees who worship thevimana (tower) derive immense and unalloyed happiness. Note that the vimana in Tirumala Tirupati is named as Ananda Vimana, whereas here it is Suddhananda Vimana. Desika's Sannidhi is located near the sanctum sanctorum. On the sides of the inner-prakara, Lord Anjaneya is on the south and Alwars' and Sri Rama's Sannidhis are located on the northern side. On the eastern side is Sri Ramanuja. Outside the main Temple is the shrine for Lord Maniappan & on the northern side is Ennappan and also the holy birth spot (avatarasthala) of Bhoomidevi. Garuda's shrine is located right opposite the main Temple. Just on the southern side of the main entrance, dancing Krishna in a niche welcomes us all with a bewitching smile. There is a shrine for Lord Rama, Lakshmana, Sita & Hanuman & then comes to the sacred bed chamber (Tiruppalliarai), full of beautiful mirrors, where during festivals, the Lord & his consort rest during nights. There is a small garden by the side of the outer prakara of the Temple. There is also a much bigger garden about ½ KM to the south of the Temple, where Tulasi & flowers are grown in abundance for weaving garlands daily for the deities. A big mandapa is located in this garden, where deities rest during the day in summer, during the Vasantotsavam celebrated for 6 days in May-June every year.

SRI KABARTHEESHWARA MANDIR AT TIRUVALANJULI - The Temple is dedicated to Lord Vinayaka. The vigraha of Lord Vinayaka is in white color and believed to have been created by Lord Indra out of sea foam during samudra Manthan and left it in a niche hoping to get it later but when he returned at this place to remove the vigraha, it would not budge. Hence it is called Swetha Vinayagar Mandir.

ARULMIGU SWAMINATHA SWAMI TEMPLE AT SWAMIMALAI, THANJAVUR - The Temple is built on an artificial hillock of about sixty foot height with sixty beautifully laid stone steps representing the Hindu cycle of sixty years - leading to the Lord. In the ground floor, there are Temples dedicated to Lord Sundareswarer and Goddess Meenakshi. The Temple has three 'Gopurams' with three 'Praharams'. The 'Gopuram' on the south side is decorated with vigrahas and contains five storeys while the other two entrances have no towers above them. The arrangement of the Praharam (also spelt as Prahar) is peculiar in this Temple. The first Praharam is at the base of the hill, the second halfway up the hill and the third at the top surrounding the sanctum. Once you pass the 'Raja Gopuram' and the 'Kalyana Mandapam', you reach the shrine dedicated to Goddess Sakti at the base. In addition to this, there are other shrines for various other deities and the well with 'Vajra Teertha'. The Temple of Swaminatha is very ancient one and it is known to have existed even in 2ndcentury. It is said that Parantaka Chola-I built the Temple. Swamimalai is fourth among the six padaiveedu or sacred shrines dedicated to Lord Muruga. The presiding deity here expounded the meaning of the pranava mantra OM to his own Father Lord Shiva himself. Mythology says that Saint Bhrigu, before commencing an arduous penance, got the boon that anybody disturbing his mediation will forget all his knowledge. Such was the power of the penance that the sacred fire emanating from the head of the Saint reached up to the heavens and the frightened Devas surrendered to Lord Shiva praying for his grace. The Lord extinguished the sacred fire by covering the Saint's head by hand. With the Saint's penance thus disturbed, the Lord became oblivious of all his knowledge and is said to have regained them by learning the Pranava Mantra from Lord Muruga at this shrine. Hymns in praise of the presiding deity have been sung by Saint Nakkeerar in Tirumurukatrupadai and by Saint Arunagirnathar in Tiruppukazh.

SRI SATCHINADESWARAR TEMPLE AT TIRUPIRAMBIYAM - The Temple is dedicated to Lord Shiva. The Temple is more than 1000 years old. The presiding deity as known as Satchinadeswarar, Satcheeswarar, Punnaivananathar. The Amman is known as Karumbanna Solli, Ikshuvani. The Tirtham is known as Brahmma Tirtham. Lord Shiva is Swayambhu Murthi here. There is a special

abhishek by honey is performed called Pralayam Katha Vinayaka on Vinayaka Chaturthi & the misery is that the honey used for the Abhishekam does not pour out. Ten days Masi Magam festival and Mahashivratri festival in addition to other festivals are celebrated here with great pomp & fervor.

CHANDRAMOULEESVARAR TEMPLE AT THAZHAMANGAI - The Temple is dedicated to Lord Shiva. This is the one of the seven sacred places of the Chakkarappalli Saptastana, worshipped by Indrani. Daksha, cursed Chandra, as he loved only his daughter Rohini and not taking into consideration others. For the children, he met Chandra. Chandra did not heed his advice. Daksha cursed him and the power of Chandra got waned. The power of Chandra got reduced. He felt sorry for what he did. He came to Thazhamangai and worshipped the presiding deity and got his curse cured. As Chandra worshipped the deity, the presiding deity is known as Chandramouleesvarar. The presiding deity in the garbhagriha is represented by the Lingam known as Chandramouleesvarar. The Goddess is known as Rajarajesvari. The Goddess is having four hands and is found in standing posture. The complete structure of garbhagriha is made of brick. The architectural style which is generally found in the Temples of Thanjavur could not be seen here. In the east of the Temple, the Temple thirtha known as Chandra thirtha. The entrance is found in the east. Balipitha and Nandhi are also there. Lord Vinayaka and Balamuruga are found on either side. In inscription, Thazhamangai is called as Nittha Vinotha Valanattu Kizhar Kutrathu Bavadhayamangalam. Very near to this place Kizhar, the town of Sangam age was found.

SHRI AIRAVATESVARA TEMPLE AT DARASURAM – It is one of the four vast Temple complexes with all stone vimanas built by King Rajaraja Chola-II. The Temple is another square plan structure completed in 1166 CE. The surviving inner courtyard is almost six stacked squares. The Nandi mandapa and the stambha are found outside of this main Temple courtyard and they are aligned with the main Temple's east-west axis. The agra-mandap is shaped like a chariot provided with stone horses and wheels. The design is similar to the Nritta-sabha (community dance hall) of Chidambaram Temple and the Konark Sun Temple. This Temple is a storehouse of art and architecture and has some exquisite stone carvings. The pedestal of the Balipitha adjoins a small shrine which contains an vigraha of Lord Ganesha. The reliefs all along the base of the main Temple narrate the stories of the sixty three Shaiva Bhakti Saints called Nayanars. In the south-west corner of the court is a mandapam having 4 shrines. One of these has an vigraha of Yama. Adjoining this shrine are large stone slabs sculptured with vigrahas of the sapthamathas (seven celestial nymphs). The construction of a separate Temple for Devi, slightly later than the main Temple, indicates the emergence of the Amman shrine as an essential component of the South Indian Temple complex. Other important sculptures of the Temple are the 108 Devara Othuvars who sung in the Temple during the time of Rajaraja Chola-II. There are sculptures for river goddesses like Cauvery, Ganges, Yamuna, Godavari and Narmada. The Temple was added to UNESCO's World Heritage Site list of Great Living Chola Temples in the year 2004.

THENUPURISWARAR TEMPLE AT PATTEESWARAM – The Temple is dedicated to Lord Shiva. Lord Shiva is worshiped as Thenupuriswarar and is represented by the Lingam. His consort Sri Parvati is depicted as Nyanambikai (Somakamalambigai). The presiding deity is revered in 7th century Tamil Shaiva canonical work, the Tevaram, written by Tamil Saint Poets known as the Nayanars and classified as Paadal Petra Sthalam. The Temple is associated with the legend of Sambandar to whose view Nandi moved to have a direct view of the presiding deity. Muthupandal festival celebrated in the Temple in associated with the legend. The entrance of Temple is through a seven tiered gopuram. The Temple has a number of shrines, with those of Thenupuriswarar, his consort Somakamalambigai and Durga, being the most prominent. All the shrines of the Temple are enclosed in large concentric rectangular granite walls. The Temple has six daily rituals and four yearly festivals. The Brahmotsavam festival is celebrated during the month of the Chittirai (April - May) is the most prominent festival. The original complex is believed to have been built by Cholas, while the present masonry structure was built during the Nayak in 16th century. Pattisvara, the presiding form of Lord Shiva manifests himself in the form of Linga, in the central mandapa of the first prakaram. Subsidiary deities like Sapthamatha, Mahalakshmi, Renuka, Navagraha, Surya, Chandra and Bhairava are housed in the inner parts of the Temple. Lord Ganesha is represented at three different places in three different forms - Anugai Pillayar, Madhavarna Pillayar and Swarna Vinayagar. In the northern part of the first prakaram, the consort Goddess Gnanambigai (Parvati) lies in a separate shrine. A sculpture of Sri Parvati doing penance is also found inside the Temple.

ARULMIGU PERUVUDAIYAR TEMPLE AT GANGAIKONDA CHOLAPURAM – The town has acquired this name because Rajendra-I, during his campaign to north, brought water from River Ganga in Golden Pot & sanctified the reservoir water body here. Hence, he was given the title of 'Gangaikondan' (the one who brought the Ganges). The popular Lord Shiva Temple was built by Rajendra Chola & devotees call it an equal of the Big Temple.

ARULMIGU PRAGADEESWARAR (PERIYA KOIL) TEMPLE AT THANJAVUR – It is popularly

known as Sri Brahadeeswara Temple [Big Temple]. The Great Chola Emperor Rajaraja Chola-I dedicated this Temple to Lord Shiva in the year 1010 AD. This Temple celebrated its 1000th year of existence in the year 2010. It is located amidst fortified walls presumed to have been added in the 16th century. The Temple is an UNESCO world heritage monument. This great Temple speaks about the architectural excellence of the region. The Tower above the sanctum sanctorum is 216 foot tall. This tower is one of the tallest tower of its kind in the

whole world. Kumbam or Chikaram, a bulbous structure above the tower cut out of one rock weighs almost 80 tons, is regarded as the show case of the architectural excellence of the period. It is believed that the Cupola / Sikaram was rolled up the incline built from the village called Saara Pallam now called as Vayalur. The majestic tower and lifting the cupola to the top is a testimony to the engineering skill of the Chola architects, who planned its construction in such a manner that the shadow of the Cupola does not fall on the ground. 12 ½ foot tall, 8 foot long and 5 foot wide sacred Bull or Nandi made out of a single rock weighing 25 tons installed outside in front of the sanctum Sanctorum. The Lingam is 13 ft tall with a circumference of 54ft.

NEELAMEGA PERUMAL TEMPLE AT THANJAVUR - The Temple is dedicated to Lord Narasimha. The Temple is 108 Divya Desams of Lord Perumal. The Temple is believed to be more than 1000 years old. The presiding deity is Neelamegar, Veera Narasimhar, Manikundrar. The Goddess is known as Senganalavalli, Thanjai Nayakai, Ambujavalli. The Tirtham is known as Amirtha Tirtham. The presiding deity has been consecrated in sitting posture. The Veera Narasimhar has been consecrated in Singaperumal Koil. Shri Yoga Narasimhar has been consecrated in the front madapam. The vigraha of Laxmi Narasimhar is in the prakara of the Temple. Abhayavaradha are Narasimhar has been consecrated on the Garudazhwar vimana and Kambathadi Yoga Narasimhar is on the pillar of Thayar Shrine. Lord Maha Vishnu had been consecrated in the discus as Chakarathazhwar. The vigraha of Lord Maha Vishnu is beautifully sculptured showing placing his hand on an elephant. Devotees offer sweet pudding - sarkarai pongal - nivedhana to the Neelamegar and Manikundra Perumal & sweet drink - panakam to Lord Narasimhar.

PANCHANATHEESWAR TEMPLE AT THIRUVAIYARU - Situated on the banks of River Cauvery, the Temple is dedicated to Lord Shiva. Surrounded by lush paddy fields and groves, the Temple has a very serene atmosphere. Devotees can also take a dip in the Cauvery River here, which is believed to absolve one of their sins. Another attraction is Thiruvaiyaru Temple, which is one of the seven Temples called Sapta Staanam. This Temple is associated with the wedding of Nandi (bull god), the mythical vehicle of Lord Shiva. Thiruvaiyaru is recognised as the place where one member of the trinity of carnatic music, Saint Thyagaraja lived and attained samadhi. The best time to visit the Temple is during a music festival held every January to commemorate the birthday of the Saint.

PUNNAINALLUR SREE MAHA MARIAMMAN TEMPLE AT MARIAMMANCOIL – Lord Shiva anointed eight Shakthis to destroy Asura Tanjan. One such Sakthi on the eastern direction is Punnainallur Mariamman. As per legend, the Maratha King Venkoji Maharaja went on a pilgrimage to have darshan of Samayapuram Mariamman. Midway, he stopped to rest. In his dream Mariamman appeared and asked him to go to the forest of Punnai Trees nearby to look for her. The King rushed to the spot indicated to him and he saw a white-ant hill (Putru) and built a Temple around it in 1680 AD. The Maratha rulers Tulja, Serfoji also worshiped and renovated the

Temple during their reign. It is believed that daughter of Tulaja Raja (1729-1735) of Thanjavur, who lost her eyesight due to illness, regained it on offering prayer worship at this Temple. The great Saint Sadasiva Brahmmendra shaped the white-ant hill (Putru) in the form of Mariamman and installed a powerful Sri Chakra here. This Temple is an existing example of Dravidian and Maratha architecture. People from all over the world visit this Temple for good health & prosperous life. As the prime deity is made out of sand, anointment (abhishekam) is not done daily. Gold and Silver shrouds are donned to the Goddess on certain auspicious days. Once in every five years for 48 days, Thil anointment (abhishegam) is done to the sand Vigraha. Yet another incredible thing is that, during summer, the Vigraha perspire, signs of perspiration can be seen on the Vigraha's body. Till date, the reason behind this perspiration is a hard nut crack. Devotees visit this Temple to get rid of all their diseases, poverty and sorrows. They offer mud replicas of body parts which has to be healed, sweet pudding, red saree and flowers to the goddess.

GAJENDRA VARADHA PERUMAL TEMPLE AT THIRUKKAVITHALAM – It is dedicated to the Lord Maha Vishnu. Constructed in the Dravidian style of architecture, the Temple is glorified in the Divya Prabandha, the early medieval Tamil canon of the Azhwar Saints from 6th – 9th centuries. It is one of the 108 Divyadesam dedicated to Lord Vishnu, who is worshipped as Gajendra Varadha and his consort Lakshmi as Ramamanivalli. The Temple is one of the five Pancha-Kannan Temples, where Lord Krishna, an avatar of Lord Vishnu is given prominence over the presiding deity. Religious scholars consider this place is a unique Lord Vishnu Temple, as he descended to rescue to an animal, while he appeared in all other places to rescue sages, celestial bodies or demons. The Temple is believed to have been built by Medieval Cholas of the late 8th century with later contributions from Vijayanagar Kings & Madurai Nayaks. A granite wall surrounds the Temple, enclosing all its shrines & bodies of water. Gajendra Varadha is believed to have appeared to Gajendra, the elephant, also called Indrajumnan, the crocodile called Koohoo, Sage Parasara & Sri Anjaneya. 6 daily rituals & 4 yearly festivals are held at the Temple, of which Gajendra Moksha Leela, celebrated during Tamil month of Aadi (July–Aug.) is the most prominent.

KALYANSUNDARESAR TEMPLE AT NALLUR - The Temple is dedicated to Lord Shiva. The Temple is believed to be 2000 years old. The Temple had been constructed by Chengotchozhan. The Temple has a misery as the Swayambhu Shivalingam changes its color five times in a day i.e. early in the morning - copper color, late morning - light red, afternoon - molten gold color, post lunch - emerald green & a very special occasion happens in the evening when the devotees could see the color of the Shivalinga which he has in mind and want to see that particular color. The middle portion of the Shivalinga alternate between shades of blue & green as this part is somewhat rough & has small spot like holes in them. The lower portion remains black at all times.

SRI MULLAIVANANATHARSWAMY & GARBARAKSHAMBIGAI AMMAN TEMPLE AT TIRUKKARUGAVUR - The Temple is dedicated to Sri Mullaivananathar & Sri Garbarakshambigai Amman. Saint Appar, Sundarar and Sambandhar, the three famous Nayanmaars have celebrated the glory of this Temple in soul stirring verses. The remarkable feature which distinguishes this Temple from the other shrines is that, Goddess Sri Garbarakshambigai Amman here cures infertility related problems to women, blesses them to conceive and also helps them for safe and trouble free delivery. Sri Mullaivananathar Swamy is worshipped for better health and well being. History says that Sri Garbarakshambigai Amman blessed her ardent devotee Vedhikai to conceive and when Vedhikai almost lost her fetus, Goddess Garbarakshambigai came to her rescue, protected her fetus and blessed her for safe delivery. Sri Mullaivananathar Swamy here is swayambhu i.e, self manifested. Even today we can see the impression of mullai creeper over him. He is made up of hardened mud and there is no Abhishegam (Holy bath) for this God. Instead Punugu sattam is being offered on the Valarpirai Pradosham day, the 13th day after new moon (Sukla Patcham Pradosham). This Punugu is believed to have healing power and it is being sent as prasadam for the peoples, who suffer due to incurable skin diseases, cardiac diseases and surgery.

DISTRICT – THENI (Railway Station – Madurai)

S. No.	Temple	Address	Type
1	Saneeswara Bhagavan Temple	Theni - 625515	Shanidev
2	Kodi Lingam Lingaparvadhina Aalayam	Suruli Falls - 625521	Shiva
3	Gowmariamman Temple	Veerapandi - 625534	Mata
4	Group of Temples	Devadanapatti - 625602	Mata, Shiva
5	Mangala Devi Kannagi Temple	Idukki - 685509	Mata

SANEESWARA BHAGAVAN TEMPLE AT THENI – The Temple is dedicated to Lord Shani (Saturn). The Lord is seen in Swayambhu (self-appeared) form. In front of this Temple, the perennial River Surabi flows which carried the waters of Periyar River & Suruliyaru. There is a separate Temple for guru which faces north direction so this Temple is known as Vadaguru Temple. There is a Lord Hanuman Temple, in which there is a Lord Ganesh vigraha installed, who has got 5 heads.

KODI LINGAM LINGAPARVADHINA AALAYAM AT SURULI FALLS - It is a hidden treasure. The Temple is housing around 30,000 Shivalingas. There is a series of thousands of Shivalingams placed in front of Amman Vigraha called Linga Parvadhini, who is an incarnation of Goddess Parvathi.

VEERAPANDI GOWMARIAMMAN TEMPLE – It is a 14th century Temple built by King Veerapandi of Pandya dynasty. It is believed that the King got back his lost sight after sincere and devoted prayer to Gowmariamman and Kanneeswara-mudaiyar. Mullai River, a perennial source of water flows close to the Temple.

DEVADANAPATTI - It is located at the bottom of the Kodaikanal Hills. The name Devadanapatti is a combination of two Tamil words: 'devadhanam' which means 'gods donated to' or 'gods gifted to' & 'Patti,' which means "village.' Therefore, the meaning is a village gifted by the gods.

Sri Kamakshi Temple - An ancient Temple called the Moongilanai Kamakshi Temple was built here. The main door of the Temple is never opened and poojas are performed only at the door. Maha Shivaratri (Tamil month of Masi) is the only festival that is celebrated inside the Temple. The story of the Temple is described in the Tamil movie "Mahashakti Mariamman". Near the Moongilanai Kamakshi Amman Temple, there is another Temple for Lord Karupannaswamy. As families, villagers from nearby Ganguvarpatti come by 'maattu vandi' (ox cart) during summer every year, cook at the Temple premises, take baths in the nearby falls and then conduct Uchchi Kaala Pooja at the Amman Temple and would often bring cooked food for all. During this Pooja, they pray for rain as well as the welfare of all villages and the neighbours. As soon as the aarthi is done, a 'Palli' will answer the prayers which can be witnessed personally.

Arulmigu Murugamalai Parameshwarar Temple - There is another Temple of Lord Shiva-Parvati located in Muruga Hill (once called Markanda Rishi hill). There are self-existed forms of Lord Shiva, Parvathi Maa and Ganga Maa. The Karthigai Deepam festival celebrated on the day of Pleiades on the Tamil month Karthigai. Married couples worship the Lord Shiva, Parvathi Maa and Ganga Maa to be blessed with a baby boy.

MANGALA DEVI KANNAGI TEMPLE - It is a historic Temple located in the Idukki district of Kerala bordering Tamil Nadu. Cheran Chenguttuvan, the King of ancient Tamilakam, had erected the Temple for Kannagi around 2000 years back at Vannathiparai and called it 'Kannagi Kottam' or 'Mangaladevi Kannagi Temple' and performed regular pujas. It sits at an altitude of about 1,337 m (4,386 ft) above sea level. It is surrounded by lush greenery and is closed throughout the year except during the Chitra Pournami festival. At other times, tourists can still view it by getting a special letter from the forest ranger. The view from the Temple premises is spectacular and one can see part of Eastern Ghats and some villages from adjacent state of Tamil Nadu.

DISTRICT – THOOTHUKUDI (Railway Station – Tiruchendur/Tuticorin)

S. No.	Temple	Address	Type
1	Ayyanarsunai	Melaputhukudi – 628201	Spring
2	Arultharum Mutharamman Thirukoil	Kulasekaranpatinam, Tiruchendur – 628206	Mata-Shiva
3	Sri Kailasa Nathar Temple	Rajapathy – 628207	Shiva (Navakailayam)
4	The Seashore Temple of Subrahmanyam	Thiruchendur – 628215	Murugan
5	Arulmigu Kailasanathar Temple	Murappanadu – 628252	Shiva (Navakailayam)
6	Sri Devi Jakkamal Temple	Fort Complex, Panchalankurichi – 628401	Mata
7	Kazhugumalai Caves, Vettuvan Koil, Kalugasalamoorthy Temple	Kalugumalai – 628552, Kovilpatti Taluk	Jain, Shiva, Murugan
8	Arulmigu Kallappiraan Temple	Srivaikuntam, Thiruchendur Taluk – 628601	Vishnu (Nava Thirupathi)
9	Azhwarthirunagari Permual Temple	Azhwar Thirunagari – 628612	Vishnu (Nava Thirupathi)
10	Sri Vaithamanidhi Permual Temple	Tirukkolur – 628612	Vishnu (Nava Thirupathi)

S. No.	Temple	Address	Type
11	Irattai Tirupati Temple	Thirutholaivillimangalam-628614	Vishnu (Nava Thirupathi)
12	Thiru Varagunamangai Permual Temple	Natham – 628620	Vishnu (Nava Thirupathi)
13	Arulmigu Kailasanathar Temple	Srivaikundam Nagar – 628621	Shiva (Navakailayam)
14	Arulmigu Kailasanathar Temple	Thenthirupperai – 628621	Shiva (Navakailayam)
15	Thiru Puliangudi Permual Temple	Thirupuliangudi – 628621	Vishnu (Nava Thirupathi)
16	Makara Nedunkuzhaikathar Temple	Thenthiruperai - 628623	Vishnu (Nava Thirupathi)
17	Sri Srinivasa Perumal Temple	Perungulam – 628752	Vishnu (Nava Thirupathi)
18	Vettrivelamman Temple	Korkai – 628801	Mata

AYYANARSUNAI AT MELAPUTHUKUDI – A natural water gushes out from the spring at this place. A Temple dedicated to the village deity is also located here.

ARULTHARUM MUTHARAMMAN THIRUKOIL AT TIRUCHENDUR - It is 300 years old Temple. It is known for the popular 'Dasara' festival where folk dance artists from all over the state participate in the festival. In this Temple, Goddess Muththaramman and Swami Nganamoorthiswarar vigraham are installed combined each other. You cannot able to see such combined vigraham elsewhere. Through Maha Mandapam, Pechiamman, Karuppaswamy and Bhairavar are showering their blessings to the devotees. Next to the Mahamandapam, you can find a 32 foot height Kodimaram, which is fully covered with Brass. At the bottom of the Kodimaram, you can see a square consists of Ambal & Swami, as one side, Astiradevar on the other side, Lord Vinayaga on the third side and on the fourth side, Lord Balasubramaniyan vigrahas are moulded in the Brass. Once upon a time, due to the curse of Saint Agathiyar, Saint Varamuni has become a man with a buffalo head. The term "Magisam" means buffalo. Since he had a buffalo head, he was called Magisasuran. With his continuous meditation and strenuous effort Magisasuran gained more power and dominated all over the world. To condemn the domination of the Magisasuran, the Saints approached the Goddess and informed the hardship done by Magisasuran. Then with the power of Goddess, there appears a female baby. The baby was named as Lalithambigai. The baby grown up within 9 days and on the 10th day, she grew as Annai Parasakthi Lalithambigai with lots of anger came strongly and destroyed Magisasuran and this day 10th day is being celebrated as Dusshera. The growth occurred by Annai Parasakthi during the nine days are resumed as Navarathiri. The first three days for Malaimagal, the second three days as Alaimagal and the last three days as Kalaimagal. After the Goddess Annai

Parasakthi demolished Mahishasuran, she was called as Mahishasura Mardhini. At last, the Goddess came to this city and settled and showered her blessing to all devotees.

SRI KAILASA NATHAR TEMPLE AT RAJAPATHY – The presiding deity in the Temple is Sri Kailasanathar and Goddess Alagiya Ponnamal and Sivakamiammai. The place is named after the palace of Pandya King belonging to the Chandra dynasty – Raja-King, Pathi-Palace. This is the place where Ketu worshipped Lord Shiva – Kailasanathar, hence praised as Kethu Parihara Sthala. There is only a disfigured Shivalinga. There are four wheel figures on all sides of the Shivalinga. It is said that there is a Temple buried under this Linga. Rahu rules 7 years in a person's life, hence, it is advised that the person do worship Lord in this Temple during this period. Devotees pray here for good farm yields, health, child boon, health of cattle, job opportunities and progress in trade and offer various farm produces as their prayer commitment to Lord and Mother. On Pradosha days, they offer various puja materials and fruits for the pujas. This place and Temple is regarded as Then Kalahasti. This Temple is praised equal in reputation to the Kethu Sthala in Keelaperumpallam Temple in Nagapattinam district. Along with Aadhi Kailasanathar, Lord Kailasa Nathar and Soundarya Nayaki bless the devotees from this holy soil.

THE SEASHORE TEMPLE OF SUBRAHMANYAM AT THIRUCHENDUR – It is one of the delightful spots sanctified and venerated by every Hindu. The rising sun bows in adoration of it each morning as he rises from the rippling expanse of the ocean and spreads light and life over every living object. Bordered by the sea on the East and the North, the Temple walls on these sides are washed by the foaming waves of the Gulf of Mannar. The date of the Temple is hidden in the Puranic past. The nucleus of the structure however has been here for more than 2,000 years. Lord Muruga's association with Tiruchendur is highly significant. It is described in extensor in his epic, the Skanda Puranam. The young Lord Muruga as the Devasenapati vanquishes evil in the form of Surapatuma. The Tamils have ever since been celebrating the event as an annual festival during Skanda Sasti. The Tamils in this part of the peninsula have such an attraction for the place and its presiding Lord Arumuga Nayinar. Tradition and Shiva-rahasya Khanda in Skanda Puranam relate that at this spot Lord Muruga encamped before and after the vanquishment of the asuras and worshipped Lord Shiva at the shrine, Mayan had built for him. The Kanda-Madana-Parvata, the red sandstone rock of this coast, had worthily received its foundations. A lofty gopuram also rose beside it. A part of the cliff some fifty foot high was bored to form the holy sanctum of Lord Subrahmanyam. The Temple was fully constructed anew in all its details and Kumbhabhishekam performed in 1941. The Temple and its gopuram of nine floors, built on the extremity of the sandstone cliff are a landmark and visible at sea for twelve miles around, looking as has been said like a brig in full sail. It is among 6 holy abodes of Lord Karthikeya. 2004 Tsunami did not touched the Temple but every thing around it was destroyed. Sea waves went back 2 KMs and saved pilgrims & Temple town from disaster. There is a square Well with circumference of 14 ft. square and has a small Well with in it. The water of the larger Well is brackish and salty in contrast to the smaller one which contains crystal clear sweet water. These two Wells despite their proximity give two completely different taste which is indeed a divine miracle.

ARULMIGU KAILASANATHAR TEMPLE AT MURAPPANADU – It is situated on the banks of River Tamirabarni and the presiding deity of the Temple is Kailasanathar and Goddess Sivakamiammal.

SRI DEVI JAKKAMAL TEMPLE AT FORT COMPLEX, PANCHALANKURICHI – The Temple is dedicated to the hereditary Goddess of Kattabomman. It is located in the fort complex. Festival is celebrated on January 15 and May second week every year which attract thousands of people. Small bullock cart race is the special attraction during festival.

KAZHUGUMALAI CAVES, VETTUVAN KOIL, KALUGASALAMOORTHY TEMPLE AT KALUGUMALAI – It is one of the important centres of the Jains. The bas-relief found here are the contribution of Jains and are among the earliest of such works. The Vettuvan Koil (Lord Shiva Temple), the rock-cut cave Temple is worth visiting. It is believed that this monolithic structure monument was established during 8thcentury by Pandya Maranchadayan King. This is a rock cut cave complex and cut out Temple on the style of the Mahabalipuram Shore Temple and cave sculptures. This monument is also nick named as "Ellora of South". It is a devotional sculptures during the Paranthaka Nedunchadaian period. In the ridge of the mountain, Vatteluthu inscription found says that "Samanar School was formed by Paranthka Nedunchadaiyan". There are lot of Jain exquisite bas-relief sculptures found with inscriptions. The main deity of the hill was called Araimalai Alwar and various other deity are Bhagwan Adinatha, Neminatha Mahaveera Parsvanatha, Bahubali. In the later days, Lord Ganesha's Vigraha was installed and worshipped. At the top of the Temple, beautiful sculpture of Uma Maheswarar, Dakshinamoorthy, Vishnu and Brahma can be found. There are around 122 sculptures in the rock cut Temple. The intricately carved vigrahas are from fine granite.

Kalugasalamoorthy Temple - The main deity of this Temple is Lord Murugan with his wife Devyanai. The main deity hall and entrance hall is excavated inside the foot hills of Kalugumalai in the south western corner of the hill and with external structural additions. The Temple has many aesthetic sculptures. The Temple dates to 18thcentury. The Temple complex also has shrines of Lord Shiva, Akilandeswari, Vinayakar and many lesser deities.

ARULMIGU KALLAPPIRAAN TEMPLE AT SRIVAIKUNTAM - The nine Vaishnava shrines hailed as Navatiruppathi are related to the nine planets or celestial bodies and the deities in these Temples are worshipped as the navagrahaas. The Navatiruppathis in the Pandya region are recognized on par with the Navagrahaa Temples in the Chola country (Surya, Chandra, Angaarakan - Putthirukku Velur, Budha Thiruvenkaadu, Guru Aalangudi, Sukra Kanjanoor, Shani Thirunallaar, Raahu Thirunageswaram, Ketu Keezhperumpallam). In these Vishnu Temples, the prime deities are worshipped as the Navagrahaas & so there are no separate shrines for the Navagrahaas, as found in other Temples. To offer worship to these deities alleviate the malignant influences of the

Navagrahaas that come about during one lifetime. Generally, in the Temples Lord Vishnu is seen reclining on Adisesha but, in this Temple, Lord Vishnu is in the standing posture under the umbrella, Adisesha. Srivaikuntam Temple is also called Kailasapuram and has Nataraja shrine with 8 artistically carved pillars. The most famous is the Kallapiran, the festival deity and presiding deity is called Vaikuntanathar. On the 6th day of Tamil month Chittirai (April), the Sun rays fall on the main deity as a token of worship. The Vigraha is most exquisitely carved with club in hand. Lions, Yalis and Elephants are carved in the pillars of the mandapam. The Temple served as a fort during the patriotic war of Kattabomman with the British. The Temple has a 9-tier rajagopuram amidst lush vegetation around the Temple. Two legends are associated with this Temple. Once an asura by the name Somakan appropriated Lord Brahma and Lord Vishnu retrieved it from the demon. Since the Lord came direct from his abode Vaikuntham and agreed to remain here, this place came to be known as Srivaikuntam. Later, Kaaladhushakan, a robber, conducted his robbery after worshipping Vaikuntanathan and surrendered to him, half of what he had plundered. He was a Robinhood of those days looted the rich and helped the poor. Once his men, while engaged in ransacking the palace were caught by the King soldiers. They had to identify their leader; when Kaladhushakan came to know about it, he prayed to the Lord of Srivaikuntam to save him. The Lord appeared before the King as Kaaladhushakan, revealed himself to the King and counselled him to protect dharma. Having had this beatific vision, the King requested the Lord to remain in this place as Kallappiraan.

AZHWARTHIRUNAGARI PERMUAL TEMPLE AT AZHWAR THIRUNAGARI – The Temple is one of the Nava Tirupathi. It is dedicated to Lord Vishnu. Constructed in the Dravidian style of architecture, the Temple is glorified in the Divya Prabandha, the early medieval Tamil canon of the Azhwar Saints from 6th – 9th centuries. It is one of the 108 Divyadesam dedicated to Lord Vishnu, who is worshipped as Adinathar and his consort Lakshmi as Athinathanayagi. The Temple is also classified as a Navatirupathi, the nine Temples revered by Nammazhwar located in the banks of Tamiraparani River. The Temple is the most prominent among the nine Navatirupathi Temples. The Temple is one of the Navagraha Temples in Vaishnavism, associated with Jupiter, the Guru. A granite wall surrounds the Temple enclosing all its shrines and two of its three bodies of water. The rajagopuram, the Temple's gateway tower, is 95 ft tall. The Temple is considered the birthplace of Nammazhwar, considered the most prominent among the twelve Azhwar Saints. The Temple follows Thenkalai tradition of worship. Six daily rituals and three yearly festivals are held at the Temple, of which the ten-day annual Brahmotsavam during the Tamil month of Chittirai (April - May) and the Nammazhwar birth celebrations with Garudasevai with all nine Temples of Navatirupathi, being the most prominent.

Alwartirunagari - Sri Nammalvar was a great Saint born about 5000 years ago in a shudra family, yet he gained the highest pedestal among the Saints in Tamil Nadu. He is one of the twelve Alvar Saints of Tamil Nadu who are known for their affiliation to the Vaishnava tradition of Hinduism. The verses of alvars are compiled as Nalayira Divya Prabandham and the 108 Temples are classified as Divya Desam. He has contributed 1352 among the 4000 stanzas in the Nalayira Divya Prabandam. As per legend, he remained speechless from his birth sitting in a tamarind tree and he first interacted with Madhurakavi Alvar, who saw a bright light shining to the south and followed it until he reached the tree where the boy was residing. His works were compiled by Madhurakavi as four different works, the Thiruvaimozhi (1,102 verses), Thiruviruttam (100 verses), Thiruvaasiriam (or Thiru Aasiriyam - 7 verses) & Periya Thiruvanthadi (87 verses). The Garudasevai festival in Nava Tirupathi and the Araiyar Sevai during the Vaikunta Ekadasi festival in Srirangam Temple are dedicated to him. The verses of Nammalvar and other alvars are recited as a part of daily prayers and during festive occasions in most Vishnu Temples in South India.

SRI VAITHAMANIDHI PERMUAL TEMPLE AT TIRUKKOLUR - It is one of the Nava Tirupathi, nine Hindu Temples dedicated to Lord Vishnu. It is located on the southern bank of Thamiraparani River. This is the eighth Temple of Nava Thirupathi and is for mars (Sevvai). It is also called as Kuberasthalam. All these 9 Temples are classified as "Divya Desams", the 108 Temples of Lord Vishnu revered by the 12 Poet Saints or Alwars.

IRATTAI TIRUPATI TEMPLE AT THIRUTHOLAIVILLIMANGALAM – The Temple refers to two Temples of the Nava Tirupathi, out of nine Hindu Temples dedicated to Lord Vishnu. It is located on the banks of Thamiraparani River. All these 9 Temples are classified as "Divya Desams", the 108 Temples of Lord Vishnu revered by the 12 Poet Saints Alwars. The two Temples are Devapiran Temple and Aravindalochanar Temple located adjacent to each other. There are two Temples, one a north Temple & other a south Temple. Both the Temples have two prakarams. It is referred to as Ketu Sthalam, a location for the snake deity, Ketu. Aravindalochanar Perumal Temple is a Rahu Sthalam.

THIRU VARAGUNAMANGAI PERMUAL TEMPLE AT NATHAM – It is one of the Nava Tirupathi Temples dedicated to Lord Vishnu. It is located on the banks of Thamiraparani River. All these 9 Temples are classified as "Divya Desams", the 108 Temples of Lord Vishnu revered by the 12 Poet Saints or Alwars. The Temple is also known as Sri Vijayasana Perumal Temple, the Chandran Sthalam. It is 2nd of the Navathirupathis.

ARULMIGU KAILASANATHAR TEMPLE AT SRIVAIKUNDAM NAGAR - It is located on the bank of River Tamirabarni. The presiding deity of the Temple is Kailasanathar and Goddess Sivakamiammai. The first Navathirupathi Temple is located here.

ARULMIGU KAILASANATHAR TEMPLE AT THENTHIRUPPERAI – The presiding deity of the Temple is Kailasanathar and Goddess Allakiyaponamal. One of the Navathrupathi Temple also located here.

THIRU PULIANGUDI PERMUAL TEMPLE AT THIRUPULIANGUDI – It is one of the Nava Tirupathi Temples dedicated to Lord Vishnu. It is located the banks of Thamiraparani River. All these 9 Temples are classified as "Divya Desams", the 108 Temples of Lord Vishnu revered by the 12 Poet Saints or Alwars. The Temple has an imposing vigraha of Lord Vishnu, a lotus stalk from the navel of the vigraha emanates the vigraha of Lord Brahma. The feet of the deity can be viewed through the passage. The Temple has two prakarams.

MAKARA NEDUNKUZHAIKATHAR TEMPLE AT THENTHIRUPERAI – It is one of the Nava Tirupathi Temples dedicated to Lord Vishnu. It is located on the southern bank of Thamiraparani River. All these 9 Temples are classified as Divya Desams, the 108 Temples of Lord Vishnu revered by the 12 Poet Saints or Alwars. The Temple is referred to as Sukra Sthalam, a location for the planet deity, Sukra. The same place hosts one of the Navakailasams, Sri Kailasanathar Temple, the seventh in the series.

SRI SRINIVASA PERUMAL TEMPLE AT PERUNGULAM – It is also known as Sri Mayakoothar Permual Temple. It is one of the Nava Tirupathi Temples dedicated to Lord Vishnu. It is located on the banks of Thamiraparani River. All these 9 Temples are classified as "Divya Desams", the 108 Temples of Lord Vishnu revered by the 12 Poet Saints or Alwars. The Temple has an vigraha of Lord Vishnu facing east direction. Kulam refers to tank in Tamil language. The name of the village is derived from the same. The Temple has two prakarams. This Temple history describes Lord Vishnu's power to perform miracles to serve his devotees. Once, one asura abducted Lord Vishnu baktha Vedasaran's wife Kumudhavalli. The asura performed magic tricks but was vanquished by Lord Vishnu who danced on his head as Koothar and he restored Kumudhavalli to her husband.

KORKAI – It is an ancient port city of Pandian dynasty in the Sangam period. The Tank of Korkai is said to be Korkai Kulam. An ancient Vettrivelamman Temple is also situated here. Many a number of tourists visit this Temple.

DISTRICT – TIRUCHIRAPPALLI (Railway Station – Tiruchchirapali/Namakkal)

S. No.	Temple	Address	Type
1	Arulmigu Thayumana Swamy Temple	Malaikottai, Trichy – 620002	Ganesh
2	Azhagiya Manavala Perumal Temple	Woriur – 620003	Vishnu

S. No.	Temple	Address	Type
3	Arulmigu Jambukeswarar Akhilandeswari Temple	Thiruvanaikkaval, Thiruvarankam Taluk – 620005	Shiva
4	Sri Ranganathar Swamy Temple	Srirangam – 620006	Vishnu-Laxmi
5	Murugan Temple	Kumaravayalur – 620102	Murugan
6	Pundarikakshan Perumal Temple	Tiruvellerai – 621009	Vishnu
7	Arulmigu Brahmapureeswarar Temple	Tiruppatur, Irrungalur – 621105	Shiva
8	Arulmigu Maariamman Temple	Samayapuram – 621112	Mata
9	Thalamalai Perumal Temple	Neeliampatti – 621208	Vishnu

ARULMIGU THAYUMANA SWAMY TEMPLE AT TRICHY – It is also known as Rockfort Pillayar Temple. It is the land mark for Trichy city. Rockfort is approximately 300 ft high and the main deity is the Lord Ganesh ("Uchchi Pillayar"). A tank and a pavilion at the foot of the Rock Fort set the scene for the Temple's Float festival. It is reached by flight of 437 steps. Halfway up is Sri Thayumanaswamy Temple, dedicated to Lord Shiva. It has a 100 pillared hall and a Vimana. There are inscription in the Temple that date back to 3rd century. Lord Shiva is worshiped as Thayumanavar and is represented by the Lingam and his consort Parvati is depicted as Mattuvar Kuzhalammai. The presiding deity is revered in the 7th century Tamil Shaiva canonical work, the Tevaram, written by Tamil Saint Poets known as the Nayanars and classified as Paadal Petra Sthalam. As per legend, when Lord Sri Rama returned to Ayodhya after rescuing Mother Sita from the captivity of Ravana, Sri Sugriva, Sri Hanuman and Sri Vibhishana accompanied the Lord to participate in the coronation function of the Lord. While returning back with the gift of Sri Ranganatha Vigraha from Sri Rama, Vibhishana came south. Seeing the beauty of River Cauvery and the scenic environment, he wanted to relax for a while. Lord Vinayaka was there in the guise of a little boy. Vibhishana asked the boy to take care of the gift Vigraha of Lord Ranganatha. After waiting for Vibhishana, the boy placed the Vigraha on the ground and hid himself in the hill. Vibhishana was shocked to see the boy missing. He applied all his energy to move the Vigraha but failed. Thus, Lord Ranganatha, bound to Sri Lanka, cut short his journey and chose Sri Rangam as his abode. Seeing the boy at the top of the hill, Vibhishana hit him on the head, the scar of which is still visible on the Lord Vinayaka Vigraha. Thus, Lord Vinayaka along with Lord Ranganatha nearby is ruling us gracefully. A furious contest arose between Adisesha and Vayu to decide the supremacy of their prowess. The condition was to shake violently Mount Kailash. Defeating Adisesha, when Vayu broke the mount, a part of it fell in this place. Demon Tirishira (demon with three heads) was on penance on Lord Shiva. Though many years passed, Lord Shiva delayed his darshan to test his purity. He threw two of his heads in fire and was about to throw the third, Lord appeared before him and restored his two heads. As requested by him, Lord Shiva agreed to stay here in the name of Thirisira Nathar (based on demon Tirishira story). The place came to be known as Tirishiramalai, now changed as Tiruchy.

URAIYUR - The spiritual town is best known for the Azhagiya Manavala Perumal Temple, dedicated to Lord Vishnu. The Temple is believed to have been built by the Medieval Cholas of the late 8th century AD with contributions from the later Pandyas, Vijayanagar Kings and Madurai Nayaks. It

is surrounded by a granite wall enclosing all the shrines. A large number of devotees visit the Temple for the annual Serthi Sevai festival observed during the months of March-April. Around 3rd century BCE when Mauryan emperor Ashoka ruled, Buddhism was quite popular in the region around Uraiyur. The town was once the capital of early Chola rulers, and among the three main kingdoms of ancient Tamil country. Inscriptions and rock edicts of Ashoka and the Satavahanas describe Uraiyur as "the citadel and centre of the Cholas".

ARULMIGU JAMBUKESWARAR AKHILANDESWARI TEMPLE AT THIRUVANAIKKAVAL - This Temple is situated in Coromandel between two Rivers - Cauvery in south & Coleroon in North. This Temple is one of the Pancha Bhootha Sthalam representing water. Hence, this Temple is also revered as "Appu Sthalam" & the Shivalingam here is called as "Appu Linga". The Shivalingam in the Sanctum Sanctorum is reported to be submerged in the water that flows from a subterranean spring into the Sanctum Sanctorum because an elephant once worshiped Lord Shiva under the holy Jambu Tree, the god gets the name Jambukeswarar. The presiding deity is Devi Akilandeswari Amman. Akhilandeshwari means 'Ruler of the Universe' (Akilam – Universe, Aanda – Ruler, Eswari – Goddess). According to the mythological scriptures, Devi Parvathi in her incarnation as Devi Akilandeswari performed penance in the Jambu forest (Thiruvanaikoil). She made a Lingam out of water from the River Cauvery and installed it under the Venn Naaval tree (the Venn Naaval tree on top of Saint Jambu) and commenced her worship. Hence, the Lingam is known as Appu Lingam (Water Lingam). Lord Shiva at last gave darshan to Devi Akhilandeswari and taught her Shiva Gnana. Devi Akhilandeswari took Upadesa (lessons) facing east from Lord Shiva, who stood facing west. Hence, this Temple is also revered as an Upadesa Sthalam. Since Devi Akhilandeswari worshipped Lord Shiva in this Temple, even today at noon the 'Archakar' (priest) dresses like a female and performs Puja to Lord Jambukeswara and the holy Cow. A specific breed of black cow called Karam Pasu is brought to the Temple for puja. As the Devi was like a student and Lord Jambukeswara like a Guru (teacher) in this Temple, there is no Thiru Kalyanam (marriage) conducted in this Temple for Lord Shiva and Devi Parvathi, unlike the other Shiva Temples. The Shrine of the Devi Akilandeshwari and the Shrine of Lord Prasanna Vinayaka opposite the Devi Shrine are in the shape of the Pranava Mantra called "OM". The Temple is one of the 275 Paadal Petra Sthalams, where all the four most revered Nayanmars (Shaivite Saints) have sung hyms in glory of the deity in the Temple. The Temple was built by Emperor Kocengannan Chola more than 1,800 years ago. The Temple has inscriptions which date from this period. Monolithic stone pillars (made from single stone) are found in the mandapam, situated at the entrance of Aariyavittan tower in 3rd Praharam. Stone chains and 12 zodiac signs are beautifully carved on these pillars. Pillars found in 1000 pillar hall and in various parts of Temple have artistic sculptural works. 'Coratham' (used for procession) and several wooden Vahanas are present in this Temple. Inscriptions of King Madurai Konda Parakesari Varman Paranthaka Cholan is the oldest. Devotees worshipping here are blessed both in this birth and in next birth. One who worships Goddess Ahilandeswari will be blessed with good education and intelligence, marriage and wishes for child are fulfilled. The Institute was presented with the prestigious "UNESCO Mandram Award" in 1970 for its commendable role in the eradication of Small pox.

SRI RANGANATHAR SWAMY TEMPLE AT SRIRANGAM - This Temple is also known as Thiruvaranga Tirupati, Periyakoil, Bhooloka Vaikundam and Bhogamandabam. It is also considered the first, foremost and the most important of the 108 Lord Vishnu Temples. Srirangam is the foremost of the eight self-manifested shrines (Swayam Vyakata Kshetras) of Lord Vishnu. This Temple lies on an islet formed by the twin Rivers Cauvery and Coleroon. "Sri Ranganathar" is the main deity of this Temple and the "Ranganayaki" is the Goddess. Srirangam is considered as the capital of Vaishnavas. To add to its pride, this Temple has the tallest Temple Tower in the world i.e. the Rajagopuram of this Temple was built in 1983 and is 236ft tall. For 'Vaikunta Yekaadesi', pilgrims come from all over the world and it is a 20 days celebration. The enclosures are guarded by thick and huge rampart walls. There are 21 magnificent and huge towers. It has seven prakaras or enclosures. This Temple underwent many changes during the rule of Cholas, Cheras, Pandiyas, Hoysalas, Vijayanagar Kings and Nayak of Madurai. Apart from the presiding deity, Lord Ranganathar, the Temple complex comprises of many other Sannathis and about 53 Upa-sannathis such as Thayar Sannathi, Chakkarathazwar Sannathi, Udayavar (Ramanujar Sannathi), Garudalwar Sannathi, Thanvanthiri Sannathi & Hygrevar Sannathi. The Temple consists of seven concentric rectangular enclosures round the sanctum sanctorum. The Temple of Srirangam is the only one in India with seven enclosures, a sacred symbolic number which for present day Vaishnava believers represents either the seven centres of Yoga or a reference to the seven elements making up the human body in the centre of which dwells the soul. The fifth enclosure contains the shrine of Manavala Mamunigal in the Cholastyle. In the fourth court, the Temple of Venugopala Krishnan exist, whose outside walls are decorated with very beautiful sculptures in high relief like young women playing the Zither (Veena) or with a parrot or putting the finishing touches (Tilaka) to their appearance before a looking glass. In the south, there exists the famous Sesharayar Mandapa. The Nazhikettan Gopura and on either side has vigrahas called Sankhanidhi and Padmanidhi, the conch and the lotus respectively, which are the attributes of Lord Vishnu. In the northwest corner are the Yagasala and the Tondaiman Mandapa of which ceiling is decorated with paintings of figures. The eastern part contains two Mandapas- Arjuna Mandapa and Kili Mandapa.

MURUGAN TEMPLE AT KUMARA VAYALUR – It is also known as Vayalur. Situated amidst lush greenery is the Murugan Temple, the highlight of the town. The Temple is dedicated to Lord Kartikeya, locally known as Murugan, the Hindu god of war. It is said that the Temple was built by the Cholas in 9th century. Legend has it that Lord Muruga created a tank with his weapon to worship his parents. It is at this place where Lord Muruga blessed the Saint Poet Arunagiri Nathar and also initiated him to compose Thirupugazh, renowned religious tamil songs dedicated to Lord Murugan. The Temple draws huge footfalls during the festivals of Panguni Utthiram, Thai Poosam and Skanda Sashti, which are celebrated with great pomp and show.

PUNDARIKAKSHAN PERUMAL TEMPLE AT TIRUVELLERAI – Located on a 50-ft-high hill of white rock, Thiruvellarai is the place where Yogi (saint) Pundarikakshan offered Tulsi (holy basil) to the Temple's God and Goddess. Pleased with his prayers, Lord Perumal blessed him. Incidentally, Perumal is also known as Pundarikakshan. The town is known for the Perumal Temple that is said to be older than the popular Srirangam Temple. The Temple has three inscriptions in its two rock-cut caves, dating back to 18th century and a swastika-shaped tank, which was built under the reign of Dantivarman, a Pallava ruler (795-846 AD), during 9th century. The entire Temple has been constructed utilising elements from Hindu mythology like the 18 steps representing the 18 chapters of the Bhagavat Gita and the entrance to the gopuram supported by four pillars signifying the four Vedas.

ARULMIGU BRAHMAPUREESWARAR TEMPLE AT TIRUPATTUR – The Temple is dedicated to Lord Shiva in the form of a Swayambhu (self-manifested) Lingam. Since Lord Shiva absolved Lord Brahma of his sins, he is known as Brahmapureeswarar in this Temple. The sanctum sanctorum is 300 ft from the main entrance. There are 7 entrances leading to the sanctum sanctorum, significant of the 7 days of the week, yet the sanctum is filled with natural light and the presiding deity can be seen clearly from the main entrance. Also, sunlight falls directly on the presiding deity three days in a year - on the 15th, 16th and 17th day of the Tamil month of Panguni. Lord Brahma installed and worshipped 12 Shivalingams at this Temple. These Shivalingams are (1) Sri Brahmapureeswarar (2) Sri Pazhamalai Nathar (3) Sri Pathala Eswarar (4) Sri Thayumanavar (5) Sri Manduga Nathar (6) Sri Ekambareswarar (7) Sri Arunachaleswarar (8) Sri Kailasa Nathar (9) Sri Jambukeshwarar (10) Sri Kalathi Nathar (11) Sri Sabthagereswarar and (12) Sri Sudharaneswarar. The Theertham from where Lord Brahma filled water to perform puja is present in the Nandavanam (Temple garden). The Sthala Vruksham is Magizhamaram which is about 150 years old. It is believed that Sage Pathanjali often left his physical body and stayed in the astral form for many days in this Magizhamaram and performed penance. Devi Parvathi gave back Lord Brahma all his sheen and hence the Devi here is called Brahma Sampath Gowri. The Vigraha of Lord Brahma is a majestic 6 foot high. It is fully decorated with Turmeric. Lord Brahma is in meditative pose sitting in Padmasana on a lotus. Lord Shanmuganathar's shrine is located near Sri Karpaga Vinayakar shrine in the inner praharam of the Temple. The Shrine of Lord Dakshinamurthy is adjacent to the shrine of Lord Brahma. The Jeeva Samadhi of the Founder of Yoga, Maharishi Patanjali is located adjacent to the shrine of Lord Brahma. The Devi is depicted seated on a Lotus, flanked on both sides by Gaja (elephant). There is a separate Sannathi for Devi Gajalakshmi in the inner praharam of the Temple. Lord Kala Bhairava's shrine is situated in the inner praharam. Sri Chandikeshwarar, known for his devotion to Lord Shiva, is believed to be the Chief of the Ghanas, guarding the abode of Lord Shiva. Lord Surya's shrine is situated in the inner praharam of the Temple. The Navagraha shrine is situated just before the entrance to the Nandavanam. Kanchi Seer (Periaval) once explained that Lord Shiva handed over the Vedas to Ambika who gave them to Lord Brahma then. Lord Brahma gave to Nandhi and they

reached the Rishis from him. It appears that this may be the place where this happened because the Temple is the home of Brhammapureeswarar, Brahmmanayaki, a gigantic Nandhi and Patanjali Rishi and gains a special significance. Lord Brahma worship should be done with 36 lamps (representing 27 stars and 9 planets) offering 108 tamarind rice balls. The devotee should walk 9 rounds.

ARULMIGU MAARIAMMAN TEMPLE AT SAMAYAPURAM – The Temple is also called as Sri Samayapuram and it lodges the Vigraha of Sri Mari Amman, Sri Ganesh and Sri Karupanna Swamy. When devotees are infected with Chicken Pox, they pray to this Goddess for relief, who immediately comes to the rescue of the ailing devotees. Pujas are performed every month in accordance with auspicious dates and the annual Temple fair is held in April/May. The Goddess is also called as 'Kamanur Mari Amman' because her consort is believed to have been brought form the village of Kamanur. The goddess is very powerful and lamps are lit during specific times to appease and please her. The powerful principle of Shakti is depicted in this Goddess. There is a legend that King Vijayaraya Chakkaravarthi built the present day form of the Temple. This Temple is situated in beautiful land scape enriched by the holy River Cauvery.

THALAMALAI PERUMAL TEMPLE AT NEELIAMPATTI - The ancient and famous Temple is situated on a unique rock on the peak of Thalaimalai Hill. It is a renowned Vaishnava Temple. This hill gets its name because it resembles the head of a person. This hill is also known as Siragiri. The presiding deity of the Temple is Nallendra Perumal, a form of Lord Vishnu. One can find shrines of Venkatachalapathy, Alamelu Mangai Thayaar, Goddess Mahalaxmi, Sri Devi, Bhudevi, Lord Anjaneya, Garudazhvar, and Karupanna Swami. If one takes a holy dip in the Kannimar Sunai and pray to Lord Nallendra Perumal, they would be void of the bad effects of Lord Shaneeswar. This Temple was built by Madurai Nayaks. There is a spring called Ramar Sunai with water flowing all the time. Devotees walk around on a narrow path around the Temple for pradakshinas. People strongly believe that going round this rock Temple would give them successful marriage, wealth and child birth. Visitors need to trek for about 4 KMs through rocky path running through steep stretches at times. Annual festival is celebrated in Tamil month of Puratasi (September / October), once in three years poojas for Edi Bhagavan (Thunder) are performed here.

DISTRICT – TIRUNELVELI (Railway Station - Tirunelveli)

S. No.	Temple	Address	Type
1	Arulmigu Kotha Parameswara Temple	Kunnathur – 627006	Shiva (Navakailayam)
2	Arulmigu Nellaiappar Arultharum Kanthimathi Amman Temple	Thirunelveli – 627006	Shiva-Parvati
3	Sri Kailasanathar Temple	Kodaganallur – 627010	Shiva (Navakailayam)

S. No.	Temple	Address	Type
4	Krishnapuram Venkatachalapathi Temple	Krishnapuram, Tirunelveli – 627011	Vishnu
5	Nambi Rayar Temple	Tirukurungudi - 627115	Vishnu
6	Arulmigu Ammanatha Swamy Temple	Cheranmahadevi – 627414	Shiva (Navakailayam)
7	Arulmigu Papanasam Temple	Papanasam, Ambasamuthiram – 627425	Shiva-Parvati (Navakailayam)
8	Sri Gajendra Varadhar Temple	Attanallur - 627426	Vishnu
9	Sri Kailasanathar Temple	Serndamangalam – 627857	Shiva (Navakailayam)

ARULMIGU KOTHA PARAMESWARA TEMPLE AT KUNNATHUR – It is located in small hillock. The presiding deity is Kothai Parameswaran and Goddess Sivakamasundari.

ARULMIGU NELLAIAPPAR ARULTHARUM KANTHIMATHI AMMAN TEMPLE AT THIRUNELVELI – This is a twin Temple dedicated to Mata Parvathi and Lord Shiva. The River

Tamirabharani referred to by poets as "Porunai" flows round the town. Rare Jewels, the Golden Lily Tank, Musical Pillars, the hall of thousand pillars are worth seeing. The Temple is also known as one of the 5 Pancha Sabhas (dance halls) of Nataraja (Lord Shiva). These two Temples are linked by a big terraced hall namely Sangili Mandapam that has life sized sculptures adoring the pillars. The main deity is a 'Swayambhu Lingam' or a Shivalingam, which erupted from underneath the earth. The Nandi Mandapam has a fairly big Vigraha of Nandi (the bull God). The unique feature of the Temple is the 'Mani Mandapam' with two giant pillars carved out of a single stone and each one is having 48 sub pillars which produce musical notes when struck. Other Mandapams include Oonjal Mandapam and the 1000 pillared hall. The 1000 pillared hall is famous for the celestial wedding of Kanthimathi Ammai with Nellaiyappar which is celebrated every year in the Tamil month of Aippasi corresponding to October-November. Car festival is the most auspicious festival of this Temple that is celebrated during Aani (June- July). Temple has 5 cars for Lord Vinayakar, Murugan, Nellaiappar, Kanthimathi, Sandikaeswarar. There are a number of stone inscriptions in the Temple. The most important of them are those Veerapandiyan who regained about 950 AD and those of Rajendran-I and Kulothunga Chola-I. The inscriptions of Maravarma Sundara Pandiyan refer to the Lord as "Woodayar" and "Wodeyanayanar" and the Goddess as

"Nachiar". Lord Shiva is said to have been worshipped by Sage Agastya in a bamboo grove and by Lord Rama after having killed Mareecha, some nine miles away at Manoor. There is also a shrine to Lord Vishnu near the sanctum signifying the belief that Nellai Govindan (Vishnu) visited Tirunelveli to officiate the divine marriage of Lord Shiva and Kantimathi. A little to the south of Swami Nellaiappar Gopuram stands the Gopuram of Arultharum Kanthimathi Ambal Temple. It was here, where composer Sri Muthuswami Dikshithar composed the Carnatic song 'Sri Kanthimatheem' in Hemavathiragam.

SRI KAILASANATHAR TEMPLE AT KODAGANALLUR – The presiding deity of the Temple is Kailasanathar and Goddess Sivakamiammai.

KRISHNAPURAM VENKATACHALAPATHI TEMPLE – The Temple is dedicated to Lord Vishnu. The presiding deity is Thiruvenkatanathar. It is constructed in the Dravidian style of architecture and the Temple is a storehouse of Nayak architecture. There are a number of life-size sculptures in this Temple with intricate workmanship. The Temple is renowned for its remarkable 17th – 18th century carvings. Along with the principal sanctuary, which houses Lord Vishnu with consorts, there are also twin Lakshmi shrines. The Temple follows Thenkalai tradition of worship. The sanctum houses the vigraha of Venkatachalapathy in standing posture 4 ft is made of granite sporting four arms. Two of his arms hold the conch and Chakra, while the other two sport Abhayamudra and Kadahasta. The vigrahas of Sridevi and Bhudevi are located on either of his side.

NAMBI RAYAR TEMPLE AT TIRUKURUNGUDI - It is located at the foothills of the Western Ghats. It is a very ancient village referred in Varaha Purana and Brahmanda Purana. The village is having history dating back more than 1500 years. Village life revolves around Nambi Rayar Temple. It is one of the 108 Divya Desams, which are sacred for the Vaishnavites. The Temple is 2300 years old. The Temple is located in the centre of the town flanked by four big Mada Veethis (Agraharams) and at the outer square by four broad and lengthy Ratha Veethis. The presiding deity of this Divya Desam was sung (Mangalasasanam) by four Azhwars, namely Thirumazhisai Piran, Nammalvar, Periazhwar and Thirumangai Azhwar. The Temple has several unique sculptures. A horse and an elephant sculpture are composed of ladies in a single granite stone. The walls of the Temple resemble a big fort and the village has been formed around these walls in a very organized manner. The interiors of the main Temple tower is covered with wood

sculptures of teak depicting most of the deities as well as other secular scenes. There are five Nambis in this Kshetram. They are Ninra Nambi (Standing posture), Irundha Nambi (Sitting posture), Kidandha Nambi (Sleeping posture), Thiruparkadal Nambi and Thirumalai Nambi. Thiruparkadal Nambi Temple is located very near to the River Nambiyaru. Malai Nambi Koil is a beautiful mountain. There are few steps that will take to the Temple entrance. Small waterfall makes devotees fresh before going to the Temple. Lord Nambi with Bhoo Devi and Sri Devi shows grace on the devotees in standing posture. Thirumalai Nambi Temple is on the Hills (Mahendragiri Mountain). Mahendragiri Mountain has abundant medicinal herbs. This mountain is mentioned in the First Chapter of Srimad Valmiki Ramayanam Sundara Kandam. Lord Hanuman while going to Sri Lanka in search of Seetha Mata set his feet here and then travelled by sky route. There are many Siddha Purushas living in this mountain observing penance. In Tamil language, the word "Nambi" means personification of all virtuous and righteous qualities blended with beauty and grace.

ARULMIGU AMMANATHA SWAMY TEMPLE AT CHERANMAHADEVI – It is located on the bank of River Tamirabarani. The presiding deity of the Temple is Sri Ammainathar alias Kailasanathar and Goddess Avudinayaki. As per local belief, it is one of the most sought Lord Shiva Temple in this district and southern India. Swayambhu Lingam known as Ammainathar, Kailasanathar and his consort Avudai Nayaki or Oppilla Nayagi Amman. The place is considered as Thingal Sthalam (Moon). Other deities in the Temple are Vinayakar, Subramanyar, Viswanadhar, Natarajar, Nalwar, Karikal Ammaiar, Nava Kanniar and Navagraham. Romesa Munivar had darshan of Lord Shiva here and was blessed.

ARULMIGU PAPANASAM TEMPLE AT PAPANASAM – The presiding deity of the Temple is Pabavinasar alias Kailasanatha and Mother Goddess is Ulagammai. Lord Papanasanatha graces the wedding darshan behind the sanctum sanctorum as Kalyanasundarar on his bull vehicle. Sage Agasthya and his wife Lopamudra are in the shrine worshipping the Lord. It is a holy place on the western ghat of Pothigai Hills. It is close to the Papanasam Falls on the banks of the Thamiraparani River, where Lord Shiva and Parvathi appeared before the great Saint Agasthiya. Hence, the falls is popularly called the "Agasthiya Falls".

SRI GAJENDRA VARADHAR TEMPLE AT ATTANALLUR - The Temple is believed to be more than 500 years old. The Temple is dedicated to Lord Vishnu known as Gajendra Varadhan and the Amman is Sri Andal. The Tirtham of the Temple is Tambiraparani. The Temple is known as Yanai Katha Nallur in the older days. Three days Thai Poosam festival is celebrated in Jan - Feb and other festivals are also celebrated with great devotion. Lord graces with Sridevi & Bhudevi, Sage Bhrigu and Markandeya from Sanctum Sanctorum. The vimana is called Indiravimanam. Pure rice is offered as nivedhana to the Lord.

SRI KAILASANATHAR TEMPLE AT SERNDAMANGALAM - The presiding deity of the Temple is Kailasanathar and Goddess Sivakami Ammai. The last and the ninth flower reached this place – Serndhapoomangalam. The Vigraha of Kubera, on an elephant, is sculpted on the Vimana above the sanctum sanctorum with his two consorts – Sanganidhi and Padmanidhi. This is the only Temple with Kubera, the Lord of Wealth in this posture. Lord Kailasa Nathar graces from the sanctum sanctorum with Shukra-Venus characteristics. Mother Azhagia Ponnammai is facing south. Those not having an advantageous aspect of Shukra in their horoscopes, pray to Shukra here. Papanasam is the first of the Nava Kailash Temples. Tambirabarani River begins its flow from the Pothigai hills here and confluences with Punnakayal Sea face in this place. On the new moon days in the months of Aadi and Thai – July - August and January - February respectively, special pujas are dedicated to Lord Kailasanathar.

DISTRICT – TIRUPATHUR (Railway Station – Tirupattur/Jolarpettai)

S. No.	Temple	Address	Type
1	Shri Sundara Veera Aanjaneya Swami Temple	Tirupattur – 635602	Hanuman
2	Athitheeswarar Temple	Vaniyambadi – 635751	Shiva
3	Sundara Varadaraja Perumal Temple	Vaniyambadi - 635751	Vishnu
4	Group of Temples	Natrampalli - 635852	Mata

SHRI SUNDARA VEERA AANJANEYA SWAMI TEMPLE AT TIRUPATHUR – It was built around 800 years ago. The Vigraha is Swayambhu (self-manifested).

ATHITHEESWARAR TEMPLE AT VANIYAMBADI – The Temple is dedicated to Lord Shiva. The Temple is believed to be more than 1000 years old. This is a special Parihara Sthalam for people born on "Punarvasu" star. The presiding deity is Athitheeswarar and Mother is called as Periyanayagi / Bruhannayaki. Lord Dakshinamurthy is also seen in the Temple, sitting on the Nandi.

SUNDARA VARADARAJA PERUMAL TEMPLE AT VANIYAMBADI – It was built by Madurantaka Cholan around 985 CE. The presiding deity is facing west. The Goddess Sundaravalli Thaayar is facing east. Other deities installed in the Temple are Dwara Ganapati, Dwara Nagarajan, Garuda, Lakshmi Narayan Perumal, Naagar, Chakrathazhwar and Bala Anjaneya. The Holy Theertham is Sheera River. The Holy Tree is Vilwam.

NATRAMPALLI –

Sri Jawathu Kali Amman Temple – The Goddess is very powerful as well as graceful. The Goddess blesses the devotees and fulfil all their wishes, who pray her in the Temple.

Mahabharata Temple At Jangalapuram - The Mahabharata is an epic narrative of the Kurukshetrawar and the fates of the Kaurava and the Pandava princes.

Mariyamman Temple - The Temple is situated on the banks of Palar River. Many devotees come from the Vellore district to worship the Goddess.

Periyandavar Temple - The Goddess is Mother Goddess for most of the people in Natrampalli. The Temple is situated on the banks of Palar River. On every New Moon day, Amavasai Pooja will celebrated very grandly.

Ramakrishna Mutt - It is the second Mutt started in India after Mylapore, Chennai. The Mutt was started in 1908. The Mutt has been sanctified by the stay of Swami Shivananda (once in 1924 and again in 1926), Swami Ramakrishnananda (in 1926) and Swami Abhedananda (in 1906), who were direct disciples of Sri Ramakrishna. Gandhiji had visited the mutt in 1933.

Shri Shamundeeshwari Amman Temple - The Temple is situated on the banks of Palar River. Many devotees come here to worship the Goddess.

DISTRICT – TIRUPPUR (Railway Station – Tiruppur)

S. No.	Temple	Address	Type
1	Arulmigu Avinashi Lingeswarar Temple	Avinashi – 638654	Shiva
2	Arulmigu Subramanyaswamy Temple	Sivanmalai Post, Kangayam – 638701	Murugan
3	Arulmigu Uthukuli Murugan Temple	Kaithamalai, Uthukuli – 638751	Murugan
4	Tirumuruganpoondi Temple	Tirumuruganpoondi - 641652	Murugan, Shiva

ARULMIGU AVINASHI LINGESWARAR TEMPLE AT AVINASHI - The famous Lord Shiva was constructed by Sundarapandiya. It is closely associated with the great Shaiva Saint Sundaramoorthy Nayanar. The word Avinashi means that which is indestructible. This is one of the seven Shivasthalams in Kongu Nadu. However, this Temple is better known as Karunaiyaaththaal Temple. Avinashi is also referred in inscriptions as Dakshina Varanasi, Tiruppukkozhiyur etc. Tirumular's Tirumantiram, Arunagirinathar's Tiruppugazh & Manikkavacakar's Tiruvacakam refer to this shrine. Inscriptions here reveal that the Cholas, Pandyas & Hoysalas have made extensive endowments to the Temples. Ambal's sanctum is to the right of Avinasiappar's sanctum. The Kasi Gangai Theertham - in the form of a well is considered to be of significance. The Kaalabhairavar shrine is held in reverence. Kaala Bhairavar is worshiped here with offerings of Vadai Maalai. The car festival is the most exciting of the festivals in this Temple. This Temple's car is second biggest in South India & is noted for its fine wooden carvings. The annual Bhrammotsavam is celebrated in the month of Chittirai. Apart from Temple car festival, 63 (Arubathi Moovar Ula) is one of the notable festival in this Temple.

ARULMIGU SUBRAMANYASWAMY TEMPLE AT SIVANMALAI – The Sivamalai of today is also known as Sivamamalai, Sivachalam, Sivathri, Sivasailam, Sivagiri and Shakthi Sivamalai. The deity is so powerful because it is supposed to be an integrated embodiment of Lord Shiva, Vishnu, Brahma, Murugan, Vinayaka and Indra. In each "yuga" (the Hindu term to mean eon),it has been referred to with special names such as Panamalai, Vellimalai, Sembumalai and now in the Kaliyuga as Kamarupa Jothigiri. Such is the antiquity of this sacred mountain. Lord Murugan is said to have gone to Vallimalai on the advice of Sage Narada and married Valli there and brought her to Sivamalai to make it their beloved abode. Like Parvathi in Kancipuram, Valli also did penance in Sivamalai, which included thirty two sacred duties. Later, Lord

Murugan went to Tiruthani and brought his consort Devayanai also to reside with him in Sivamalai. Innumerable Tamil Scholars have immortalized Sivamalai with their songs of praise. The most important annual festival celebrated in this Temple is the Thai Poosa Thiruvizah which lasts 18 days. Kandha Shasti, Soorasamharam, Karthigai Deepam are the other important festivals that are celebrated grandly.

ARULMIGU UTHUKULI MURUGAN TEMPLE AT KAITHAMALAI, UTHUKULI - Once the famous Saint Agastiyar came to this place for meditation but was not able to find water. He prayed to Lord Muruga to help him. Soon, Lord Muruga appeared before him and thrust his lance (Vel) in the sand and water spring came from the spot. The Important things is that only in Kaithamalai that is Uthukuli, the Temple car is in the hill and devotees pull the Temple car in the slopes. No place in the world, where a Temple car is pulled in the hill. Then the God is called as "Vetri Velayudha Swami" and the Temple is called "Kaithamalai Murugan Temple".

THIRUMURUGANPOONDI TEMPLE - The name of the village is derived from the famous Murugan Temple located here. The Temple dates back to 9th century. The origin of the Temple is rooted in legendary antiquity. Soorapadma, the scourge of the Gods with his retinue of demons, struck terror in the celestial world with his sudden depredations and campaigns. The persecuted Gods approached Lord Shiva and implored him to save their lives. Lord Shiva sent Lord Subramanya with a huge army headed by the valiant Veerabhahu to destroy Soorapadma and his retinue. Lord Muruga accomplished the arduous task but he was afflicted with the mortal sin of mass killing. In order to absolve himself, he installed a Shivalinga in Thirumuruganpoondi and worshipped it. As Lord Muruga himself adored Lord Shiva, the latter assumed the appellation "Thirumuruganathaswamy" which means "Master of Muruga". The holy shrine is also associated with Sundaramurthynayanar, one of the most celebrated Saints of Shaivism. He did a pilgrimage to the holy shrines of Lord Shiva in Kongunadu. Now Lord Shiva, the Lord of Thirumuruganpoondi, who wanted to hear the Saints melodies & compositions way laid Sundaramurthynayanar, in the guise of a hunter & robbed him of all his belongings and disappeared into the Temple, Sundaramurthynayanar's sorrow burst out in the form of soul full song expressing his anguish & chiding the Lord that his divine presence in such a notorious place was mere mockery.

DISTRICT – TIRUVALLUR (Railway Station - Tiruvallur/MGR Chennai Ctl/Avadi/Tiruttani)

S. No.	Temple	Address	Type
1	Vadivudaiamman Thygarajaswamy Temple	Thiruvotriyur – 600019	Mata
2	Devi Karumariamman Temple	Thiruverkadu – 600077	Mata
3	Arulmigu Periyapalaiyath Bhavani Amman Koil	Tiruvallore, Periyapalayam – 601102	Mata
4	Sri Viswaroopa Panchamukha Anjaneya Swami Ashram	Devi Meenakshi Nagar, Periakuppam Village – 602001	Hanuman
5	Veera Ragava Perumal Kovil	Theppakulam, Thiruvallur – 602001	Vishnu
6	Bhaktavatsala Perumal Thirukovil	Tiruninravur - 602024	Vishnu
7	Arulmigu Subramanya Swamy Thirukoil	Tiruttani – 631209	Murugan

VADIVUDAIAMMAN THYGARAJASWAMY TEMPLE AT THIRUVOTRIYUR – Vadivudaiamman is the form of Gnana Sakthi, who blesses the people with wisdom and knowledge to survive in this world. It is important that visiting the Temple at noon and participating in the mid-day pooja with a red colour saree and jack fruit as a humble offering to Amman will bless the needs of the devotees stepping in to the Temple. The Temple is said to be the first Temple created in this world hence the name for Lord Shiva is known as Aadhipurishwarar (the first form of Shivan). Thygaraja Swami in the Temple resemble Thygaesar of Thiruvaaroor. The Temple is preserved with its ancient touch and on entering the Temple, the divine silence welcomes you. It's rare to have sand floor in the Temples in Chennai which makes our legs soothing and pleasant walk. Elephant God, Vinayagar Sanidhi is here at the entrance of the Temple. Vadiudaiamman means Vadivu (divine beauty) + Udai (with) + Amman (Mother) hence, Amman stands in the Temple facing south with divine beauty with four hands and merciful eyes. Kungama Archanai is also special for Amman and visiting Thyagarajaswami Sanidhi and Aadhipurishwarar Sanidhi are also divine experience. The Lord is also known as Kaarani Vidangar. Padambakka Naadhar in the inner praharam of Aadhipurishwarar, 63 Nayanmars, Dhakshina Murthy, Durgai Amman, Vishnu, along with Aadishankarar, Vattaparai Amman stay here to bless us. The outer praharam of the Temple has many surprises, 27 Lingams for 27 stars of astrology and people perform prayers for the Lingam corresponding to their birth star, Valar Kali, Aagaya Lingam stands in the open air, Annamalaiyar, Naagalingam, Infant Shiva, Kaalahastheeswarar, Bhairavar, Subramaniyar have separate Sanidhi's here. Next to the Temple tank is the Kalyana Sundareswarar Sanidhi and the Temple tree, the Maghizhamboo tree stands here beneath which Sundarar, one amongst the four Shaivite married to Sangiliyar the marriage was conducted by the blessings of Lord Shiva and still the marriage occasion is celebrated every year as a big carnival in the Temple.

DEVI KARUMARIAMMAN TEMPLE AT THIRUVERKADU – One day Devikarumari took the vigraha of old nomadic lady and went to Lord Sun to forecast his future. Without realising her as Devikarumari, he simply neglected her. Devikarumari immediately vanished and Lord Sun has lost its brightness and its glory started declining. Realising his mistake, he begged Devikarumari to forgive and excuse him. Lord Sun also requested Devikarumari to celebrate Sunday as the day of Devikarumari. Devikarumari accepted it. Lord Sun got permission from her to pour on her sunrays twice in a year in the month of Panguni and Purattasi. Once upon a time, Lord Thirumal came to Thiruverkadu to witness the grace rule of Umadevi. When Thirumal personally met his sister Karumari, she requested him "to seat there as Srinivasan of Thirumurai and assist her and bless the devotees who worship Navagraham and stand towards southern direction". He was happy and promised her that he would sit by her side and protect the position of Nine Planets. Veda Viyasar was extremely happy to see Annai Parasakthi and Lord Venkatesan together.

Vedapureeswarar Temple at Thiruverkadu - The Temple is dedicated to Lord Shiva. Lord Shiva is worshipped as Vedapureeswarar and is represented by the Shivalingam. His consort Goddess Parvati is worshipped as Balambigai. The presiding deity is revered in the 7th century Tamil Saiva canonical work, the Tevaram, written by Tamil saint poets known as the Nayanars and classified as Paadal Petra Sthalam. The Temple complex is very huge & it houses two gopurams each facing the Vedapureeswarar and Balambigai shrine. The Temple has a number of other shrines. The Temple has six daily rituals from morning to evening and four yearly festivals. The Brahmotsavam festival is celebrated during the day of the Magam (February - March) which is the most prominent festival. It is believed that the original Temple complex have been built by The Cholas. The Temple had been reconstructed in 1973 with the blessings of Sri Swamiji Ramadoss.

ARULMIGU PERIYAPALAIYATH BHAVANI AMMAN KOIL AT PERIYAPALAYAM - Bhavani Amman is the main deity of the Temple. According to legend, people refer Amman as the sister of Lord Krishna, who managed to escape from the clutches of Kansa (Demon King) and after warning Kansa about his death, she decided to settle in this place in name of Sri Bhavani. The Temple has Vinayagar Sannidhi as Sri Arpudha Sakthi Vinayagar followed by Sri Sarva Sakthi Mathangi Amman. In the Moolasthanam, Amman seen with Sangu Chakram in the upper hands while sword and Amirtha Kalasam on her lower hands, a thousand watts vision (be ready to withstand the power of Amman eyes). Crossing the Moolasthanam, Utsavar Amman welcomes us sitting in a well-decorated seat, Kungumam and Theertham is offered as Prasadham, which is known to cure many ailments in human body. After having Darshan people can now visit Sannidhis of Sri Subrammaniyar, Srinivasa Perumal with Mahalakshmi, Anjaneyar and Sri Prasuramar (one among the ten incarnations of Lord Vishnu) and Naga Sannidhi. Nearest Railway Station is Gummidipundi.

SRI VISWAROOPA PANCHAMUKHA ANJANEYA SWAMI ASHRAM AT PERIAKUPPAM VILLAGE - The origin of Sri Panchamukha Hanuman can be traced to a story in the Ramayana. During the war between Lord Rama and Ravana, Ravana took the help of Mahiravana who was the king of patala. Lord Hanuman in order to protect Lord Rama and Lakshman formed a fortress with his tail but Mahiravana took the form of Vibheeshana and took Lord Rama and Lakshman to patalaloka. Hanuman entered patalaloka in search of Lord Rama and Lakshmana. He found out that to kill Mahiravana, he had to extinguish 5 lamps at the same time, so he took the Panchamukha form with Hanuman, Hayagriva, Narasimha, Garuda and Varaha faces and extinguished the lamps. Mahiravana was killed immediately. The story apart, Sri Panchamukha Hanuman was the upasana deity of Sri Ragavendra Tirtha, the Saint of Mantralaya. The place where he meditated on Panchamukha Hanuman is now known as Panchamukhi, wherein a Temple for Panchamukha Hanuman has

been built. There are various holy features which makes the installation of Sri Viswaroopa Panchamukha Anjaneya Swami at Tiruvallur Ashram, a unique and exceptional venture in the whole world. There are five faces of Sri Viswaroopa Panchamukha Anjaneya Swami. The face towards the East is "Sri Anjaneyaswami Mukha" which removes all blemishes of sin and confers purity of mind. The South facing mukha of "Sri Narasimhaswami" removes fear of enemies and confers victory. The West facing mukha of "Sri Mahaviragarudaswami" drives away evil spells, black magic influences and removes all poisonous effects in one's body. The North facing mukha of "Sri Lakshmi Varahamurthyswami" wards off the troubles caused by bad influences of the planets and confers all prosperity Ashta Aishwarya. The face looking upwards of "Sri Hayagreevaswami" confers knowledge, victory, progeny and mukthi. Here, Mahapradishtai of tallest (40 ft) Sri Panchamukha Anjaneyswami in Viswaroopa form installed, which is magnificently sculpted out of a massive monolithic green granite stone transported from Hassan, Karnataka. It is the only pradishtai in the whole world under Mantra Shastra and the place of pradishtai was known as Rudhra Vanam in legendary times where great Sages like Agasthya have done penance. It is believed that Lord Hanuman, while carrying the Sanjeevani Parvatha to Sri Lanka, stopped here for a while to see Sage Agasthya performing poojas to a Shivalinga. This place was called Rudravanam at that time and was abode of Sages and Siddha Purushas. As per the "scrolls", the Shivalinga worshipped by Sage Agasthya will surface as the appropriate time.

VEERA RAGAVA PERUMAL KOVIL AT THEPPAKULAM - The legend connected with the origin of this Temple shows that once upon a time in Kritayuga, a Sage Purupunyar lived with his wife Satyavathi in Badarikashram. They had no children. He performed a Sali Yajna (Putrakameshti Yagya) with great fervour and devotion. Lord Narayana was pleased with the austerity of the ritualistic observances of the Sage and appeared in the sacrificial fire in a blissful mood to offer boons. The Sage prayed for a noble son. The boon was granted with the condition that he should be named after the name of the Yajna as Salihotran. In the tenth month after that, a glorious son was born to Sage Purupunyar. The child was named Salihotran as ordained by Lord Narayana. With the growth of years, the child showed signs of precocity and started on a pilgrimage-visiting Temple after Temple. On Tai Amavasya day (New Moon day in January-February), he reached Tiruvallur, where he found that Lord Brahma, other Devas and great Sages like Vasishtha were engaged in taking bath in the Hrittapanasini tank. The sacred tank here is known as Hrittapanasini. The tank is so holy that evens a sight or a touch or a bath would immediately dispel all anguish of heart. The local tradition attaches greater importance to this tank than to the Ganga, the Godavari etc. As usual, at the centre of the tank, there is a mandapam, where seasonal Festivals are performed. Tiruvallur was also known as Bhikshwaranyam (the forest where Sages lived on alms) in ages gone by. During January 1999, Kumbhabhishekam was performed in this Temple after all the gopurams were renovated and repainted. It is a marvellous sight to see the glorious specimens of Dravidian art in sculptures depicting the mythological legends of Hindu scriptures in the pinnacles of the gopurams.

BHAKTAVATSALA PERUMAL TEMPLE AT THIRUNINDRAVUR - The Temple is dedicated to Lord Vishnu. The Temple is one of the 108 Divyadesams which are dedicated to Lord Vishnu. Lord Vishu is worshipped as Bhaktavatsala Perumal and his consort Goddess Lakshmi as Ennai Petra Thayar in

the Temple. The Temple has been constructed in the Dravidian style of architecture. The Temple had been glorified in the Divya Prabandha, the early medieval Tamil canon of the Azhwar saints from the 6th–9th centuries CE. It is believed that the Temple had been built by The Pallavas of the late 8th century CE. In the Temple, there were contributions from Medieval Cholas and Vijayanagar kings. A granite wall surrounds the Temple which is enclosing all the shrines and two bodies of water. There is a four-tiered rajagopuram. It is believed that Sri Bhatavatsala Perumal have appeared to Lord Kubera here. Six daily rituals and three yearly festivals are held here. The Krishna Janmasthami festival is the most prominent festival in the Temple.

ARULMIGU SUBRAMANYA SWAMY THIRUKOIL AT TIRUTTANI – The town constitutes one of the 6 padaiveedu shrines of Skanda and it represents the site where Lord Subramanyar stayed after destroying the demon Surapadman. It has been revered by the Tiruppugazh hymns of Arunagirinathar, Tirumurugatruppadai of the Sangam period, Tanikaipuranam by Kachiappa Munivar & Ramalinga Adigalaar is also associated with this shrine. Legend has it that Subramanyar married Valli who hailed from the Vallimalai hills. The same legend is associated with Velimalai in Kanyakumari district. Another legend has it that Indra presented a sandal stone as a part of his daughter's dowry. The sandal paste made on this stone is applied to the vigraha of Lord Subramanya & the applied paste is said to acquire medicinal value. Legend also has it that Skanda bore the discus thrown by the demon Tarakasuran on his chest and hence there is a hollow in the chest of the vigraha of Lord Subramanya in this Temple. Legend also has it that Skanda gifted the discus to Lord Vishnu. Legend also has it that Skanda imparted knowledge of Tamil to the Sage Agasthyar & he is regarded as Veeramurthy, Gnanamurthy & Acharyamurthy in this shrine. The Temple has 4 prakarams & a series of towers. There is a shrine to Aabat Sahaaya Vinayakar who is said to have come to the aid of Skanda in winning Valli's hand in marriage. The processional vigraha of Skanda is housed in a Rudraksha vimanam with his consorts. The shadkonapadakkam or the hexagonal medallion is adorning the vigraha of Skanda is decorated with green stones & is of great beauty. Also of significance here is a golden vilva garland. Lord Muruga is not holding the Vel weapon which is closely associated with him but Vajra Hastam in his right hand that would produce a sound as thunder. His left hand is on the hip representing wisdom. There are separate shrines for Valli and Deivanai. The festival Sura Samhara - destroying demon Sura in Tiruchendur being celebrated in all Murugan Temples on Skanda Sashti in Oct.-Nov. is not followed here because the Lord is in pleasant mood without war plans. Instead, on this day, flowers weighing 1000 KGs are used to please the Lord. In the place of peacock, the elephant is the vahan for Lord Muruga. Daughters of Lord Vishnu, Amudavalli & Sundaravalli performed penance seeking Lord Muruga's hands. Deivanai was under the care of Indira while Nambirajan took care of Valli. They realized their aim & became consorts of Lord Muruga. They wished to show that they were one & took the form of Gajavalli. Gajavalli holds the Lotus in her right hand attributed to Valli & the Neelotpala flower in the left representing Deivanai. She graces from her parrot vehicle. It is believed that Indira worshipped here on the Kruthika star day in the month of Aadi (Jul.-Aug.). Lord Muruga comes in procession to the sacred spring Saravana Poigai at the foot of the hill. As Indira used the Kalhara flowers for his puja, the tradition of carrying Malar Kavadi - flower Kavadi is devotionally followed by the devotees in the Temple. Sri Aadhi Balasubramania graces on the wall behind the sanctum sanctorum as a child. He was the Lord with Akshara Mala and a Kamandala (a small pot with a handle to carry water usually held by Gods and Sages) before his wedding with Valli. Lord Bhairava graces in Temple with 4 dogs vehicle representing 4 Vedas, Rig, Yajur, Sama and Atharvana. Those aspiring to achieve academic excellence pray here. During the final puja at night, Lord Muruga graces with Valli on a day and Deivanai the next day. As Lord Muruga wedded Valli in the guise of a hunter, he graces on a Tiger Vahan on the sixth day of Brahmmotsavam and then on the Elephant Vahan. A Muslim gentleman had the luck of being graced by Lord Muruga in this Temple. Remembering the event, during festival days, when the Lord comes in procession, a Muslim devotee plays the drum even today.

DISTRICT – TIRUVANNAMALAI (Railway Station – Tiruvannamalai/Walajah Road)

S. No.	Temple	Address	Type
1	Gangaikonda Choleeswarar Temple	Koozampandal, Cheyyar – 604407	Shiva
2	Vedapureesshwarar Temple	Thiruvatoor, Cheyyar – 604407	Shiva
3	Shiva Temple	Seeyamangalam, Vandavasi – 604408	Shiva, Jain
4	Arulmigu Raghumayi Sammetha Pandurangan Temple	Thennakoor Village, Vandavasi – 604408	Mata
5	Yoga Ramachandra Perumal Temple	Chetpet, Vandavasi – 604408	Vishnu
6	Thadagapureeswarar Koil	Matam – 604502	Shiva
7	Pachaiyamman Temple	Munugupattu – 604504	Mata
8	Annamalaiyar Temple	Thiruvannamalai – 606601	Shiva
9	Arahanthgiri Jain Math	Ganesapuram, Tiruvannamalai – 606601	Jain
10	Javadhu Hills	Tiruvannamalai – 606601	Shiva
11	Parvathamalai	Polur - 606803	Shiva
12	Arulmigu Periyanayagi Thirukovil	Devikapuram – 606902	Mata
13	Sri Endhira Shani Bhagvan Temple	Erikuppam, Kalambur – 606903	Shani
14	Jain Temple	Tirumalai - 606907	Jain
15	Parvathamalai	Kadaladi – 606908	Shiva
16	Cave Temples	Mamandur – 631702	Vishnu, Shiva
17	Sri Valeeswarar Temple	Dhusi Post, Kuranganilmuttam – 631702	Shiva
18	Poondi Arugar Temple	Arani – 632301	Jain
19	Arulmiku Renuka Kampal Amman Tirukoil	Padavedu Village, Arni Taluk – 632315	Mata
20	Shiva Temple	Brahmadesan - 632511	Shiva

GANGAIKONDA CHOLEESWARAR TEMPLE AT KOOZAMPANDAL - This Temple was built by Isana Siva Pandita, the spiritual Guru of Rajendra Chola-I. This village used to be known as Ganfaikonda Cholapuram and the deity as Gangaikonda Choleeswarar. This stone Temple consists of a three storeyed vimana, an ardhamandapa and a mudkamandapa. All the sculptures adorning the niches belong to the period of Rajendra Chola-I.

VEDAPUREESSHWARAR TEMPLE AT CHEYYAR – This Temple is 2000 years old. It has 7 tier Rajagopurm. One has to cross 9 entrances to have the darshanam of Vedapureeswarar. There are separate shrines for Pancha Boothams. Hence, we can have the darshan of all Pancha Bootha Lingams together. We can also have the darshan of all the 8 Gopurams from one spot. Here, Lord Shiva is in Swayambhu Lingam form. Daily Sun rays falls on the deity in the Sanctum. While worshiping one can stand in one place and see Swamy, Ambal, Ganesan, Murugan, Navagraham and Sthala Viruksham. This is another speciality of this Temple. Ambal has been portrayed so beautifully with Ruthraksha Malai in one hand, Lotus flower in another, the third is Abhaya Hastham and the forth is Varatha Hastham. She is blessing the devotees with her sathurpujams. Lord Shiva explain in detail about Vedham to Devas and Rishis in this place. Hence, this place is called Thiruvothur. Here, Gnanasambandar and Thirunavukkarasar have sung Thevara Pathigam on Vedapureeswarar. Arunagirinathar sung about Lord Murugan of this Temple. Lord Shiva danced in this place. The dance is called Veera Nadanam. Lord Vinayakar here is Narthana Vinayakar and Lord Murugan is Shanmugar. Lord Murugan created the theertham "Cheyaru" for this Temple. Hence this town is called Cheyyaru. Vinayakar, Murugan, Vairavar, Thirumal, Brahma, Suryan and Thondaman were worshiped Vedapureeswarar in this Temple. The Nandhi in this Temple will not be looking towards Sannadhi, It is facing outside, as Lord Shiva teaching Vedam to all the Devas and Rishis, he had instructed the Nandhi not to allow anyone except Devas and Rishis.

SEEYAMANGALAM CAVE TEMPLE - This rock cut Lord Shiva Temple was built by Mahendra Varman-I in 7th century. The main deity Lord Shiva is called here as Thoon Andar in Tamil and Sthambeshwara in Sanskrit. "Thoon" means pillar and "Andar" refers Lord and hence Thoon Andar means Lord of Pillars. This name is because of the presence of two pillars in front of this cave Temple. Two dvarapalas are located on the either side of the entrance of sanctum sanctorum of the shrine. Unlike other Temples, here the main deity is facing the west direction. Lord Shiva was carved in the Temple Pillars as Natarajar and Vrishbhantika. This is the first Temple in Tamil Nadu having the vigraha of Lord Natarajar. Also, the dwarf Muyalaka is missing from the Natarajar vigraha. This Temple was renovated and extended by various kings as it is evident from the presence of various inscriptions in Tamil and Grantha characters by Pallavas, Chola and Vijayanagara empires. This rock cut Jain Temple was built by Western Ganga King Rajamalla-II during the end of 9th century. This Temple is seen in a hillock named Vijayadri (as per inscription of Rajamalla-II) located northern side of Thoon Andar Shiva Temple. Inside the rock cut, a new Lord Mahaveerar Vigraha is kept and worshipped by nearby Tamil Jains. On the top of the rock facing east, relief sculptures of Lord Mahaveerar, Parshavanthar and Bahubali are seen. On the either side of Lord Bahubali, his sisters Brahmi and

Saundari are seen. On the top, left side of Lord Bahubali, Indra sitting on elephant and right side, two Gandharvas are seen. The head of Lord Parshavanathar is surrounded by five headed snake. The left and right side of Lord Parshavanathar, his attendants Padmavathi and Daranendran can be seen. Both the vigrahas of Lord Bahubali and Parshavanathar were carved in standing posture. The vigraha of Lord Mahaveerar, sitting in Sukhasana position on a Simhasana with his attendants on either side, is seen at the extreme southern direction.

ARULMIGU RAGHUMAYI SAMMETHA PANDURANGAN TEMPLE AT THENNAKOOR VILLAGE – The Temple is 500 years old. The Temple is also known as Sri Pandurangan Temple. Resembling the design of Puri Jagannath Temple, this Temple stands majestically with a 120 ft. tall tower and Gold Kalasas of 9.5 ft. with Sudarsana Chakra above. The saffron flag flying above the tower invite the devotees with blessings of the Lord. There is a 16 pillared mahamandapa. Bhagwan Garuda is in the centre space as a Gem. The Temple follows both the orthodox sampradaya of south and bajan sampradaya of north. The Brindavan of HH Gnanananda Swamigal adds more sanctity to the Temple. Made of Salagrama stone, Lord Panduranga 12 ft. tall standing in the Sanctum Sanctorum & mother Raghumayee is nearby & it is noteworthy that all the dieties related to Srichakra - Mahashodasi, Raja Rajeshwari, Saraswati, Laxmi, Brahma, Vishnu, Rudra, Iaswara, Vinayaka, Bala, Annpoorani, Ashwaruda, Raja Madhangi, Varahi, Pratyangara, Sarabeswra, Chakkarathazhwar, Yoga Narsimha, Agoramurthy, Vana Durga, Para Saraswati, Medha Dakshinamurthy, Subramanya, Chandi Mahalaxmi, Brahmi, Maheshwari, Gaumari, Vashnavi, Mahendri, Chamunda, Mahalaxmi are in the Temple in Vigraha forms. Lord Panduranga showers his blessings as a King of Mathura on Sunday. Vishukani Utsav on tamil year day, Muthani Sevai are major festivals of the Temple. Nearest Railway Station is Melmaruvattur.

YOGA RAMACHANDRA PERUMAL TEMPLE AT CHETPET VANDAVASI - The statues of Lord Perumal has his left hand over his heart and Lord Hanuman reading Vedas opposite to him. Very artistic Dwarabalagars statues can also be seen here. The front mandapam has Ramayanan, Dasaavathars of Lord Vishnu, Gishnalelai and Krishnadevarayar statues. Special Structure of Krishnadevarayar is notable are seen. Hanging lotus Vigraha, Raman – Valli fight scenes, Krishnalelai, Vigraha of Sukkirivan Valli are few notable structures. The Temple was constructed during Vijayanagar reign is famous for great architectural & historically important stone inscription.

CHANDRAPRABHA NATHAR JAIN TEMPLE AT VANDAVASI - The moolavar of the Temple is Sri Chandraprabha Nathar, white marble Vigraha fully engraved, in the sitting posture resides upon a plinth under a decorated vimana. The Vigrahas of all 24 Tirthankaras are engraved at the entrance of the Temple. There was a reference to a Jain Temple located in this village before 745 AD in the inscriptions located on the Perumal Rock near this Temple. Pallava King Nandi Varman has granted grants for repair work in the Jinalya and in Chola regime. The Temple was adorned. The Temple has a separate shrine for Goddess Dharma Devi.

THADAGAPUREESWARAR KOIL AT MATAM - This Temple was constructed during the Chola period and the main deity is Thadagapureeswarar. The place was mentioned as Jeyankonda Cholamandalathu Palkundrakottathu Thennattur Nattu Kulathur in the Temple stone inscription. The main deity is mentioned as Agneeshwaramudaiyar during Kulothunga-I, as Mudal Kulanthai Aandar during Rajarajan-II and currently as Thadagapureeswarar. The Rajagopuram is erected as a remembrance of the victory of Vijayanagar emperor over Sambuvarayars. The Temple is a unique one which contains Sahastralingam which has more than 1000 Lingams on it.

PACHAIYAMMAN SAMEDA MANNARSAMY TEMPLE MUNUGAPATTU – It is one of the oldest Temple. It functions as family Temple for thousands of families. Thousands of devotees gave their offerings from first 10 Mondays of Tamil month of Aadi. The east facing Goddess Pachiyamman blesses her devotees with a graceful face and in standing posture. Sudai structure in sitting posture can be seen at the backside. The Mahamandapam has the Goddess along with her friends and angels. Kaval Deivangal are seen at the entrance.

ARULMIGU ANNAMALAIYAR TEMPLE AT TIRUVANNAMALAI – Lord Shiva is known by the devotees as Annamalayar or Arunachaleswarar and this is believed to be the largest Temple in the world dedicated to Lord Shiva. Annamalaiannal is the most sacred of the names of the manifestation of Lord Shiva. It is located at the base of Annamalai Hills. In most of the holy places, the deity is found atop the Hill but here the Holy Hill itself is the deity (Lord Annamalaiyar). "Arunam" means Sun and denotes the red colour of fire, "Asalam" means "Giri" or "Malai" (mountain) and thus "Arunachalam" means the Holy Hill which is red in colour. The Holy Hill is 2668 ft high. The Annamalai Hill was Agni (fire) during Krithayugam and was Manikkam (Emerald) during Threthayugam and was pon (Gold) during Dwaprayugam and rock during Kaliyugam. The Temple has the third-tallest Gopuram (216.5 ft) in the world. The Temple is very unique as it is one among Pancha Bhoota Sthalam and sung by Shaiva Kuravargal. It was built before 1100 years and the architecture of the Temple has its contribution from various Kingdoms from Cholas, Pandians, Sambuvarayars Posalas, Vijayanagar Kings, Nayaks, Nagarathargal,

Chieftains and Zamindars. The Temple possesses more than 1000 statues and 450 stone inscriptions. The Temple has more than 100 Sannidhis. Various vigraha, bronze statues, paintings, thirusutrugal, thirtakulangal, 1000 pillar mahal and towering gopurams are the specialties of the Temple. The Temple consists of Vallala Maharaja gopuram, Kiligopuram and Ammani Amman gopuram which are of historic important. The main deity of the Temple is Annamalaiyar and Unnamalai Amman. On the request of Thirumal and Brahma by their devout prayer, Lord Shiva who was in the form of a fire column, took the form of a Shivalingam at the foot of the hill here. There are eight Lingams located at the eight directions and provides an octagonal structure to Thiruvannamalai Town. The eight Lingams are: Indra Lingam, Agni Lingam, Yama Lingam, Niruthi Lingam, Varuna Lingam, Vayu Lingam, Kubera Lingam and Esanya Lingam. The Adi Annamalai Temple glorified in Dhevaram, is located on this path. The Ezhuthu Mandapam situated in Girivalam path is an excellent art gallery. Kanthashram. Pavazhakundru. Ramanashram and Astalingas around the Girivala path are few notable tourist spots. Siva Puranam identifies four sacred places for obtaining salvation. Thiruvannamalai is one among them. The significance of this place is that by mere remembrance of Lord Arunachaleswarar at this place gives salvation to all souls (Ninaithale Mukthi Tharum Thiruthalam). Thiruvannamalai is the "Manipooraga Sthalam", which is one among six atharasthalams. Thiruvannamalai is so sacred that even Gods and celestials offered their prayers. Tradition has it that Sun, Moon, Eight Vasus, Brahma, Vishnu and so on have worshipped here. Thiruvannamalai has been the abode of Siddhars. Idaikkattu Siddhar, one of the eighteen Siddhars, belongs to this sacred soil. Thiruvannamalai has the honour of providing an abode for Saints such as Arunagirinathar, Vitpatchathevar, Gugai Namachivayar, Guru Namachivayar, Deivasigamani, Arunachala Desikar, Mahan Seshadri Swamigal, Bagawan Ramana Maharishi, Sri Yogi Ram Surathkumar and the like.

Girivalam – It is a popular religious practice in Tamil Nadu in which devotees circle around the Annamalai Hill on the occasion of full moon every month. Thousands of devotees gather at the Arunachaleswarar Temple to walk all the way round the 14 KMs path around the hill. The word Girivalam has been derived from the Tamil words giri meaning hill and valam meaning coming around. The practice is said to bring peace to one's mental and physical health. The Arunachaleswarar Temple has eight Lingams known as Ashtalingam which are positioned at different locations facing different directions. Each Lingam signifies different directions of the earth and is believed to bless the devotees who undertake Girivalam, with various benefits. Girivalam is usually practiced barefoot and devotees must look at the top of the hill throughout their walk and chant the Om Arunachala mantra. This practice is akin to the Govardhan Parikrama taken by devotees in Mathura, Uttar Pradesh.

ARAHANTHGIRI JAIN MATH AT THIRUMALAI VILLAGE - It is an ancient Jain Math in Tamil Nadu. The Village is also known as Arhatsugiri or Arihantgiri. This Jain Math is also known as Shri Kshetra Arihantgiri Digambar Jain Mandir. History of Arahanthgiri Jain Math starts from the period of 322–185 BCE as the Last 'Shrutkevali' Bhadrabahu expected to stay at this place. He stayed at this place to practice meditation and "Swadhyaya" along with 8000 other saints. We can see various ancient caves existing in this Jain Math along with 18 foot Vigraha of Tirthankara Neminath and

hundreds of Religious books. It is a Jain Temple and cave complex dating from at least 9th century. The complex includes 3 Jain caves, 2 Jain Temples and a 52 foot sculpture of Tirthankara Neminatha thought to date from the 12th century that is the tallest Jain vigraha in Tamil Nadu. Nearest Railway Station is Polur.

JAVADHU HILLS - The Kovilur Shivan Temple built during Chola dynasty is of historic importance.

PARVATHAMALAI AT POLUR - The holy place is dedicated to Lord Shiva. It is believed that while returning from Himalyas, Lord Shiva stepped on this place and from here, he went to Arunachala. The Temple had been setup by Saints to meditate and attain enlightenment and the devotees who gets the darshan of these Saints are believed to be very lucky. It is believed that this place is having hidden supreme powers and there were lots of miracles happens. It is also believed that many Gods & Goddesses visit this place to worship Lord Shiva on various festivals and on full moon day.

ARULMIGU PERIYANAYAGI THIRUKOVIL AT DEVIKAPURAM - It is the best example for Vijayanagar architecture. The consort of Sri Kanakagiriswarar installed at the hill Temple is Sri Periyanayagi Amman, found at the bottom. She is also otherwise known as Sri Brahanayagi and Sri Brahadhambal. There is no Shivalingam here. Periyanayagi Amman Temple located at the foot hill and Ponmalainathar Temple is located at the hilltop. It has more than 10000 statues and 60 stone inscriptions. The compound walls, marriage hall, Garbhagriha were inscribed with the stories of shaivism and vaishnavism. Devara statues, avatars of Lord Vishnu and sthalapurana statues are few notable ones. Thirukameshwarar Sammeda Kokilambal Temple and Ponmalainathar Temple are known for their architectural beauty. After entering the Temple, one would find Sri Veerabadrar on the south and Sri Bairavar on the north. The Brahma Theertham is on the southern side of the Temple. The Kalyana Mandapam is found in the north facing south. This is designed in the shape of the two wheeled car drawn by horses which is very impressive and attractive. There are several architectural carvings on the pillars of this mandapam depicting the history of the King Sri Manu Needhi Cholan. There are several sacred Theerthas in this shrine. The Brahma Theertham is inside the Temple while the Navagraha Theertham is located at the foot of the hill which is now known as Periayappan Kulam. To the south east of this Sthalam is the Agni Theertham with Neerazhi Mandapam at its centre. People call this Agni Theertham as Kaatan Kulam. There is a Lord Murugar Temple at the top of a hilllock on the bank of the Agni Theertham and to the west corner is the Devaraidyar Theertham and to the west the seyyyankulam or seeyankulam. There are also several other small Theerthams here all round the hill. On all Tuesday, it is customary for the devotees to come around the hill and offer worship to Sri Kanakagiriswarar. By doing so, it is believed that the devotees who are suffering from incurable diseases are easily cured. Nearest Railway Station is Polur.

SRI ENDHIRA SHANI BHAGVAN TEMPLE AT ERIKUPPAM - This is a famous Navagraha Temple dedicated to Sani Bhagavan/Shani Bhagavan (Planet Saturn). Usually, Sri Sani Bhagwan appears in the Vigraha form, but in the Erikuppam Temple, Sri Sani Bhagwan graces in the form of the Shivalinga. Long before, a king built the Temple for the Saturn planet installing him as Shivalinga with the yantras. Yantra is a diagrammatic representation of the power of the deity we worship. In due course of time, the Temple disappeared leaving the Linga alone in the open space. Later, people built this Temple. As he graces as a Linga with Yantras, He is known as Enthira Saneeswarar. In the sanctum sanctorum, Sri Saneeswara appears in the 6.5 feet tall Shivalinga form placed on a peeta of 2.5 feet width. As in Shivalinga, Moon and Sun have their places on the head. His crow vehicle is in the middle. The six faced (Shatkona) yantra with Namashivaya, basic mantras as Beejakshara and Mahalakshmi mantras are inscribed in the Linga. The entrance sculpture shows Sani Bhagwan in a Rath which is driven by the crows. There are also paintings of all planets with their vahana in the front hall. It is suggested to offer archanas with Vilva leaves for Shiva worship. On the next day of the Pongal, mattupongal day, abishek is performed with 108 pots of milk. For the people to have a good look, the Sun, Moon, the Crow, the hexagon & the triangles have been covered with metal plates carved to the shape. We can see the figures and letters on the deity, if we watch with concentration. He is on a Peeta and near Him is the Yanthra of Chaya Devi which was found buried near the Lord. These designs on Sri Saneeswara were carved more than thousand five hundred years ago by the evolved souls. Our ancient Rishis had academic and spiritual facts on all the planets, even before the scientists discovered them. Nearest Railway Station is Arni Road.

Jain Temple at Tirumalai - The Temple is rare of its kind in which Panchkula Devatas are worshipped under a single roof facing different directions. The Temple is dedicated to Jain Yakshini (Goddess). There are five Yakshinis worshipped in the Temple. The first Yakshini is Varahi Amman, also known as Hindu & Buddhist Goddess. There is a interesting iconography of Varahi Amman that is the Tirthankara is sitting on her forehead. The second Yakshini is Kushmandini Amman. She is also known as Ambica Devi and is dedicated attendant deity of Sasana Devi, who is protector Goddess of twenty second Tirthankara Lord Neminatha. The third Yakshini is Jolamalini Amman, who is protector Goddess of eighth Tirthankara, Lord Chandraprabhu. She was one of the most widely popular Yakshini during the early medieval period and Jain Literature also recognise her as Vahni Devi. The forth Yakshini is Chakreshwari Amman who is the protector Goddess of first Tirthankara Lord Adinatha. She is one of the most popular Goddess in Jainism. The fifth Yakshini is Padmavathi Amman who is protector Goddess of twenty third Tirthankara, Lord Parshvanatha. According to tradition, Padmavathi Amman with her husband Dharanendra protected Lord Parshvanatha during Upsarg of Kamath.

Jain Temple at Dadapuram - Sister of great Rajaraja Chola, Kundavai Pirattiyar is credited with building to Jain Temples, one at Dadapuram and other at Tirumalai. The Jinalaya is in existence since last so many 100 years and is one of the major Jain Temples in Tamil Nadu.

PARVATHAMALAI - It is present in the foothill of Javadi hills and Abidagujambal – Maligarjunar Temple is located in the hill top. The Temple is a boon for mountain trekkers with natural sceneries and gentle breeze. This hill is known as Thenkailayam and worshipped by many Saints. One of the legends associated with Parvathamalai states that when Lord Hanuman carried Sanjeevini hill to revive Lakshmana, a piece of Sanjeevenimalai fell at this spot. For this reason, this particular area is famous for various herbs and shrubs which can cure the deadliest disease. It is not just herbs that can cure disease but it is thought that the breeze alone from the Hill wafting through the plants and shrubbery is enough to affect cure of sickness. This place can be reached either from Thenmadhimangalam or from kadaladi.

MAMANDUR CAVE TEMPLE - This Temple is one of the biggest Cave Temples of Tamilnadu. There are 4 Cave Temples located in Narasamangalam – Mamandur Village hill. The 1st and 2nd cave present at the extreme right are for Lord Vishnu and Shiva respectively. Sri Valeeswarar and Bairava Temples are situated at the hill top.

SRI VALEESWARAR TEMPLE AT KURANGANILMUTTAM – The Temple is situated on the southern bank of Palaru River. The Temple is more than 1000 years old. The Moolavar of the Temple is Lord Valeeswarar and Koyyamalarnathar and Amman is Irayarvalai Ammai. The Theertham is Kakkaimadu Theertham and Vayasai Theertham. The presiding deity is graces in the form of Svayambhulinga facing west. The sunrays falls on the presiding deity on certain days during Chithirai month. Shrines of Kasi Viswanathar, Bhairavar, Navagrahas, Sapthamadas, Nagadevadha are on the corridor. Lord Mahavishnu is behind the sanctum sanctorum with his discus.

POONDI ARUGAR TEMPLE AT ARANI - Ponnezhilnathar Temple is now called as Poondi Arugar Temple by the local people. It was constructed with the architectural style of Chola period. Even though it is a Jain Temple, it has been built with the southern cultural style. The song inscription of Sambuvarayan denotes this Temple named as "Veera Veera Jeenalayam".

ARULMIKU RENUKA KAMPAL AMMAN TIRUKOIL AT PADAVEDU VILLAGE - The Temple is one of the famous Sakthisthalas. The Amman Vigraha in Garbhagriha is self-existing and the presence of Lord Brahma, Thirumal and Shiva beside her proves that Lady Shakthi is predominant in the

universe. Amman as Suthai Thirumeni is present at the backside along with Banalingam and Janakarshanachakaram established by Adhisankarar. The Vibhuti Prasatham given here was collected every year in the tail month of aani from the place of yajna done by Saint Jamathkanni and it is believed that this vibhudi prasadam will cure disease and avoid evils. Apart from the presence of many number of Temples and the place is surrounded by mountains, coconut groves and banana sheds, the head of the Goddess Renuga Devi was present as self-exiting in the Garbhagriha and festivals celebrated on every Friday in the month of Aadi is very special. This is one of the Shakti Peethams. Worshipping Ambica means worshipping all the Gods and 30 crore Devas of the celestial world. Padavedu is the place where Sage Jamadagni, an incarnation of Lord Shiva, lived with his wife Renuka, an incarnation of Parvathi and son Parasurama, the avatar of Lord Vishnu. Sage Jamadagni and Sage Vishwamitra grew together. The Sage used to perform Yagna daily to which mother Renuka used to bring water in a pot just made that day. One day the Mother saw a Gandharva flying and lost her mind on that due to the maya or the play of the great Shakti, she was late for the yagna and felt ashamed. The Sage, knowing this, asked his sons to chop off mother's head but none came forward. Only Parasurama to abide his father came forward and did it and also cut his head. Nearby Dobis (Cloth washers) came to rescue the mother but Parasurama killed all of them. The Sage was pleased and asked Parasurama's wish and he rightly wanted his mother back. Sage agreed and asked Parasurama to join the head and the body and sprinkle holy water over them. Parasurama did so and his mother came to life and also the dobis who died in the fight. But, alas, his mother's head was attached to a dobi woman's body and vice versa while doing it in an anxiety but then Universal mother might have wanted this way only and she then made that dobi woman, her close maiden. She is also worshipped here. All these happened in Padavedu. There is a river nearby where dobis washed the clothes. The Holy ash given in the Temple is the one from the Sage Jamadagni's yagagonda which still exists.

BRAHMADESAM - Lord Prakadiswarar Temple is the oldest Temple built by Simhavarman of Pallava dynasty in circa 6th century. It is now maintained by Tamil Nadu State Archaeology Department. Specialty of this Temple are pillars that can produce seven different types of musical notes (or seven swaras or sapthaswara). The sanctum sanctorum of this Temple is also one of a kind.

DISTRICT – TIRUVARUR (Railway Station – Thiruvarur)

S. No.	Temple	Address	Type
1	Sri Kiruba Samudra Perumal Temple	Sirupuliyur - 609403	Vishnu
2	Lalithambigai Temple	Thirumeyachur - 609405	Mata
3	Sri Brahmapureeswarar Kovil	Ambal - 609503	Shiva
4	Paampuranathar Temple	Tirupampuram - 609503	Shiva
5	Sithalapathy Muktheeswarar Temple	Punthottam – 609503	Shiva, Ganesh
6	Maa Saraswathi Amman Temple	Koothanur - 609503	Mata
7	Veezhinathar Kovil	Thiruveezhimizhalai - 609503	Shiva
8	Arulmigu Thiyagaraja Swamy Temple	Thiruvarur - 610001	Shiva
9	Bhaktavatsala Perumal Temple	Tirukannamangai - 610104	Vishnu
10	Vanchinadha Swamy Temple	Srivanjiam – 610107	Shiva
11	Sri Nellivananathar Thirukoil	Tirunellikaval - 610205	Shiva

S. No.	Temple	Address	Type
13	Arulmighu Subramanya Swamy Temple	Engan - 612603	Murugan
14	Arulmigu Abathsagayeswarar Temple	Alangudi, Valangaiman Taluk – 612801	Jupiter
15	Varatharajan Pettai Maha Mariamman Temple	Valangaman – 612804	Mata
16	Sri Rajagopalaswami Temple	Mannargudi – 614001	Krishna
17	Kothandaramar Temple	Thillaivilagam – 614706	Rama

SRI KIRUBA SAMUDRA PERUMAL TEMPLE AT SIRUPULIYUR - The Temple is more than 1000 years old. The historical name of the Temple is Chalasayanam, Bala Vyakra Puram. The Temple is dedicated to Lord Vishnu who is known as Krubhasamudra Perumal & the Amman is Thirumamagal Nachiar. The Thala Virutcham is Vilwa and the Theertham is Tiruvananda Theertham, Manasa Theertham. The Temple is one of the 108 Divya Desams and Lord Perumal blessings the devotees in reclining posture. The vimana is Nandiyavardhana. Saint Tirumangai Azhwar has sung the glory of the Lord forming part of the celebrated Naalayira Divya Prapandham. There are various festivals celebrated in the Temple with great fervour.

LALITHAMBIGAI TEMPLE AT THIRUMEEYACHUR – The Temple is about 1000 years old. The Temple has many history and myths which is famous all over India. This Temple is the 56th Temple of Lord Shiva situated near the southern banks of River Cauvery flowing by the Thevaram hymns. Rathasapthami is one of the grand festivals that are celebrated in this very Temple during the month of January & February. The priests believe that the history which is linked to this place is, once a dreaded devil Pandasura was troubling the Sages. The Sages went to Mother Parasakthi so that she can give them safety. In response to their plea, Devi took rise from the Yaga, climbed over Sri Chakra as Lalithambika, started the war alongside the devil and at last she ruined him. She was angry and Lord Shiva asked Mother Parasakti to come to earth with the name of Manonmani so that she could calm down her anger. She became pliable and kind after coming to this very Temple. She formed the Vak Devathas - deities to rule words and asked them to chant her commend with about 1000 names. This is believed that it is the confinement place of Aruna, Garuda, the Sun's charioteer and Saneeswara. Therefore, people carry out the Mrutyunjaya Homam and the Ayush Homam at this very Temple in many festivals. Mother Kali is also worshiped in this very Temple. Lord Brahma, Vishnu is also worshiped as the myth about this Temple also says a lot about existence of them. This age-old Temple is one of the finest Temples that is popular across the country and believed as one of the great Shiva Temple of India.

SRI BRAHMAPUREESWARAR KOVIL AT AMBAL - The Temple is dedicated to Lord Shiva. The Temple is believed to be the last among the sixty maadakoil built by Kochengat Chola. Lord Shiva is known as Brahmapureeswarar here and Goddess Parvati is known as Poonkuzhalammai. The Lord Shiva as Sri Brahmapureeswarar is revered in the 7th century Tamil Saiva canonical work, the Tevaram, written by Tamil saint poets known as the Nayanmars and classified as Paadal Petra Sthalam. The Temple has a three-tiered rajagopuram and all other shrines are enclosed in rectangular walls. The Temple has four daily rituals. The Temple is celebrating three yearly festivals. As per legend, Lord Brahma had worshipped Lord Shiva here to regain his original form. Lord Brahma was cursed by Lord Shiva to be a swan. Lord Brahma is believed to been propitiated from his curse, after have taken a holy dip in Annam Poigai, the Temple tank, before worshipping Lord Shiva.

PAAMPURANATHAR TEMPLE AT TIRUPAMPURAM - It is one of the shrines of the 275 Paadal Petra Sthalams - Shiva Sthalams glorified in the early medieval Tevaram Poems by Tamil Saivite Nayanar Tirugnanasambandar Sundarar and Appar. This Temple is also known as Urakapuram and Seshapuri. The name of the Lord Siva here is Paampuranathar (also referred as Seshapureeswarar) and Sarpeswararand. The Goddess is Vandaar Poonkuzhali (also referred to as Pramarambikai). Lord Brahma and Saint Agasthyar are said to have worshiped Lord Shiva here. Also, the Kings of Serpents Nagarajan and Karkotakan are said to have worshiped Lord Shiva here. Pooja's for Rahu-Ketu doshas is done here. In order to get relieved from Nagadosham, people who do not have children and for Rahu-Kethu Dosham, people come here and offer prayers to the Lord. As per belief, people troubled by Sarpa-dosha or malefic effects Rahu-Kethu seek a relief by offering prayers in a single day to Kudanthai or Kumbakonam Nageshwarar in the morning, Thirunageshwaram Naganathar at the noon, Thirupamburam Pambureswarar in the evening and Nagoor Nageshwarar or Naganathar Temple at night.

SITHALAPATHY MUKTHEESWARAR TEMPLE - The presiding deity is Lord Shiva. He is called as Muktheeswarar. His consort is known as Porkodi Nayagi. It is one of the shrines of the 275 Paadal Petra Sthalams - Shiva Sthalams glorified in the early medieval Tevaram poems by Tamil Shaivite Nayanar Tirugnanasambandar. In the Temple Complex, there is unique Temple of Ganpati Bappa where Lord Ganesha is worshipped in human face, which is known as Nara Mukha Vinayaka.

MAA SARASWATHI AMMAN TEMPLE AT KOOTHANUR - The Temple is dedicated to Goddess Saraswathi. As per local belief it is the only Temple of Goddess Saraswathi. The glow of Goddess and the way of her sitting has attained popularity.

VEEZHINATHAR KOVIL AT THIRUVEEZHIMIZHALAI - The Temple is an ancient Temple dedicated to Lord Shiva. This Temple is 61st Padal Petra Kovil also known as Paadal Petra Sthalams in the Chola Naadu, South of Kaveri. Goddess Parvati is said to have been reborn as Katyayani and married Lord Shiva here. Lord Vishnu received the cosmic weapon Chakrayudam from Lord Shiva here in lieu of the 1000 flowers worship to Lord Shiva. A panel depicting the divine marriage is seen behind the Shivalingam. The Moolvar vimanam is believed to be brought to here by Mahavishnu. When Sambandar and Thirunavukarasar visit this place, there was a severe drought all around. They prayed to Lord Shiva who gave Padikasu (Gold Coin) one each every day to both of them. Sambandar gets Padikasu at the Pedam in front of Mahamandapam. Navukarasar gets gold coin in the Pedam in Merkku (west) prakaram (closed precincts of a Temple). Using these gold coin, they offered food to the needy people. The Math where they did anandanam is located on Vadaku Therodum Veedhi (North car Street).

ARULMIGU THIYAGARAJA SWAMY TEMPLE AT THIRUVARUR - It is one of the ancient heritage sites of India and is a representation of the religious-socio-cultural history of the Tamil region for a period spanning over a millennium and a half. Vanmikanathar represents the Moolavar while the shrine dedicated to Lord Thiyagaraja is the better known shrine in the Temple. Legend has it that Lord Thiyagaraja (Somaskanda) vigraha at Thiruvarur was created and worshipped by Lord Maha Vishnu. Lord Thiyagaraja represents the Somaskanda manifestation of Lord Shiva at Thiruvarur and at a few other shrines. Lord Thiyagaraja is said to have arisen from the navel of Lord Vishnu. Lord Vishnu in his yoga stage breaths and when Adisesha also breaths, there are waves found in the parkadal, the milky ocean at the Vaikuntha, where Lord Vishnu resides. The valorous Chola King brought back 7 vigrahas of Somaskanda from Lord Indra. Sapta Vitanka shrines refer to seven Temples in the Chola Kingdom enshrining vigrahas of Lord Thiyagaraja brought to earth by Mucukunda Chakravarti. This causes tilting and Lord Thiyagaraja is always visualised like doing a rhythmic dance which is known as "Ajaba Natanam". Devaram hymns dedicated to Thiruvarur describe festivities in the Temple town during the 1st millennium CE. 62 of the Nayanmaar preceding Sundarar are mentioned in Tiruttondattokai. The vast Temple complex at Thiruvarur with several shrines has many spacious mandapams and towering gopurams. There is another separate shrine for Goddess Nilothpalambal. The Goddess with two hands is Aadi Parasakti. Alongside the Goddess, an assistant is seen carrying on her shoulder Lord Muruga- an interesting feature and the Goddess is shown touching the head of Lord Muruga. In all Temples, there's only one Chandikesvarar but here, there are two Chandikes-varars, one known as Chandikes-varar and the other called as Yama Chandikesvarar with curls of hair and beard. It is said that all those born at Thiruvarur are Shivaganas and Lord Yama does not have any work to do.

BHAKTAVATSALA PERUMAL TEMPLE AT TIRUKANNAMANGAI - The Temple is dedicated to Lord Vishnu. The Temple finds mention in Skanda Purana and Brahmanda Purana. Constructed in Dravidian style of architecture, the Temple is glorified in the Divya Prabandha, the early medieval Tamil canon of the Azhwar Saints from 6th – 9th centuries AD. It is counted as one among the 108 Divya Desams dedicated to Lord Vishnu. Lord Vishnu is worshipped as Bhaktavatsala Perumal and his consort Lakshmi as Kannamangai Nayagi. The Temple is believed to be of significant antiquity and is believed to be initiated by the Medieval Cholas of the late 8th century AD with later contributions at different times from Thanjavur Nayaks. The Temple has three inscriptions dating from the Chola period. The Temple has a five-tiered Rajagopuram and enshrined within a granite wall. The complex contains all the shrines and the Temple tank is located outside the main entrance of the Temple. Bhaktavatsala Perumal is believed to have appeared to marry his consort Goddess Lakshmi in the place. As per legend, Varuna, the guardian deity of the west and Sage Romasa are believed to have worshipped Lord Vishnu at this place. The beehive in the Temple is believed to be Devas worshipping Lord Vishnu and in modern times, has special rituals performed for it. Lord Shiva is believed to guard the four corners of the Temple. This shrine is also referred to as Saptamrita Kshetram (seven celebrated elements of nature), referring to seven of its elements such as Vimanam, Mandapam, Aaranyam, Theertham, Kshetram, River and Town. A rare vigraha of Lord Buddha, vigraha of Lord Vaikunta Natha and Vishnu mounted on his eagle mount Garuda are the major vigrahas in the Temple. There is a pillared hall leading to the shrine of Kannamangai Thayar shrine that has pillars with Nayak architectural representation. The Temple observes six daily rituals and three yearly festivals. The chariot festival, celebrated during the Tamil month of Chittirai (March–April) is the most prominent festival of the Temple.

VANCHINADHA SWAMY TEMPLE AT SRIVANJIAM - The Temple is dedicated to Lord Shiva. Lord Shiva is worshiped as Vanchinadha Swamy and is represented by the Lingam. His consort Goddess Parvati is depicted as Mangalambigai Amman. The presiding deity is revered in the 7th century Tamil Saiva canonical work, the Tevaram, written by Tamil Saint Poets known as the Nayanmars and classified as Paadal Petra Sthalam. The Temple houses two gateway towers known as Gopurams. The tallest is the eastern tower with 11 stories and a height of 108 feet. The Temple has numerous shrines, with those of Vanchinadhaswamy, Yama and Mangala Nayagi Amman being the most prominent. The Temple has six daily rituals and twelve yearly festivals on its calendar with the Masi Magam festival celebrated during the Tamil month of Maasi (February - March) being the most prominent. The present masonry structure was built during the Chola dynasty in 11th century, while later expansions are attributed to Vijayanagar rulers of the Thanjavur Nayaks of 16th century. The Sthalavriksham is Sandalwood tree. The sacred tank is called the Gupta Gangai. It is one of the rare Temples where there is a separate shrine for Yama, the God of Death. Lord Yama is sported in seated posture with Chitragupta by his side. Gupta Ganga, Yama Theertham, Agni Theertham and Lakshmi Theertham are the various bodies of water associated with the Temple. The Temple has two Nandhis facing both sides of Vanchinadha. Rahu-Ketu, carved out in a composite sculpture. There is a separate sannathi for Lord Shani.

SRI NELLIVANANATHAR THIRUKOIL AT TIRUNELLIKAVAL - The Temple is dedicated to Lord Shiva. Lord Shiva is worshiped as Nellivaneswarar and Aanlavaneswarar. Goddess Parvati is worshiped as Mangala Nayagi. The Sthala Vriksham in the Temple is known as Nellikka, as King Chola was also called Amlakesha Chola. Lord Shiva is Swayambhu here. As per Sthala Puranam, Surya Dev, Chandra Dev, Lord Vishnu, Lord Brahma & Sage Durvasa worshiped Lord Shiva here. Sage Durvasa, who was famous for cursing due to his anger, was relieved from it after worshiping here. Lord Brahma created Theertham here which is called Brahma Theertham. Surya Puja is very famous here. Maha Shivratri festival is celebrated here with great pomp & fervor.

ARULMIGHU SUBRAMANYA SWAMY TEMPLE AT ENKAN - Rajaraja Cholan-I created a permanent endowment for the requirements of the daily poojas and festivals. In praise of the glory of Lord Subramanya, the Saint Poet Arunagirinathar dedicated his famous hymns of Thiruppugazh. The divine sculpture of the presiding deity Lord Arulmighu Arumuga seated on his peacock inside the sanctum sanctorum in this Temple is a marvellous work of art. The Thaipoosam festival celebrated in the middle of January in this Temple attracts devotees in large numbers every year.

ARULMIGU ABATHSAGAYESWARAR TEMPLE AT ALANGUDI - Alangudi is the divine place where Lord Guru can be propitiated in the form of Sri Dakshinamurthy. This sacred shrine of Jupiter is renowned for its tri-glories i.e. Moorthy (The Presiding Deity), Sthalam (Place of divinity) and Theertham (The Holy Water). Lakhs of people throng this place particularly on the day of Jupiter's transit to the next sign and to solicit Jupiter's protection from afflictions. Lord Jupiter's benign look can shower a lot of blessings from him. He is Devaguru. He is also known as Brihaspathi due to his excellence in education and fine arts, possessing supreme intelligence. Lord Shiva is manifested here in the form of Lord Guru. 274 Sthalams of erstwhile Chola Country have been sung in Devaram and Alangudi is one among the 127 Sthalams situated on the southern banks of Cauvery River. Sage Sukha, Rishi Viswamithra, Sage Agastya, Adisankara and several other holy men have worshipped at this shrine. The Lord of this Sthalam is Swayumbhu (Natural origination of the Vigraha). This Temple was believed to be constructed by an ardent of Lord Shiva. 'Amuthokar', the minister of the King Masukuntha Chakravarti. He was beheaded by the Chakravarti, as he refused to give half of his Punya (merit) to the King. On his death, the Sthalam reverberated with the sound 'Amuthokar'. The King got frightened at this constant diabolic echo, realizes his mistake and worshipped the Lord Abadsahayeswarar with ardent devotion. Then, he was relieved from all Doshas. Poolai Shrub is the holy tree of this Sthalam and it is an object of worship here. Alangudi is surrounded by three holy Rivers. They are Cauvery, Kolidam and Vennaru. Fifteen Theerthams are around this Temple, among which the Amrita Pushkarani encircling the Temple is very famous. Chakra Theertham is in front of the Temple. It is said that this Theertham was created by Lord Maha Vishnu's Chakra (Disc). Once a Chola Raja, who ruled over Thiruvarur, was fascinated by the Vigraha of Sundaramurthy at Alangudi and desired to have it installed at Thiruvarur for worship. On learning this, Temple priest at Alangudi become panic stricken. He disguised the Vigraha as a child affected with chicken-pox, hid it inside a swing and brought it back safely to Alangudi. The traces of Chicken-pox can still be seen on this vigraha.

VALANGAIMAN VARATHARAJAN PETTAI MAHA MARIAMMAN TEMPLE - This Temple is popularly known as Paadaikavadi Mariamman. The Temple has front mandapa, arthamandapa, sanctum sanctorum and prakara. In the mahamandapa, at the south Vinayaka and at the north Irulan, Pechiamman, Veeran with consorts are found. In the arthamandapa processional deities are kept. Sanctum sanctorum is in square size. In the south of the Temple, Temple tank is found. During the Tamil months of Avani (Aug-Sep) and Panguni (Sep-Oct) festivals are celebrated in this shrine.

SRI RAJAGOPALASWAMI TEMPLE AT MANNARGUDI - Shri Raja Gopalaswamy Temple is considered as the King of the Temples in the state. The presiding deity is Rajagopalaswamy, a form of Lord Krishna. The Temple is called Dakshina Dwarka (Southern Dwarka) along with Guruvayoor by Hindus. Its Rajagopuram (main tower) is 154 foot high and inside the Temple, there are 16 gopurams or towers, 7 mandapams or halls, 24 sannathi or thresholds and 18 vimanas. Lord Krishna appears as a shepherd boy with a whip on hand and turban wearing a dhoti. He has butter on the right hand, an ornament around the hip, key bunch, bangles in hand and jewels of children. There is cow and two calves by his side. His life in Gokhulam as a shepherd was the 32nd Leela. Based on these events, the presiding deity is Vaasudeva and procession deity as Rajagopala. While opening the Vaasudeva shrine in the morning, Gopuja-cow puja and Gaja puja-puja to elephant are performed. Procession deity is also called Rajamannar, hence the name of the place Mannargudi. The speciality of this Sthalam is that it is said that if we stay for a night in this Sthalam, we will get the credit, which is equivalent to donating 1000 cows to someone. Prayers to Lord Rajagopalar-Vaasudeva would bless them with prosperity in life, happy wedding, removal of adverse aspects on children, health of cattle and all happiness. A small golden Navaneedha Krishnan Vigraha on Garuda close to the Perumal and a small Vigraha of Santhana Gopalan is also found. It is believed that if any person who doesn't have children, are blessed with the worship of this Perumal.

KOTHANDARAMAR TEMPLE AT THILLAIVILAGAM - The Temple is dedicated to Lord Rama, the seventh avatar of Lord Vishnu. The presiding deity is known as Kothandaramar and also Veera Kothandaramar. There are also vigraha of Mata Sita, Lakshmanan and Lord Hanuman. The vigraha of Lord Hanuman with four feet height, in standing posture, is the speciality of the Temple. This Temple is one of the Pancha Rama Kshetrams and considered the foremost among the five Temples. Pancha means five and Kshetrams refers to holy places. All the five Temples are situated in Tiruvarur district, Tamil Nadu. Other Pancha Rama Kshetrams are located at Adambar, Mudikondan, Paruthiyur and Vaduvur.

DISTRICT – THE NILGIRIS (Railway Station – Metupalaiyam)

S. No.	Temple	Address	Type
1	Bhavani Amman Temple	Upper Bhavani, Udagamandalam - 643001	Mata
2	Arulmigu Vetrivel Murugan Temple	Kotagiri - 643217	Murugan

BHAVANI AMMAN TEMPLE AT UPPER BHAVANI - The Temple is also known as Lakshmi Temple. The Temple is located in the Nilgiri Biosphere Reserve. The Temple had been originally built during the construction of Upper Bhavani Dam. The Bhavani River originates in Nilgiri District & has origins in the Shola forest beyond this Temple. The stream running behind the Temple is the main feeder of Upper Bhavani Dam. Devotees worship this Temple on regular basis and specially on new moon days.

ARULMIGU VETRIVEL MURUGAN TEMPLE AT KOTAGIRI - The Temple is dedicated to Lord Murugan. The place is located on the Somas Kanda Scorpion & it has so many special features. The vigrha of the Lord Murugan usually carved as if Lord Murugan is standing with a mace but here the vigraha of the Lord Murugan is carved as if it is Murugan Velu which is rare. Peacock feathers on the left side of the head of Lord Murugan are also seen here which is rare. There are various other shrines of Lord Adi Ganesha, Somapuriswarar, Somamabiki, Byravar, Chandikeswarar Nagar. There are also Dakshina Murthi & Linkodpavar Brahma are in the trio form. Vaikasi Visakam and Panguni Uttiram Surasamaharam are the main festivals. The annual festival of the Temple is eleven day Thaipusam festival.

DISTRICT – VELLORE (Railway Station – Vellore/Katpadi/Arakkonam)

S. No.	Temple	Address	Type
1	Valleswarar Temple	Takkolam – 631151	Shiva
2	Jalakandeswarar Temple	Balaji Nagar, Vellore – 632004	Shiva
3	Sri Lakshmi Narayani Golden Temple	Sri Narayani Peedam, Thirumalaikodi, Vellore – 632055	Mata
4	Sri Margabandeswarar Temple	Virinjipuram – 632104	Shiva
5	Sri Vana Durga Devi Temple	Erayangadu - 632104	Mata
6	Sri Vilvanatheshwarar Temple	Tiruvalam - 632515	Shiva
7	Arulmigu Balamurugan Tirukkovil	Rathinagiri, Kilminnal, Walajah Taluk – 632517	Murugan
8	Murugan Temple & Jain Temples	Vallimalai – 632520	Murugan, Jain
9	Pallipadar Temple	Melpadi - 632520	Shiva
10	Cave Temples	Vilapakkam - 632521	Jain
11	Sundara Kamakshi Mandir	Sirukarumbur - 632531	Mata

VALLESWARAR TEMPLE AT THAKKOLAM - An inscription of Rajendra Chola-I registers the gift of 32 cows for the abhisheka with milk for the welfare of the King's mother named Tribhuvana Maadeviyar and another inscription informs the bronzes of Umamaheswara and Vinayaga were being worshipped in this Temple. The village used to be known as Tiruppamudhal and the deity Mahadevaraya Mummalai Easwaran.

JALAKANDESWARAR TEMPLE AT VELLORE FORT - The Temple is dedicated to Lord Shiva. According to legend, Chinna Bommi Nayaka, a Vijayanagar chieftain, who was controlling the Fort had a dream where the Lord Shiva asked him to build a Temple at that location. Nayaka proceeded to demolish the anthill and build the Temple in 1550 CE and since the Lingam was surrounded by water (called Jalam in Tamil). The deity was called as Jalakandeswarar (translated as "Lord

Siva residing in the water"). The Temple also has the Vigraha of Sri Akhilandeshwari Amma, the consort of Jalakandeswarar. The Jalakanteshwara Temple is a fine example of Vijayanagaram Architecture. The Temple has exquisite carvings on its gopuram (tower), richly carved stone pillars, large wooden gates and stunning monoliths and sculptures. The Gopuram of the tower is over 100 ft. in height. The Temple also has a Mandapam, with the hall supported by carved stone pillars of dragons, horses and yalis (lion like creature). The Temple itself built in middle of a water tank (called Agazhi in Tamil) and there is water surround the Temple like a garland. The wedding hall (Kalyana Mantapam) inside the Temple has a 2 faced sculpture that of a bull and an elephant. The water used for bathing the deity (abishekam) is drawn from an ancient well called the Ganga Gouri Thertam within the Temple. Behind the Nandi Vigraha, there is an earthen lamp, which is said to revolve when some people place their hands on it. Some devotees of the Temple worship the golden and silver lizard sculptures and the snake sculptures in order to get relief from 'sarpadosham'.

SRI LAKSHMI NARAYANI GOLDEN TEMPLE AT THIRUMALAIKODI - The Temple is located on 100 acres of land and has been constructed by the Vellore-based charitable trust, Sri Narayani Peedam, headed by its spiritual leader Sri Sakthi Amma also known as 'Narayani Amma'. The Temple with its gold (1500 KGs) covering has intricate work done by artisans specialising in Temple art using gold. Every single detail was manually created including converting the gold bars into gold foils and then mounting the foils on copper. Gold foil from 9 layers to 10 layers has been mounted on the etched copper plates. Every single detail in the Temple art has significance from the Vedas. The Temple is in the middle of a star-shaped path, such that it absorbs maximum energy from nature, which creates enormous peace and brings relaxation to the devotees who walk through the starpath. The star-shaped path with twelve 'auspicious' vertices creates a divine energy form on the Earth akin to the sacred Srichakra. Holy water from all the major rivers of the country was brought together into one holy pond called 'Sarvatheertham,' as a major source of evolution. A traditional & Vedic-style Temple architecture, 'Sri Lakshmi Narayani Golden Temple' is the world's largest Golden Temple and is one of the most visited holy shrines in the world. In alignment with this mission, Sri Sakthi Amma created a solid Vigraha of Sri Mahalakshmi with gold, weighing about 70 KGs. Sri Sakthi Amma has consecrated Sri Swarna Lakshmi Vigraha in the mandapam facing the Golden Temple enabling devotees to perform abhishekam to the Vigraha by themselves. Sri Sakthi Amma consecrated the Temple of Sri Srinivasa at Sripuram on 9th December 2016 and aptly named it as 'Sri Sripuram Srinivasa'. The main Vigraha of Sri Srinivasa stands at 10 ft in height with four hands viz. Abhaya Hastha, Varadha Hastha, Shanku (conch in one hand) and Chakra (Wheel) in the other hand.

SRI MARGABANDEESHWARAR TEMPLE AT VIRINJIPURAM – The main deity of this Temple is Swayambhu Lingam known as Margabandeeswarar. The Simha Teertham, the tank with the lion faced sculpture, located inside the Temple complex is nicely built. The most sacred Lord Shiva Temple at Virinchipuram is popularly known as "Bhaskara Kshethiram" because the Lord Sun is said to worship the Linga when its rays fall on it in the month of Panguni. As one enters a little distance into the eastern gate of the gopuram, he is attracted by a beautiful lion faced sculpture in the left side of the Shrine.

SRI VANA DURGA DEVI TEMPLE AT ERAYANGADU - The Temple is dedicated to Goddess Durga. Goddess Durga is known as Vana Durga. Devotees visit the Temple from far & wide to get the blessing of the Goddess. During Navratri festivals, large congregation gathers here to celebrate the festival with great pomp & fervor.

SRI VILVANATHESHWARAR TEMPLE AT TIRUVALAM - The Temple is also known as Bilvanathesvara Temple. Lord Shiva is worshipped as Vilwanatheswarar and is represented by the Lingam. His consort Parvati is depicted as Vallambigai. The presiding deity is revered in the 7th century Tamil Saiva canonical work, the Tevaram, written by Tamil saint poets known as the Nayanars and classified as Paadal Petra Sthalam. The Temple has a five-tiered gopuram. The Temple has a number of shrines. All the shrines of the Temple are enclosed in large concentric rectangular granite walls. Unlike other Temples, where the Nandi is located axial to and facing the sanctum, in this Temple the Nandi faces the opposite direction. The sanctum is structured in the form of a moat. The central shrine is approached through the flagstaff and Mahamandapam, both which are located axial to the gateway. The Temple has many historic inscriptions from the 8th-century Nandivarman-II era and later. The north wall of the Temple is notable for one of the earliest inscriptions that mention Tevaram singers. Many parts of the Temple complex is attributed to the Cholas, while the present masonry structure was built during the Nayak in the 16th century. The Temple has four daily rituals & four yearly festivals on its calendar. The Brahmotsavam festival is celebrated during the month of the Magam (Feb. - Mar.) is the most prominent festival.

ARULMIGU BALAMURUGAN TIRUKKOVIL AT RATHINAGIRI, KILMINNAL – It is an ancient Lord Murugan Temple. It is situated in south side of River Palar on the top of a hill. Ancient Hindu scriptures says where there is a hill, there is Lord Murugan. Over the passage of time, an ordinary sand structure was converted into a stone shrine. The 14th CE Poet Arunagirinathar has sung about this Temple as 'Rathinakiri Vazh Murukanellaya Vaaramarar Perumaley', which means 'Murugan, the God of Devas resides in Rathinagiri'. It is believed that the divine power in the Temple manifests its blessings in three forms: In the form of the Lord Murugan; In the form of the Guru Swami Balamurugan Adimai & in the form of the devotee.

LORD MURUGAN TEMPLE AT VALLIMALAI - This is the place where Valli performed penance on Lord Vishnu to have the hands of Lord Muruga, hence the Sadari blessing with Lord Vishnu Pada (feet) is offered to Devotees in the Temple.

JAIN CAVES - The Jain Vigraha is a noteworthy valuable monuments of Vallimalai. These are of 9th & 10th CE. The stone inscription of the Rashtrakuda King. Krishna-III is found here. The silver coins of Rajaraja Cholan was found in this place is considered to be yet another interesting part of the monumental artefacts.

GROUP OF TEMPLES AT MELPADI - The great King Rajaraja Cholan raised a Temple here for God Somanathar. He raised a Pallipadar Temple for his grandfather Arinjaya Cholan over his cemetery. It is named after the King as Arinjaya Choleeshwaran. The commendable aspects are that both the Temples are located near the banks of the River Nuga. The history of Rajaraja-I, Rajaraja-II, Koperunsingan, Sambuvarayargal, Kings of Vijaya Nagar could be found in the stone inscription of the Temple, which is yet another unique feature of this monument. The Seven Mothers statues and other statues of Somanathar Temples serves as a best example of sculptures found in Melpadi.

VILAPAKKAM - Thirupar Malai is being preserved by the Archaeological Survey of India. A Pallava period Cave Temple is found in the southern part. The cave is built (engraved) with 6 fully sculptured pillars and two partially sculptured pillars. The roof of the Cave is filled with the paintings of Jain Tirthankarar. The stone bed Jains and the debris of age old brick constructions are found here. A beautiful Goddess Ambigai – Yakshini vigraha is engraved here. This sculpture is proud to have sculptured during the period of King Thanthivarman. The King Rajaraja Cholan had offered the village named Koorambadi to the Jain monks as an offering which is inscribed in the stone engravings. The protruding statues are beautifully seen sculptured here.

SUNDARA KAMAKSHI MANDIR AT SIRUKARUMBUR - The Temple is dedicated to Lord Shiva & Goddess Kamakshi Devi. The stone inscriptions suggest the existence of the Temple since 10th CE Chaulakyan period. The Mandir is built in green granite stone and has rare Murthis and carvings on the walls. There is a sculpture of a foetus in the mother's womb. The legend says that the Temple was covered with sand due to mughal invasion and it was uncovered in 1958.

DISTRICT – VILUPPURAM (Railway Station – Villupuram)

S. No.	Temple	Address	Type
1	Sivankoil & Vishnukoil	Olagapuram – 604154	Shiva, Vishnu
2	Singavaram Ranganatha Temple	Gingee – 604202	Vishnu
3	Gingee Venkataramana Temple	Gandhi Bazaar, Gingee – 604202	Vishnu
4	Arulmigu Angalamman Thirukoil	Melmalayanur, Gingee – 604204	Mata
5	Jinakanchi Matha	Mel Chittamur – 604206	Jain
6	Mukthiyaleeswarar Koil & Seetha Cave	Perumukkal – 604301	Shiva, Sita
7	Arulmigu Subramaniya Swami Temple	Mailam - 604304	Murugan
8	Matri Mandir	Auroville – 605101	Peace
9	Sivankoil	Kandamangalam – 605102	Shiva
10	Panchavatee Jayamangala Panchamukha Sri Anjaneyaswamy	Vanur - 605109	Hanuman
11	Sri Saneeswarar Temple	Moratandi - 605111	Shani
12	Mandagapattu Rock-Cut Temple (Lakshitha Yathanam)	Vanniyapuram – 605203	Trinity
13	Sri Abiramaeshwarar Temple	Thiruvamathr – 605402	Shiva
14	Ennayiram Malai	Vikravandi - 605652	Jain
15	Atulya Nadheswarar Temple	Arakandanallur - 605752	Shiva
16	Ulagalandha Perumal Temple	Tirukkoyilur - 605757	Vishnu
17	Tirumoolanathar Temple	Perangiyur - 607107	Shiva
18	Kripapureeswarar Temple	Tiruvennainallur – 607203	Shiva

OLAGAPURAM –

SIVANKOIL - This Temple was built by Ambalavanan Kandrarathiyan, a local King under Rajaraja-I. The name of the Village itself in the name of Rajarajas wife "Ulagamadevi".

VISHNU KOIL – The Temple is also known as Devaraja Perumal Koil. This stone Temple is constructed with unique style of Rajendra Chola-I, facing eastern side and consists of Sanctum Sanctorum, Ardha Mandapam & Maha Mandapam. Inscriptions of Rajendra Chola-I is mentioned about the names of the Lakes as "Kaalakanda Pereri", "Kandarathiththa Pereri".

GINGEE SINGAVARAM RANGANATHA TEMPLE – The Temple is also known as Singavaram Perumal Temple. It is a Cave-Temple dedicated to God Ranganatha and Goddess Ranganayaki Thayar. The Temple is a Pallava period structure and was patronized by subsequent rulers. The 24 foot long Vigraha of Ranganatha, carved from living rock, is in a reclining pose on the coils of the serpent Ananta. A panel in the rear wall depicts the Gandharvas and Lord Brahma, in which Lord Brahma is born from the navel of Lord Vishnu. Besides Garuda, the demons Madhu and Kaitabha who were killed by Lord Vishnu are depicted. Goddess Bhoomidevi graces the feet of the Lord while Prahlada sits near his knee. Maa Durga with 4 hands holding the Shankha, Chakra and two arms resting on her thigh and waist, stands on the head of Mahishasura. The Sthalapurana of the Temple associates it with the

legend of Prahlada, born to the demon-king Hiranyakashipu. The Shashti Poorthi celebration in this Temple is associated with a legend of Desing Raja. This Temple was his tutelary deity (Kuldev).

SRI RAMANATHA ESWARAR TEMPLE AT ESALAM - Built by Rajendra Cholan-I, the Temple is dedicated to Lord Sri Ramanatha Eswarar. The legend found in sanskrit & in grantha character. A shrine dedicated to Kamalakkani Amman (Goddess Durga), a local deity, is found on the way to the citadel on Rajagiri Hill. It contains a sacrificial altar & well-preserved mural paintings belonging to the Nayak period.

GINGEE VENKATARAMANA TEMPLE - This sprawling Temple, dedicated to Lord Venkateshwara, with its striking sculptures and carved pillars, narrates the aesthetic skills of the Nayaka dynasty. Built by Muthialu Nayaka, this is the largest Temple of Gingee. The Temple abounds in gopuras, mandapas and sculptured panels depicting gods and goddesses in scenes from the Hindu epics. Many Tamil inscriptions are also found in the walls of the Mandapas. The Temple's most admirable carvings are found in the panels located on either side of the entrance gateway depicting Ramayana scenes, Lord Vishnu's incarnations and the puranic legend of samudramanthan. To the east of the Temple is the Kalyanamahal, an architectural treasure piece. Shrines of Goddesses are placed in the western corners of the Temple, each with a small mandapa with a pier having multiple colonettes while another shrine with Lord Narasimha and Krishna carvings is placed away from the middle of the western wall. It is a remarkable piece of sculpture in bold relief in which is carved a panel of Lord Krishna, Rukmani and Satyabhama and two other female figures. The Pattabhirama shrine (aka Pattabhiramaswami Temple) situated at the foot of the Chakkali Durgam hill also has several carvings of interest.

Gingee Fort or Senji Fort (also known as Chenji, Chanchi, Jinji or Senchi) is one of the surviving Forts in Tamil Nadu. The site is so fortified that Chhatrapati Shivaji, the Maratha king, ranked it as the "most impregnable fortress in India" and it was called the "Troy of the East" by the British. The Gingee Fort complex is on three hillocks: Krishnagiri named after Krishna Kon to the north, Rajagiri or Anandagiri named after Ananda kon to the west and Chandrayandurg to the southeast. The three Hills together constitute a fort complex, each having a separate and self-contained citadel. The complex has a seven-storeyed Kalyana Mahal, granaries, prison cells and a Temple dedicated to its presiding Goddess called Chenjiamman. The fortifications contain a sacred Pond known as Aanaikulam. On the top of the hillock, there are minor fortifications. The fort, in modern times, is maintained and administered by the Archaeological Survey of India.

ARULMIGU ANGALAMMAN THIRUKOIL AT MELMALAYANUR - The deity of the Temple is Sembadavars. There is an ancient snake pit in the inner sanctum. Goddess Parvathi took birth on her as hive. The purpose of the birth is to clear Lord Shiva from certain sin and give blessings to all people in Kaliyugam. The birth took place her before the start of Kaliyugam. The specialty in this Temple is Mother in Angala Amman faces north while blessing devotees. A festival celebrated here during February-March is famous for Simimasana Kollai. During the festival, many pilgrims cook large quantities of various kinds of grain and set it out in the burning ground. This offering to the Goddess is believed to grant wishes. The great dazzling brightest light is mother Sri Angala Parameshwari, who was ruling the world even before inhibition started. According to legend of

Daksha Yagya & Sati's self-immolation, the right hand of Dhakshayani fell in Dhandakarunyam. Malayanoor is a part of Dhandakarunyam. People took sand from snake hive as prasad and got relief from diseases. The Angala Parameshwari was taken in procession in car to subside her anger. Angels, Sages and Saints became wheels, wheel latch and throne of the car.

JINAKANCHI MATHA AT MEL CHITTAMUR - It is Headquarter of Digambara sect in Tamilnadu presided over by the Pontiff. Two Temples, one dedicated to Lord Parsvanatha and other known as Mailanatha Temple was originally a boulder containing rock-cut vigrahas of Lord Bahubali, Parsvanatha, Adinatha, Mahavira and Ambikayakshi carved in 9th century. Raja Gopuram is a seven storeyed tower with a total height of more than 70 foot. vigrahas of Tirthankaras are carved on Temple walls. Main Vigraha of Lord Parsvanatha is a black coloured 14 foot Vigraha in Padmasan posture. The 52 foot manasthambha in Temple is a monolith. Malinatha Temple is also known as Thiruvooram Palli or Kattam Palli.

24 THEERTHANGARARGAL - The hillock on the western side of the road has two Jain caverns and a huge boulder containing sculptures of all the 24 Theerthankaras in 9th century style. It is the only place where all the 24 Theerthankaras are shown in a single large composition. An open rock nearby was the place where Monk Chandranandi observed 57 days of fasting and died (5th-6th century). Another Monk, Ilayabhattara observed 30 days of fasting and died. The pathway leading to the caves at the ground level has an vigraha of Lord Adinatha and at the top of a figure of Lord Mahavira.

MUKTHIYALEESWARAR KOIL & SEETHA CAVE AT PERUMUKKAL - The 10th century Chola Heritage Temple is located at the peak of Perumukkal Hill with a vast area covered by fortress. Mukthialeeswarar Temple was built by Kulothunga-I and covered in to stone structure during the Vikrama Chola period. Seetha Cave inscription in Tamil Vatteluthu form and belongs to 6th - 7th century. Local people worshiped here Lord Shiva, Seetha and Anumar. 60 inscriptions available here.

MAILAM - Arulmigu Subramaniya Swami Temple is located on a small hillock. It is a famous place for pilgrimage. The Panguni Uthiram festival held in March – April fascinates a large crowd of devotes from all over Tamil Nadu.

THIRUVAKKARAI - There is a Temple for Lord Siva constructed by the famous Chola queen Sembiyan Madheviyar. Arulmigu Chandramoulisvarar and Tenambikai are the presiding deities here. Arulmigu Vakkaralingam and Arulmigu Vakkrakali for whom every full moon day and night of the year special prayers are conducted and thronged by pious devotees throughout the night. The Temple was sung by the Thirugnana Sambandar. Excellent sculptures and car/chariot like Mandapam is also existing here with huge Nandhi and Ganesha.

MATRI MANDIR AT AUROVILLE – The place is called the 'soul of the city'. The MatriMandir is situated in a large open area called 'Peace'. The MatriMandir can be viewed as a large golden sphere which seems to be emerging out of the earth, symbolising the birth of a new consciousness. The central MatriMandir, which is not a Temple but a place for individual silent concentration, is seen as "a symbol of the Divine's answer to man's aspiration for perfection and as a Union with the Divine manifesting in a progressive human unity." The spacious inner chamber in the upper hemisphere of the MatriMandir is completely white with white marble walls and deep white carpeting. In the centre, sits a pure crystal-glass globe which suffuses a ray of electronically guided sunlight that falls on it through an opening at the apex of the sphere. The Inner Chamber is devoid of vigrahas, organised meditations, flowers, incense, religion or religious forms. The concept of Auroville – an ideal township devoted to an experiment in human unity – came to the Mother, the spiritual collaborator of Sri Aurobindo. On 28th February 1968, some 5,000 people assembled near the Banyan Tree at the centre of the future township for an inauguration ceremony attended by representatives of 124 nations including all States of India. The representatives brought with them some soil from their homeland, to be mixed in a white marble- clad, lotus-shaped urn, now sited at the focal point of the Amphitheatre. At the same time, the Mother gave Auroville its 4-point Charter. Architecturally speaking, the buildings are a combination of modern, western and traditional Indian elements, set in a rural landscape of deep red earth and widespread forestation, with narrow earth roads linking the settlements.

SIVANKOIL AT KANDAMANGALAM – This village was called Srikandaradhitha Mangalam in the Chola period. The Lord Shiva Temple has been constructed in the early Chola architectural style. The small Shivalingam in this Temple has facial features. According to the inscriptions found on the southern side of the sanctum sanctorum, this Temple used to be called Thirunareeswaram.

PANCHAVATEE JAYAMANGALA PANCHAMUKHA SRI ANJANEYASWAMY AT VANUR - The Temple is dedicated to Lord Hanuman. It is known as Panchvati Kshetran. As per local belief, the Temple has the world's second largest Lord Anjaneya Vigraha. The Temple is in a big complex. The consecration ceremony was performed on 31st January, 2007. Devotees offer a garland of Ulundu Vadais to the Lord which is popularly known as Hanumar Vadais. It is believed that people suffering from incurable diseases and ceasless struggles are advised to visit this Temple for six consecutive

saturdays and chant the mantra of Jai Ram 108 times. There are various festivals which are celebrated here with great pomp & fervour.

SRI SANEESWARAR TEMPLE AT MORATANDI - The Temple is dedicated to Navagrahas. The main Vigraha of Saniswaran Bhagwan is about 27 ft tall and each Vigraha of Navagraha is 15 ft. tall. The speciality of the Temple is that the Vigrahas of all the Navagrahas are with their Vahanas. There is also a huge Vinayagar Vigraha of about 34 ft tall and made of gold painting. Lord Shiva is known as Kalyana Sundareshwarar in the Temple and there is also Vigraha of Vasthu Bhagwan. Each Navagrahas have a distinct tree and there is also certain trees which denotes the zodiac signs. Devotees with various zodiac signs worship the tree that belong to their star.

Poothurai Village - The village is having a very big cashew forest wherein app. 1000 Shivalingas exist. All the Shivalingas are in different shapes and some of them are having sculptures. Devotees visit the forest with great devotion specially on Monday and Mahashivratri festival.

MANDAGAPATTU ROCK-CUT TEMPLE (LAKSHITHA YATHANAM) AT VANNIYAPURAM – It is a famous Archaeological Temple site. It is a 100 ft hillock Cave Temple called Mandagapattu Cave Temple, which is a Hindu Temple. This shrine, called the Trimurti Temple, is generally considered as the first of the PallavaCave-Temples and was commissioned by King Mahendra-I in the early 7th century on a 100 ft hillock. The Temples were a significant architectural innovation as they marked the transition from wooden structures to stone. An inscription on the Temple calls it the Laksitayatna and dedicates it to Lord Brahma, Isvara and Vishnu.

THIRUVAAMATHOOR - An ancient Chola Temple, which is dedicated to Lord Sri Abiramaeshwarar. It is 1500 years old Temple. The Amman is called Muththambigai. The Temple is also called as Thiruvamathur Temple. The Temple is dedicated to Lord Shiva. The presiding deity is revered in the 7th century Tamil Saiva canonical work, the Tevaram, written by Tamil saint poets known as the nayanmars and classified as Paadal Petra Sthalam. The Temple has a number of shrines, with those of Abirameswarar being the most prominent. There is a Temple opposite to the premises that houses the shrine of Muthamman, the consort of Abirameswarar. There are many yearly festivals celebrated here & Navaratri during the month of Purattasi (September - October) is the most prominent festivals celebrated in the Temple.

ENNAYIRAM MALAI AT VIKRAVANDI - The place is an ancient site belongs to Jainism. There are important Tamil inscriptions, Jain beds & Jina Parshvnatha vigraha carved on the rock. Among the various inscriptions, one inscription belong to the period of Pallava Dynasty of 7th CE and other inscriptions belongs to the period of Chola Dynasty.

ATULYA NADHESWARAR TEMPLE AT ARAKANDANALLUR - The Temple is dedicated to Lord Shiva. Lord Shiva is worshiped as Atulya Nadheshwara and Goddess Parvati is worshiped as Azhagiya Punnazhagi here. The Temple is one among the Paadal Petra Shiva Sthalam. Lord Shiva is Swayambhu here. It is believed that the Pandavas stayed near a cave during exile period and Bheema created a small pond here which is known as Bheema Tirtham. As per Sthala Puranam, Lord Vishnu wanted to relieve himself from the sin done against Mahabali during Vamana Avtaram, hence Lord Vishnu prayed Lord Shiva in this Temple and he was relieved from all sins. Sambandar wished to worship Lord Shiva here but the Temple was locked, hence Sambandar sang about Atulya Nadheshwarar outside the Temple and it is believed that Lord Shiva opened the door of the Temple by himself for Sambandar. Mahashivratri festival is the main festival here which is celebrated with great pomp & fervor.

ULAGALANDHA PERUMAL TEMPLE AT TIRUKKOYILUR - The Temple is also known as Trivikrama Temple. The Temple is dedicated to Lord Vishnu. Constructed in the South Indian style of architecture, the Temple is glorified in the Divya Prabandha, the early medieval Tamil canon of the Azhwar saints from the 6th–9th centuries AD. It is one of the 108 Divyadesam dedicated to Lord Vishnu, who is worshipped as Ulagalantha Perumal and his consort Lakshmi as Poongothai. The Temple is believed to have been built by the Medieval Cholas, with later contributions from Vijayanagar kings and Madurai Nayaks. The Temple has a Temple tower that is the third tallest in

Tamil Nadu, measuring 192 ft in height. As per legend, Lord Vamana, a dwarf and an avatar of Lord Vishnu, appeared here to quell the pride of Asura king Bali. The Temple is believed to be the place where the first three Azhwars, the Vaishnava saints, namely, Poigai Alvar, Bhoothathalvar and Peyalvar attained salvation. The Temple is one of the Panchakanna (Krishnaranya) Kshetrams, the five holy Temples associated with Lord Krishna, an avatar of Lord Vishnu. Six daily rituals and a dozen yearly festivals are held at the Temple, out of which the chariot festival, celebrated during the Tamil month of Chittirai (March–April), is the most prominent.

Parikkal Lakshmi Narasimha Swamy Temple - The Temple is dedicated to Lord Narasimha & Goddess Lakshmi. The Temple is very ancient. Many Madhva Brahmin families of the Shri Vyasaraja Mutt (Sosale) order owe allegiance to Parrikal Lakshmi Narasimha as their Kula Devata. It is believed that the vigrahas of Lord had been consecrated in 1500 BC by Lord Brahma himself. It is also believed that the Chola kings had great reverence towards this Temple.

TIRUMOOLANATHAR TEMPLE AT PERANGIYUR - This Temple is facing east belong to Paranthaka period. In the inscription, 'Perangiyur' mentioned as 'Perankoor'. The Temple is called 'Mulasthanamudayar' or 'Tirumulasthanmudaya Mahadevar'. There are number of inscription of the King Paranthaka Chola to look under administration of the Temple. 'Sri Rutragana Perumakkal' are appointed during the period of Rajaraja-I. In the beginning, there was only sanctum sanctorum and Arthamandapa in the Temple. Mukamandapa was the later development. From Adhistanam to Kapothagam, they used granite stones and later, Vimana portion were constructed with brick and mortar.

THIRUVENNAINALLUR - It is the birth place of Sadayappar, the patron of Kambar (The greatest Tamil poet and author of the Tamil Epic Kambaramayanam). There is also an ancient Temple dedicated to Lord Shiva, known as Kripapureeswarar Temple. The presiding deity is revered in the 7thcentury Tamil Shaiva canonical work, the Tevaram written by Tamil Saint Poets known as the Nayanmars and classified as Paadal Petra Sthalam. The Temple is closely associated with Sundarar, the Shaivite Saint of 8th century, who started composing his Tirumurai starting with "Pitha Piraisudi" verse in this Temple. Constructed in the Dravidian style of architecture, the present structure of the Temple is believed to have been built during the Cholas period in 10thcentury. The Temple has received gracious endowments from the Chola Queen Sembiyan Mahadevi. Lord Shiva is worshipped as Kripapureeswarar and his consort Parvathi as Mangalambigai. The Temple has a five-tiered rajagopuram, the gateway tower.

DISTRICT – VIRUDHUNAGAR (Railway Station – Virudunagar)

S. No.	Temple	Address	Type
1	Ayyanar Falls	Rajapalayam – 626117	Sastha
2	Sathuragiri Hills	Srivilliputtur – 626125	Shiva
3	Srivilliputtur Andal Temple	Srivilliputtur – 626125	Vishnu

AYYANAR FALLS AT RAJAPALAYAM - Ayyanar Falls are a part of the eastern slopes of the Western Ghats of the south. The name Ayyanar is given to these falls because there is a small Forest Temple named Ayyanar Temple beside the falls.

SATHURAGIRI HILLS AT SRIVILLIPUTTUR – It is also known as Chathuragiri. There is a Sundara Maha Lingam. The name Sathuragiri came from Chathur (4) Veda (Vedas) Giri (Hill), where all the four Vedas met and formed the hill. Another meaning is that the whole mountain is in square (Chathuram) in shape so the name Chathuragiri. Sathuragiri is the Abode of God. It is otherwise also called as Mahalingam Hill. This is also called as "Siddhargalbhoomi". 18 Siddhas were said to live here. This is a mysterious hill where it is believed that Siddhars still worship the Lord Shiva. Public are allowed only Six days in a month, 3 days each during New Moon & Full Moon days (i.e. Day before & Day after, with Full moon or New moon days).

SRIVILLIPUTTUR ANDAL TEMPLE – It is a popular and old Temple and considered to be the holiest among the 108 Divya Desams of Lord Sri Vishnu. This is the birth place of Andal & also the birth place of Periyazhvaar (Andals Father). To the devotees and vaishnavites, Srivilliputtur is synonymous with Lord Vishnu, Periyalwar and Andal. It is an interesting place to any aesthetic person for enjoying the sculpture and ancient drawings in the Temple. It gave –'Thiruppavai' of Andal and 'Tirupallandu' of Periyalvar - the hymns on Lord Vishnu to Tamil Literature. These Tamil hymns – Tamil Vedam-Alwar Pasurams- are recited every day at this Temple. Thousands of people from the state participate in the "Aadi Pooram" festival celebrated in the Temple. The Temple consists of two parts. The first part is called Vadabadra Sayanar Temple and the second part is known as Andal Sannadhi. The Alwars lived in 8th century, so we can say that the existence of the Temple can be traced even before. Vadabadrasayanay Temple was constructed by the King Villi who ruled the place. The tall tower was constructed by Peria Alwar with the help provided by the Pandia King Vallabadevan as per Guru Parambara traditions. The Rajagopuram is the tallest in Tamil Nadu. It is also the Emblem of Tamil Nadu Government. It has eleven stages. The great poet Kamban has praises it in lofty terms and the poem finds a place in the Tower. As the Lord took rest here in the form of pig, It was called Varaga Kshetram.

TELANGANA

Telangana is the 29th state of India, formed on 2nd June 2014. The Telangana region was part of the Hyderabad state from Sept 1948 to Nov 1956 until it was merged with Andhra state to form the Andhra Pradesh state. Megalithic stone structures like cairns, cists, dolmens and menhirs found in several districts of Telangana shows that there were human habitations in this part of the country thousands of years ago. Remnants of iron ore smelting found at many places demonstrate the hoary roots of artisanship and tool making in Telangana for at least two thousand years. The reference to AsmakaJanapada, part of present Telangana, as one of the 16 Janapadas in ancient India proves that there existan advanced stage of society. Located on the uplands of Deccan plateau, Telangana is the link between the North and South of India. It is thus no surprise that the region on the whole came to be known for its Ganga-Jamuna Tehzeeb and the capital Hyderabad as a 'miniature India!'

Capital City	Hyderabad
Total Population	35,193,978 (2011)
Districts	33
Official Language	Telugu
Emblem	Kakatiya Kala Thoranam, Charminar
Motto	Satyameva Jayate
Animal	Jinka
Bird	Palapitta
Fish	Korameenu
Tree	Jammi Chettu
Flower	Tangedu
Fruit	Mango
Sport	Kabaddi
Festival	Dasara
Song	Jaya Jaya He Telangana
Airport	Hyderabad

N
80 km
40 mi
© d-maps.com
Adilabad
Komaram Bheem
Nirmal
Mancherial
Jagtial
Nizamabad
Peddapalli
Jayashankar
Rajanna Sircilla
Kamareddy
Karimnagar
Mulugu
Siddipet
Medak
Warangal Urban
Warangal Rural
Bhadradri Kothagudem
Sangareddy
Jangaon
Mahabubabad
Medchal-Malkajgiri
Yadadri Bhuvanagiri
Vikarabad
Hyderabad
Khammam
Ranga Reddy
Suryapet
Nalgonda
Mahabubnagar
Narayanpet
Wanaparthy
Nagarkurnool
Jogulamba
Mercator

DISTRICT – ADILABAD (Railway Station – Adilabad)

S. No.	Temple	Address	Type
1	Kuntala Water Falls	Babjepet - 504203	Shiva
2	Siva Temple	Gudihatnur, Boath – 504304	Shiva
3	Mahadev Temple	Bela – 504309	Shiva
4	Jainath Temple	Jainath – 504309	Vishnu-Laxmi
5	Hemedpanti Temple	Ootnur – 504311	Shiva
6	Nagoba Jatara	Keslapur – 504346	Nagnath

KUNTALA WATER FALLS AT BABJEPET - At Kuntala, the Kadem River cascades 45 meters down and rushes deep into the Jungles. Kuntala, the highest waterfalls in the State, offers a spectacular sight particularly when the River is flush with copious inflows. There is an vigraha of Lord Shiva near the water falls known as Someshwara Swami. Many devotees congregate here for Mahashivaratri festivities.

SIVA TEMPLE AT GUDIHATNUR, BOATH - The Temple is dedicated to Lord Shiva. The Temple belongs to 17th century CE. The Temple consisting of a garbhagriha and antarala with pillared mandapa. Nandi is placed in the centre of the mandapa facing the Shivalinga.

MAHADEV TEMPLE AT BELA - The Temple is dedicated to Lord Shiva. It is believed to be of 11th – 12th century CE. The Temple consists of garbhagriha and antarala with pillared mandapa. The shikhara which forms the main backdrop for the Temple is built in Nagara style, surmounted with amalaka. The location of this Temple in pristine surroundings adds to the charm.

JAINATH TEMPLE - The Temple has a prakrit stone inscription depicting the 20 slokas which establishes that it was constructed by the Pallava chief. The Temple boasts of impressive features resembling the Jain style of Temple architecture. The village gets the name from the famous Temple which is an abode of Lord Lakshmi Narayana Swami. Every year from October-November,Bhramotsavalu is held from Karthika Sudda Astami to Bahula Saptami attracting a large number of devotees. The Lord's Vigraha in the sanctum sanctorum is six-foot tall and is made entirely of black stone.

HEMEDPANTI TEMPLE AT OOTNUR - The Temple is dedicated to Lord Shiva. The Temple is believed to be of 16th – 17th century CE. The Temple and koneru are archaeological sites. The Temple complex consists of Lord Shiva, Rama and Sai Baba shrines. There is a beautiful rectangular step well (Koneru) in the Temple complex. Hemadpanti is an architectural style followed in the state of Maharashtra. It is named after its founder, the Prime Minister Hemadpanth who had served in the Court of Yadavas of Devagiri, who ruled from 850 – 1334 CE from their capital city Devagiri (present day Daulatabad in Maharashtra).

NAGOBA JATARA AT KESLAPUR - The famous Nagoba Temple, which has stone vigraha of Lord Seshanag (Serpent God), attracts large numbers of devotees. During Pushya month (December-January), devotees belonging to various castes and creeds participate in the Keslapur Jatara. People from all parts of the district as also Gonds and other tribes from the neighbouring Maharashtra state take part in large numbers.

DISTRICT – BHADRADRI KOTHAGUDEM (Railway Station - Bhadrachalam Rd)

S. No.	Temple	Address	Type
1	Sree Seetha Ramachandra Swamy Vaari Devasthanam	Bhadrachalam - 507111	Ramayana Circuit
2	Nava Bharath Temple	Paloncha - 507115	Vishnu
3	Peddamma Talli Temple	Jagannadhapuram - 507115	Mata
4	Buddhist Sites	Ramavaram - 507118	Buddhist
5	Parnasala	Parnasala - 507137	Rama

SREE SEETHA RAMACHANDRA SWAMY VAARI DEVASTHANAM AT BHADRACHALAM – It is situated on the banks of Godavari River. The town is synonymous for its famous Temple devoted to Lord Rama. The town has a documented history of Lord Sri Rama Temple, which was constructed in 17th CE. According to mythology, the present town was once part of the Dandakaranya forest, which Lord Sri Rama, Sita & Lakshmana had visited during their exile. The forest was the place for Lord Rama's retreat and a place called Parnasala was the location where Lord Rama had built a dwelling for himself and Sita. Agastya Muni helped Lord Rama in selecting this spot. It is believed that from this place, Mata Sita was abducted by Lanka ruler, Ravana. The name Bhadrachalam is derived from the word Bhadragiri (The Mountain Abode of Bhadra, the child of Meru and Menaka). The famous Temple is home to the Archa Murthy's of Lord Rama, Sita & Lakshmana and their vigraha are believed to be swayambhu i.e. self-manifested ones. There is picturesque display of few scenes from vanavasa at Parnasala. Pilgrims enthral when they see the footprints of Mata Sita, the mosaic of Maarecha who appears in the guise of golden deer & Ravana who appears in the form of Sanyasi. One can see Sita Vaagu where Sita had bathed & gathered turmeric & Kunkum from the nearby stones. Yetapaka has a history where the bird Jatayuvu, an ardent devotee of Lord Rama tried to obstruct Ravana when he was proceeding on a chariot after kidnapping Sita. A fierce battle ensued & a wing was believed to have found at Rekkapalli. Lord Rama is worshipped as Atmarama here, where according to Purana, Lord Rama killed app. 14,000 demons belonging to Khara & Dushana. The place is called Dummugudem as it was built on the ashes of these demons. At Gundala, one can see hot water springs after digging a pit on the riverbank & it is said that the divine trio of Lord Brahma, Vishnu and Maheshwara dipped in the holy water here during winter season. There are other places too like Sree Rama Giri, Venkatreddipeta, Gannavaram etc. The puranic & historic facts relate that Lord Rama had shed his mortal coils, manifested himself, to save his devotee Bhadra Maharshi, whom he promised 'moksha' after intensive prayer. That is why the village is named after Bhadra as Bhadradri or Bhadrachalam. Lord Rama appeared in a dream to a woman called Pokala Dammakka & informed here about the existence of vigrahas on Bhadragiri hills. To her surprise, she found the "Vigrahas" & put up a modest structure. This was the origin of the present Temple. Thus, the moorthies of Lord Rama (having four hands) - Shanku on the right, Chakra at his left & Dhanurbhana, Sita had condescended on the left lap of Lord Rama & Laxman are existed & the hill place was the head place of Bhadra - achalam, thus this shrine was transformed into Bhadrachalam.

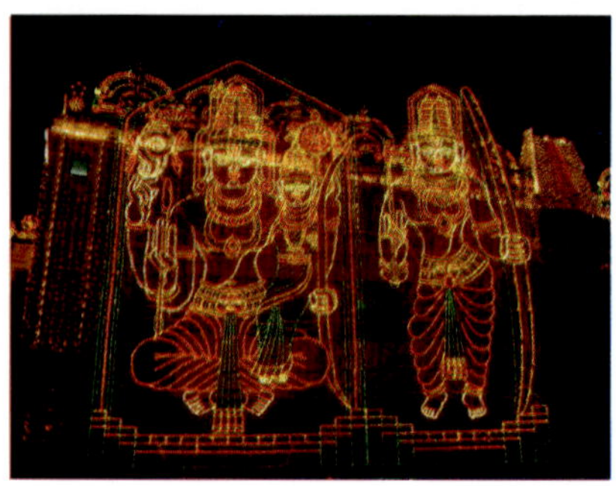

NAVA BHARATH TEMPLE AT PALONCHA - The Temple is also known as Sri Venkateswara Swamy Temple. The Temple is dedicated to Lord Vishnu. The Temple is located in a peaceful place and is having a big garden.

PEDDAMMA TALLI TEMPLE AT JAGANNADHAPURAM - It is a very famous Temple. People come across from the Khammam District to get the darshan of the Goddess Kanaka Durga (Peddamma Talli). Long ago, this was a thick forest area with wild animals. As per legend, one tiger lives here under the Tamarind Tree. Even people used to walk via that way but it won't hurts or kill anyone. Villagers considered that tiger as Goddess Peddamma Talli and they constructed a small Temple with placing her vigraha inside. Day-by-day Temple has been developed and became as a Village Goddess.

BUDDHIST AND ANDHRA SITES AT RAMAVARAM - The place belongs to 1st – 3rd century CE.

There are two Buddhist monuments on Karukonda Hillock. One is a big boulder with Lord Buddha sculptures in niches on the four sides. On each cardinal side, there is a niche in which a figure of Lord Buddha is carved (relief), seated in padmasana (lotus throne) in a meditative mood. The second one is, two cells cut in a single piece of rock and the walls are sculpted with the figures of Lord Buddha, a chauri bearer on each side and dwarapalakas. Despite not having a large number of sculptures, the art showcased at Karukonda is extremely developed. The Lord Buddha figures and the chauri bearers in the rock cut caves are typical examples of conventional and graceful curves of the body, an example of refined Mahayana art.

PARNASALA - It is a small village in a remote location. According to the legend, Lord Rama spent some of his fourteen years of exile at this place. The little stream stands as a testimony to the belief that Sita Mata took her bath in the stream and that place is called Sita Vaagu. Every belief is justified one such proof is the imprints in "Radhagutta" in Parnasala. Another story accounting to the history of this historical village is that Maricha Rakshas was killed by Lord Rama in the same place when he came in disguise as a golden deer to deceive Sita Mata. It is believed to be the place where the evil-minded King Ravana abducted Sita Mata. This place unfolds this part of the epic Ramayana by exhibiting the primary events with beautifully canvassed sculptures of Shri Ram, Sita, Laxman and Ravana.

DISTRICT – HYDERABAD (Railway Station – Secunderabad)

S. No.	Temple	Address	Type
1	ISKCON	Nampally Station Road, Abids, Hyderabad – 500001	Radha-Krishna
2	Sitaram Bagh Temple	Sitaram Bagh, Hyderabad – 500001	Hanuman
3	Sri Mahankaleshwara Temple	Mir Alam Mandi, Hyderabad – 500002	Mata
4	Sri Bhagyalakshmi Temple	Charminar, Hyderabad - 500002	Mata
5	Sri Ujjaini Mahakali Temple	General Bazar, Secunderabad – 500003	Mata
6	Birla Mandir	Khairtabad, Hyderabad – 500004	Vishnu
7	Buddha Vigraha	Khairtabad, Hyderabad – 500004	Buddha

S. No.	Temple	Address	Type
8	Sri Swayambhu Chennakesava Swamy Temple	Keshogiri - 500005	
9	Mahabodhi Buddha Vihara	Mahindra Hills, Secunderabad - 500026	Buddhist
10	Ramakrishna Math	Domalguda, Valmiki Nagar, Lower Tankbund Road, Hyderabad - 500029	Ramakrishna
11	Peddamma Temple	Road No. 55, Jubilee Hills, Hyderabad – 500033	Mata
12	Lord Jagannath Temple	Road No. 12, Banjara Hills, Hyderabad – 500034	Jagannath (Vishnu)
13	Sri Lakshmi Narasimha Swamy Temple	Road No. 12, Banjara Hills, Hyderabad – 500034	Narasimha (Vishnu)
14	Ashtalakshmi Devalayam	Vasavi Colony, Kothapet, Hyderabad – 500035	Mata
15	Balkampet Yellamma Pochamma Temple	Balkampet, Hyderabad – 500038	Mata
16	Sri Subrahmanyaswamy Devalayam	Skandagiri Secunderabad - 500061	Subrahmanya
17	Kali Bari	Vivekanandpuram, Secunderabad – 500094	Mata

ISKCON TEMPLE - Hyderabad is the South Indian headquarters for ISKCON in India. It is magnificent Sri Sri Radha - Madana - Mohana Temple, which was inaugurated by Swami Prabhupada. Deity worship accompanied by the constant chanting of the holy names will be a special feature at the centre. Besides, there will be daily classes in Sanskrit, Bhagavad - Gita, Bhagavatam and the Upanisads. There is be a Vedic library consisting of Swami Prabhupada's books and various books on a comparative study of religion. Devotees will travel into towns and villages and do sankirtana for the uplift of the masses. Besides regular free nutritional food distribution program, ISKCON is also planning to set up a model high-yielding 600-cow dairy farm, handloom centres, nature-cure hospital, and gurukula school project.

SITARAM BAGH TEMPLE AT MANGALHAT, HYDERABAD – It was built by Seth Puranmal Ganeriwala in 1830. Its architecture style is a mixture of Rajasthani, Mughal and European. The Temple is classified as a heritage building by INTACH. The Temple has a 50-foot wall giving the Temple a fort like look. The Temple is equipped with six step wells. The Temple has a shrine dedicated to Lord Hanuman. The vigraha that you see now is a discovery even for the family members. "We had been worshipping Hanuman only till the knee," said Arvindji, "not knowing that the rest had been buried over a period of time." The major sanctum sanctorum of Lord Rama and Sita is carved through marbles and there are also shrines dedicated to Lord Shiva, Lord Hanuman, Goddess Lakshmi and Varadarajaswamy within the Temple. The smaller Garudas placed on the top.

SRI MAHANKALESHWARA TEMPLE AT MIR ALAM MANDI, HYDERABAD – It is an ancient Temple dedicated to Goddess. The deity never look the same to a devotee, as the expression of Goddess changes every minute.

SRI BHAGYALAKSHMI TEMPLE AT CHARMINAR - It is an ancient Temple located adjacent to the Charminar. The city of Bhagyanagar, viz today's Hyderabad was named after Devi (Goddess) Bhagyalakshmi. This fact has also been established by famous social historians. In the past, attempts have been made to destroy this Temple. It has been a practice in the Temple to have special decorations during festivals like Ganesh Chaturthi, Dushera and Deepavali. During the fortnight preceding Deepavali, lamps (diyas) are lit and women in large numbers come to the Temple.

SRI UJJAINI MAHAKAALI TEMPLE AT GENERAL BAZAR, SECUNDERABAD – It is a popular Temple devoted to Goddess Mahakaali. It is more than 200-years old Temple. According to legend, in the year 1813, a Military Battalion was transferred to Ujjaini. This was a time when there was Cholera outbreak and thousands of people had reportedly perished. Suriti Appaiah, who was part of the Military Battalion and his associates reportedly went to Mahankali Devasthanam at Ujjaini and offers prayers that if the people were saved from this epidemic, they would be installing the Vigraha of Mahankaali at Secunderabad. Promptly after his return from Ujjaini, Sri Suriti Appaiah and his associates went ahead and installed the Vigraha of Goddess Mahakaali which was made of wood at Secunderabad in July 1815. During the construction of sanctum sanctorum, a stone Vigraha of Manikyalamma was reportedly found and even that Vigraha was reportedly installed beside Sri Mahankaali Ammavaru. The Goddess is seen in a Padmasana posture with four hands along with a sword, spear and also a vessel of amrut, damaru in the form of a beautiful stone Vigraha. The Vigraha is covered with silver and devotees make sacrifices after fulfilment of their wishes. There are two main Goddess residing in the Garbhagudi, namely Sri Ujjaini Mahakali Mata on the right and Sri Manikyalama Mata on the left. Apart from these vigraha

there are two utsava vigraha (murtis) namely Chandi Devi Mata and Bala Devi Mata. A Shivalingam also adorns the Gabhaalayam. Right opposite to the Garbhagudi, there is another Goddess called Mathangeshwari Mata.

BIRLA MANDIR AT KHAIRTABAD – It is located towards the southern end of Hussain Sagar Lake. It is situated atop the Kala Pahad, which is a twin hillock of Naubat Pahad. The Birlas built the Hyderabad Temple in 1976 and constructed it with white marbles imported from Rajasthan. The hillock is at a height of 280-foot. The construction took almost a decade to complete and was consecrated in the same year by Swami Ranganathananda of Ramakrishna Mission. The Temple is dedicated to Lord Vishnu present in the form of Sri Venkateswara. One can find the kirtanas of Tyagaraja, Annamayya, and Ramadasu reverberating against the backdrop of a blue sky in the morning. The Temple combines the architectural styles of Utkal (Oriya) and South Indian style. The Rajagopuram represents South Indian architectural style while the tower over the main shrine also called the Jagadananda Vimanam represents the Oriyan style. The Temple also boasts of finely sculpted marbled vigrahas depicting the great epics of Ramayana and Mahabharata. The 42-foot high sanctum sanctorum (garbhagudi) is an impressive replica of Sri Venkateshwara Temple at Tirumala. The presiding deity is made of granite, 11-foot tall. Swami Venkateswara's consorts Padmavati and Andal are worshipped in the adjoining separate shrines. The Birla Mandir complex also houses a Temple dedicated to Lord Buddha along with fresco paintings describing his life. The Temple also has separate shrines for other gods such as Lord Shiva, Ganesh, Saraswati, Hanuman, Brahma, Lakshmi and Saibaba. In the evening, Birla Mandir presents a spectacular sight upon illumination.

BUDDHA VIGRAHA AT KHAIRTABAD – It is the world's tallest monolith of Lord Gautama Buddha erected on Gibraltar Rock in the middle of Hussain Sagar. Between 1983 and 1989, Sh N. T. Rama Rao served as the Chief Minister of Andhra Pradesh. During his visit to New York, he saw the Vigraha of Liberty and was inspired by the efforts to restore it. Sh Rama Rao chose to depict Lord Gautama Buddha. After a long search, he found a solid white granite rock near Raigiri, Bhongir (Nalgonda District) on a mountainside 46 KMs outside Hyderabad. In October 1985, NTR inaugurated work on structure. After five years, the Vigraha stood at 59 foot and weighed 350 tons making it the world's tallest monolithic Vigraha of Lord Buddha. A concrete platform measuring 15 foot was constructed in the middle of Hussain Sagar to aid in erecting the Vigraha. This Vigraha is located at Lumbini Park in the Hussain Sagar Island. The Vigraha was ready for erection in 1990. ABC Limited, a local company, was given the responsibility of transferring the Vigraha onto the concrete platform. Using a trailer vehicle, the Vigraha was brought to the shore of Hussain Sagar. On 10 March 1990, company workers shifted the Vigraha on top of a barge. After traveling only 100 yards (91 m), the Vigraha tripped and fell into the Lake. After a two-year salvage operation, the

Vigraha was pulled out of the lake. On 1st December 1992, the Vigraha was installed on the platform successfully. In 2006, the Dalai Lama consecrated the Vigraha after performing a ritual.

SRI SWAYAMBHU CHENNAKESAVA SWAMY TEMPLE AT KESHOGIRI - This Temple is built on the flat top of a hillock (nearly 50 to 60 feet tall) locally known as Chandrayana Gutta or Kesavagiri Gutta. The vigraha of Chennakesava Swamy at this Temple is carved on a boulder. The Temple consists of garbhagriha and antarala, connected with 28 pillared mandapa which has entrances on both the south and north sides. On the door jambs of the garbhagriha, Vaishnavite dwarapalas i.e., Jaya and Vijaya are carved. On the lintel portion of antarala, the vigrahas of Sheshasai Vishnu, Sanka, Chakra and Vaishnavite marks are carved. Based on the architectural features, the Temple is believed to have been built during 18th Century CE.

MAHABODHI BUDDHA VIHARA AT MAHINDRA HILLS - It is a Buddhist complex with meditation halls and a Temple site atop the Mahindra hills. The complex offers splendid views of the city. The hall of the Temple has a large golden Vigraha of Lord Buddha and another smaller Vigraha of Lord Buddha is placed in a mini garden outside. The Vihara was inaugurated in 2002 by the 14th Dalai Lama, Tenzin Gyatso. It was started in 1974 and aims at spreading Buddhist values and reviving the culture. On April 6, 2003, the Dalai Lama dedicated the Vigraha of Lord Buddha in a position called the Dhamma Desana Mudra. Anand Buddha Vihara is considered to be the hub of Buddhist activities that take place in the city.

RAMAKRISHNA MATH AT HYDERABAD - The Math is a branch center of Ramakrishna Math & Ramakrishna Mission, Belur, West Bengal. Prior to shifting of the Math complex to the present site in 1979, the institution was functioning on the Market Street, adjoining the Mahaboob College in Secundrabad in a much smaller building from 1973. That Math at Begumpet was built in 1922 by one Swami Yogeshwaranandaji, a disciple of Sri Ramachandra Datta who was a householder disciple of Sri Ramakrishna. The Math has a beautiful Temple dedicated to Bhagawan Sri Ramakrishna Paramahamsa. This is a universal Temple in the sense that all people, irrespective of religion, caste, creed, race, sex and nationality are welcome here. They can participate in the worship, bhajans, arati etc, or engage themselves in silent prayer or meditation. This Temple is a place where anyone who needs a favourable atmosphere to dive deep into oneself through meditation or prayer or vichara (self-enquiry). As part of the 125th Anniversary of Swami Vivekananda's Chicago Addresses, the 1st phase of the Gita Darshan pictorial Museum in the Math which has been renovated and upgraded into a Digital Museum was inaugurated by Revered Srimat Swami Gautamananda ji. The Math has set up a beautiful and permanent museum where the oil paintings of some selected Saints are displayed.

PEDDAMMA TEMPLE AT JUBILEE HILLS – It is one of the most revered Temples of Hyderabad. People consider that it has been here since 150 years. The Temple is dedicated to Ammavaru who is seen as the mother and people coming to this Temple believe that the Goddess is their saviour. The Telangana festival Bonalu is celebrated once in a year, but at this Temple, the Bonaluutsavam is celebrated every Sunday. The supreme power and the mother of all Gods and Goddesses, Maa Peddamma is the

ultimate primordial being and the demon slayer. This Devi with lush black hair, beautiful eyes and ten hands dawned on earth to establish the supremacy of goodness over evil.

LORD JAGANNATH TEMPLE AT BANJARA HILLS – It is a magnificent creation of Kalinga

Cultural Trust to provide a sacred place for worship and to arouse divine thoughts in mind and hearts of the people. More than 100 devoted workers toiled for about five years and the construction of the main Temple and Temple for Lord Ganesh, Anjaneya Swamy, Maa Vimala, Maa Laxmi, Lord Shiva and Nabagrah was completed in March 2009. The Temple replicates the Puri Jagannath Temple with Vimana/Deula (Garbhagruha), Mukhashala (Jaganmohan), Nata Mandir (dancing hall) and Bhogamandap (offering enclave). The intricate stone carvings, craftsmanship, sculptures of the Temple arouse unique aesthetic feelings in devotees. The Upa-Devalayams are equally spectacular and arouses spiritual feelings. The mythological and religious murals on the boundary wall consisting of history of construction of the Jagannath Temple at Puri, Dasha Avatar and mysteries and miracles of God and Goddesses in different form and stage are educative and enlightening. The lighting of the Temple has been artistically planned and gives a spectacular appearance at night. Lord Jagannath, Balabhadra and Subhadra adorn the sanctum sanctorum of the main Temple. Several important festivals like Mahabishuva Sankranti, Deba Snana Purnima, Ratha Jatra, Janmashtami, Ganesh Chatruthi, Vijaya Dashami, Makara Sankranti, Basanta Panchami, Sivaratri, Ramnavami etc. are celebrated with great religious fervour. The main Temple is curvilinear and crowing the top is Srichakra or Nilachakra (an eight spoke wheel of Lord Vishnu) made out of Ashtadhatu and is considered sacrosanct. The pyramidal roof of surrounding Temple rise in steps towards the tower like a ridge of mountain peak. The upa-devalayams resembles the architectural beauty of the main Temple like a mountain with ridges like steps. Some devotees find resemblance of these Temples with pagoda shape of remains of the famous Sun Temple of Konark in Odisha.

SRI LAKSHMI NARASIMHA SWAMY TEMPLE AT BANJARA HILLS -

This Temple is one of the ancient Sri Lakshmi Narasimha Swamy Temple of the city located on a hillock. The Temple's presiding deity Sri Lakshmi Narasimha Swamy is an ancient Swayam Vyakta Deity (Swayambhu) that appeared on an Udbhava Shila in a standing posture which is very rare. The deity is said to be dating back to 7th or 8th century and discovered by devotees about 400 years back. In the year 1907, Maharaja Sri Krishna Prasad Jagirdar donated land to the Presiding Deity and the Temple has come under the purview of the endowment department since 1993. The Temple was adopted by Yadagiri Gutta shrine in the year 2002. The management of this

Temple was handed over to the Hare Krishna Movement in the year 2011. The magnificent Golden Temple was, therefore, built in the last few years. Devotees have donated a unique Saligramam to this shrine. It is one of the largest Saligramas in this world and it is believed to contain the water of River Ganges. The name of this unique Shila is "Jala Garbha Narayana Saligrama Shila" which reportedly took millions of years to form in a River called Gandaki (in Nepal) and it is a unique blessing that it has arrived at this Holy Kshetram.

ASHTALAKSHMI DEVALAYAM AT KOTHAPET - This magnificent Temple is dedicated to Goddess Lakshmi. Here, Goddess Lakshmi is in her eight splendorous forms. It is also a place of architectural beauty. The Temple is a two-storey building. The deities are situated on the top-floor. The right staircase leads to the Lord Ganapathi Temple. Then we reach the Dhhwajasthambham (a tall holy pillar) and the Vigraha of Garuda. According to the Vaishnava tradition, it is customary that devotees have a darshan of either God Hanuman or God Garuda before having the darshan of the main deities in the sanctum sanctorum (Garbhagudi). At the sanctum sanctorum, we have the darshan of Lord Narayana with his consort Sri Adhilakshmi. Lord Narayana is seen having 4 hands. He holds the sacred conch (Shankha) and the sacred disk (Chakra) in two hands. He uses the other two hands to bless his devotees - one hand shows the Abhaya Mudhra (security) and the other shows the Varadha Mudhra (protection). His consort Sri Adhilakshmi is seen beautifully clad in silk clothes decorated with jewels and garlands. Lord Srimannarayana (Narayana) and Sri Adhilakshmi are surrounded by the other 7 forms of Sri Lakshmi. The 8 forms of Lakshmi are: Sri Adhilakshmi, Sri Santhanalakshmi, Sri Gajalakshmi, Sri Dhhanalakshmi, Sri Dhhanyalakshmi, Sri Vijayalakshmi, Sri Aishwaryalakshmi and Sri Varalakshmi. The holy feet of the deities can remove all our difficulties. Their holy hands grace us for our wealth and prosperity. Their faces are seen illumining with divine consciousness. The wish to have children for barren women (women without children) will be fulfilled if they take the Garuda Prasaadham during the Brahmotsavas. The deities grace the devotees with all kinds of prosperity such as knowledge, fame, wealth, happiness, courage etc. and also help them to overcome difficulties. The priests worship Lord Ganapathi according to the Smaartha system and Ashtalakshmi and Lord Narayana in the Vaishnava system. Every day in the morning, the cow is worshipped. The cow is considered sacred because all the deities reside in the different parts of the cow. This cow is a descendent of the Kamadhenu (the sacred cow in Heaven). The Temple is a marble structure and it illumines gloriously in the moon - light of the full-moon night. In the spacious compound of the Temple, there is a flower garden with a water pond.

BALKAMPET YELLAMMA POCHAMMA TEMPLE – It is one of the old and among the most revered Temples of Hyderabad. The Temple is thronged by heavy crowd on Sundays and Tuesdays and is quite famous for the annual Bonalu Jathara festivity that takes place in Hyderabad. This Temple is dedicated to Goddess Yellamma that literally means 'mother of the universe'. There is also an alternative name called Jagadamba who is considered the same as Goddess Renuka. According to a legend, Renuka, the daughter of Raja Renuka had married Jamadagni, the son of Satyawati and had five sons, one of them being Parashurama. One day, Renuka couldn't perform one of her regular household chores and this enraged her husband who then asked her to leave the house. Dejected Renuka was reportedly suggested by Saints to perform pujas near a Shivalinga and feed Brahmins for her penance. Jamadagni was reportedly furious at her and demanded his sons as well to punish their mother Renuka. Others refused and they were burnt to ashes by the father's gaze while Parashurama searched for his mother who was hiding in a village, beheaded her and even the poor woman who helped her.

Jamadagni who was pleased by his son's obedience, gave him a boon and in turn Parashurama asked his father to restore the lives of his brothers, his mother and the village woman. However, during the process, the head of Renuka was restored on the other woman's head and vice versa. While Jamadagni accepted the woman who had Renuka's body, the other form came to be popularly known as Yellamma, which means mother to all and is being devoutly worshipped from then by the people of Telangana people. Balkampet Yellamma Goddess is also considered as an incarnation of Goddess Kali. Devotees offer animal sacrifice here. The most important event here is the celestial marriage ceremony of the Temple Goddess, Yellamma Kalyanotsavam. Bonalu Jathara Festival at Balkampet Yellamma Temple falls in the calendar only after Golconda Bonalu Jathara followed by Ujjaini Mahankali Bonalu Jathara each year. The Temple was first constructed in 15th century and later renovated in the early 20th century. The Vigraha of the Goddess here is seen 10 foot lower than the ground level and the devotees believe that the water in the well here can cure all ailments. The holy water is treated as Theertham. The Temple also has Akhand Jyothi, which was lit during the renovation.

SRI SUBRAHMANYASWAMY DEVALAYAM AT SKANDAGIRI - The Temple is dedicated to Subrahamanya Swamy. In 1968, the shankusthapanam for Sri Sundara Vinayagar & Sri Subrahmanyaswamy Temples was done by Pujya Sri HH Mahaswamigal Jagadguru Sri Sri Sri Chandrasekarendra Saraswathi Swamigal. The Sundara Vinayagar Temple was completed and the Maha Kumbhabhishekam was done by HH on 26/08/1968. The Mahakumbhabhishekam of Sri Subrahmanyaswamy Temple was performed as ordained by HH, on 22/01/1970 - Thai Poosam day. Later, Sri Kamakshi Amman, Sri Ekambareshwarar & Navagraha sannidhis were constructed. There was Sri Jaya Durga vigraha also installed in the Temple. Virgaham of Sri Varadarajaswamy with Sridevi & Sri Bhudevi have also been consecrated. The Mahakumbhabhishekam of Rajagopuram built in Chola style & in line with the Brihadeeswara Temple at Tanjavur, the Aarupadaiveedu (the six holy shrines of Sri Subrahmanyaswamy viz. Thiruparankundram, Thiruchendur, Palani, Swamimalai, Thiruthani and Palamudhircholai – depicted at the front elevation and the installation of the Dwajasthambam was performed on 22/06/1989. A sannidhi for Sri Sivakami sameda Sri Nataraja and the vigrahas of Sri Lakshmi, Sri Saraswathi, Sri Bhairavar and Sri Idumbhar were also consecrated later. Sri Shanmugar with his consorts Sri Valli and Sri Devasena made in panchaloha, was consecrated in the year 2002. The Brahmotsavam of the Temple is being performed during the month of Vaikasi (May-June) every year on a large scale. The Temple celebrates many other important festivals throughout the year.

Sri Kanchi Kamakoti Sankar Mandir & Hanuman Mandir - The Temples are dedicated to Lord Hanuman & Adi Sankaracharya & were established more than 20 years ago. Lord Hanuman's imposing Vigraha is a unique one of its kind in the twin cities. In addition to everyday puja, Visesha Abhishekam and Archana are offered to the Lord on Tuesdays and Fridays. In addition to the Adi Sankar and Hanuman Temples, shrines for Sri Ganesha, Guru Paduka and Naga Devatas are also present in the Temple. Various religious festivals are observed & festivals like Navaratri, Hanuman Jayanthi, Sankara Jayanthi & Jayanthis of Pujyasri Acharya Swamijis of Sri Kanchi Kamakoti Peetam are celebrated in a grand manner. Distribution of Prasadam & annadaanam is performed on various occasions.

KALIBARI AT SAINIKPURI, SECUNDERABAD - In the year 1972, quite a few Bengali settlers, who were mostly from Army/Railways, had decided to set up a Temple of Goddess Kali in Vivekanandapuram. Foundation Stone was laid by Late Swamy Ranganathananda, the then president of Ramakrishna Mission, Hyderabad on 11th August 1974. In the year 1976, premises of Kalibari has been inaugurated and the Vigraha of Maa Kali has been installed by Tantrik Gostha Bihari Bhattachrya of Chunagali Kali Temple of Kolkata. The Lord Shiva Temple was founded on 22nd May 1997. There is also a Lord Ganesh Temple in premises. The vigraha of Dasha Mahavidya has been installed around the Temple of Maa Kali.

Sri Ranganatha Swamy Temple at Jiyaguda - The Temple is a 400 year old Vaishnavite Temple dedicated to Lord Ranganatha, a form of Lord Vishnu. Situated on the banks of the Musi River, the Temple was built by the Nanganur Prathama Peetham. It initially followed the Thenkalai tradition, but later adopted the more specific Vanamamalai sampradayam. Vaikuntha Ekadashi is the major festival celebrated here, attracting lakhs of devotees every year.

DISTRICT – JAGTIAL (Railway Station - Lingampet Jagit)

S. No.	Temple	Address	Type
1	River Godavari	Dharmapuri - 505425	River
2	Sri Anjaneya Swami Vari Devasthanam	Kondagattu, Muthyampet - 505452	Hanuman
3	Bugulu Sri Venkateswara Swamy Temple	Chilpur - 506145	Vishnu
4	Sri Siddeswara Swami Temple	Kodavathur - 506221	Shiva

DHARMAPURI - The place is situated on the banks of River Godavari. This River flows west to east except in Dharmapuri where it flows north to south, hence, the River is termed as Dakshina Vahini (South Flowing).

SRI ANJANEYA SWAMI VARI DEVASTHANAM AT KONDAGATTU – It is situated on the hill. It is an ancient Temple stated to have been coming in to existence at about 500 years ago. The presiding deity, Sri Anjaneya Swamyvaru is said to be Swayambhu as seen from the Silasasana which is available on the external wall of the main Temple. Sri Venkateswara Swamy, Alwar and Laxmi Ammavaru deities are situated at the left and right of main deity. Sri Anjneya Swamy faced to the north side of the Temple along with Narasimha Vaktram Amburilla and Shankhu Chakra. The presiding deity Sri Anjaneya is believed as 'Sanjeeva' for the diseased, mentally retarded and for childless for progeny. Lord Shiva incarnated as Sri Anjaneya. Here pilgrims perform Abhishekam to fulfil their vows and worship Kondagattu

Anjaneya and Sri Anjaneya Swamy. The pilgrim visiting this Temple must invariably take Chandanam as Prasadam.

HANUMAN VIGRAHA AT KONDAGATTU – There is a Vigraha of Sri Anjaneya Swami of 56 foot height installed in 2003. It is five faces Vigraha having ten hands standing on a lotus pedestal.

BUGULU SRI VENKATESWARA SWAMY TEMPLE AT CHILPUR GUTTA - The Temple is dedicated to Lord Venkateswara (Vishnu). This is the parihara Temple for loans, debts, enemy problems, sorrow, worries, fear. The Temple is situated on a rocky mountain called Chilpur Gutta. It has been the preferred place of Lord Venkateshwara Swamy himself when he was feeling burdened under the weight of the wedding loan he had taken from Kubera, the God of Wealth. Legend has it that Lord descended upon this little pleasant elevation, washed his feet in the cold water and rested here till he gathered enough courage to face the world and work out an action plan to clear his debt. The Temple has been popular as a place to seek refuge when burdened with debts and enemy threats. Bugulu means fear and nervousness in Telugu language. Devotees affirm they have got freedom from the credit card bills, housing loan payments, personal loans and EMI circles and even enemy threats after visiting the Temple.

SRI SIDDESWARA SWAMI TEMPLE AT KODAVATHUR - The Temple is dedicated to Lord Shiva. The Temple is located in the rocky hills. The Temple is ancient and famous. There are various pillars in the Temple. There is also a Banyan Tree and a Pond. There is a deep cave in the Temple complex.

DISTRICT – JANGAON (Railway Station – Jangaon)

S. No.	Temple	Address	Type
1	Someshwara Temple	Palakurthi - 506146	Shiva
2	Sri Ramachandra Swamy Devasthanam	Jeedikal - 506201	Rama
3	Bammera Pothana	Bommera - 506252	Saint Pothana

PALAKURTHI - It is said that the Rishis practiced penance here about 1200 and 1300 years ago. Another story is that Lord Someshwara was revealed here on the wish of the Sapt Sages. The cave can also be visited by devotees. At the bottom of the hill is the tomb of famous poet ruler Someshwar. This is his birthplace. His poems are titled Dashama Purana and the history of scholars. Somesvara poet's parents named the Swami after the birth of his son. The poet's life span dates to

1160 – 1240 AD. This great poet also worshiped the Someshwar. It means that from the very beginning, Someshwaraswamy was worshiping the devotees here.

SRI RAMACHANDRA SWAMY DEVASTHANAM AT JEEDIKAL - It is a famous Lord Sri Rama Temple. According to a local lore, the Temple's existence dates back to 'Tretayuga' as it was here that Lord Rama, while in exile, is said to have shot demon Maricha with an arrow, who comes in the guise of a golden deer. When Maricha asks for Lord Rama's forgiveness and promises to worship him, the latter agrees to emerge as 'Swayambhu' on the hillock here in this Temple. Lord Sri Rama's Paduka's or the spot at which the golden deer met its death, locally famous as "Lady Banda", every edifice, be it made of a stone or mud or the pond that's inside the natural stone rock, throws evidence of Lord Sri Rama visiting this place on his chase for the golden deer. In the chase for the golden deer by the Lord, the Lord shoots an arrow at it, hurting and making it fall on a rock. The deer after falling down transforms itself into a human form which makes the Lord furious and upon his explanation understands that his name was Chitraradha and was cursed by Koushika Maharashi and got liberated by Lord's arrow and praises the Lord for his kindness. Lord Sri Rama delighted by this asks Chitraradha if he had any wish. Chitraradha asks for the water that has touched the Lord's holy feet. Lord Sri Rama there upon presses a small rock nearby with his thumb and pray the Goddess Ganga to flow through it, making it famous as "Uttar Ganga". Even today, upon clearing the dust from the hole, one can experience the fingers getting wet. Also it is observed by the local people that the colour of the rice changed to yellow at the Temple premises exactly at the time when the priests at Bhadrachalam were preparing "Thalambralu" for Lord Sri Rama and Mata Sita's wedding. God also blesses a Sage nearby, who was in great penance by keeping Lords Vigraha in front of him and asks him to wish something. The "Veera = great" Sage asks for an opportunity to perform "Pada Seva" (Padaseva - offering prayers to ones feet) until his life on earth. Lord Sri Rama happy with his devotion grants him that wish by entrusting life into the Vigraha what he has made and leaves behind his foot wear at this place and tells him that this place will be famous as Veerachalam. Even today if you step at this place, one will notice a pond that's with in a rock and Lord Sri Rama's Paduka under worship. Even though the water is being used at the Temple premises, the water level neither has gone down nor risen up, in the history so far. The Temple is built on a pond that never goes dry even during peak summer.

BAMMERA POTHANA – He was a Telugu and Sanskrit Poet & Scholar, who is best known for his translation of the Bhagavata Purana from Sanskrit to Telugu. His work, Andhra Maha Bhagavatamu, is popularly called as Pothana Bhagavatam in Telugu. Pothana was born into a Niyogi Brahmin family at Bammera Village in 1450 AD. His father was Kesana and his mother Lakkamamba. He was considered to be a 'Sahaja Kavi' (natural poet), needing no teacher. He was known to be very polite and was an agriculturist by occupation. Though he was a great scholar, he never hesitated to work in the agricultural fields. At a very early age, Bhogini Dhandakam, a poem written by him in the praise of King Sri Singa

Bhoopala's concubine Bhogini. This was his first poetic venture which had the seeds of his great poetic talents. Bhogini Dhandakam is the earliest available Dhandaka (rhapsody which uses the same gana or foot all through) in Telugu. His second work was Virabhadhra Vijayamu which describes the adventures of Lord Virabhadhra, element of Lord Shiva. The main theme was the destruction of 'Daksha Yagna' performed in the absence of Lord Shiva by Daksha Prajapathi. The great Poet was died in 1510 AD.

DISTRICT – JAYASHANKAR BHUPALPALLY (Railway Station - Ramagundam/Warangal)

S. No.	Temple	Address	Type
1	Sri Kaleshwara Muktheeshwara Swamy Devasthanam	Kaleshwaram Village, Mahadevpur Mandal – 505504	Shiva
2	Nainpaka Temple	Warangal – 506168	Narasimha (Vishnu)
3	Ghanpur Group of Temples	Ghanpur – 506345	Shiva

SRI KALESHWARA MUKTHEESHWARA SWAMY DEVASTHANAM AT KALESHWARAM - This is a revered Temple and dedicated to Lord Shiva. The most iconic aspect in this ancient Temple is the presence of two Lingams holding on to a single pedestal or the Panavattam. The Temple gets its name Kaleshwara Mukteswara Swamy Mandiram because of the duel presence of Lord Shiva or the Mukteshwara and the other is the Lord Yama or Kaleshwar. It is also believed that the Kaleshwara Mukteswara Swamy Temple is one of the three Temples of Lord Shiva of Trilinga Desham. All the three Temples are considered as Jyotirlingas that ornament the three corners of Telugu Land. The Temple boasts of several unique features, one of which is the hole in the Mukteshwara Linga which can never be filled with water. The reason behind it is still a wonder. Many researchers have failed to provide any explanation for this. Another special attraction of this Temple is the interesting sculpture of the fish Vigraha. This place is also called Dakshina Triveni Sangamam, as two Rivers meet here along with a third, the illusionary flow of Antarvaahini. It is said that long time back, one of the Vaishyas had performed an abhisheka to Kaleshwara Mukteswara with hundreds of milk pots and the milk evolved at the sangamam of River Godavari and Pranahita. Hence, the name Dakshina Gangotri (the other being Allahabad or Prayaga).

NAINPAKA TEMPLE AT WARANGAL - It is believed to have built in the 15th or 16th century on a pink stone rock, which is unique in style and touted as the one and only in southern India. This lesser-known rock-cut Temple, a prototype of Sarvatobhadra architecture, has four deities carved out on a protruded boulder, is a revelation of sorts. Inside the sanctum sanctorum, the carvings of Yoga Narasimha Swamy, Kaleeya Venugopala Swamy, Sri Rama and Balarama, one on each side of east, south, north and west respectively, on a boulder that is a part of the pink stone bedrock on which Temple is located is a visual fiesta. The shrine, which has four functional entrances on cardinal directions could be accessed from all sides. The vimana (upper part) of the ornately sculpted 50-foot gopuram (tower) was made of bricks while the Adhishtana (base) was constructed with the pink stones sliced from the bedrock. Local lore has it that once upon a time Bakasura ruled the land. He protected his subjects but killed those outside his kingdom. While he came to be known as a demon, his subjects considered him their god and as a tribute, this Temple was built. The structure reflects excellent sculpture. The whole of sanctum sanctorum was carved out of single huge boulder. The 'shikhara' was built with bricks.

GHANPUR TEMPLES - Being locally termed as "Kota Gullu", the Ghanpur Temples were

established by King Ganapathi Deva during Kakatiya reign. Portraying these amazing architectural skills, Ghanpur Temples are a group of beautiful Temples. It was built in the late 12th and early 13th century and reflects a great deal of culture from that era. The Ghanpur group of Temples comprise of more than 20 Temples. All of them vary in size as well as design. All of these Temples were enclosed by a two layered brick walls. A museum which exhibits the art and architecture of the Kakatiya dynasty was contained by the Temple. The main Temple is dedicated to Lord Shiva. Tourists can come across many mythical sculptures in these Temples like half human half lion riding on the elephant, Gaja-Kesari, Horse head lion back elephants in the porticos of the Temple. The sight of ancient Temples beneath the towering and lofty palms entices you. The other inscription slab refers to certain Ganapathi Reddy, who installed Lord Ganapeswara and donated land.

DISTRICT – JOGULAMBA GADWAL (Railway Station – Gadwal)

S. No.	Temple	Address	Type
1	Beechupally Hanuman Temple	NH-44, Beechupally – 509125	Hanuman
2	Lord Sri Venkateswara Swamy Temple	Korakondaiah Hill, Revulapalli Village – 509125	Venkateswara (Vishnu)
3	Shiva Temple	Poodur - 509133	Shiva
4	Sri Jogulamba Devi Temple, Navabrahma Temple & Sangameshwara Swamy Devasthanam	Alampur – 509152	Shakti Peetha

BEECHUPALLY HANUMAN TEMPLE - Beechupally is one of the famous shrines of Lord Hanuman (Anjaneya Swamy). It is located on the banks of Krishna River. The shores of Krishna River at this location are noted for carrying out obsequies to the departed souls as per the Hindu custom. Initially, the shrine consisted a Lord Hanuman Temple about 200 meters away from the River and a Shivalingam Temple near the River. During the rainy season, the water flow becomes high enough to touch the Shivalingam

Temple. A Temple for Lord Rama was also built in the area in 1992. For the convenience of devotees, several ghats were built for Pushkara Snanam, a sacred bath that takes place every 12 years.

LORD SRI VENKATESWARA SWAMY TEMPLE AT KORAKONDAIAH HILL – The Lord is also known as Korakondaiah Swamy. Sri Seshadasula Swamy find Lord Sri Venkateswara Swamy lying on the Korakondaiah Hill through his power and told about Lord Sri Venkateswara Swamy to Sri Timmaiah, who was a Patwari of Revulapalli Village and ordered to perform special pujas on every Karthika Pournima (during November), Pallaki Sevas and 'Jathara (Brahmotsavam)' on the Padyami Day. The Temple is one of the oldest Temples in that area and is surrounded by many villages. According to tradition, a devotee who used to visit Tirupati every year could not do so due to economic conditions, ill-health, far distance etc. visits this Temple and perform their pujas, tonsure ceremonies and other functions. The unique feature of this Vigraha is that the Lord Sri Venkateswara is between two hillocks.

SHIVA TEMPLE AT POODUR - There are inscriptions of 11th century CE in the Temple. The Temple has Garbhagriha connected to Mandapa with entrance porch with steps on south and north. There is a seated Nandi facing Garbhagriha. The shikhara of the Temple has a shukanasi surmounted with stupika. There are two Temples here, one before the main Temple and another Temple is on the northern side. There are other sculptures and inscriptions near the Temple.

MAHASHAKTIPEETHAM - SRI JOGULAMBA DEVI TEMPLE, NAVABRAHMA TEMPLE & SANGAMESHWARA SWAMY DEVASTHANAM AT ALAMPUR – It is situated on the banks of Tungabhadra River and is considered as the western gateway of Srisailam. Here, the marvellous Temple and remains of some ancient Temple signify Badami Chalukyan architecture. The principal deities at the Temple are Goddess Jogulamba and Balabrahmeshwara. Goddess Jogulamba is considered as 5th Shakti Peetha among 18 Shakti Peethams in the country. It is believed that "Upper jaw with tooth" Oordhvadanta Pankti of Devi fell here. Here, Goddess Jogulamba is seen seated on the corpse with scorpion, frog and lizard on the head. She is seen in a naked avtar with her tongue stretched outside, an avtar of fierce goddess that grants Siddhi in Yoga and hence called Jogulamba. This word is a changed form of Yogula Amma in Telugu which means Mother of Yogis. As per the local people, Alampur Sri Jogulamba Devi is in Ugra Rupa (highly powerful and onerous to worship) and therefore the water pool nearby makes the cool atmosphere. vigraha of Saptamatrikas, Vighneswara and Veenapani Veerabhadra vigraha are also installed in the Temple. According to a popular legend, there was a great Saint in 6thcentury called Rasa Siddha who had the power to convert base metal into gold and he was considered close to Chalukya King Pulakesi-II, instrumental in constructing many Temples called 'Nava Brahmas'. According to the legend, the nine names of Lord Shiva are actually the names of medicinal herbs put forth by Rasa Siddha and there are nine Temples here. They are the Swarga Brahma Temple, Padma Brahma Temple, Vishva Brahma Temple Arka Brahma Temple, Bala Brahma Temple, Garuda Brahma Temple and Taraka Brahma Temple. The Siddha Rasarnavam is a tantric work, which states that if upasana is performed as per the prescribed Tantra, then Mercury oozes from the Linga of Bala Brahma, Thighs of Subramanya, Navel of Ganapati and Mouth of Mother Jogulamba, which can be converted into Gold by using the medicinal herbs. The popular Temple stands as a testimony to Chalukya Art and Culture. The Tungabhadra and Krishna Rivers are seen in a confluence near

Alampur and hence it is also known as Dakshina Kailasam. It is also said that Lord Brahma had performed a great penance here for thousands of years and he pleased Lord Shiva who conferred the powers of creation for him. Hence, the deity is also called Brahmeswara and the Goddess as Yogini or Jogulamba, a synonym for Mother Parvathi. On entering into the Temple, we see Nandeeswara Vigraha in the hall. In the prakara, Veerabhadra Swamy, Navadurgas, Navagrahas, Trimoorthy Gods (Dakshinamoorthy, Yoganarasimha Swamy and Brahma), Kumaraswamy, Kalabhairava, Vighneswara are present. In pradakshinamarg, Parvathi Mata, Yoga Narasimha Swamy, Ugra Narasimha Swamy, Siddhas are present. In the Garbhagriha, Lord Shiva Bala Brahmeswara Swamy is present. The Shivalinga has an irregular shape and Panapatta is slightly slanted towards left. The Temple has extraordinary sculptures. Several Shivalingas are also present in the campus of the Temple.

SANGAMESHWARA SWAMY DEVASTHANAM – The Lord of the confluence, the Sangameshwara Devasthanam is located at a short distance from the Papanasi group of Temples. You can see this Temple on the way to the Papanasi (Papavinasanam) Temples.

DISTRICT – KAMAREDDY (Railway Station – Bodhan/Kamareddi)

S. No.	Temple	Address	Type
1	Sri Sidhi Rameshwara Swami Temple	Bhiknoor Mandal - 503101	Shiva
2	Santana Venugopal Swamy Temple	Chinnur, Nagireddypet – 503108	Vishnu
3	Trilinga Rameshwara Temple	Tandur, Nagireddypet – 503108	Rama
4	Sri Lakshmi Narasimha Swamy Temple	Chukkapur - 503111	Narasimha
5	Sri Bugga Rama Lingeswara Temple	Maddikunta Village, Machareddy – 503112	Rama
6	Sri Raja Rajeshwara Swamy Temple	Machareddy – 503112	Shiva
7	Sree Kalabhairava Swamy Temple	Issannapalle - 503144	Bhairav
8	Sri Sai Baba Temple	Kamshetpalle - 503301	Sai Baba
9	Somalingeswara Temple	Durki – 503301	Shiva
10	Kowlas Yellamma Temple	Kolas, Jukkal – 503305	Mata
11	The Ayyappa Swamy Temple	Bichkunda – 503306	Ayyappa
12	Mirzapur Hanuman Temple	Shahapur - 503309	Hanuman
13	Lord Venkateshwara Temple	Timmapur - 503321	Venkatesh

SRI SIDDIRAMESWARA SWAMY TEMPLE AT BHIKNOOR MANDAL – It is very old Temple & famous for its reverse position of the Shivalinga in garbhalaya. This Temple is one of the rare Temples of Lord Shiva in South India. Devotees believe that Lord Siddheswara Swamy is the most powerful deity here. There is a Well near the Temple and water is available throughout the year. A big bell is present in the Temple and attracts every visitor. The Temple has a beautiful Mukhamandapa with well-sculptured pillars. There is also a Rajagopuram at the entrance of the Temple with 7 kalasas. At the same time, the construction structure of Temple has good architectural values. Mahashivaratri festival is celebrated as the most important festival.

SANTANA VENUGOPAL SWAMY TEMPLE AT CHINNUR, NAGIREDDYPET - 700 years ago in the dream of King Gary, who ruled the region during the reign of the Nizam Kings, a man in the form of Bhagwat appeared in the pool at the end of the village in the form of an vigraha of Venugopal Swami and told him to find it and build a Temple. Next day, the King ordered his army to visit the pool and search there. After much effort, they found a beautiful two and a half foot Venu Gopala Swami vigraha with Rukmini and Satyabhama. According to local belief, the vigrahas of Sri Sudarshan Perumal and Srimannarayana were found along with the vigrahas of the Swami and the King built a magnificent Temple and erected the vigrahas of Swami, along with the vigrahas of Nammalwar and Bhagwad Ramanuja. According to the Agama Shastras, the worship of the Swami and the activities on the special festivals are very beautiful and a festival of the eyes. Devotees have always believed that whoever worships the Swami in this Temple will give them good offspring. Swami's marriage takes place in the glory of the genitals. Devotees believes that the wishes of those who participate in Swami's marriage ceremony will be fulfilled.

TRILINGA RAMESHWARA TEMPLE AT TANDUR, NAGIREDDYPET - The Temple is dedicated to Lord Shiva. It is believed that Lord Rama has installed this Shivalingam and the Lord Shiva is known as Bheemeshwara Swamy. The Temple is white in colour. There is another old Mandapa, which is of its own architectural importance. On the entrance of the Temple, one can find the vigrahas of two females of the Kakatiya times besides that one can find the designs in green colour. This Temple is constructed only with stone and no cement or mud is used for the construction of this Temple. It is said that Chalukyas have constructed this Temple and later on Kakatiyas have completed the construction of this Temple. From whichever side you see, one can see that this Temple looks like a Shivalinga itself. As per architectural beauty of this Temple, it is believed that this Temple belongs to 11th century. The 3 Lingas are called Rama, Bheema and Soma, which are installed here by Lord Rama, Lakshmana and Seetha Mata. One can find the vigraha of Nandi in front of this Temple, architecture of which is extraordinary. The Nandi when touched gives you feeling of touching a real Nandi. The sunlight falls directly on this Shivalinga in the morning. On opposite of this Temple, there is a Hill called Veeranna Gutta and it is believed that from this Temple, there is a pathway to reach that Hill. There are vigrahas of Lord Shiva and Goddess Parvathy made with black stone inside the Temple. The special Poojas performed in this Temple is Laksha Bilwarchana and there are special Poojas which are conducted on Mahashivaratri and Karthika Purnima.

SRI LAKSHMI NARASIMHA SWAMY TEMPLE AT CHUKKAPUR VILLAGE - During the Chola dynasty, the Temple was built around 400 years ago. Every year, Narasimha Swamy Kalyanothsavam in Vaishaka month is celebrated.

SRI BUGGA RAMA LINGESWARA TEMPLE AT MADDIKUNTA VILLAGE, MACHAREDDY - The Temple is located in the forest area. The Temple is dedicated to Lord Shiva.

SRI RAJA RAJESHWARA SWAMY TEMPLE AT MACHAREDDY - The Temple is also known as Sri Mallikarjuna Swamy Temple and Banda Rameshwara Swamy Temple. The main presiding deity here is also fondly called as Sri Raja Rajeshwara Swayambhu Kshetram. This is a very ancient Temple. The Temple was built during the Kakatiya period on the orders of King Rajeshwara, a devotee of Lord Shiva. The Temple and pillars are carved on the large rock. The Temple is thronged by thousands of devotees during festivals especially Shivaratri and other auspicious occasions.

SREE KALABHAIRAVA SWAMY TEMPLE AT ISANNAPALLY VILLAGE – As per local belief, this is the only Kalabhairava Swamy Temple situated in South India after the Kashi-kshetra. Sri Kalabhairava Swamy Jayanthi is grandly celebrated here on Karthika Bahulashtami and huge crowd of devotees visit here from all over Telangana State on this occasion.

SRI SAI BABA TEMPLE AT NEMLI VILLAGE – The Temple is also known as "Mini Shirdi". The Temple was built by Shri Mohan Reddy Patalolla from New Jersey (USA) and surprisingly, within few months, the Temple has become major tourist place for Northern Telengana and also border districts of Maharashtra. Thousands of tourists & devotees visiting Temple every day. In this Temple, a 23 foot Sai Baba's cooking Vigraha has been installed. Temple is surrounded by beautiful and attractive garden, peaceful nature and mesmerizing statues of Sai baba.

SOMALINGESWARA TEMPLE AT DURKI - Durvasa Maharshi, one of the Sapta Rishis, lived in the village of Durki and practiced penance. That is why it is said that this town was also named Durki after Sage Durvasu. Somalingeswara Temple is located on the outskirts of Durki village. Historians date the Temple to the time of the Kalyani Chanukyas. During the Kakatiya period, the region of Banswada, Kotagiri and Varni was ruled by a King named Somnath. As the King had no son, Lord Shiva appeared while performing penance at the present Temple site & gave birth to a child. History has it that the King named his sons Someshwars after him. It is believed that the Temple was built by Someshwar-III. The Temple is built entirely of stone. The entrances to Temples are usually on the east side but the entrance to the Temple is on the west side. Locals say that the main Shivalingam in the Temple was about the size of a fist 50 years ago and is growing day-by-day. The Temple also has vigrahas of Goddess Parvati and Lord Ganesha. In addition to the Ashtamukhi Lingam, there are several other Lingams in different shapes in the Temple premises. Shivaratri celebrations are held in this Temple every year. The festival attracts thousands of devotees not only from the district but also from neighbouring districts as well as other states like Maharashtra, Karnataka etc. The Temple is filled with devotees on the Monday In the months of Karthika & Magha.

KOWLAS YELLAMMA Temple AT KOLAS, JUKKAL - It is very old and famous historical Temple. Devotees not only from the district but also from neighbouring districts as well as other states like Maharashtra, Karnataka etc. visit here to seek the blessings of the Goddess. The Temple is filled with devotees on Sunday, Tuesday and Friday. Devotees have always believed that whoever worships the Goddess in this Temple will give them good offspring.

THE AYYAPPA SWAMY TEMPLE AT BICHKUNDA - It is one of the largest pilgrimage Temple in the District with many devotees visiting every day. The Temple is dedicated to Lord Ayyappan also known as Dharma Shasta, who according to belief is the son of Lord Shiva and Goddess Mohini, the feminine incarnation of Lord Vishnu.

MIRZAPUR HANUMAN TEMPLE AT MADNOOR MANDAL – It is a famous Temple and devotees come here from Maharashtra, Karnataka and Telangana. On the occasion of Hanuman Jayanthi, a Jathara will be conducted for 3 days.

TIRUMALA VENKATESWARA SWAMY TEMPLE AT TIMMAPUR – It is popularly known as Telangana Tirumala. The Venkateswara Swamy Vigraha was installed at the Temple 74 years ago. During the past decade, the Temple has seen a rise in its popularity.

DISTRICT – KARIMNAGAR (Railway Station – Ramagundam)

S. No.	Temple	Address	Type
1	Gauthameswara Temple	Manthani – 505184	Shiva
2	Jain Temple	Kurikyal - 505445	Jain

MANTHANI GAUTHAMESWARA TEMPLE - It is located in the heritage place of Manthani and it is known for its great historical, archaeological and religious evidence. This Temple is dedicated to Lord Shiva and some parts of Jain and Buddhist cultures are also located within this segment. The main deity over here is Gautameswar. The Kakatiya kings renovated this old Temple during their reign and its sculpture. The Manthani Temple has Godavari River in its surroundings and to its north, there is Bokkala Vaagu. This place is considered to be the oldest example of Vedic learning with a growing knowledge platform for the vacationers. The old people here say that "Manthani" refers to a pot of buttermilk. Just like butter-milk gets churned into a pot so were the Vedic Mantras that used to churn in this village. According to an inscription of Sri Jagadguru Shankaracharya at Dwarakapeetam and Pushpagiri Peetam, Adi Shankara had visited Mantrakootam, now known as Manthani, during early sixth century and praised the Vedic customs and Vedic literacy of the people of this place. The other Temples in Manthani are Laxmi Narayana Swamy Temple, Saileshwara Temple, Mahalaxmi Temple, Vinayaka Temple, Dattatreya Temple, Ramalayam Temple, Saraswati Temple, Omkeshwara Temple and Panchayatanam Temple. The festival of Shivaratri is celebrated with zeal and enthusiasm and people from different places gather here in large numbers to seek 'darshan' of their Lord. The devotees consider this as a sacred place. There is a huge Shivalingam which is formed of black stone used in the 'Garbhagudi' i.e. sanctum sanctorum on an amazingly carved 'Panawatika', a pedestal or platform on which there is fixation of phallic emblem as per 'Somasutra'. There is a small room located in between the room for entrance and Garbhagudi where the Vigraha of Lord Vigneswara was kept in the right corner. One can see a huge 'Nandi' Vigraha placed in the entrance room. People coming to this Temple also visit the three Teerthams found adjoining to this place which are referred to as 'Brahmateertha', 'Vishnuteertha' and 'Rudrateertha' are regarded as holy places to take a dip in the Godavari River.

JAIN TEMPLE AT KURIKYAL - It is also known as Bommalagutta. An excellent vigraha of Chakresvari (Jain Sasanadevi in seated posture with eight hands) is flanked by lady attendants along with Jain Tirthankaras on either side in Kayotsraga pose, which is carved here. Above the vigraha of Chakresvari, Adyanta Tirthankaras i.e. Vrishabha and Vardhamana are carved. An inscription of Arekesari-II (930-955 CE) of Chalukyas of Vemulawada is inscribed below the vigraha of Chakresvari, which gives valuable information regarding the genealogy and the origin of Pampa, the great Kannada poet and author of Vikramarjunavijaya and Adipurana. This inscription is in three languages i.e., Sanskrit, Kannada and Telugu. The last three verses are in Telugu Kanda metre, which is the earliest of its kind in the Telugu language. Since the Bommalu (figures) are carved on this hillock, this hillock has got the name "Bommalagutta".

DISTRICT – KHAMMAM (Railway Station – Khammam)

S. No.	Temple	Address	Type
1	Shivalayam	Kusumanchi – 507159	Shiva
2	Sri Bhakta Ramadasu Smaraka Mandiram	Nelakondapalli - 507160	Saint Ramadasu
3	Venkateswara Swamy Temple	Jamalapuram - 507201	Venkatesh (Vishnu)
4	Venu Gopala Swami Temple	Kallur – 507209	Vishnu

KUSUMANCHI – It is home to Sri Ganapeshwaralayam and Mukkanteswaralayam, the two Lord Shiva Temples built by the Kakatiya rulers during 12th and 13th centuries. These Temples stand as testimony to the architectural skills of the Kakatiya Kings. The Shivalingam in the Temple is three meters high with a radius of two meters and it is one of the biggest Shivalingas in the state. Built on an elevated platform facing east, the Temple consists of pillared rangamandapa and antarala followed by the sanctum. With entrances on three sides, the Temple is a beautiful structure. There is a 15 ft high Vigraha of Lord Venu Gopala on the southern side of the Temple. Mukkanteswaralayam is located a few meters away from Ganapeswaralayam. It is a trikutalaya with three shrines having common mandapa. Each shrine has a portico, garbhagruha and antarala with a common 16-pillared mandapa. The pillars in the common mandapa are wonderfully carved with vigrahas of swans and floral designs.

SRI BHAKTA RAMADASU SMARAKA MANDIR AT NELAKONDAPALLI MANDAL - It is known as the birth place of Sri Bhaktha Ramadasu. His childhood name was Sri Kancherla Gopanna. He was posted as Tahsildar at Bhadrachalam and constructed the famous Sri Seeta Ramachandra Vari Devasthanam. Hence, after his death, the villagers constructed a Temple and vigraha of Lord Sri Rama, Seeta, Laxmana along with Sri Bhakta Ramdas were installed and performing daily rituals. Sri Bhaktha Ramadas Memorial Festival is celebrated every year between 28 April and 2 May.

NELAKONDAPALLY – It is a historic site encompassed by a mud fortification wall. Excavations have unearthed foundations of brick built viharas, wells cisterns, a mahastupa, terracotta figurines, a bronze Vigraha of Lord Buddha, a miniature stupa carved in lime stone and other early historic materials belonging to 3rd and 4th centuries. According to a myth, the Pandavas spent a year of

unknown (agyatvas) here after twelve years in exile, working incognito in the palace of Virata Raju, the King of Viratanagaram.

JAMALAPURAM – There is a very old Venkateswara Swamy Temple, which is also called Telangana Chinna Tirupati. "Swayambhoo" and "Swayam Vyakta", this Temple is believed to be over 1000 years old and visited by a large number of devotees especially every Saturday. The Temple is considered to be very holy and it's believed that pujas and darshan here lead to fulfilment of desires and wishes.

VENU GOPALA SWAMI TEMPLE AT KALLUR - The famous Temple, built 400 years ago by Queen Rudramma Devi, is situated here. Nearby is a Lord Shiva Temple constructed by the Kakatiya ruler Prathapa Rudra with five Lingas and a huge water tank.

DISTRICT – KUMURAM BHEEM ASIFABAD (Railway Station – Sirpur Kagazngr/Asifabad Road)

S. No.	Temple	Address	Type
1	Lord Venkateshwara Temple	Gangapur - 504292	Venkatesh (Vishnu)
2	Siva Temple	Wankidi – 504295	Shiva
3	Sri Siddi Hanuman Temple	Tonkini – 504299	Hanuman

GANGAPUR - The Lord Venkateshwara Temple is a major religious place. The Vigraha is Swayambhu (self-manifested) recovered from the rocky hillock. This Temple was built in the 16th century by Vishwabrahmin Mummadi Pothaji and large number of devotees come from all over Telangana and Andhra Pradesh as well as from Maharashtra and Chhattisgarh to Gangapur Jatra held on Magha Poornima every year.

SIVA TEMPLE AT WANKIDI - The Temple is dedicated to Lord Shiva. The Temple belongs to the Kakatiya period of 13th - 14th century. It is a triple shrine Temple complex facing east. It is located on the right banks of the Wankidi River. The Temple consists of three shrines in a row with a common rangamandapa and a stepped pyramidal type of shikhara. The central four pillars in front of the central shrine are polished. Sculptural motives of elephants, dancing figures, mithuna etc. are carved on adhisthana and all around the mandapa. The entire complex is located within stone prakara with an entrance mandapa.

SRI SIDDI HANUMAN TEMPLE AT TONKINI VILLAGE – It is a very famous Temple dedicated to Lord Hanuman. During Kartheeka Masam, devotees of Lord Hanuman set out on a 'mahapadayatra' or walkathon from various parts of the district to the Temple. They will take a holy dip in Wardha River flowing by the Temple before having darshan of Lord Hanuman.

DISTRICT – MAHABUBABAD (Railway Station – Mahbubabad)

S. No.	Temple	Address	Type
1	Veerabhadra Swamy Temple	Kuravi – 506105	Veerabhadra
2	Siva Temple	Katrepalli – 506112	Shiva
3	Bheemuni Paadam Waterfalls	Seethanagar – 506134	Mahabharata Circuit

KURAVI SRI VEERABHADRA SWAMY TEMPLE - It is a historic Temple dedicated to Lord Sri Veerabhadra Swamy. The deity has fierce look with three eyes and ten hands. According to local lore, the Kuravi Temple was said to have been built during 900 AD by Bheema Raju of Vengi Chalukya dynasty. Later, the renovation of the Temple was taken up by Kakatiya ruler Betharaju-I. Kuravi is unique for its culture. There is also a famous Bhadrakali Temple. So many tribal and non-tribal people comes to the Temple to get blessings of the Lord. Mahashivarathiri Festival is the biggest event in Kuravi. Other festivals celebrated here are "Bathukamma", "Bonalu" etc.

SIVA TEMPLE AT KATREPALLI - The Temple is dedicated to Lord Shiva. The Temple belongs to 13th century AD. The Temple is datable to Kakatiya period. The Temple faces east, preceded by an antarala, a closed mandapa and an entrance porch towards east. The Temple reflects the archaeological significance. The shrine doors have Poornakumbhas on either sides of the bottom of the doorjambs and its upper portion is divided into number of facets consisting of a row of flowers, slender ornate pilasters accompanied by dancing figures on its middle square portion. The Temple shows the importance of religious structures which were built widely during those times at several places, where the deity was installed with care. This Temple has been constructed with attention to detail and shows the skill of the workers in those times. The lintel has Gajalaxmi figure as its Lalata Bimba. Miniature shikhara motifs filled the space of the horizontal lintel. Four central pillars here bear the carving of pairs of hamsas, depicting elephants, kirthimukhas and there is a pearl garland design on the central square. The Temple is popular with devotees during festivals and other important occasions.

BHEEMUNI PAADAM WATERFALLS AT SEETHANAGAR - The place is hidden inside a dense forest. It is a picturesque waterfall known as Bheemuni Padam (Bheema's step). Here, water falls from a hillock in a semi-circular enclosure. Apart from the sound of falling water, it is quiet all around. It has not been conclusively established that from where the water comes. When sun rises and sets, the water shines in rainbow colours, which is an amazing sight. The water drops down from a height of about 70 ft to form a pool at the bottom. The flow of water is heavy in monsoon season. A cave beside the falls, which is believed to be 10 KMs long, is the other attraction here. Apart from the waterfall, there are several Lakes nearby which can be visited as well. There are vigrahas of Lord Shiva and Nagadevatha in a small enclosure near the falls where visitor perform poojas. As per legend, a person named Yadava Raju get married with two women and Raju blessed with a daughter from first wife. When Yadava Raju visited Papameda Gutha (Hills), his second wife planned to put an end to first wife and daughter. So she planned to build a house named as "Lakha Medha" with wooden sticks, which can easily burns. Pandava legend goes that Bheema set foot here to make way for water to save her with daughter. On the Foot of Lord Bheema, the water get flows. The floating of water from Bheema Padam connects and fills three Lakes nearby. This place is so beautiful. It is ideal for family picnics.

DISTRICT – MAHABUBNAGAR (Railway Station – Mahbubnagar)

S. No.	Temple	Address	Type
1	Manyamkonda Sri Lakshmi Venkateshwara Swami Temple	Mahabubnagar – 509001	Venkatesh

S. No.	Temple	Address	Type
2	Jagadguru Sri Dattatreya Maha Samsthana Peetham	Paspul – 509208	Dattatreya
3	Aishwarya Ganapathi	Avancha - 509301	Ganesh
4	Sri Lakshmi Chennakeshava Temple	Gangapuram – 509302	Vishnu
5	Sri Krishna Dwaipayana Theertha Math	Kusumurthy – 509352	Swamy Krishna
6	Sri Ksheera Lingeswara Temple	Krishna – 509352	Shiva
7	Swayambhu Sri Lakshmi Venkateshwara Swamy Temple	Gudeballur – 509352	Vishnu
8	Nivruthi Sangam	Tangadgi - 509352	Triveni Sangam
9	Sri Yadavendra Swamy Temple	Mudumal – 509352	Yadavendra Swamy
10	Sri Ramakonda Temple	Koilkonda – 509371	Ramayana Circuit
11	Sri Ramalingeswara Swamy Temple	Bhutpur – 509382	Rama
12	Sri Venkateswara Swamy Temple	Kurumurthi Rayadu – 509409	Venkatesh

MANYAMKONDA SRI LAKSHMI VENKATESHWARA SWAMI TEMPLE - In the ancient days,

Sages / spiritual gurus like Narasimha Yogi, Ettepu Ramayogi, Kasirayalu, Veerappaiah, Yanumaddhasu were meditated here so that it is known as Munulakonda. During a passage of time, it has been transformed to Manyam Konda. The main deity of this place is Sri Venkateswara Swamy & it is a Harihara Kshetra. This Temple is located in a cave and it is perched on the top of three hills. Famous singer, Sri Narayana Konda Hanumaddhas is having connection with this place. Annual festival of this place is held on the day of Magha Purnima.

JAGADGURU SRI DATTATREYA MAHA SAMSTHANA PEETHAM AT PASUPULA - It belongs to Datta cult & is connected with Lord Dattatreya. 700 years ago, the place is named as Srikshetra Sri Vallabhapuram by HH Sri Sri Sri Swamy Vittalananda Saraswati Maharaj. He has constructed a Datta Temple in this holy place. Sripada left the house after taking the permission of his mother & visited many Kshetras on foot, took a dip in many Thirthas. In his tour, he reached Gokarna Kshetra and stayed there for few years performing penance. Then he proceeded to Srisailam and performed penance for some time. Afterwards he came to Kuruvapuram Agraharam, which is existing in the riverbed of Krishna. He selected that place for his abode and for his penance. Sri Vallabha used to go to the other bank of River Krishna daily from Karuvapuram and was sitting on a huge stone & performing Surya Namaskara during the dawn. Even today, the devotees are clearly seen & prostrating to the impressions of his feet and hands. This particular place is called Sri Kshetra Sri Vallabhapuram today.

AISHWARYA GANAPATHI AT AVANCHA - Ancient Ganesha vigraha sculpted on a big granite boulder is believed to be built in 12th Century by a king of western Chalukya dynasty. It is believed to be the tallest Ganesh vigraha in India in sitting posture. The vigraha depicts the Western Chalukya Empire. The vigraha is 9.144 meters tall – 7.62 meters including pedestal.

SRI LAKSHMI CHENNAKESHAVA TEMPLE AT GANGAPURAM - It is one of the important Temples existing in South India & it is mentioned in Skandha Purana. The Chalukya King of Kalyani, Sri Thrailokya Malla Someswarudu built Kesava Swamy Temple. The main deity of this Temple is Sri Kesava Swamy & the sculpture here is very attractive. There is an evidence of Jaina Kalamukha & Shaiva religions spread here. Every year, festival of this Temple will be celebrated on the day of Radhasapthami and people participate in this event on a large scale.

SRI KRISHNA DWAIPAYANA THEERTHA MATH AT KUSUMURTHY – This southern flowing Bhima River is very pure and having special significance in Hindu culture. Swamy Krishna Dwaipayana Theertha belongs to Uttaradhi Math of Madhva cult. He was disciple of Swamy Vedavya Sateertha. After taking Sanyasasrama, he moved to many places in the country. He was good scholar and studied vedas & puranas, having good command on Hindu mythology. He got Vairagya on physical life and entered into philosophical life. He was principle disciple of his Guru. According to the order of God Swamy, he came on the bank of Bhima River near to Kusumurthy Kshetra. He ended his life with "Sadhana" towards God and got Moksha.

SRI KSHEERA LINGESWARA TEMPLE AT KRISHNA VILLAGE - This is the first village after the Sangam Kshetram of Krishna & Bhima Rivers. Many people from Karnataka & Andhra Pradesh come here & completes their elders' ceremonies. The oldest railway bridge was constructed across the Krishna River by the Nizam Govt. & located here. It was an engineering wonder & strongest bridge till today. Ksheera Lingeswara Matham is also one of the greatest landmark. Swamy Ksheera Linga was the great devotee sacrificed his life & went for Samadhi here & he established Lord Shiva Temple here. This Math is a faithful place for many people. In the Sankranthi season, the festivals of Temple will be performed every year. Nearly two lakhs people visit during festival period. On every Wednesday, local sandy is available in this village from past 100 years.

SWAYAMBHU SRI LAKSHMI VENKATESHWARA SWAMY TEMPLE AT GUDEBALLORE – Previously, this village was known as "Gundilapuram". Lord Venkateshwara Swamy along with Lakshmi Devi came to this hill to fulfil the desire of Mandavya Maharshi. Once Mandvya Maharshi is going to Tirupathi to participate in Brahmotsava, when he reached to Krishna River, it was flowing fully and he received a message from the God to stop here and the God will come to him. He went for Tapas for 8 Months then he got the mercy of Lord Venkateshwara and during the period of Tapas, the cowboys has given the cow milk for Maharshi as food, so here all types of Pujas will be done by that particular family, who called as Golla. Every year in Chaitra Masa, Brahmotsavas will be conducted for 15 days (from Chaitra Padyami to Pournima). Lakhs of People come from surrounding areas and participate in these festivals, especially from Karnataka, Maharashtra. The devotees feel that because of the God, this area is covered with good crops and protected from natural calamities.

NIVRUTTI SANGAM AT TANGADGI - Sangam is a place of confluence of Krishna & Bhima Rivers, which is located at the border of Karnataka. River Bhima merges with Krishna here. According to Guru Charitra (Dattatreya Charitra), this merging point is known as Nirvruthi Sangamam. River

Bhima flows to south side. This is equal to Ganga River at Kashi and it is also sacred, as Dattatreya Swamy moved on the bank of this River. It is the entry place of Krishna River in to Andhra Pradesh.

SRI YADAVENDRA SWAMY TEMPLE AT MUDUMAL – It is located on the Bank of Krishna River. The historical Math of Yadavendra Swamy is belongs to Madhva cult. He was the contemporary of Raghavendra Swamy of Mantralayam. Yadavendra Theertha Swamy was principle disciple of Pudenda Swamy of Madhva cult and he left for tour to north India. At that time, Sudhendra Theertha want to give the charge to his Uttaradhikari. He selected Raghavendra Swamy and given the charge as Mathadhikari. After return of Yadavendra Swami, Raghavendra offered the charge but he did not accepted that and left towards Mudumal Village. He did Tapas and ended his life with 'Sadhana'. Every year, Aradhana Ustavas for one week is celebrated here and lakhs of people of Madhva cult come and offers their devotions to Swamiji. Now, we can see the "Brindavana" of Yadavendra Theertha Swamiji at Mudumal Village. We also find a Lord Shiva Temple having 4 dwaras. Four types of people visit Lord Shiva from 4 sides i.e. from East-Human beings, from West-Gods, from North-Yakshas and from South-Rakshsas. We also find Hathiram Baba Math here, which belongs to Tirupathi, having one Mandir. Here, Krishna River flows in angular manner & looks very beautiful.

SRI RAMAKONDA TEMPLE AT KOILKONDA – It is one of the reputed historical monuments of the district. Lord Sri Rama put his leg in Thretayuga along with his wife Sita and brother Lakshmana, when he is in Aranyavasa (forest dwelling), so this Hill is known as Sri Ramakonda. Lord Rama has stayed here for some time and we can witness the foot print of Lord Rama till today. A stone is known as Sitamma Gundu on the top of the hill on which Sitadevi sat. Many Sages did penance or meditation on this hill after the advent of Lord Rama and we can see their dwellings till today and it has become very sacred. Lakshmana became unconscious during Rama-Ravanawar so Lord Hanuman brought Sanjivani Hill to make Lakshmana conscious. A small piece of this Sanjivani Hill fall in Koilkonda area, which has gradually became Sri Ramakonda.

SRI RAMALINGESWARA SWAMY TEMPLE AT BHUTPUR - The Temple is dedicated to Sri Ramalingeswara Swamy of 12th century CE. The Temple has a garbhagriha connected to 16 pillared mandapa facing east. The Vimana of the Temple is in stepped pyramid form. In the inscriptions, the place is referred to as Budupur, Budhapuri. The inscription records the construction of a Shaivite Temple by Kuppamambika, the wife of Malayala Gumda after the death of her husband and also the fact that she had given a gift of some land to the Temple. This Temple is of archaeological significance and represents the fine skill of sculptors during that period.

SRI VENKATESWARA SWAMY AT KURUMURTHI RAYADU – The place is under Chinna Chita Kunta Mandal. Kurumurthi is a hill Temple and the main deity is Lord Sri Venkateswara Swamy. In olden days, the Temple was in a cave in between two mountains. The Temple was constructed during 1350 AD. At present, the cave has been removed and the Temple was reconstructed. To reach the Temple, there are steps from the foot of the Hills. Sacred Water Pushkarni is located at the foot hills.

DISTRICT – MANCHERIAL (Railway Station – Manchiryal)

S. No.	Temple	Address	Type
1	Sri Satyanarayana Swamy Temple	Gudem Gutta - 504215	Satyanarayan
2	Gandhari Khilla	Bokkalagutta - 504301	Mata

SRI SATYANARAYANA SWAMY TEMPLE AT GUDEM GUTTA - It is a popular Temple. Lots of pilgrims visit this place during 'Karthika Masam' to have a holy dip in Godavari River and perform "Satyanarayana Vratam/Puja".

GANDHARI KHILLA AT BOKKALAGUTTA – It is also called Gandhari Kota. It is a hill fort having sand rock hills. The fort was built within a thickly forested area, which has a wealth of plant species which includes many medicinal herbs. Mahankali Jatara (Quarry Jatara) is conducted every year which attracts more than 10,000 people. Gandhari Maisamma Jatra is done in the Temple on the fort of Gandhari for every 2 years and tribal people from Vindhya region i.e. Maharastra, Chattisgarh on the other bankside joins it. Gandhari Maisamma Temple is located at the fort. The fort was built in the 12th century by Gondu Tribal with the help of the Kakatiya people of Warangal. Archaeological work suggests that construction of the fort was begun early as the Rastrakuta era (prior to 1200 AD) and continued until 16th century.All the sculptures, gate (thoranam) and pillars were constructed in Kakatiyas style. By observing the decorations, the Shanku and Chakra, beside every sculpture, we find that they are dedicated to Lord Vishnu, while Kakatiyas worshipped Lord Shiva.

DISTRICT – MEDAK (Railway Station – Akanapet)

S. No.	Temple	Address	Type
1	Kuchanpally Venkateshwaraswami Temple	Kuchanpally – 502130	Vishnu
2	Sri Chamundeshwari Devi Temple	Chitkul, Medak-Jogipet Road – 502270	Mata
3	Joginath Swami Temple	Jogipet – 502270	Shiva
4	Durga Devi-Sapta Prakarayuta Bhavani Mata Temple	Ismailkhanpet – 502296	Mata
5	Shri Sahakara Anjaneya Swamy Temple	Chakarimetla, Narsapur - 502313	Hanuman
6	Shri Shanishwara Temple	Yerdanur, Rudraram - 502329	Shani
7	Edupayala Durga Bhavani Temple	Edupayala Road, Nagsanpally – 502331	Mata

KUCHANPALLY VENKATESHWARASWAMI TEMPLE - It is an abode of Sri Venkateshwara Swamy and considered a holy divine destination by worshippers and visitors. It is located on a hillock. It is locally called as "Kuchadri". One of the highlights of this Temple is that the visitors need to slightly crawl between two massive rocks to reach the sanctum sanctorum where priests perform daily

rituals. Lord Venkateshwara (Srinivas) is the presiding deity along with his consorts Sridevi and Bhudevi. Towards the North East side of the hillock, there is a sacred tank (Koneru) which is square on plan with steps in eastern and southern directions. The Koneru consists of water all through the year and the devotees believe that there are many springs that release fresh water into this sacred tank. The ruins of this Temple in Medak district is of archaeological importance and represents the various methods used in the construction of religious structures centuries ago. Although there are no proper records of the Temple but based on iconographical features of loose sculptures and pillared mandapams, it is dated back to 10th– 11th century.

SRI CHAMUNDESHWARI DEVI TEMPLE AT CHITKUL - The family of Ailavajjala of Bhardwaja Gotra in Patakoduru village in Nellore district was well known for several great men who were experts in the Shakta cult of worshipping Mother Goddess. In 1917, Shree Venkataramanayya was born in this family. He was blessed by the Goddess Mukkantamma, who was the family deity and also the village deity. He was a great scholar in Ayurveda, Astrology, Telugu, Sanskrit, Vyaakarana and others. He was called as Ayyagaaru by the disciples with great respect and affection. Ayyagaaru started a group called Sri Chamundeshwari Seva Samithi Shaktamandal in 1968. From its inception onwards a programme of worship of Sri Chamundeshwari is performed once in a month of Telugu calendar with the name Samavesham. In this program, the deity is worshipped in the form of a photo and a holy vessel i.e. Kalashamand Shreechakram. Recitation of Holy Scriptures, Homam (fire sacrifice) of Saptashati, Kumaripooja and Mahapooja in the night are performed. He joined the goddess on Jan 31, 1988. After him, his son Shree Subrahmanya Shastry is managing efficiently the Samithi and the Temple. While the monthly celebrations were going on for several years, Ayyagaru thought of establishing a Temple for Sri Chamundeshwari Devi. He visited several places and selected the eastern bank of Manjeera near Chitkul village. The land was first purified by ploughing and by performing sacred rites. The stone for the Vigraha was selected from the rocks near Dharmapuri in Karimnagar district. The Vigraha of Sri Chamundeshwari Devi was carved by the sculptors of Tamilnadu. The nine foot high Vigraha with eighteen arms and a flaky crown is very attractive and impressive. The Vigraha was consecrated on 2nd January 1983 corresponding to Ananda year Pushya month and seventh day black fortnight. Thousands of people thronged for the installation ceremony, though it was in the night. Normally, the Temple is fully constructed and then the Vigraha is installed but here the Vigraha was installed initially and then the work of construction of the Temple and other facilities is still going on. The pace of work of different buildings, the continuation of the arrangement of free food to the visiting devotees and the increasing number of devotees day by day are surprising. Opposite the Chamundeshwari Devi, three other vigraha of Brahmi, Kaali & Vaishnavi are installed. Devotees get their desires fulfilled by worshipping the Goddess in different ways. Taking bath overhead and directly circumambulation, without wiping the body & without changing the dress, the Temple, eleven to more number of times according to one's capacity or tying a coconut in a cloth & offering it as mudupu are some methods to get the desires fulfilled.

JOGINATH SWAMI TEMPLE AT JOGIPET – It is a highly revered shrine. The Temple is dedicated to Goddess Joginatha. The most attractive feature of this holy shrine is that both Lord Shiva and Goddess Parvathi stand side by side in the form of Lingam (Shivalinga) without the Panivattam (pedestal). Of the Temples at the place, Jogipet, the Temple of Lord Joginatha is the most worshipped one. The Joginatha festival is celebrated on a grand scale here for eleven days during the months of March and April. Thousands of devotees from all parts of the state throng the Temple at this time.

DURGA DEVI-SAPTA PRAKARAYUTA BHAVANI MATA TEMPLE AT ISMAILKHANPET – The Temple is the 800-years old. The Temple was renovated by Swamy Madanaananda Saraswathi, the spiritual Head of Basava Kalyana Peetham based in Karnataka. The Temple comes under the control of Sri Sringeri Jagadguru Mahasansthan, Dakshinaamnaaya Sarada Peetham. One cannot view the Temple from outside as it is surrounded completely by the fort but it is easy to spot the gopuram from outside. The Temple's speciality is that deity is made of a single stone with a majestic height of 15 foot and it is said that this is second biggest Vigraha of Durga Mata in the world.

SHRI SAHAKARA ANJANEYA SWAMY TEMPLE AT CHAKARIMETLA – The Temple is surrounded by a dense forest. It gives immense pleasure after visiting the main deity of "Sahakara Anjaneya Swamy" who is self-manifested some thousand years ago while Saints & Monks were doing penance in the middle of the dense forest. The Temple has quadrangular space. The Satyanarayana Swamy Temple is west of it. Now, it has become one of the famous holy places in Telangana.

SHRI SHANISHWARA TEMPLE AT YERDANUR - The Temple is dedicated to Shri Shani Dev who is known as God of Justice. The vigraha of Shri Shani Dev is of black stone and it is more than 20 ft. in height along with peacock who is the vehicle of Shri Shani Dev. The vigraha has been consecrated on a big platform which is also made from black stone. Devotees visit the place in large number specially on Saturday and various other festivals.

EDUPAYALA DURGA BHAVANI TEMPLE AT NAGSANPALLY – Built in 12th century, the Temple is one of the most famous and powerful pilgrimage destinations in the region dedicated to Goddess Kanakadurga. This is a picturesque shrine located amidst the lush green forest and natural stone formations inside a den. The location marks the confluences of seven rivulets into the Manjeera River and hence the name Edupayala, which means Edu (seven) and Payalu (streams). The destination attracts around 30 lakhs devotees annually not only from Telangana but also from neighbouring states such as Karnataka and Maharashtra to worship to the Goddess Durga. According to the legend, Maharaja Parikshit (the grandson of the great warrior Arjun of

Mahabharata) performed "Sarpa Yagya" to get rid of a curse. When Garuda, the eagle, was transporting the snakes used in the Yagna, their blood is said to have fallen at seven different places and place where blood spilled became streams. Recently, while constructing a bridge, a layer of ash was found below the Manjeera Riverbed. The Temple is also famous for Jatara (fair), a three-day grand affair celebrated during Shivaratri in the month of February. With hundreds of devotees pitching up their makeshift tents around the Temple, the stage is set for a three-day event attracting more than 5 lakh pilgrims. In the rainy season, the River water flows in heights and reaches the foot of the Goddess and thousands of devotees come to Edupayala to watch this amazing event.

DISTRICT – MEDCHAL-MALKAJGIRI (Railway Station – Ghatkesar)

S. No.	Temple	Address	Type
1	Sri Ramalingeswara Swamy Temple	Keesaragutta – 501301	Shiva

SRI RAMALINGESWARA SWAMY TEMPLE AT KEESARAGUTTA - It is dedicated to Lord Shiva and his consorts Goddesses Bhavani and Sivadurga. Legend has it that Lord Sri Rama installed the Shivalingam in the revered shrine to atone for the sin of killing Ravanasura. Lord Rama chose this lovely valley with green pastures surrounded by magnificent hills and ordered Lord Hanuman to bring the Shivalingam all the way from Varanasi but Lord Hanuman could not arrive on time and as the auspicious hour was approaching, the Lord Shiva himself appeared before Lord Rama and presented him a Shivalingam for installation. For this reason, the Shivalingam in this Temple is called Swayambhu Linga. The Lingam is also called Ramalingeswara, as it was installed by Lord Sri Rama. Lord Hanuman came with 101 Lingams for choice from Varanasi and felt aggrieved at not having his Lingam installed. Thus, he threw all over the area. Even to this day, many Lingams are also found scattered outside the Temple. To mollify Lord Hanuman, Lord Sri Rama ordained that precedence would be given to him for worship at the Temple. He also said that the hillock where the Lingam was installed would bear his name Kesarigiri that is, Hanuman, the son of Kesari. Over a period of time, it has colloquially transformed and is now known as Keesara and the hill as Keesaragutta. Ever since, the rituals follow the command of Lord Sri Rama. Exploration and Excavations were conducted by the archaeological department in the surroundings of Keesaragutta Temple. Many remnants of brick structures and Shivalingas were found on the Hill. The remnants belonged to Chalukyan Empire reign. Some vestige remnants and rock cut cisterns were found on the hills as an indication of Jainism and Buddhism flourished contemporarily. On 18th October 2014, twelve vigraha of Jain Tirthankaras dating back to the 4th-5th century were found near the Temple steps at a depth of one foot which proves that Jainism co-existed along with Hinduism at Keesaragutta during the time of Vishnukundins in 4th-5th century. It is a different experience altogether if you happen to visit during the festivals of Sri Rama Navami, Hanuman Jayanti, Mahashivratri, Shiva Kalyanam and Ramalingheshwara Brahmotsavam. It is the

best time to visit during these festivals as the fervour and the dedication of devotees on these days add on to the overall charm of this Temple.

DISTRICT – MULUGU (Railway Station – Warangal)

S. No.	Temple	Address	Type
1	Sri Hemachala Laxmi Narsimha Swamy Devalayam	Mallur – 506172	Narasimha
2	Ramappa Temple	Palampet – 506345	Shiva

SRI HEMACHALA LAXMI NARSIMHA SWAMY DEVALAYAM AT MALLUR - This Temple has many specialities. The height of Moollaviraat Sri Narasimha Swamy is upto 10 foot. It is located in the midst of forest. The Belly part of Moolavirat Vigraha is soft as human skin. Malluru famous for Sri Ugra Narasimha Swamy Temple. The dhwjasthambha here at the Temple is nearly 60 foot in height. There is a rock formed Ugra Anjaneya Swamy Vigraha near to the Temple. It is the first of its kind known in South India. There is a continuous water flow near the Temple from the top of the hills. The Temple has been renovated during Godavari Pushkarams in 2003. There will be an annual proceeding here in the month of Apr-May every year.

RAMAPPA TEMPLE AT PALAMPET - The Ramalingeswara Temple is an amazing piece of art that stands as a testimony of the royal Kakatiyas. The Temple got its name Ramappa because of its chief sculptor Ramappa. It's probably the only Temple in the country to be known by the name of its sculptor. The medieval Deccan Ramappa Temple which dates back to 1213 AD was built by the patronage of the Kakatiya ruler Kakati Ganapathi Deva under the authority of his Chief Commander Rudra Samani at the place known as Ranakude in the Atukuru province. The Ramappa Temple is the right destination for people who admire architectural brilliance and have a panoramic view of true scenic beauty. Another striking feature of this Temple is that it is built with bricks that are so light that they can easily float on water. The Temple which is situated in a valley took nearly 40 years to be completed. Elaborate carvings line the walls and also cover the pillars and ceilings of the Temple. The Ramappa Temple finds its hold on a 6 foot high platform on a cruciform plan. The Temple's chamber is crowned with a shikharam and is surrounded by pradakshinapatha. At the entrance of the Temple, we can find a Nandi mandapam. An imposing Nandi vigraha stands on it. It is worthy to mention here that the Temple is the latest monument to be included in the UNESCO'S World Heritage List.

DISTRICT – NAGARKURNOOL (Railway Station – Jadcherla)

S. No.	Temple	Address	Type
1	Uma Maheswaram Temple	Rangapur - 509201	Shiva
2	Sri Bhaktha Laxmi Narasimha Swamy Temple	Mahbubnagar - 509235	Narasimha

UMA MAHESHWARA SWAMY TEMPLE AT RANGAPUR – It is located in a picturesque Nallamala forest range. The Temple dates back to 2nd century and belongs to the reign of Maurya Chandragupta. The Temple houses a Shivalinga, which has two colours – white on one side and red on the other. The deity in this Temple is believed to have spotted in naturally formed cave. The continuous flow of water from the hillocks on this beautiful Temple gives an impression as if Goddess Ganga is bestowing her purity here. There is a huge tank near the Temple. It is the northern gateway of Srisailam – one of the Jyotirlingas. It is atop the hill covered by huge trees. The hill ranges shields the Temple. Papanasanam is around 200 m away from the sanctum sanctorum, where water comes out underneath the huge rocks all through the year.

SRI BHAKTHA LAXMINARASIMHA SWAMY TEMPLE AT MAHBUBNAGAR – The place is known as Punya Kshetra. The Vigraha is Swayambhu. The Moolavar is Ugrah Narasimha Swami. The Sthalvruksha is Neem, Ashwata. All festivals are celebrated here with religious fervour.

DISTRICT – NALGONDA (Railway Station – Nalgonda)

S. No.	Temple	Address	Type
1	Pachala Someshwara Temple	Panagal – 508001	Shiva
2	Sri Chaya Someshwara Temple	Nalgonda – 508004	Trinity
3	Sri Rajarajeswari Devi Temple	Gudivada – 508211	Mata
4	Group of Temples	Nagulapahad - 508217	Shiva
5	Sri Narasimhar Temple	Mattapalli – 508218	Narasimha
6	Sri Parvathi Jadala Ramalingeshwara Swamy Temple	Cheruvugattu - 508254	Shiva
7	Sri Lakshmi Narasimha Swamy Temple	Vadapalle – 508355	Narasimha
8	Sri Meenakshi Agasteswara Swamy Temple	Vadapalle – 508355	Shiva, Sangam

PACHALA SOMESHWARA TEMPLE AT PANAGAL - The ancient Temple looks very casual from the outside but once you step in, the architecture tells you the actual story. The Temple has 70 pillars with intricate carvings depicting stories of Lord Vishnu and Shiva. Main shrine is dedicated to Lord Shiva, who is in the form of Linga made out of Green Onyx stone, hence the name Pachhala Someswara. There is huge beautifully carved Nandi who seems to come to life any moment. There is an archaeological museum on the site and many ruins around. The ground plan of Pachala Someswara Temple is markedly different from other shrines in Telangana. It has four shrines and these shrines are arranged three on the western side while there is only one on the eastern side with a common and large rectangular mandapam. Locals throng the Temple during festival occasions. From the inscriptional evidence found at Panagal and architectural style of the Temple, it is dated back to 11th-12th century. The other ruins located close by and the sculptures are highlights of this Temple which shows the glory of ancient dynasties which ruled the region and their patronage towards religion.

SRI CHAYA SOMESHWARA TEMPLE AT NALGONDA – It is a wonderful Temple. This is an interesting pilgrimage and historical site. The Temple was built during 11th– 12^{th}centuries by Cholas. This amazing Temple, engineered by the Kunduru, testifies the fantastic creative thinking and scientific knowledge of its architects. The complex houses three deities – Lord Brahma, Vishnu and Shiva facing three different directions connected by common mahamandapa. The Temple also demonstrates wonderful sculpture and art work. The Temple got the name as it is believed that one of the garbhagrihas situated in the west and facing east contains relentless shadow (Chaya in Telugu) of a pillar falls over the main deity of Shivalingam throughout the day. This mysterious shadow is a huge attraction of the Temple. The pillars of the Temple are decorated in great detail with relief sculpture of episodes from Ramayana and Mahabharata. Several sculptures collected from this area are preserved at the museum constructed in the compound of Pachala Someswara Swamy Temple. Some of the ancient Shivalingas preserved in the museum were collected from a village called Yelleswaram, which was submerged during the construction of Pachala Ramalingeshwara Temple lies 1 KM from the Temple.

SRI RAJARAJESWARI DEVI TEMPLE AT GUDIVADA - The Temple consists of garbhagriha, arthamandapa and pillared mandapa, which have central four pillars with rangasila and ten short pillars on kakshasana with entrance on southern side. In garbhagriha, a Shivalinga is enshrined. This is a typical example of Temple with entrance on southern side along with a flight of steps, whereas the Shivalinga in the shrine is located on western side. Purnakumbha motifs are carved on either side door jambs of garbhagriha. A typical Kakatiya Nandi carved in black basalt is kept in the mandapa facing Shivalinga. In front of the Temple, on the southern side, there is a double storied mandapa. On stylistic grounds, this Temple can be dated back to 12th – 13th century AD.

GROUP OF TEMPLES AT NAGULAPAHAD - The place is famous for many ancient Temples out of which Trilingeshwara Aalayam & Veerabhadreshwara Aalayam are most famous. These Temples were built during the reign of Kakatiya Kings who used their signature style of using black stone to carve beautiful vigrahas in the Temple. Both the above Temples resembles in architectural style with the Pillalamari Temple in Suryapet & Thousand Pillar Temple of Hanamkonda.

SRI PARWATHI JADALA RAMALINGESWARA SWAMY DEVASTHANAM AT CHERUVUGATTU – It is situated on the hillock. It is ancient and historical Temple. The Temple is dedicated to Lord Shiva. The Lord Ramalingeswara Swamy erected by "Lord Parashurama in Trethayugam". An interesting fact about this Temple is Muddu Gundlu, on which the Shivalinga is situated. Muddu Gundlu is located on three large rocks. You can only get there in stages, which are really very complicated and tricky. Devotees must be careful while entering in to the rock pass.

SRI NARASIMHAR TEMPLE AT MATTAPALLI – It is a famous and ancient Temple, which is one of the Pancha (five) Narasimha Kshetras on the banks of River Krishna. The Temple is more than 1000 years old. Sri Narasimha Jayanti is devotionally celebrated at the Temple. The Vigraha is one foot tall and carved on the rock. Devotees pray here for child boon, wedding and cure from prolonged illness.

SRI LAKSHMI NARASIMHA SWAMY TEMPLE AT VADAPALLE – It is a famous and ancient Temple, which is one of the Pancha (five) Narasimha Kshetras on the banks of River Krishna. The specialty of the Deity there is the Lord breaths in and out. Two lit lamps are at place before the Vigraha. The one at the face of the Lord quivers to testify this while the other kept below remains resolutely. This is an 'akhanda' Deepam and devotees are seen offering oil to the priests.

SRI MEENAKSHI AGASTESWARA SWAMY TEMPLE AT VADAPALLE - This Temple is located at the confluence of River Krishna & Musi (Muchikunda). The Village was earlier known as Wazeerabad. This is an ancient Lord Shiva Temple with a huge Shivalingam of 6000 years old. The Lingam was installed by Sage Agasthya. Lord Shiva & Maa Parvathi are worshipped here as Agastheeshwara and Meenakshi. The Temple was built in 12th CE by Kakatiya rulers. It attracts large number of devotees in Kartika month and on Shivaratri days. There is a crevice at the top of Shivalinga. This is always with full of water and even on removal, it maintains the same level. There is no logical explanation for this phenomenon as the Temple is located at a height of about 120 metres from the river water level. For thousands of years, the Temple remained in dense forest. Once a hunter was chasing a bird and the bird hid behind the Shivalinga to save its life. Lord Shiva appeared before the hunter & asked him not to kill the bird & offered him to take his brain and the hunter inserted his fingers on the head of the Linga for the purpose and in the process the crevice was caused.

SANGAM - There are quite number of steps / slope to the Sangam where River Musi joins River Krishna.

DISTRICT – NARAYANPET (Railway Station – Krishna)

S. No.	Temple	Address	Type
1	Sri Padamati Anjaneya Swamy Temple	Makthal - 509208	Hanuman

SRI PADAMATI ANJANEYA SWAMY TEMPLE AT MAKTHAL – It is located near Krishna River. This Holy Vigraha of Lord Hanuman was instantiated by Lord Jambavantha, who lived at the time of Lord Hanuman and was also a Bhakth to divine Lord "Rama" who is the incarnation of Lord Vishnu. The Vigraha of Lord Hanuman is faced towards west, which is the only one of its kind in south India. The word "Padamati" means "west side facing".

DISTRICT – NIRMAL (Railway Station – Basar)

S. No.	Temple	Address	Type
1	Sri Gnana Saraswathi Devasthanam	Basara – 504101	Mata
2	Gopaliji's Temple	Bhainsa - 504103	Krishna
3	Kadile Papahareshwar Temple	Malegaon – 504306	Shiva
4	Kalwa Narsimha Swamy Temple	Kalwa – 504306	Narasimha (Vishnu)

SRI GNANA SARASWATHI DEVASTHANAM AT BASARA – It is located on the banks of Godavari River. It is very close to Maharashtra border. This Temple is an abode of Goddess Saraswathi, Lakshmi and Kali considered as the Holy Trinity. Legends says that Veda Vyasa, his followers and Sage Sukha had desired to stay in a serene environment after the Kurukshetra War. Searching for a peaceful abode, they then moved into the Dandakaranya forest and finally chose this place owing to peaceful climate. Maharishi Vyasa was known for performing his regular ablutions in the Godavari River. Each day after this process he used to get sand in fists and made them into vigrahas of Goddess Saraswathi, Lakshmi and Kali by means of his mystic power and offered prayers. The place derives its name from Vyasa and called Vasar or Basar (Basara in local dialect). It is also considered to be among the three Temples created near the holy confluence of the Manjira and Godavari Rivers by the Ashtrakutas. A Karnataka King by the name Bijialudu reportedly constructed this Temple. It is decorated with turquoise and sandstone statues. It is widely believed that one can eat this turmeric and get the most knowledge. The Brahmanda Purana relates that the Adi Poet Valmiki wrote the Ramayana here with the presiding deity of Goddess Saraswati. The ashram of Valmiki Maharishi is located near this Temple. Here in Goddess Saraswati Temple, people give utmost importance to literacy of child girls. The specialty of this is because the trident vigraha here are dedicated to the essay. There is a special eye for literacy. People come with relatives and spell it out for children. Literature is conducted in a special shrine in the Temple premises. Devotees are interested in bowing to the Akhanda Jyoti in the hands of Jnaprasunamba in the Temple premises.

GOPALIJI'S TEMPLE AT BHAINSA - The Temple consists of garbhagriha, antarala and pillared mandapa that adorn the various directions of the Temple. The central four pillars show some of the best sculptural representations. Shaivite dwarapalas (carrying damaru, trisula, gada etc. in their hands) are carved here on antarala doorjambs and dwarapala sculptures at the entrance of the Temple. Due to this evidence, it was once considered to be a Shaiva Temple but there was no presence of Shivalinga in the garbhagriha. Presently, it is known as Gopalji Temple/Gopalkrishna Mandir since the Temple now has a Lord Krishna vigraha which is kept here in the garbhagriha and worshipped by the local people.

KADILE PAPAHARESHWAR TEMPLE AT MALEGAON - There is a stream that emerges from high hills and flows in to the beautiful valley towards north. On the either side of this fresh stream, we can see huge trees of about 50 metres height. The well-known Temple has entrances on three sides excluding the east. One can see the statues of Shringi and Bhringi on either sides of the entrance on the north. While doing the pradakshanas around the Temple, we can see vigraha of Lord Gajanan, Brahma, Varaha, Uma Maheswari and Vishnu. On the north-east side, there is a Temple of Lord Annapurna. There is an Vigraha of Nandi in front. According to

a legend, the devotees can hear 'Om Namahshivaya' if they place an ear against Nandi's ear. The Shivalingam in this Temple has a special significance. It is believed that the Shivalingam slightly swings. According to the legend, Bhagvan Parshurama killed his mother on his father's order and to wash off his sin, he installs thirty one Shivalingas in other places and installs the thirty second Linga here.

KALWA NARSIMHA SWAMY TEMPLE AT KALWA – It is a holy shrine located in the city of Koneru. The Temple authorities also organize 'Vana Bhojanam' as part of their many rituals. On this occasion, the authorities serve the devotees meals beneath the lush green trees. This is a very popular ritual and many people visiting the Temple to participate in this ritual. Moreover, the dedication and the excitement of the people turns this event into a family picnic, especially children are seem enjoying this ritual to the fullest. At the Temple, we can see the deity seated in a yogic posture. To his side, we see Narsimha Swamy's consort Goddess Lakshmi. This is a rare form of the God, as we see that most of the other Temples usually house the more furious avatar of Narsimha Swamy. We can also see a Ratham or the holy chariot in the Temple premises. The Ratham is decorated with different types of colourful flowers on special occasions and it carries the vigraha of gods and goddesses.

DISTRICT – NIZAMABAD (Railway Station – Nizamabad)

S. No.	Temple	Address	Type
1	Quilla Ramalayam	Mujahed Nagar, Nizamabad – 503001	Rama
2	Sarangpur Hanuman Temple	Nizamabad – 503001	Hanuman
3	Kanteshwar Temple	Kanteshwar, Nizamabad – 503002	Shiva
4	Dichpally Ramayalam	Ramalayam Killa – 503175	Rama
5	Ashok Sagar	Jankampet – 503186	Saraswati
6	Sri Apuroopa Venkateswara Swamy Temple	Gutpa - 503213	Venkatesh
7	Sri Navanatha Siddeshwara Temple	Armoor – 503224	Shiva
8	Indur Tirumala Temple	Narsingpalli - 503230	Venkatesh
9	Sri Laxminarasimha Swamy Temple	Janakampet - 503307	Narasimha

QUILLA TEMPLE AT NIZAMABAD - Raghunatha Temple is located on the top of the Nizamabad Fort. It is believed to have been built by Chatrapathi Shivaji Maharaj. Lord Rama Temple, which is also called the Quilla Raghunathalayam, is very huge and magnificent. Visitors can observe that the entrance of the Temple is very similar to the entrance of the Quilla. The Vigraha of Lord Shri Rama is in the shape of Kurma (tortoise). According to legends, this is the place where the great Saint Maharshi Raghunatha Swami sat down for tapasya. There is a very beautiful meditation hall where Raghunatha spent years meditating to gain salvation. The meditation hall has a unique system of ventilation which is the reason that the hall is always cool. The Quilla is also adorned by a beautiful and spacious kalyanamandapam.

SARANGPUR HANUMAN TEMPLE AT NIZAMABAD - The popular Lord Hanuman Temple of Sarangapur is dedicated to the greatest devotee of Lord Shri Ram. According to the localities, the foundation stone of this shrine is believed to be laid by a Saint called Samartha Ramadas, who was the guru of the great Indian leader Chatrapati Shivaji Maharaj. The ancient Temple of Lord

Hanuman is spread over a total of 1400 acres land and the Temple is situated on a beautiful and serene hillock.

KANTESHWAR TEMPLE - There is an ancient Temple, which is dedicated to Lord Shiva. It is the Neela Kanteshwar Temple. The Temple attracts a large number of devotees coming from different corners of the state and the district. This famous Temple was constructed for the Jains by the Satavahana King, Satakarni-II. The structure has a lot of resemblance with the North Indian architectural style. The festival of Ratha Sapthami is an annual event celebrated on a grand scale with a lot of pomp in this Temple. It is revered shrine located on a beautiful hillock. The deity Lord Shiva gains the name of Neela Kanteshwar due to the presence of blue throat.

DICHPALLY RAMAYALAM - Constructed in the 14th century, the Dichpally Ramalayam, which is also called the Khilla Ramayanam, is one of the oldest and most known Temples in Nizamabad. The Temple is dedicated to Lord Rama, the seventh incarnation of Vishnu. It is believed to have been built by the generous Kakatiya kings. As the Temple has a lot of resemblance in its style and structure, it is also called the Indhoor Khajuraho or the Khajuraho of Nizamabad. The Temple is one of the finest examples of the ancient stone architecture.

It was built in white and black basalt stone and is embellished with vigraha of goddesses, devils, animals and also has Khajuraho style erotic structures engraved on each of its pillars, ceilings and door frames. Each year, during the monsoon season, the surrounding area of the Temple is filled with water and at this time of the year, the Temple assumes the look of an island. The Ramalayam has 105 steps which the visitors have to walk in order to offer prayers to the deity. Each carving on the walls inside and outside of the Temple stand as strong reminders of the Kakatiya glory. The Temple got its first Vigraha of the great Lord Rama and his consort Goddess Sita, his brother Lakshmana and his greatest devotee Hanuman in the year 1949. The Vigraha was gifted to the Temple by a local devotee Gajawada Chinnaiah Gupta.

ASHOK SAGAR AT JANAKAMPET - It is a huge reservoir comprising of a beautiful Rock Garden, octagonal shaped restaurant, swinging bridge, boating facilities and children park. There exists a 15 foot marble Vigraha of Goddesses Saraswathi in the middle of the lake. The lake is scenic with a backdrop of hilly landscapes. Landscaped rock garden with winding path in the midst of rocks gives a memorable experience to the visitors.

SRI APUROOPA VENKATESWARA SWAMY TEMPLE AT GUTPA - The Temple is dedicated to Lord Venkateswara. The Temple complex is big. The Temple is having a flat post. Sculptural motives of elephants, dancing figures, mithuna etc. are carved in the Temple. The Temple has been constructed on an elevated platform.

SRI NAVANATHA SIDDESHWARA TEMPLE AT ARMOOR - There are beautiful rock formation around this Temple which extends up to 2 KMs. Legend says that as it is on this hillock, hence it is called as Navanathapura. There are many Temples on the hillock namely Shivalayam, Ramalayam, Hanuman Temple, Durga Devi Temple and all these Temples are believed to be Swayambhu Temples. Inside these caves, is a Shiva Temple, where the Shivalingam is said to be Swayambhu or self-manifested.The entrance to this cave Temple is a door that is barely three feet. Just outside the exit point of this narrow cave is a Ramalayam and the Temple tank, Jeeva Koneru.

INDUR TIRUMALA TEMPLE AT NARSINGPALLI - The Temple is dedicated to Lord Venkateswara. The Temple is having a five tiered Gopuram at the entrance with carvings on it. The Temple complex is constructed with a prakara wall. The Temple is having a flag post. There are various sub-shrines in the Temple complex.

SRI LAXMINARASIMHA SWAMY TEMPLE AT JANAKAMPET - The principal deity is Sri Narasimha Swamy. The Temple belongs to 17th century. The Temple is consisting of garbhagriha and pillared hall enclosed within a prakara wall. By the side of this Temple, there is a Puskarini, which is constructed in octagonal (Astamukhi) plan. Though the Puskharini here and the Temple was built during the Rashtrakuta times, it undergone continuous renovations during the period of Chalukyas, Kakatiyas and later period. The plan of the Temple consists of a central mandapa, a chamber and pillared hall. It is also a popular learning centre i.e. Vidyapeeth / Vedapathasala.

DISTRICT – PEDDAPALLI (Railway Station – Peddapalli)

S. No.	Temple	Address	Type
1	Buddhist Stupa	Gattusingaram - 505174	Buddhist
2	Siva Temple	Guttepalli - 505185	Shiva

BUDDHIST STUPA AT DHULIKATTA - The Buddhist Monastic complex is located on the right and left banks of Hussaini Vagu. The excavations brought to light a Buddhist Stupa, fortification walls etc. One of labels inscribed in Brahmi over a slab in this Stupa is Palaeographically datable to 2nd century. The Stupa belonged to the Hinayana Sect of Buddhism in which the anthropomorphic representation of Lord Buddha was taboo. Here, Lord Buddha is showed in symbols such as his Chatra, Padukas, throne with Swastika, Pillar of fire etc. The Stupa consists of lower pradakshina path, circular drum with ayaka platforms on four cardinal directions i.e. on east, west, north and south and a dome. These ayaka platforms project from the main drum. This Stupa was beautified with carved lime stone slabs during the early Satavahna period and this embellishment is contemporary to the Barhut Stupa dated to the early Sunga period. Among the lime stone slabs Naga Muchilinda (a snake guarding the Buddha) is prominent.

SIVA TEMPLE AT GUTTEPALLI - The Temple consists of garbhagriha, arthamandapa and pillared mandapa, as well as central four pillars with rangasila and ten short pillars on kakshasana with an entrance on southern side. In Garbhagriha, a Shivalinga facing east is enshrined. This is a typical Temple having the entrance on southern side with a flight of steps with ornamental balustrade, whereas the Shivalinga is in the shrine which is located on western side. Purnakumbha motifs are carved on either side of the door jambs of Garbhagriha. A typical Kakatiya Nandi carved in black basalt is kept in the mandapa facing Shvalinga. On stylistic grounds, this Temple can be dated back to 13th century A.D.

DISTRICT – RAJANNA SIRCILLA (Railway Station – Karimnagar)

S. No.	Temple	Address	Type
1	Group of Temples	Sirsilla - 505301	Venkatesh, Shiva
2	Lakshmi Narasimha Temple	Nampally Gutta – 505302	Narasimha, Nagnath
3	Sri Raja Rajeswara Swamy Devasthanam	Vemulawada – 505302	Shiva

GROUP OF TEMPLES AT SIRSILLA - Sircilla once ruled by Chalukyas of Vemulawada is an important town. There are a number of Temples of historical importance located in this town, of which the Venkateswaralayam and Sivalayam are important, dating back to 18th - 19th century A.D.

Venkateswaralayam - This is a single shrine Temple dedicated to Lord Vishnu. The Temple consists of garbhagriha, antarala and an open pillared mandapa. The spire is in stepped pyramidal type. Lord Vishnu in the form of Sri Venkateswara Swamy is housed and daily rituals are being carried out.

Shivalayam - There is a Shiva Temple consisting of garbhagriha and antarala with small mandapa. Important sculptures such as Shivalinga, Nandi and Ganesha are housed in the Temple and are worshipped.

LAKSHMI NARASIMHA TEMPLE AT NAMPALLY GUTTA - Sri Raja Rajanarendra was the ruler of this area. One day, Lord Shiva came in his dream, when he was a leper, and told to build a Temple for him at the middle of Vemulawada and gone. Then Raja Rajanarendra has constructed the Temple more than 100 years ago. On the path to the Lord Narasimha Temple, there is a Temple for Naga Devatha. The Temple has worked in a model of Snake. There are statues portraying the episode of Prahalada and Hiranyakashipu. At the end of the passage, the Vigraha of Lord Narasimha, ending the life of demon Hiranyakashipu, is installed. At the top of the hill, there is another Temple dedicated to Lord Lakshmi Narasimha Swamy. The Vigraha was carved out of the rock around which the Temple was built. At the entrance of the Temple, one can find a Vigraha of Lord Narasimha breaking his way out of a pillar.

SRI RAJA RAJESWARA SWAMY DEVASTHANAM AT VEMULAWADA - The Temple of Lord Shiva in the form of Raja Rajeswara Swami is very famous. The presiding deity of the Temple is Sri Raja Rajeswara Swamy, who is locally popular as Rajanna. The deity is adorned on both the sides by the Vigraha of Sri Raja Rajeswari Devi on the right side and to the left is the Vigraha of Sri Laxmi Sahitha Siddi Vinayaka. There is a Dargah inside the Temple complex where all devotees offer prayers, irrespective of caste and creed. Pilgrims have divine bath in a holy tank called Dharma Gundam before proceeding for darshanam and these holy waters are believed to have medicinal properties. Every year at the time of Mahashivaratri, devotees in large numbers flock to Vemulawada to offer prayers to Lord Shiva. This Temple also has a very special offering made by devotees called 'Koda Mokku'. It is a ritual where the devotee makes the pradakshinam of the Temple with a Koda (bull) which is vahanam (Nandi) of Lord Shiva. Inside, there is a massive Shivalinga installed. The Temple was built by King Rajaraja Chola. The shrine deserves a special mention in terms of its architectural grandeur and spiritual sanctity. Existence of this shrine is lost in the mists of antiquity and even Puranas mention the existence of the Deity. The presiding Deity – Lord Raja Rajeshwara in the form of "Neela Lohitha Siva Lingam is known for his boundless benevolence in fulfilling the wishes of the devotees. This Shrine is popularly known as 'Dakshina Kasi' [Southern Banaras] and also as "Harihara Kshetram" for their being two Vaishnava Temples in main Temple complex i.e. Sri Anantha Padmanabha Swamy Temple & Sri Seetharama Chandra Swamy Temple. Sri Anantha Padmanabha Swamy is Kesthra Palaka of this Temple being consecrated with Pujas/ festive rituals [both Shivate & Vaishnavite festivals] and Sree Rama Navami is the 2nd major festival in this Temple. Bhavishyothara Purana mentions that the Sun-God [Surya Bhagavan] recovered from disability by praying at this shrine and so this shrine is termed "Bhaskara Kshethram" and Indra- the King of Astadikpalaka, by devoutly worshipping Lord Sri Raja Rajeshwara, purified himself from Brahmahatya Dosham. Further, it is said that during 750 to 973 AD, this Temple was built by Raja Narendra - the grandson of Parikshit, who in turn, the grandson of Arjuna, was not only cured of Leprosy by which he was afflicted by virtue of killing Muniputra accidentally, by taking bath in Dharmagundam but also seen Lord Sri Raja Rajeshwara & Goddess Sri Raja Rajehwari Devi in a vision & received blessings with directions to build a Temple & install' Shivalingam' which was laying in the bed of the Pushkarni. The Temple picturesquely stands on the bank of a large Tank which is called Gudicheruvu. The Garbhagriha has "Sri Lakshmi Ganapathi"; Lord Raja Rajeshwara in the form of Neelalohitha Shivalinga; Goddess Sri Raja Rajeshwari Devi & Nandeeshwara facing the Lord. The sanctum sanctorum encloses Sri Anantha Padmanabha Swamy Temple; Sri Seetharama Chandra Swamy Temple; Sri Anjaneya Sahitha Kasi Visweswara Swamy Temple; Sri Dakshina Murthy Temple; Sreeevalli Devasena Sametha Subramanya Swamy Temple; Sri Bala Tripura Sundari Devi Temple; Sri Someshwaralayam; Sri Uma Maheshwaralayam; Sri Mahisasura Mardhani Temple; Kotilingalu; Sri Kala Bhairava Swamy Temple.

DISTRICT – RANGAREDDY (Railway Station – Kacheguda/Budvel)

S. No.	Temple	Address	Type
1	Chilkoor Balaji Temple	Himayat Nagar, Hyderabad – 500075	Vishnu
2	Karmanghat Hanuman Temple	Padma Nagar Colony, Champapet, Hyderabad – 500079	Hanuman
3	Ananthaswamy Temple	Anantagiri Hills – 501102	Vishnu

S. No.	Temple	Address	Type
4	Ammapally Ramachandra Swamy Mandir	Shamshabad - 501218	Rama
5	Sri Saneeswara Swamy Temple	Shamshabad - 501218	Shani
6	Sri Vendikonda Siddheswara Swamy Temple	Shamshabad - 501218	Shiva
7	Maheshwaram Group of Temples	Maheshwaram – 501359	Shiva
8	Sri Ananta padmanabha Swamy	Chevella - 501503	Vishnu
9	Paramanandagiri	Sanghinagar – 501511	Vishnu, Rama, Mata
10	Jiva Asramam & Divya Saketam Temple	Sriramnagaram, Palamakula Post, Shamshabad - 509325	
11	Maisigandi Maisamma Temple	Kadthal - 509358	Mata

CHILKOOR BALAJI TEMPLE AT HIMAYAT NAGAR, HYDERABAD - The Temple is located on the banks of Osman Sagar Lake. It is a popular site for the devotees of Lord Balaji Venkateswara. It is believed that prayers offered after 11 pradakshanas (rounds) of the Temple come true on the condition that once the prayer is fulfilled, devotees have to come back and do an added 108 pradakshanas (circumambulation). The Temple is also known as visa Temple, as it is said that people attempting to obtain a visa to any country are never disappointed if they pray here. The Temple has beautiful architecture and it is believed that it was built more than half a millennium ago. The main deity is Lord Balaji Venkateswara, who is accompanied by Sridevi and Bhoodevi. Legend has it that the Temple was built by a devotee who couldn't visit the famous Tirupati Temple due to his health condition. Pleased by his devotion, the Lord himself appeared to him and asked him to build his Temple at this spot. The Temple has a pleasing architecture too, boasting of being one of the oldest Temples in Telangana. The Temple is also visited by many great spiritual and religious gurus also. To name a few, the Temple is often visited by Jeer of Sri Ahobila Mutt, Tilakayaths of Shri Vallabhacharya Sampradaya, Jagadguru Sri Sankaracharya of Sringeri Mutt and many others.

KARMANGHAT HANUMAN TEMPLE AT CHAMPAPET, HYDERABAD – The Temple was built during 12th century by Kakatiya kings. One of the renowned legends of this historical Temple is that while on a hunting trip, a king of Kakatiya dynasty heard thunderous chanting of Lord Rama's name as "Ram Ram" from Lord Hanuman's self-manifested Vigraha. The King took the blessings of Lord Hanuman and returned to his kingdom. On the same night, the king was advised by Lord Hanuman in his dream to build a Temple at that place where he found the Vigraha. Subsequently, he constructed a Temple with the divine blessings of Lord Hanuman. The Mughal Emperor Aurangzeb sent out his Army troops around the country to destroy all the Hindu Temples. Neither the troops nor the Emperor Aurangzeb could enter through the compound wall of this Temple. When they tried to enter into this Temple, they heard the warning "Karo Man Ghat" which means make your heart stronger to destroy this Temple. Hence, this Temple got to be popular as Karmanghat Hanumanji Temple.

ANANTHASWAMY TEMPLE AT ANANTAGIRI HILLS – It comprises ancient cave like structures and several bathing ghats. The Temple is located in the forested area. It is the origin of Musi River. The Musi River is also called as Muchkunda River, which flows through Hyderabad. The Temple is dedicated to Lord Ananta Padhmanabha Swamy and is considered to have been built many centuries ago by a Muslim king. According to the Sthala Purana, Markandeya Swami (a devotee of Lord Shiva) did penance for nearly 1400 years for the Darshan of Lord Vishnu. Pleased by his penance, Lord Vishnu appeared to him as Ananta Padmanabha Swami in Shaligrama form, which is installed in the cave. Even now pilgrims need to have a darshan of the Lord by going inside a small cave.

AMMAPALLY RAMACHANDRA SWAMY MANDIR AT SHAMSHABAD - The Temple is dedicated to Lord Rama, Goddess Sita & Lakshman. The Temple is also known as Shree Sita Ramachandra Swamy Temple. The Temple is believed to be built in 13th CE. In the Garbhagriha, there are vigrahas of Lord Rama, Mata Sita & Lakshman. Interestingly, vigraha of Lord Hanuman has not been consecrated in the Grabhagriha which represents the exile period of Lord Rama when he & Lakshman had not met with Lord Hanuman. The Temple is having a magnificent seven storied, 80 ft. high Gopuram. On the festive occasion of Shri Ramnavmi, divine wedding of Lord Rama & Mata Sita is celebrated with great fervor.

SRI SANEESWARA SWAMY TEMPLE AT SHAMSHABAD - It is said that Shani Deva advised a devotee named Shri Shankararaju Koyadora to construct a Temple in his dream. Later, he started the Temple construction work and installed the Lord Shani's Vigraha on 29th December 2012. The main deity Lord Shani Vigraha is installed here along with his wife Goddess Jeshta Lakshmi Devi. Lord Shani's Vigraha is of 22½ foot ekashila Vigraha height. This Temple has no rooftop for the Vigraha. The main deity appears openly to all. Generally, Lord Shani Temples do not have bells to ring but this Temple has bells in the Temple. On Saturday, Shaneeshwara Mahahomam is being performed at the Temple. Large number of devotees' visits on Saturdays, Shani Trayodashi and Amavasya days and offer poojas.

SRI VENDIKONDA SIDDHESWARA SWAMY TEMPLE AT SHAMSHABAD - The Temple is located on the terrace of a hill and is dedicated to Lord Siva. There are two subsidiary shrines namely Ammavari Temple and Bhavani Matha Temple which are connected by a mahamandapa supported by 32 pillars. In the Temple complex, there are also other Temples dedicated to Lord Vinayaka, Anjaneya and Shiva located on either side of the complex. There is a stepwell called "Gundam" with perennial water. In front of the gundam, a Shivalinga and Nandi dating back to 7th century CE are installed. There are two pillars inside the mahamandapa in typical Rastrakuta style datable to 9th century CE. Inside Shiva Temple and Ammavari Temple, Shivalinga and Parvati datable to 10th century CE are installed. The Kalyana mandapam and Anjaneya Swamy Temple located on the left side of the complex are datable to the Kakatiya period. The Lord Ganesha vigraha in the Vinayaka Temple is in seated posture and is in typical Kakatiya style.

MAHESHWARAM – It is a popular pilgrimage centre. The main attraction of the place is the ruins of an ancient Lord Shiva Temple. Apart from this Temple, the place also comprises two fortresses namely Shiva Ganga and Vishnu Ganga along with a Kacheri House of Akkanna and Madanna and four ministers of the Bhaktha Ramdas era; as well as the Kodanda Ramalayam and the Shivaji Durgam. Every edifice present at this place can be dated back to more than 500 years. The smaller Temples of Maheshwaram are known for their exquisite sculptures and detailed carvings. This Temple is built on the Pushkarani which is known as Shiva Ganga. It has a big holy bath with a few steps leading down under the water and one can see sixteen small sanctums built around the Pushkarani. The small Temples have little Shivalingams in them. These Lingas are Shodasalingas around main Goddess. Near the Temple, one can notice three main trees at one place and a Lord Ganesha Vigraha in a small sanctum.

SRI ANANTA PADMANABHA SWAMY SCULPTURE AT DEVARAMPALLY, CHEVELLA - The vigraha of Sri Anantha Padmanabha Swamy Sculpture is carved in black granite stone measuring (2.20 m x 1.00 m) on a boulder. A 32 hooded snake is also beautifully carved behind him. The upper right hand is kept below, head and lower right hand is kept near his chest. The upper left hand is holding Sankha while the lower left hand is kept on the folded left leg. Sri Brahma is seen seated on a lotus which is raised from the navel of Sri Anantha Padmanabha. His consorts Sri Devi and Bhu Devi are carved near his feet portion. Above the deity, Sankha, Chakra & devotees vigrahas are also carved. On the basis of the iconographical features, this sculpture dates back to 12th - 13th CE A.D.

PARAMANANDAGIRI AT SANGHINAGAR - It is a Temple complex built by the Sanghi Family. This Temple has been built completely in marble and was sculpted by the renowned craftsman, Sri Ganapathy Stapathy. This Temple complex, collectively called as `Paramanandagiri, comprises Temples of Lord Hanuman, Lord Rama, Lord Ganesha, Lord Venkateshwara, Lord Kartikeya, Goddess Durga and Goddess Ashtalakshmi. Many Telugu films have been shot in this Temple. It takes its position on a hillock known as the Paramananda Giri. The Raja Gopuram is 15 foot tall. The first thing that catches your eye is the heavy & beautifully carved door that forms the main entrance. The majestic Temple is built in the flawless Chola-Chalukya style of architecture. You can find three Gopurams at the foot of the hillock, which stand tall as if entering into the heavens.

JIVA ASRAMAM AT SRIRAMNAGARAM - JIVA or Jeeyar Integrated Vedic Academy was established in 2008 to protect and promote Vedic literature and values. JIVA was established to commemorate HH Srimannarayana Pedda Jeeyar Swamiji's centennial celebrations. To commemorate Vaishnavaite Saint Bhagavad Ramanujacharya's millenial appearance, a new structure at the height of 216 foot called "Vigraha of Equality" has been installed. It is an iconic memorial in honour of the greatest Acharya. Bhagawad Ramanuja was an icon treating everyone as equal before God and was the first Saint to allow the downtrodden to enter Temples. Covering an area of 53 acres, it

contains not only a Vedic Gurukulam but also computer labs, JIMS hospitals, a gosala, Nethra Vidyalaya (school for visually challenged) and a Homeopathic Degree College.

DIVYA SAKETHAM TEMPLE – It has three floors, where three different avatar of Lord Vishnu reside in the form of deities. The first floor has the main deity in the form of Lord Rama (Kondanda Ramaswamy), who beautifully dwells along with his retinue –Vishwaksena, Alwars, Acharyas and others. The very sight of the deity reminds one of the grace, love and affection, which Lord Rama had in his heart for his parents and in turn filling our hearts with those same virtues. On the second floor, one would get to witness the whole of universe in one sight. This floor has the original form of the Lord, Lord Ranganatha along with his consorts Lakshmi and Goda. Lord Brahma is also depicted here praying to Lord Ranganatha and it is through his prayers, the Lord protects the living entities of the world. The divine-body of Lord Sri Ranganatha is in colour, constituted with salagramas that have been acquired in worship from all the Divyadesams. Worshipping Lord Ranganatha, in Divya Saketham, is equivalent to worshipping the God in all Divyadesams. In the third floor, the almighty dwells in the form of Lord Vaikunthanatha, who came down on earth as Vyuha, who in turn happens to be the incarnation of Lord Ranganatha. This avatar of the Lord carries out the task of creation, sustenance and destruction. From this Vyuha Lord Ranganatha, the Lord further came down as human incarnation of Sri Sitha Ramachandra Prabhu who is the presiding deity of the Temple. At the top of these altars, there is the sanctum-tower called Sri Vimanam which has taken the shape of eight-structured-tower. The dazzling divine discus Sri Sudarshanam is installed on top of the primary tower. Beneath this, there are eight other towers. Each of the eight towers is embellished / consecrated with one syllable from the Narayana Ashtakshari, Manthram and the presiding deities regularly accept the propitiations. A similar type of eight-tower sanctum is found only in one other known as Goshtipuram in South India. This also happens to be the first Divyadesam sung by the Alwars and also the place where the great Sri Ramanujacharya – the preceptor of Visisht Advaitha Philosophy and also a great social reformer, climbed the Temple tower and proclaimed the essence of the Narayana Ashtakshari to all interested devotees irrespective of caste, creed and gender. There are 108 altars (each dedicated to the presiding deity of each Divyadesam) in the sanctum-enclosure. These altars have been consecrated by the sacred Tulasiplant procured from 106 Divyadesams.

MAISIGANDI MAISAMMA TEMPLE AT KADTHAL - The Temple is dedicated to Maisamma (local name for Goddess Mahakali). It reflects the cultural and mythological sentiments of the local Banjara people. The vigraha of Maisigandi Maisamma is around 20 ft. tall and the Gopuram is also huge and different from all South Indian Temples, as it is open at the top. Legend has it that the presiding deity of the Temple needs the Temple to be open at the top. The priests of this Temple are from the Banjara or Lambada caste. On weekends, the Temple surroundings get a festive look with tourists and devotees, and particularly during Bonalu, and "Jatara" (fair). Mahakali is considered a powerful goddess and the locals feel that she fulfills the wishes of devotees & the devotees offer "bonam"

(food offerings to the goddess) after their wishes are fulfilled. In the back side of Temple, several Temples of Lord Rama, Lord Anjaneya, Lord Shiva, can also be found. The very large "Koneru" (a stone-faced tank with steps) is also a good place to visit.

DISTRICT – SANGAREDDY (Railway Station – Vikarabad)

S. No.	Temple	Address	Type
1	Sri Veerabhadra Swamy Temple	Bonthapalle - 500043	Shiva
2	Sri Rechanna Swamy Temple	Badampet, Kohir - 502210	Rechanna
3	Sri Venkateswara Rukmini Panduranga Temple	Gadi Mohalla, Zaheerabad - 502220	Venkatesh
4	Sri Swayambhu Siddhi Vinayaka Temple	Rejinthal - 502249	Ganesh
5	Sri Ramalingeswara Swamy Temple	Nandi Kandi, Sadasivpet – 502291	Shiva
6	Kasivisweswaralayam	Kulabgoor – 502294	Shiva
7	Shree Kethaki Sangameshwara Temple	Jharasangam - 502318	Shiva
8	Sri Bhramarambhika Mallikharjuna Swamy Temple	Beeramguda, Patanchery Mandal – 502319	Shiva
9	Trikutalayam Kakatiya Temple	Nidigonda - 506244	Shiva

SRI BHADRAKALI SAMETHA VEERABHADRA SWAMY TEMPLE AT BONTHAPALLE - This Temple of Lord Shiva and Goddess Bhadrakali is a very ancient one and is said to be in existence from times before the Kakatiya Empire. The main Temple is of Lord Veerabhadra Swamy and just behind it to the right is the Temple of Goddess Bhadrakali. Priests of Jangama and Thambali castes serve the Lord here.

SRI RECHANNA SWAMY TEMPLE AT BADAMPET, KOHIR - The Temple faces east consists of garbhagriha, antarala and mukhamandapa. In front of the Temple, dhwajasthamba and deepa sthamba are erected. There is a step well (koneru) in the north-western direction of the main Temple. The main Temple was reconstructed recently and inside the garbhagriha, Temple walls are cladded with marble. The architectural features of Temple very much resembles the Temple styles of Maharashtra, datable to 18th – 19th century A.D.

SRI VENKATESWARA RUKMINI PANDURANGA TEMPLE AT GADI MOHALLA, ZAHEERABAD - The Temple consists of garbhagriha and mukha mandapa supported by pillars of Kakatiya style. Inside the garbhagriha, the vigraha is carved in black granite stone which is in standing posture with four hands holding shanka – chakra in upper two hands while the lower two hands are with varada and katyavalambita posture. The sanctum sanctorum is in circular in plan but conical in elevation. Behind this, there is another Temple with garbhagriha and antarala, dedicated to Lord Panduranga and Rukmini. These Temples have north indian style of shikhara and the veranda is with dwarf pillars and arches. Though the Temples were constructed much earlier but subsequently renovated in 18th century A.D.

SRI SWAYAMBHU SIDDHI VINAYAKA TEMPLE AT REJINTHAL - The Temple is dedicated to Lord Ganesha. The Temple is ancient & famous. The vigraha of Lord Ganesha is in Padmasana Posture giving blessings to the devotees from the Garbhagriha. Devotees visit the Temple on Wednesday & during festivals, large congregations held here.

SRI RAMALINGESWARA SWAMY TEMPLE AT NANDIKANDI – The Temple is most important monument in the village. It has a star shaped ground plan and four profusely sculptured pillars in the navaranga mandapa depict the figures of the Brahmanical deities such as Lord Brahma, Vishnu, Shiva, Narasimha, Varaha, Nataraja, Mahishasur Mardini, Saraswati and Gaja Lakshmi etc. The Temple is built in the Kalyani Chalukya style and the inscription found in the place indicates that it was constructed in the year 1014 AD during the rule of Vikramaditya-V. It records a gift of Kovuru village by Mahamandaleswara Pampa Permanadi to God Nameswara of Kiriyakandi. The Temple consists of garbhagriha and antarala and a hall with porches on the east, north and south with a Torana entrance. The Temple is locally known as Rameshwara or Ramalingeshwara Temple.

KASIVISWESWARALAYAM AT KULABGOOR - There is a Trikuta Temple which consists of a porch in the east, a hall and shrines to the west, north and south of the hall. Each shrine has an antarala and a garbhagriha. Lord Venugopala, Vishnu as Anantasayana and Lingam are the icons housed in the three shrines. The walls of the shrine are constructed of large blocks of stone. The shrines have the stepped pyramidal type of shikharas. These Temples belong to the Kakatiya period.

SHREE KETHAKI SANGAMESHWARA TEMPLE AT JHARASANGAM – It is one of the old Lord Shiva Temples. It is said that the Shivalingam was consecrated by "Lord Bramha". The king of Surya Vamsha Raja Kupendra during "Kruthayuga" suffered from a skin disease which did not have a remedy. One day while in forest for hunting, he reached Kethaki Vanam where he found a stream and washed his body, he was surprised to see his body cleansed and the same night Lord Shiva showed up in his dreams and asked him that he wanted the king to construct a sanatorium on the Shivalingam. Raja Kupendra constructed a Temple and dedicated it to Lord Shiva to show his gratitude. Pushkarni (holy pond) which came to be known as "asthatheerthaamruthagundam" and is called as "Dakshina Kasi". Gundampooja is performed by followers from Karnataka, Maharashtra and Telangana due to its religious and historical importance and pay homage to the Lord Shiva. According to the Hindu mythology, it is believed that Lord Bramha came to this propitious spot for meditation after the creation of world. As the present, Shivalinga was installed by Lord Bramha and the pooja's are being performed by Kethaki flowers (Kethaki flowers are generally

not used for pooja's) and also the water of that stream which the king converted into pushkarni consisting of 8 theerthas (narayana, dharma rushi, varuna, soma, rudra, indira, and datha). Here Lord Shiva is called as Kethaki Sangameshwara.

SRI BHRAMARAMBHIKA MALLIKHARJUNA SWAMY TEMPLE AT BEERAMGUDA - It is a famous Temple. It is also called as second Srishilam. This Temple was established in 13th century. Five days of festivities are held here on Shivaratri.

TRIKUTALAYAM KAKATIYA TEMPLE AT NIDIGONDA - This Temple was constructed in 11th century by Kakathiyas. It is a famous Temple and dedicated to Lord Shiva. The speciality of the Temple is that it is an ancient 500 pillared Trikutalayam.

DISTRICT – SIDDIPET (Railway Station – Karimnagar)

S. No.	Temple	Address	Type
1	Sri Renuka Ellamma Temple	Siddipet – 502103	Mata
2	Sri Umaparthiva Kotilingeshwara Swamy Kshetram	Siddipet – 502103	Shiva
3	Siva Temple	Duddeda – 502277	Shiva
4	Wargal Saraswati Temple	Wargal – 502279	Mata
5	Sri Kondapochamma Temple	Teegul Narsapur – 502301	Mata
6	Sri Saraswathi Kshetramu	Ananthasagar – 502306	Mata
7	Sri Lakshmi Narsimha Swamy Temple	Nacharam – 502334	Narasimha
8	Sri Trilingeswara Alayam	Yellareddypet – 502372	Shiva
9	Lakshmi Narasimha Swamy Temple	Bejjanki – 505528	Narasimha
10	Mallanna Swamy Temple	Komuravelli – 506223	Shiva

SRI RENUKA ELLAMMA TEMPLE AT SIDDIPET - The Temple is dedicated to Goddess Renuka Yellamma. The Temple is big. The black stone vigraha of the Goddess with five hoods of Nagdevtha gives solace to the devotees. There are daily rituals held in the Temple and special rituals during festivals.

SRI UMAPARTHIVA KOTILINGESHWARA SWAMY KSHETHRAM AT SIDDIPET - This Temple was built in late 1970s and there is an independent Vedic school running in the premises. The Temple got its name Koti Lingeswara due to the presence of 10 million Shivalingas in the Temple. Sri Sri Sri Madananada Swamy's preashrama (earlier) name was Laxminarayana. He was born in 1902 at Tekmal. Ravi Koti Narsamma and Narahari were his parents. Shreethi Koundinyasa was his Gothram. Since childhood Swamiji possessed with Vairagya features & thinking (detachment). Daily, he used to do 'Anna Danam' (Free Feeding). He entered into "Thuriyashramam" with the blessings of Sri Madhavananda Swamy, the head of Sri Sadananda Ashramam of Basava Kalyan. Lord Vaishnava Murthulu ordered him in a swapna (dream) to construct and establish Temple of Parthiva (Earth) Lingams. In Kaliyuga, worship of Parthiva Lingams is important and significant. Therefore, Swamiji started searching for suitable place to establish and construct Kotilingeshwara Temple. At the same time, one devotee from Siddipet accidentally had Swamiji's darshan at Koppole village. He asked his devotees to write the name of village (place) where they want Temple on a paper and keep at the feet of Lord Sangameshwara Swamy. Then he ordered one devotee to pick up one piece of paper. As per the wish of Bhagvan that piece of paper contained the name of Siddipet. In the Garbhalaya (Sanctum Santorum), more than one crore Parthiva (Earth) Lingams, Shiva Panchakshari written manuscripts were placed one feet deep inside the earth under the main Lingam. On these, the main Vigraha of Lingam brought from Varanasi was installed. In the Garbhalaya along with Shiva Pachayathanam, Maha Ganapathi, Nandeeshwar, Dwara Palakas and vigraha of Adishankara Charya, Dathathreya, Raja Rajeshwari Devi and Gayathri Matha were installed on both sides of the entrance to sanctum sanctorum. There are 12 Temples & 148 vigraha in this Kshethram. The broad and well-built wide mukhamandapam with 36 pillars is a special attraction to the Temple.

SIVA TEMPLE AT DUDDEDA - The Temple has a garbhagriha connected to 14 pillared mandapa with a renovated vimana. The entrance to the mandapa is connected with a flight of steps with balustrades on either side. The door jamb of garbhagriha is flanked by two Shaivite dwarapalas on both sides. On the basis of architectural features, the Temple belongs to late Kakatiya period of 14th century.

SRI VIDYA SARASWATHI SHANEESHWARA TEMPLES AT WARGAL - The Temple is situated on a hillock. It is the most famous Temple in the state after Basara. This Temple is famous for Aksharaabyasa for children. It is one of the popular pilgrimage sites around Siddipet & Hyderabad. It was built by Sri Yamavaram Chandrashekhara Sharma. The Temple foundation stone was laid in 1989. On 1992, Sri Vidya Nrusinha Bharati Swamy has laid the foundation to the statues of Goddess Sri Vidya Saraswathi Devi and Lord Shani. Now, it is maintained by Kanchi Mutt. The garbhagriha is located at a level nearly equivalent to the third floor. The Goddess is seen to be in full glory decorated with a lot of jewels and garlands and adorned in a saree. There is an Vigraha of Goddess about 10 foot high in front of the Temple, which is a magnificent piece of art. The other Temples in the complex are Sri Lakshmi Ganapathi, Lord Shanishwara and Lord Shiva. There are two Vaishnava Temples here, which are almost in ruins as of now. A huge victory pillar is also located nearby. With a height of about 30 foot, it has statues of Lord Rama, Sita, Lakshmana and Goddesses Lakshmi over it. The Temple has a Veda Paathashaala in its premises where many students learn Vedas. Meals are provided for free for all the devotees at the Temple premises called as Nitya Annadanam. Vasantha Panchami, Navartri Mahaotsavams and Shani Tryodasi festivals are being celebrated in a grand manner in this Temple. Moola

Nakshatram (Birth star of Goddess Saraswati) is the most auspicious day for worshiping Saraswati Devi. During this day, special rituals are performed at the Temple.

SRI KONDAPOCHAMMA TEMPLE AT TEEGUL NARSAPUR - Kondapochamma Sagar was named after Kondapochamma Temple, which is located on the borders of erstwhile Medak, Warangal and Nalgonda districts. It is a famous Temple and various Yagya & Pooja rituals are held here.

SRI SARASWATHI KSHETRAMU AT ANANTHASAGAR – The Temple is dedicated to Goddess Saraswathi. The Temple was built on 2nd May 1980 by Astakala Narasimha Rama Sharma (Astavadhani). This is the first Temple having standing Vigraha of Goddess Saraswathi. Saraswati Puja is performed on the 5^{th}day of Magha month of Vedic Calendar (also known as Basant Panchami).

SRI LAKSHMI NARSIMHA SWAMY TEMPLE AT NACHARAM - The Nacharam Gutta houses a revered Lakshmi Narshima Swamy Temple. The Temple is believed to be 600 years old. The Temple is a cave Temple, situated on a beautiful hillock. Inside the sanctum, we can see Swayambhu Narashima Swamy along with his consort Lakshmi Thayar beautifully carved in the rock. The Temple also has some more vigrahas. According to mythology, Naradha forfeited here. The place got its name Nacharam Gutta after a devotee by the name Nacharam. As we go round the Temple, we can find a flight of stairs to the left side, these stairs lead us to the darshanam of Shri Surya Narayana.

SRI TRILINGESWARA ALAYAM AT YELLAREDDYPET - The Temple is a trikuta Temple. The Temple faces south and has a common mandapa consisting of 16 pillars and three shrines on east, north and western sides. All the three shrines consist of Lingas in garbhagriha. The door Jambs of garbhagriha are carved with dwarapalakas flanked by female chowri bearers at the bottom. The lintel is carved with Gajalakshmi in the centre. Over the lintel, miniature Temple models are noticed on the western side shrine, while the remaining is of plain type. There is a tank locally known as Bollakka Cheruvu, existing on the southern side of the Temple. The Temple belongs to the Kakatiya times of 12th – 13th Century A.D.

LAKSHMI NARASIMHA SWAMY TEMPLE BEJJANKI - The Temple is situated on the top of the hill. The Temple faces south. It consists of garbhagriha, antarala and mandapa with porches on south, east and west. Originally, the sanctum sanctorum is a cave, converted into the present form of garbhagriha. As the Temple stands on a hill, the garbhagriha does not contain any adhisthana and the walls rise directly from the surface of the rock. The central four pillars are exquisitely carved. The stories of Bhagavata, Bharata and other puranic episodes are carved on the pillars. As both Chalukya and Kakatiya styles are apparent in this Temple, this Temple may be assigned to 12th Century A.D.

KOMURAVELLI MALLIKARJUNA SWAMY TEMPLE – It is located on a hill. The primary deity is Mallanna or Mallikarjuna Swamy, who is an incarnation of Lord Shiva. The deity is also called as Khandoba by the Maharashtrian people. Mallanna along with his consorts Golla Kethamma, Goddess Ganga and Medalamma, Goddess Parvati are at the main Temple. The Oggu Katha singers sing the tale of Mallanna here. Devotees offer prayers to Mallanna with the help of Oggu Pujaris who draw a Rangoli called as Patnam (A form of offering prayers to Lord) in front of Lord Mallanna inside Temple and also in Temple's verandah. Another Temple, Konda Pochamma Temple is nearby which is visited by the devotees who visit Mallanna Temple.

DISTRICT – SURYAPET (Railway Station – Khammam)

S. No.	Temple	Address	Type
1	Sri Amaralingeswara Swamy Temple	Amaravaram – 508204	Shiva
2	Group of Temples	Huzurnagar – 508204	Mata, Shiva
3	Sri Adi Varaha Laxmi Narasimha & Venugopala Swamy Temple	Booruggadda – 508204	Vishnu
4	Peddagattu Jathara	Durajpally – 508213	Shiva
5	Sri Undrugonda Laxminarasimha Swamy Temple	Undrugonda - 508213	Narasimha
6	Pillalamarri Temple	Pillalamarry - 508214	Shiva

SRI AMARALINGESWARA SWAMY TEMPLE AT AMARAVARAM - The Temple belongs to 14th – 15th century CE during Kakatiya period. The Temple is dedicated to Lord Shiva. The Temple consists of garbhalaya & eight pillared mandapa facing east. The Shivalinga is enshrined in the garbhalaya and a Nandi is kept in the mandapa facing Shivalinga.

GROUP OF TEMPLES AT HUZURNAGAR

Kanaka Durga Ammavari Temple - Inside the garbhagriha, Goddess Kanakadurga is worshipped. The Temple has been completely renovated.

Sri Parvathi Bhimeswara Swamy Temple - The Temple belongs to 13th century CE. The Temple consists of garbhagriha and antarala with opened pillared mandapa. This Temple has been completely renovated without disturbing the garbhagriha.

SRI ADI VARAHA LAXMI NARASIMHA AND VENUGOPALA SWAMY TEMPLE AT BOORUGGADDA - Burugadda village is a historical one having inscriptional evidence of Chalukya and Kakatiya kings. A stone inscription is located in the premises of Venugopala Swamy Temple which is dateable to (1268 AD and belongs to Rudradevamaharajulu (Queen Rudramadevi). The inscriptions states that while Srimanmaha Mandalesvara Kakatiya Rudradeva Maharajulu were ruling the kingdom, Devakiputradasa, the younger brother, Satram Bollamraju set up in the middle of the village Burugadda, the Temple Chenna Gopinatha along with his two pirattis (wives) Sridevi and Bhudevi for the good of all the people and granted gifts for the anga and ranga bhogas etc. This is an important Temple of historical importance and represents the historical significance of this district. Locals throng the Temple during festival occasions. The Temple consists of garbhagriha, antarala and closed mandapa with a pillared porch within stone prakara. A large Lord Vishnu vigraha in the sleeping posture is an important object of worship in this Temple. This Temple is dateable to 13th century A.D.

PEDDAGATTU JATHARA AT DURAJPALLY - Peddagattu or Gollagattu Jathara is the festival done in the name of Lord Lingamanthulu Swamy and Goddess Choudamma every 2 years. The presiding deities, Sri Lingamanthula Swamy, believed an Incarnation of Lord Shiva and his sister – Choudamma are offered various pujas during the five-day fete. Peddagattu (Gollagattu) is the second biggest religious congregation or Jathara in the state of Telangana after Sammakka Saralamma Jatara in Jayashankar Bhupalapally. Though primarily the Yadava community takes part in huge numbers, people from all castes and religions from across Telangana, Andhra Pradesh, Chhattisgarh, Madhya Pradesh, Maharastra, Odisha, Karnataka and Tamil Nadu come to the place. According to history, this religious congregation has been celebrated since 16th century.

SRI UNDRUGONDA LAXMI NARASIMHA SWAMI DEVASTHANAM - It is an ancient Giridurgam (hill forte) constructed initially by Vishnukundinulu in 5th century and later developed by various dynasties. It is a magnificent archaeological and spiritual pilgrimage centre hosting different Temples of which Sri Undrugonda Laxmi Narasimha Swamy is best worshiped adored by local public. Many fortifications, hillocks, valleys, lakes and greenery of the forest also make a very beautiful eco-tourist destination. Local philanthropic organizations have been trying to revive the name and fame of Undrugonda since 2002.

PILLALAMARRI TEMPLE - The Temple is dated back to almost 1000 years and is considered to be one of the oldest ancient Temples in the District. It is dedicated to Lord Shiva. In addition to the Pillalamarri Temple, the village also houses several other ancient Temples built during the Kakatiya period. This helps to enhance the historical and religious value of the village. Built on the banks of Musi River, the Temple belonged to the Kakatiya era and stands testimony to the architectural craftsmanship displayed by the Kakatiya rulers. It houses beautifully carved pillars and walls where each intricate sculpture is poetry in stone. Beautiful paintings are also found to adorn the walls of the Temple. A grand and regal Nandi bull is seen gracing its portals. The detailing in the architecture is an indication of the touch of excellence which the craftsmen of the Kakatiya period have been able to impart on Telangana art and culture. In addition to the historical and aesthetic value of the village, it is also a culturally significant area. This is the birthplace of the famous Telegu Poet Pillamarri Pina Virabhadrudu.

DISTRICT – VIKARABAD (Railway Station – Vikarabad)

S. No.	Temple	Address	Type
1	Sri Anantha Padmanabha Swamy Devasthanam	Ananthagiri Hills - 501102	Vishnu
2	Bugga Rameshwaram Temple	Ananthagiri Hills - 501102	Shiva
3	Mahalakshmi Venkateshwara Swamy Temple	Kodangal - 509338	Venkatesh

SRI ANANTHA PADMANABHA SWAMY DEVASTHANAM AT ANANTHAGIRI – The Temple is dedicated to Lord Vishnu. According to Skanda Purana, it is believed that the Temple is installed by Rishi Markandeya in Dwapara Yuga. Attracted by the peaceful atmosphere of Ananthagiri Hills, Markandeya Rishi came here for yoga sadhana. Every day Markandeya Rishi used to go to Kashi from Ananthagiri to take a holy bath in the Ganges through a cave due to his yoga sadhana. On one day, he was not able to go to Kashi. Lord gave Darshan in a dream and arranged the Ganges to flow to perform a holy bath for Rishi.

BUGGA RAMESHWARAM TEMPLE AT ANANTAGIRI HILLS - The Ramalingeshwara Swamy Temple is dedicated to Lord Shiva. This Temple has more than 500 years of history. There is an underground stream which originates beneath the Shivalinga of the Temple and flows continuously throughout the year. The water collected into a pond near the Temple. River Musi which flows through Hyderabad is originated from this place. Maha Shivaratri is the major festival here and it is celebrated pretty well. A major number of pilgrims visit this Temple on this special occasion.

MAHALAKSHMI VENKATESHWARA SWAMY TEMPLE AT KODANGAL - The Temple is dedicated to Lord Venkateshwara Swamy. The Temple is ancient & famous. The vigraha of Shri Venkateshwara Swamy is in standing posture having Sridevi & Bhudevi on either side of the vigraha. Devotees visit the Temple with full devotion & faith and Lord fulfils all their desires when worshiped with pure heart.

DISTRICT – WANAPARTHY (Railway Station – Gadwal)

S. No.	Temple	Address	Type
1	Sri Ranganayaka Swamy Temple	Srirangapuram Village, Pebbair Mandal - 509105	Vishnu

SRI RANGANAYAKA SWAMY TEMPLE AT SRIRANGAPURAM – The Temple was built during 18th century. According to legend, Krishnadevaraya, the Vijayanagar ruler, went to Srirangam and was enthralled by the Sri Ranganayaka Swamy Temple there. He desired to construct a Ranganayaka Swamy Temple in his kingdom. Later, Ranganayaka (Lord Vishnu) appeared in his dream and told the King that his Vigraha is lying in the kingdom and an eagle will direct him to that place. The succeeding day, Krishnadevaraya followed the eagle and found the Lord's Vigraha between Kothakota and Kanvayapally mountains. The King constructed the Sri Ranganayaka Swamy Temple near Ratna Pushkarini Lake. The Temple is a classic example of Vijayanagar architecture. The Temple was built by the Rajas of Wanaparthi

Samsthanam on the bund of Ratna Pushpakarini Lake. During Navaratrulu, the flow of tourists is more than 20,000 per day for 9 days. The Temple celebrate 'Kotai Vutsavalu' on the occasion of Sankranthi Festival for a period of one month. In addition, the Temple celebrates 'Rathotsavam' during March for a period of 15 days and the flow of tourists to this destination is more than 20,000/day on an average. During Shravana Masam, the flow of tourists is more than 5,000 per day on an average as the destination is having water body beside the Temple.

DISTRICT – WARANGAL (Railway Station – Warangal)

S. No.	Temple	Address	Type
1	Warangal Fort	Warangal – 506001	Shiva
2	Sri Rama Satya Narayana Swamy Temple	Mulugu Road, Warangal - 506002	Satya Narayan

WARANGAL FORT - The Fort was the capital city of Kakatiya dynasty and Musunuri Nayakas. It appears to have existed since 12th century. The Fort has four ornamental gates, known as Kakatiya Kala Thoranam. There is a Shivalinga which was on unearthed from the Fort by the archeologist and the Shivalinga is made out of Basalt Rock, which is very hard and it is unbelievable that the said Shivalinga with a hard Basalt Rock can be polished and finished with common tools more than 800 years ago. The Kakatiyan Arch has been adopted and officially incorporated into the emblem of Telangana after the bifurcation of Andhra Pradesh.

Shambhuni Gudi - The Temple consists of garbhagriha, antarala and ranga mandapa. The square shaped ranga mandapa has porticos on its three sides, while the main entrance faces east. There is an inscription, which mentions the installation of the deities of Veyilingala Devara and Ganadhipathi by a person called Chaviki Buddayya for the merit of the world. On architectural grounds, this Temple can be dated back to 13th century AD.

SRI RAMA SATYA NARAYANA SWAMY TEMPLE AT MULUGU ROAD - The Temple is dedicated to Bhagwan Sri Satya Narayan. The vigraha of Bhagwan Satya Narayan is made out of single stone and is in black color. The said vigraha has been crafted in standing posture. Devotees visit the Temple in large numbers on every Friday & on various festive occasions.

DISTRICT – WARANGAL URBAN (Railway Station – Warangal)

(Now known as **HANUMAKONDA**)

S. No.	Temple	Address	Type
1	Padmakshi Temple	Meerpet, Hanamkonda – 506001	Mata
2	Sri Siddeshwara Temple	Meerpet, Hanamkonda – 506001	Shiva
3	Mettugutta Temple	Madikonda, Kazipet – 506003	Shiva, Rama
4	Trikuta Temple	Kondaparthy - 506003	Shiva
5	Sri Bhadrakali Temple	Tadkamalla Village, Warangal – 506007	Mata
6	Thousand Pillar Temple	Brahmanawada, Hanamkonda – 506011	Shiva
7	Sri Mallikarjuna Swamy Temple	Inavolu - 506143	Shiva
8	Sammakka Saralamma Temple	Medaram – 506344	Mata

PADMAKSHI TEMPLE AT HANAMKONDA – It was built during the Kakatiya reign in 12th century. The Temple is one among the oldest Temples in Hanamkonda. Dedicated to Goddess Padmakshi, also known as Padmakshamma, this Temple is especially visited by women devotees during the Bathukamma festival. The major attraction of this Temple is the pillar Annakonda. Annakonda Pillar is made up of granite and is built in quadrangular shape. The walls of the pillar showcase carvings and inscription related to Jain religion, especially dedicated to Goddess Kalalaya. Goddess Padmakshi is fondly referred as "Amma" by locals. The word Amma means mother in Telugu and the Goddess Padmakshi is considered as the Mother of Mothers. The Padmakshiamma resides on the top of a Gutta (hill).

SRI SIDDESHWARA TEMPLE AT HANAMKONDA – The Temple is dedicated to Lord Shiva. It was constructed in 3rd century and is one of the Paschimadwara Mukha Temples. The Temple is popular for its intricately carved pillars and architectural work, which is similar to the Chalukyan style of architecture. A huge number of devotees visit this Temple during the festival of Maha Shivaratri. The Siddheswara stands tall and has a majestic appearance. Its real beauty lies in its pillars which are adorned with intricate carvings. The uniqueness of the Temple lies in these intricate designs which are scattered liberally throughout the Temple. It is owing to these marvels that the Siddhewara Temple is regarded as one of the most beautiful Temples of Warangal.

METTUGUTTA TEMPLE AT MADIKONDA – It is a famous Temple. This place is also known as Manigiri. The Linga in this Temple has many similarities with Varanasi Visveswara. There are two Temples on Mettugutta. One Temple is for Lord Shiva and other one is for Lord Sri Ram. Local people call this Temple as Mettu Rama Lingeshwara Swamy Temple. Lord Shiva Temple is constructed during the Kaktiya regime. The Temple is located on a hillock, there many small water bodies located within the area, there are various rock formation which can be found near the site, which have very important significance.

Swetharka Moola Ganapathi Temple at Kazipet - The Temple is dedicated to Lord Ganesha. It is one of the rare and only one Temple in Telangana where the vigraha of Lord Ganesha is of milky color. It is believed that Lord Ganesha came in dream of his staunch devotee and instructed him to consecrate this vigraha in the Temple. The devotee obeyed the instructions of Lord Ganesha and this miraculous vigraha of Lord Ganesha had been consecrated by the priest in the present Temple. Devotees from far and wide visit this Temple in large numbers specially on Wednesday & Sunday and there are so many festivals celebrated with great pomp & fervor and in one of the grand festival, celestial wedding of Lord Ganesha is performed with full devotion.

TRIKUTA TEMPLE AT KONDAPARTHY - The village has witnessed its heyday during the Kakatiya period when it bore the name "Sri Kondiparthy Nagare" and served as the headquarters of the feudatory chiefs of Malyala family. Three inscriptions were reported from this village. The earliest inscription datable to 9th century AD in archaic Telugu is on a boulder locally known as "Kokkera Gundu" situated in a big tank of the village. The second inscription datable to 1203 A.D. gives an account of Malyala family and records the construction of a Shiva Temple called Chandesvara and excavation of a tank named Chanda Samudra by Chanda Senapathi, the Commander of Kakatiya ruler Ganapathi deva. The third inscription datable to 1242 AD, records the construction of two Temples to Rudresvara and another to Kesava and installation of deities as well as the construction of prakara wall to the above Temples including Prolesvara Temple which was already in existence. This is a Trikuta Temple which has three shrines on the south, west and north along with garbhagriha and antarala while a common rangamandapa has an entrance facing east. The shikharas of the shrines are built with brick and are of the stepped pyramidal type.

SRI BHADRAKALI TEMPLE AT TADKAMALLA VILLAGE - The Temple is believed to be built in 625 AD by the King Pulakeshin-II of Chalukya dynasty to commemorate his victory over Vengi region of Andhra Desham, as per the writings on the Temple wall. Kakatiya Kings later have adopted the Temple & considered Goddess Bhadrakali as their "Kula Devatha". This Temple regained its glory in 1950s when Sri Ganapathi Sasthri along with other locals started renovations of this Temple. During renovation, changes were made to the main Vigraha as well. It is said that the deity was in fierce form, which was later changed to subtle & calming Vigraha. The Goddess Bhadrakali is in a sitting position here. She is shown with 8 hands, each with one weapon. 2.7 meters long stone Vigraha of the deity is wearing a crown as well. One of the inner pillars of the Temple has a Sanskrit inscription on it. That particular pillar is called the Antralaya Sthambam. High point of Bhadrakali Temple is an artificial lake of 2 ½ KMs radius in the vicinity of the Temple. Number of natural rock formations in the surroundings add to the spiritual charm of the Temple & are the most dominant feature of the Temple. Some of the unique shaped rocks are said to carry immense spiritual powers.

THOUSAND PILLAR TEMPLE AT HANAMKONDA – A UNESCO World Heritage Site, the Thousand Pillar Temple is among the oldest Temples of South India It is located at the base of Hanamkonda hill. It was built in 12th century by the Kakatiya King Rudra Deva. Dedicated primarily

to Lord Shiva, this Temple is also known by the name of Sri Rudreshwara Swamy Temple. At this Temple, three deities - Lord Shiva, Lord Vishnu and Lord Surya are worshipped. They are known as Trikutalayam. There are three shrines, one for each deity. Currently under the maintenance of Archaeological Survey of India, Thousand Pillar Temple is known for intricately carved pillars. A massive sculpture of Nandi, carved out of a single rock, is another attraction of this Temple. Rock cut elephants and exquisite engravings at the Temple are also worth noticing. Every part of the Temple depicts the typical Chalukya style of architecture. The Temple stands as a statement of the finest of arts of the Kakatiyas. The Temple has a star shaped architecture, which stands as a testimony to the expertise of the wonderful craftsmen of the glorious period.

SRI MALLIKARJUNA SWAMY TEMPLE AT INAVOLU - The name Ayanavolu seems to have been derived from Ayyanavole means 'Priest's Holy Village'. The name Ayanavolu first appeared in the inscription of western chalukya King 'Satyasraya Irivabedanga' in 1007 A.D in Punnavolu. The earliest inscription noticed in this village is datable to Tribhuvanamalla Vikramaditya-VI (1118 A.D.) which records a gift to Lakulesvara Pandita by a subordinate of the King. There is a stone inscription in the Temple premises setup by Anapotanayaka, Velama chief of Recharla family datable to 1369 A.D. in which the name of the God is mentioned as 'Mailarudevara'. Sri Mallikarjuna Swamy or Mallanna is worshipped here as Mailarudeva. The vigraha of Mailarudeva is 6 feet in sitting posture facing east, sand-witched between the vigrahas of his consorts, Balija Medalamma and Golla Kethamma. The Temple is constructed in the center of massive toranas with in a rectangular prakara with openings on south, east and northern sides. This is a sandhara type of Temple having inner pradakshanapatha. In front of the Temple is a massive 24 pillared ranga mandapa. On the southern and eastern cardinal directions, two massive toranas resembling the Kakatiya gates of Warangal are located. On the northern side, the remnants of fallen torana is seen on ground. From the architectural point of view, it appears that the Temple was constructed in the early Kakatiya period and the mandapa and toranas were added during the period of Kakatiya Rudradeva (1158 – 1195 A.D.). Recently the Department has re-erected the northern side fallen torana in its original place.

SAMMAKKA SARALAMMA TEMPLE AT MEDARAM – It was built during 12th century. This Temple has no mythological background relating to the construction of the Temple; instead, it is believed to be built in the memory of two tribal women. The main deity(s) of the Sammakka Saralamma Temple are two brave women who stood up for their community and its betterment. They became Martyrs in the battle. According to the legend, once a troop from the Koya tribal community was returning from a trip, when they saw a little girl playing with the tigress. The head of the troop saw the girl and inspired by her bravery, he adopted her and named her as Samakka. Later, she married a headman of a neighbouring tribal group and had a daughter, Sarakka. Both the mother and daughter protested the Kakatiya kings, who forced the tribes to pay taxes. Both the women fought bravely and reportedly lost their lives. The Koya community constructed this Temple as a token of gratitude. Annually, an event called Sammakka Saralamma Jatara is held which is considered as one of the largest tribal festivals of the world. The deities are brought from the forest to a spot for a period of 10-12 days when more than one crore devotees offer prayers and gift 'bangaram', which is pure jaggery to the deities.

DISTRICT – YADADRI BHUVANAGIRI (Railway Station – Aler/Rayagiri/Bhongir)

S. No.	Temple	Address	Type
1	Kulpakji Temple	Kolanpaka – 508101	Jain
2	Sri Someswara Temple	Kolanpaka – 508101	Shiva
3	Basavanna Temple	Kuravaram Village, Rajapet – 508105	Shiva
4	Kunda Satyanarayana Kaladhamam	Surendrapuri – 508115	Sapta Lokas
5	Sri Lakshmi Narasimha Swamy Temple	Yadagirigutta – 508115	Narasimha (Vishnu)
6	Bhuvanagiri Fort	Bhongir – 508116	Mata, Shiva
7	Shiva Shakthi Anugraha Mahapeetam	Tekulasomaram - 508285	Shiva

KULPAKJI TEMPLE AT KOLANUPAKA - The Temple is popular for its incredible architecture. The Temple has been a gift for over two thousand years. Inside the Temple, there are some wonderful pictures of the Jains, the great achievers of final knowledge. The Temple is decorated with beautiful vigrahas of Tirthankaras and it's one of the important Jain pilgrimage sites in the country. Kulpakji is an important pilgrimage centre for Swetambara Jains of South India. According to the mythological legend, the main Temple of Kolanupaka is said to have been built by Emperor Bharata, son of King Dushyanta and Queen Shakuntala. Jainism was prevalent in Andhra Pradesh & Telangana before the 4thcentury and Kolanupaka was one of the prominent centres of Jainism from early times. About 20 Jain inscriptions have been found there. It is said that Kolanupaka flourished as Jain centre during the Rashtrakutas period. This Temple has three main vigraha of Gods, called as Tirthankars. These are of Lord Rishabha, Lord Neminath and Lord Mahavir. The Vigraha of Lord Mahavir has been made out a single jade. The Vigraha of Lord Rishabha, who is also known as Lord Adinath, has been carved out of a green stone. Historically, it has been popular as Manikya Swami. There are eight vigraha of various other Tirthankaras placed on both sides of the Temple. Every Tirthankara has been built with their own unique style. The Vigraha of Lord Mahavira has been carved with an vigraha of Lion, while there is a bull on the pedestals of Lord Rishabha. A cobra with multi heads has been carved as an umbrella over the Vigraha of Lord Parshawnath. The architecture of the Temple is stunning with wonderful carvings on the Temple walls. The Jain Temple of Kolanupaka was made using red sand stone and the pillars of Temple are made out of white marble.

SRI SOMESWARA TEMPLE AT KOLANPAKA – It is an ancient Temple dedicated to Lord Shiva. This Temple is also called as Veyi Lingala Gudi (Thousand Lingas Temple). The Temple was built around 12th century by Kakatiya Kings. Here, Lord Shiva is found in human form unlike the common Linga form. Poojas are still being performed in this Temple. The Temple complex also houses the Archaeological Museum with several hundreds of wonderful sculptures dating back to 10th century to 14th century found in this region. A life size Vigraha of Lord Mahavira is the first exhibit that you come across as soon as you enter the Temple. There is also a victory pillar belonging to king Thribuvanamalla, the same kind associated with the Bhuvanagiri Fort. At the end of the corridor, the site museum leads to the Someswara Temple. The pillars inside the main Temple are ornate with rich, trademark sculpture of the Kakatiyas. Noteworthy are the miniature sculptures of stories from Ramayana and Dasavataras of Lord Vishnu. There are other shrines around the main Temple, a shrine for Sahatsralinga, where hundreds of small Lingas are carved on the main Shivalinga. There are two Nandis and a tiny Shivalinga, looks like one of the Nandis was originally located elsewhere in the Temple.

Veeranarayana Swamy Temple at Kolanpaka - According to an inscription, on the inner wall of the mukhamandapa, during the western chalukya period, Kumara Mahamandaleswara Jagaddeva, a subordinate of Tribhuvanamalla, offered gifts to Lord Jagaddevanarayanadeva, consecrated by him for anga, ranga and bhogas. In front of the Temple, a monolithic Garuda pillar is erected.

BASAVANNA TEMPLE AT KURAVARAM VILLAGE, RAJAPET - The Temple has been built on high adisthana with entrance from southern side. The grabhagriha is located on western side with antarala and pillared mandapa. In the centre of the shrine, a Shivalinga is enshrined. In front of the Temple i.e. on southern side, a big Nandi (Basavanna) is placed on a pedestal. Hence, this Temple is known as Basavannagudi.

KUNDA SATYANARAYANA KALADHAMAM AT SURENDRAPURI – The place is a unique one-stop destination, which is an epitome of artistic as well as sculptural excellence. The museum known as Kunda Satyanarayana Kaladhamam is also called the mythological awareness centre, which was established to create awareness regarding Hindu mythology. It is a one-of-its-kind spiritual theme park, which features a sprawling 3 KMs length walkways and more than 3000 statues offers a delighted tour of the Hindu epics. Here, Kunda Satyanarayana has made use of artistry extensively for depicting mythology forms in an interesting and artistic manner. The museum is home to full sized replicas of most of the Hindu Temples in India. The architecture of the Temple and the sculptures lend an aura of spiritual bliss. The sculptures and paintings depict stories from Hindu epics like Ramayana, Mahabharata and Bhagavatam. Visit the holy "Sapta Lokas" – the seven divine worlds at this destination, according to Hindu mythology. The place is also home to unique 'Navagraha Temple' with a separate Temple for each of the Navagrahas in their relative positions. The deities appear along with their divine consorts and vahanas. The dramatic war scenes between Rama and Ravana in Ramayana and between Kauravas and Pandavas in Mahabharata are carved and portrayed in great detail. The wonderful marvel of mythology is a brain child of a great visionary Sri

Kunda Satyanarayana. The other major attractions of Surendrapuri are Nagakoti (101-foot Shivalinga) as well as 60-foot double-sided Panchamukhi Hanuman (one of the tallest vigraha of Hanuman) and Lord Shiva Vigraha located at the entrance, which captures the attention of visitors. The museum is a unique concept based on astounding Vedic knowledge.

SRI LAKSHMI NARASIMHA SWAMY TEMPLE AT YADAGIRIGUTTA - It is the most unique, beautiful and pleasant Hillock with moderate climate in all seasons. The Temple is a popular Temple of Lord Narasimha Swamy, an incarnation Lord Vishnu. The Lord appeared in the dream of a devout lady among the tribe, directing her to a large cavern wherein he revealed himself to all as five majestic Avatars. Pleased with his deep devotion, Lord Narasimha, an incarnation of Lord Vishnu appeared before him in five different forms as Sri Jwala Narasimha, Sri Yogananda, Sri Gandabherunda, Sri Ugra and Sri Lakshminarasimha. All these five forms (roopas) are presently worshipped within the Temple. They later manifested themselves into finely sculpted forms that later came to be worshiped as Pancha Narasimha Kshetram. There are Purana and traditional accounts of this Shrine, which are widely popular among the devotees. There is mention about the origin of this Temple in the Skanda Purana. Glowing bright atop the shikharam of garbhagriha (Sanctum Sanctorum) of this cave Temple is the golden Sudarshana Chakra of Lord Vishnu, the adornment as well as the weapon is a symbol. It is said that many years ago, the chakra moved in the direction from which the devotees came as if like a compass guiding them towards the Temple. The Chakra considered to possess mystic power and value at times turns on its own; no human hand is capable of turning it. Another Legend also has it that Sriman Narayana, pleased with Yada's penance, sent Sri Anjaneya to direct the rishi to a holy spot, where the Lord appeared to him in the form of Sri Lakshmi Narasimha. This spot is marked by a Temple located at the foot of the Yadagiri hillock. There, the Sage worshiped the Lord for many years. The Aradhanam and Puja in this Temple are performed according to Pancharatra Agamam. As the belief goes, Lord Narasimha has taken on the role of a "doctor" and is known as "Vaidya Narasimha" by his devotees at this shrine to cure many chronic diseases and the role of a 'do gooder' to those who are under the influence of bad planets, witch craft and black magic. A mandala (40 day) pradakshina is very popular made by many devotees to get cured of a long standing ailment or chronic disease.

BHUVANAGIRI FORT AT BHONGIR - The Bhuvanagiri Fort stands as a testimony to the history of Telangana state, which is the epitome of many battles. This magnificent fort, which dates back nearly 3000 years, is home to many astonishing structures. Sarvai Pandu who was born in Telangana to a common Kalu Geetha family won the Orugal in 1708 and later took over Bhuvanagiri. Prior to his conquest of Golconda, he had hid his vast treasures here at the Kalika Mata Temple in the interior of the hill. There are many caves and tunnels that have not yet been discovered in the hill. Historians claim that the coins

of the Vishnu Kundi period were found here. The hill is 610 meters high and is the tallest mountain in Telangana. The mountain is an oval monolithic mountain and from the south it looks like a tortoise and a sleeping elephant from the west. Bhuvanagiri Fort has the first steel gateway. There is a Lord Shiva Temple on the hill of Bhuvanagiri, a Vigraha of the black Nandi, Someshwara, Bammadevara Temple and a monastery under the hill.

SHIVA SHAKTHI ANUGRAHA MAHAPEETAM AT TEKULASOMARAM - The Temple is dedicated to Lord Shiva. There is a 54ft. tall Shivalinga. There are various Gods & Goddesses consecrated at the Mahapeetam. It is a ancient place of worship.

❖ ❖ ❖ ❖ ❖

प्रो.(डॉ.) आलोक शर्मा

निदेशक

भारतीय पर्यटन एवं यात्रा प्रबंध संस्थान
(भारत सरकार के पर्यटन मंत्रालय के अधीन स्वायत्तशासी निकाय)
INDIAN INSTITUTE OF TOURISM AND TRAVEL MANAGEMENT
(An Autonomous Body under Ministry of Tourism, Govt. of India)

No. 138.DIR/IITTM/2024 **Date: 22.08.2024**

प्रति,
राधाकृष्ण प्रकाशन
नई दिल्ली

विषयः आपके द्वारा प्रकाशित पुस्तक में संस्थान की जानकारी समाहित करने हेतु निवेदन।

महोदय,

भारत में पर्यटन मंत्रालय, भारत सरकार के अधीन भारतीय पर्यटन एवं यात्रा प्रबंध संस्थान अपने पांच केन्द्रों द्वारा पर्यटन के सांस्कृतिक, आध्यात्मिक, ग्रामीण, साहसिक आदि क्षेत्रों में औपचारिक शिक्षा प्रदान करने में अपनी महती भूमिका अदा कर रहा है साथ ही एमबीए, बीबीए एवं पीएचडी पाठ्यक्रमों का संचालन करता हैं एवं केन्द्रीय नोडल एजेंसी एवं आईआईटीएफसी के द्वारा टूर गाइडिंग, प्रशिक्षण, ऑनलाईन प्रशिक्षण कार्यक्रमों का आयोजन करता है। सांस्कृतिक एवं आध्यात्मिक पर्यटन भारतवर्ष की आत्मा रही है तथा भारत में पर्यटन क्षेत्र के हितधारक पर्यटन संबंधी सर्वश्रेष्ठ जानकारी हेतु आईआईटीटीएम से सम्पर्क करते हैं। आईआईटीटीएम युवाओं के सुरक्षित भविष्य के दृष्टिगत संस्थान रोजगार परक कार्यक्रमों के साथ ही पर्यटन विकास की दिशा में महत्वपूर्ण कार्य कर रहा है।

आपके संस्थान द्वारा चार खण्डों में प्रकाशित टेम्पल टूर नामक पुस्तक में भारत के मंदिरों की जानकारी का संकलन पर्यटकों की जिज्ञासाओं को हल करने का एक महत्वपूर्ण प्रयास है तथा आईआईटीटीएम ने आपकी संस्था के इस प्रकाशन का शासकीय नियमानुसार क्रय किया जा रहा है। इस विषय में आपसे निवेदन है कि भारतीय पर्यटन एवं यात्रा प्रबंध संस्थान की संक्षिप्त जानकारी का एक पृष्ठ आपकी ओर प्रेषित किया जा रहा है जिसे आपके प्रकाशन 'टेम्पल टूर' नामक पुस्तक के सभी खण्डों के आगामी मुद्रण में उचित स्थान पर दर्शाने का कष्ट करें, ताकि मंदिरों से संबंधित विस्तृत मूर्तिशास्त्र, वास्तुकला, आध्यात्मिक महत्ता से संबंधित अतिरिक्त जानकारी प्राप्त करने के लिए जिज्ञासु आईआईटीटीएम से सम्पर्क कर सकें। आईआईटीटीएम आपका आभारी रहेगा।

(आलोक शर्मा)

गोविन्दपुरी, ग्वालियर, म.प्र. (भारत) 474 011 Govindpuri, Gwalior, M.P. (INDIA) 474 011
टेली. /Tel.: +91 751-2345821 **ई.मेल** /e-mail: iittm@sancharnet.in
वेबसाइट /Website: www.iittm.ac.in

सांस्कृति एवं आध्यात्मिक पर्यटन, भारत वर्ष की आत्मा रही है। भारत में पर्यटन मंत्रालय, भारत सरकार के अधीन भारतीय पर्यटन एवं यात्रा प्रबंध संस्थान अपने पांच केन्द्रों द्वारा पर्यटन के सांस्कृतिक, आध्यात्मिक, ग्रामीण, साहसिक आदि क्षेत्रों में औपचारिक शिक्षा प्रदान करने में अपनी महती भूमिका अदा कर रहा है। भारत में पर्यटन क्षेत्र के हितधारक पर्यटन संबंधी सर्वश्रेष्ठ जानकारी हेतु आईआईटीटीएम से सम्पर्क करते हैं। चार खण्डों में प्रस्तुत इस पुस्तक में संकलित भारत स्थित मंदिरों की जानकारी पर्यटकों की जिज्ञासाओं को हल करने का एक महत्वपूर्ण प्रयास है। मंदिरों से संबंधित विस्तृत मूर्तिशास्त्र, वास्तुकला, आध्यात्मिक महत्ता से संबंधित अतिरिक्त जानकारी हेतु आईआईटीटीएम से सम्पर्क किया जा सकता है। भारत सरकार के पर्यटन मंत्रालय के अधीन यह संस्थान एमबीए, बीबीए एवं पीएचडी पाठ्यक्रमों के संचालन के साथ ही केन्द्रीय नोडल एजेंसी एवं आईआईटीएफसी के द्वारा टूर गाइडिंग, प्रशिक्षण, ऑनलाईन प्रशिक्षण कार्यक्रमों का आयोजन करता है। युवाओं के सुरक्षित भविष्य के दृष्टिगत संस्थान रोजगार परक कार्यक्रमों के साथ ही पर्यटन विकास की दिशा में महत्वपूर्ण कार्य कर रहा है।